W9-ADR-340

WITHDRAWN

The American Adventure

1957 EDITION

BERTRAND M. WAINGER has enjoyed a long career in teaching young people and in writing for them. At present he edits and writes social studies books for junior and senior high school pupils and is Research Professor of American Civilization at Union College, Schenectady, New York. As a writer, he coauthored *Exploring New York State*—a seventh-grade social studies textbook—combining history, geography, industries, and government.

BUENA JACKSON STOLBERG, *Consultant,* teaches the social studies–English core curriculum in the junior high school of Webster Groves, Missouri. Currently, she also serves as a consultant for teachers engaged in the core program. Her experience includes teaching in a one-room rural school, teaching junior high school social studies, and teaching the core curriculum in college summer sessions. In addition to acting as a consultant for *The American Adventure,* she is also the author of *Tests for The American Adventure* and *Teacher's Guide to The American Adventure.*

The American

Drawings by Aldren Watson *Maps and Charts by* Harold K. Faye

Adventure

1957 EDITION

Bertrand M. Wainger

Buena Jackson Stolberg, Consultant

McGRAW-HILL BOOK COMPANY, INC.

New York *Chicago* *San Francisco*

Dallas *Toronto* *London*

Contents

II
67724

Library of Congress Catalog Card Number: 57–12595

The American adventure
is the story of settling the continent.

The first little groups of settlers landed on the coast at Jamestown and Plymouth and hung on for dear life. Gradually pioneers opened up the vast and beautiful land. They moved westward on foot, on horseback, in covered wagons, on river rafts and canalboats, in railroad cars, and in automobiles. For more than three centuries moving westward has been part of the American adventure for men and women, boys and girls.

CHESAPEAKE & OHIO RAILWAY CO.

UNITED STATES STEEL CORP.

STANDARD OIL CO. (N.J.)

The American adventure is the story of building a great nation.

In every generation Americans plowed the soils, tended machines, kept store, served others. Every man earned a living in freedom.

Builders opened up the land for traffic first with roads and canals. Then they built railroads that span the continent and crisscross the land, carrying goods

CATERPILLAR TRACTOR CO.

BETTMANN ARCHIVE

STANDARD OIL CO. (N.J.)

MONKMEYER

to and from cities and countryside. Ocean liners exchanged products with the rest of the world.

Lumberjacks cut down forests for lumber, out of which carpenters built homes. Steel poured from huge furnaces and was molded into beams, out of which skyscrapers were constructed. Factories across the land produced enormous quantities of goods. With tractors, combines, and other machines, farmers raised large enough crops to help feed the free world. Today the American nation is the most prosperous on earth.

UNION PACIFIC RAILROAD CO.

The American adventure is the story of expanding opportunity.

In the 1800s the vast unsettled lands beyond the frontier, the spreading railroads, the rising factories, and the growing cities offered opportunity to get ahead to the millions already here and to the millions more

who came from across the oceans. In the eyes of the world the United States was the land of opportunity.

For you the United States is still a land of expanding opportunity. The doors of education are open to every American boy and girl. You can be trained for any one of thousands of skilled jobs in industry. You can prepare for the life of a modern farmer. You can aspire to a career in the arts or the sciences. In whatever way you choose to earn a living, you can look forward to a life of comfort and friendship.

WIDE WORLD

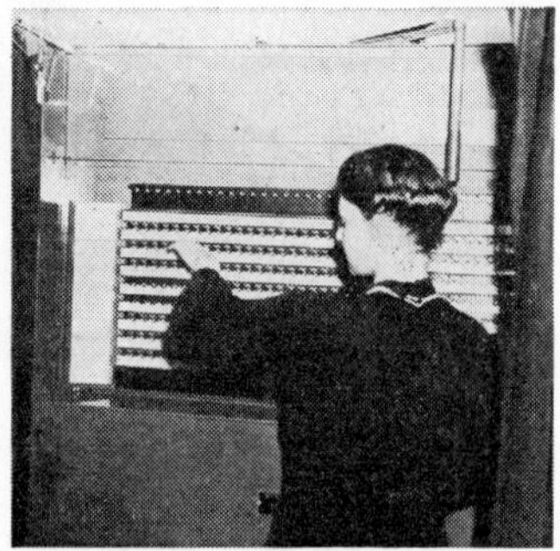

WIDE WORLD

The American adventure is the story of strengthening democracy.

INTERNATIONAL HARVESTER CO.

When our nation began, only property owners voted. Gradually all men won the right to vote. After a long struggle the suffragettes won the right for women, too.

Wherever Americans get together in groups, they talk politics. They love the turmoil of political conventions and campaigns. On election day the people make their choice, every voter casting his ballot in secret.

ACME

WIDE WORLD

WIDE WORLD

WIDE WORLD

Stronger democracy means greater freedom and greater security for every person, for the man in the street. He is free to worship in his own church, to read the newspaper of his choice, to stand up in community gatherings and express his opinions. He has the right to join a union and go on strike. He is insured against unemployment and against poverty in old age. The courts protect him in his rights—even against his own government. The schools prepare his children for the rights and duties of democratic citizenship. In a democracy the individual comes first.

ANSEL ADAMS—THE UNIVERSITY OF ROCHESTER

MONKMEYER

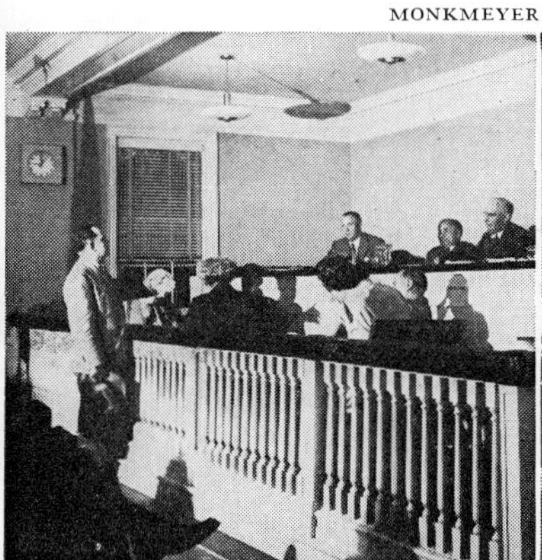

MONKMEYER

The American adventure is the story of folk tale, dance, and play.

The American people make up tales, sing songs, dance, play, have fun. They tell whopping stories about Paul Bunyan, the

mighty lumberjack, and his big blue ox named Babe. They tell about Joe Magarac, the giant steelworker, who bends steel rails with his hands. They sing about John Henry, who drove a steel drill faster than any other man and who died trying to outlast an automatic steam drill.

Americans square-dance in their barns and swing to jazz orchestras. Americans play games. They root for their favorite teams. Great athletes are among their heroes. Sportsmanship is a rule of the American way of life.

"All the News That's Fit to Print."

The New York Times.

NEW YORK, SATURDAY, DECEMBER 14, 1918. TWENTY-FOUR PAGES. TWO CENTS

THE WEATHER

PRESIDENT WILSON WELCOMED AT BREST, STARTS FOR PARIS; WANTS THE SEAS RESTRICTED ONLY BY UNITED CONTROL; FAVORS CAREFUL INQUIRY BEFORE FIXING INDEMNITIES

TESTIFIES BER… SENT SPIES HE… BEFORE WAR BE…

130 Propagandists Mobili… from Official Ranks, Capt. Lester Tells Senators.

HEARST FILM HIT AT JAPAN

Then Shifted to Mexico When President Wilson Criticised Certain Parts.

FOX'S CONFESSION IS TOLD

…den Frontier Villages Ask Annexation to Switzerland

…NGS BANK; …YLIGHT

BURLESON TAKES CONTROL OF CABLE FROM C. H. MACKAY

Newcomb Carlton, Western Union Head, Is Made Director of All Lines.

LAND WIRE BOARD NAMED

Will Control Telegraph and Telephone Lines Under Wire Control Committee.

PURCHASE BILL INTRODUCED

Find Edith Cavell's Grave and Hold Service There

…NT AMERICA …CH TURKEY

NEW LIGHT ON PEACE POINTS

President Said to Favor Sea Regulation by All Nations, Not One.

WANTS CLEAR DEFINITION

Believes the Key to Peace Rests with Peoples Rather Than with Governments.

FIRM FOR LEAGUE OF NATIONS

Regards Reported Agreement of Premiers on Indemnity as Only Tentative.

Must End All Conscription or Peace Conference Fails, Says Lloyd George, in Final Word to Electors

LONDON, Dec. 13.—Premier Lloyd George, in a statement to Reuter's, Limited, tonight on the subject of conscription, said: "On the eve of this important election, which means so much to the country, I wish to make it clear beyond all doubt that I stand for the abolition of conscript armies in all lands. Without that the Peace Conference would be a failure and a sham. "These great military machines are responsible for the agony the world has passed through, and it would be a poor ending to any peace conference that allowed them to continue. Any delegate that represents Great Britain at that conference must labor to the end I have stated."

LONDON PREDICTS HARMONY AT PARIS

High Authority Pins Hope … Agreement on Wilso… Heart-to-Heart…

HIS IDEAS …

FLEET MET WILSON BEFORE DAYLIGHT

GREETED BY HIGH OFFICIALS

French Ministers and Americans Board the President's Ship.

SPLENDID HARBOR DISPLAY

French and American Warships and Gayly-Garbed Throngs Form Picturesque Setting.

The American adventure is the story of growing into world leadership.

The United States began as a weak little country. The big European nations showed little respect for it. In the 1800s the United States grew strong and prosperous. The American people sought trade and friendship with the other peoples of the world.

In the 1900s the United States fought in two great world wars. It threw its strength on the side of England and France and helped them emerge victorious. In the 1950s the American people used their wealth and power to support the free world against the danger of communism. The United States rose to world leadership.

After many failures to achieve long-time peace, the United States led in organizing the United Nations. The UN headquarters stands in New York City. Here the representatives of 60 countries meet to debate their problems. Here the many agencies associated with the UN come to report on their work. They improve health and living standards around the world. They prepare groups for self-government. They strengthen understanding among the peoples of the world. The UN builds for peace. For the sake of peace and freedom, the American people share in the work of the United Nations.

UNITED NATIONS

Unit *1 Europeans Build the Foundations of a New World 1492–1750*

ONLY IF space ships succeed in landing on another planet will men ever again enjoy the thrill of discovering and exploring a new world. Until that day comes, we can try to share the adventures of the Europeans who, 300 and 400 years ago, discovered and explored and settled the new world that we call America.

They stumbled on America, so to speak, while looking for a sea route to Asia. As they continued to search for a water passage, they filled in the map of the Atlantic coast with its islands, its long shore line, and the broad rivers leading inland. But no one dreamed of two continents stretching 3,000 miles and more to the west.

Spanish explorers on the Caribbean islands met strange natives wearing ornaments of gold and silver. In their search for the mines from which the precious metals came, they conquered Central America, Mexico, and Peru. They put the Indians to work digging gold and silver and raising food.

Farther north, around the mouth of the St. Lawrence River, French fishermen came ashore to dry their fish. They met friendly natives eager to exchange valuable furs for knives, mirrors, fishhooks, pieces of cloth, and other articles made in Europe. The fishermen found the exchange very profitable. Soon Frenchmen settled on the river to collect cargoes of furs and to raise food.

Most settlers in the English colonies were refugees from religious oppression and poverty in Europe. In their eyes America was a haven where they would be free from persecution. They wanted freedom to worship in their different churches and opportunity to make a better living for themselves and their children. From the forest they cut the timbers to build their homes. On soil never tilled before, they raised crops. By the sweat of their brows they earned freedom and opportunity.

The first settlers in the English colonies depended completely on the mother country even for food and medicines. Three years after Jamestown, Virginia, was founded, the half-starved, fever-ridden, discouraged survivors had actually abandoned the settlement and were on their way home. Only the arrival of ships with supplies and new settlers saved the colony.

Gradually Virginia and the other English colonies became less and less dependent on the mother country for their basic needs. The people raised their own food and made most of their own clothes. They traded their surplus crops and bought manufactured goods. They governed themselves in their local communities and played an important part in the colonial governments.

But, so far as conditions permitted, colonists who came to the New World tried to live as they had lived in Europe. They built their houses like those they had known in Europe. They imported European furniture and clothes. They brought their ideas from Europe—their religious faiths, their political beliefs, and their social customs. Though they lived in the New World, they remained Spaniards, Frenchmen, Englishmen, Dutchmen, Swedes, Germans, Scotch-Irish.

Gradually, however, conditions in the New World changed these Europeans into Americans. The changes that took place in the English colonies were the beginnings of a truly American way of life. That is the story of the colonial period of the American adventure, as told in Unit 1.

1 *Europeans Explore and Settle the New World*

Tony and Niccolo, 14-year-old cousins, sailed from Venice on the vessel *Lucia,* of which their Uncle Marco was the captain. He took them along to teach them the life of a trader. The ship, loaded with European furs, lumber, and some gold and silver coins, lifted anchor at Venice, moved down the Adriatic to the Mediterranean Sea, and then turned eastward.

One day the boys caught sight of a fleet of Venetian spice galleys sailing toward home. They were sleek, handsome ships, with banks of oars on each side. Huge sails were spread to catch the wind. Their valuable cargoes of spices and silks made the galleys attractive to pirates. For that reason they were required by Venetian law to sail in groups, called convoys, protected by ships of the Venetian navy. For further safety each galley carried a company of archers to fight off pirates who might slip past the warships.

The *Lucia* visited Alexandria, Constantinople, and other strange ports in the eastern Mediterranean and the Black Sea. The captain traded his cargo for gems, perfumes, and other goods brought from the East. The boys looked and learned.

Part of the way home, along the coast of Greece, the *Lucia* also traveled in a convoy. The many small inlets that dent the Greek shore line were especially dangerous because they provided good hiding places for pirates. On this voyage, however, the *Lucia* met no pirates, somewhat to the disappointment of the boys.

Now the excitement of the voyage was past, and the *Lucia* was coming into home port with its valuable cargo. Tony and Niccolo, tanned and happy, had learned many lessons on their first voyage. Perhaps the one they would remember most clearly was that trading in the Mediterranean had its risky side.

The story of Tony and Niccolo is imaginary, but there were many vessels like the *Lucia* sailing the Mediterranean during the 1400s. They carried the goods of the East to the cities of Italy, and their crews often met danger, hardship, and adventure. There is a connection between this Mediterranean trade and the discovery of America. You will see what it is as you read on.

1 *Christopher Columbus Discovers the New World*

Although Columbus first saw the New World in 1492, the story of the discovery of America really begins much earlier. For centuries before Columbus's great voyage, European merchants had been carrying on a valuable trade with Asia.

Some of the products of this trade were luxuries that only the very

Trade routes with the East. By trading with Asia along the routes shown, Europeans obtained spices and luxuries. Today we speak of India, China, and the Pacific islands off Asia as the Far East; and we speak of the lands around the eastern Mediterranean, including Persia and Arabia, as the Middle East.

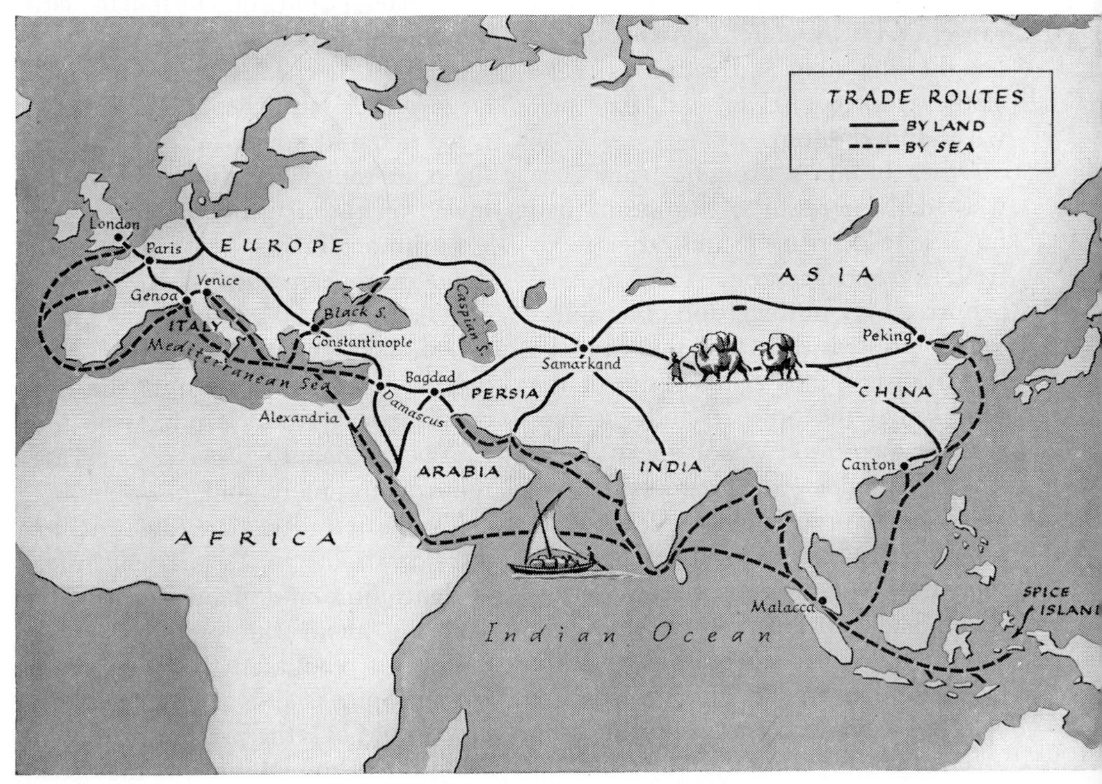

Venice Harbor. The harbor at Venice was a busy place in the 1400s. It was a main center of the rich trade between Europe and the East.

wealthy could afford to buy. Kings and nobles purchased rubies, diamonds, and other precious stones. They bought carpets and draperies to brighten and warm up the cold, dark rooms of their castles. Wealthy merchants and nobles bought fine silks and satins to make clothes for themselves and for their wives and children.

Other products brought from Asia were daily necessities. Europeans had no way to keep meat and other foods fresh by refrigeration. They needed pepper, cloves, nutmeg, and other spices to help preserve their food and to make it tasty. Europeans called some of the East Indies the Spice Islands because that is where most of the spices grew.

Asian products are very expensive. Whether luxuries or necessities, by the time the products of Asia reached Europe they were very expensive. Merchants had to bring them a long, long way by slow caravan or ship or both. In Asia one trader after the other bought them, each transporting the precious goods part of the way and then selling them. After a long journey, the silks and spices reached Bagdad, Constantinople, and other cities of the Middle East. There merchants from Venice, Genoa, and other Italian cities bought the goods and sold them in western Europe. These merchants made large profits, and the Italian cities became rich and powerful. You can trace the trade routes that the merchants followed on the map on page 5.

European traders seek a sea route to Asia. Europeans paid for the products of Asia mainly by sending gold and silver to Asia, and their supply of these precious metals was running short. To continue to buy the products of Asia, Europeans had to discover a cheaper route or find more gold, or do both.

European traders were eager to find a direct sea route to Asia. Then, instead of depending on a chain of merchants to bring them the products of the East, they would go to India, China, and the Spice Islands themselves. There they would buy the precious wares and bring them home by sea. If they could do that, they could sell the goods at lower prices and still make big profits.

The Europeans of the early 1400s knew only a small part of the world—the part lying around the Mediterranean Sea. They had only the most hazy notion of the mysterious lands from which the silks, spices, and other luxuries came. Very few of them had ever traveled so far from home. But Marco Polo, of Venice, was an exception. He followed the overland trade routes to Asia in 1271 and spent many years there. When he returned to Italy, he wrote a book about the Far East. In it he described China as a land of great cities and much wealth. Japan, said Marco Polo, was an island off the coast of Asia that had an immense amount of gold—so much that the roof, floors, and ceilings of the emperor's palace were covered with it. He described the many other islands near the coast of Asia where spices and jewels were abundant.

When they read about the exciting travels of the young Venetian, some Europeans could not believe the amazing story. Others, however, were eager to get to the Far East in order to see its wonders and to share in its fabulous wealth. By 1450 men who studied geography believed that the best way to reach Asia directly was by sea.

New inventions help explorers. At that time, however, to look for a sea route from Europe to Asia required great courage. It is true that several new inventions had made sea travel safer. Sea captains had learned to use the compass. With its miraculous needle, they could tell in what direction they were traveling. They had other instruments to tell where a ship was at any moment

Ignorance and knowledge. Sailors of the 1400s (*above*), in their ignorance, were afraid of the ocean. They told fanciful tales of boiling seas and monsters that swallowed ships. Modern seamen (*below*), thanks to scientific knowledge, embark on long ocean voyages as confidently as you go to and from school.

—how far north or south of the equator or how far east or west of a particular place. They were learning more about using maps, and more accurate maps were being made for them.

But in spite of these helps, most people of Europe still feared the unknown. In their imaginations they had filled the unexplored parts of the world with dangers of all kinds, including boiling seas and monsters that devoured sailors and maybe whole ships. Sailors were afraid to sail far from familiar shores into unknown waters. Thus superstition and fear held back progress, as they always do.

Just the same, the reward would be great. The country that found a sea route to Asia would become rich and powerful. Its merchants would bring silks and spices to sell to the other countries for gold. With the gold it would build a larger army and navy. It would become the strongest nation in Europe. Men in every country of western Europe were eager for their nation to be the first to find a sea route to Asia.

The Portuguese sail around Africa. In the 1400s Portugal was ahead in the race to find a sea route to the East. For this success the Portuguese could thank Prince Henry, a member of the ruling family. He was called "the Navigator" because he had established a training school for seamen. After their training many of these seamen explored the unknown oceans. One after another they ventured farther and farther along the west coast of Africa, trying to sail around that continent and on to the East. In 1486 one of them, named Bartholomew Dias (dē′ăs), sailed around the Cape of Good Hope. He would have gone on to India, but his frightened men refused to go farther and he had to turn back.

Twelve years later another Portuguese, Vasco da Gama (dȧ gä′mȧ), reached India by this route and brought back to Portugal a valuable cargo of silks, spices, jewels, and rugs. Thereafter Portugal became rich from its Far Eastern trade. Notice that Vasco da Gama reached India in 1498, six years after Columbus's first voyage.

Columbus sails west. While the Portuguese were still feeling their way along the coast of Africa, a tall, redheaded sailor from Genoa was trying to interest the king of Portugal in a plan. It was a plan that the sailor had been turning over in his mind for a long time. If someone would supply him with ships, he said, he would reach the Spice Islands and China and Japan with their fabulous wealth by a water route. But he would not sail eastward; he would sail to the west.

Failing to interest the Portuguese king in his plan, Christopher Columbus moved on to Spain. There the Spanish queen, Isabella, after much hesitation finally agreed to help raise the money for ships and men to carry out Columbus's plan.

On August 3, 1492, three tiny ships—the *Niña,* the *Pinta,* and the *Santa Maria*—sailed out of the harbor of Palos (pä′lōs), Spain. Columbus was in command. On September 9 the ships sailed out of sight of known land and into the unknown and uncharted ocean.

For 30 days the fleet moved westward. The farther they sailed, the more frightened the sailors became. On October 10 they refused to sail farther, but

THE NEW-YORK HISTORICAL SOCIETY, NEW YORK CITY

"Look! Is that land?" Columbus and his men, in unknown seas, eagerly watch for land. These figures were made by John Rogers, popular American sculptor of the late 1800s.

Columbus persuaded them to give him a little more time. The three days he asked for proved to be enough. At 2 A.M. on Friday, October 12, 1492, the small cannon on the prow of the *Pinta* boomed. Sailors on the other ships cheered as they saw a pennant raised to the top of the *Pinta's* mast. This was the signal that a sailor had seen land. In the distance the dim moonlight shone on a line of white surf where the sea beat against sand.

When daylight came, Columbus went ashore on what proved to be an island. He took possession of it in the name of the king and queen of Spain. He named the place San Salvador, which means "Holy Saviour."

The greatest voyage. Columbus had completed his greatest voyage. But he did not realize how truly great it was. He did not know that he had discovered two new continents. He believed that he had landed on one of the islands called the Indies, which lie off the coast of Asia. Therefore he called the red-skinned people that he found there Indians. Today we call them American Indians to distinguish them from the people of India.

Columbus was bitterly disappointed that he did not find the gold and spices that Marco Polo and others had said were plentiful in the Indies. After a few days he set sail again to look for Japan and the mainland of Asia, which he was sure were near. Remembering Marco Polo's story, he hoped to see the golden palace of the Japanese emperor. He carried with him a letter from the king and queen of Spain to the ruler of China and he wished to deliver it. How could he know that Asia was still far off? Sailing from San Salvador, he discovered a number of other islands, including Cuba and Haiti. Leaving Haiti, he turned back to Spain to tell the queen that he had reached the Indies by sailing west.

Columbus made three more voyages, during which he sailed along the coast of South and Central America. When he died in 1506, he still believed that he had reached Asia.

The Line of Demarcation. The voyages of Columbus started a great rivalry between Spain and Portugal. Spanish spies reported to their king that the Portuguese were sending a fleet to take over the islands that Columbus had found. The king asked the Pope to decide the ownership of the new lands. The Pope did so by drawing on the map a north-south dividing line, called the Line of Demarcation. In the Western Hemisphere the line, as finally agreed on by the two countries, ran 370 miles west of the Azores (*ȧ* zōrz′). All discovered lands east of that line were to belong to Portugal; all west of it, to Spain. Since Brazil was east of the line, it became a colony of Portugal. The Line of Demarcation, however, did not prevent other nations from making voyages of discovery and claiming ownership of parts of the New World.

2 *Europeans Explore the New World*

After a great man has shown the way to a new world or to a new idea, many others will follow his lead and reveal the full importance of his discovery. So it was with Columbus. His voyages had shown the Europeans that their superstitious fears about ocean monsters were silly. After he had crossed the Atlantic Ocean, the countries of western Europe sent out many expeditions to explore the New World. At first the explorers were not much interested in the lands that Columbus had found. They were searching for a short route to the wealth of Asia. Sailing up and down the Atlantic coast, they turned the prows of their little vessels into every bay and harbor, looking for a waterway to Asia through or around the New World. They were unaware that the continents of North and South America blocked their way. It took many years and many expeditions by sea and by land to reveal how big the New World really is.

Ponce de León discovers Florida. Using the islands of the Caribbean (kăr ĭ bē′*ă*n) as a base, the Spaniards explored the American mainland. Several captains who had sailed under Columbus undertook voyages of their own. They sailed their ships along the coast line of South America, looking for gold and pearls. One of these captains, Ponce de León (pŏns′ dē lē′*ŭ*n), conquered Puerto Rico for Spain. There an Indian told him a story of an island on which there was a magic fountain. According to the story, if an elderly person drank from that fountain, he became young again. Ponce de León was over 50 years old at the time and was eager to be young again. In 1513 he set out in search of the Fountain of Youth. Landing on what he thought was an island, he named it Florida. Here he looked for the famous fountain, but never found it. On his second voyage to Florida eight years later, Ponce de León was killed by Indians. He was one of many Spaniards who were to meet the same fate in the New World.

Balboa discovers the Pacific Ocean. In 1509 a large number of gold-seeking Spaniards tried to make a settlement on the coast of Central America. Most of them died of hunger or from poisoned Indian arrows. Vasco Nuñez de Balboa (băl bō′*ȧ*) took command of the survivors. Organizing them as a fighting force, he conquered the neighboring Indians and compelled them to bring him gold. One day Balboa's men were weighing gold brought by conquered Indians. The son of an Indian chief suddenly struck the scales, scattering the gold.

"Why do you bother with this little gold?" he asked, according to the story. "In that direction," he said, pointing

Strait of Magellan. Magellan's ships fight their way through the strait later named for him. Does the artist make you feel that the ships were tossed about by violent storms?

south, "lies a great ocean. On its shore there is a land that has more gold than Spain has iron."

A short time later Balboa set out to find that ocean and the golden land. You can follow his route on the map on page 18. In weeks of desperate effort, he and his men, cutting a path through 60 miles of jungle, sweated and fought their way across the Isthmus of Panama. On September 26, 1513, Balboa climbed a hill and looked down upon a vast expanse of water, which he called the South Sea. It was what we now know as the Pacific Ocean. Reaching the shore, he waded into the water and took possession of the sea and all the lands that bordered on it for the king of Spain.

Balboa could scarcely wait to start his search for the rich country that he had been told about. But before he could sail, he was arrested by order of the Spanish governor of Panama. Balboa was accused of plotting against the government and was executed. But the story of the golden land had spread like wildfire. Soon Spaniards were searching for it along the entire western coast line of the Americas.

Magellan's expedition circles the globe. Before many years passed, Spanish ships crossed the Pacific Ocean. In 1519 Ferdinand Magellan set out from Spain with five old, unseaworthy ships. He hoped to find what Columbus had looked for—a westward sea route to Asia. He followed the coast of South America southward until he discovered the strait that is named for him. After six weeks of perilous sailing through storms and the floating ice of the strait, he came out upon the Pacific Ocean. One of his ships had been wrecked; another had deserted. The three remaining vessels sailed over the Pacific for 98 days, but there was no sight of land. Little did Magellan realize that the ocean he was exploring covered a third of the globe. Food gave out, and the

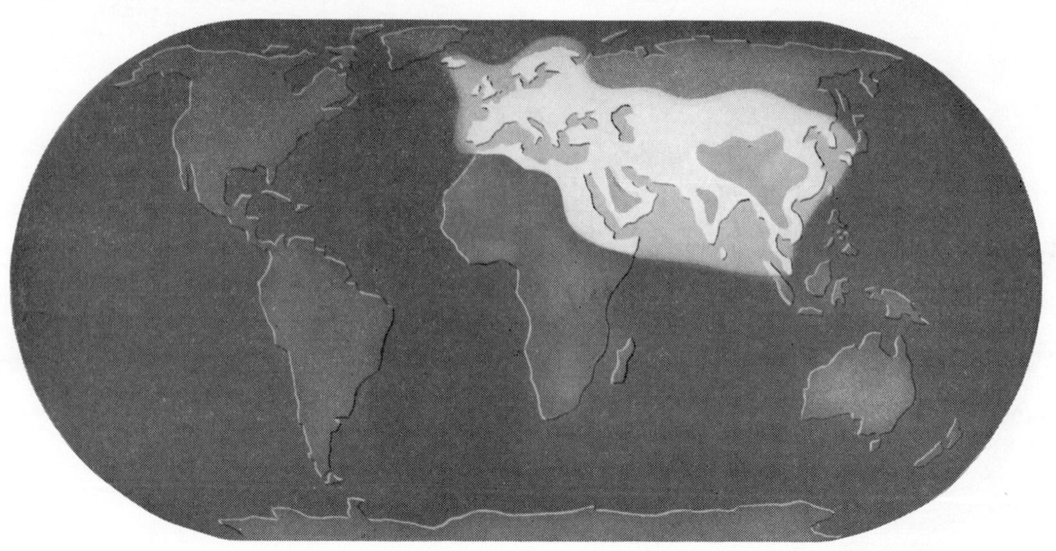

Explorers throw light on the world. These maps show how Europeans came to know more and more of the world. In the time of Marco Polo (*above*), Europeans knew only Europe, part of Asia, and northern Africa. By 1498 (*below*), the Portuguese had sailed around Africa and Columbus had discovered America. The shadow had been pushed back, and Europeans knew a larger part of the world.

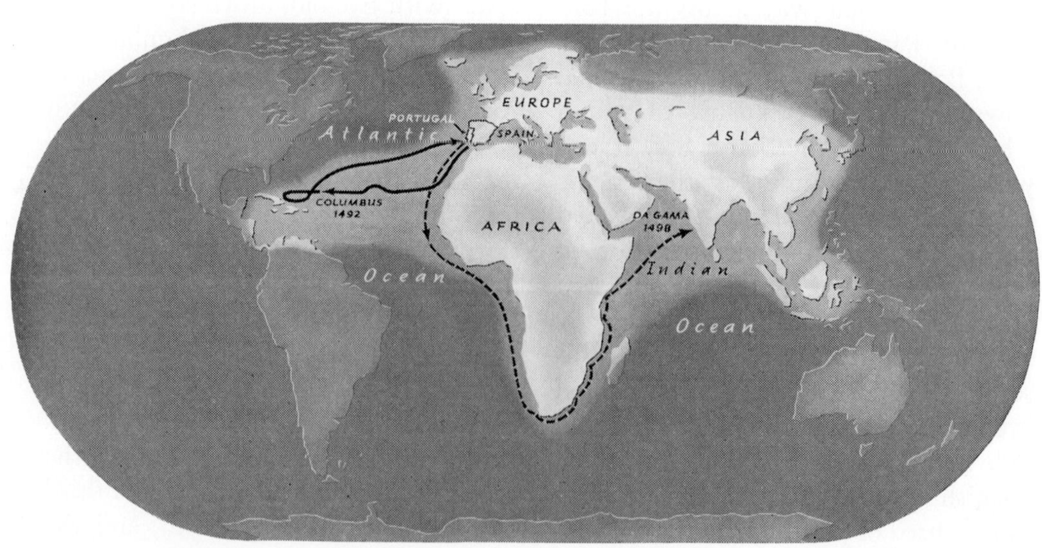

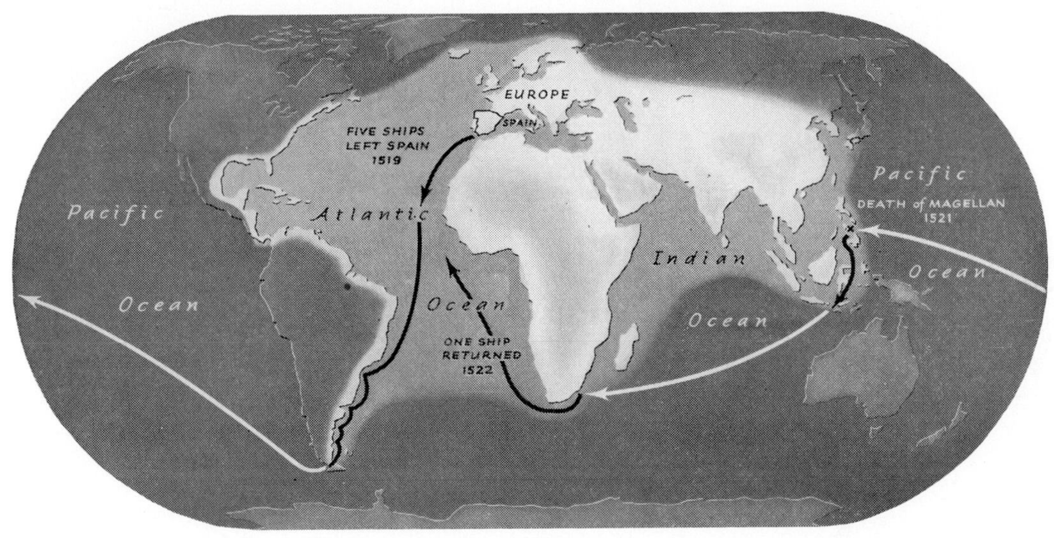

By the time of Magellan's voyage (*above*), European explorers had brought the entire Atlantic coast line of America into the light. And circumnavigation of the globe proved that the world was round. By 1580, after Drake's voyage around the earth (*below*), the known world was much bigger. Notice, however, that most of North America was still unknown.

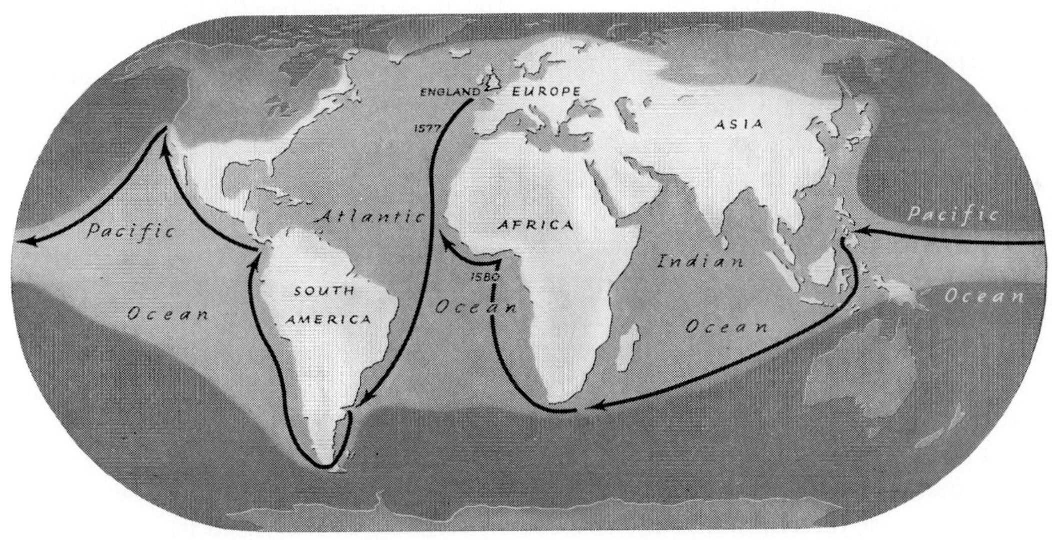

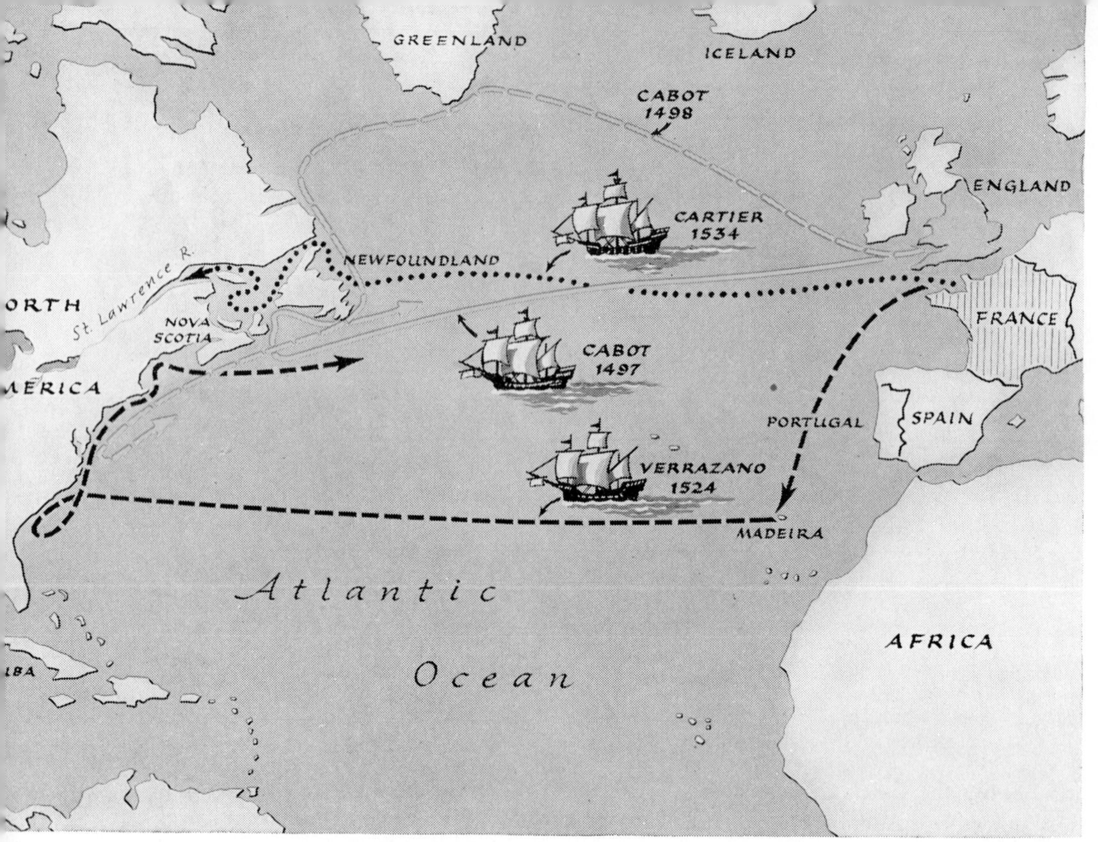

Early explorers of the North Atlantic. What country sponsored each of the voyages shown? What was the importance of each?

men ate sawdust and chewed leather to keep alive. Many died of scurvy, a sickness caused by lack of vitamins in the diet. Finally the three leaking ships reached the islands that are now called the Philippines. Here, in a battle with the natives, Magellan and a number of his officers were killed. The survivors sailed in two ships to the Spice Islands. There the one vessel that remained seaworthy took on a cargo of spices and followed the Portuguese route around Africa. (See map on page 13.)

In September, 1522, with a crew of 18 exhausted men, after a voyage of three long years, the one surviving ship got back to Spain. Thus ended the first voyage to circumnavigate (sûr kŭm-năv′ĭ gāt), or travel around, the globe. It proved once and for all that the earth is round. It proved that Asia could be reached by sailing west. It proved that the land discovered by Columbus was not Asia but a new world.

John Cabot discovers the mainland of North America for England. Spanish explorers continued to learn more and more about the Caribbean islands and Central and South America. At the same time, other nations hired explorers to sail farther north in search of a way to the East that would be shorter than Magellan's. The plan was to find a water route through North America or around it to the northwest and so reach the riches of the Far East.

John Cabot, like Columbus, was born in Genoa. He was hired by a group of

Hudson's voyages. What parts of America did the Dutch and the English claim as a result of Hudson's voyages? Did he succeed in the main purpose of his explorations?

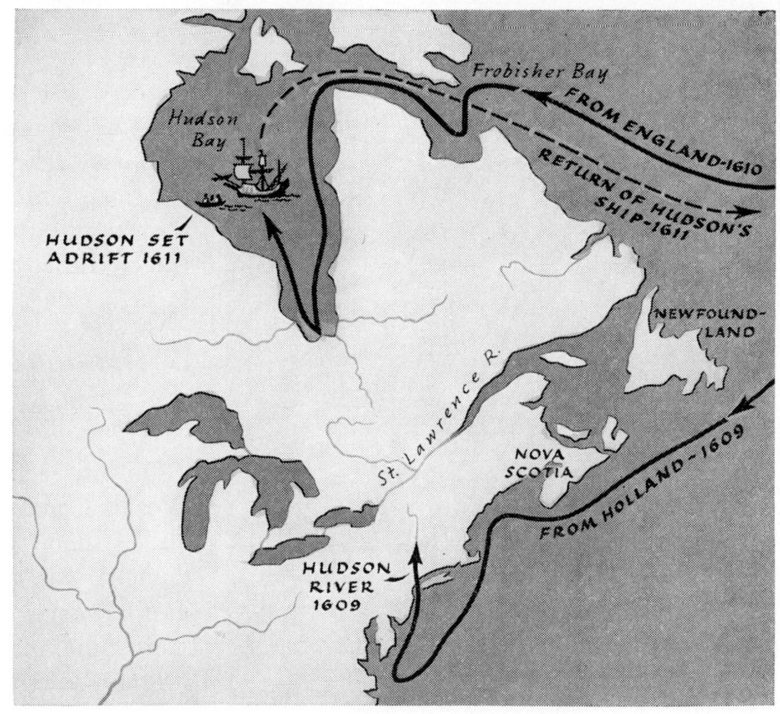

merchants of Bristol, England, to make a voyage to the New World. The merchants hoped to make their city a center of trade with the Far East. In 1497, in a small ship manned by a crew of 18, Cabot crossed the North Atlantic. He sailed along the North American coast from Newfoundland to Nova Scotia and then returned home. He did not find the wealth of Asia. He found only snow and ice, a wild, wooded shore, and some strange-looking people who painted their faces and bodies. The next year he came back with four ships and sailed farther south. (See map on page 14.) But he found no passage to the East.

Cartier discovers the St. Lawrence River for France. Giovanni Verrazano (vär rä tsä′nō), exploring for France, sailed along the coast of North America in 1524. Ten years later a Frenchman named Jacques Cartier (kär′tyā) discovered the St. Lawrence River. The next year he tried, but failed, to establish a settlement where Quebec now stands. The cold winters and scurvy discouraged the settlers and they returned to France. A few years later Cartier again attempted to make a settlement, and again he failed. More than 60 years passed before another French explorer came to the St. Lawrence.

Henry Hudson explores for Holland and England. In 1609 the Dutch sent Henry Hudson, an Englishman, to look for a water route to Asia. (See map on this page.) He crossed the North Atlantic and, entering what is now New York Harbor, sailed his ship the *Half Moon* 150 miles up the Hudson River.

The next year, on a voyage for the English, Henry Hudson braved the icebergs of the North Atlantic to discover Hudson Bay. He explored its shore line and spent a winter on land. It was a bitter winter for his men. They were wet, cold, and hungry. The next spring they

FLORIDA STATE NEWS BUREAU

Relic of the conquistadors. Castillo de San Marcos is the oldest standing fort in the United States. It was built by the Spaniards at St. Augustine. Over it have flown the flags of Spain, Great Britain, the Confederacy, and the United States.

wanted to go home, but Hudson insisted on sailing farther west along the rocky shore. The crew mutinied and set him, his son, and several others adrift in a small boat to perish.

Thus a procession of courageous explorers from several European nations followed Columbus to the New World in one adventurous voyage after another. In these pages only a few of them have been mentioned. While searching for a new route to Asia, they explored the entire Atlantic coast line of the Americas and sailed up the great waterways that lead into the continents. Each European king claimed the lands that his expeditions discovered. Each country established colonies on the coast and along the rivers. From these colonies settlers began to explore the interior of the New World. Little did they imagine the extent and richness of the land that lay waiting for them.

3 *Spaniards Conquer a Great American Empire*

On his second voyage to the New World, Columbus started a settlement on the island of Haiti. In 1496 this settlement was moved to where Ciudad Trujillo (syōō dhädh′ trōō hē′yō) now stands, making that city the oldest European settlement in the New World.

Using Haiti as a base, the Spaniards spread over neighboring islands and onto the mainlands of North and South America. A number of hardy adventurers called conquistadors (kŏn kwĭs′-tȧ dôrz), conquerors, won a huge empire for Spain in the New World. Their conquests extended from Argentina to California. From this empire they sent large quantities of gold, silver, pearls, and other wealth to Spain.

Cortes conquers Mexico. One of the most brilliant of the conquistadors was Hernando Cortes (kôr′tĕz). The governor of Cuba chose him to lead an expedition to what is now Mexico. The governor had heard rumors that Indians of great wealth lived in that part of North America. In 1519 Cortes landed on the coast of Mexico with about 600 Spanish troops, a number of muskets and small cannon, and 16 horses. Some additional Spanish soldiers arrived later. With his small force Cortes conquered the great Aztec (ăz′-

tĕk) empire with its 100,000 people, powerful army, and cities of stone towers and temples.

How was that bold victory possible? The Spaniards had several advantages over the Indians. Their steel swords and their cannon that shot round stones were much better weapons than the Aztec arrows and slingshots. The Indians had never seen horses before and were terrified by soldiers on horseback. They thought the horses were monsters with human bodies growing out of their backs. Some of the Indians believed that Cortes was a god and were afraid of him. Furthermore, when he landed on the coast, Cortes found Indian tribes that were forced to pay heavy taxes to the Aztecs. When he promised to free them of their taxes, they gladly became his allies and helped the Spaniards defeat the Aztecs.

In spite of these advantages, however, the Spaniards had no easy time in conquering the Indians. The big battle was fought in the Aztec capital, which stood where Mexico City stands today. Many Spanish soldiers lost their lives in the attacks. But at last the Spaniards captured the city after destroying most of it.

Cortes set up headquarters in the Aztec capital and sent his men to conquer neighboring tribes. They collected gold, silver, and jewels and took charge of gold and silver mines. Before long the Spaniards controlled most of southern Mexico. Cortes divided the land among his Spanish followers and gave each Spaniard a number of Indians as slaves. He sent a part of the booty to the king of Spain. As a reward, the king made him a general and a member of the Spanish nobility. Cortes died in Spain about 25 years after his conquest of Mexico.

LIBRARY OF CONGRESS

De Soto in Florida. This is an imaginary picture of De Soto landing in Florida. Conquistadors brought to the New World horses as well as weapons and other equipment that the Indians had not seen before.

Pizarro wins Peru. Another of the rugged conquistadors was Francisco Pizarro (pĭ zär′ō), who conquered Peru for Spain. Peru was the center of an Inca (ĭng′kȧ) empire that included half of South America. Like the Aztecs, the Incas had developed a superior civilization. Among other things, they had built a system of roads to keep their empire together. Those roads made the Spanish conquest easier.

Pizarro started from Panama. It took him eight years to establish a base on the coast of Peru from which he could march on the Inca capital in the mountains. In November, 1532, he entered the city. There, in a battle that lasted half an hour, 200 Spaniards killed several thousand Indians and took the Inca emperor prisoner. In that one battle the Inca empire fell. Without weapons to match those of the Spaniards and without their ruler to lead them, the people were unable to fight off the newcomers.

The Inca emperor promised a huge ransom for his release. Pizarro agreed. But after the Indians delivered the gold and silver, he had the emperor killed. Pizarro and his men divided the gold and became rich men.

Pizarro had won riches, but he had to spend the rest of his life defending himself against Indian uprisings and threats from Spanish rivals. The city of Lima (lē′mȧ), which he founded in 1535, became one of the important capitals of Spain's colonial empire in America. Pizarro was murdered by enemies less than 10 years after his conquest of Peru.

De Soto and Coronado explore interior North America. Mexico and Peru proved to be rich prizes. Every year these colonies sent millions of dollars' worth of gold and silver to Spain. Spanish conquistadors who came later

Spanish conquerors. Each of the voyages of exploration and conquest shown on this map has an interesting story. How many of the stories can you tell?

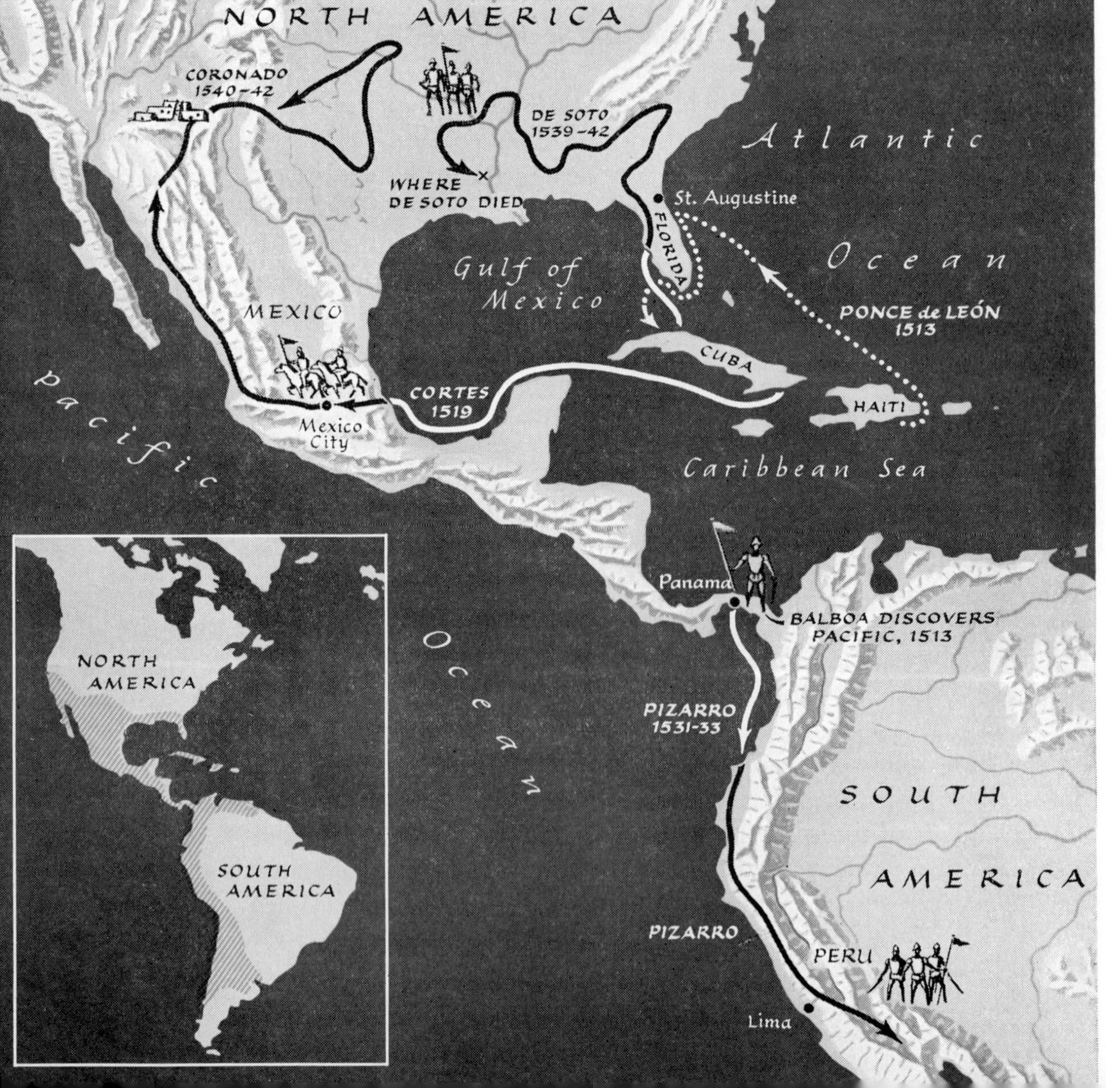

were led on by the hope of finding other places as rich as Mexico and Peru, or even richer. They conquered Central America and most of South America. Two of them, De Soto and Coronado, explored large parts of what is now the United States.

De Soto. Hernando de Soto had served under Pizarro in the conquest of Peru. In 1539 he left Cuba with 600 men and landed in Florida. He planned to explore the interior for gold and hoped to find a waterway to the Pacific. He and his men wandered through most of the present southern states on both sides of the Mississippi River. (See map on page 18.) They found no water route to the Pacific and no gold. Many of the men were killed in fights with the Indians. De Soto took sick and died. Now the Spaniards were in real trouble. They had told the Indians that De Soto was a god. If the Indians found out that he had died, they would know that he had been only a man. Then they would probably kill all the Spaniards. To keep De Soto's death a secret, the men wrapped his body in furs, weighted it with sand, and let it sink into the Mississippi River. They told the Indians that De Soto had gone to the sky for a visit. But their troubles were not over. Only after four years of painful wandering in the wilderness did the survivors of the expedition manage to find their way to a Spanish settlement in Mexico.

Coronado. About this time Francisco Vásquez de Coronado led an expedition north from Mexico. He went into the region now called New Mexico to conquer the Seven Cities of Cibola. The Spaniards had heard that these cities contained vast stores of gold and precious stones, but they turned out to be ordinary Indian villages. The Indians who lived in them were farmers. They watered their fields by irrigation. They lived in well-built adobe (*ȧ* dō′bĭ) houses. They raised cotton for clothing. But they had neither gold nor precious jewels. The Coronado expedition continued the search, going as far north as present-day Kansas before returning to Mexico. As an exploring trip it was remarkable for the amount of territory it covered. But as a search for wealth it was a failure.

After the failures of De Soto and Coronado to find gold, the Spaniards explored and conquered mainly in Mexico and Central and South America. In these regions they continued to find great wealth. They thought of the land north of Mexico as the frontier of the Spanish empire. In this area, from Texas to California, and also in Florida, they built forts and missions for the Indians. Around some of these, agricultural towns grew up. One of them was St. Augustine, Florida, where Spanish colonists in 1565 made the first permanent settlement in what is today the United States.

Summary

The story of the discovery and exploration of the New World is the story of a search for trade and gold. Christopher Columbus hoped to win wealth for himself and for Spain by discovering a westward sea route to Asia. Instead he discovered two new continents. After him, many explorers looked for a water passage through or around the newly discovered lands. While searching, they mapped out the coast lines of the New World and sailed up its rivers into the interior. Magellan circumnavigated the globe.

Spaniards were the first Europeans to settle in the New World. They made their first settlements on the Caribbean islands. Using these islands as bases, they seized Central America. Cortes conquered Mexico and Pizarro won Peru. The conquistadors divided among their followers the immense wealth in gold and silver, the land, and the inhabitants of great Indian empires. De Soto and Coronado led expeditions into the interior of North America, searching for riches. But the survivors of these two explorations returned to Mexico with no gold or silver—only with memories of hardships and tall tales about a strange, wild land. After these failures the Spaniards turned to the job of gathering more and more riches from the lands of South and Central America.

For a Quick Review

1. Why were western Europeans eager to find a new route to Asia? What difficulties did the explorers of the 1400s face?
2. For what explorations do we remember each of the following: Balboa, Cortes, Pizarro, De Soto, Coronado?
3. What other explorers of the New World can you name?
4. What parts of North and South America did the Spaniards eventually control?
5. Which parts of their American possessions did the Spaniards prize most?
6. Why did the Spaniards drop their efforts to explore and occupy a larger part of North America?

Learning to Study More Easily

SOME SPECIAL HELPS FOR YOUR YEAR'S WORK

Books are like people. They are alike in many ways; yet they also differ. For example, this history textbook is like other books in having a title page, a table of contents, and an index. At the same time, this book is different from other books in a number of ways. As you discover its special features, you will be able to get more out of it. Perhaps you have already discovered some unusual features of *The American Adventure*.

The authors have included several features to help you see how various parts of our nation's story fit together. Preceding Chapter 1 you found a preview of Unit 1. You will find a similar account at the beginning of each new unit. (See page 106 for the next one.) The unit preview will give you a general picture, a sort of airplane view, of the unit. Then, as you read each of the chapters that make up the unit, you will be able to fit each event into this picture. If you read the nine previews one after the other, you will have a short short history of our country. Clearly in such a short account you would hit only the high points. You may wish to do that, however, either now for an advance view or at the end of the year for review.

Cross references help you see connections between events. Occasionally, as you read, you will find the words "see page 000." Such a cross reference guides you to an illustration or a paragraph that tells more about the topic under discussion. To get the most out of your reading, take time to look up the cross references.

At the close of each chapter you will find a summary of the important events discussed in the chapter. The summary will help you keep in mind what you read in the chapter.

At the end of each unit you will find a group of suggestions, called High Points of the Unit, to help you tie together related facts and ideas that you have studied. (See page 100 for the first example.)

Other features of the book have different uses.

Following the summary of each chapter you will find a group of questions. These will help you review quickly the information and ideas that you have gathered from reading the chapter.

At the end of each chapter, also, there are sections like this one, Learning to Study More Easily. They contain suggestions that will help you to improve your work in this class. Try them in other classes, too, wherever they fit. They include tips on using books, preparing and giving talks, taking part in class discussions, and doing many other things that are a part of your everyday work. You will have to practice making use of these suggestions, of course. Just reading the learning-to-study sections without actually using them will not help you much toward successful studying.

At the end of each unit you will find a section called Unit Roundup. It contains many suggested activities from which you, consulting with your teacher, may choose. Some of the activities will provide interesting assignments for the entire class; others are more suitable for individuals. Form the habit of checking through these suggested activities as you begin each unit. You can then choose one to be working on while you are studying the unit.

Many books about Americans, their customs, and their lives have been written for people of your age. At the end of each unit in this book you will find the names of some of the best books that tell about America during the years covered by the unit. In the appendix you will find another list of books that cover many periods of our history. This list will be useful for almost every unit.

As you use *The American Adventure,* you will find in it other interesting features—for example, the time line and table of main events after each unit and the maps that have been specially prepared for this book. All these features will help you understand and enjoy *The American Adventure.*

2 *French and English Plant Colonies in North America*

Some years ago a Canadian farm boy was plowing a field. Suddenly the plow scratched metal. The boy pulled on the reins and stopped the horse. Digging into the soil with his fingers, he uncovered several silver cups and copper kettles. He gathered them in his arms and ran home, excited at his find.

It took a long time before the boy learned who had left the cups and kettles there. Important people came from the nearby city to examine them. At last the boy knew the whole story. The cups and kettles had been in the ground for hundreds of years. They were left there by the French explorer Samuel de Champlain in the year 1613.

It seems that Champlain had been in Paris, France, in 1612 getting supplies for his new settlement of Quebec. While he was there, a young fellow named Nicholas Vignau (vē nyō′) arrived from Quebec. Vignau had spent the previous winter with Algonquian (ăl gŏng′kĭ ăn) Indians deep in the Canadian wilderness, and he had an interesting tale to tell. He said that he had reached the northern sea. "You go up the Ottawa River," he told anyone who would listen, "and you come to a lake, and the lake empties into the northern sea." He had seen the wreck of an English ship on the frozen shore of that sea.

The story excited Champlain. He had recently heard of Henry Hudson's discovery of Hudson Bay. Perhaps Vignau had reached the same body of water. Perhaps it would prove to be a water passage to the East. He would go there and claim it for France, and then the French would control all trade that passed between Europe and the Far East!

Vignau told his story to make himself important. He enjoyed being talked about in Paris. He did not expect Champlain to make the hard journey up the Ottawa River. But Champlain took him

The beginnings of New France. Champlain, often called the father of New France, founded Quebec. He also led several early French explorations westward. The dotted lines show his various journeys.

back to Canada, and in the spring of 1613 with three other Frenchmen and an Indian they started up the Ottawa River in canoes.

It was hard traveling. Often the water was so rough that they had to carry the canoes, paddles, clothes, food, and guns on their backs through the thick forests. On one of these carries Champlain decided to lighten his load by leaving some silver cups and copper kettles behind. He buried them and marked the place so that he would be able to find them on the way back.

The party finally reached the Indian village where Vignau had spent the winter. Champlain told the chief he wanted to go on to the northern sea. The chief said it was impossible; the distance was so great that he would never get there.

"But," said Champlain, "Vignau was there the winter before last."

The chief turned to Vignau. "That is not true," he said. "You know very well that every night you slept in my lodge. If you went to the sea, it was in your sleep."

Vignau confessed his lie. Champlain was embarrassed and angry. The Indians wanted to kill Vignau, but Champlain decided that death would be too severe a punishment. Champlain and his companions returned to the St. Lawrence with a large fleet of canoes carrying Algonquins (ăl gŏng′kĭnz) and their furs down to Quebec to trade with the French merchants. Champlain forgot to stop for the silver cups and copper kettles.

1 *The French Explore the Interior of North America*

As French and English explorers worked their way along the North Atlantic coast, they frequently came upon Indians. These natives of the New World were quite different from those

PUBLIC ARCHIVES OF CANADA

Welcome to the New World. In the early days, American Indians warmly welcomed European explorers and traders. They were eager to exchange valuable furs for the white men's cloth and trinkets.

that the Spaniards conquered in Central and South America. The northern Indians did not have permanent cities with stone buildings. They lived in the woods in small villages of bark huts, and they moved their villages to new locations every 20 years or so. From the villages as their headquarters the hunters of each tribe wandered over a large hunting ground in search of game, which provided them with both food and skins. From the skins the Indian women made clothing. In addition to the meat brought home by the hunters, the Indian families lived on corn, beans, and squash, which the women raised.

The northern Indians had no gold, silver, or precious stones. Their most cherished possessions, which they used as money in trading, were strings of sea shells called wampum. They seemed to have nothing that the gold-hungry Europeans could turn into money.

The French find wealth in the fur trade. The northern Indians were not completely without valuable products. John Cabot and other early explorers of North America brought back to Europe reports that the waters off Newfoundland and Nova Scotia swarmed with fish. European fishermen began visiting these American fishing grounds every year. When they landed on the coast to dry and salt their catches, they met Indians. These Indians were eager to obtain knives, hatchets, kettles, mirrors, blankets, beads, pieces of cloth, and other articles that the fishermen brought with them. Such articles the Indians did not know how to make. To them, mirrors in which they could see their faces were magical. They were attracted by the bright colors and the warmth of European cloth and blankets. The white men's hatchets and other iron products were far superior to their own stone implements.

In return for these European goods, the Indians traded beaver pelts. When the fishermen returned to Europe, they sold the furs for high prices. From the beaver pelts Europeans manufactured hats and furs for clothing. The pelts were so valuable that French merchants began sending men up the St. Lawrence River to trade with the Indians for them. In northeastern America the treasure that first attracted Europeans was not gold but the beaver pelt.

BUREAU OF PUBLIC ROADS

La Salle pushing to the Mississippi. La Salle is making his way through the winter wilderness to the upper Mississippi River. Note that his party includes an Indian guide and a missionary. The men are carrying their canoe and their packs around a waterfall. Modern highways now run along many of these early portage paths.

In order to make bigger profits from the fur trade, the French started a settlement on the St. Lawrence River. In 1608 Samuel de Champlain brought 18 men to Canada and founded Quebec on a rocky height above the river. There the men could trade with the Indians the year round and collect cargoes of furs for French ships to take home. A second trading place, Montreal, was founded in 1642. It soon became the great center of the fur trade in New France.

Missionaries and trappers. From Montreal and Quebec two kinds of men went out into the woods to live with the Indians. They were the missionaries and the trappers.

French missionaries lived with the Indians, learning their languages and teaching them the Christian religion. Some Indians did not understand the purpose of the missionaries. When the missionaries began teaching that Indian gods were false and Indian ways were wrong, the Indians became angry. They treated the missionaries cruelly and even burned some of them at the stake. But other missionaries arrived from Europe to take the places of those who died. They patiently preached their faith and slowly won over many Indians to Christianity.

The fur trappers were mainly young Frenchmen attracted by the adventurous life of the forest. They wanted to make money from furs. They lived in the woods, where they trapped beaver and other fur-bearing animals. Each spring they led the Indians down to

French trapper. Some Europeans in the New World became fur trappers in the forest.

Montreal to sell furs to the traders at the great fair. (See page 64.)

These trappers were the first of a long line of Europeans who became men of the forest in the New World. They went into the wilderness and learned to live as the Indians did. They put up bark huts for shelter, warmed themselves at the campfire, hunted game and raised corn for food, and made their own clothing out of animal skins and furs. Many of them married Indian girls and were adopted into Indian tribes. They followed the Indian trails through the woods farther and farther into unexplored regions. They were the first pioneers, the trail breakers who showed the way to the settlers who followed. You will come across many more of these woodsmen in the story of the American adventure.

The French explore the Great Lakes and the Mississippi. When Champlain came to the St. Lawrence, he had another purpose in mind besides carrying on the fur trade. Like many other explorers, he hoped to find a water route to the Pacific. When the Indians described Lake Huron to him, he thought it was the Pacific Ocean. When he reached that lake in 1615, he realized his mistake. The French missionaries and fur traders also kept in mind the search for a waterway to the Pacific as they traveled farther west to reach distant Indian tribes. From Lake Huron they entered Lake Superior and Lake Michigan. They were led on still farther by Indian stories of a great river that flowed to a salt sea many miles away. Every trader who heard the river described thought that perhaps this was the river that led to the Pacific. The question to be answered was: does this river flow into the Pacific Ocean or into the Gulf of Mexico?

Marquette and Joliet. In 1673 a missionary named Father Jacques Marquette (mär kĕt′) and a fur trader, Joliet (jō lĭ ĕt′), explored this great river, which we know as the Mississippi. You can trace their route on the map on page 27. They paddled and drifted down its swirling current as far south as the mouth of the Arkansas River. By that time they knew that the Mississippi must empty into the Gulf of Mexico. Since there was no reason to go any farther and run the risk of being taken prisoner by the Spaniards, they turned back.

La Salle. By taking possession of the Mississippi, the French could control the rich interior of North America. The fur trade of the entire continent would be theirs. This was surely worth striving for. One man who thought so was Sieur de La Salle (lȧ săl′), an active, ambitious Frenchman who had come to Montreal as a young man. Accompanied by a few French and Indians, in the spring of 1682 he drifted down the winding brown waters of the Mississippi to the Gulf. Paying no attention to the Spanish claims to the region, he boldly claimed the entire territory drained by the river and all its tributaries for the King of France, Louis XIV. He named the region Louisiana in honor of his monarch.

Two years later La Salle started a colony on the shore of the Gulf of Mexico in the region that is now Texas. His purpose was to gain control of the Gulf. Then he would be able to seize the Spanish silver mines in Mexico in case of a war between the French and the Spaniards. But Fort St. Louis, as the colony was called, was in an isolated place, and the settlers suffered from hunger. While exploring the territory around the colony, La Salle was murdered by his own discontented men. The colony soon disappeared.

Thus the French explored the St. Lawrence River, the Great Lakes, and the Mississippi River. To hold the immense territory drained by these great waterways, they established a series of forts, missions, and trading posts. Their chief interest in the New World was the fur trade.

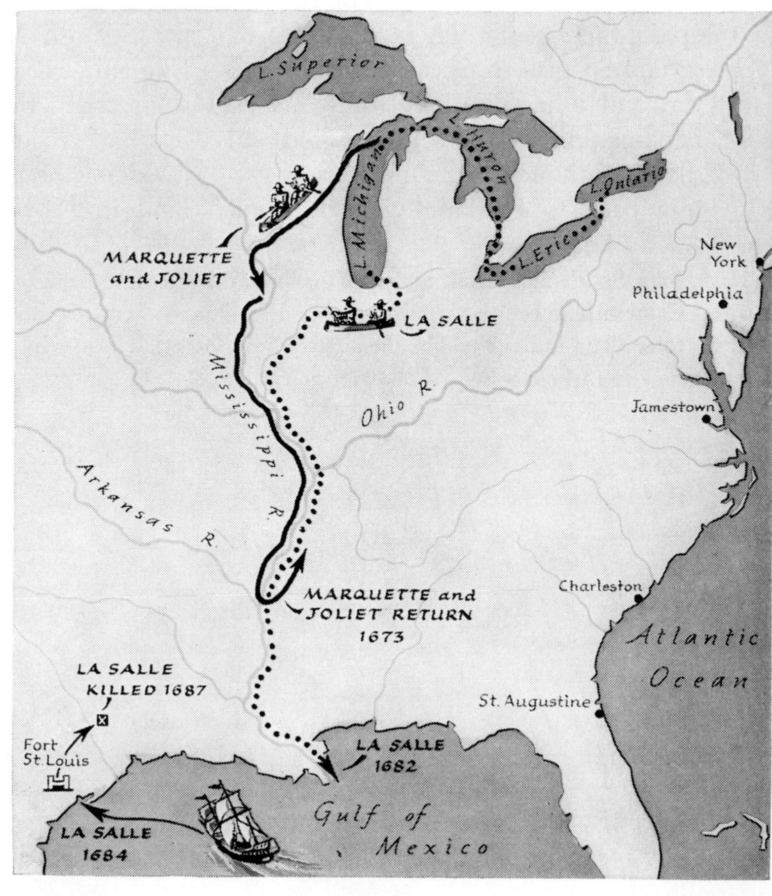

The French explore the Mississippi. Here you can follow the routes of Marquette and Joliet and La Salle. Which of the settlements along the Atlantic coast had been established before Marquette and Joliet reached the Mississippi?

2 *The English Establish Thirteen Colonies*

The Spanish empire in America was so big that Spain was unable to protect it. Even in time of peace, many Englishmen, Frenchmen, and Dutchmen raided settlements in the Spanish colonies and captured Spanish treasure ships in American waters.

Around the world with Drake. One of the most famous of these freebooters was the Englishman Francis Drake. He set out on his greatest voyage from England in 1577. He sailed around South America through the Strait of Magellan and surprised the Spaniards by turning up in the Pacific. There he captured several Spanish ships carrying gold, silver, and other treasure from Peru to Panama. His ship laden with gold and silver, Drake faced the problem of getting back to England without being captured. Since he knew that Spanish warships would be lying in wait for him in the Atlantic, he decided to go home the long way around. He sailed his ship with its valuable cargo up the western coast of North America and struck out across the Pacific. Continuing west through the Indian Ocean and then around the southern tip of Africa, he reached England in 1580. He was the first Englishman to circumnavigate the globe. (See the map on page 13.)

The Spanish king demanded that the English Queen Elizabeth return his treasure and punish Drake. Instead, she took her share of the wealth and made Francis Drake a knight. Partly to end such raids on his colonies and his ships, the Spanish king decided to conquer England. He built a huge fleet of warships called the Spanish Armada. The Spaniards believed that their fleet was invincible. But when it attacked England in 1588, the English navy sank

John Smith makes friends with the Indians. Because he was friendly with the Indians, Captain John Smith was able to obtain food from them for the starving colonists at Jamestown. The Indians taught the settlers how to get along in the New World—for example, how to make a boat by hollowing out a log.

BUREAU OF PUBLIC ROADS

many of the Spanish ships and scattered the rest. With that great victory England won from Spain control of the seas.

Early English settlements in North America fail. The earliest attempts to found English colonies in North America failed. One reason was the trouble with Spain. For example, in 1587 Sir Walter Raleigh sent a group of settlers to Roanoke Island, off the coast of what is now North Carolina. After landing the colonists, the ship returned to England. In England every ship and every sailor were needed to fight the Spanish Armada. Not until 1590 did a ship with supplies reach Roanoke. By that time the settlers had disappeared. No one has ever found out what happened to them. Among those who vanished was Virginia Dare, a little girl born on Roanoke—the first English child born in North America.

Another reason for the failure of the earliest English colonies was that individuals tried to provide all the money needed. The English learned that planting a colony cost more money than one man could supply. To obtain the money needed, they formed companies. A company could sell stock and so collect money from many people. The company would pay the expenses of setting up a colony. The colonists might find gold or they could send to England other products of the New World to be sold. Then the stockholders of the company would share in the profits. Two English colonizing companies were formed—one for Virginia, called the London Company, and one for New England, called the Plymouth Company.

Virginia becomes a tobacco colony. In 1607 the London Company sent a group of colonists to North America. They settled Jamestown in what is now Virginia. That was the first English settlement in the New World that lasted a long time.

The men who started Jamestown did not plan to remain there permanently. They intended to find gold and return home to live as rich men. Instead of growing food to have enough to eat, they immediately began to search for gold. As a result they suffered a great deal. When food from England did not arrive on time, they starved. Furthermore, Jamestown was built on swampy land, and there was no fresh water for drinking. In the summer almost everyone in the colony was sick with malaria or typhoid fever. By the end of the first year more than half of the settlers had died and those who had survived were discouraged. Fortunately, Captain John Smith, who became the leader of the colonists, had made friends with the Indians. They brought corn, fish, and game to the white men. Smith finally had to order the colonists to provide their own food by planting corn and other crops.

The starving time. The settlers of Jamestown had their worst troubles during the winter of 1609–1610, after Captain John Smith had returned to England. That period was known as the starving time. The settlers were hungry, sick, and cold. By this time the Indians, not always well treated by the settlers, had become less friendly. Rather than helping, they attacked the colonists every chance they got. The settlement was almost wiped out. Of

PLIMOTH PLANTATION, INC.

Pilgrim home. Houses in early Plymouth looked like this modern reconstruction. The boards were hewn from logs by hand. Notice the steep thatched roof.

Indian friendship. When white men were friendly to the Indians and treated them fairly, they in turn became loyal friends. That was the experience of Roger Williams and of many other settlers.

400 men only 60 were still alive in the spring. The survivors decided to give up the colony and go home. They were actually on their way down the James River when they met ships bringing supplies, a new governor, and more colonists. The old and new settlers returned to Jamestown and the colony was saved.

Thereafter Jamestown grew, slowly but surely. The early settlers became accustomed to the climate. They raised more food. Women and children arrived from England, and the settlers built homes for them. A real community grew up. New colonists started other settlements nearby. Thus Virginia became the first permanent English colony in America.

Tobacco. Though the firstcomers had hoped to find gold and return to England, Virginia became an agricultural colony. In Jamestown, as elsewhere in the New World, colonists learned many things from the Indians. One of the most important was how to grow tobacco. When the first tobacco had been brought to Europe from America, Sir Walter Raleigh had made its use fashionable in the English royal court. The people of Europe bought more and more of it.

John Rolfe, who married Princess Pocahontas, learned how to improve the taste of Virginia tobacco and sold his crop in London at a high price. Soon everyone in Jamestown was growing tobacco. So important did tobacco become that it was used as money. Virginians paid public officials, teachers, and ministers their salaries in tobacco. The people paid their taxes in tobacco instead of money.

The Pilgrims settle Plymouth. You have just read that the first settlers of Jamestown came to America with the hope of finding gold and returning to England to enjoy their wealth. The pioneers of the other English colonies came to the New World with the purpose of making their homes here. Many of them belonged to small religious groups that were persecuted in the Old World. They came to America to be free to worship as they believed. All of them hoped to make a better living in America than they had made in Europe.

In northern England, in the early 1600s, there was a group of poor farmers who refused to worship in the Church of England, the official church in that country. Because they organized their own church and worshiped separately from the members of the English church, they were called Separatists. They were frequently punished for their religious beliefs. They fled to Holland in 1607 to be free to worship in their own way. After more than 10 years in Holland, they became dissatisfied with life there and decided to move to North America. We know them today as Pilgrims because they wandered from place to place in search of a permanent home.

Sailing from England in the *Mayflower,* about a hundred Pilgrims reached the shore of New England. They knew that after they landed they would have no government to keep order. While still on board ship, therefore, all the men signed an agreement to make their own laws and obey them. This agreement is known as the Mayflower Compact. Again and again, in later years, groups of pioneers in the West would find themselves without governments. And, like the Pilgrims, they would set up governments of their own, which they promised to obey.

PUBLIC BUILDINGS ADMINISTRATION

Puritan explorers. Puritan settlers rapidly spread over New England, exploring and settling. This painting in the post office at Holyoke, Massachusetts, shows a group of them in the Connecticut River Valley.

The Pilgrims landed at what is now Plymouth in December, 1620. As at Quebec and Jamestown, the first winter at Plymouth was a time of suffering and death. After that, however, the Pilgrims got along more easily. They made friends with the Indians and signed a treaty with them that remained unbroken for more than 50 years. The Indians taught them how to keep alive in the wilderness—how to grow corn and how to fish and hunt. Seventy years after it was founded, Plymouth became part of the larger colony of Massachusetts Bay.

The Puritans in Massachusetts Bay. The colony of Massachusetts Bay was settled by Puritans from England. Like the Pilgrims, the Puritans were not satisfied with the Church of England. But they continued to belong to that church, hoping to change it. For many years the English government allowed

Geography influenced early English settlement. Locate each settlement that is named on the inset list. Which are near the seacoast? Which are inland on rivers? Why did the settlements spread along the coastal plain instead of pushing far into the West?

the Puritans to worship as they wished. But in the 1620s the government began to compel everyone to worship exactly as the bishops of the Church of England ordered. Puritan ministers were not allowed to preach. Puritans who held government positions were discharged. Puritans were forbidden to practice law.

A group of Puritans decided to settle in New England. There they planned to set up the kind of church they believed in. In the New World they hoped to be able to live and earn a living without the disadvantages that they suffered at home. Many of them were well-to-do people. Some of their leaders were rich enough to bring servants with them. Some, including the ministers, were university graduates. Salem was settled as early as 1626. In June and July, 1630, about a thousand Puritan colonists reached Massachusetts Bay and settled on the coast. The largest settlement they named Boston. It became the capital of the colony.

The Puritans started towns up and down the coast and inland along the rivers. In many cases a group of 50 or 60 neighbors arrived from England together with their minister to establish their own town and church. To such a group the government of the colony gave a piece of land. Their leaders divided the land among the settlers. The houses were built around a town square. Each family had a garden lot of about half a dozen acres close to its house and a much larger farm farther out. Land not given to anyone was held in common and was generally used as pasture. That is how the New England town started.

Roger Williams founds Rhode Island. The leaders of Massachusetts Bay insisted that all churches in the colony carry on worship in the same way. They forbade any person to express ideas different from the official ones. But many settlers refused to obey such laws. Some returned to England; others left Massachusetts Bay and made new settlements nearby. In this way several other New England colonies were started. By the harsh policies of its leaders, the Massachusetts Bay colony lost some of its most active, independent citizens.

A young minister named Roger Williams came to Massachusetts in 1631. He soon began to disagree with the leaders of the colony. For example, he denied that the English government had the right to give the Indians' land to settlers. He believed that the colony should pay the Indians for it. Williams also insisted that the government should not force a person to attend one church or another but rather should leave every individual free to worship in his own way. Today we in the United States enjoy freedom of religion. In Roger Williams's time, however, it was not allowed in most European countries or in their American colonies.

The Puritan leaders of Massachusetts Bay would stand for no differences of opinion. They warned Roger Williams to stop expressing his views. When he continued to speak his mind, he was banished from the colony. In January, 1636, he made his way south through the heavy snows to friendly Indians. He bought land from the Indians. With a handful of friends who believed as he did, he settled Providence, now the capital of Rhode Island. Williams and his friends established a democratic community. In the new settlement all men had equal rights. Everyone was free to worship in his own way. Everyone was free to express his ideas.

Roger Williams was not the only person who was dissatisfied with the lack of freedom in the Puritan colony. Anne Hutchinson was another. Her religious views, which she freely expressed, were different from those of most Puritans. Fearing that others would take up her beliefs, the authorities ordered her to leave Boston. At first she went to Providence to live. Later she and her husband with a group of friends founded the nearby settlements of Portsmouth and Newport. These two settlements and Providence were united in 1643 to form the colony of Rhode Island.

New Hampshire. Reverend John Wheelwright was still another who was forced to leave Massachusetts Bay. He was Anne Hutchinson's brother-in-law and believed in her religious ideas. In 1638 he, with others, founded Exeter, New Hampshire. The first settlement in what is now New Hampshire had been made 15 years earlier at present-day Portsmouth.

Connecticut. Connecticut also was settled by people who were dissatisfied with the government of Massachusetts Bay. In May, 1636, Reverend Thomas Hooker and his congregation of about a hundred persons started out from Cambridge, Massachusetts. They followed Indian trails overland to the Connecticut River, driving their livestock before them and sleeping out in the open. After about two weeks they reached the place where Hartford now stands and settled there. Soon other settlements were made along the river and on nearby Long Island.

New York. As the English spread into the Connecticut Valley and Long Island, they clashed with the Dutch who were already there. The Dutch claimed the land east and west of the Hudson River on the basis of Henry Hudson's discovery of the river in 1609 (see page 15). They had established a lively fur-trading post at what is now Albany and had made a settlement on Manhattan Island. They had started other settlements on Long Island and up the Hudson. The entire colony was called New Netherland.

England, however, also claimed the land on which the Dutch had settled. In 1664 Charles II granted to his brother, the Duke of York, the entire territory between the Connecticut River and the Delaware River. England and Holland were at war at the time. Four English warships entered what is now New York Harbor and demanded the surrender of the Dutch colony. Peter Stuyvesant (stī′vĕ s'nt), the peppery Dutch governor, stomped about on his wooden leg and threatened to fight. But the people refused to support him. The Dutch company that owned the colony had not treated them well. They also felt that Stuyvesant had been a harsh governor. The English took control without firing a shot. They gave the name New York to the colony and also to the principal settlement at the southern tip of the island of Manhattan.

New Jersey. To pay a debt, the Duke of York turned over to two of his friends, Sir William Berkeley and Sir George Carteret, the part of his land that is now the state of New Jersey. They divided it between them. English settlers soon joined the Dutch and Swedish colonists who were already there.

Maryland. Roman Catholics, like Puritans, were persecuted in England and in some other European countries. Lord Baltimore, a Catholic English nobleman, established Maryland as a place where Catholics would be able to live in peace and be free to worship in their own way. In 1633 he sent the first settlers to the colony.

Lord Baltimore wanted the Catholics in his colony to enjoy religious freedom. He was also eager to attract more settlers to Maryland. To provide religious freedom and to attract settlers, he persuaded the legislature of the colony to pass the Toleration Act in 1649. According to this law, any Christian, whether Catholic or non-Catholic, had the right to worship God in the way he believed he should. Thus Maryland, like Rhode Island, took a great step toward religious freedom. Puritans, Quakers, Episcopalians, and members of other churches settled in Maryland. Soon they outnumbered the Catholic settlers and for a time denied freedom of worship to Roman Catholics.

North and South Carolina. In 1663 the king of England granted the Carolinas to a group of his friends. Seven years later the owners sent the first boatload of English settlers to South Carolina. Other early settlers came from older English colonies in the West Indies. Charleston soon became the most important settlement. People from Virginia made the first settlements in what is now North Carolina. These settlements were near the coast in the region called Albemarle. The two groups of settlers were so far apart that each had a separate government.

Pennsylvania. William Penn had learned the religious beliefs of the Quakers while he was a student at Oxford University. The Quakers taught that religion was a personal matter, something a person felt inside himself. There was no need for church ceremonies. The best way to worship was to sit silently and think about God. All men, the Quakers said, should be able to live together in peace and happiness. They believed it was wrong to take an oath or to fight in a war. They considered all men equal; and to show their equality, they refused to take their hats off to anyone.

Because they were so different from people of other religions, the Quakers were persecuted in almost all the countries of Europe. Like many other persons before and since his time, Penn knew that the New World was a place to which people could go to escape persecution. He decided to establish a colony in America in which Quakers and other persecuted people could live in freedom. Charles II had owed Penn's father a large sum of money. In pay-

Cave shelters. Some of the earliest settlers of Philadelphia lived in caves in the riverbanks until they could build houses.

LIBRARY OF CONGRESS

Philadelphia in 1702. Twenty years after the first settlers had dug cave shelters, Philadelphia was a bustling place with many homes and streets and wharves.

LIBRARY OF CONGRESS

ment of this debt, Penn accepted the land that is now Pennsylvania. The name means "Penn's woods."

In 1681 Penn sent the first Quaker settlers to his colony. They made their homes among Swedish and Dutch people already there. Penn himself came to the colony in 1682 and remained for two years. Because he and the members of his colony treated the Indians fairly, there was no warfare between Indians and whites for 70 years.

Pennsylvania prospered from the start. Penn advertised it all over western Europe. Swedes, Dutch, Welsh, and Germans, as well as Englishmen, settled in the colony. Within a few years Philadelphia (where Penn himself had laid out the streets) became a large town with many brick and stone houses.

Delaware. The first settlements in the colony of Delaware were made by people from Sweden. Later many Dutch settled among them. However, the land was claimed by England and was included in the grant made by the king to William Penn. That is why the governors of Pennsylvania governed Delaware until 1776, when it became a separate state.

Georgia. Georgia was the thirteenth colony to be founded by the English on the mainland of North America. It was established in 1732 by James Oglethorpe. In England at the time, people who could not pay their debts were put in prison. Oglethorpe wanted to start a colony where such poor persons could start life over again. He persuaded the king to make a grant of land on which to build a colony for debtors. The colony was named Georgia in the king's honor. Oglethorpe himself led the first group of 130 settlers to their new home.

At Savannah they set to work erecting shelters and clearing fields. A few years later a fort was built at Augusta. Although the colony had been founded for debtors, few of the colonists after the first shipload actually were debtors. Oglethorpe's generous dream and his personal sacrifices failed to do much for the poor people whom he tried to help. But Georgia grew, along with the other English colonies.

3 *The English Colonies Expand to the Appalachians*

Trace the Atlantic coast line of our country on the map on page 32. See how irregular it is. That coast line made it possible for the English to establish their string of colonies on the Atlantic seaboard. The small vessels of the 1600s and 1700s could unload passengers and freight only where they were protected from winds and storms. In the Gulf of St. Lawrence, Cape Cod Bay, Long Island Sound, Delaware Bay, and Chesapeake Bay, as well as in the many harbors along the coast, ship captains found the shelter that they needed for their vessels.

The numerous rivers that flow into the Atlantic were even more helpful. The forests in the New World were so thick that overland travel was just about impossible. The colonists had to depend upon the waterways for transportation. The rivers were ready-made, natural highways through the impassable wilderness.

Early colonists remain near the Tidewater. In the southern colonies—that is, those south of Pennsylvania—settlers moving inland found that for some distance the rivers are broad and quiet. Their waters rise and fall with the ocean tides, as if they were arms of the sea reaching into the land. At a certain point in each river, the quiet water gives way to waterfalls and rapids. Above the waterfall the river is a swift stream with a one-way current rushing to the sea.

This change in the streams, from the quiet water near the sea to the swift water farther inland, corresponds to a change in the land itself. Where the rivers rise and fall as the tide moves in and out, the land is low and level and is called the Tidewater. Where the rivers flow one way, the land is hilly and is called the Piedmont. The imaginary line between the Tidewater and the Piedmont is called the "fall" line, meaning the line where the rivers break into waterfalls and rapids.

In the early years of settlement, colonists stuck close to the Atlantic coast and to the banks of the rivers in the Tidewater. The Atlantic was their highway to Europe, their link with civilization, and they did not wish to lose contact with it. Since the small vessels of the seventeenth century could sail up the rivers as far as the fall line, settlers along the Tidewater felt as close to Europe as those who lived on the coast. But above the fall line only canoes and small boats could be used. Anyone who settled above the fall line left behind him the ocean and the ships that sailed the ocean. In other words, he was in a way breaking contact with home.

This geography of the Atlantic seaboard explains why the early colonists did not settle above the fall line. They preferred to spread along the coast and

HISTORICAL COMMISSION OF CHARLESTON, S.C.

French Huguenot church. Services are still held regularly in this Huguenot church in Charleston, South Carolina. It reminds us of the French settlers who fled religious persecution in Europe.

A farm of their own! As soon as the official signs that paper giving them the land, they're off to settle on their own 50-acre tract at the edge of settlement.

on the islands. As a result the English settlements formed a thin line along the Atlantic coast. But as more people settled in the Tidewater area, the price of land went up. Newcomers who could not afford to pay the price had to go to the Piedmont, where land was inexpensive or even free. By taking this big step from the Tidewater and onto the Piedmont, these pioneers began the westward movement of the American people that continued until the entire continent was settled.

New settlers. Before 1700 most of the settlers were English. After 1700 many Scotch-Irish, German, and French people moved to the English colonies.

The Huguenots (hū′gẽ nŏts) were French Protestants. They came to America to escape religious persecution. In France they had been businessmen and skilled workers, and they became successful in the same occupations in the New World. Most of them settled in colonial towns. In South Carolina some of them established plantations.

The early German settlers in America came from the Rhine Valley. In wars that seemed to have no end, armies had marched across their fields over and over again, destroying their crops. In spite of their poverty, their rulers made them pay heavy taxes. Many of them belonged to small religious groups that were being persecuted for their beliefs. These people came to America to enjoy religious liberty and to obtain land that they could own, cultivate in peace, and pass on to their children.

From Ireland came the Scotch-Irish. Their ancestors had moved from Scotland to northern Ireland in the early 1600s. They were so poor in Ireland that

PEOPLING THE COLONIES

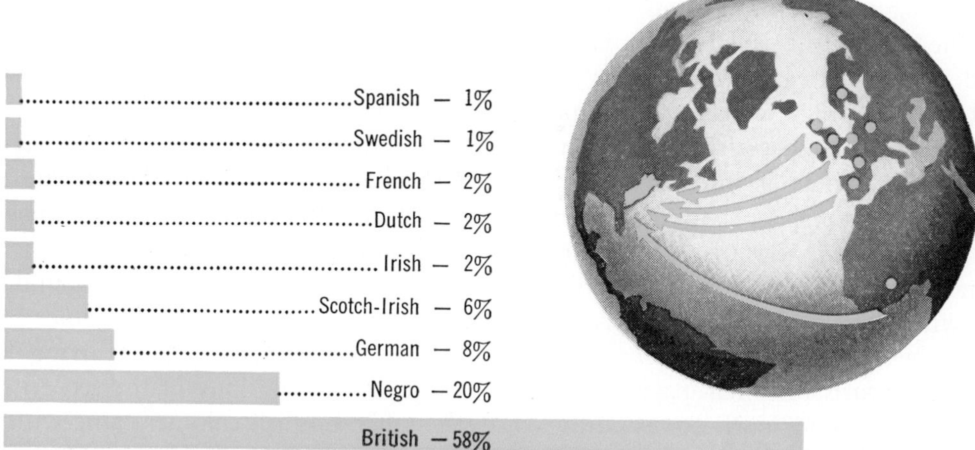

People from many lands, speaking many languages, settled the American colonies and fought to win American independence.

Large families grew up in the colonies. More people came from Europe and Africa. Pioneers pushed the frontier westward.

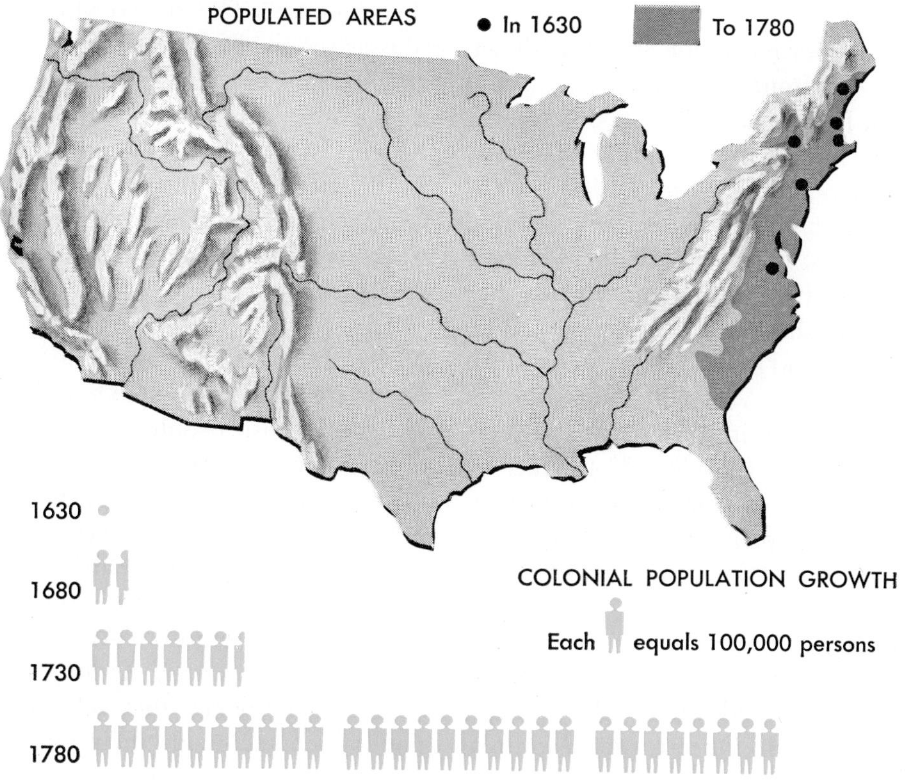

they were eager to come to the colonies. The Scotch-Irish proved to be excellent colonists. They were hardy and courageous and unafraid of the wilderness. They valued liberty. English laws had done much to keep them poor in Ireland. Now they were suspicious of any government, especially the English government, when it interfered with the efforts of the people to earn a living.

Indentured servants. Some of the new settlers were unable to pay their own way to the New World. These people became indentured servants. That is, in return for their passage money, they agreed to work for wealthy colonists for a number of years. After an indentured servant had worked for the period of his contract, he was free. In some colonies, when he became free, he received 50 acres of land on which to start out on his own.

Many Germans and Scotch-Irish settle on the frontier. The Germans and Scotch-Irish usually struck out for the frontier, where they were the first white settlers. Some of them settled on the New England and New York frontier. The largest number settled in Pennsylvania. From southern Pennsylvania they spread farther south. Some settled in Maryland and in the broad Shenandoah (shĕn ăn dō′ȧ) Valley of Virginia. Others moved on into western Carolina. (See the map on page 32.) Thus by 1750 settlements reached across the Atlantic coastal plain and up to the Appalachian Mountains.

Summary

Early French settlers came to North America to trade with the Indians for furs. Both Quebec and Montreal were started as fur-trading centers. But Champlain and other French leaders were interested also in looking for a water route to the Pacific. In this search they traveled up the St. Lawrence, through the Great Lakes, and down the Mississippi. La Salle claimed the entire Mississippi Valley for France and named it Louisiana. He died trying to establish a French colony on the coast of Texas.

The English settlers who founded Jamestown came looking for gold, but those who survived made a living by raising tobacco. Many of the settlers of the other English colonies came with a somewhat different purpose. They all wanted to earn a better living, of course. But they had another reason for coming to the New World—to be free to set up their own churches and to worship in them in peace. The Puritans first settled Massachusetts. From Massachusetts dissatisfied groups moved out to found the three other New England colonies: Rhode Island, New Hampshire, and Connecticut. In Pennsylvania it was the Quakers, and in Maryland the Roman Catholics, who made the first English settlements.

The English took over New York, New Jersey, and Delaware after they had been started by Dutch and Swedish settlers. English people settled the Carolinas. James Oglethorpe established Georgia as a home for people who were in trouble in England because they were unable to pay their debts.

The early settlers in the English colonies stayed close to the Atlantic shore and to the Tidewater. As long as they could see the ocean, they felt they had not lost contact with their old homes in Europe. But as more people settled near the coast, the price of land went up. Newcomers without money had to settle in the interior, in the Piedmont.

Large numbers of settlers came to the colonies as indentured servants. After working off their time, they settled mainly in the Piedmont where land was cheap.

For a Quick Review

1. Why were furs important in the history of New France?

2. Where and when were the first colonies founded in Virginia and Massachusetts?

3. Why were settlements begun at Providence, Exeter, and Hartford?

4. What was an unusual and important fact about each of the following colonies: Maryland, Georgia, New York?

5. What was there about the coast line of North America that made it a help to the early settlers?

6. Before 1700 from where did most of the settlers in the English colonies come? What groups came in large numbers after that year?

Learning to Study More Easily

HOW A BOOK INTRODUCES ITSELF TO YOU

"Mother, this is Jack," you may say when a new friend comes home with you for the first time. That is Jack's introduction to your mother. The title page of this book is its introduction to you. On the title page you find the name of the book, the names of the persons who wrote it and made the maps, charts, and drawings, the name of the publisher, and the place of publication. In most books the copyright date is on the back of the title page. Why is all this information important? Let us see.

The title is important because it tells you the general subject discussed in the book and something about how it is presented. Thus the title *The American Adventure* lets you know that this book tells about the history of our nation, with particular attention to the many exciting and important happenings along the way.

The names and experience of the persons who wrote and illustrated the book are important because this information tells you whether they were qualified to make the book.

The name of the publisher and the place of publication tell you where you can order other copies of this book and where you may send any questions or comments you may have about the book.

The copyright date shows when the book was published. In some books you will find more than one copyright date, telling you that, since the book was first published, it has been revised—that is, changed in some parts. The most recent date marks the latest revision.

The title page, although it gives you much information, is only your first introduction to a book. Another important part is the table of contents, where you will find the titles of the main divisions of the book. From studying it, you can find out how the book is planned and what major topics it includes.

This book is divided into units, and the units are divided into chapters. As you look at the table of contents, you will see that each unit deals with a particular period. You will see, too, that each chapter within a unit discusses one thread that runs through the entire story—how the people lived, how they earned a living, how they ran the government, and so on.

In addition to the titles of the units and chapters of a book, the table of contents usually gives the page numbers for any special materials to which you may wish to refer. If there is a list of the maps in the book, for example, the table of contents will tell you what page it is on. Important documents, such as the Declaration of Independence and the Constitution, are listed in the table of contents.

Consult the opening pages of this book and then answer the following questions:

1. Who wrote and illustrated the book? What experience have they had to qualify them to make the book?
2. In what year was this book published? Has it been revised? How do you know?
3. How many units are in this book? How many chapters?
4. In which unit will you find an account of the Revolutionary War? Of the Second World War?
5. Where would you write to ask a question about the book or to report any misprints so that they might be corrected before more copies of the book are printed?
6. Which pages contain the text of the Constitution of the United States?

3 The Old World Governs the New

One day in the 1670s a ship dropped anchor at Quebec, in New France. We can imagine that soon the townspeople and the settlers farther up the St. Lawrence were buzzing with gossip. Always there was excitement when a ship came, but this time there was even more interest than usual. On the ship were young women sent out by the French king to be married to bachelors in New France. Probably the older men teased the young unmarried men somewhat like this: "Now, Jacques, you'll be settling down. If you're not married in two weeks, you'll lose your license to go into the forest to hunt. That's the law, you know."

That was indeed the law. Another law required the boys of New France to be married by the time they were 20 and the girls by the time they were 16, or their fathers would be fined. The settlers themselves had nothing to say about making or enforcing these laws or the many others that tried to control their daily lives. The French king and his representatives in New France made the laws for the colonists.

During the 1500s and early 1600s, we must remember, people did not govern themselves as we do today. Democracy as we think of it was unknown. Kings ruled and made any laws they considered necessary. When a king made a law, he might think of the welfare of his subjects but it would never occur to him to ask whether they approved the law. Even in England, where the people governed themselves in part, the king had a great deal of power. Since they governed their people at home, it was only natural for the rulers of Spain, France, and England to govern their colonies in the New World.

1 *Spain Controls Its American Colonies*

The king of Spain looked upon Spanish colonies as his own private property and as a source of income. The income was a good one indeed. If anyone today owned land as valuable as the Spanish colonies in the Americas, he would be the richest man in the world.

At first the Spanish king made the rules that regulated the daily life of the colonists. But he soon found that the job was too big for one man. Therefore he set up two committees to do the work of governing for him. One committee was called the House of Trade. It made the rules under which the colonists could carry on trade. The other was called the Council of the Indies. It made all other laws for the colonies and sent officers to America to enforce them.

Viceroys rule the Spanish empire. As the conquistadors conquered more and more of Central America, Mexico, and South America, the Council of the Indies divided Spanish America into two (later four) parts and placed an officer called a viceroy (vīs′roi) over each. (Roy means "king"; viceroy means "in place of the king.") The area over which a viceroy ruled was called a viceroyalty.

The viceroy carried out all the laws that were made in Spain for the colonies. He also appointed colonial officials and commanded the army. He collected the taxes for the king of Spain.

As you can see, a viceroy had a great deal of power. The Spanish government at home was always afraid he might break away from Spain and set himself up as king of an independent country. To keep him under control, the Council of the Indies limited his power in various ways. Usually he was allowed to hold office for not more than five years. He was required to write daily reports, giving an account of everything he did down to the smallest detail. Inspectors were frequently sent to America to check up on him. If he were found guilty of doing wrong, he might be made to pay a large fine.

The Spanish government tries to protect the king's wealth. The king's chief interest in his American empire was the enormous amount of money it brought him. The money came from many sources. He was supposed to receive one-fifth of all the gold, silver, and other metals mined. Every adult Indian up to the age of 50 was required to pay a yearly tax. There was a tax on imports and a tax on exports. Every time something was sold, whether it was a tract of land or a piece of bread, the buyer had to pay a sales tax. Only the king had the right to sell quicksilver, a shiny, liquid metal that was used to separate silver from ore. The king also kept for himself the right to sell all tobacco, salt, and gunpowder, as well as the ice that was brought from the mountains for use in iceboxes. There was a stamp tax: no business deal was legal unless it was written down on official stamped paper. Anyone who wanted a government job had to buy it, and the money went to the king. The king also sold titles of nobility. A Spaniard in the colonies could become a noble if he could afford to pay $20,000 for the title. By the year 1800 there were more than 60 different ways in which

Spanish empire in North America. Study this map for facts about Spanish America. It shows the four viceroyalties: New Spain, New Granada, Peru, and Rio de la Plata. It also shows the main trade routes to and from Spain. Find the capitals of the viceroyalties and the centers of trade, mining, and education. Which cities shown here became capitals of Latin-American countries?

money for the king was raised in the colonies.

The Council of the Indies made rules to protect the money collected for the king. Every safe in which it was kept had three separate locks, each opened by a different key. The door of the room in which the safe stood was locked in the same way. The keys were held by the three chief treasury officials, and the room and the safe could be opened only if all three were present.

In spite of precautions like these, there were graft and theft among the officials. The Council of the Indies might send an inspector and then, not sure of him, might send another to check on the first. Soon there were spies

Protecting the king's treasure. The gold and other treasure collected for the Spanish king were carefully protected by his officials in the colonies.

spying on spies. But there seemed to be no way to stop officials from cheating because investigators and spies could be bribed.

Cruelty to Indians. The king of Spain was concerned about the Indians in the colonies. One of the duties of the viceroys was to protect the Indians. Special officials were appointed to carry on trade with them and to collect taxes from them. These officials were instructed to treat the Indians kindly, but many of them were extremely cruel. Some of them forced Indians to pay more taxes than the law required and kept the money for themselves. Others compelled Indians to pay high prices for things they did not need. For example, one official bought a stock of eyeglasses. He announced that no Indian would be admitted to church services during festivals without a pair of eyeglasses. He soon sold the entire stock at a huge profit.

So you see how difficult it was for Spain to run good governments in its colonies. There is, however, another side to the story. The Council of the Indies passed many wise laws to help the colonists. Many officials obeyed the laws and served the colonists well. And many Spaniards, especially church leaders, tried hard to get better treatment for the Indians. By one test the government of the Spanish colonies was certainly successful. Spain held its colonies for 300 years—twice as long as France and England held theirs.

2 *French Colonists Have No Share in Their Government*

When Champlain founded Quebec in 1608, he was working for a group of French businessmen. The French king had given them complete control of the fur trade. In return they were required to send settlers to Canada. These men were eager for profits from the fur trade, but they had no desire to spend their own money to settle French farmers and workers in Canada. The result was that in 1665, after 57 years of control by fur companies, all of Canada had only 3,215 French people, or about

500 families. It was about this time that the king of France took control of the colony into his own hands in order to make it grow faster. Hundreds of settlers were sent to Canada, with the king paying the bill.

The Sovereign Council. One of the first things the king did was to organize a government for the colony. He set up a Sovereign (sŏv′ĕr ĭn) Council, which was to rule Canada under his direction. The leading member of the Council was the governor, who was appointed by the king. His main duty was to be military head of the colony. It was his job to prevent New France from being destroyed by the Indians or seized by some other country.

The second most important member of the Council was the bishop. He was important because the Roman Catholic Church was the official church in France and its colonies. The church played an important part in the life of Canada.

The third leading member of the Council was the intendant (ĭn tĕn′-dănt). He did nearly all the work of governing. He was chairman of the Council at its meetings, and he told the Council what laws were necessary to carry out the orders of the king. He also enforced the laws after they were passed. He sent the king long reports covering everything that happened in the colony, including the actions of the other officials.

New France, like Spanish America, was ruled by the king through his representatives. As in France itself, the people had no voice in the government. The colonists were forbidden to get to-

Official visit. The intendant of New France visits a home to find out how the family is getting along and whether it is obeying the laws. Can you guess what they might be talking about? The government closely watched over the everyday lives of the French colonists.

PUBLIC ARCHIVES OF CANADA

PUBLIC ARCHIVES OF CANADA

Church in French Quebec. The king of France paid for building this old church in Quebec. Building churches was one of the many ways in which the king supported his American colony.

gether in meetings to discuss any problem. They were expected to obey orders without asking questions.

The king in France and the intendant in Canada, between them, tried to control every detail in the lives of the colonists. You read on page 43 of the laws they issued about the marriage of young people. That was just one example. The king, or the intendant speaking in the king's name, decided the prices for which goods were to be sold and the amount of profit the merchants were to make. The intendant forbade children to sleigh down the steep hills at Quebec. He made rules for taking care of stray hogs and mad dogs. He even tried to patch up quarrels between husbands and wives.

The king tries to do everything for the colonists. The king was so eager to make the colony succeed that he tried to solve all its problems. He found settlers for it in France. He shipped them across the ocean. He gave them land. He practically supported them for the first year or two. He built homes for some of them, and he even supplied them with wives. He sent cattle, horses, and sheep to the colony. He sent money and supplies to start new industries, to support the poor, and to build churches, roads, and other public works. In short, he did everything for the colonists. He did not give them a chance to do things for themselves. He treated them like children.

The government of the French colony did not always work well. The king and his ministers had never been in Canada and did not fully understand many of the problems to be solved. Furthermore, the distance from Paris to Quebec was great, and mail was sent only once a year. When the governor or the intendant sent a message to the king, he received an answer the next year—if the king replied promptly. If the king happened to be busy with other affairs, the reply would be delayed another year. Meanwhile in Canada some important matter remained unsettled because the government was unable to act.

The three leading members of the Council caused much trouble in Canada with their quarrels. The governor and the intendant jealously spied on each other. They wrote the king long letters in which each said that the other was

PUBLIC ARCHIVES OF CANADA

Ship from home. People of New France happily welcome a ship from the mother country. It may bring word from friends, news of the world, orders from the king, and new settlers.

disloyal and dishonest. The bishop and the governor also quarreled, mainly over the question of selling liquor to the Indians. The bishop protested that, by selling them liquor, the traders undid all the good work of the missionaries.

The king read about these quarrels in the long reports sent to him. He patiently tried to settle them but could not always do so from a distance of more than 3,000 miles. Nor did he always succeed in preventing his officials from being dishonest. In many ways the problems that the French king faced in ruling his American colonies were like those of the Spanish ruler.

3 *Self-government Increases in the English Colonies*

The Spaniards and the French in America, as we have seen, had no share in their government. The English colonists, on the other hand, had something to say about how they were governed.

One reason for this difference was that Englishmen at home had for a long time taken part in running their local governments. Another reason was that in the 1600s, while the colonies were being founded, the government of England went through two revolutions. One king was beheaded for resisting Parliament, and another had to scurry out of the country to save his life. English officials were so busy with these quarrels that they were unable to keep full control over the colonies, and the colonists were left to manage many of their own affairs. By the time the English government was ready to take over full control again, the colonists had grown accustomed to ruling themselves and were unwilling to take orders from the king and his officers.

Our oldest representative assembly. The Virginia House of Burgesses is shown in session. The room in which it met has been restored in Colonial Williamsburg.

Development of colonial governments. The colonists in Virginia began taking part in their government early. At first the colony was ruled by a governor and his council of advisers, all of whom were appointed in England. Then in 1619 property owners in each of the Virginia settlements chose two representatives called burgesses (bûr′jĕs-ĕz). The burgesses met with the governor and the governor's council to make laws for the colony. They passed laws about such matters as the planting of crops, the prices of tobacco, and relations with the Indians. For the first time in the New World a group of elected representatives took part in government. Since representative government is the basis of our democracy, 1619 is an important year in our history.

As the Virginia government developed, the council and the burgesses formed the two houses of the legislature, which made the laws. A law passed by the legislature could be vetoed, however, by the governor or by the king. (To veto is to forbid; thus the governor or the king could forbid the passing of any law that the king disliked.)

By 1750 seven other colonies had the same kind of government as Virginia. Each had a governor and a council appointed by the king and an assembly (in Virginia the House of Burgesses) elected by the property owners. These were called royal colonies. In Pennsylvania, Maryland, and New Jersey, the three colonies originally granted to individuals, the governor was appointed by the proprietor, or owner. These were called proprietary (prō̇ prī′ĕ tĕr′ĭ) colonies. Connecticut and Rhode Island had charters from the king that gave each the right to elect its own governor and legislature. These two were called charter colonies.

Colonial assemblies gain powers from the royal governors. In most of the colonies, especially the royal colonies, the governor and the assembly quarreled. Those quarrels are important in the story of United States independence.

Why did they quarrel? Remember that the governor represented the king, while the assembly represented the colonial property owners. The governor could not govern without money, and only the assembly had the power to give him the money. The king said that the assembly should vote the governor as much money as he asked for and leave him free to govern: to appoint officials and pay them, organize and pay the militia (citizens making up the colonial army), direct the building of forts and the buying of military supplies, and so on. On the other hand, the assembly wished to control the spending of the money, in order to have more say in the government and in order to keep taxes down.

In New York the quarrel between governor and assembly was especially strong. The New York assembly began passing laws that granted the governor money for only one year and appointed a committee to watch over the spending of the money. What was the governor to do when the king ordered him to veto such laws? Since he needed money to defend the colony against French and Indian attacks and since he wanted to receive his own salary, he disobeyed the king and gave in to the assembly. Gradually the assembly took over many of the governor's powers. For example, it named the men to be appointed to the various offices. It decided what military supplies were to be bought. It directed where the militia was to be sent. As the power of the assembly increased, the power of the governor, and therefore of the king, decreased.

This clash between governor and assembly was repeated in most of the other colonies. In every case the assembly, because it alone could pass laws for collecting taxes and spending money, took away much of the power of the governor. The assembly simply told the governor that there would be no money to spend if he did not cooperate with it. By 1750 the assembly was by far the strongest part of the government in each colony.

Only property owners vote. Although the assemblies gained more

The right to vote. In colonial times (*above*), men in the English colonies who did not own property did not have the right to vote. They could only look on as property owners voted. Today all American citizens, women as well as men, have the right to vote (*below*). Giving the right to vote to all citizens has been one of the ways in which democracy has grown in the United States. Should citizens exercise their right to vote?

ENOCH PRATT FREE LIBRARY

Cecil Calvert. The first proprietor of Maryland, whose title was Lord Baltimore, urged the Maryland assembly to adopt the Toleration Act of 1649. Here he is shown with his grandson, a later Lord Baltimore.

power, most of the colonists did not share in the government. Those who did not own property did not have the right to vote for members of the assembly. To give but one example: in order to be a voter in Pennsylvania, a man had to own 50 acres of land, with 12 of them cleared of trees, or other property worth about $250. The result was that in the rural areas about 1 person in 10 could vote, while in Philadelphia only about 1 in 50 could do so. In all the colonies, to hold an important office like member of the assembly, a man had to own a great deal of property. The members of the assembly were therefore wealthy property owners.

English colonists run their local governments. Besides their interest in the colonial governments, many people in the English colonies took part in the government of their local communities. In New England the unit of local government was the town. (A town in the New England colonies consisted of a village and the farms that surrounded it. See page 33.) The people met in town meetings to discuss local problems and elect local officials. They elected overseers of the poor; town clerks; and constables, who were police officers. They also elected fence viewers, who saw to it that fences were kept strong and in good repair, and surveyors of highways, who kept roads and bridges in good condition. Almost every family in a town owned pigs, which were allowed to wander about the streets. The pigs were good garbage removers, but they tore up the streets and became a dangerous nuisance. For this reason many towns elected hogreeves, whose duty it was to keep the pigs off the streets. Towns that had too many stray dogs appointed dogcatchers.

In the South the main unit of local government was the county. A county was much larger in area than the New England town because plantations were large and the population was scattered. The county was governed by the county court, which was made up of justices of the peace (or judges) appointed by

METRO-GOLDWYN-MAYER

Zenger's arrest. John Peter Zenger published a newspaper in colonial New York. When his newspaper criticized the royal governor, he was arrested and placed on trial. His lawyer argued that, if the press is not free to publish the truth about government, then the liberties of the people are not safe. Zenger was set free. His acquittal was an important victory for freedom of the press.

the governor. Besides the duties one might expect justices to perform, the members of the county court collected taxes and looked after highways.

In the middle colonies—New York, New Jersey, Pennsylvania, and Delaware—local government was a combination of town and county governments. In the local governments throughout the colonies, early Americans learned how to carry on public business and became accustomed to having some voice in making the laws under which they lived.

Summary

The king of Spain ruled his colonies in the New World through the House of Trade and the Council of the Indies. The colonies were divided into viceroyalties, and the Council appointed a viceroy to rule each one. New France, like the Spanish colonies, was ruled directly from the mother country. The king sent a governor and other officials to Canada.

While the English king claimed the power to approve or veto laws passed in his colonies, he did not try to rule them by sending orders about everything. In each of the English colonies, by 1750, the government was carried on by a governor, a governor's council, and an assembly. Property owners in each colony elected the members of the assembly. In all but two of the colonies the king or the English proprietor appointed the governor. In these eleven colonies the assembly and the governor frequently quarreled. As a result of these quarrels, the assemblies gained a great deal of power.

It is interesting to compare the colonial governments in the New World. The kings of Spain and France did not give their colonists any share in government. They tried to rule through officials, most of whom they sent over from Europe. But they could find no way to make sure that the officials would carry out their orders. As a result the governments were often poorly run.

In the English colonies, on the other hand, the colonists had a large share in their government, especially in local matters. Since officials were elected by their neighbors, they had to give good service or they would lose their jobs.

Here we have one difference between democratic government and government by one man who has all the power. In a democracy the people elect the officials and the officials are responsible to them. If the people see that an official does not do his job well or is dishonest, they can, in the next election, elect someone else in his place. Of course, the people must take an interest in their government in order to have it well run.

Under one-man government the ruler appoints the officials, and they are responsible to him alone. But he cannot keep a close watch over them all, and there is always the danger that they will govern badly and the people will suffer.

For a Quick Review

1. What were the duties of the Council of the Indies, the House of Trade, and the viceroy in the Spanish colonies?

2. In what ways was the government of New France like that of Spanish America? In what ways was it different?

3. Why did the English colonists have a larger part in their government than did the French or the Spanish?

4. What did governors and assemblies in the English colonies quarrel over? Why were these conflicts important?

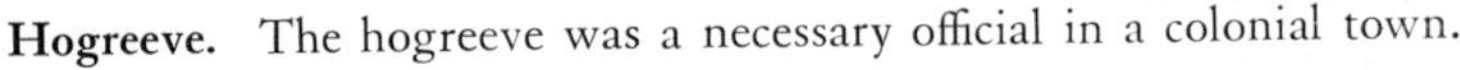

Hogreeve. The hogreeve was a necessary official in a colonial town.

Learning to Study More Easily

USING HEADINGS

As you read the chapters of this book, you will find four kinds of headings in each chapter. First comes the chapter title, which states the subject of the entire chapter. Next in importance is the numbered section heading. There are three section headings in this chapter. They divide the chapter into its main parts and tell you the subject of each. Notice the heading of the second section (page 46), for example; it lets you know that the paragraphs that follow discuss the government of the French colonies. Each section is subdivided into topics. A topic is introduced by a side heading; for example: English colonists run their local governments. Finally, some of the topics are divided by subtopic headings. Each of the four kinds of headings is printed in a different kind of type.

The headings have been put into the book to help you read it easily and quickly. You can use them in two important ways. When you read the chapter for the first time, they serve as introductions. From them you learn, in general, what is coming and what are the most important ideas and facts that you should look for. Then, after you have read the chapter and are discussing it with your classmates, you may want certain information in a hurry. The sections headings will help you find the pages that you are looking for. Instead of reading through each page to find the paragraphs where the needed information is given, use the side headings as guideposts to help you locate the paragraphs you want.

Use the headings in Chapter 3 to answer these questions:

1. In which section would you look for information about the government of the Spanish colonies in America? About the government of the English colonies?
2. On which page would you find information about how the Spaniards treated the Indians in their colonies? About taxes collected by the Spanish king? About quarrels between the governors and assemblies in the English colonies? About the Sovereign Council of Canada?

4 Colonists Make a Living in the New World

Jonathan Franklin opened his eyes when he heard his father putting wood on the fire. He knew he should be getting up. He had to help clear a new field this spring, but his father had promised to go hunting for wild turkey today after they finished the corn planting.

In a few minutes Jonathan's mother called him. "It is time to get up, Jonathan. You have a pile of work to do today. You'll go hungry early in the winter if you sleep late in the spring!"

Jonathan's mother was eager to get breakfast over and begin her many daily tasks. With some help from other members of the family, she cooked meals, baked bread, raised vegetables in the garden, made her own soap, washed the family laundry by hand, dipped candles, spun flax and wool, wove cloth, and sewed all the clothes for the family.

Jonathan Franklin lived on a partly cleared farm in Massachusetts in the 1650s. He and his parents and three sisters had come from England to make their home in the New World.

John Franklin opened his eyes for a moment, then rolled over in bed for another nap. He knew he should be getting up, or he would be late for school. Home-room period started at eighty-thirty at Jefferson Junior High. John could tell from the noises in the kitchen that his mother had breakfast about ready. Just then she came to the door. "Hurry, John," she said. "Your toast and eggs are ready, and I've sliced an orange for you. Dad's already gone—he's on the early shift in the factory this week. You'll have to hurry to get to school on time."

John Franklin lives in a city in the

1950s. His father earns a living for his family by working as a machinist in a tractor factory. His mother takes care of the family, keeps the apartment clean, shops for groceries at the nearby supermarket, cooks the meals, takes care of John's younger brother and sister, and has time to serve as president of the Parent-Teacher Association at John's school.

Both Jonathan and John are imaginary characters, but these paragraphs about them are true to the time in which each is supposed to have lived. Jonathan Franklin's boyhood was different from that of John Franklin. Can you point out some of the ways in which it was different? Why was it different? Here are some suggestions.

To the early settlers in the New World, earning a living meant something different from what it means to us today. They could not go out and find jobs in factories or on farms. They could not buy groceries, clothing, and furniture in stores. There were, of course, no factories, no farms, and no stores.

The early settlers had to work fast to build some kind of shelter against the weather and to obtain food before they starved. Even after the settlements were established, all the colonists had to work hard to clear more land on which to grow enough food; to build real houses of wood, brick, or stone; and to make their own clothing of wool and flax.

But the settlers were not satisfied to have just enough food, shelter, and clothing. They wanted to enjoy many things that they had been accustomed to in the Old World—fine clothes, beautiful furniture, books, jewelry, and other luxuries. Of course, they had to pay for these imports (goods brought in from another country). They had to grow crops larger than they needed for themselves and sell the surplus, that is, the part that was left over. They also produced other goods they could sell abroad, such as furs, lumber, and naval stores (tar, pitch, and turpentine). With the money received for these goods they paid for the articles they imported from Europe. Thus, gradually, by hard work the colonists made their life in the New World easier and more enjoyable.

1 *People in Spanish America Live by Farming or Mining*

In the Spanish parts of America most of the people earned their living by farming and mining. Only a few were busy in manufacturing and trade. Indians did all the hard work.

Indians work hard. After conquering Haiti, Columbus demanded gold from the Indians. He believed they had great stores of it. Since they had none, he made them work. He gave each Spaniard a number of Indians to work for him. The Spanish master was supposed to feed and clothe them and teach them religion, but most of the masters did little for them.

As the Spanish conquerors spread over Central and South America, they followed this plan of making the Indians do their work. Indians worked on plantations, in sugar mills and cloth factories, and in gold and silver mines. In the factories they were locked up like prisoners. At the end of the day, if they failed to complete the assigned work, they were beaten. In the mines they suffered even more, standing day after day knee-deep in water and breathing foul air. Many thousands of Indians died of starvation, disease, and overwork.

Some Spaniards in the colonies, especially missionaries, were shocked by these conditions and appealed to the king to free the Indians. The king ordered that the Indians should be paid wages. But the wages were so small that most Indians fell deeper and deeper into debt. To pay their debts, they had to continue to work for their masters as before. In thinking about the suffering of the Indians, however, we must remember that in most parts of the world in the 1500s and 1600s life was very hard for the ordinary people, and the conditions under which they worked would seem bad today.

Mines produce great riches. In spite of the fact that the king took one-fifth of the metal, the mine owners of Spanish America became extremely wealthy. One owner is especially remembered for his extravagant living. When his daughter got married, he paved the street with silver tiles for the wedding party to walk on. At another time he presented the king of Spain with a completely equipped battleship.

In the eyes of the Spanish rulers, mining was the most important activity in their American colonies because it produced an enormous treasure of silver and gold. But only a small number of Spaniards owned mines. Most people in Spanish America had to be content with earning a living by farming.

Farmers grow New World and Old World crops. Upon coming to the New World, the Spanish colonists learned from the Indians how to grow

A silver mine in New Spain. Indians did all the hard work connected with mining.

LIBRARY OF CONGRESS

Spanish mission in California. In the Spanish missions Indians were taught to farm, to make cloth, and to do other work, as well as to be Christians. This picture was made in the 1840s.

corn. It became the basic food crop in Spanish America. They found the Indians using other native products that were unknown to Europeans, although they are well known to us today. Among these were cocoa, potatoes, tobacco, and vanilla. The colonists learned to cultivate these products and exported them to Spain.

The Spaniards brought many of the plants of the Old World with them to the New World: grains, fruits, sugar cane, and most of our garden vegetables and flowers. These plants grew well in America, as we know today. The American Indians had no domesticated animals except the dog. The Europeans brought with them cattle, horses, sheep, and hogs. These multiplied rapidly on the broad plateaus of Spanish America, and grazing became a major industry.

The planters on the Spanish islands in the Caribbean produced one crop—sugar. At first the Indians did the hard work on the sugar plantations, but they

Spanish galleons. Ships like these carried manufactured goods to the Spanish colonies and brought gold and silver back to Spain. Usually they sailed in convoys to protect them from the English, Dutch, and French.

BANCROFT LIBRARY, UNIVERSITY OF CALIFORNIA

BANCROFT LIBRARY, UNIVERSITY OF CALIFORNIA

Mule train. Over the long distances of Spanish America, goods could be carried only in wagons or on the backs of mules. In most places there were no roads, only wheel tracks made by wagon caravans or paths made by mule trains.

died off by the thousands. In order to have enough workers, the planters imported Negro slaves from Africa. Because the planters in the West Indies grew sugar only, they had to import almost everything else they needed, even food for the slaves.

On the other hand, a big ranch on the mainland made everything it needed. The Indian workers produced food and clothing. Some of them soon learned the handicrafts of the Spaniards and became carpenters, bricklayers, shoemakers, and tailors.

Farming in the Spanish colonies in America did not progress rapidly. This lack of development is not surprising when you consider how great were the distances in Spanish America. South America alone stretches 4,600 miles from north to south and 3,500 miles across its widest part. There were few roads. Transportation was slow and expensive. It cost so much and took so long to transport goods that owners of ranches far away from cities could not sell their surplus products. One product they could export was hides. They slaughtered their cattle for the hides and let most of the meat go to waste. Year after year each ranch produced enough for its own people and no more.

The government restricts commerce and manufacturing. There was another reason for the lack of progress in Spanish America. The House of Trade (see page 44) regulated the trade of the colonies so that the Spanish king and Spanish merchants would make all the profits. It tried to keep all foreigners out of the colonies. To make control easier, all cargoes from the colonies had to be landed at a single port in Spain and all shipments to the New World had to be shipped from that same port. Ships were permitted to sail to and from the colonies only once a year. They traveled in convoys protected by warships. The convoys were needed to prevent the valuable cargoes from falling into the hands of English, French, and Dutch pirates who roamed the sea watching for the wealth-laden Spanish ships called galleons (găl′ē ŭnz).

In the colonies, commerce was restricted to two ports. Veracruz was the port for goods that were being shipped to or from Mexico. Porto Bello, on the Isthmus of Panama, was the port for the trade of the viceroyalty of Peru. You can find these ports on the map on page 45. When the annual fleets arrived from Spain, colorful fairs, which lasted about a month, were held in the two towns. At these fairs almost the entire year's business of the colonies with the mother country was transacted.

Fair at Porto Bello. The fair at Porto Bello was the larger. For 11 months of the year Porto Bello was an unhealthy, unimportant little town. For one month it was the trading center of a continent, crowded with merchants, soldiers, sailors, and laborers. Prices went sky-high. For the month of the fair, a tiny room for sleeping cost $100 or more and a store might rent for $1,000. Food prices multiplied a hundred times.

During the fair, merchants gathered together at Porto Bello the exports of South America: cocoa, indigo, vanilla, quinine, and other colonial products. They piled bars of silver and gold in the streets like stacks of brick. Money collected in taxes for the king of Spain was brought from the farthest districts of the viceroyalty to be shipped under heavy guard to the royal treasury in Spain.

From the ships were unloaded silk and cotton goods, religious articles, expensive clothing, jewelry, iron products, wine, olive oil, and quicksilver. The merchants bought and sold, and the ships took on their new cargoes. After the fair everyone deserted the unhealthy spot as soon as possible.

Slow development. Just as Spain limited trade, she restricted manufacturing in the colonies. Considering the size and the population of Spanish America, its trade and manufacturing were small. The geography of South America was partly to blame for this. But the strict laws of the Spanish government did much to hold back the development of Spanish America for 250 years. Everywhere except in the few cities, the people existed upon what food they could supply for themselves, and they had to get along with the few articles they could make.

2 *French Colonists Live by Farming and Fur Trading*

In New France, as in Spanish America, most of the colonists were farmers. The government granted large tracts of land to leading persons in the colony. They were usually retired army officers. Such an owner of a tract of land was called a seignior (sēn′yẽr) and his estate was called a seigniory (sēn′yẽr ĭ). The seigniories varied in size from 12 to 200 square miles.

The farms of New France. The seignior was required to clear the land and grow crops on it. But he did not do the work himself. He divided up the land among tenants, called habitants (hăb′ĭ tănts). The habitant cut down the forest, built a house, plowed the land, and grew crops. He paid the seignior a small annual rent for the use

Plowing in New France. The French-Canadian habitant plowed his fields with a crude ox-drawn plow. Notice that the farms fronted on the St. Lawrence River.

of the land—usually a few bushels of wheat and a fat hen or two in addition to a small sum of money. The habitant also had to take his grain to the seignior's mill to be ground and paid one-fourteenth of the flour for the service. He had to work for the seignior without pay six days a year—two in the plowing season, two at seedtime, and two at harvest. The habitant also gave one twenty-sixth of his grain crop for the support of the local church.

River farms. Most of the farms were along the St. Lawrence River. It was the main highway between the farms and the towns and between the colony and the outside world. When a road was built, it ran along the riverbank. Naturally everyone wanted to live close to the river.

Each seigniory was laid out with one side along the river. When it was divided into farms for the tenants, each farm had a narrow frontage on the river, from which it ran back in a long narrow strip. Each owner built his house close to the water. A person who paddled down the St. Lawrence could see almost every house in Canada.

French Canadian farmers grew wheat, corn, rye, barley, peas, beans, flax, hemp, and other crops that do not require a long growing season. They raised cattle, pigs, poultry, horses, and sheep. They cut lumber. The little surpluses that they produced were sold in the market that was held in Quebec every Tuesday and Friday.

Farming unsuccessful. For years the colony did not produce enough to feed its population. If what the colonial farmers produced had been the colony's only value to France, the king would probably have thrown up his hands and refused to spend any more money on New France.

There were several reasons for lack of success in farming. One was the cold climate with a short growing season. Farmers never knew whether they would be able to harvest their crops before the heavy frosts set in. To see the result of a whole summer's work destroyed by an early frost discouraged many a hard-working Canadian farmer.

Another reason for lack of progress in farming was that the habitants used the same backward methods that were used all over colonial America. With their wooden plows they could do little more than scratch the surface of the soil. Because they did not know how to keep up the fertility of the soil by rotating crops and using fertilizer, the land produced less and less each year.

The final and most important reason for the slow development of farming in New France was that many of the habitants and seigniors were more interested in furs than in farming. Hundreds of them, especially the young men, found the life of a fur trader much more exciting and more profitable than that of a farmer.

Fur fair. White traders often drove hard bargains with the Indians for their furs.

The fur trade. Although only a minority of the colonists traded in furs, that trade was the most important business in New France. It was important for the colonists because with furs they paid for imports from the mother country. It was important for the king because most of his colonial income came from furs. He took as his share one out of every four beaver skins and one out of every ten moose hides.

At first the government did not allow the French colonists to go into the forests to trap or trade for furs. Instead, the

Fur trader. A French trader, with an Indian companion, is on his way to an Indian camp to buy furs.

Indians had to come to the settlements to sell the skins of beaver, otter, and other animals that they trapped. They came mainly to Montreal, where a great fair was held every summer. The Indians arrived in large numbers, drifting down the Ottawa River or the St. Lawrence in fleets consisting of anywhere from 200 to 1,000 canoes, each with its bundles of skins. As soon as they landed, the Indians set their pots of food to boil over campfires and unpacked their furs.

The first day of the fair was given over to ceremonies and flowery speeches (see page 109 for an example of the kinds of speeches that were made when Indians and white men met in council). On the second day the trading began. In their booths the merchants displayed articles that the Indians were eager to buy—cloth, blankets, knives, guns and ammunition, beads, looking glasses, and many other things. The Indians paid for these products with their furs, which the French traders, in turn, sold in Europe.

As the fur trade grew more prosperous, the government permitted the colonists to go into the forest to trade with the Indians. Many of the Frenchmen became trappers. (See page 25.) Some of them became as skilled at living in the forest as the Indians. They penetrated farther and farther west into the wilderness to reach more distant tribes.

Since many of the Indians lived too far away to take their furs to Montreal every year, the traders established trading posts in the interior where the Indians could sell their furs. Later, as the French came to realize that they must protect themselves against the English, the trading posts became forts. The forts, in turn, became the centers of settlements.

The fur trade not only brought the French large profits, but it also was a way of gaining mastery over the American continent. It led to friendship with the Indians, and friendship led to control of the territory they inhabited. French and English traders competed for furs and for control over the Indians and their land everywhere, from Hudson Bay to the mouth of the Mississippi.

Farmers on the Mississippi. Not all French colonists settled in Canada. In the Illinois country there was a group of little settlements on the west bank of the Mississippi River. The largest was Kaskaskia (kăs kăs′kĭ ȧ). Here, as in Canada, there were seigniories. Here, too, the farms had narrow frontages on the Mississippi and the fields stretched back into the woods. Many of the same crops were grown. French travelers used these settlements as stopover places on the long voyage between Canada and New Orleans.

The French founded New Orleans, near the mouth of the Mississippi River, in 1718. It was the capital of French Louisiana, which included the Illinois settlements. As you have read on page 27, La Salle had claimed this vast territory for France.

Around New Orleans, farming was different from farming in Canada. The principal crops were indigo, rice, and cotton. On the large plantations the work was done by Negro slaves. Owners of small farms did their own work. In the state of Louisiana today, as well as in the St. Lawrence Valley, French names and the use of the French language by many persons remind us that the Mississippi Valley was once a part of the French empire.

3 *Most English Colonists Earn a Living by Farming*

If you were to visit the English colonies in the early 1700s, you would be surprised to find how completely the forest still covered the countryside. On the typical farm of several hundred acres, five or ten acres were cleared and the rest was wild forest land. Between settlements the wilderness was unbroken. It seemed to swallow up the small settled areas.

In some ways the forest was of benefit to the settlers. From it they obtained lumber and naval stores to sell in the West Indies and in Europe. From it they obtained timber for homes and fences and nuts and wild berries for food. Hogs and cattle were able to find forage in the woods almost the year round. The wilderness provided cover for the game that the colonists hunted and trapped for food and clothing.

Forest causes hardships. But the forest was the cause of as much hardship as of good. As the soil in one field wore out, the settler had to clear another; and clearing a field was a long, slow, hard, backbreaking job. The colonist might hew the trees down, one by one, with his ax, or he might use the Indian method of cutting a circle through the bark of a tree and letting it die standing up. In either case it took several years to clear an acre of standing timber and deeply rooted stumps.

The forest slowed up settlement by making transportation by land almost impossible. Settlers had to make their clearings near the coast or along a riverbank until they found time and labor to build roads through the wilderness (see page 119). You can understand why it took a hundred years for pioneers to push the thin line of settlements from the Atlantic coast to the foothills of the Appalachian Mountains.

20TH CENTURY-FOX

Living on the frontier. In this scene from the film *Drums Along the Mohawk,* you can see the kinds of tools early settlers used. Notice the rail fence and the cabin.

Until the forest was cut down, it was a source of danger and disease. It concealed wolves and other animals of prey that seized sheep and poultry that were not well guarded. Even children had to be careful not to wander out of the little clearings around the homes. Large areas in the woods were swampy breeding places for mosquitoes, which kept the settlers ill with fever much of the time. Pioneers had to be people with brave hearts as well as strong backs.

Farm families work hard. In the early years all the farmers in the English colonies, north and south, grew corn as their main crop. They could grow corn between stumps on half-cleared fields. It was an excellent food for the farmer and his family as well as for his livestock. From the Indians the white men learned to roast it and to make corn bread, corn-meal mush, and other dishes.

As the years went by, the colonists found time to clear bigger fields and to remove stumps and roots from them. Then they raised many additional kinds of crops, including grain, vegetables, and fruits. They also raised livestock. You will recall that the early settlers brought hogs, cattle, sheep, and poultry from Europe. The colonists added to their diet by picking wild berries and nuts and by hunting and fishing. Thus they were able to enjoy a variety of foods.

On a typical small farm anywhere in the 13 English colonies, the farmer and his family did all the work. In the South some were helped by a few slaves; in the North, by an indentured servant or two. While the men worked in the fields, the women and children looked after the dairy, the poultry, and the garden. Whenever they were needed—especially at harvesttime—women and children helped in the fields.

With only crude hand tools, the colonial farmer had to work hard and long. He turned the soil with a heavy wooden hand plow and planted seed by hand. He cut wheat with a sickle and threshed it with a flail. He husked

Mount Vernon. George Washington's Mount Vernon was laid out like many other large plantations of the late colonial period. The gardens, sheds, storehouses, and slave quarters were clustered near the planter's house. Field hands lived farther from the house.

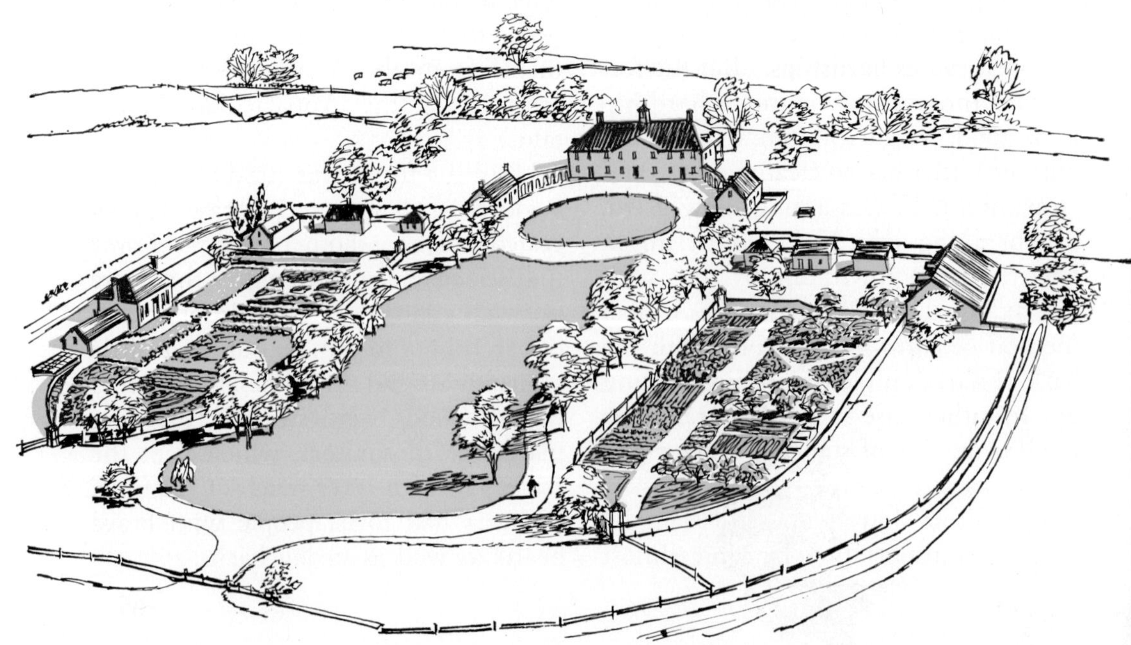

and shelled corn by hand. He did not have the tractors, reapers, threshers, and other machines that farmers use today.

Many small colonial farms did not produce very much food. To get even a bare living, a farmer had to make use of every resource at hand. He kept a swarm of bees and used the honey for sweetening. In March he collected maple sap and boiled it down to make maple sirup and maple sugar. When he cleared a new field, he piled up and burned the logs. Then he collected the ashes and made potash by letting water soak through them. Some of the potash he used at home to make soap and dyes, and the surplus he sold. Good, straight logs that he did not burn the farmer floated down the river to the nearest sawmill, where he sold them for lumber. In winter he put in time profitably by cutting firewood to be sold in the towns or by cutting shingles, barrel staves, and hoops. There was always a good market for these wood products. Some farmers, especially those near the seacoast, added to the family diet by catching fish.

Whenever they were lucky enough to have potash, butter, eggs, vegetables, or salted meat to sell, the farmer and his wife delivered the products to the country store. In return they received such necessities and little luxuries as salt, sugar, spices, powder and shot, iron bars for making nails, iron pots, knives, and pipe tobacco. The goods bought in a store were treasured and made to last as long as possible.

The southern plantation system. As the English colonies grew, farming began to differ from one region to the other, according to the different soil and climate. The southern colonists grew mainly staple crops. (A staple crop is one grown in large quantity for sale.) In Virginia, Maryland, and parts of the Carolinas, the staple crop was tobacco.

BETTMANN

Tobacco wharf. A southern plantation usually had a wharf. There English ships delivered goods the planter had ordered and loaded his tobacco, rice, or indigo for export. With such wharves, few cities were necessary.

The growing and curing of tobacco takes a great deal of hard manual labor, requiring many hands. In the 1600s it was done by the farmer himself, working alongside a few indentured servants. Beginning about 1700, Negro slaves were brought from Africa in large numbers and were put to work in the tobacco fields. The use of slaves to grow staple crops was the beginning of the southern plantation system.

After three or four crops of tobacco had been grown on a field, the soil lost its fertility. Little was known about how to care for soil to prevent its wearing out, and there was so much unsettled land that no one thought that all of it would ever be used. Instead of rotating crops or using fertilizer to build up the soil, a planter would clear a new field in the forest whenever he needed more land. Some of the land, used up by tobacco crops year after year, was ruined forever.

In South Carolina a plantation system grew up with rice and indigo (ĭn′-dĭ gō) as staple crops. Rice was grown in drained swamps, which had to be flooded two or three times while the plants were growing. The rice plants were hoed and weeded in the mud. A great deal of tiresome hand labor was also needed to prepare the rice grains for market. This work was done by Negro slaves because a slave could be forced to do work no matter how unpleasant it was. Indigo, a plant from which blue dye was made, was also grown by slave labor.

Family farms in the Piedmont and in the North. The majority of southern farmers were not wealthy plantation owners. Instead, they were men who cultivated small farms with the help of their families alone and without slaves. Most of these farmers lived in the hilly Piedmont Region above the fall line, which you read about on page 37. The Piedmont farmers generally did not grow staple crops. It would have cost too much to transport the crops to market, for there were no good roads. The farmer and his family, like the families described on page 66, tried to provide for their own needs as far as possible.

In the colonies north of Maryland there were not many large estates. Negro slaves were few and usually worked as household servants. The farms of the North were small. In New England the soil in the narrow river valleys was fertile; elsewhere it was thin and stony. A farm usually contained about a hundred acres. The soil in the middle colonies was generally more fertile than in New England, and the typical farm was somewhat larger. The middle colonies were famous as a great wheat-producing area. They exported large quantities of flour and other farm products to the New England seaboard towns, to the West Indies, and even to Europe. The middle colonies were called the "bread basket" of the English colonies.

Hard life on the frontier. We have been picturing colonial farm life in the settled area near the seacoast. At the western edge of settlement was the frontier. The pioneers there met all over again the problems of the first set-

Corn Dodgers
A Frontier Recipe to Try

Mix 1 cup of corn meal, 1 teaspoon of salt, 1½ tablespoons of sugar. Add 1 tablespoon of bacon drippings (or butter). Pour 1¼ cups of boiling water over the first four ingredients, beat well. Put the batter by spoonfuls onto a greased cookie sheet, smoothing each spoonful into a flat cake. Bake in a hot (preheated) oven (400° to 425°) until brown—about 20 minutes. Makes about 12 corn dodgers.

¶ A colonial mother probably cooked corn dodgers on a griddle over an open fire. Few frontier kitchens had ovens. To prevent the family from tiring of corn, she also prepared it in other ways: pone, hoecake, johnycake (journey cake), hominy, and Indian pudding.

tlers. They practiced the crudest kind of farming, partly because they did not know better methods and partly because they and their families had to do all the work of clearing as well as farming. As a result they lived from hand to mouth. To clear the land, the pioneer cut or burned down trees and underbrush. On his little clearing he planted corn and built a rough log cabin. The earth was its floor, a slab of wood hanging on leather hinges was the door, a hole cut in the logs was the window. The pioneer and his family made what they needed, and what they could not make they did without.

Gradually, as more people settled nearby, life in a frontier region became easier. But these farmers had to continue to supply most of their own needs for a long time. There were no roads and usually no waterways to link their lonely homes in the wilderness with the older settlements on the seacoast. When such links were formed, the region was no longer on the frontier.

4 *Some English Colonists Carry on Commerce*

The people of the 13 English colonies carried on a large trade with the mother country. By means of this trade the wealthy colonists obtained tea, spices, iron products, fine clothing and furniture, and other manufactured goods. Because commerce was so important, shipbuilding became a leading industry in many of the colonies, and many boys and young men earned a living and saw the world as sailors and traders.

THE NEW-YORK HISTORICAL SOCIETY, NEW YORK CITY

Commerce in early New York. Barrels of flour are being loaded on a vessel. The houses, with gables rising in steps, were built by the original Dutch settlers.

Another important industry made necessary by colonial commerce was cooperage, or the making of barrels. Loading and unloading cargo were hard jobs since there were no derricks. The colonists made the work as easy as possible by packing most products in barrels, which could be rolled in and out of wagons and up and down gangplanks. Wherever goods were in transport, there were barrels. Notice the many barrels in the illustrations in this chapter.

Great Britain regulates colonial trade. Like other nations of Europe, England believed that colonies should help make the mother country rich and strong. In order to make sure that the English people would profit from the colonies, the government enforced strict trade laws. All goods shipped to or from colonial ports had to be carried in British ships with British crews. Certain goods, such as furs and tobacco, could be exported only to England. Goods shipped from Europe to the colonies had to be sent by way of England, where a tax was collected.

The purpose of these laws was to prevent any foreign shipowner or merchant from profiting from the American colonial trade. The sale of goods to the colonies helped make English manufacturers prosperous. Thousands of English workers were employed in making and transporting the goods sent to the colonies.

Colonial trade is prosperous. Southern planters found that it was easy to sell their staple crops in England. Tobacco, rice, and indigo were not grown in any great amounts in England or in western Europe. The large-scale planter sent his crop directly to a merchant in England. The merchant sold the crop, taking a commission for himself. Then he bought manufactured goods ordered by the planter, taking another commission, and had the goods loaded on a ship. The ship crossed the Atlantic and tied up at the planter's wharf. The cargo of manufactured goods was unloaded. Tobacco, rice, or indigo was taken on for shipment to England.

Triangular trade. In the colonies north of Maryland, people had no staple crops to sell in England. Northern merchants sent furs, potash, lumber, whale oil, and naval stores to the mother country. These products, however, did not begin to pay for the goods imported from England. The merchants made up the difference by carrying on a triangular trade between the northern colonies, the West Indies, and the mother country.

Rum manufactured in Massachusetts and Rhode Island was used in another kind of triangular trade. New England merchants carried rum to the west coast of Africa. With it they paid tribal chiefs for captured Negroes, whom they carried off to the West Indies and sold as slaves. From the islands they took molasses home to be distilled into rum. With the profits they bought manufactured goods.

Molasses Act. Northern merchants and ship captains were naturally eager to increase their business. They began to trade with the planters in the French, Dutch, and Spanish West Indies as well as with those in the British West Indies. But in 1733 the English government passed the Molasses Act, which placed high duties on sugar and molasses imported from foreign colonies.

The merchants of the northern colonies were not willing to pay the duty. They called the law unfair. When they saw that their complaints had no effect on the British government, the merchants decided to ignore the Molasses Act. Many of them took to smuggling. They landed the foreign sugar or molasses secretly at out-of-the-way places along the coast. Just as often, some merchants brought their cargoes in openly at the large ports, where the small number of British officials were too busy to examine every ship.

Thus by a complicated triangular system of trade, including smuggling, the people of the northern colonies were able to sell their surplus products and to buy the manufactured goods they needed. On the map on page 71 you can study all these trade routes and the products carried.

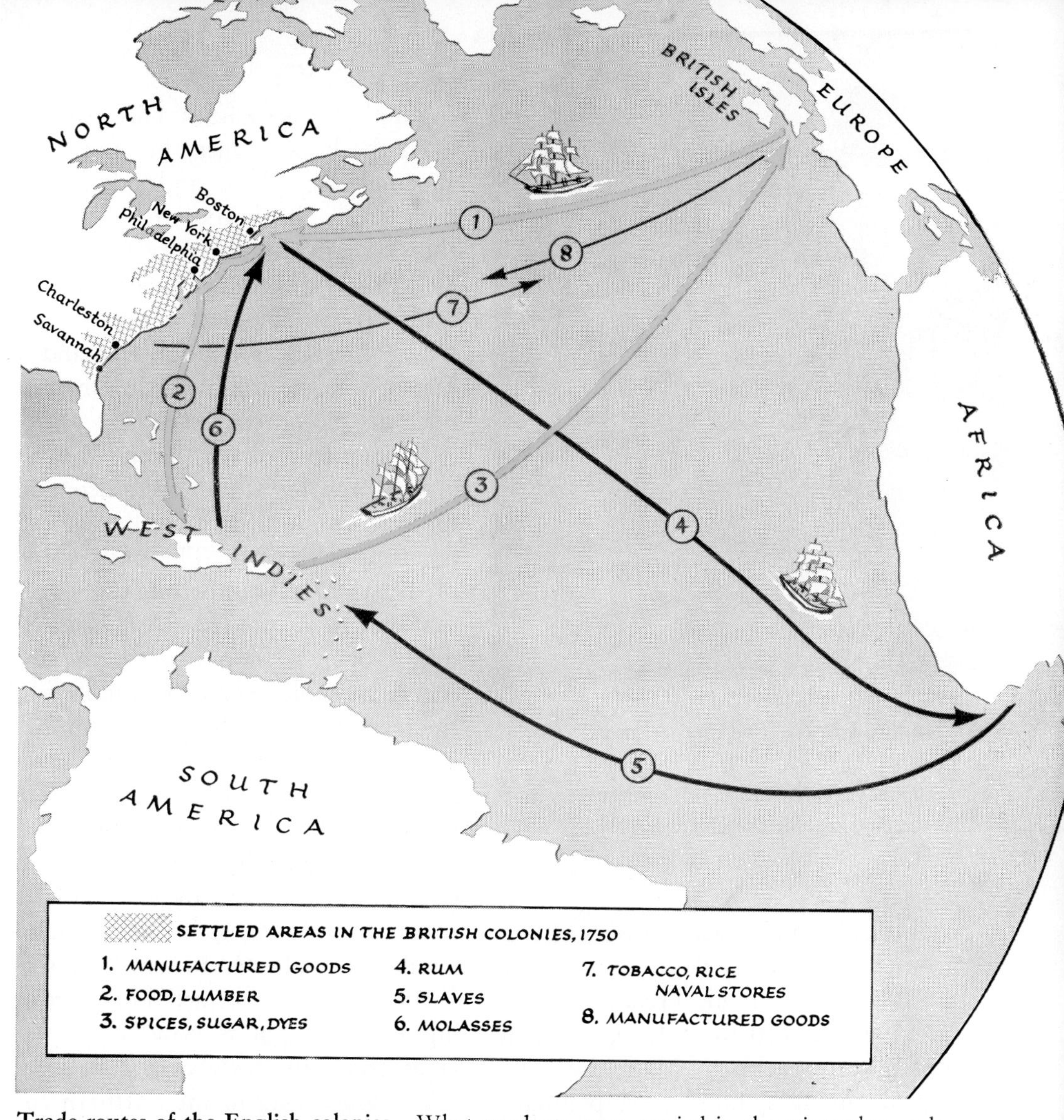

Trade routes of the English colonies. What products were carried in the triangular trade between the northern colonies, the West Indies, and England? What was carried in the triangular trade with Africa and the West Indies? What products were exchanged between the southern colonies and England?

Trading towns in the northern colonies. In the southern colonies, as we have seen, plantation owners shipped their crops and received imported goods at their private wharves. Many of them sold goods to their neighbors. Therefore only a very few towns like Charleston, South Carolina, grew up. In the northern colonies trade gave rise to a number of seacoast towns. For a living, most of the townspeople depended in one way or another on shipping.

Trade required many kinds of workers. There were the carters, who used carts or wagons to do the work our truck drivers do today. They hauled farm products from the surrounding

THE NEW-YORK HISTORICAL SOCIETY, NEW YORK CITY

Spinning wheel. The mother and daughters of the colonial family spun wool and flax into yarn, wove yarn into cloth, and sewed most of the clothing for the entire family.

countryside to city warehouses. Millers ground wheat into flour, and out of the flour bakers made bread. Butchers salted and packed meat. Coopers made barrels for packing. Many workers earned a living by building ships; many others earned a living by sailing them. Others served as shoemakers, barbers, tailors, carpenters, and silversmiths.

As the towns grew, they attracted teachers, preachers, physicians, and other professional people. By 1750 life in the seaboard towns had come a long way from the time when the first settlers lived in makeshift shelters and sometimes did not know where their next meal was coming from. People could live easier lives. They could enjoy a few luxuries. They had time for visiting and playing games. (See page 86.)

As the back country became settled, shoemakers, tailors, and other craftsmen from the seaboard towns went there to earn a living. A craftsman traveled from farm to farm, working at his trade. If he found a country village where there was enough demand for his services, he might settle down and open his shop there.

A country village often grew up around a waterfall where someone had built a flour mill, a sawmill, or a combination of the two. The miller probably began to sell on the side the supplies that farmers needed. A blacksmith might open a shop next to the mill, where he could repair farm tools while the farmers waited for their grain to be ground or their boards to be sawed. Next someone would open a tavern, where the farmers could gather to eat and drink and talk. Thus the place became a crossroads and a gathering place. Soon a church and a school would be built. Craftsmen and shopkeepers would be attracted to the growing village. That is how country villages gradually developed.

Manufacturing in the northern colonies. We have already seen that the people in the northern colonies made such products as rum and flour and built ships. Other kinds of manufacturing were carried on in the colonial homes, in towns as well as in the country. The clothing industry is one example. The colonists made most of their own clothes in their own homes. Only the well to do could afford to import cloth from England and to have their clothing made by a tailor.

The colonial tailor who was just start-

Colonial ironworks. This drawing shows an iron furnace in colonial Saugus, Massachusetts. The ore was tossed into the top opening. Bellows at the bottom forced air through the fire to keep it hot. The bellows were operated by the waterwheel at the right.

ing out in business made clothes to measure from cloth brought to him by the customer. After he became established, he might import a stock of cloth out of which to supply his customers. Besides selling imported cloth, he might set up a number of looms in his shop and hire weavers to make cloth, or he might buy surplus cloth woven by farm families in their homes. The manufacture of hats from beaver fur and the manufacture of shoes also became important industries in the New England towns.

Still other industries grew up in the colonies. For example, in several colonies, especially New York, New Jersey, and Pennsylvania, companies were formed to build iron furnaces and make iron products.

England did not stand by and permit her colonies to manufacture goods that would compete with those made in English factories. In addition to the trade laws, the government passed laws to limit manufacturing. One law forbade the colonists to export wool and woolen cloth. They could not ship such goods even from one colony to another. Another law similarly prohibited them from exporting hats. Because the products could not be sold away from home, the industries could not grow. Still another law, passed in 1750, tried to limit the colonial iron industry by forbidding the colonists to manufacture nails, tools, pots and pans, or other articles made from iron. But the colonists did not obey these laws any more than they observed the Molasses Act.

The English colonies become firmly established. By 1750 the oldest English colony—Virginia—was almost 150 years old. The youngest—Georgia—was almost 20 years old. Already the people in the settlements along the coast had overcome the hardships connected with obtaining food, clothing, and shelter in a wilderness. They were producing larger crops than they needed for themselves, and with the surplus they were buying luxuries from Europe. They were even beginning to manufacture some products for themselves. They had built cities. In short, a permanent branch of European life had been established in the New World.

Summary

The vast majority of European colonists in America, whether Spanish, French, or English, lived by farming. From the land and by the work of their own hands, most colonists produced almost everything they needed. In Spanish America much of the land was divided into large estates, and the work was done by Indians. Because of poor transportation, agricultural products were usually not shipped far and each estate took care of its own needs. In New France the habitants did most of the farm work and paid the seigniors a small annual rent for the use of the land. The farmers of New France usually did not raise enough food to feed the colony.

In the English colonies farming not only provided the colonists with their daily living but also supplied most of their exports. In the northern and middle colonies there were small farms, each one worked by the farmer and his family with little outside help. There were many such family farms in the southern colonies, too. But the southern colonies also had large and small plantations on which Negro slaves did most of the work.

Each mother country wanted its colonies to send home products not easily obtained in the homeland. The king of Spain prized his American colonies mainly for the gold and silver that were mined there. The French king prized New France mainly for the wealth that came from the fur trade. The English colonies were important for their large trade in many products.

All the 13 English colonies exported such products as naval stores, but in their most important exports each region was different. By trading directly with English merchants, southern planters sold tobacco, rice, and indigo and bought manufactured goods. By means of a triangular trade that included the West Indies, New England and the middle colonies exported grain, meat, and other products and imported manufactured goods.

Spain, France, and Great Britain tried to control the trade of their colonies. Spain and France prohibited their colonists from trading with foreigners. The British government placed a tax on most colonial trade with foreign countries. Since the mother countries wished to sell their own manufactured goods in the colonies, they passed laws prohibiting colonial manufactures. Thus the mother countries—Spain, France, and Great Britain—used their colonies to make themselves richer and stronger.

For a Quick Review

1. How did transportation conditions affect farming in Spanish America?

2. How did the Spanish king control trade in his colonies?

3. Compare the system of farming used in Spanish America with that used in New France.

4. Why was the fur trade important in the growth of New France? How was it carried on?

5. What were the important staple crops of the southern colonies?

6. Compare farm work in New England, in the Piedmont, and on large southern plantations.

7. Why have the middle colonies been called the "bread basket" of the English colonies?

8. To pay for goods that they bought in Europe, what goods did the New Englanders trade? With whom did they trade?

Learning to Study More Easily

READING FOR MAIN IDEAS

An author builds a chapter around certain main ideas. He supports these main ideas with other ideas and with facts. For example, one main idea in Chapter 4 is that the fur trade was very important to the colonists of New France. The chapter gives facts showing that the idea was true and explanations of why it was true.

Similarly, an author usually builds a paragraph around one thought, and he often expresses that thought in a single sentence, called the topic sentence.

One way to learn to study more easily is to look first for the big, important ideas in a reading assignment. Then fit the facts and other ideas into place under the main ideas. You can form the habit of studying this way by first reading an assignment to get the main ideas.

Try this exercise for practice in reading for main ideas. (Remember to use the headings in the text as suggested on page 55.) Turn to page 65 and skim the section that begins on that page to decide what is the main thought of each paragraph or group of paragraphs. Then test how well you have selected main ideas in the section by answering these questions:

1. Which is the main thought of the paragraph beginning, "In the early years . . ."? (*a*) Corn was a good food for the early settlers. (*b*) The Indians taught the settlers how to raise corn. (*c*) The early settlers raised corn more than any other crop, because it could be used for many purposes.
2. Which is the main thought of the paragraph beginning, "As the years went by, the colonists . . ."? (*a*) Later colonists learned to use wild fruits and to hunt wild animals for their food supply. (*b*) By combining the crops and livestock of the Old World and the New World, the later colonists improved their food supply. (*c*) The colonists gradually increased the size of their clearings.

Work through the rest of the section, stating the main idea of each paragraph or group of paragraphs in one sentence. If the entire class is doing this exercise, perhaps you can all compare your main-idea sentences and choose the best ones.

5 *Life in the New World Is Varied*

You are in Lima, Peru, at three o'clock in the afternoon one October day in the 1750s. The streets are practically deserted. Everyone is at home asleep or just waking up. But siesta (sĭ ĕs′tȧ) time, the time when everyone takes a nap during the hottest part of the day, is about over. Gradually people appear on the streets. They seem to be waiting for something, and their interest is centered on the plaza (plä′zȧ), or city square. By four o'clock there are many people walking slowly around the plaza or standing in groups talking. The crowd murmurs as it turns to stare down the main avenue leading into the plaza. "Here comes Don Diego's coach," someone shouts. "And Don Alberto's, just behind," says another voice. The afternoon promenade (prŏm ē̈-näd′) has begun. The wealthy gentlemen and ladies of Lima are on display.

By four-thirty the big show is at its height. Two long lines of gilded coaches, one coming from each direction, roll along the main avenue and across the plaza. Some coaches are drawn by two horses, some by four. Each coach is accompanied by four or five slaves dressed in colorful uniforms. Inside sit the ladies, dressed in rich evening gowns and glittering with jewels. They nod and bow as they recognize friends in the passing coaches. The men, dressed in velvet and satin clothes with gold and silver decorations, ride on horseback. The saddles and bridles on their horses are covered with silver and gold. Here is the time and place for ladies and gentlemen to show off a new costume and to win the admiration of friends and the envy of others. The less fortunate enjoy the show from a distance, just as you are enjoying it on an October afternoon 200 years ago.

1 *Spanish Customs Influence Life in Spanish America*

The people of Spain, like those of other European nations at the time of Columbus, were divided into groups called social classes. The members of each social class had certain privileges that made them different from the members of other social classes. Nobles, for example, were not required to obey the same laws that governed other persons. A master could change his place of residence as he wished, but his servants could not choose where they would live. People placed great importance upon the differences between social classes.

It was difficult for a person to rise into a higher social class than the one in which he happened to be born. The accident of birth usually decided what opportunities a person would have for education, for making a comfortable living, and so forth. The idea that every person has a right to equal opportunities was not accepted at all.

Social classes in Spanish America. The Spaniards brought to America the custom of dividing people into social classes. At the top of the social ladder in the Spanish colonies were the Spaniards who had been born in the mother country. Only those Spaniards who had proved their loyalty to the king and the

City plaza. The plaza of a colonial Spanish-American city was the center of activity. The cathedral and the government buildings gave it great dignity. In the broad square, soldiers marched, businessmen carried on trade, and people gathered to walk and talk.

BANCROFT LIBRARY, UNIVERSITY OF CALIFORNIA

Spanish colonial plantation. A plantation in Spanish America was an almost self-supporting community. Compare this plantation with the sketch of Mount Vernon, in the southern English colonies, on page 66.

church were allowed to come to the New World. They held all the chief offices in the government. They held all the highest ranks in the army. The most important men in the church were Spanish-born. Though not a very large group, they owned much of the wealth of the colonies. A Spaniard who came to America was almost sure to make a fortune in a few years.

Next in social rank were the Spaniards born in the colonies. They were called Creoles (krē′ōlz). Many of the Creole families were rich, but even the most wealthy ranked below the Spaniards born in Europe. To make up for their lower rank, many of them spent money extravagantly.

Although these two white groups made up only a small fraction of the population, they enjoyed all the wealth and honors of Spanish America. It was the men and women of these groups who joined in the daily promenade in Lima and the other cities of Spanish America. They did none of the hard hand labor. They owned the plantations and the mines. They carried on the commerce. They were the doctors, lawyers, and teachers. All the high and honored offices in the army and the church were theirs. If a person happened to be a member of one of these groups, his life was easy compared with the life of others in Spanish America.

At the other end of the social ladder were the Indians and the slaves. The Indians, who made up the mass of the population, worked hard and lived in poverty. On about the same level were the Negro slaves. For the most part the Negroes worked as household servants. If a person happened to be born in one of these groups, his life was hard.

Besides these three separate racial groups—Spaniards, Indians, and Negroes—there were several mixed groups in the population. Some had white and Indian or white and Negro parents. Others had Indian and Negro parents.

Most of them worked in humble jobs in the cities and on the plantations.

City life is colorful. The cities of Spanish America were much alike because they were modeled after the cities of Spain. The heart of the city was the plaza. Around it stood the public buildings, including the church, the town hall, and the prison. In a capital city the church was a cathedral. The most elaborate dwellings on the plaza were the palaces of the bishop and the governor. On the streets near the plaza were the homes of the wealthy. The slums of the poor were not far away.

The cities were not large. Lima, the capital of the viceroyalty of Peru, had a population of 80,000 at the end of the eighteenth century and covered an area one mile square. Compare this population and area with that of the largest city in your state today.

City houses were generally built of adobe, or sun-dried bricks. They were whitewashed so that they would reflect the heat of the sun and remain cool. The home of a well-to-do family was built around a series of courtyards, or patios (pä′tĭ ōz). This method of building around courtyards brought the sunshine right into the house. The children were able to play out of doors without leaving their homes. Less wealthy families lived in homes built around a single courtyard. A poor family, together with its pigs and poultry, might live in a hut with a single room.

City streets were busy in the morning hours. Every morning a market was held in the square for the sale of farm products. Officials and merchants went to their offices and carried on their affairs. At noon all the people went home

NATIONAL GALLERY OF ART, INDEX OF AMERICAN DESIGN

Spanish influence. The Spanish missionaries taught the Indians to carve wooden figures for the church. This carving was made in what is now New Mexico.

City home in New Spain. The city home of a wealthy colonist in New Spain was built around several courtyards. The family could be outdoors and have privacy at the same time.

and ate the heavy meal of the day. Immediately after that, silence fell over the city as everyone went indoors for the siesta.

After the siesta the city returned to activity. Then came the promenade of which you read as you began this chapter. In the smaller towns there were few, if any, coaches. For their promenade the people walked up and down the main street.

Country life is quiet. Such was life in the city. Country life did not have so much glitter and glamor. The owner of a plantation had a large house built around several courtyards. Storehouses, stables, and gardens were nearby. There was usually a church in which services were held regularly. Because of the long distances and the poor transportation between plantations, there was little social life with other aristocrats. That is why every plantation owner who could afford to do so spent most of his time in a city.

Most of the country people were Indians and other humble folk. They tilled the soil, planted, and harvested for their masters. They found time to grow food for themselves on the land they were allowed to use. They paid taxes and they went to church. It was a hard life that did not change from year to year, from generation to generation.

Holidays. For all the people in the Spanish colonies there were many breaks in the dull routine. Out of the 365 days of the year 159 were holidays. Some of them were observed in some places, some in other places, while a large number were celebrated throughout Spanish America. Most of the holidays were religious, and on a religious holiday no one worked. Every holyday was celebrated with a special Mass in the church, feasting in the homes, and dancing in the streets. Some celebrations lasted as long as a month.

The church in the life of the Spanish colonies. The Catholic Church played an important part in the life of the Spanish colonies. All the inhabitants belonged to it and accepted its teachings. Education in Spanish America was almost entirely in the hands of the church. There were no public schools. Only the sons of the well to do were expected to have more than the most elementary education. They were taught at home by private tutors until they were ready to attend a university. As in Spain, girls—even daughters of the wealthy—learned only to read and write. In the colonies, as in the mother country, the church tried to keep out any ideas that were contrary to its teachings.

The priests were the best friends the Indians had. They protested to the king of Spain against the cruel treatment suffered by the Indians. They taught the Indians how to raise crops and how to make cloth, furniture, candles, soap, and other products. As a result the Indians were able to better their lives.

The Catholic Church was an important force in holding the people of Spanish America together in one society.

2 *French Colonists Live a Simple, Friendly Life*

It is not difficult, from what we already know, to picture the life of the habitants of New France in their little

PUBLIC ARCHIVES OF CANADA

Bake oven. Close to the house of the Canadian habitant was the bake oven, where the housewife baked a whole week's supply of bread at once.

homes along the St. Lawrence River. The simple houses were built low, tight, and snug against the winter cold. The house contained one, two, or three rooms, depending on how well off the family was. In any case the door from the outside opened into the large main room, which served as kitchen, dining room, sitting room, and usually bedroom, too.

The furniture was simple and homemade. A table made of hand-hewn pine, chairs with frames of pine saplings and woven seats, a colorful wool rug or two, a spinning wheel and a loom, a few chests in which to store clothing, and a bench for the water buckets were the usual furnishings. On the walls were a crucifix and pictures of saints. From the rafters hung slabs of cured meat, smoked eels, and the father's gun and powder horn.

Summer work and winter play. From May to October the habitants worked hard in the fields, but everyone took time off to celebrate the many saints' days and other church holidays. On these occasions, as on Sundays, the men dressed in their Sunday homespuns and beaver hats. The women wore their best homemade dresses touched off with a bit of imported lace and perhaps ribbons in their hair.

On ordinary summer days women and children wore dresses of homespun. Children wore sleeveless, straight-cut dresses that reached to the knees. Men wore homemade shirts and trousers. Women and children went barefoot. The men wore cowhide clogs (rough shoes) to protect their feet in field and forest. All wore hats of braided straw, made by the women in the winter.

After harvest, and before winter set

LIBRARY OF CONGRESS

Habitant's living room. The furnishings of this room suggest the simple life of the habitant in New France.

in, each family filled its root cellar with potatoes, peas, beans, beets, carrots, cabbages, apples, and salted or smoked meat. With this food reserve, the family was ready for the winter.

In the winter the family wore heavy clothing made at home out of tough, drab woolen homespun and out of furs, which were often as cheap as cloth. The men wore long, loose coats reaching to the knees and tied around the waist with a knitted belt; warm, baggy trousers; two or more pairs of woolen socks; and oiled moccasins laced up almost to the knees. They wore home-knitted woolen gloves and toques (tōks), or brimless hats, that could be pulled down over the ears.

Aside from cutting firewood and doing other chores, the men had little to do during the long winter months except to keep warm and to enjoy themselves. Neighbors spent much of their time at one another's houses gossiping and playing cards.

The habitants ate heartily. There was not much variety in the menu, especially in the winter, but the meals were nourishing. They ate stacks of pancakes. In the winter they thawed out and cooked the hard-frozen smoked meat or salted fish. The vegetables came out of the root cellar, where they had been protected from the frost. However, many a family frequently made a meal of a bowl of thick pea soup and a wedge of dark bread.

If you were to enter the house of a habitant, the host would rise, take off his cap, and invite you to sit. When you were seated, he would put his cap on and sit down, too. If you stayed for a meal, you would find that the smaller children ate separately at a little table. The hostess would remain standing behind your chair to serve you throughout the meal. With such courtesy did the habitants treat their guests.

The church in the French colonies. The church was the center of the French-Canadian farm village. The parish priest was with his people in their time of need, in their work, and in their play. As a rule he was the only educated person in the village. The people respected him for his knowledge as well as for his spiritual leadership.

The habitants were pious (pī′ŭs) folk who attended church regularly on Sundays and holydays. One outstanding church holiday was Michaelmas (mĭk′ĕl măs), November 11. That day was also important in their lives because it was the day for paying their rent to the seigniors.

Michaelmas came soon after harvest, and all the village farmers, together with their families, gathered in the yard of the seignior's house. They were dressed in their holiday best, with a few coins in their pockets and fat hens and bushels of wheat in their little carts. They followed one another into the house to pay their rent. After the business was done, the seignior provided refreshments. Then the people scattered to their homes for visits and parties.

The entire population of the seigniory again gathered before the seignior's house on the morning of May Day. The men planted a Maypole in the yard, and the people danced around it. The seignior and his family greeted them and invited them in for wine and cake.

Aristocratic life in Quebec. Not all seigniors were wealthy. Many of them were little better off than the habitants. They and their families worked in the fields side by side with the tenants. Only in Quebec was there a group that stood out as a social aristocracy. This group included the governor, the intendant, and other government officials; army officers stationed in the city; the wealthy merchants; and the seigniors who could afford to spend their winters in town.

These people tried to create, around the governor's palace on the rock overlooking the St. Lawrence River, a small-scale imitation of the glittering royal court in Paris, France. The men wore coats trimmed with gold lace, silk stockings, bright-colored shoes with high heels and silver buckles, wigs, and swords. The women wore elaborate dresses of heavy brocade imported directly from Paris. They had complicated hairdos ornamented with ribbons, feathers, and jewels. The houses of the aristocrats were modeled after houses in France, with two full stories, slate roofs, and courtyards.

After Midnight Mass. Church is out, and the French-Canadians, bundled in furs, crowd into their sleighs for the merry ride home in the moonlight.

We must not think of the lives of the aristocrats as typical of life in Quebec. Most of the people in the capital lived much like their country neighbors. We should remember that until the end of French control Quebec was little more than a village. In 1661, 50 years after it was founded, it had a population of 547. Most of the houses in Quebec resembled those of the habitants along the river, though they were generally somewhat larger and better furnished. Like the habitants, the people of Quebec made their own clothes, cured meat and eels, and stored vegetables in their root cellars against the long winter. The difference between the lives of wealthy and poor in the French colonies was not so great as in the colonies of Spain.

New England room. This is a room in a colonial home in Springfield, Massachusetts. Compare its furnishings with those in the home of the Canadian habitant (page 82).

SMITHSONIAN INSTITUTION

3 *In the Northern English Colonies Town Life Changes Faster Than Farm Life*

As in England and as in other colonies in the New World at the time, class divisions were important in the life of the English colonists in America. The settlers took it for granted that all men were *not* created equal, that some were born superior to others and therefore were more deserving. The aristocrats of the colonies showed their superiority in their education, manners, splendid homes and clothes, and fine food. A gentleman had opportunities that ordinary people did not have. He had special privileges. For example, if he committed a crime for which the usual punishment was whipping or standing in the pillory, he did not receive such punishment but paid a fine instead.

The well to do enjoy an easy life. In the northern colonies most of the aristocrats were prosperous merchants and shipowners who lived in the towns. They built stately mansions in what we call the Georgian style, then popular in England. These homes were richly furnished. The walls were paneled; the floors were covered with soft rugs. The furniture was mainly of delicately carved mahogany. Tables were set with expensive silver, imported linens, and fine china and glass. The ladies and gentlemen and children who lived in these mansions wore clothes as rich and showy as their homes.

The daily life of the family of a wealthy merchant was usually easy and pleasant. The father went to his place of business at ten o'clock in the morn-

BETTMANN

A game at Bowling Green. Bowling was a popular sport in colonial New York. The game was especially popular with the Dutch. They brought it with them from the Old World. Do you remember that bowling played a part in the story about Rip Van Winkle? What details in the picture—clothing, buildings, and so on—suggest colonial times? The spot where this game is being played is still a park at the tip of Manhattan Island, and it is still called Bowling Green.

ing. At two in the afternoon he called it a day and drove back home for dinner. Dinner consisted of several kinds of fish, half a dozen meat dishes, vegetables, imported wines, pies, puddings, fruits, and nuts.

In the middle colonies the men found recreation in horse racing, fox hunting, and card playing. Dancing was popular. So was the theater. When young people got together for an evening visit, they often entertained themselves by singing.

In New England horse racing, fox hunting, and other sports were frowned upon. In the early days the Puritans had prohibited dancing, music, and the theater as well. But by 1750 dances were held and music was heard in Boston. The theater was still forbidden.

The middle class live comfortably. The skilled workers made up the large middle class in the colonial towns. They included many kinds of craftsmen: butchers, bakers, tailors, shoemakers, hatmakers, blacksmiths, jewelers, printers, carpenters, coopers—it is impossible to list them all. They were not only craftsmen, making and repairing the products of their trade; they were also storekeepers, selling the articles they made and other things as well.

The homes of the skilled craftsmen were plain wood or brick houses, usually two stories high, with small, low rooms. The kitchen, which contained the great fireplace in which the food was cooked, also served as living room, dining room, and bedroom. The furniture was simple but strong. In some cases the workshop occupied a room on the first floor with a door opening directly on the street. In other cases the shop was a separate little building ad-

ADRIANCE MEMORIAL LIBRARY, POUGHKEEPSIE, N.Y.

Colonial street. The departing stagecoach, man on horseback, and flock of sheep made up a typical scene in a colonial town. How would you describe the clothing worn by the people? This painting is in the Poughkeepsie, New York, post office.

joining the home. Over every shop door hung a sign indicating the trade of the owner.

The craftsman's family wore inexpensive clothing and ate plain, nourishing food. The diet had little variety, but included fish, meat, and vegetables. Dresses and suits were made of homespun. Father's and mother's clothes were often cut down to make them fit the children. Apprentices and servants wore coarse shirts and large, loose leather breeches.

The men of the middle-class families spent many an evening in their favorite inns, where they played such games as billiards, shuffleboard, and cards. Children had games and toys. In the winter they went skating. In the summer the boys went swimming in the harbor off the wharves. The women attended quilting parties and other social gatherings. A great to-do was made over weddings and christenings. People of the craftsman group, for the most part, did not approve of dancing.

Wage earners have opportunities to advance. Below the middle class in the social ladder were those who were not skilled and owned no property. They included sailors, fishermen, porters, dock workers, and manual laborers. When times were bad and there was no work for them, some of these people had to be supported by charity. But workers in the colonies were much better off than workers in Europe. They received higher wages; and in their rapidly growing communities there were many opportunities for themselves and their children to become craftsmen, merchants, and professional persons. Those who wished to become farmers could easily acquire land.

Indentured servants and slaves. At the lowest social level were the indentured servants and the slaves. They had few, if any, rights. We can judge the hardships they suffered from the large numbers that ran away. Almost every issue of colonial newspapers contained advertisements seeking the return of runaway servants. But once an indentured servant had served his time, he faced all the opportunities of an expanding country. In some colonies he received 50 acres of land to start him off. Many indentured servants became successful citizens and leaders of their communities.

Towns face problems of city life. By 1750 the largest towns in the northern English colonies were big enough to be faced with some of the same problems that cities must solve today. One problem was to get the streets paved. In most cities each citizen had to pay half the cost of paving the street in front of his property; the town paid the rest. Then there was the problem of keeping the streets clean. Each citizen was expected to sweep the street in front of his home. The town governments had to threaten the people with fines to make them keep the streets clean.

To preserve law and order, each town had constables, or policemen, in the daytime and a watch at night. Members of the night watch walked the streets with their lanterns from nine o'clock at night until five o'clock in the morning. They stopped at street corners and in loud voices announced the time and the state of the weather. "Two o'clock. The night is clear" might be the call. They questioned anyone who was out late at night, and they were always on the lookout for signs of fire.

Fire was one of the greatest dangers in colonial towns. The large cities had many disastrous fires. After each one the towns passed stricter laws to help prevent fires and to fight them after they started. For example, to prevent the many fires that started in chimneys, they appointed chimney sweepers to keep chimneys clean.

Water was essential for fire fighting as well as for household use. To obtain water, the towns permitted private persons to dig wells in the middle of the streets. By 1750 pumps were almost as close to one another down the middle of Philadelphia streets as street lights are on city streets today.

The three largest towns—Philadelphia, Boston, and New York—had traffic problems 150 years before the coming of the automobile. The narrow streets were jammed with men on horseback, coaches, wagons and carts drawn by oxen, peddlers, porters pushing wheelbarrows, porters carrying packs on their backs, stray dogs and hogs, people walking, and children playing games. In those days there was no curb separating sidewalk from road. Pedestrians walking along the side were liable to be spattered with mud or even be knocked down by horses and wagons. Accidents were frequent, espe-

Fireman's hat. This leather fireman's hat, made in Philadelphia in the 1830s, was used by members of the Franklin Hose Company. Why does it bear Franklin's portrait?

NATIONAL GALLERY OF ART, INDEX OF AMERICAN DESIGN

cially to children. To meet this problem, men on horseback were forbidden to gallop their horses. Carters were ordered to lead their horses through the streets by the reins.

Philadelphia and its famous citizen. In the middle years of the eighteenth century (the 1700s), Philadelphia was the largest city in the English colonies and the second largest in the British Empire, being surpassed only by London. It was a busy, prosperous port with much trade and shipbuilding. Many immigrants landed at its wharves.

Philadelphia's leadership in this period was due in large part to one man—Benjamin Franklin. We can think of Franklin's career in Philadelphia as beginning in 1726, when he returned from his first trip to England at the age of 20. The next year he organized a club called the Junto (jŭn′tō). The members held debates and helped one another to learn how to speak in public. Under Franklin's leadership the Junto started the first circulating library in Philadelphia. Several of its members joined with Franklin in founding the American Philosophical Society, the first scientific organization in the English colonies.

Franklin was responsible for many improvements in Philadelphia. He formed the first volunteer fire company. He campaigned for a paid night watch because it would be more reliable than one made up of volunteers. He persuaded Philadelphia to pave its streets and light them at night. He shamed people into keeping the streets clean in front of their houses by printing in his newspaper the names of those who failed to do so. He took the lead in organizing the academy that later developed into the University of Pennsylvania. And he helped found the Pennsylvania Hospital, the first hospital in the 13 colonies.

At the same time Franklin was gradually building a fortune. He became official printer for four of the colonial governments. He issued a newspaper and published books. He wrote and printed *Poor Richard's Almanac.* The sayings of "Poor Richard" were known and repeated in all the colonies. In 1748, at the age of 42, Franklin was able to retire from business and devote his time to other interests, especially science and politics.

He made electrical experiments. He built one of the earliest batteries. By his famous kite experiment he proved that

Benjamin Franklin Said:

Savages we call them because their manners differ from ours.

To find out a girl's faults, praise her to her girl friends.

If you would keep a secret from an enemy, tell it not to a friend.

Work as if you were to live one hundred years, pray as if you were to die tomorrow.

The way to be safe is never to be secure.

The most acceptable service of God is doing good to man.

Where liberty dwells there is my country.

They that can give up essential liberty to obtain a little temporary safety deserve neither liberty nor safety.

¶ Here are a few of the sayings credited to "Poor Richard." Can you find others?

lightning is electricity, and he made a practical application of that discovery by inventing the lightning rod. He also invented an improved stove. These achievements made him famous, and his personal fame brought glory to the city in which he lived.

Franklin also became active in politics. He was elected city alderman and then member of the colonial assembly. In 1754 he was a Pennsylvania delegate to the Albany Congress, which you will read about in the next chapter. He helped defend Pennsylvania against the French and Indians. In 1757 he was sent to England to represent the Pennsylvania assembly before the British government. With that journey began the international part of his career. You will be reading more about Franklin's work for his country.

Northern farm life does not change much. Public-spirited citizens like Franklin helped make town life in the colonies about as comfortable as it was in the cities of England. But farm life in the colonies remained simple and hard, more like life during the early years of settlement. As you read on pages 66–67, each family produced for itself almost everything it needed.

The New England farm family usually lived in a village. The village was the population center of the town. (You will remember that the New England town consists of the village, or sometimes more than one village, with the surrounding farms. It is like the township in other parts of the country.) In the center of the village was the common, or village green.

The middle colonies had farm villages and some large, isolated farms. The villages reminded one of New England. The large farms, on the other hand, suggested the southern plantations.

The middle colonies are the great melting pot. While there were non-English settlers in all the colonies, there were more in the middle colonies than in New England or the South. The smaller groups, like the French, Swedes, and Welsh, were soon absorbed by intermarriage with their neighbors. Others, especially the Dutch in New York and the Germans in Pennsylvania, gathered in separate communities where they kept their Old World customs and taught their children the ways of life of their European mother countries.

The Dutch. In 1750 the older section of New York City still looked like a Dutch town. Country villages like Albany and Schenectady (skĕ nĕk′tȧ dĭ) were almost entirely Dutch. Most of the houses built by the Dutch were of brick. Everything inside the houses was shiny with cleanliness. In her spic-and-span kitchen the Dutch housewife made cookies, doughnuts, sausage, and other foods that have become part of the American diet.

The Germans. The Germans who settled in Pennsylvania became prosperous farmers and skilled craftsmen. German craftsmen were responsible for the perfection of the Kentucky rifle and the Conestoga (kŏn ĕs tō′gȧ) wagon, later famous as the "covered wagon" that carried many settlers to the Far West.

The Germans kept many of their Old World living habits. They ate favorite German foods like sauerkraut, potato soup, and frankfurters. They brought a

Colonial postman. The colonial postal service was slow, irregular, and expensive. Mail was carried by postriders, who often made extra money by delivering packages—or even a flock of sheep—along the route.

love of music with them and made many of their own musical instruments. The best music in the colonies was heard in some of the German communities in Pennsylvania. Such customs of the non-English settlers gave to life in the middle colonies the charm of variety.

In time, of course, these non-English groups blended with the English colonists to form the American nation. Because of this mingling of many groups, our country has been called a melting pot. Each group contributed some of its customs and skills to the American way of life. Each group learned from the others. American life was full of variety and change and adventure.

4 *In the Southern English Colonies Life Centers in the Plantations*

Life in the colonial South centered chiefly in the plantations. In their large homes in Virginia or Carolina, the great plantation owners copied the ways of living of the wealthy English landlords of the day. They kept in close touch with the mother country through trade, as you discovered in reading pages 69–71. Clergymen came from England to preach in southern churches. Many planters had been educated in England and sent their sons to be educated there. When these boys returned home, they brought back the latest London books, fashions, and dance steps. Families and friends eagerly learned from these returned travelers. The southerners desired to keep up with everything new in English life.

The planter and his family enjoy many pleasures. In the 1700s some of the planters of the South lived even more luxuriously than the wealthy merchants of the North. The southerners, like the northern merchants, also built magnificent mansions in the popular English Georgian style. (Many of these large brick homes still stand in Virginia.) Inside they were furnished at least as richly as in the North. The southern planter dressed in the same style as, but more lavishly than, the northern merchant.

The well-to-do planter and his family enjoyed life. About once a month the boys and girls of a region gathered in one of the mansions for a whole day's dancing. The older people had parties that lasted for days. Sunday was especially the day for visits, though every planter's home was always open to guests. The planters enjoyed horse racing, fox hunting, cockfighting, and other sports. The height of the social season came when the planters moved to the capital of the colony for the meeting of the legislature. Charleston, South Carolina, was known in the eighteenth century as the gayest city in the colonies. Williamsburg, Virginia, was another brilliant social center.

Plantation life includes hard work. We must not, however, think of the southern planter and his family as enjoying one continuous round of fun. Their time was divided about equally between pleasure and work.

On each plantation, besides 50 or 60 slaves, there were a number of white workers, including some indentured servants and others hired by the month or year. Counting all the persons on the plantation, young and old, black and white, there might be from 100 to 300 people subject to the orders of the planter.

Some planters owned two or more plantations besides the one on which they lived. Such a planter ran a big, complicated business. He had to attend to his affairs much of the time. He frequently had to act as judge in disputes between Negroes and in complaints by Negroes against their overseers. When we add to these many activities the planter's duties as member of the parish vestry (the group that ran the local church), the county court, and the colonial legislature, we must conclude that he had to spend much of his time in serious work.

The planter's wife supervised a large household. Under her control usually were the slaves who did the spinning, weaving, and sewing for all the slaves. She also directed those who cured meat and prepared other foods. Of course, she also played a large part in bringing up her children, especially in training

THE MARYLAND HOUSE AND GARDEN PILGRIMAGE

Georgian architecture. The Hammond-Harwood House, Annapolis, Maryland, was built in 1774. It is a famous example of the Georgian style. Notice the beautiful doorway and the four windows on the first floor and five on the second.

Benjamin Franklin, postmaster. As postmaster for the northern colonies after 1753, Franklin improved the service. Soon a person in Philadelphia could send a letter to New York and receive a reply the next day.

the girls. The girls had to learn how to manage a plantation home in preparation for the day when they would become the wives of planters.

The Negro slaves did not, of course, share in the luxurious living and merry parties on the plantation. The servants who worked in the mansion enjoyed better clothing and food than those who worked in the fields. Those who were personal servants to members of the master's family received special consideration.

The slaves lived in small one- and two-family cabins. In the summer they wore very few clothes. For the winter they were given enough clothing to keep them warm. Besides small weekly rations of corn and meat, each family had a small piece of land assigned to it on which the men could work on Sundays to grow vegetables.

The small farmers of the South could not afford the luxuries of the large plantations. They lived in small frame houses furnished with articles that they made themselves. The social life of these farmers was similar to that of the farming people in the North.

George Washington: Virginia planter. George Washington grew up in the plantation society of Virginia and was a plantation owner. He was 11 years old when his father died. Thereafter he spent most of his time with his two older brothers. His teacher was a clergyman, who taught him arithmetic, spelling, and grammar. Later Washington learned surveying. That was the extent of his schooling, but he continued to study by himself.

After his brother Lawrence died, George Washington inherited a plantation called Mount Vernon and became a planter. In 1759, when he was 27 years old, he married Martha Custis, a widow with two children. He enlarged the mansion at Mount Vernon and equipped it with imported furniture. He increased the size of the plantation to more than 8,000 acres.

Washington took an active part in Virginia society. Whenever he was in Williamsburg, the colonial capital, he attended concerts and went to the theater as often as possible. He was especially fond of dancing.

Like other planters, Washington devoted much of his time to managing his plantation. He was a progressive farmer and followed the improved farming methods of his time. Realizing that tobacco ruined the soil, he planted less of it and raised wheat, which he manufactured into flour and sold. He learned to rotate crops in order to keep

A Medical Prescription

In the month of March place live toads into an iron pot until it is half full. Set a charcoal fire around it. After the fire has burned itself out, pound the toads into a black powder. Give a dose of this powder to a patient with any infection and put him to bed to sweat it out.

¶ An English doctor sent this prescription to a colonist, assuring him that the medicine would cure smallpox, poisoning, and fevers. Many medicines of colonial days were mixtures of herbs, snakes, snails, and the like.

the soil fertile and grew large crops of hay, clover, buckwheat, turnips, and potatoes. He imported the newer types of farm tools and machinery.

Washington was away from Mount Vernon for long periods, first in the colonial army and then in the Revolutionary army. While he was away, his estate was not well taken care of in spite of weekly letters he wrote to his plantation manager. Nothing could make up for the absence of the owner himself. The property lost much of its value, and Washington received little income from it. Thus Washington performed his public services at a personal sacrifice.

Washington was a member of the small group of wealthy southern planters. They were the leaders of southern life, and the less wealthy people looked up to them.

5 *English Colonial Life Is Backward in Many Ways*

Even after the English colonies had become firmly established along the Atlantic coast, colonial life was in some ways still rough and hard. Many colonists had to struggle with the hardships of the wilderness. And the people were limited by the lack of knowledge in their time.

Backwardness in treatment of disease. There were no medical schools in the colonies until 1765. Physicians did not have to obtain licenses as they do in the United States today. Anyone who wished could practice medicine. In colonial days almost every educated person dabbled in medicine, and those who were not educated had their favorite remedies. Many people believed that disease was caused by evil spirits in the body and used all kinds of superstitious practices to chase them out. Often they made the sick person more severely ill. Doctors believed that to draw blood from the patient would cure almost any illness. Actually, of course, it weakened him just when he needed his strength most.

Knowing so little about the causes and cure of disease, the colonists suffered severely. The diseases that caused the most deaths among adults were smallpox and yellow fever. These two diseases have been just about wiped out in the United States today by the use of scientific knowledge of their causes and cure. Many people in the colonies suffered from typhoid fever, cholera (kŏl′ẽr *ȧ*), malaria, and tuberculosis, other diseases that can be controlled today. Children died in large numbers from "stomach complaint," diphtheria, and measles. Infections spread rapidly in colonial towns because people knew nothing about hygiene. They drank water from shallow wells, which were often polluted. Since there was no plumbing, people bathed very rarely. In the summer men and boys went swimming in the creek.

Even in the colonial period, however, there was some improvement in the prevention of disease. Inoculation for smallpox was first used in Boston in 1721. As has often happened when people do not understand a new idea, the doctor who used it was attacked by other doctors, by many ministers, by the colonial assembly, and by mobs of peo-

Inoculating a soldier. By the time of the Revolution, people had learned that inoculation against smallpox saved lives. American soldiers reported willingly for inoculation.

ple in the streets. But after its value in saving lives was proved to the people, inoculation was slowly accepted.

Education for the few. Perhaps one reason the colonists resisted a new idea such as inoculation was that many of them could not read and so could learn of new developments only through word of mouth. Most children received very little schooling, and many received no schooling at all—never learning even how to read and write. The early settlers could hardly have started schools while they were struggling to survive. Furthermore, the people of the time, in the colonies as in Europe, did not believe that children should be educated at the expense of the government. Parents were expected to pay for the education of their children. For those who were willing to pay, there were schools. In all the colonies there were dame schools, so named because they were conducted by women. Here little children learned their letters.

In 1647 Massachusetts passed a now famous law that required every town of 50 families to keep an elementary school and every town of 100 families to keep a Latin school. Parents still had to pay for their children's education. Many of the Massachusetts towns did not obey the law, especially in regard to the Latin school. They found it difficult to get a teacher or to pay one. Besides, most parents felt that they needed the children at home to help with the work.

The Puritans established Harvard College in 1636, only six years after they had founded the Massachusetts Bay Colony. The number of students was small. Almost all of them went to college to prepare to become ministers.

In the middle colonies a smaller proportion of children went to school than in New England. Most of the schools were run by churches. Parents who could afford to pay for the education of their children did so. The other boys and girls who attended were educated as a matter of charity.

In the cities of the middle colonies, businessmen demanded an education for their sons that would prepare them for trade and commerce. To meet this demand, private schools were opened. They taught their students such subjects as arithmetic, bookkeeping, surveying, and navigation.

The plantation homes of the South were so far apart that it was difficult to bring the children together. As a result schools did not develop there so rapidly as in the other colonies. Wealthy planters had tutors for their children or sent them to private schools. In the towns there were a few charity schools for a limited number of poor children and orphans. The pupils were taught how to earn their living as soon as possible.

Many sons of rich planters went to England to attend the universities. A small number were sent to college in the North. In the 1700s many of them went to the College of William and Mary in Williamsburg, Virginia, which was founded in 1693.

Travel is dangerous and communication is slow. Travel in the New World was slow, hard, and dangerous. Early settlers traveled mainly by water. A person who decided to travel overland had to follow Indian trails on foot. Gradually the branches of the bordering trees were broken off, and the trails became wide enough for a man on horseback. Riding on horseback remained the principal mode of land travel throughout the colonial period.

The colonists developed roads very slowly. They improved a few for short distances around the cities. Elsewhere there was seldom more than a set of winding wheel tracks through the woods. A traveler had to ford small streams, that is, drive through the water itself. Frequently he had to hunt up and down a stream for a safe place to ford. Ferries often could not run because of wind, ice, or high water.

In 1704 a woman traveled from Boston to New York on horseback and kept a diary of her trip. The trail was so narrow that the branches of the trees on both sides scratched her face. Bridges were rickety. Several times, while crossing a bridge, her horse stumbled on a loose board and almost toppled over with her into the stream below. At night she was terrified by the pitch-darkness. The meals in the taverns were

Colonial Boston Post Road. Compare this road, which was one of the main colonial highways, with highways you have traveled.

BUREAU OF PUBLIC ROADS

unappetizing. The bedding was usually dirty. It took the woman seven full days of travel to reach New York.

Summary

By 1750 European settlers had established themselves firmly in the New World. They kept in touch with life in the Old World and tried to imitate it as closely as possible. The more prosperous colonists, whether Spanish, French, or English, imported European clothes and furniture. They sent their sons to Europe to be educated. They danced, played cards, went fox hunting, or attended bullfights, just as European aristocrats did. But the great majority of the people of the New World could not afford such luxuries. They lived more simply, using homemade clothes and furniture, and enjoyed simpler pleasures in one another's company.

In all the colonies of the New World, roads were so bad that long-distance travel was actually dangerous. There were no free public schools, and most children received very little education—or none at all. Because people were afraid of anything they did not understand, they opposed new discoveries and ideas that would have helped them. The people knew nothing about hygiene, and diseases that were carried by germs spread rapidly. Even doctors did not know much about the causes and cure of disease.

But when we call the colonists backward, we are comparing their life with our life today. We must remember that they lived in a period when people knew little science and did not believe in the need of education for all. In such matters, the American colonists were not far behind the best that was known in Europe in their own time.

On the whole, the English colonies had deeper roots in the New World than had the Spanish and French, although they occupied less territory. The English settlers had won a voice in their own government. They had cleared large areas of land for farming. They grew enough crops to feed themselves and to have a large surplus to sell. They built ships to carry the surplus products abroad and to bring back manufactured goods. They had begun to manufacture things for themselves. They had advanced far enough to begin to feel independent of the mother country.

For a Quick Review

1. What social classes were found in Spanish America? What determined the class to which a person belonged?

2. Compare the everyday life of the French habitant with that of the Quebec aristocrat. Consider such things as the work they did, the clothing they wore, their recreation.

3. Compare New France and Spanish America as to social classes, importance of church, imitation of European customs.

4. What social classes existed in the English colonies? Describe the life of each class.

5. What problems did colonial towns have to solve? Compare their solutions with the ways our modern cities meet the same problems.

6. What conditions endangered the health of the people of the English colonies?

7. What conditions in the English colonies made travel hard?

Learning to Study More Easily

USING THE INDEX

Many times you will need to find information about a particular topic in a book you are using. The index of the book can help you locate this information quickly, provided that you know how to use it. In this text, as in most books, the index is at the end. Turn to it now and see what it looks like. You will find that it is a list of the most important topics, subjects, events, and persons discussed in the book. The list is arranged alphabetically, in the same way that words are arranged in a dictionary or names in a telephone directory. After each entry you will find the numbers of the page or pages on which that particular subject is discussed.

Sometimes after the entry and its page numbers you will find the words *"See also"* and a list of other topics. These topics are cross references. Look them up also, because they are related to the topic on which you are seeking information. Often you will find page numbers printed in italics rather than in regular type. These are references to illustrations, including maps, that tell something about the topic.

Sometimes, when you turn to the index, you will not find the particular topic you are looking for. It may be that the book does not discuss the topic. In that case you should find a book that does. It may be, however, that the authors have used a different but related heading to refer to the information. For example, you may be looking for information about recreation in the English colonies. You may turn to the "R" section, expecting to find "Recreation" as an entry. If it is not there, try "English colonies" or the names of individual colonies to see if there is a reference like this: "English colonies, recreation in." In other words, if you do not find the entry you first look for and you think the book contains the information you need, try to think of other ways the topic might be listed in the index.

Answer these questions, using the index of this book:

1. On what page can you find information about indentured servants? Is there more than one reference for this topic?
2. Are there any pictures of indentured servants? How do you know?
3. On what page is there a map showing Philadelphia?
4. Locate and skim rapidly all the references to Benjamin Franklin. Are there any pictures of him?
5. Is there an index entry "Schools"? Under what other headings might you look for information about colonial schools? On what pages can you find information about schools in the Spanish colonies? In the English colonies?
6. What index entries can you use to locate information about how people dressed in the English, French, and Spanish colonies?
7. In Chapter 5 you read about transportation in the English colonies. On what pages will you find information about transportation in the United States today?
8. If you want to compare home life in the English colonies with that in the United States today, how will you use the index to find the information?

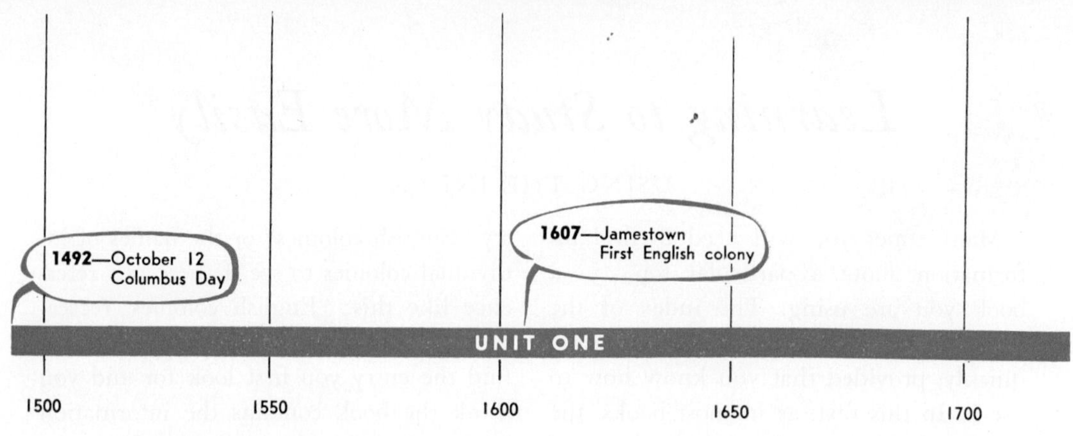

MAIN EVENTS OF UNIT 1, 1492–1750

Building and governing the nation	*Earning a living*	*Science, arts, and the people*	*The nation and its neighbors*
1492 Discovery			
1607 Jamestown			
			1608 Quebec
	1612 Tobacco raised in Virginia		
1619 First representative assembly in America, Virginia	**1619** First Negro slaves, Virginia		
1620 Plymouth			
1630 Massachusetts Bay			
1636 Providence, R.I.			
1636 Connecticut		**1636** Harvard College	**1642** Montreal
		1647 Massachusetts school law	
		1649 Maryland Toleration Act	
	1651 British Navigation Act regulated colonial trade		
1664 New York seized from Dutch by English			
1670 Charleston, S.C.			

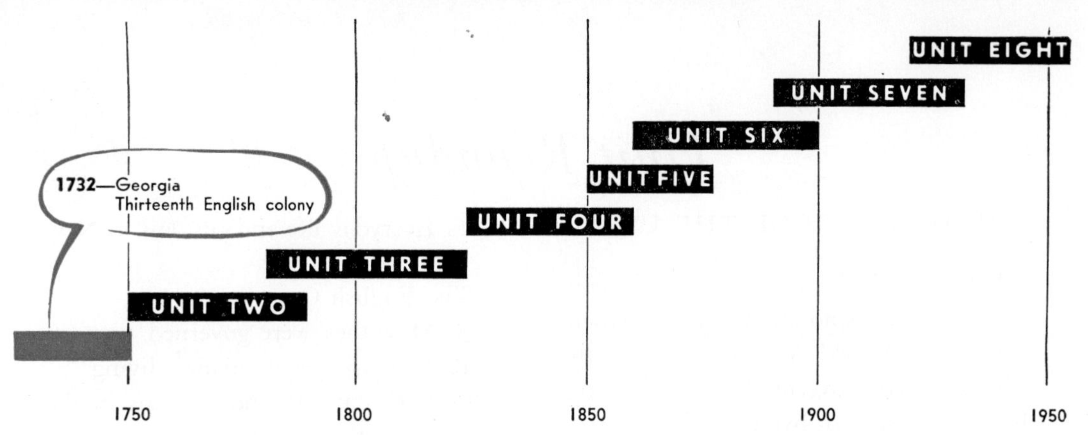

MAIN EVENTS OF UNIT 1, 1492–1750

Building and governing the nation	*Earning a living*	*Science, arts, and the people*	*The nation and its neighbors*
1682 Philadelphia			
			1689–1697 War, English *vs.* French (see p. 110)
	1690s Rice raised successfully, South Carolina	**1690** Estimated population of English colonies 213,500	
		1693 William and Mary College	
		1701 Yale University	
			1702–1713 War, English *vs.* French
	1716 First lighthouse, Boston	**1716** Theater built, Williamsburg	
			1718 New Orleans
1732 Georgia		**1732** *Poor Richard's Almanac*	
		1735 Zenger trial (freedom of the press)	
	1741 Indigo introduced, South Carolina		
			1744–1748 War, English *vs.* French colonies
	1750 Coal mine opened near Richmond, Va.	**1750** Estimated population of English colonies 1,207,000	

Unit Roundup

HIGH POINTS OF THE UNIT

As you studied Unit 1, you read about the discovery, exploration, and settlement of the New World. You learned how the colonists were governed, made a living, dressed, worshiped, lived in their town or country homes, and did all the other things that make up everyday living in any time or place. You read about differences and likenesses of the French, Spanish, and English colonies.

Here, at the end of Unit 1, is a good place to select the most important facts about the colonial period. These facts will help you understand how the European settlers changed the New World and how the New World changed the settlers from Europeans to Americans. Below is a skeleton outline to help you organize the facts and ideas that you select as being most important. Fill it out by writing a brief paragraph about each of the subheads.

I. The discovery and exploration of the New World
  A. Explorations made in the name of Spain
  B. Explorations made in the name of France
  C. Explorations made in the name of England

II. The Spanish Colonies
  A. How they were governed
  B. How the people made a living
  C. Everyday life and customs in Spanish America

III. The French Colonies
  A. How they were governed
  B. How the people made a living
  C. Everyday life and customs in New France

IV. The English Colonies
  A. How they were governed
  B. How the people made a living
  C. Everyday life and customs in the English colonies

EXPAND YOUR VOCABULARY

1. As you studied Unit 1, you probably discovered several new words and phrases. Can you explain each of the following and give an illustration, either in words or by a drawing on the board, to show what it means?

charter	inoculation
circumnavigate	isthmus
coastal plain	Piedmont
convoy	promenade
county court	proprietor
fall line	strait
homespun	Tidewater
indentured servant	tradition

2. There are several ways to add to your vocabulary. You may learn the meanings of words that are new to you. You may learn new meanings of words with which you are already acquainted. "Estate," for example, has more than one meaning. How many of them can you give? "Fertilizer" and "fertility" are examples of words that are closely related in meaning. You will find it helpful, when looking up the meaning of a word, to notice what related words mean as well.

Copy on a sheet of notebook paper the following list of words, leaving a line or two after each one. Check the spelling of each word as you copy it. After each word write a sentence that makes its meaning clear. Can you find a second meaning for it? Is there a word that is closely related to it?

assigned	laborer
duties	rotate
exports	smuggle
fertilizer	staple
imports	transport

3. Draw pictures or bring to class examples to illustrate each of these:

brocade	quilting
fair	satin
frame house	shuffleboard
patio	toque
plaza	velvet

HISTORY IN THE MOVIES

1. *Colonial Expansion* will help you review the exploration and settlement of North America from 1492 to 1763, especially the areas claimed by each nation. Look for answers to the following questions, discuss them, and, if there is time, study the film a second time to clear up any points that may not have been clear: (*a*) What early settlements are shown in the film, and where is each located? (*b*) What industries are mentioned, and where did each grow up? (*c*) What information does the film give about the French and Indian War and the treaty that ended it? The film *Discovery and Exploration* is a good one to study along with *Colonial Expansion*.

2. To learn more about the early days in New England, study the films *Early Settlers of New England* and *Colonial Children*. As you see the films, look for answers to these questions and be ready to discuss them: (*a*) In what ways did the settlers depend on one another? (*b*) How did the kind of land affect their everyday lives? (*c*) How did the settlers' lives change as the settlement grew?

3. Study the film *Planter of Colonial Virginia* for answers to these questions: (*a*) How did the family's life in the country compare with its life in the city? (*b*) Why was Williamsburg important to the entire colony of Virginia? (*c*) What can you learn from the film about medical treatment of that day?

4. Study the film *The Story That Couldn't Be Printed,* looking for answers to these questions: (*a*) Why was John Peter Zenger put in jail? What was unfair about the way he was arrested? (*b*) Why did a famous colonial lawyer consent to defend Zenger when he came to trial? (*c*) Do you think the verdict in Zenger's trial has made any difference in your life today?

WITH CRAYON, RULER, AND PASTE

1. Prepare a comic-strip history of any one of the English colonies. The first steps will be to choose the events that you think should be included and to decide how many pictures you will need. Your comic strip will be more interesting if you use several pictures to illustrate each of a few important events than if you try to crowd too many happenings into one picture. Remember that you are more interested in telling the story than in perfecting each picture. Stick figures and quick sketches will serve your purpose. Probably you will want to write a caption (a brief description or explanation) beneath each picture or group of pictures. Give your comic-strip history a title that will tell the readers

what it is about. You can think of many topics for comic-strip histories. Here are three suggestions: "The life of a French fur trader," "Mining in Spanish America," "Conflict between governor and assembly in the English colonies."

2. Begin a "Time Line of Our Nation's Growth." It should be one that your class can use through much of the year. Perhaps you can place a long strip of brown paper across the front of your room above the blackboard or the bulletin board. Use crayons to divide the space into six equal parts for the centuries from 1400 to 2000; then divide each century into 50-year periods and each 50-year period into quarter centuries.

When you have finished the time scale, place the dates of these events on it:

The discovery of America by Columbus
The conquest of Mexico by Cortes
The founding of St. Augustine, Jamestown, Quebec, Plymouth, Massachusetts Bay, Georgia
The adoption of the Toleration Act

Consider what other important events of the colonial period should be placed on the time line. Perhaps the class as a group can select the events to be listed.

3. Draw a plan of a typical town in Spanish America or a sketch of a Canadian habitant's home. Make it large enough for display on the class bulletin board.

4. Make a picture chart entitled "Food Exchange—What the New World and the Old Taught Each Other." Divide your sheet of paper in half. On one side draw or paste pictures of the foods brought to the New World by the Spanish, French, and English settlers. On the other side show the foods that Europeans found here and learned to eat. Each side of the chart, of course, must be labeled.

PUT ON A PLAY

No doubt you have enjoyed many thrilling historical plays in the movies and on radio and television programs. There are many subjects for historical broadcasts or plays that a committee of your class could prepare and perform. If one of these plays is done well enough, it might be suitable for a program at an assembly or a Parent-Teacher Association meeting. There are various techniques that you can use, separately or in combination, in developing your broadcast or play:

You can have a roving reporter interviewing participants in an event or getting the comments of spectators.

You can have a commentator who furnishes the framework for spots of dialogue.

You can conduct an interview with a person, using flash backs to tell the story of his or her life.

You can prepare a script for a radio or television play.

You can use music for continuity or background.

Keep in mind these suggestions and others that are given on pages 226–227 as you consider the following topics:

Conversation piece (You might imagine the conversation that might have taken place if the governor of New France, a viceroy of Spanish America, and the governor of an English colony had met to discuss their problems.)
The fair at Montreal
Governor *vs.* assembly: the struggle for control

Life in colonial Virginia (The early life of George Washington, for example, may be used.)
May Day celebrations in New France
The Porto Bello fair
Sail ahoy! (An English ship is arriving at the wharf of a southern plantation.)
A visit to the home of a habitant
You are there: the surrender of New Amsterdam (You may substitute any other event discussed in the unit.)

STORIES THERE WAS NO ROOM TO TELL

Choose one of the topics listed below, or another one on which you and your teacher agree, and prepare a report on it. Decide with your teacher whether you should give it orally before the class or prepare it as a written composition. In either case you will find helpful suggestions on pages 162, 207, and 258 about collecting information and preparing your report. Perhaps your English teacher will help you with the organization of the report. In giving your report, let the class know where you found your information.

The adventures of Sir Francis Drake or another of the explorers mentioned in Unit 1
Art and artists in the English colonies
The Aztecs of Mexico
Commercial ships of the colonial period (Spanish caravels, Yankee ships, etc.)
The founding of St. Augustine or Quebec
New World homes (English, Spanish, or French)
Marco Polo's travels
Recreation in Spanish America or New France
Travel in the English colonies

USE YOUR IMAGINATION

1. If you had lived on the frontier in one of the English colonies, describe in a diary how your family would have made its living. Be sure to tell where your imaginary home is located and make your descriptions accurate for that location. Write 10 entries in your diary and scatter them throughout a year. In each one describe some of the chores you would have done, the food your family would have eaten and the clothing it would have worn, the work your father and mother would have done, and other facts about making a living.

2. The life of the French-Canadian habitant was different with each season of the year. Prepare a diary-letter that you might have written to a friend in France if you had been living with a French-Canadian family in the early 1700s. Scatter the entries through one year so that you will record typical happenings for each season.

3. Imagine that you are a cabin boy on the flagship in a convoy of Spanish cargo ships during the middle 1500s. Prepare 10 diary entries to report the events of one journey from Spain to the colonies and back. Your entries should show how the convoy system operated and why it was needed.

4. Imagine that you are the son of a wealthy family in Spanish America. Write to your cousin in Old Spain, telling about your schooling.

SHOW IT ON A MAP

1. Study the maps of North and South America on pages 14 and 45, noticing the shape of the coast line and the location

of the mouths of the important rivers. With the eraser end of your pencil, follow the coast line of North America. In the same way follow the coast line of South America. Using one of the world maps, study the way in which North and South America are located in relation to each other. Now make a freehand sketch map of the two continents, showing the coast line. Consult the maps in your book but do not trace them or try to make your freehand map the same size. To draw this freehand map will help you to study more carefully the coast line of the New World continents.

2. On the map on pages 672–673, find these rivers: Mississippi, St. Lawrence, Rio Grande, Hudson, Columbia. Place the eraser end of your pencil at the source of the Mississippi, then trace the river to the spot where it flows into the Gulf of Mexico. In the same way trace the course of each of the other rivers mentioned. Draw the course of each of the five rivers on an outline map of North America, beginning at the spot where the river rises and following its course to the sea or the Gulf of Mexico. Locate and name each of the Great Lakes and show the Appalachians and the Rockies.

3. Locate the following settlements on a map of North America, showing by color or symbol whether each one was French, English, Spanish, or Dutch:

Baltimore	New Amsterdam
Boston	New Orleans
Charleston	Philadelphia
Exeter	Providence
Jamestown	Quebec
Hartford	St. Augustine
Kaskaskia	Savannah
Montreal	Schenectady

FURTHER READING

In addition to the books listed below, the general list in the appendix contains books that you can use in working out projects. Most of the books that are mentioned in these lists you can probably find in your school library or your public library. Use the library card catalog to locate them. If you do not know how to use the catalog, see pages 146–147 or ask your teacher or librarian to help you.

Some of the books listed at the end of this and the other units are easy to read; others are more difficult. The symbol † means easy reading; †† means more difficult reading. If there is no symbol, the book is of average reading difficulty.

Remember that this information applies to the reading list in each Unit Roundup.

Books about Interesting People

Champlain, Northwest Voyager by Louise Hall Tharp. Little, Brown, 1944.

Hudson of Hudson's Bay by J. M. Scott. Schuman, 1951.

Lone Journey: The Life of Roger Williams by Jeanette Eaton. Harcourt, Brace, 1944.††

New Found World by Katherine B. Shippen. Viking, 1945. Stories of Columbus, Drake, and other early explorers.††

Penn by Elizabeth Janet Gray. Viking, 1938.

Vast Horizons by Mary S. Lucas. Viking, 1943. Stories of great explorers, including Marco Polo and Prince Henry the Navigator.

Stories of Adventure and Everyday Life

Beppy Marlow of Charles Town by Elizabeth Janet Gray. Viking, 1936. An English girl comes to live in Carolina in the early 1700s.

Border Iron by Herbert Best. Viking, 1945. Adventures connected with one of the first iron mines in the English colonies.

Golden Horseshoe by Elizabeth Coatsworth. Macmillan, 1935. Life in colonial Virginia.†

He Went with Christopher Columbus by Louise Andrews Kent. Houghton Mifflin, 1940. Adventures of a boy who was in Columbus's company. You can get other books by the same author about boys who went with Marco Polo, Vasco da Gama, and Ferdinand Magellan.

Jeremy Pepper by Frances Rogers and Alice Beard. Lippincott, 1946. Jeremy was apprenticed to Baron Steigel to learn glass blowing.

Jonica's Island by Gladys Malvern. Messner, 1945. New Amsterdam in the last days of Dutch control.

Matchlock Gun by Walter D. Edmonds. Dodd, Mead, 1941. New York frontier, 1750s.†

Mayflower Boy by Stanley Young. Rinehart, 1944. The first year at Plymouth.

Peter Hale by Julia Davis. Dutton, 1939. A boy makes his way from Jamestown to Boston in the 1640s.†

Puritan Adventure by Lois Lenski. Lippincott, 1944. Life and adventure in early Massachusetts.

Sign of the Golden Fish by Gertrude Robinson. Winston, 1949. Early days of settlement in Maine.

Traveler's Candle by Florence Maule Updegraff. Harcourt, Brace, 1942. Rhode Island in the 1680s.

Other Interesting Accounts

Americans before Columbus by Elizabeth C. Baity. Viking, 1951. Indian life in America before discovery.

Everyday Things in American Life 1607–1776 by W. C. Langdon. Scribner, 1937. Descriptions and pictures of houses, tools, and so on.††

Half a Hemisphere by Delia Goetz. Harcourt, Brace, 1943. An interesting history of Latin-American nations.

Home Life in Colonial Days by Alice M. Earle. Macmillan, 1948. Customs in the English colonies. Your library may also have other books on colonial life by the same author.

In Good Old Colony Times: A Historical Picture Book by Louise Andrews Kent and Elizabeth Kent Tarshis. Houghton Mifflin, 1941. Boston's first 200 years.

Unit 2 *The English Colonies Become an Independent Nation 1750–1783*

WRITING ABOUT the Revolutionary War, John Adams said that the true revolution had taken place "in the hearts and minds of the people" long before the war began. What did he mean?

By 1750 the colonists were able to make a living without help from England; and they were playing a large part in their own government. They still considered themselves Englishmen. But powerful forces were separating them more and more from the mother country.

The very conditions of space and time helped weaken the feeling of dependence. A wide and stormy ocean that took two months to cross separated the colonists from the mother country. By 1776 many people in the colonies were the grandchildren and the great-grandchildren of the first settlers. They

had never seen England. By simple subtraction you can prove that, to the children of 1776, the settlement of Jamestown was about as far away and long ago as the signing of the Declaration of Independence is to you.

Then think of the many ways life in America was different from life in England. Since only a handful of titled aristocrats settled here, the English colonies did not have the class system of Europe. Most of the settlers were middle-class people who found ample opportunity in America to better their lives. By his own efforts a poor boy like Benjamin Franklin could rise to become the most distinguished man in all the colonies.

Franklin is only one outstanding example of the way Americans were achieving success all the time. In the colonies, poor people like wage earners and indentured servants rose to become independent farmers, businessmen, and community leaders. In England they would have remained poor. These men and their children had found opportunity and had won success in America. If they ever had to choose between loyalty to England and loyalty to America, which do you believe they would choose?

In the 1760s and 1770s the English colonists were being pulled two ways. On the Atlantic coast many people wore English clothes, lived in English-style houses, and read English books. They faced east across the ocean and were loyal to the mother country.

Inland, on the frontier, pioneers met all over again the problems that had faced the first settlers. They learned how to repel an Indian attack and how to grow crops between tree stumps. They learned to make garments out of deerskin that would stand the rough wear of the wilderness. They learned to paddle canoes, to follow forest trails, and to trap game. By solving their own problems, they learned to be self-reliant and independent. They faced west across the continent, and they were loyal to their new country. The future of America was with those who faced west.

After 1763 England passed new laws that turned eastern and western colonists against her. Since England had taken over Canada, the colonists no longer needed English protection against the French and the Indians. They felt that they were able to fight their own battles and govern themselves. When England would not permit them to enjoy their rights, they declared their independence and won it on the field of battle. Unit 2 tells the story of the War of Independence and the early growth of national unity.

6 *The British Conquer North America*

If you were to attend a council meeting of Indians in the northern English colonies, you would be impressed with the way the Indians carefully followed old customs. First they lighted the council fire, which they kept burning throughout the meeting. At the end they put out the fire to show that the meeting was over.

Once the council fire was lighted, the leader of each group took his turn making flowery speeches. The topics, and even the words, of the speeches were determined by custom. His people, one leader might say, wished to clear the path between friends, to strengthen the chain of friendship, to sweep away the clouds of suspicion. As he made each statement, he presented to the other leader (or leaders) a belt of wampum. The wampum was a pledge that he spoke truthfully and sincerely.

After one leader had spoken, another stood up and replied, expressing the same ideas in almost the same words and giving belts of wampum in return. These speeches might take a day or two. Only after the ceremonial speeches were over was the council ready to get down to business.

The white settlers soon learned that, if they wished to settle important matters with the Indians, they had to follow these customs. We can imagine a council between white men and Indians:

Scene: Albany, New York. A group of men have gathered in the open around a newly lighted council fire.

Time: July, 1754.

Characters: Colonial delegates and Indians who have come to attend the Albany Congress at the request of the British.

A colonial delegate steps forward to speak.

COLONIAL DELEGATE: Brothers, we

welcome you. The path between your villages and ours is overgrown with weeds because it has not been used. With this belt of wampum I make the road clear and smooth so that you will come to us more often. (Hands the Indians a belt of wampum.)

Brothers, the chain of friendship between us has grown weak. With this belt of wampum I renew the chain of friendship and make it bright and strong. (Hands the Indians a belt of wampum.)

Brothers, the clouds hang heavy over us. With this belt of wampum I clear away the clouds so that we may speak plainly to one another as friends. (Hands the Indians a belt of wampum.)

The colonial delegate sits down. An Indian chief steps forward.

INDIAN CHIEF: Brother, we thank you for your welcome. With this belt we clear the path between us. With this belt we renew the chain of friendship and make it strong and bright. With this belt we clear away the clouds and are ready to listen as friends. (After each sentence he hands the colonists a belt of wampum.)

COLONIAL DELEGATE: Brothers, we shall speak plainly to you. A long time ago your fathers won a great country to the north and west and put it under the protection of the king of Great Britain. Now the French are trying to take possession of that country. They are building forts between Lake Erie and the Ohio River. Some of your people have visited the French. Tell us: Are you aware of this? Are you willing that the French should take your land? Open your hearts to us.

INDIAN CHIEF: I speak plainly to you. It is true that the French have won over some of our people. Why? Because you have neglected them while the French have given them many presents.

It is true that the French are building forts. We see that the French and the English are fighting over who should own our land. What can we do? The French are strong and win victories. The English are weak and are in retreat. The French could easily come down and capture this city and turn you out of doors. With this belt of wampum I tell you that I speak the truth. (Hands a belt of wampum to the colonists.)

COLONIAL DELEGATE: We are happy that you do not support the French. The English king, your father, will now attack the French and protect the

Indian council. The Indian is handing a belt of wampum to the white man, whom he is addressing. What did this act mean?

PUBLIC BUILDINGS ADMINISTRATION

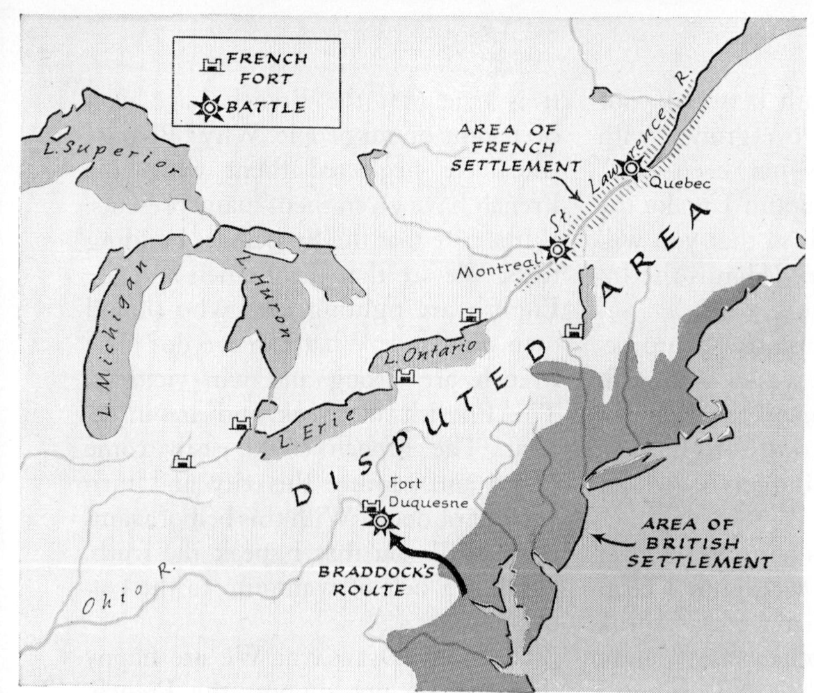

The French and Indian War. Why was the control of Fort Duquesne important? Why was Montreal almost certain to fall to the British once they had captured Quebec?

land for you. We need your help. Together we can defeat the French.

After this meeting you will receive presents. And now I cover up this council fire.

1 *The British Win Canada*

The meeting described above took place when the French were threatening to push the English out of North America. For many years after 1688 Great Britain and France were almost continuously at war in Europe. Other countries, it is true, were also involved, but the long conflict was actually a struggle between Great Britain and France. Each was trying to become the leading power in Europe, to rule the seas, and to win a great colonial empire.

Every time the two mother countries engaged in war, their American colonies also fought one another. From 1688 to 1748 there were three colonial wars. The fourth war, 1754 to 1763, we call the French and Indian War. It was part of a much larger war, called the Seven Years' War, in which France and England fought in Europe and India as well as in America.

The French and English clash on the Ohio. Unlike the three earlier wars, which began in Europe, the fourth war was started by the French and the English colonies in America. Both sides claimed the Ohio Valley. In 1753 the French crossed Lake Erie and began to build forts in what is now western Pennsylvania. At that time Virginia claimed that region as part of its territory. The governor of Virginia sent a 21-year-old major named George Washington to the French to warn them to leave the region because it belonged to the king of Great Britain. But the French refused to budge. Next the Virginia governor sent men to build a fort at the head of the Ohio River, where Pittsburgh now stands, in order to hold

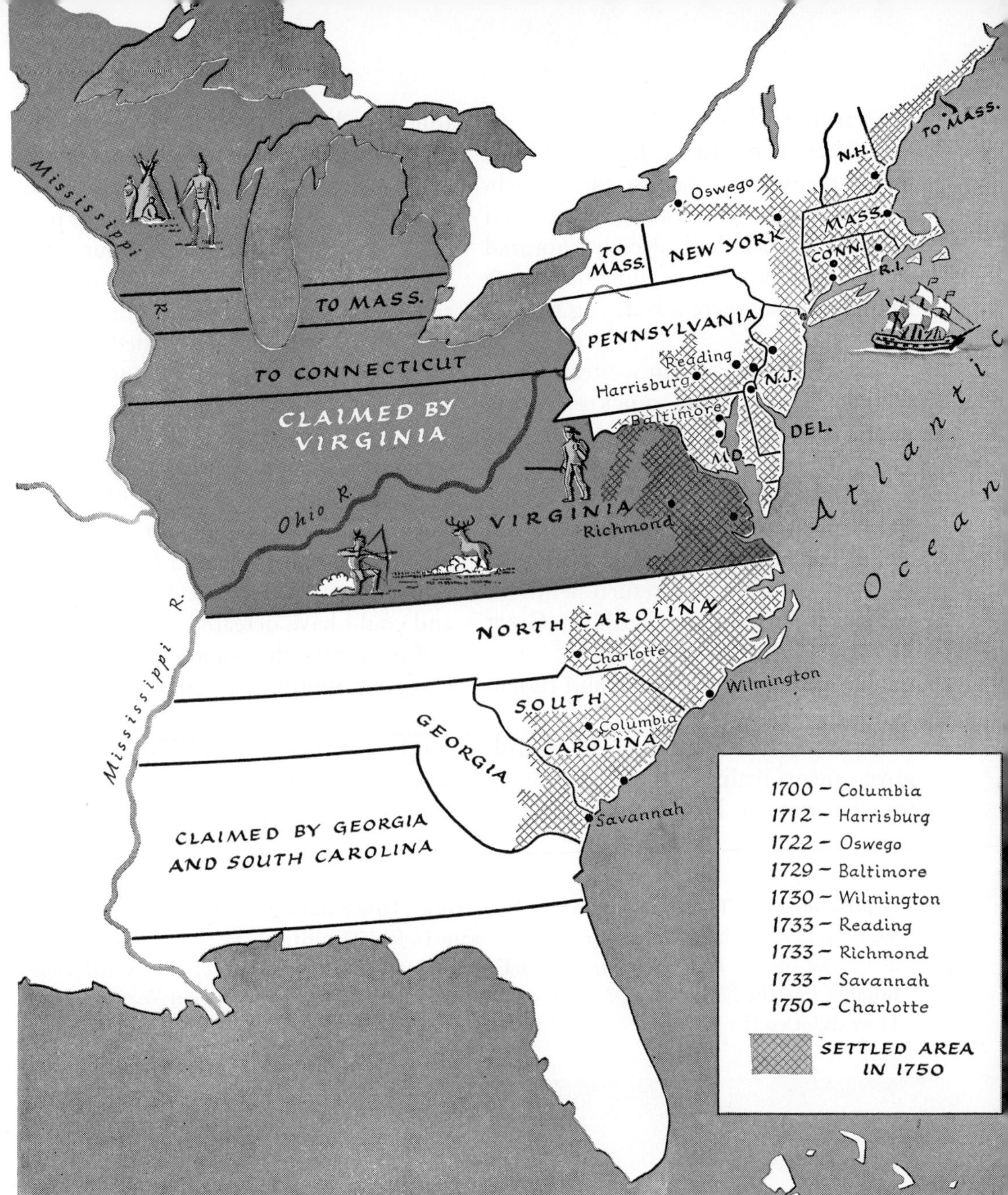

The English colonies in 1750. Locate each settlement on the inset list, in the order of founding. Which ones are near the seacoast? Which is the farthest inland? Can you name the towns that are marked but not named on the map? If you cannot, see page 32. Notice that several colonies claimed land west of the Alleghenies. Which colony had the largest claim? How did its efforts to protect its claim help cause the French and Indian War?

the territory. He sent Washington with a number of militia to help build the fort and protect it against the French. But on the way Washington learned that the French had already captured the partly built fort and that some French soldiers were advancing toward him.

At Great Meadows, in western Pennsylvania, Washington quickly built a small fortification, which he named Fort Necessity, and prepared to fight. The French force was too strong for his small group of militia. Washington was defeated and forced to surrender, but was permitted to return with his men to Virginia. The battle at Great Meadows, which occurred in 1754, was the beginning of the French and Indian War.

The Albany Congress. The British government realized that, to prepare for the war in North America, two things had to be done. It was necessary to persuade the colonies to cooperate against France. It was also necessary to gain the aid of as many Indians as possible. To achieve these two purposes, the British ordered the colonies to send representatives to a meeting in Albany in 1754. This meeting is called the Albany Congress. Seven colonies were represented.

One reason why the French had won so many victories in previous wars was that each English colony had been interested mainly in defending itself. If all of them had combined forces in one army, they would have been stronger and could have defeated the French.

For uniting the colonies, the Albany Congress approved a plan drawn up by Benjamin Franklin. It would set up a single government over all the colonies. The new government would control relations with the Indians and would di-

A prize of war. This is a painting of New York Harbor during the French and Indian War. Notice the flags flying over the large ship (*left*). The British flag has been hoisted above the French flag. The ship was a French vessel that the British had captured and brought into the harbor as a prize of war. When was the French and Indian War fought? How did it end?

THE NEW-YORK HISTORICAL SOCIETY, NEW YORK CITY

LIBRARY OF CONGRESS

Washington in the wilderness. Young George Washington, accompanied by a backwoodsman, is crossing the Allegheny River on a log raft. As surveyor and soldier on the frontier, Washington endured the hardships of life in the wilderness.

rect the settlement of the West. The existing colonial governments would continue to deal with affairs inside the separate colonies. Although the members of the Albany Congress favored the plan, it was never adopted. The colonies rejected it because they did not wish to give up any part of their power. The British government was dissatisfied with the plan because it wanted the colonies to give up more of their power. During the French and Indian War, each English colony acted, for the most part, independently.

Importance of Indian allies. The second purpose of the Albany Congress was to strengthen friendship with the Indians. Both the French and the English armies in the colonies were small. A few hundred Indian warriors on one side or the other might make the difference between winning and losing the war. Each side had Indian friends. The French had the Hurons (hū′rŭns) in Canada. The English had the Iroquois (ĭr′ō kwoi) in New York and others farther south.

In the 1730s and 1740s the French had won to their side many of the Iroquois. They sent missionaries among them. They gave the Indians presents. French fur traders treated the Indians more fairly than English fur traders did. Most important, the French won victory after victory in the colonial wars and it looked as if they would finally defeat the English. The Indians wanted to be on the winning side.

Braddock's march. Braddock's troops, marching in military formation, were easy targets for Indian warriors, who hid in the woods and shot from cover.

The English were losing their Indian allies. That is why the English government invited the Iroquois to the Albany Congress. About 150 chiefs and warriors with their families were there. The chiefs had many complaints to make. The English were stealing their land. English fur traders made their people drunk with rum and then cheated them of their furs. The English neglected their Indian allies, did not give them presents, while the French were friendly and generous. The French were building strong forts along the Great Lakes and the Ohio, said the Indian spokesmen, while the English had no defenses. The French could come right down and capture Albany.

The leaders of the Congress promised to take care of these complaints and gave the Indians presents. Some of the Iroquois fought on the British side in the war that followed.

Thus the Albany Congress was only partly successful in its two purposes. The colonies did not cooperate completely, and only some of the Indians remained loyal to the English. But the Albany Congress gave colonial leaders experience in meeting together and discussing their problems, so that it was valuable for the future cooperation of the colonies.

The British win the war. In 1755 the British government sent Major General Edward Braddock and an army of 1,500 men to drive the French out of the Ohio Valley. George Washington joined Braddock's staff as a volunteer. Washington warned Braddock that the British troops marching in close ranks, as they had been trained to do for fighting in Europe, would be slaughtered by the enemy firing from the protecting woods on both sides of the road. But Braddock ignored the warning. He led his army into a French and Indian ambush in which half his men were killed or wounded. Braddock himself was wounded and died a few days later. Washington helped to organize the retreat of those who survived.

Braddock's defeat was the first in a long line of defeats that the British suffered during the next three years. As these defeats piled up, almost all the Indians turned to the French side and attacked English frontier settlements. Things looked bad for the British. But the tide turned in their favor in 1758 when they began to use their great power in North America. In that year the British recaptured from the French the fort on the present site of Pittsburgh and renamed it Fort Pitt. The French had called it Fort Duquesne (dōō kān′). In 1759 the great victory was General James Wolfe's capture of Quebec. In 1760 the French surrendered Montreal, and with that surrender all of New France fell to the English. In these same years the English also defeated the French in India.

The treaty of peace was signed in Paris in 1763. France turned Canada over to Great Britain and gave up her claims to any land east of the Mississippi River. Because Spain had aided France against the English, the Spanish government had to give Florida to Great Britain. To make up to Spain for her loss of Florida, France gave her Louisiana. Louisiana included New Orleans and all French territory west of the Mississippi. In the New World, France kept only the right to fish along the coasts of Newfoundland, two small islands in the Gulf of St. Lawrence for fishing stations, and two islands in the Caribbean. On the maps on page 119 you can see how the treaty of peace in 1763 changed the ownership of North America.

Victory in the Seven Years' War won for Great Britain a large empire in North America and in India. It also helped to make her the ruler of the seas and a great power in Europe.

The farmer defeats the fur trader. How can we explain the victory of Great Britain over France in North America? The French had explored a vast territory in the interior of the continent. French traders and explorers had traveled from the Great Lakes to the Gulf of Mexico and from the St.

Capture of Quebec. British troops are preparing to attack Quebec. Why was the capture of Quebec important?

Lawrence River to the Rocky Mountains. But they did not settle this area. They used it only for the fur trade. Except for some farms along the St. Lawrence, the entire region remained a wilderness with widely scattered forts and trading posts. In all of New France there were less than 100,000 white inhabitants. The fur trade brought immediate profits but was a weak foundation for building an empire.

The English, on the other hand, had settled on the narrow Atlantic coastal plain to the number of 1,500,000. They had cleared broad areas for farms. They had built large towns and established industries. Their ships carried their products to distant ports. They had laid a strong foundation for a new civilization.

In the fight for the continent of North America, the English colonies were bound to win in the long run. They had many more men to serve in the army. Their farmers could provide more food, horses, wagons, and other army supplies than the French could. The English colonies had more money to spend for war. In the struggle between the two unequal sides, the farmer was victorious over the fur trader.

The Indian Point of View

Our forefathers had a castle on this river. One day one of them walked out and saw something on the river. He took it at first for a great fish. Two of our forefathers went to see what it was and found it to be a vessel with men in it. They immediately joined hands with the people in the vessel and became friends. At this time the white people were few, but we were very numerous and strong. We defended them in that low state. But now the case is altered. You are numerous and strong; we are few and weak. Therefore we expect that you will act by us as we did by you.

¶ In this speech an Indian orator at the Albany Congress summarized the history of Indian-white relations along the Hudson River.

2 *English Settlers Cross the Appalachian Mountains*

Before 1763 the dangers of French and Indian raids kept many people from settling along the frontier. During the wars with the French some settlers on the frontier actually left their homes and sought safety farther east. But after 1763 there was no longer any danger from French and Indian war raids. In 1763 large numbers of settlers were on the move westward.

Moving westward. People from eastern New England, in search of more fertile soil, went north into Maine, New Hampshire, and Vermont and west into New York. In New York, settlements reached northward as far as Lake Champlain. The English government gave farms around Lake Champlain to British soldiers as a reward for fighting in the French and Indian War. Germans, Scots, Dutch, and English filled in the Mohawk Valley as far west as Fort Stanwix, where Rome, New York, now stands.

In Pennsylvania, Virginia, and North Carolina, westward-moving settlers came to rivers that flowed into the Ohio and the Tennessee. During the French and Indian War the English cleared two roads from the Atlantic coast to the Ohio Valley. Over these roads they carried supplies for the armies attacking Fort Duquesne. As soon as the British captured that fort, English settlers, using the military roads, moved into the upper Ohio Valley. By the 1770s there were as many as 30,000 people in the valleys of the Ohio and its tributaries. (See the map on page 213.)

The corner where Tennessee, Virginia, and North Carolina meet is a mountainous region. A number of streams flow through the mountains and join to form the Tennessee River. As early as 1769 pioneers from Virginia and North Carolina began to settle along these streams and create a new frontier. By 1772 there were 13 little settlements in the valleys. The people of these settlements were without a regular government. Therefore, like the Pilgrims on the *Mayflower,* they got together and formed a government. They called it the Watauga (wŏ tô′gȧ) Association, taking the name of one of the rivers. The Watauga settlements became a base for the pioneer settlers who crossed the last range of mountains.

Crossing the mountains. So far the frontier had not yet crossed the Appalachian Mountains. There was still no permanent English settlement in the territory west of the mountains. Traders and trappers had, however, visited the land. Fur traders from South Carolina and Georgia had traded with the Indians as far west as the Mississippi itself. The backwoodsmen of Virginia and Carolina had gone hunting and trapping in the mountain valleys and in the open country beyond. They were called long hunters because of the long distances they covered and the long periods of time they were away from home.

There were rich men in the East who wanted to invest their money in western lands. They sent out parties to explore the western country and to bring back information about it. One such party discovered the Cumberland Gap. It was an easy pass through the last high mountain ridge that barred the way to the open country of Tennessee and Kentucky (see the map on page 213). One of the eastern investors hired Daniel Boone to explore Kentucky for him.

Boone was born in 1734 near Reading (rĕd′ĭng), Pennsylvania, then on the frontier. He was one of 11 children. Daniel was given his first rifle at the age of 12 and soon became a crack shot. Every fall and winter he went on exciting hunting trips and brought back meat and furs. Many boys of his age today would envy Daniel.

In 1750, much to Daniel's delight, the Boone family joined the great flood of settlers moving from Pennsylvania south along the Shenandoah Valley (see page 40). They settled in what was then the farthest frontier, the hilly country in western North Carolina. Here Daniel hunted for months on end, shooting deer, bear, and wild turkey. He became an explorer as well as a hunter. Every mountain was a challenge to him. He could not rest until he had climbed it or had found a way around it to see what was on the other side.

Long hunter. A long hunter is making ready for the trail.

In 1756 Daniel Boone married, built a log cabin, and made a clearing in the woods for a farm. But the adventurous life in the woods appealed to him much more than the monotonous life on a frontier farm. He left the farming to his wife and children while he roamed farther and farther on longer and longer trips into the mountains. He became a long hunter.

The Wilderness Road. In 1769 Boone and five other men started out on a hunting and exploring expedition into Kentucky. They wore long, fringed hunting coats, leggings, and moccasins —all of deerskin. Around their waists they wore large belts, from which hung their powder horns, hunting knives, and tomahawks. The packs on their horses were filled with ammunition, traps, blankets, and salt. They were as much at home in the woods as the Indians were. They lived chiefly on the game that they shot and cooked over campfires.

The purpose of this expedition was to bring back information about the western country. The men traveled by way of the Watauga settlements and the Cumberland Gap and reached the open

Stockade fort. Inside the stockade, settlers felt safe from Indian attack. Pioneers lived in such stockades until frontier communities were strong.

North America changes hands. The 1750 map shows how North America was divided by the European nations before the French and Indian War. The 1763 map shows how North America was divided by them after the war. Which nation lost its colonies?

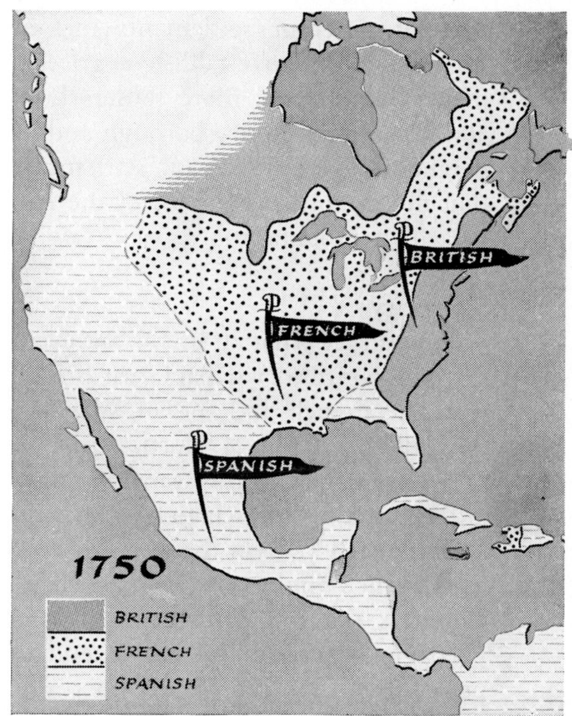

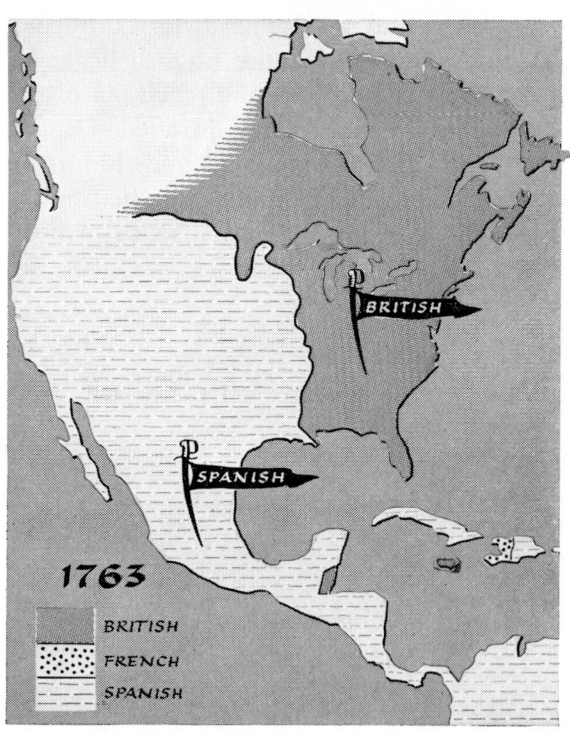

country beyond. After the other members of the expedition had gone back east, Daniel Boone explored the land of Kentucky alone. He liked the looks of the country and decided to settle in Kentucky someday.

That day came in 1775. An eastern investor bought from the Indians the land between the Kentucky and the Cumberland rivers. He intended to start settlements there and hired Daniel Boone to cut a path for the settlers to follow. Boone led a party of 30 men. West of the Watauga settlements they blazed the trees, cut the underbrush, picked out the best places to ford creeks, and made a way through the wilderness to the Kentucky River. This path became known as the Wilderness Road.

The first settlements west of the mountains. Boone's hardy trail blazers were followed by more settlers. They brought supplies and tools and erected a typical frontier fort on the Kentucky River. They built their cabins in a line so that the rear walls formed part of a stockade. (A stockade is a fort with walls made of logs.) At each corner of the stockade they built a two-story blockhouse. They called their settlement Boonesborough.

Another group of settlers came down the Ohio River from Pittsburgh and built another stockade nearby, which they called Harrodsburg. Soon there were two more forts, and representatives of the four settlements met at Boonesborough to establish a government. Before long, more settlers built additional forts. Boonesborough and its neighbors were the first settlements that the English made west of the Appalachian Mountains.

Summary

You can see what an important event it was in our history when Great Britain won the French and Indian War and pushed France out of North America. If France had won the war, we might all be speaking French today.

In the early years of the war, it looked as if France might win. In the Albany Congress the English succeeded only partly in obtaining Indian aid and in persuading the colonies to cooperate with one another. With their Indian allies the French defeated Braddock's army and won other victories. But beginning in 1758 the English began to win. They drove the French out of the Ohio Valley. They invaded Canada and captured Quebec and Montreal. France was so badly beaten that, in order to make peace, it had to give up Canada and India to Great Britain, and its ally Spain had to give up Florida.

The defeat of the French removed for the time being the fear of Indian attacks west of the Appalachian Mountains. Soon English settlers were living along the Ohio River, and Daniel Boone blazed the Wilderness Trail into Kentucky. The settlement of the West had begun.

For a Quick Review

1. In the colonial period were the French or the English generally more successful in holding the friendship of the Indians? Why?

2. Why did the French and the English come into conflict with each other in North America? Where were important battles fought during the conflict?

3. Explain why the English were able to win North America from the French.

4. How did the outcome of the French and Indian War affect the English colonists?

5. How did Daniel Boone and the other long hunters prepare the way for settlement west of the Appalachians?

Learning to Study More Easily

USING PHYSICAL MAPS

Maps can be a great help in studying history if you know how to use them. In this book you will find several physical maps, that is, maps that show the natural features of the land—mountains, plains, rivers, coast lines, and so on (see pages 672–673). Probably there are large physical maps on the wall of your classroom. In order to get the most information from physical maps, large or small, you must know how to interpret the scale and the symbols that you find on them.

Each map is drawn to a scale; an inch on the map represents a given number of miles on the earth's surface. With the scale you can measure the distance between any two points on the map. Suppose you want to measure the distance between Philadelphia and Boston, using your classroom wall map. Measure the space between the two cities with the straight edge of a piece of paper. Mark the distance with pencil dots. Then move the paper to the scale to measure the distance. You must remember, of course, that a map of this size cannot be exactly accurate. Therefore this is an approximate distance.

On large wall maps that show physical features, geographers have agreed to use certain colors to show elevation of land (distance above the level of the sea). On most physical maps (not all, to be sure) the lowlands, lands below sea level or up to 1,000 feet above sea level, are shown in various shades of green. The deeper shades are used for the lower elevations. As the land rises higher and higher above sea level, the colors used are yellow, tan, brown, and red, each showing greater elevation in that order. Most maps have in one corner a legend, or key, that shows what each color means. If you wish to know the elevation of western Kentucky, for example, you look to see the color of that region on the map. From the key you can learn what elevation the color stands for. What is the elevation of western Kentucky, according to your classroom wall map of the physical features of the United States?

Rivers flow from higher lands into lowlands and finally into the sea. On a map you can tell the direction in which a river flows by studying the elevation of the land through which it flows. When tracing the route of a river, start at the river's headwaters, where it rises or is formed. It may be formed by water flowing from a lake, in the case of the St. Lawrence River, or from smaller streams that unite to form a larger one, as in the case of the Ohio River.

Prepare an answer sheet in your notebook with space for your answers to the following 10 statements. Read each statement through; then consult your classroom wall map. Decide whether the statement is true or false. If it is true, place a *T* in the proper space on your answer sheet; if it is false, use an *F* to record your answer.

1. The Hudson River flows, in general, from north to south.
2. The Ohio River rises in the western ranges of the Appalachian Mountains.
3. A man in a canoe could travel more rapidly from Albany, New York, to New York City than from New York City to Albany.
4. If a man could travel in a straight line from one place to another, he would have a longer journey from Hartford to New Haven, Connecticut, than from Philadelphia, Pennsylvania, to Wilmington, Delaware.
5. The distance from New York to Boston, in a straight line, is about 250 miles.
6. The St. Lawrence River flows in a northeasterly direction.
7. The eastern coastal plain extends about 75 miles west of Columbia, South Carolina.
8. The Savannah River rises at Savannah, Georgia.
9. Fort Oswego, New York, was built near the headwaters of the Mohawk River.
10. The Hudson River flows into the Mohawk River.

7 *Thirteen English Colonies Win Their Independence*

The American colonies won their independence in the Revolutionary War. Great leaders like George Washington and Benjamin Franklin helped to win it: we all know of them. Thousands of others helped, too, thousands of persons whose names are unknown to many Americans today. There was Haym Salomon (săl′ō mŭn), who helped raise money to pay for supplies for Washington's army. His story is told in the movie *Sons of Liberty*. There was Thaddeus Kosciusko (kŏs ĭ ŭs′kō), the military engineer who came from Poland to enlist in Washington's army. He went back to his own country after the war and earned the title "the George Washington of Poland." There was Deborah Sampson, who posed as a man and served in Washington's army for two years under the name of Robert Shurtleff. Of course, there were no WACS then. Therefore, when it was discovered that she was a woman, she was sent home—with an honorable discharge.

Then there were the thousands of men who stayed with Washington through the hardships and defeats the army had to endure. And there were the thousands of women and children who did the best they could at home while the men were away at war. Someone had to do the work of farming and keeping the businesses going. Abigail Adams, whose husband John was to be the second President of the United States, was one of these women. "If many more men are called away," she wrote to her husband in 1776, "the women must reap the harvests. I am willing to do my part. I believe I could gather corn, and husk it; but I should make a poor figure at digging potatoes."

At the end of the French and Indian War, most of the people who later took part in the Revolution had no idea that they would soon be working for independence from England. Even to think about breaking away from the mother country would have seemed ridiculous to some and frightening to others. To understand how the people in the colonies gradually came to feel that they wanted independence and that it was worth fighting for, we must trace the story from 1763.

1 *Colonial Opposition to British Laws Leads to War*

In the year 1763 the 13 English colonies on the mainland of North America were a prosperous and important part of the British Empire. Although the colonial assemblies were cutting down the power of the royal governors (see page 50), the people were loyal to England. As they celebrated the victorious end of the French and Indian War, they proudly expressed their loyalty to the British king and Parliament. They had good reason to be grateful. For almost a hundred years the French in Canada and the Spanish in Florida had attacked their settlements and had stirred up the Indians to attack them. In 1763 England took over Canada and Florida. Now the people in the English colonies could look forward to living in peace and expanding their settlements.

England makes new laws for the colonies. After the victory over the French, the mother country decided to govern its colonies more strictly. To make the colonies pay the cost of governing them, the English government passed new tax laws. Besides the old duties (taxes on trade), it laid new ones on many imported products. It reduced by half the duty on molasses brought from the foreign West Indies (see page 70). But now the English government was determined to collect this tax. It appointed more tax collectors and stationed warships in the colonial harbors to put an end to smuggling. If a ship was caught trying to smuggle its cargo in, the owner lost both the ship and the cargo.

The English government added a new stamp tax. The stamps cost from 10 cents to $10 and more. The colonists had to attach stamps to all court documents, business papers, newspapers, and pamphlets. In other words, a colonist could not take a case to court, complete a business transaction, receive a diploma, or buy a newspaper without paying a stamp tax to the English government.

The English government also faced the problem of protecting frontier settlements from the Indians. The Indians were threatening to make war on the settlements because the whites were taking more and more of their land. The English government decided to prevent the colonists from moving west, for the time being at least, in order to quiet the Indians.

In 1763 the English government stopped the sale to colonists of land west of the Allegheny Mountains. It sent an army of 10,000 men to America to protect the settlers from Indian attack. The soldiers could also be used, if needed, to enforce the new laws.

Most colonists oppose the new measures. As you can see, this new program meant that the English government would play a much larger part in the life of the colonists than formerly. And, as you can guess, most of the colonists were strongly opposed to the new program.

Many people objected to the law that stopped the sale of western land. Wealthy men who had planned to buy land in the West and then sell it at a profit had to give up their plans. Persons who wished to settle in the West could not do so.

Merchants resented the whole tax program. They had to pay the new taxes as well as the old ones. Smuggling, so easy before, no longer paid. Too many smugglers' ships were caught, the owners losing their ships as well as the cargoes.

The new program hit the people of the northern colonies hardest of all. The English government now collected the duty on molasses imported from the foreign West Indies. Rather than pay the duty, many merchants stopped trading with the islands. Since fewer ships were used, fewer were built and many workers in shipyards lost their jobs. As we have seen, the islands had been the market where farm products had been sold. Now farmers could not sell their surplus crops.

The stamp tax especially angered lawyers, printers, and businessmen because they had to put stamps on every legal paper, every newspaper, and every kind of business document.

Colonial opinions. If an inquiring reporter had traveled through the colonies in 1765 asking people the question, "What do you think of England's new laws?" he would have received answers something like these:

From a frontiersman: "They can't keep us off the western lands. Nature meant for us to clear and plow that fertile soil so that we can produce food for all. I made this clearing with my own hands. And when I get ready, I'll make another farther west, king or no king, law or no law."

From a farmer: "All I know is that I'm being pushed against the wall. The merchants tell us that they can't sell our produce in the West Indies because the molasses duty takes away their profit. If we can't sell what we grow, we can't buy English cloth and hardware. They can't take the bread out of our mouths for long. We'll do something about it."

From a merchant: "England's policy is selfish and shortsighted. We can't pay the tax on molasses and stay in business. If we go out of business, English traders will suffer, too, because we'll stop buying manufactured goods from them. It seems to me that England is about to kill the goose that lays the golden eggs."

From a southern planter: "The entire policy is completely wrong. The English compel us to sell our tobacco, rice, and indigo in England, where we receive less for them than we would in other countries. They compel us to buy goods manufactured in England or to pay England a tax on goods we buy from other countries. I have been running into debt for years. Now they have increased the duty on many imports. This must come to an end sometime."

From a lawyer: "The trouble is that laws are being made to govern us by a parliament in which we are not represented. One way out would be for the colonies to send representatives to the

British Parliament. But London is too far away, and our representatives would be a small minority without influence. Each colony has a parliament of its own—its legislature. Let the British government agree that the colonies are to be taxed only by their own legislatures."

From a worker: "The new British policy isn't a policy; it's slavery. If they can tax us any way they want to, then they can take our homes and everything else away from us. We didn't ask them to send an army here. We don't want any fat redcoats in our town, high-hatting us and pushing us off the sidewalks. When the redcoats come, maybe we'll give them something they don't expect. Why, if King George himself comes over, we'd just as soon give him a bloody nose."

Besides these individual objections, there was one complaint upon which almost everyone in the colonies agreed. The colonists were used to running their own governments to a large extent. The mother country had not controlled them very strictly. Now, when England began to exercise full control, the colonists felt that they were being wronged. Many years after the War for Independence, an old veteran of the war was asked why he had fought against the English. "We always had run our own affairs," he said, "and we always meant to. They didn't mean that we should."

Opposition to the stamp tax. But whatever Americans thought later, in 1765 most of the colonists aimed their opposition at the Stamp Act. The British Parliament had passed that law without the consent of the colonial assemblies. If the colonists paid the stamp tax, the assemblies would lose the control over taxes that they had struggled so hard to gain. If the colonists buy the stamps, said colonial leaders, they will soon lose the right to govern themselves.

In October, 1765, representatives of nine colonies met in New York City. This meeting was called the Stamp Act Congress. The Congress declared that the colonists were loyal to the king. At the same time it insisted that free people could be taxed only by their own representatives. Therefore, the Congress said, only the colonial assemblies, and not the British Parliament, had the right to tax the colonists.

To make the English government give up its plan for a stamp tax, the colonists attacked the British where it hurt the most—in the pocketbook. Colonial merchants stopped importing English-manufactured goods, and the people stopped buying English products. The colonists manufactured their own cloth. People agreed not to eat lamb so that there would be more sheep to provide wool for cloth. The colonists who resisted England in these various ways called themselves Patriots.

After the Stamp Act went into effect, business almost came to a stop because the people refused to use stamps. Ships lay idle at the wharves. Sailors and waterfront workers had no jobs. Under the leadership of men like Samuel Adams, of Boston, the discontented workers organized secret clubs and called themselves Sons of Liberty. They set up liberty poles, or trees, under which they met to sing songs, drink

Patriot women. In support of the colonial boycott of British goods, colonial women met to spin yarn, weave cloth, and sew homemade clothes.

toasts, and make their plans. They punished persons who bought English goods. They broke into the homes of the men appointed to sell the stamps and frightened them into resigning or running away. Soon they insisted that the colonists carry on business without the use of stamps.

England repeals the Stamp Act. Meanwhile, in London, the English government received protests against the Stamp Act from English merchants as well as from the colonists. The merchants pointed out that the colonial boycott of (agreement not to buy) English goods was hurting business. Parliament found a way out. It repealed, or canceled, the Stamp Act. But at the same time it passed the Declaratory Act. This law declared that the colonists were subjects of Great Britain and that Parliament had full power to govern them and intended to do so.

When news of the repeal of the Stamp Act reached the colonies, the people broke out in joyous celebrations, pledging their loyalty to Great Britain. They ended the boycott. They paid no attention to the Declaratory Act. Even most of the Patriots joined in the celebration.

New taxes cause new troubles. The colonists soon learned, however, that the British government had meant what it said in the Declaratory Act. It had not given up any of its authority. Parliament passed new laws, called the Townshend Acts, that placed duties on paper, paint, glass, and tea imported by the colonists. Once again the colonial merchants agreed not to import any goods from England except certain necessities. Especially they would not buy paper, paint, glass, and tea. The Sons of Liberty became active once more. They frightened merchants who were slow to join the new boycott and they made life unpleasant for royal officials. In

Boston, customs officials were unable to carry on their work. The English government stationed British soldiers in that city to protect officials and help enforce the law.

The presence of British soldiers in the colonial towns naturally caused bad feeling among the people. The colonists resented the idea of being compelled by force to obey laws they did not like. Fighting between soldiers and civilians broke out in New York and Boston. In Boston, one evening in March, 1770, some boys threw snowballs at a British sentry. The soldier chased them away. A crowd gathered, armed with clubs. More soldiers were called out. One soldier was knocked down by a brickbat. He got up and shot into the crowd. The other soldiers fired. Five civilians were killed. The colonists called the incident the Boston Massacre, although the British said that the soldiers were defending themselves. Samuel Adams and other Patriot leaders began to talk of war.

The English government now yielded again by abolishing the new taxes except the one on tea. They kept the tea tax as proof that the government had the right to tax the colonies. The colonial merchants were satisfied. They began to trade with England again, and before long that trade was larger than ever. For the next three years, until 1773, the colonies were fairly quiet.

But many Patriots had their hearts set on independence. Samuel Adams organized the Boston Committee of Correspondence and persuaded other Massachusetts towns to appoint similar committees. Patriots set up committees of correspondence in other colonies. The committees kept in touch with one another by writing letters. Through these groups Adams worked to keep alive the opposition to England.

The colonists refuse to buy tea. The English government soon gave Samuel Adams the chance he was waiting for, to arouse the people against the mother country again. The East India Com-

Debating the issues. In the 1770s men debated the rights of the colonies against England in country stores and wherever they met.

METRO-GOLDWYN-MAYER

A Patriot speaks. In this scene from the film *Land of Liberty,* Thomas Jefferson (*left*) looks on approvingly as a Patriot argues with the royal governor of Virginia (*center*). What were some questions about which the governor and the Patriots disagreed?

pany had a vast amount of tea in its storehouses in London. The government permitted the company to sell the tea in the colonies at a very low price. The company was to sell it directly to local storekeepers, so that colonial merchants who imported goods from England would make no profit. The price of the tea would be so low that the colonists would forget that they were paying a tea tax.

Immediately the merchants joined the Patriots in opposing the sale of tea by the East India Company. Not only did they resent losing their profits on the tea; they were afraid that the company would begin selling other products directly to storekeepers. In time the company might force the merchants out of business altogether.

The colonial leaders decided not to permit the tea to be landed so that the people would not be tempted by its low price. In New York and Philadelphia, officials turned the tea ships back before they entered the harbors. In Charleston the tea was landed and placed in a storehouse. In Boston, Samuel Adams refused to allow the tea to be unloaded from the ships. The governor, on the other hand, refused to permit the ships to sail back to England with their cargoes.

Boston has a tea party and is punished. On the evening of Thursday, December 16, 1773, while the tea ships lay in Boston Harbor, about 8,000 people attended a meeting in the city to consider what to do about the tea. Samuel Adams was the chairman. He sent a message to the governor, asking him for the last time to let the ships sail. When he refused, Adams announced, "This meeting can do nothing more to save the country."

Those words were the signal. A mob of men disguised as Indians rushed to the wharf, boarded the three ships, and dumped all the tea into the harbor. The crowd gleefully watched from the shore. To this day no one knows exactly who took part in the Boston Tea Party. Some people believed that the Boston Patriots, by destroying private property, had gone too far.

The next step taken by the English government united the colonies for all time. The government passed four measures, known as the Coercive (kō-

Lexington. The first battle of the Revolutionary War was fought at Lexington. What events led up to the battle?

ûr′sĭv) Acts because they were meant to punish Boston for the tea party and to force the city to yield to English authority. The most severe of these acts closed the port of Boston so that no ship could sail in or out. The purpose was to starve the people into submission.

The other colonies support Massachusetts. The English government probably expected the other colonies to stand by and watch Massachusetts being punished. Instead, the colonies supported Massachusetts. They realized that, if Massachusetts were forced to give in, then they also would have to give in. The other colonies showed their sympathy by sending aid. Virginia sent money and food. Philadelphia sent flour. Charleston sent rice. From Connecticut came a flock of sheep. Massachusetts did not stand alone.

To decide on what united action to take, representatives of 12 colonies—all except Georgia—met in Philadelphia in September, 1774. This meeting was called the First Continental Congress. It demanded that Parliament repeal all laws passed against the colonies since 1763. It declared that thereafter the colonists would be taxed only by their own legislatures.

To make Britain pay attention to its demands, the Congress again called for a boycott of English goods. The Patriots signed an agreement not to buy any English products. Persons who refused to sign the agreement had their names published in the newspapers as Enemies of American Liberty. Some of them were attacked by mobs. The boycott was so successful that from 1774 to 1775 imports from Great Britain were reduced by 97 per cent. Before adjourning, the First Continental Congress called for the Second Continental Congress to meet in 1775.

Patriots and British fight at Lexington and Concord. Local committees of Patriots, especially in Massachusetts, began to train men to be prepared to take up arms at a minute's notice. These citizen-soldiers were called minutemen. The committees also stored guns and gunpowder for use in case of attack.

The Boston Patriots feared that the British might try to seize their ammunition. During the cold winter nights of 1774–1775, Paul Revere and his friends walked the streets of Boston, keeping watch on the British soldiers. Finally the Patriots learned that the British general planned to seize the arms and ammunition that were stored at Concord. On the night of April 18, 1775, Paul Revere and two other messengers rode out on horseback. They cried the alarm at houses in the countryside on the way to Concord, arousing the minutemen to prepare to meet the British.

On the morning of April 19 a British force, marching to Concord, came upon 60 or 70 minutemen lined up on the Lexington village green. The British shot at the minutemen, killing eight Americans and wounding ten. At Concord, British and Americans exchanged shots across a bridge. The British destroyed the small amount of stores that they found and started back. By that time minutemen had gathered along the road. From behind fences and trees, they kept shooting at the British all the way to Boston. An army of New Englanders held the British bottled up in that city.

The Battle of Bunker Hill. On the evening of June 16 the Americans occupied Breed's Hill, north of Boston. From the top of the hill they could shoot down on the British in the city. When the British discovered them the next day, they decided to attack the minutemen immediately. As the ranks of British redcoats came up the slope of the hill, the Americans mowed them down with gunfire. The Americans held their position until they had shot their last bullet. Then they moved back to Bunker Hill, from which they were also driven by the redcoats. From this second hill the battle took its name.

The British had planned to pursue the colonists into the country, but now they were content to remain where they were and lick their wounds. On Breed's Hill they had lost more than 1,000 men, a larger loss than in any battle of the French and Indian War. The Americans had lost about 400.

Washington drives the British out of Boston. At this time the Second Continental Congress was holding its secret meetings in Philadelphia. Even before the Battle of Bunker Hill, it had decided to organize the colonies for defense against British attacks. Now it enlarged the army surrounding Boston, named it the Continental Army, and appointed George Washington, of Virginia, its Commander in Chief.

In the spring of 1776 Washington seized the highest hill south of Boston and placed cannon on the summit. From the top of the hill the cannon could shoot into the city and its harbor. Rather than run the risk of another battle, the British gave up Boston and sailed away to Halifax, Nova Scotia. They took with them about a thousand colonists, who preferred to go with the English rather than remain in the rebellious colonies.

Words and events lead to war and independence. The military events of 1775, beginning at Lexington, marked a great turning point in our history. The American colonists had started out to persuade the mother country not to impose any new taxes on them and not to

SONS OF THE REVOLUTION

Adams names a commander in chief. John Adams proposes to the Second Continental Congress that George Washington be appointed Commander in Chief of the Continental Army.

interfere with their trade. They had resisted efforts to collect the new taxes. But there had been no armed conflict. Now the colonists found themselves carrying on a real war against the mother country. Resistance to a few laws, with no thought of independence, had gradually turned into rebellion against the British government.

The Olive Branch Petition. The colonists had not yet decided, however, that their aim was independence. Even after appointing General Washington as Commander in Chief of the Continental Army to defend the colonies against Great Britain, the Second Continental Congress tried to avoid war. It sent a petition to the king, seeking peaceful agreement. This document is known as the Olive Branch Petition (the olive branch is a symbol of peace). But the king refused even to receive the petition.

Arguments concerning independence. There were two sides to the question of independence. Some people argued that colonial trade had been prosperous because of the connection with England; if that connection were broken, the trade would decline. Others said that the weak colonies would never be able to defeat the powerful British Empire; let them wait 50 years or so, when they would be stronger. Still others feared that, if the colonies should win independence, they would be unable to unite and establish a government that would be strong enough to protect life and property.

On the other hand, the events of the past 10 years had done much to prepare many colonists for independence. They had learned to work together. They had cooperated in enforcing the boycotts against English products. Colonial leaders had met in congresses and had

A serious, exciting moment. This scene from the film *The Declaration of Independence* re-enacts what probably happened as soon as the Second Continental Congress adopted the Declaration. Can you pick out the actors who represent Franklin and John Adams?

acted together. The shedding of blood at Lexington and Bunker Hill had made many people bitter against England. The success of the colonial troops in those battles had made them proud and sure of themselves.

Weighing the arguments for and against independence, most people hesitated. Tom Paine brought many of them over to the side of independence by writing *Common Sense*. That pamphlet was published in January, 1776. Tom Paine had come from England only a few years before, but he had already caught the spirit of liberty. In his pamphlet he answered the arguments against independence and even proposed a whole plan for a new government. "The period for debate is closed," he wrote. "Arms, as the last resource, must decide the contest."

The Continental Congress declares independence. While the colonists hesitated, the British king took steps that made it easy for the people to decide in favor of independence. He announced that the colonists were in rebellion. He treated them like enemies.

In reply the Continental Congress also took warlike actions. It advised the colonies to throw out the old royal governments and to set up new ones. In other words, it urged the colonies to become independent states. Congress also appointed a committee to prepare a plan for uniting the new states.

On July 2, 1776, the Continental Congress voted in favor of a resolution that was offered by Richard Henry Lee, of Virginia. That resolution declared the colonies to be independent of Great Britain. On July 4 Congress adopted the document that we know as the Declaration of Independence.

The Declaration of Independence was written by Thomas Jefferson. It officially declared the colonies independent and gave the reasons for separating from England. In the Declaration, Jefferson presented this argument: People organize governments to help make their lives prosperous and free. When a government turns against its own people and oppresses them, the people have the right to overthrow the government and set up a new one. Jefferson then gave a long list of instances in which Great Britain had oppressed the colonies. Therefore, he concluded, the colonies were justified in declaring their independence and in establishing new governments.

With this argument for independence, the members of the Congress hoped to win the support of the colonial people. By actually declaring independence, they hoped to obtain help from European countries. They were sure that England's rivals in Europe would be glad to weaken her by helping her colonies break away.

2 *The Colonies Win Their Struggle for Independence*

The 13 colonies declared themselves independent, as you have just read. Great Britain refused to admit their independence and sent an army and a navy to America to put down the rebellion and to force the colonies to obey her. When the colonies fought back, the Revolutionary War began.

British fight under difficulties. Great Britain fought the war under several disadvantages. She had to send an army 3,000 miles away from home and keep it supplied. Since not enough Britishers would enlist, the government hired German soldiers to fight the Americans. They were Hessians from the German kingdom of Hesse.

With her navy England planned to blockade the colonies, that is, to keep them from sending their products to or bringing supplies from other countries. But even the British navy could not blockade a coast line a thousand miles long, and American ships were able to bring in supplies from Europe.

American difficulties. The Americans had to overcome far greater handicaps. Congress and the states found it difficult to raise an army and to keep it in the field. Congress itself enlisted and paid the Continental Army. It was the best trained American force, but it was small. Each state enlisted its own militia, or citizen-soldiers. But the men signed up for only a short time, usually three months, and so were not well trained. When their time was up, many of them picked up their guns and went home. It is true that they were often urgently needed to harvest crops or to protect their frontier homes against Indian attacks. But, whatever the reason for their leaving, the result was that one day Washington might have a sizable army and in a few days it might dwindle to a fraction of its former size.

Lack of supplies and money. Congress and the states were unable to provide enough food, clothing, and munitions (guns, ammunition, and so on) for even a small army. Congress had no power to tax the states or the people. It could only request the states to contribute money and supplies, and the states were free to send as much or as little as they pleased. More than once Washington had only one day's food supply in camp.

The Americans were handicapped in the war by the lack of gold and silver money. Congress printed paper currency, called Continental money. But this rapidly lost its value until it was worth practically nothing. George Washington wrote that it took a wagonload of paper money to buy a wagonload of flour. After the Revolution, when an American wanted to say that something was worthless, he said that it was "not worth a Continental."

Foreign aid. Conditions improved in the later years of the war, however, thanks to foreign aid. Many individual Europeans came on their own to help the Americans. There was the German General Steuben (stū'bĕn), who trained Washington's men how to march and fight. There were the Polish Pulaski (pụ lăs'kĭ) and Kosciusko. The Frenchman Lafayette became Washington's close friend and helped to get important help from France. France helped the Americans from the beginning. After 1777 her aid increased tremendously, and Spain and Holland joined her. These countries sent gold and silver money, arms and ammunition, clothing, blankets, and tents. This foreign aid was very important to the states in their fight for independence.

Patriots and loyalists. Another disadvantage of the Americans fighting for independence was that the people in the states were divided. About one-third of the people remained loyal to England. These loyalists helped the English cause whenever they got a chance. They regarded the Patriots as traitors to England. The Patriots regarded the loyalists as traitors to America.

Fights between Patriot and loyalist

Declaration of Independence Is Read in Boston

Last Thursday, after hearing a very good sermon, I went with the multitude into King Street [Boston] to hear the proclamation for independence read and proclaimed. Some fieldpieces . . . were brought there. The troops appeared under arms, and all the inhabitants assembled there (the smallpox prevented many thousands from the country), when Colonel Crafts read from the balcony of the State House the proclamation. Great attention was given to every word. As soon as he ended, the cry from the balcony was, "God save our American States," and then three cheers rent the air. The bells rang, the privateers fired, the cannon were discharged, the platoons followed, and every face appeared joyful. . . . After dinner, the King's Arms were taken down from the State House . . . and burnt in King Street. Thus ends royal authority in this State. And all the people shall say Amen . . .

¶ This eyewitness account was written by Abigail Adams to her husband, John Adams, on July 21, 1776.

neighbors were often more cruel and bloody than battles between the American and the British armies. The bitterest strife between Patriots and loyalists took place on the frontier because there each party stirred up Indians to attack the other. With bases at Fort Niagara and Detroit, bands of Indians under loyalist leaders attacked outlying settlements in New York, Pennsylvania, Virginia, and Kentucky. General Washington sent an expedition into central and western New York to destroy the villages and crops of hostile Indians in order to put an end to their attacks.

Washington retreats across New Jersey. You will recall that in the spring of 1776 Washington placed cannon on a hill overlooking Boston and the British left the city (see page 130). Washington was now free to move his troops to New York. He expected that the British would soon attack this important center in an attempt to divide the northern states from the southern ones. Nor was he mistaken. The British arrived in New York City in July, 1776, with 32,000 soldiers and 30 warships. Even with the militiamen who had joined from nearby states, Washington had fewer than 20,000 men.

Washington tried to defend New York. But the British general, Sir William Howe, pushed him out of Long Island and Manhattan to the mainland. Howe had several chances to surround Washington's army and destroy it, but he moved too slowly. Washington crossed the Hudson and began a long retreat across the state of New Jersey with Howe at his heels. As the British hurried in at one end of a town, the Americans hurried out at the other.

LIBRARY OF CONGRESS

Kosciusko. This Polish soldier came to America to help in the War for Independence. He was the chief engineer in the building of the fortifications at West Point.

You can trace the retreat on the map on page 136. Finally, on December 7, Washington crossed the Delaware River into Pennsylvania. The British had no boats in which to follow him.

Today we recognize the long retreat of Washington's army as a master feat of generalship. The American army was weaker than the British and could not meet it on anything like equal terms. If Washington's army had been destroyed, the Revolution would have been ended. Therefore Washington's great achievement in 1776 was that he kept an army together.

To the people of the time, however, retreat meant only weakness and defeat. Nothing is so disheartening to an army, especially to untrained militia, as continual retreat. As Washington moved back across New Jersey, his men deserted individually and in groups. By the time he got across the Delaware, early in December, he had about 3,000 men. Most of these would be leaving on January 1 because their term of en-

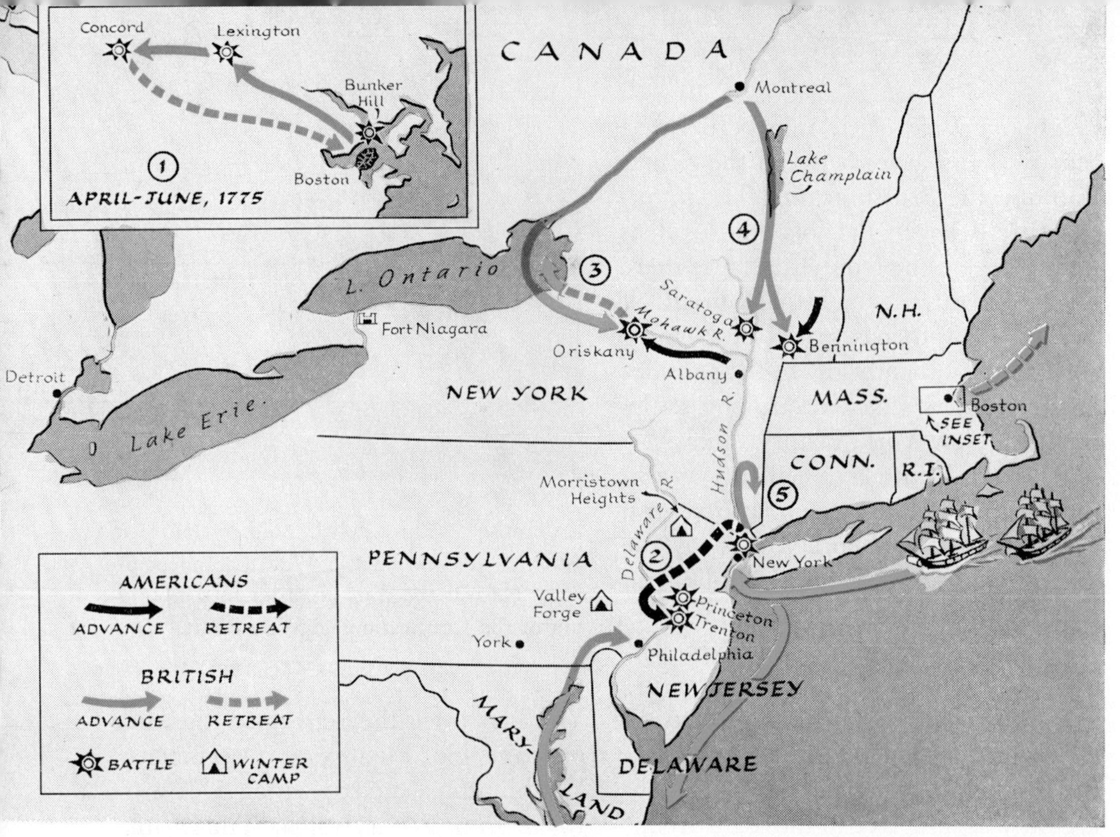

The Revolutionary War in the North, 1775–1777. As you read about military events of the Revolution, follow the action on this map. Where did major battles occur? What was the importance of each?

listment would be over on that day. "I think," Washington wrote, "the game is pretty near up."

It was at this despairing time that Tom Paine contributed his second great piece of writing to the American Revolution. It was the first of his series of papers called the *Crisis*. Washington ordered these papers read to the soldiers, and Tom Paine's words encouraged the men.

Victories at Trenton and Princeton. But action was more necessary than words. Washington watched eagerly for an opportunity to win a victory over the British. After Washington had crossed the Delaware, General Howe returned with his main army to New York. He left 1,400 Hessians at Trenton, New Jersey. Washington, with about 2,400 men, came back across the Delaware into New Jersey on Christmas night. Early the next morning the Americans attacked and captured about 1,000 Hessians at Trenton together with a large amount of supplies. Then they immediately crossed the Delaware back into Pennsylvania to avoid a possible counterattack by the British.

The victory at Trenton gave the army confidence and gave the Patriots hope. On the last day of the year Washington's army again crossed the Delaware into New Jersey. On January 2 the British attacked, and again Washington seemed to be in a trap, with his back to the Delaware River. But that night the American army, leaving its campfires burning brightly, stole silently around the main British army. The next day the Americans attacked the British rear guard at Princeton. In the Battle of Princeton the Americans lost about 40 men, the British about 400. Washington had won a second important victory.

But Howe was not beaten. In October, 1777, he captured Philadelphia, the American capital. Congress moved to York, Pennsylvania, and the Revolution went on. Washington had to stay around Philadelphia to watch what Howe would do. The most important events of 1777 were taking place farther north, in New York State.

The British plan for 1777 fails. Having failed to destroy Washington's army and so end the rebellion with one blow, the British planned a threefold campaign for 1777. One British army under General Burgoyne (bûr goin′) was to move south from Canada along Lake Champlain and down the Hudson River. Another British army was to travel up the Hudson from New York City. A third was to come around from Canada and go down the Mohawk River from the west. The three forces were to meet at Albany. By gaining control of the Hudson Valley, the British would cut off New England from the other colonies. Then they could end the rebellion in New England first, and afterward in the other colonies.

Oriskany. The plan failed. The army from New York City started too late. The troops from the west had to stop to take Fort Stanwix by siege. When they heard of the fighting at Stanwix, about 800 Patriot volunteers started up the Mohawk Valley to relieve the fort. They were ambushed at Oriskany (ō rĭs′kȧ nĭ) by a force of Indians and loyalists who had been their neighbors in the valley. The battle was the bloodiest of the war. Discouraged by their heavy losses, the Indians deserted. The British had to give up the siege and return to Canada.

Bennington. Burgoyne reached the Hudson River without much trouble. Being short of supplies, he sent some men to seize the horses, cattle, and flour that the Americans had gathered at Bennington, Vermont. On August 16 the New Hampshire militia under General John Stark wiped out this small British force.

Saratoga. Burgoyne then started down the Hudson toward Albany, but he moved too slowly. As time passed, his army grew weaker from defeats and desertions while the American army was made stronger by reinforcements. Finally, on September 19, 1777, the two armies met in a sharp battle on Bemis Heights, overlooking the Hudson River. This was the first Battle of Sara-

Tom Paine Wrote

These are the times that try men's souls. The summer soldier and the sunshine patriot will, in this crisis, shrink from the service of their country; but he that stands it *now* deserves the love and thanks of man and woman.

¶ When he wrote these words in the *Crisis,* to what times was Tom Paine referring?

PUBLIC BUILDINGS ADMINISTRATION

Continental soldiers fight. A small group of American soldiers holds off a British army while the main American forces reorganize. In the center is Colonel "Light Horse" Harry Lee, of Virginia. Still in his twenties, he was already a famous cavalry officer.

toga. The British held the field but lost twice as many men as were killed on the American side. Burgoyne did not dare attack again immediately.

Soon the British supplies were so low that Burgoyne had to push his way through to Albany or go back to Canada. On October 7 he attacked and was thoroughly beaten in the second Battle of Saratoga. On October 17 Burgoyne surrendered his entire army to General Horatio Gates at Old Saratoga, now Schuylerville, New York.

Saratoga is the turning point. The victory at Saratoga was the turning point of the American Revolution. A professional army, the pride of the British service, had surrendered to an American army made up mostly of militia. This surrender changed everyone's outlook on the war.

The English had learned that they were in a full-scale war. For the Americans, Saratoga meant that independence had become, not a forlorn hope, but a great expectation. Most important, Saratoga proved to the French that the former colonies were determined and able to fight the war through to final victory. Within 24 hours after receiving the news of Burgoyne's surrender, the French government decided to recognize the independence of the United States. In Paris, Benjamin Franklin signed a treaty with France in February, 1778, and the two countries became allies. France was soon at war with Great Britain.

Other European countries, jealous of England's size and power, were eager to strike a blow at the British Empire. Spain declared war in 1779, and Holland in 1780. Countries like Russia, Denmark, and Sweden did not declare war, but they were definitely unfriendly toward England and friendly toward the United States.

What had started as a quarrel between the English and some discontented colonists had now become a world war. Great Britain was fighting a large part of Europe. She found herself fighting in India, in the West Indies, and on the high seas. The French were even making plans to attack England itself. With so much on her hands, Britain could not give full attention to her rebellious colonists. England's world-wide troubles gave the Americans their great opportunity for victory.

Washington's army suffers at Valley Forge. At the end of December, 1777, Washington's army established winter quarters at Valley Forge, near Philadelphia. More than any other name, Valley Forge reminds us of the suffering of the American soldiers of the Revolution. The men in the camp did not have enough food or clothing or any other necessity. The most regrettable part of the story is that there were enough food and clothing in the states to supply the army. But Congress had no power, individuals were selfish, and means of transportation were lacking. Merchants who owned stocks of clothing preferred to hold them for higher prices. Continental money was rapidly losing its value. Many farmers hid their produce from the Americans. They preferred to sell it to the British, who paid in gold. Many Americans still were not convinced that liberty was worth fighting for.

End of important fighting in the North. General Howe had hoped to dishearten the Patriots by capturing their capital (see page 137). But hold-

Nathan Hale, American Patriot. While the British were in New York, Hale secretly entered the city in an attempt to learn their plans. He was caught and was hanged as a spy. This picture shows him being questioned by the British General Howe.

MUSEUM OF THE CITY OF NEW YORK

ing Philadelphia brought the British no advantage. In June, 1778, they moved out of Philadelphia and went back to New York City, which was their main base throughout the war.

There was no more important fighting in the North. The British in New York City were too strong for Washington to attack. The Americans had fortified West Point, up the Hudson River to the north, and had made it so strong that the British could not hope to capture it. In the remaining years of the war, each side kept watch on the other without attacking while the most important fighting took place in the Northwest and the South.

George Rogers Clark conquers the Northwest. The English had won the Northwest, you will remember, in the French and Indian War. The important settlements in the area were Detroit, Vincennes (vĭn sĕnz′) on the Wabash River, and Kaskaskia and Cahokia (kȧ hō′kĭ ȧ), the old French towns on the Mississippi. From these places the British were sending out parties of Indians to raid American settlers along the frontier. To end these raids and to capture the Northwest for the Americans were the purposes of George Rogers Clark.

With a commission from the State of Virginia and a force of 175 men, Clark captured Kaskaskia and Cahokia in July, 1778 (see the map on this page). Vincennes surrendered without a blow. The French inhabitants were glad to be

The Revolutionary War in the West and the South. On this map follow the events of the Revolutionary War in the West and the South. How did geography play a part in the campaigns—for example, in the surrender at Yorktown?

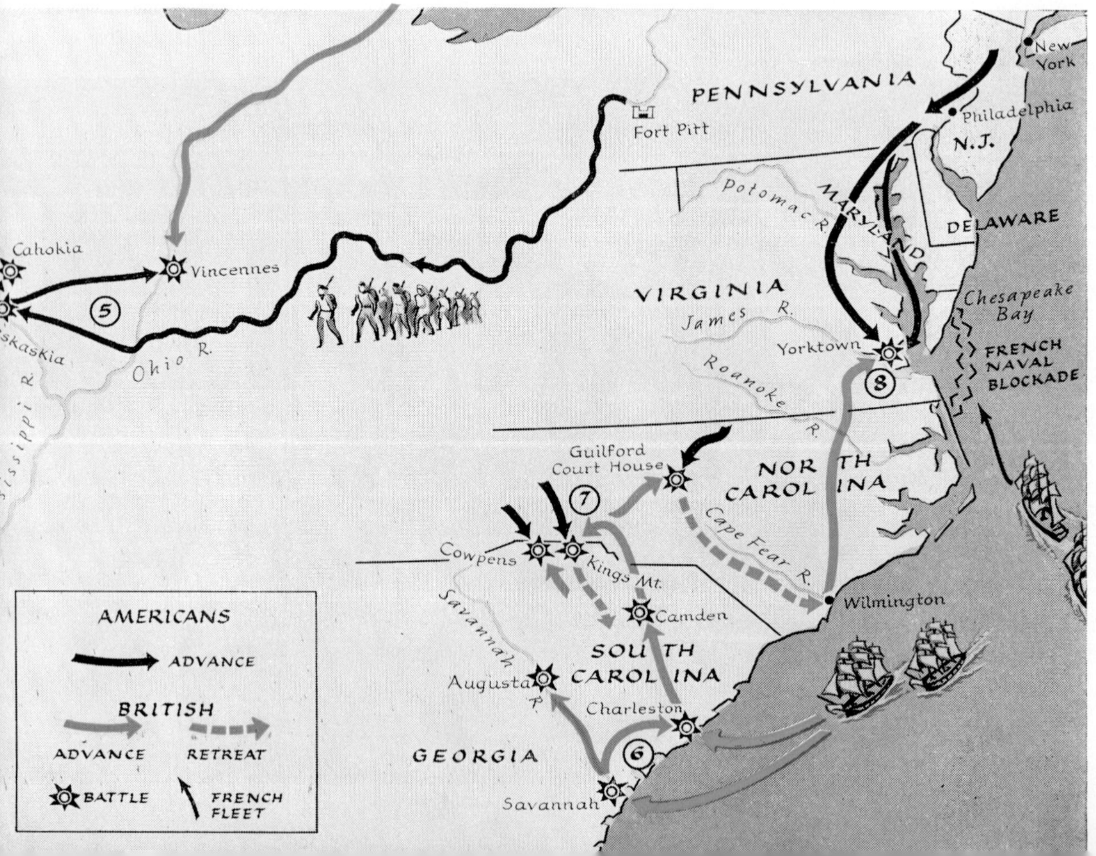

INDIANA HISTORICAL BUREAU

British surrender to George Rogers Clark. Clark was only 26 years old when he led the Virginia militia to capture Vincennes, but he was a powerful man and an inspiring leader. Notice the stockade and corner blockhouse in the background of this painting.

on the American side since France had just made an alliance with the states. From these villages as a base, Clark planned to attack Detroit, the strongest British settlement in the Northwest. But the British did not wait for his attack. They sent a force of 175 whites and 500 Indians down from Detroit to recapture Vincennes.

The British might have gone on to take Kaskaskia, where Clark had his headquarters, but they considered the trip impossible in winter. However, George Rogers Clark thought differently. He collected 150 men and led them over the cold, swampy prairies to Vincennes. For 18 February days Clark's band waded through the icy water of these "drowned lands," eating little food and sleeping on low hills that rose just above the freezing mud. With the promise of victory, George Rogers Clark inspired his men to carry on. They reached the goal of their 230-mile march on February 23, 1779, making the final rush through water that was breast-high. They surprised the small garrison of Vincennes and captured the place two days later.

This campaign involved only a few hundred men. But great results often come from little events. Clark's conquest of Kaskaskia and Vincennes later gave the United States a reason for demanding the Mississippi River rather than the Allegheny Mountains as its

LIBRARY OF CONGRESS

Marion's Brigade. Francis Marion crosses the Pee Dee River in South Carolina on his way to attack the British. He was called the "Swamp Fox" because, as often as the British drove him into the swamps, he appeared again where least expected.

western boundary. The British agreed to the demand for other reasons, but Clark's victory helped.

Guerrilla warfare in the South. The most important battles of the final years of the war were fought in the South. The British planned first to conquer the southern states and then to move up north. In the last days of 1778 a British force captured Savannah and, a short time later, Augusta. By these victories the British won control of Georgia. A year later a British army from New York landed in Savannah. Two months later it marched overland to Charleston and surrounded the city. On May 12, 1780, the Americans surrendered Charleston to the British, together with 7,000 American troops. This surrender was one of the worst disasters of the war for the Patriots.

From Charleston the British extended their control over all South Carolina. For a time only guerrilla (gĕ rĭl′ȧ) bands upheld the Patriot cause in South Carolina. Guerrillas hid in the swamps and forests, marched under the cover of night, swooped down on scattered British or loyalist troops, and vanished again, leaving behind death and destruction. Their weapons were anything from hunting knives to pitchforks. They did their best fighting with the long-barreled rifle. The most famous of the guerrilla leaders were Francis Marion, Thomas Sumter, and Andrew Pickens. In a number of battles, as at King's Mountain, Cowpens, and Guilford (gĭl′fẽrd) Court House, the Americans defeated the British. By these victories the Americans drove the British out of the Carolinas.

Cornwallis is trapped at Yorktown. In the spring of 1781 Cornwallis, the British commander in the South, moved his army from North Carolina into Virginia to join the British troops already in that state. With an army of 7,000 he settled down at Yorktown, Virginia, and fortified his position. He was on a peninsula, a piece of land joined to the mainland by a narrow neck. It was a convenient place to get supplies and reinforcements from the ships of the British navy, which controlled the sea.

Now, in the summer of 1781, the French played a star part in the last great action of the Revolutionary War. A French army was encamped at Newport, Rhode Island. A large French fleet arrived in the West Indies. Washington carried out a careful plan that would make use of this aid. The French fleet sailed for Chesapeake Bay. The French army joined the American army on the Hudson River, and the combined force marched south. The army crossed Chesapeake Bay in boats, landed upon the Yorktown peninsula, and dug in. The French fleet drove off an English fleet and won control of Chesapeake Bay.

Washington's army and the French fleet both arrived at the right place at the right time and shut a tight trap around Cornwallis. At his back, the French fleet prevented all possible aid by sea. In front, Washington at the head of an army of 16,000 men cut off escape by land. On October 19, 1781, four years and two days after Burgoyne's surrender at Saratoga, Cornwallis surrendered his entire army.

At Yorktown, Great Britain's effort to keep her colonies by force of arms came to an end. The British had lost two armies in America. They were busy with problems in other parts of the

American marines, 1779. John Paul Jones reviews American marines aboard the *Bonhomme Richard*. The Marine Corps, oldest of our armed forces, was organized in 1775. Compare the uniforms of these marines with those worn in the Corps today.

OFFICE OF NAVAL RECORDS AND HISTORY

world. British leaders decided to give up the war in America and call their soldiers home.

An outstanding victory at sea. The effectiveness of the French fleet at Yorktown showed the value of naval power in fighting Great Britain. The principal American fighting forces at sea during the Revolutionary War had been ships owned by private citizens. These ships were licensed by Congress to attack enemy vessels. Such private warships were called privateers. In the course of the war, more than 2,000 of them seized many British supply ships.

Throughout the war there was no regular American navy to speak of. Congress depended on the French and Spanish navies to oppose Britain on the sea. But one memorable battle was fought by an American warship during the Revolution.

One day in September, 1779, John Paul Jones, in command of the *Bonhomme Richard* (bô nôm′ rē shär′), attacked the more powerful British warship *Serapis* (sė rā′pĭs). To overcome the enemy's advantages in fire power and speed, Jones ran his ship against the enemy's and lashed the two vessels together. At such close quarters each ship threw murderous fire into the other. When the British captain asked Jones whether he was ready to surrender, Jones replied, "I have just begun to fight." The *Bonhomme Richard* was full of holes and on fire. The *Serapis* also was burning and had lost all of its rigging. But Jones and his crew stuck it out, and the British captain finally surrendered. More than half the men in the two ships were either killed or badly wounded. This spectacular victory had no effect on the result of the war, but Americans took pride in it and it made John Paul Jones popular in Europe as well as at home.

The thirteen states become independent. Cornwallis's surrender at Yorktown in 1781 marked the end of the actual fighting between Great Britain and her former colonies. But the peace treaty was not signed until 1783. The Americans who took part in writing the treaty were Benjamin Franklin, John Adams, and John Jay.

The treaty favored the Americans. The king of Great Britain recognized the independence of the 13 states. The British gave the Americans the right to fish off Canada and Newfoundland just as they had always done as colonists. The Americans promised that Congress would urge the states to restore the property of loyalists. They also promised that no laws would be passed to prevent British citizens from collecting debts in the United States. The British gave the vast territory between the Alleghenies and the Mississippi to the United States. Great Britain gave Florida back to Spain.

Summary

The fundamental cause of the American Revolution was that Great Britain insisted on governing the colonies while the colonies insisted they had the right to govern themselves. Even for that cause many colonists refused to fight against the mother country. But the Patriots took over control in the colonies. They declared independence and won it on the battlefield in spite of many difficulties.

At the beginning of the war, General

Washington saved the American cause by retreating before the stronger British forces and, at the same time, keeping an American army together. The British general called him an "old fox." In 1777 the British plan was to divide the states by winning control of Lake Champlain and the Hudson River. But the plan failed and, after the Battle of Saratoga, Burgoyne surrendered his entire British army to the Americans.

Saratoga was the turning point of the war. That victory encouraged France to come out openly and declare war on Great Britain, and other European countries did the same. Great Britain

The new nation and its neighbors, 1783. What boundaries were set for the United States by the Treaty of Paris? What nations held territory bordering the United States?

had to fight, not only in America, but also in Europe and India.

In 1778–1779 George Rogers Clark drove the British out of most of the Northwest. At the same time the British started winning victories in the southern states and moving northward. But at Yorktown in 1781 Washington, with the help of a French fleet and a French army, caught the British in a trap; and Cornwallis surrendered another British army to the Americans.

The victory at Yorktown marked the end of the fighting. The peace treaty, signed in Paris in 1783, gave the states their independence and all the land west to the Mississippi River.

For a Quick Review

1. What policies did the British follow in governing the American colonies after the French and Indian War? What reasons did they give for their policies?

2. What were the American objections to the British policies?

3. Trace the steps by which the Americans came to declare their independence.

4. What were the advantages and disadvantages of Great Britain and the American colonies in fighting the Revolutionary War?

5. What were the major battles and campaigns of the Revolutionary War? Why were Saratoga and Yorktown important?

Learning to Study More Easily

USING THE CARD CATALOG

From time to time in your school work, you will be looking for information to prepare a report or some special program. The card catalog in your school library or in the public library can help you find the information you will need.

The card catalog is a guide to the books in the library. The cards are arranged alphabetically, like items in an index or words in a dictionary. Each card contains (1) the author's name, (2) the exact title of the book, (3) a *call number,* by which you can ask for the book, and usually (4) a brief description of the contents.

For each book there are at least three cards. The *author card* lists the book under the author's name. The *title card* lists the book by its title. One or more *subject cards* list the book under the main subjects with which it deals. Take, for example, the book *Americans and Their Songs* by Frank Luther. The author card would be listed under "L" and the title card under "A." The subject cards would be listed under (1) Ballads, American, (2) American Ballads and Songs, and (3) Folk Songs, U.S.

These several cards for each book make it easy for you to find the book you need. You can find a book if you know only the author's name or only the title or if you have only a general subject in mind and are looking for books on that subject.

Having found the name of the book you want, your next step is to get the book from the library shelves. In some libraries you must write the author's name, book title, and call number on a call slip and give it to the librarian. Then the librarian will get the book for you. In other libraries you may go to the shelves and get the book yourself. To do so, you need to learn how the books are arranged on the shelves according to their call numbers. What is the system in your school library? In the public library you use?

For more detailed information about the card catalog in your school library, ask your teacher or the librarian to demonstrate how to use it and to answer your questions. You may also consult one of these books: *Social Studies Skills* by Forrest E. Long and Helen Halter or *Basic Social Science Skills* by J. Wayne Wrightstone, Dorothy Leggitt, and Seerley Reid.

To begin using your library's card catalog and, at the same time, to locate useful information for your study of this unit, do one or both of these exercises:

1. Consult the following subject headings in the card catalog of your library and make a list of the books that are available under each: Revolutionary War, Military campaigns of the American Revolution, George Washington, Continental Congress.
2. Consult the list of books given at the end of Unit 2. See how many of them you can find in the card catalog of your library. Perhaps each member of the class can look up one book and report whether or not it is in your library.

8 Americans Form a National Spirit

In Charleston, South Carolina, one day in August, 1780, Dr. David Ramsay's patients missed him. "Dr. Ramsay isn't here," his patients were told. "He's been sent to St. Augustine by the British commanders. He's exiled because of his work for the Patriots." David Ramsay really had been exiled for Patriot activities. But after the British troops had left Charleston, he came back home and again began treating his patients.

When the Revolutionary War was over, Dr. Ramsay was proud of his new country. Like many other Americans, he was proud of the part he had played in the winning of independence. He was an educated man, one who liked to study and write. The great events of the Revolution should not be forgotten, he decided, and he wrote a book about them. It was published in 1789.

Dr. Ramsay wrote that many good things came out of the Revolution. One was that the people from different states got acquainted with one another. "The Americans knew but little of one another previous to the Revolution," he wrote. "Trade and business had made the inhabitants of their seaports acquainted with each other, but the bulk of the people in the interior country were unacquainted with their fellow citizens." Then came the war, and men from all the states came into the army and to Congress. They learned to know people from other states. Sometimes, as Dr. Ramsay pointed out, a soldier far from home married a girl who lived where his company was stationed. When this happened, new family ties brought together people from different states. What was the result of these new ties and new friendships? As Dr. Ramsay saw it, "Unreasonable jealousies had existed between the inhabitants of the eastern and of the southern states; but on becoming better acquainted with each other, these in a great measure subsided." (Subside means to become smaller, less important, to quiet down, or even to disappear.)

In the very year that Dr. Ramsay's book was published, 1789, a new federal government was put in operation. You will read that part of the story in Chapter 9. But setting up a government does not in itself make a nation. To be a nation, people must look up to the same heroes, celebrate the same holidays, share the same ideals. To say it in another way, they must have a common patriotism. They must feel that they belong together. Today, when we know some of the problems our nation faced after 1789, we can see that Dr. Ramsay overestimated how well the people of the various states understood one another and how much the jealousies between them had subsided. But we can see that he was right in saying that by the end of the Revolutionary War the people were beginning to share a national spirit. They continued to think of the problems of their home states, but they also began to think of the problems of the nation as a whole. They were becoming Americans as well as Virginians, New Yorkers, or Marylanders.

1 *The People of Each Section Follow Their Own Ways*

In 1773 Josiah Quincy, Jr., of Boston, took a trip through the colonies for his health. He traveled through the southern colonies like a person visiting a foreign country for the first time. He noticed the differences between New England and the South.

Differences between the sections. In New England property was pretty equally divided. Each farmer owned his land. He had a voice in the town meeting and in church affairs. He felt independent. He respected the merchants for their wealth and the clergymen for their education. But in most ways the New England farmer considered himself as good as any man.

In the South, Quincy found, property was unequally divided. A few planters owned so much land and so many slaves that the small-scale owners could not hope to catch up with them in property and wealth. The large planters controlled the government and the church. They passed laws to suit themselves and did little to help the rest of the people. The result was, Quincy believed, that the small farmers and the poor whites were ignorant and poor in comparison with the farmers of New England.

Quincy contrasted other conditions in the South with life as he knew it in New England. In New England the people lived in small, compact villages. Each village had a church and was required by law to support a public school. The lives of the people were strictly regulated by the church and by public opinion. Dancing, attending the theater or concerts, card playing, even reading novels were frowned on. Sunday was a day of prayer and meditation; no work or pleasure was allowed. On all other days everyone was expected to keep busy, for idleness was considered to be a sin.

COLUMBIA PICTURES

On a southern plantation. This scene from *The Howards of Virginia* suggests the rich way of life that Josiah Quincy noticed as he traveled through the southern colonies.

Since the plantations of the South were large, homes were long distances apart. There were few schools. Churches were hard to get to. Negro slaves did most of the manual labor. Many white people, Josiah Quincy thought, considered themselves above doing any kind of work. By Quincy's New England standards, the southern planters enjoyed too much luxury and idleness. Within a short time after arriving at Charleston, South Carolina, Quincy attended a concert, two merry meetings of men's clubs, and the horse races. Thus, though he had a good time there, Quincy's opinion of the South was distinctly unfavorable.

Southern opinion of New England was equally unfavorable. Southerners considered New Englanders too narrow-minded in religion and too democratic in politics and social life. The New Englanders were too much concerned with trade. They were not to be trusted. They talked a great deal about their grievances against England, but when the time to act came, they would do nothing. That, Quincy found, was the southern opinion of New England.

Of course, we now know that the southerners were partly wrong about New England, just as Josiah Quincy was partly wrong about the South. People with different ways of living and different ideas often misunderstand and mistrust each other. That is as true today as in Quincy's time, whether we are thinking of groups of people in our own country or of groups in other parts of the world. By knowing more about one another's lives and by working together on important projects, people with different customs learn to understand one another. That was one truth colonial Americans soon found out.

As Josiah Quincy, Jr., on his return trip north, entered the middle colonies, he found the scene more familiar than it had been in the southern colonies. Fields of wheat and corn, cow pastures, and apple orchards were more homelike to him than rice and tobacco plantations. He found that in the middle colonies there were some large estates but that, in general, property was more equally divided than in the South.

Villages in the middle colonies were not so compact as in New England; yet there was more village life than in the South. There was much wealth and luxury, especially in the large towns, but life was not so free and easy as in the South. There was no one official church. A number of churches existed side by side—Presbyterian, Episcopalian, Roman Catholic, Quaker, Baptist, and those of various German sects.

Each church had rules for its own members. There was no one strict church rule for all, as in New England. From what you know about the settlement of these colonies, how would you explain these differences?

People from the different sections do not mix. The groups of colonies differed from one another and misunderstood one another. And it looked as if this condition would not improve. One way to overcome misunderstanding was for people to travel from section to section and to learn to understand and sympathize with one another. But not many people traveled far in the colonies.

Most people did not have time or money for travel. Unless they moved west to establish new homes on the frontier, they never took a long journey. The wealthy people in each colony were interested first of all in the affairs of their own colony and in its relations to England. Therefore they either remained at home or traveled to the mother country. Josiah Quincy, Jr., was an exception.

Benjamin Franklin was another exception. He knew many colonial leaders, and he in turn was known in all the colonies. He thought of the colonies as being closely related to one another. But not many people thought as he did. Most colonial leaders were unacquainted with one another. When the delegates to the First Continental Congress arrived in Philadelphia in 1774, many of them met one another for the first time. When John Adams later met the delegates from Georgia, he had to ask them how big Georgia was, how it was governed, and what kind of courts it had. If an educated and well-read

THE NEW-YORK HISTORICAL SOCIETY, NEW YORK CITY

Sailboat ferry. In 1746 the ferry from Manhattan to Long Island, shown in this picture, was a flatboat with sails. Passengers never knew how long it would take such a ferry to reach its destination.

person like John Adams knew so little about another colony, we must conclude that most of the people knew very little indeed about other colonies.

Travel is slow and difficult. The main reason why people in the colonies did not travel much was that transportation was slow and difficult, even dangerous. In the North there were wagon roads leading a short distance out of the large towns. Except for these, the only road on which wagons could be driven in 1760 was the main coastal road connecting Boston, New York, and Philadelphia. Regular stagecoach lines covered the distance from Boston to New York in about a week and from New York to Philadelphia in three days. That was the schedule in summertime; in the winter the trips took longer.

To accomplish this miracle of speed, travelers got up at three o'clock in the morning and dressed by candlelight.

BUREAU OF PUBLIC ROADS

Speed record. The stage wagon called the *Flying Machine* traveled about 90 miles in two days. It made the trip between New York and Philadelphia twice a week. What does the picture suggest about the discomforts of travel in the late 1700s?

With their eyes still heavy with sleep, they climbed up the steps of the covered stage wagon and stumbled to their wooden seats. As the horses galloped over the rough road, they bounced and rattled around like corn in a corn popper.

After three or four hours of rough travel, they stopped for breakfast and then climbed back on the wagon for more torture. When the wagon went uphill, the men passengers got out and walked to lighten the load. After rain the road was likely to be a mudhole at many points, and the men frequently had to put their shoulders to the wheels to help the horses pull the wagon out. The wagons crossed small brooks at fording places. The larger streams they crossed on ferries like the one shown on page 151. Ferries were known to overturn, and the passengers and horses often drowned.

After 18 or 19 hours of bouncing around and pushing and hauling and waiting, at nine or ten o'clock at night the travelers finally stopped at a tavern for supper. They were 50 miles or so nearer their destination. Soon after supper they dropped into bed to rest their weary limbs, only to be awakened again at three o'clock the next morning for another day of the same rough treatment.

By the time of the Revolution, travel had become faster, but it was no more comfortable. As the result of improved roads, faster ferries, and more frequent changes of horses, people could go from New York to Philadelphia in two days. They could go from Boston to Philadelphia in about eight days. The stage wagons that traveled so fast were called "flying machines."

Bad as roads were in the North, in the South they were much worse. There were no regular stage lines. In fact, it was almost impossible to travel in a wagon, even on the main coastal road. It was difficult even to cover that road on horseback, as Josiah Quincy, Jr., found out on his journey. The road was level, but his horse had to wade through deep, heavy sand and was soon tired out. After rain the road was one long mudhole. For long stretches it was a corduroy road, made up of logs laid across swampy fields. The logs were covered with mud and the horse sometimes sank down to the stirrups. The few bridges were unsafe; the ferries were bad. Towns were long distances from one another. The uncomfortable taverns were far between, and they charged very high prices for poor accommodations.

Such was the main road through the colonies. Other roads were no more than trails or, at best, rough cart tracks through the woods. Almost all traveling was done on horseback.

Of course, it was possible to travel from colony to colony by sea. But there was no way to tell when a ship would leave or when it would arrive. Since there were no lines of passenger ships that sailed on schedule, a traveler had to wait for a trading vessel bound for his destination. Once at sea he was at the mercy of wind and weather, and the voyage might be long or short.

Communication is difficult. As it was difficult for people in the colonies to travel from place to place, so was it difficult for them to communicate with one another. Benjamin Franklin, as colonial postmaster, had improved the postal service somewhat, but it was still unreliable. Even this service was provided in the North only. In the South there was no regular mail delivery. From New York it took five or six weeks for a letter to be delivered in Virginia, and three months in North Carolina.

Off the main coastal road there were no postal routes and no post offices in the North or in the South. The postrider dropped off a letter at the post office nearest its destination. From there its delivery depended more or less on chance. It was picked up by any stranger "going that way" and was again left at the nearest point. After months, or a year, it might reach the person addressed. A letter sent by boat was left by the ship's captain at a tavern in the port where he landed, and from there its delivery depended on chance.

2 *Bonds of Unity Tie the Colonies Together*

We see, then, that the colonies differed in their ways of living. Since travel and communication were difficult, people could not easily learn to know and sympathize with one another. We can understand how a person in 1763 might conclude that the colonies would not be able to get along together. However, as we look back now, we see that there were many bonds of unity between them, and these proved to be stronger than the differences.

Leaders see the need for cooperation. Now we can appreciate how important it was that the colonial leaders met together in congresses. Here they worked on matters that concerned all of them. When they began to discuss their prob-

"THE POUGHKEEPSIE NEW YORKER"

Franklin and his printing press. The newspapers, almanacs, magazines, and books that Franklin printed were read in many of the colonies. They encouraged cooperation among the colonies against England.

lems, they found that they had much in common. Have you noticed that this is often the case when people (or nations) begin to work together to solve common problems?

The colonial leaders were as a rule the wealthy men of the colonies. Many of them had been educated in the colonial colleges. They had read the same books. They had absorbed the same ideas about the right of people to govern themselves. When they talked over their problems, they found that all the colonists had the same kind of complaint against the mother country. They saw that the colonies would have to cooperate to obtain their demands. When the leaders returned to their homes, they spread the idea of colonial cooperation among the colonists.

The colonists speak the same language. One bond that united the colonies is so easy to see that it is often overlooked. The people of the 13 colonies spoke the same language. In the Revolutionary period most of the people were of English descent or came from some part of the British Isles. (See the chart on page 39.) Most of the Dutch, Germans, Swedish, and French had learned to speak English. The Negroes spoke the language of their masters. Because they had a common language, the people in the colonies were able to exchange ideas and agree upon common grounds in their opposition to England.

The principal means of exchanging ideas was the weekly newspaper. In the 12 years of controversy (kŏn′trō̍ vûr sĭ) with the mother country before the Revolutionary War, the colonial newspapers were a powerful bond of unity. From 1763 to 1775 the number of papers in the colonies increased from 21 to 42.

The colonial newspaper was not much to look at. It consisted of four small pages, hardly bigger than the pages of this book. There were three columns to a page. The paper contained very little news, and that was likely to be a month or more old. Two pages were filled with advertisements, lists of ships arriving and departing, and tables giving business information such as the values of the different kinds of money then in use. The editors filled the remaining space with articles sent in by readers or copied from other newspapers or from books. Compared with our newspapers today, the colonial papers seem very dull indeed.

Many colonial papers did not sell more than 300 copies a week. A circulation of 1,000 was large. (How does this compare with the circulation of the paper your family reads?) These small circulation figures for colonial newspapers, however, do not indicate the number of readers. In colonial times a paper was handed from person to person until it was almost worn out. Only about half of the men and about one-fourth of the women of the Revolutionary generation could read. It was a common custom in those days to read aloud so that those who did not know how to read could listen and learn.

Newspapers unite the Patriots. Beginning about 1763, every colonial newspaper printed more news of the other colonies and in this way helped to produce a new feeling of continental unity. Each time the colonies and Great Britain had a disagreement, most papers printed articles attacking Great Britain.

The Patriot arguments in the newspapers prepared the people for independence. Most of these arguments came from Boston, where Samuel Adams wrote many of them. In the *Boston Gazette* he printed an endless stream of articles to stir up feeling against Great Britain, especially against the British soldiers stationed in Boston.

After the Boston Tea Party and the Coercive Acts, the newspapers attacked Great Britain more fiercely than ever before. They published protests made by towns, counties, and colonial assemblies. They printed patriotic songs and poems. They reprinted Tom Paine's *Common Sense* and other documents of the fight for liberty. These items were copied from one paper to another. As a result, the people throughout the colonies read the same ideas and the same arguments against Great Britain. All that Thomas Jefferson had to do in the Declaration of Independence was to restate the case and to draw the conclusion. The Patriots understood, agreed, and gave their support.

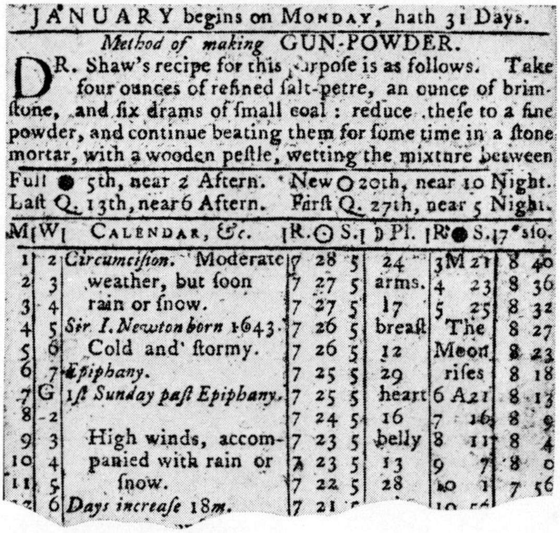
JANUARY begins on MONDAY, hath 31 Days.

Method of making GUN-POWDER.

DR. Shaw's recipe for this purpoſe is as follows. Take four ounces of refined ſalt-petre, an ounce of brimſtone, and ſix drams of ſmall coal: reduce theſe to a fine powder, and continue beating them for ſome time in a ſtone mortar, with a wooden peſtle, wetting the mixture between

Full ● 5th, near 2 Aftern. New ○ 20th, near 10 Night.
Laſt Q. 13th, near 6 Aftern. Firſt Q. 27th, near 5 Night.

M	W	CALENDAR, &c.	R. ☉ S.	☽ Pl.	R. ● S.	7* ſto.
1	2	*Circumciſion.* Moderate	7 28 5	24	3 M 21	8 40
2	3	weather, but ſoon	7 27 5	arms.	4 23	8 36
3	4	rain or ſnow.	7 27 5	17	5 25	8 32
4	5	*Sir I. Newton born* 1643.	7 26 5	breaſt	The	8 27
5	6	Cold and ſtormy.	7 26 5	12	Moon	8 23
6	7	*Epiphany.*	7 25 5	29	riſes	8 18
7	G	*1ſt Sunday paſt Epiphany.*	7 25 5	heart	6 A 21	8 13
8	2		7 24 5	16	7 16	8 9
9	3	High winds, accom-	7 23 5	belly	8 11	8 4
10	4	panied with rain or	7 23 5	13	9 7	8 0
11	5	ſnow.	7 22 5	28	10 1	7 56
	6	*Days increaſe* 18*m.*	7 21			

NEW YORK PUBLIC LIBRARY

New England almanac. Published in 1776, this almanac contained a gunpowder recipe. Why? Weather forecasts, schedules of tides, and articles on anniversaries were the main features of an almanac.

Almanacs support the Patriot cause. Another kind of publication that helped to make the colonists think alike was the almanac, which came out once a year. Almanacs were first of all calendars, but they were much more than calendars. They contained all sorts of reading matter for information and entertainment. There were bits of humor and wisdom tucked away in the corners of the pages: for example, "Wood burns faster than it grows" and "Better men, better times."

After 1763 the writers of almanacs, like newspaper editors, discussed the differences with Great Britain. Their

LIBRARY OF CONGRESS

Down with George III! After the Declaration of Independence was signed, many statues of the British ruler were pulled down by Patriots. Sometimes the statues were melted, and the metal was used to make bullets for the American soldiers.

short sayings had to do with politics: for example, "The sole end of government is the happiness of the people." (Why do you suppose they used that one?) Essays in the almanacs supported the colonial cause. The writers urged the people to stand up against Great Britain and to support the boycott of English goods. They urged the people to save rags for making paper. An almanac for 1775 told its readers how to make gunpowder!

Almanacs were more widely read than newspapers. They reached places where a newspaper was never seen, like backwoods settlements and frontier log houses. In such isolated spots the almanac was often the only reading matter the people had. During the year they read the pages over and over again and absorbed the idea of opposition to the mother country.

A common enemy. Few things will unify a people as fast as a common enemy. When the Americans began to look upon Great Britain as their common enemy, everything else—common problems, a common language, common ideas—worked to bring them together into a single nation. On the very first day of the First Continental Congress, Patrick Henry, of Virginia, said: "The distinctions between Virginians, Pennsylvanians, New Yorkers, and New Englanders are no more. I am not a Virginian, but an American." Of course, people did not change their loyalty in one day or in one year or even in one decade (10 years). But Patrick Henry's words became true for more and more people as the Revolutionary War went on.

Once independence was declared, the Patriots tried to tear down and root out everything that reminded them of England and their dependence upon England. They removed the British lions from their door knockers and replaced them with eagles. They took the king's picture off their walls. Streets, taverns, and other places named for the king had their names changed to those of new American heroes, especially George Washington. In New York City, King Street was renamed Liberty Street. Even nursery rhymes were rewritten. What lines were changed in this stanza of "Four-and-twenty Blackbirds"?

When the pie was open
The birds they were songless.
Was not that a pretty dish
To set before Congress?

Patriotic songs and poems. The Americans expressed their strong patriotism in songs and poems. The most popular song of the Revolutionary War was one you have often sung, "Yankee-Doodle." A British officer had written the words originally to make fun of the colonial militia. The soldiers of the Revolution adopted the song and gave it new words. Then everybody sang it.

Revolutionary poets made fun of British leaders and the British army and praised the Americans. In the spring and summer of 1777, Americans were very much afraid of Burgoyne. He was coming down from Canada with a large army, a great reputation,

Reading the news. Newspapers, eagerly read by the American colonists, helped to form public opinion in favor of independence.

and complete confidence in himself. After he surrendered, the people laughed with a feeling of deep relief. What was the joke in this rhyme, which was popular after Saratoga?

Burgoyne, alas, unknowing future fates,
Could force his way through woods, but
not through Gates.

If you do not see the joke, reread page 137 and page 138.

Philip Freneau (frē nō′) is known as the poet of the American Revolution. He wrote poems in praise of America's fight for liberty. He celebrated American victories in battle. He attacked George III, Burgoyne, and other British leaders. After he spent six weeks on a British prison ship, his poems were filled with bitter hatred for the British. As always in time of war, the Patriots

NATIONAL GALLERY OF ART, INDEX OF AMERICAN DESIGN

The eagle, symbol of patriotism. Common symbols to express love of country help to make a people a nation. The greatest such symbol is the flag. Since 1776 Americans have also used the eagle as a symbol of patriotism. It has appeared on our coins, for example, and unknown folk artists used eagles to decorate many objects. You will find several of these eagle designs reproduced in this book. The first, shown above, was part of a wall painting done in Connecticut about 1779.

were ready to believe the worst of the enemy.

Freneau wrote one of his most humorous poems after the American victory at Yorktown. It is called "The Prophecy." After the war was practically won, Freneau could safely prophesy the events that had already happened. He wrote, in part:

When a certain great king, whose initial is G,
Shall force stamps upon paper, and folks to drink tea;
When these folks burn his tea and stamped paper, like stubble,
You may guess that this king is then coming to trouble . . .
But when B(urgoyne) and C(ornwallis) with their armies are taken,
This king will do well if he saves his own bacon.

The poem is not great literature, but the reader cannot help sharing the happiness of the poet over the victory won by his countrymen. The American Patriots read these lines and laughed with Freneau.

3 *Independence Strengthens National Feeling*

By the 1770s many colonists were beginning to think of themselves as Americans rather than as Europeans. They were beginning to be proud of the vast, rich continent that was their home. Some colonists, especially those of English descent, could look back to American-born great-grandparents. The more recent French, German, and Scotch-Irish settlers never had a strong love for Great Britain. Their children thought of themselves as Americans first of all. The farther west settlers went, the weaker became their contact with the Old World and the more they felt themselves to be Americans.

As they fought together in the Revolutionary War, the people of the new states thought of themselves more and more as belonging together. When they achieved independence, the feeling of nationalism became stronger. In other words, the American people began to think of themselves as one nation and to feel strong loyalty for their country. Persons who shared this feeling of nationalism were eager to see America become independent of England in language, literature, and art, as well as in government.

Americans change the English language. In most nations one bond that unites the people is a common language. The colonists, as we have seen, spoke English. Even in the colonial period American English was different from London English. In expressing their experiences in the New World, the colonists gradually changed the language they had brought with them.

One way in which they changed the language was by borrowing foreign words. The Americans took over many words from the Indians, like hickory, squash, moose, tomahawk, succotash, and wigwam. They also translated Indian expressions into English. As a result an American could make a statement that an Englishman would not understand. An Englishman would not understand, for example, if he were told that the Indians had decided not to go on the warpath against the palefaces, that the medicine men had buried the hatchet, or that the tribal chiefs had smoked the peace pipe.

From the Spaniards, who in turn had taken the words from the natives of the West Indies, Americans adopted words like tobacco, mosquito, tomato, banana, tapioca, cannibal, and barbecue. Americans also adopted words from foreign immigrant groups: for example, cruller, waffle, and stoop from the Dutch.

The Americans made new combinations of old words to name the new objects and new experiences of the New World. Thus they coined words like bullfrog, catfish, garter snake, ground

raiſed to beat out his brains, when Pocahontas, a beautiful and compaſſionate daughter of the Chief, ran to him, and taking his head in her hands, laid her head upon his, and moſt tenderly intreated the king to let him live. The king conſented, and his life was ſaved. Capt. Smith found means afterwards to return to his companions at James Town, and ſeveral times, ſaved the people from ſtarving.

NEW YORK PUBLIC LIBRARY

Page of a Noah Webster book. Webster's schoolbook *The Little Reader's Assistant* was printed soon after the Revolution. Webster's books were studied by children throughout the nation and strengthened national unity.

hog, polecat, muskrat, potato bug, and peanut. When they found small trees and bushes growing in a tangle between the large trees in the forest, they called the tangled growth underbrush. The undeveloped or partly developed area beyond the settlements they called the back country. They got light from what they called a pine knot. A sled that could be pulled by hand was to them a hand sled. From the Indians they learned to make a contraption for walking on snow and called it a snowshoe. These were all new combinations of English words.

The entire story of the settlement of the English colonies is suggested by four such new word combinations or new uses of old words. When a pioneer selected a piece of frontier land for a home, he marked it off by slashing some of the trees along the boundary with an ax or a tomahawk; and he

"A hoop for the barrel." Without the hoops, which this cooper is fitting, the barrel would fall apart. A slogan of the colonists who wanted a united nation was "a hoop for the barrel."

called the land his tomahawk claim. After the settler had chopped down the trees on his land and had burned the underbrush, he called the open area a clearing. The shelter he built out of the fallen logs was his log house. After his farm was cultivated and a farmhouse and outbuildings were erected, he called the property his homestead.

Noah Webster strengthens American nationalism. After the Revolution, Noah Webster determined to establish an American language. It was to be based, not on the way the English people spoke and wrote, but on the way the American people spoke and wrote. A uniform language, he believed, would help to keep the states together as one nation. He began by writing American textbooks to replace English textbooks in American schools. In the 1780s he published a *Speller,* a *Grammar,* and a *Reader*. Later he published his famous dictionary.

In his *Speller,* Webster changed the spelling of a large number of words. He taught Americans to write "color" instead of the English "colour" and "center" instead of the English "centre," and so on with many other words. In his *Reader* he printed American patriotic selections in order to teach children to love their country. Webster's books sold by the millions and in all parts of the country.

The postal service is improved. The postal system was improved after the Revolution. This was another channel for strengthening national unity. As early as 1773 the Patriots set up their own postal service. In July, 1775, the Continental Congress established a post office and appointed Benjamin Franklin to be postmaster general. This post office kept Congress, the state governments, and the army in touch with one another during the war.

After the war the postal service grew rapidly. Beginning in 1786, on the main line from Portsmouth, New Hampshire, to Savannah, Georgia, the mail was carried by stagecoach three times a week in the summer and twice a week in the winter. Besides this principal seaboard route, there were a number of roads, called crossposts, to towns off the main line. The only route that crossed the Allegheny Mountains was the one to Pittsburgh, over which mail was carried every two weeks.

Holidays and heroes. After the Revolution the people expressed their patriotism by celebrating the anniversa-

PUBLIC BUILDINGS ADMINISTRATIONS

Postal service expands. The first postal delivery in Kennebunk, Maine, in June, 1775, is pictured in this painting. The mail was carried in the saddlebags, which the rider moved to a fresh horse at each relay station.

ries of great events of the war. Congress itself began the custom of celebrating Independence Day. The people also honored the leaders of the Revolution, especially George Washington. Artists painted many portraits of Washington and other leaders of the time. They also made paintings of the outstanding events of the Revolution. (See page 252.)

The officers and men of the Continental Army were a binding force that made nationalism stronger. They had enlisted under Congress and had been paid—when they were paid at all—by Congress. They had served under Washington, who was responsible only to Congress. They had made sacrifices, not for one state, but for all states together. Their favorite saying was "A hoop for the barrel," that is, a single government to unite the 13 states into a single nation. When peace came, the soldiers scattered to their homes and spread the idea of unity among the people.

Thus by 1783 the people in the 13 states were beginning to think of themselves as Americans belonging to one nation. But, as we shall see, the spirit of unity had not yet won a complete victory. There was still a long, hard climb ahead before the people of the United States could be said to be knit into one indivisible nation.

Summary

Before the Revolutionary War the groups of colonies were very different from one another. That was especially true of New England and the South. New England was a region of farm villages. Almost every farmer owned his farm, took part in his government, and felt independent. His life was in many ways strictly controlled by the church and by his neighbors. The South was a region of scattered farms and plantations, with few cities. On the large plantations Negro slaves did the work. The wealthy planters spent their leisure having a good time. They ran the government and the church. The small farmers looked up to them and followed their leadership. In the middle colonies, ways of living were a mixture of those of New England and those of the South.

Because their ways of life were so different, people in the various regions did not understand one another very well. It was hard to overcome this misunderstanding because travel and communication were difficult and slow. Thus there was good reason to believe that the colonies would never be able to cooperate.

But they did cooperate. When colonial leaders met in congresses, they found that they had much in common. Because the people in the colonies spoke the same language, they could exchange ideas through newspapers and almanacs. These publications helped the people to unite in their opposition to Great Britain. Once they faced Great Britain as a common enemy, the people were brought together even more closely by a common patriotism.

After they became independent of England politically, the American people were encouraged to become independent also in language, education, and art. Noah Webster published American textbooks for American schools, with American ways of spelling and American readings to teach children to love their country. The people celebrated national holidays and revered Revolutionary leaders as national heroes. The American people began to think of themselves as one nation.

For a Quick Review

1. Contrast the ways in which people lived in New England, in the middle colonies, and in the southern colonies just before the Revolutionary War.

2. How did such differences work against unity among the Americans?

3. In spite of differences that existed among the colonists before the Revolutionary War, certain conditions and events helped to make them feel united. What were these conditions and events?

4. How did events of the Revolution cause Americans to share in a growing feeling of unity?

5. After the Revolution how did each of the following help the Americans to think of themselves more as citizens of the United States than as citizens of a state: national holidays, the work of Noah Webster, improved postal service?

Learning to Study More Easily

OUTLINING A READING ASSIGNMENT

An outline is a framework, or skeleton, of a piece of writing or a talk. It shows the main topics and the important facts that explain each topic. To make an outline of a chapter or an article that you have read, you first write down the main ideas. These you label with Roman numerals or capital letters. Then you put down the details that support each of the major topics and label them with Arabic numerals or small letters.

If we set about outlining Chapter 8, we would find three big topics for which we would use Roman numerals.

1789 Postal Rates

MILES CARRIED	CHARGE (*cents*)
under 40	8
40 to 90	10
90 to 150	12½
150 to 300	17
300 to 500	20
over 500	25

¶ Compare these postal rates for one-sheet letters with the rates in effect today. In 1789 about 75 post offices and 2,400 miles of post road served 3 million people. How does that compare with our postal service today?

I. Different ways of living kept colonists of the different sections from understanding one another.
II. In spite of differences, certain forces helped the colonists to unite.
III. Winning independence caused greater unity to develop among Americans.

For each topic we find main thoughts and facts that explain each main thought. Thus an outline of the second major topic, for example, would begin like this:

II. In spite of differences, certain forces helped the colonists to unite.
  A. Leaders in most of the colonies realized that cooperation was necessary and possible.
    1. The colonial leaders had much in common.
    2. They saw that most of the colonies wanted the same things.
    3. Their experience in intercolonial meetings made them see that the colonies could cooperate.
  B. The English language, spoken and written, was a bond of unity.
    1. People from different colonies could talk with each other whenever they met.
    2. People in all the colonies read the same newspapers.
      a. The colonial newspapers were small and very different from ours today.
      b. In most cases each copy of a colonial newspaper was read by many people.
  C. American attitudes toward the Revolution were influenced by newspapers and almanacs.
    1. During the disagreements with Great Britain and during the Revolutionary War, colonial newspapers printed the views of the Patriots.
    2. People in all the colonies read the same almanacs.
      a. Almanacs contained many kinds of information, including comments on politics.
      b. Almanacs were read, and even memorized, by many people in every colony.

Compare this outline with the paragraphs on pages 153–158. You can see that, although the same ideas are given, the words of the text are not copied into the outline. When you outline, always put the ideas into your own words. If you do so, you can be more certain that you understand the ideas.

Complete the outline of Chapter 8. Check it with your teacher to see whether you have included the main ideas in the capital letter topics, placed the less important details under the main ideas they support, and used your own words in the outline.

MAIN EVENTS OF UNIT 2, 1750–1783

Building and governing the nation	*Earning a living*	*Science, arts, and the people*	*The nation and its neighbors*
		1752 Pennsylvania Hospital, first in colonies	
1754 Albany Congress, Plan of Union	**1754** Semiweekly stages, New York to Philadelphia	**1754** King's College (Columbia) founded	**1754** French and Indian War began **1755** Braddock defeated **1756–1763** Seven Years' War **1763** Treaty of Paris
1765 Stamp Act; Stamp Act Congress **1767** Townshend Acts **1769** Nonimportation agreements	**1765** Stiegel glass factory, Pennsylvania		
1770 Townshend Acts repealed, except tea tax **1773** Boston Tea Party **1774** First Continental Congress		**1770** Estimated population of English colonies 2,205,000	
1775 Second Continental Congress	**1775** First Continental money		**1775** April 19, Battles of Lexington and Concord
1775 Boonesborough **1776** Declaration of Independence		**1776** Thomas Paine's *Common Sense* and the *Crisis*	**1775** June 7, Battle of Bunker Hill
1777 Stars and Stripes adopted as American flag **1778** Clark wins Northwest			**1777** Battle of Saratoga, Burgoyne surrendered **1778** Alliance, United States and France
1781 Articles of Confederation			**1781** Yorktown, Cornwallis surrendered 1783 Treaty of Paris, independence of U.S. recognized by Great Britain

Unit Roundup

HIGH POINTS OF THE UNIT

Using the chapter topics (put into your own words) as the three major headings, prepare an outline of the important facts in Unit 2.

EXPAND YOUR VOCABULARY

1. Write a sentence explaining the meaning of each of the following:

back country	loyalists
blockhouse	Patriots
committee of correspondence	Sons of Liberty
	stamp tax
Continental Army	tomahawk claim
long hunter	Valley Forge

2. Arrange with one or two of your classmates to present brief skits that illustrate the following words:

ambush	retreat
boycott	smuggle
guerrilla	surplus
repeal	trail blazer

HISTORY IN THE MOVIES

1. *Sons of Liberty* tells a dramatic story of events in the Revolutionary War, especially of the help that Haym Salomon gave in raising money to support Washington's army.

2. Study the film *Our Declaration of Independence* to see what answers it gives for these questions: (*a*) What were the steps through which most members of the Continental Congress progressed in their thinking before they favored independence? (*b*) What persons played the most important parts in writing the Declaration?

WITH CRAYON, RULER, AND PASTE

1. Let a committee prepare a true comic-strip history of the American Revolution.

2. Decide as a group what events should be placed on the large class time line and have a committee record them there.

3. Draw cartoons to show the differences between northern, middle, and southern colonies in recreation, transportation, and ways of earning a living about 1770.

4. Show, in three cartoons, three of the forces that helped to unite the people of the 13 English colonies before, during, and immediately after the American Revolution.

PUT ON A PLAY

1. Present an opinion roundup that might have been made in 1765 on the topic "What I think of British tax policies." In-

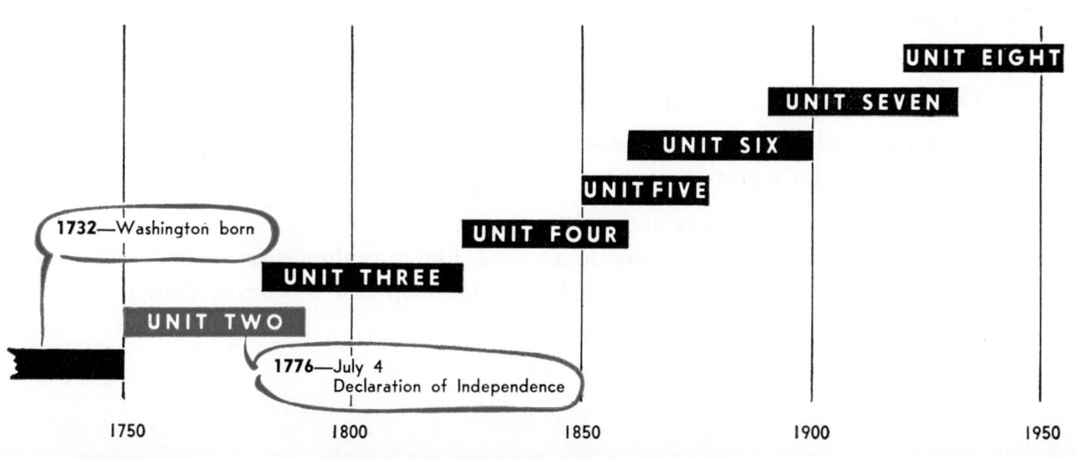

clude interviews with people giving British as well as American points of view.

2. As a committee project, plan and present a dramatization entitled "Saratoga, the Turning Point of the Revolution."

STORIES THERE WAS NO ROOM TO TELL

Some of the topics suggested below are so broad that a committee might choose one of them and assign different aspects of the subject to individuals on the committee. In preparing a report on one of these topics, you will need to apply some of the skills you have studied in Unit 2, especially the use of the card catalog to find information and the ability to outline the information you find.

Early days of settlement in Kentucky
Events leading to the British surrender at Saratoga
George Rogers Clark and the war in the West
How Philip Freneau contributed to American life (You may substitute another leader mentioned in Unit 2.)
How the Sons of Liberty influenced the Revolution (Committees of correspondence, Green Mountain boys, or another such group can be substituted.)
Music of the Revolutionary War period (A small group can learn some of the songs to sing for the class.)
Poems about the Revolutionary War
Why Valley Forge has become a national shrine

USE YOUR IMAGINATION

The topics listed in this exercise would also be interesting for reports.

1. Choose one of these topics and write an editorial that might have appeared in a newspaper of the Revolutionary period. Express a definite opinion or urge action and give reasons to support the view expressed. Give the date and the place of publication of the imaginary newspaper.

Activities of the Sons of Liberty
The appointment of Washington as Commander in Chief of the Continental Army
The Boston Tea Party
The British surrender at Saratoga
The closing of the port of Boston
The First Continental Congress
The Declaration of Independence
The Stamp Act
Washington's victory at Trenton

2. Prepare the diary of a traveler in which you describe the conditions of travel in the United States during the years immediately after the Revolution.

3. Write a series of entries for the diary that might have been kept by one of the following, telling of the events in which the individual would have participated:

A soldier in Washington's army from 1775 to 1777
A member of the Second Continental Congress
A member of George Rogers Clark's expedition
A loyalist during the American Revolution
A member of a group following the Wilderness Trail to settle in Kentucky

SHOW IT ON A MAP

1. On three maps show the ownership of territory in North America in 1750, 1763, and 1783. The information is given on maps in this text. Use the map list to find them.

2. On an outline map of the world or a sketch map that you draw, show the chief

trade routes of the English colonies in the late colonial period. Show the most important articles of trade on each route by placing symbols on the map, or write short paragraphs listing them. What title will you give the map?

FURTHER READING

Books about Interesting People

America's Ethan Allen by Stewart A. Holbrook. Houghton Mifflin, 1949.

America's Paul Revere by Esther Forbes. Houghton Mifflin, 1946.

I Have Just Begun to Fight! The Story of John Paul Jones by Edward Ellsberg. Dodd, Mead, 1942.

Paul Revere and the Minute Men by Dorothy Canfield Fisher. Random House, 1950.

Poor Richard by James Henry Daugherty. Viking, 1941. Benjamin Franklin.

Son of Thunder, Patrick Henry by Julia Margaret Carson. Longmans, 1945.

That Lively Man, Ben Franklin by Jeanette Eaton. Morrow, 1948.

The Youngest General: A Story of Lafayette by Fruma Gottschalk. Knopf, 1949.

Washington: The Life of a Patriot by André Maurois. Didier, 1946.

Stories of Adventure and Everyday Life

Battle Lanterns by Merritt Parmelee Allen. Longmans, 1949. Adventures with Marion's South Carolina militia.

Black River Captive by West Lathrop. Random House, 1946. French and Indian War on the New Hampshire frontier.

Coat for a Soldier by Florence Maule Updegraff. Harcourt, Brace, 1941. Life in New England during the Revolution.

Hoof-Beats of Freedom by Helen Fuller Orton. Stokes, 1936. Life on Long Island in the time of the Revolutionary War.†

Indian Captive: The Story of Mary Jemison by Lois Lenski. Stokes, 1941. True story of Mary's capture by Indians.

Liberty for Johanny by Adelaide Wonsetler and John C. Wonsetler. Longmans, 1943. Story about American courage at Valley Forge.

Mounted Messenger by Cornelia Meigs. Macmillan, 1943. Events of 1775 in Pennsylvania.

Red Heritage by Merritt Parmelee Allen. Longmans, 1946. Battle of Oriskany, Mohawk River Valley.

Silver for General Washington: A Story of Valley Forge by Enid La Monte Meadowcroft. Crowell, 1944. Hardships and courage at Valley Forge.

War Belts of Pontiac by William H. Bunce. Dutton, 1943. Frontier dangers during French and Indian War.

Wilderness Clearing by Walter D. Edmonds. Dodd, Mead, 1944. Settlers of the Mohawk Valley during the Revolution.††

Other Interesting Accounts

Birthday of a Nation, July 4, 1776 by Frances Rogers and Alice Beard. Lippincott, 1945. The colonies declare independence.

George Washington's World by Genevieve Foster. Scribner, 1941. Important events around the world during Washington's lifetime.

Old Liberty Bell by Frances Rogers and Alice Beard. Stokes, 1942. From London, where it was cast, to Independence Hall.†

Unit 3 *Americans Build a Strong Nation 1780–1824*

WHEN A new nation is born out of revolution, there is always the danger that no strong government can be established to keep the peace. The United States passed that danger successfully by establishing a strong government under the Constitution.

The young republic grew larger and stronger. Jefferson seized the opportunity to buy Louisiana and double the country's size. American merchants traded in faraway markets. After remaining neutral in European conflicts for more than 20 years, the United States fought England in the War of 1812. Neither side won the war, but out of it the United States obtained national heroes and slogans, a national anthem, and a stronger spirit of national unity.

During the war, merchants could not import manufactured goods. Americans had to do more of their own manufacturing. They made woolen and cotton goods, iron products, shoes, and other products. The people of the

United States became less dependent on Europe for their needs.

Most of the new factories were in the northern states. Northern farmers continued to raise wheat, corn, and other food crops. Southern planters, thanks to Eli Whitney's cotton gin, raised larger and larger crops of cotton to feed the spindles of New England and Europe.

The country prospered and grew stronger. Improved roads and canals speeded up transportation and increased trade. Settlers moved west in large numbers and built new states to be added to the Union.

The Monroe Doctrine expressed the feeling that the young republic had of its own strength and unity. President James Monroe announced that the United States would protect the independence of the Latin-American republics. With that announcement the United States became an equal among the nations of the world.

In the arts the United States moved more slowly toward independence than in other fields. Jefferson introduced his favorite style of European architecture into the young republic, and it spread across the country. American painters studied in Europe and came back to paint Revolutionary heroes and events. American writers imitated English writers. But in some of the stories of Washington Irving, the novels of James Fenimore Cooper, and the poems of William Cullen Bryant, the American way of life was beginning to express itself.

Unit 3 tells how the young American republic grew in size, in wealth, in unity, and in the respect in which it was held by the other countries of the world.

9 The States Set Up a National Government

What is democracy? It is a hard word to define exactly because the idea behind it is different for different people. Even the members of your own American history class may define the word in several ways. Democracy is hard to define because its meaning has been changing and growing throughout American history. Americans living at different times defined it differently.

In a democracy every person should be free. Of course, he cannot be free to do just anything at all. He cannot be free to smash a jeweler's show window and grab watches and fountain pens to pass around to his friends. He must obey the laws against robbery. And he must obey many other important laws.

People must obey the law under any kind of government. But the important difference is that in a democracy the people decide which laws are to be passed. They decide by electing the officials who make the laws. Elections are held frequently. If the people do not like the laws that are passed by one group of officials, they can elect another group. In a democracy the people are free because the laws that they obey are made by their own representatives.

In a democracy people should not only be free; they should also be equal. In electing government officials, they are equal since no citizen has more than one vote. They are likewise equal before the law. Equality before the law means that everyone is required to obey the same laws. It also means that a person who is charged with a crime has an equal chance to defend himself before a jury, whether he is rich or poor, famous or unknown. If he is found guilty, he receives the punishment required by law, whether he is rich or poor, famous or unknown.

In a democracy people should be free and equal, not only in relation to government and the law, but in the "pursuit of happiness" as well. In other words, all persons should be free to choose the occupations they wish to follow—to become doctors, miners, electricians, businessmen, baseball players, and so on—and they should have an equal chance to succeed in their chosen occupations to the best of their ability. They should have an equal opportunity to obtain the education they need.

Freedom, equal rights, and equal opportunities for each citizen are the accepted goals of our democracy today. When we read about the new constitutions at the time of the Revolution, however, we must remember that democracy was then a new and radical idea. People did not understand it then as we understand it now. Therefore the new nation was not fully democratic. (See pages 51–52 and 182.) In later chapters we shall see how our country gradually became more democratic. We shall see that we are still working for freedom, equal rights, and equal opportunities for every American citizen.

1 *Our First Government Is Based on the Articles of Confederation*

The states lost no time in setting up new governments even while the Revolutionary War was being fought. In each state a constitution was written. The new governments set up under these constitutions were very much like the old colonial governments. Each one included a legislature (to make the laws), a governor (to see that the laws were put into effect), and courts (to apply the laws fairly in specific cases).

The new state governments were not fully democratic. They still followed the colonial idea of granting suffrage, or the right to vote, only to men who owned property. Many years passed before all white male citizens obtained the right to vote. In those days no one thought of granting suffrage to women.

Every state constitution, however, contained a bill of rights. The bill of rights listed certain rights that every individual possessed and that the government could not take away from him. These rights are described on page 184.

Maryland delays approval of the Articles of Confederation. About one month after the Declaration of Independence, the Second Continental Congress began to discuss a plan for setting up a government of the United States. The plan was called the Articles of Confederation (kŏn fĕd ẽr ā′shŭn). Congress sent the plan to the states for their approval. The Articles did not go into effect until 1781 because Maryland waited until that year to approve them.

Maryland delayed because of the western land question. Seven states claimed lands west of the Appalachian Mountains because of the way their colonial charters read. (See the map on page 111.) Their charters gave them all the land between their northern and southern boundaries reaching to the Pacific Ocean. The area under discussion at the time was the land north

METRO-GOLDWYN-MAYER

The road home. In this scene from a historical film, Revolutionary soldiers are resting as they return home after the war. Their worn-out clothing indicates the government's shortage of money for equipment. Why did the shortage exist?

of the Ohio River from the mountains to the Mississippi. It was later called the Northwest Territory.

The six states without claims were afraid that the western lands would make the other seven states too big and powerful. Maryland argued: Since the West would be won by all the states cooperating in the war, the land should belong to all the states. Maryland waited until New York, Connecticut, and Virginia gave up their claims and then accepted the Articles of Confederation. Virginia gave up the most, since it had a claim to the entire Northwest Territory.

Within a few years nearly all the Northwest was turned over to the national government. It was called the public domain (dō mān′); that is, it was owned by all the people through their government. Since it was owned by all the states together, the public domain became another bond of unity. It helped keep the states together in the difficult years after the war.

Under the Articles, Congress lacks important powers. The Articles of Confederation set up a new Congress to take care of the common problems of the 13 states, such as the postal service and relations with foreign countries. But Congress did not have enough power to deal with many of the problems that came up.

Congress did not have power to collect taxes from the people. The only way that it could raise money was to ask each state to pay its share of the expenses. Most of the states contributed only a small part of their shares. As a result there was not enough money in the national treasury to pay the interest on the nation's war debts. Since Congress could not even pay the interest on the money it already owed, naturally it could not borrow any more.

Congress could not raise enough money to pay the army. Of course, the officers and men were angry not to receive their pay when the time came to go home. In March, 1783, in the camp near Newburgh, New York, General Washington had to plead with the officers not to lead a rebellion. In June of the same year, 80 Pennsylvania soldiers marched from Lancaster to Philadelphia to demand their pay. Congress, helpless and frightened, fled to Princeton. It lacked all the authority and the respect that a government should have.

Under the Articles of Confederation, Congress was unable to control commerce among the states or with foreign countries. Several states collected taxes on goods brought in from other states as well as from foreign countries. Because of these taxes, the states did not sell their products to one another as much as they might have. Businessmen in the various states wished to have these taxes removed so that they could trade with one another more easily.

Some of the states had a special objection to the tariffs, as such taxes on imports are called. New Jersey, for example, obtained her imported goods through New York City and Philadelphia. Duties were collected in both ports. Therefore the people of New Jersey were really paying taxes to New York and Pennsylvania. And New Jersey was not happy to be paying taxes to her neighbors.

The states also quarreled over boundaries, paper money, and the use of rivers for transportation. Congress was unable to settle any of the arguments.

Congress could not even carry out some of the terms of the treaty it had made with Great Britain. Under the treaty British merchants were to be allowed to collect prewar debts and loyalists were to be permitted to return to their homes. But the states made it impossible to collect the debts and passed laws against the loyalists. In return Great Britain refused to give up the forts at Niagara, Detroit, and other posts on the Great Lakes in American territory.

The Confederation makes plans for the public domain. Under the Articles of Confederation, then, Congress was too weak to do many of the things that a government ought to do. But it did solve one problem so well that its method has been used ever since. It worked out the rules for settling and governing the public domain.

By 1781, as we have seen, the states had turned over to the central government their claims to most of the Old Northwest. Connecticut kept a tract, called the Western Reserve, along Lake Erie and just west of Pennsylvania. Virginia kept a larger tract in which to grant land to her Revolutionary veterans. The rest went to the United States.

Before the land could be sold, it had to be surveyed so that every buyer would know the exact location of the land he bought. Also, a plan was

JOHN HANCOCK MUTUAL LIFE INSURANCE COMPANY

One-room schoolhouse. The boy in the center is reciting the day's assignment. Schools like this one sprang up in the Old Northwest as fast as that region was settled. How did the Ordinance of 1785 help American education?

needed for governing the territory after it was settled. For these purposes the Confederation Congress passed two important laws: the Ordinance (ôr′dĭ-năns) of 1785 and the Ordinance of 1787 (an ordinance is a law).

Under the Ordinance of 1785 the land was divided into square townships, each six miles square, and the townships were divided into sections one mile square. The land was to be sold to the public. Section 16 in each township was set aside for the support of public education; that is, the land in that section was to be sold and the money used for education.

The Ordinance of 1787 made plans for the government of the Northwest Territory. In the beginning the territory was to have a governor and other officials named by Congress. As soon as there were 5,000 men in the territory, they were to elect their own assembly.

Out of the Northwest Territory from three to five states were to be formed. As soon as a future state had a population of 60,000, it was to write a constitution, establish a government, and apply for admission into the Union. When admitted, the new state would take its place as the equal of all the other states.

The Ordinance also included a bill of rights for the people, and it prohibited slavery in the Northwest Territory.

The Ordinance of 1785 and that of 1787 are important for several reasons. The first law set up the pattern followed in surveying and selling almost all the rest of the continental United States. The other decided that the new settlements would not remain colonies but, as soon as possible, would become equal partners with the other states. Thus, instead of being a nation of 13

FAIRCHILD AERIAL SURVEYS, INC.

Section lines. This modern aerial view of Iowa shows that the section lines surveyed under the Ordinance of 1785 are still followed by many roads and farm boundaries.

states with colonies beyond the Appalachians, the United States has become a nation of 48 equal states reaching across the continent.

First settlements in the Northwest Territory. As soon as Congress passed the Ordinance of 1787, the frontier took another long step westward. Settlers began to move rapidly into the Northwest Territory. In April, 1788, 48 pioneers from New England floated down the Ohio River and settled on its northern bank. They called the place Marietta in honor of Marie Antoinette, Queen of France. The settlers laid out a town on the New England model, with streets leading from a central square. Each settler received a town lot for a house and garden and a lot outside of town for a farm. Before the end of the year, 132 more settlers arrived.

In the same year a company of investors from New Jersey bought a tract of land farther down the Ohio River. In November the first settlement was made on this land, and two years later it was named Cincinnati. Most of the settlers were from New Jersey. Other settlements soon took root nearby.

At Manchester, Ohio, in 1791, Virginians made the first settlement on the land reserved by Virginia for her war veterans. Thus in the first few years of settlement the Old Northwest already contained settlers from New England, the middle states, and the South.

2 *The Federal Constitution Is Written and Approved*

We can easily see today that the Congress of the Confederation performed a valuable service by setting up the plan for organizing the public domain.

HISTORICAL AND PHILOSOPHICAL SOCIETY OF OHIO

Cincinnati in 1800. This drawing shows Cincinnati when it was 12 years old. Its rapid growth was only beginning. (See page 210.) The flatboat in the lower right-hand corner is probably carrying a family on its way to settle in the Old Northwest.

At the time people did not appreciate its value. They were more concerned with the weakness of the Confederation. After 1784 many persons feared that the union of the states might break up.

But, as we have seen in Chapter 8, the feeling of nationalism was growing. The leaders who had fought and sacrificed to win independence for the United States hoped to establish a strong, united country. They succeeded in persuading the states to send delegates to a Constitutional Convention for the purpose of setting up a stronger national government that would make the union permanent. The Convention met in Philadelphia in May, 1787.

Experienced young leaders write the Constitution. Since the members of the Convention wrote the Constitution of the United States, we should know something about them. In all, 55 men attended the meetings at one time or another; but generally about 30 attended any one session.

The chairman of the Convention was George Washington, then 55 years old. He knew better than any other American the need for a strong central government. When he was Commander in Chief of the Revolutionary army, he almost lost the war because the government was not strong enough to support his army. Although Washington took almost no part in the debates, his presence gave the people confidence in the Convention.

Next to Washington the most important member of the Convention was

James Madison, then 37 years old. Madison was the son of a Virginia plantation owner. He was a graduate of Princeton University and a lawyer. He knew a great deal about how a government should be organized and how it should work. He had prepared himself for the Convention by studying the constitutions of other nations. He was a small, thin man and not a great speaker, but when he arose to talk, the delegates listened. He, too, wanted a strong union. Many of his ideas were included in the Constitution.

Independence Hall. Delegates to the Constitutional Convention arrive at Independence Hall, Philadelphia.

Although Alexander Hamilton did not play a large part in the Convention, his influence was important in getting a stronger central government. He was then 30 years old. Like Madison, he was a lawyer. Hamilton admired the British form of government and wanted the United States to establish one like it—even with a king. He was not altogether satisfied with the Constitution as finally written, but he did as much as any man to persuade the people to accept it.

These leaders were typical of the whole group of delegates. They were mainly young men who had already played an important part in winning independence from England and in establishing the new state governments. Most of them were lawyers; others were plantation owners, merchants, and bankers. They were men of wealth and ability. They wanted a strong central government that would protect property, help commerce, and keep the states united.

The Convention met in an upstairs room in a building in Philadelphia now called Independence Hall. The members had to wrestle with many problems that caused long and bitter debates. More than once the Convention seemed to be on the point of breaking up. However, the aged Benjamin Franklin was present, and he was able to restore calm at some of the most difficult moments.

A strong central government with limited powers. Some delegates believed that it would be enough to change the Articles of Confederation to give the old Congress more power. The majority of the delegates, however, wanted a different kind of government. We have seen earlier in this chapter that the Confederation Congress could not collect taxes, regulate commerce, or exercise other powers that governments usually have. The delegates decided to set up a central government with more power. It would pass laws and would be able to compel the people to obey them. Its laws would be more important than laws made by the states.

Now, if the new government were to have such power, it might seem that

METRO-GOLDWYN-MAYER

Rising sun. In this movie scene of the Constitutional Convention, Washington invites Franklin to sign the Constitution. After signing, Franklin pointed to the sun carved on the chair. He said that he had wondered, during the convention, whether the sun was rising or setting, but now he knew it was rising. What did he mean?

there would be no need for state governments at all. Yet probably no one in the Constitutional Convention wished to do away with the state governments altogether. Certainly the people would not have accepted such a plan. The problem of the Constitutional Convention, therefore, was to find a way to combine national and state governments.

The delegates solved the problem by dividing the powers of government between the nation and the states. The Constitution listed certain powers that were to be given to the national government; all the rest were to be kept by the states. A citizen of the United States would live under two governments. He would be ruled by the national government in matters having to do with the country as a whole. He would obey national laws in such fields, for example, as foreign and interstate commerce, coinage of money, the post office, the Army, and the Navy. In all other matters he would be ruled by his state government. We call such an arrangement a federal system of government.

Differences of opinion are settled by compromise. After the delegates decided on the federal system, they were able to settle other differences of opinion by compromise, that is, by meeting one another halfway.

One problem was: how will the

states be represented in the new Congress? The large states said: According to population. It would be unfair for a small state to have as much voice in the government as a large state with three or four times the population. The small states said: Equally. If each state is represented according to population, the large states will have so many votes in Congress that they will control the government. Then they will pass laws for their own benefit, and the small states will suffer. Let each state have an equal number of representatives.

A compromise was finally reached. Congress would have two houses. The members of the House of Representatives would be divided up among the states according to population. This part of the compromise favored the large states. In the Senate each state would have two Senators. This part of the compromise favored the small states.

Since the population would have to be counted in order to determine how many Representatives each state would have, the question arose whether Negro slaves were to be included. Here another compromise was reached. Following the plan already used under the Articles of Confederation, three-fifths of the total number of slaves were to be counted.

Many delegates, including some from the South, wished to have the Constitution stop the importation of slaves. Under the compromise arrived at, the federal government was forbidden to prohibit the slave trade before 1808, but could do so after that date.

There were many debates on these problems and on many others. The

NATIONAL GALLERY OF ART, INDEX OF AMERICAN DESIGN

Eagle, 1792. This eagle was painted on a leather fire bucket. (See page 158.)

Convention was busy all through the summer. Finally, on September 17, 1787, the complete Constitution was signed and made public.

In spite of opposition the Constitution is adopted. When the Constitution was sent to the states for their approval, a large part of the American people were opposed to it. Most persons at the time had a strong pride in their own state. They were suspicious of the proposed central government that would take so much authority away from the states. Many of the ordinary people—workers in the towns, small farmers, the poor everywhere—feared this new "foreign" government that would have the power to tax them, to coin their money, and to send them to war. Many people were opposed to the Constitution because it did not include a bill of rights. (See page 184.)

Thus those men who favored the Constitution had to overcome strong opposition. But they had several factors

The democratic way. These men are settling a problem democratically. Each one explains his views and listens to the views of the others. Then they work together to find a reasonable solution.

in their favor. Conditions under the Confederation were so bad that many people were eager to adopt any plan for a stronger government. The states were tied together by trade with one another. The feeling of unity was strong, and most people wanted the Union to be preserved. Finally, the Constitution was supported by most of the leading men of the country—by many of the best thinkers and writers and speakers.

The supporters of the Constitution made haste to get it approved before its opponents could be fully organized. The states called special conventions to vote on the Constitution. Delaware gave its approval first. Then came Pennsylvania, New Jersey, Georgia, and Connecticut. After nine states had accepted, the other four found it impossible to stay out.

In several states there were bitter debates, especially in Massachusetts, Virginia, and New York. In these states the Constitution was finally adopted, but by a very close vote. In New York, for example, the vote was 30 for the Constitution and 27 against. Although the Constitution went into effect in 1788, North Carolina did not join the new government until 1789 and Rhode Island did not join until 1790.

Seven states accepted the Constitution with the understanding that amendments would be added to protect the rights of the individual. Accordingly, in 1791 the first 10 amendments were added. They make up the federal Bill of Rights. (See page 184.)

3 *The Constitution Provides for a Strong, Balanced Government*

Let us take a closer look at the Constitution to see what kind of government it set up. As you read this explanation, you will wish to check each point by referring to the Constitution itself (pages 680–693).

Perhaps we should first ask: what is a constitution? A constitution is a kind of outline of a government. It might be called a blueprint of government, since it shows the parts of the government and how they work together.

A constitution can be changed. When it is changed, we say that it is amended. The Constitution of the United States, in Article V, gives four methods by which it may be amended. For 21 of 22 amendments made so far, one method was used. Congress proposed the amendment by a two-thirds vote in each house, and the legislatures of three-fourths of the states approved it. The Twenty-first Amendment was approved by special conventions held in the states.

The Constitution of the United States tells what duties and powers the government has. In Article I, Section 8, for example, it lists the powers of Congress. But our Constitution also tells what duties and powers the government does *not* have. In Article I, Section 9, for example, it lists some of the powers that Congress does not have.

According to Article I, Section 9, Congress does not have the power to lay a tax, or duty, on articles exported from any state. Suppose Congress were to pass a law to collect such a tax. What would happen? The matter would be brought before the Supreme Court,

The undemocratic way. In contrast to the men on the opposite page, these men are not following the democratic way. They are trying to win the argument by anger and force instead of by reason and compromise. Do you use the democratic way? How can you help keep discussions democratic?

After New York had ratified. Governor George Clinton (*left*), opponent of the Constitution, shakes hands with Alexander Hamilton, who was mainly responsible for ratification. John Jay, later the first Chief Justice of the United States Supreme Court, is at Hamilton's left. This painting is in the post office at Poughkeepsie, New York.

PUBLIC BUILDINGS ADMINISTRATION

and the Supreme Court would decide that Congress did not have the power to pass the law. In other words, it would declare the law unconstitutional. Then the tax would not be collected. The law would be erased from the list of laws.

Congress passes the laws. Article I describes the make-up of Congress and its powers. Congress consists of two parts, or houses: the House of Representatives and the Senate. Members of the House of Representatives are elected for two years. The number from each state depends on the size of its population. The Senate is composed of two members from each state. A Senator is elected for six years. As the Constitution was originally written, Senators were chosen by the state legislatures, but since 1913, under the Seventeenth Amendment, they have been elected by the people of the states.

Congress passes the laws by which the people are governed. It performs the legislative work of government.

The President enforces the laws. Article II describes how the President is elected and what his duties are. The President is elected every four years. Voters do not vote for President directly. They vote for Electors. Each state has as many Electors as it has Representatives and Senators in Congress. The Electors of each state meet and vote for their choice for President. The votes are counted in Congress. If no candidate receives a majority of the electoral votes, the House of Representatives chooses the President from the three highest candidates, with each state having one vote.

While the President is still elected by Electors, this method of election no longer serves the purpose for which it was intended. The men who wrote the Constitution expected the voters to choose as Electors the leading citizens of their communities. After they were chosen, the Electors were to meet and elect the best qualified man in the United States to be President.

The idea of having Electors elect a President did not last long. Soon Americans divided into political parties. Each party selected a candidate for President and named its own list of Electors in each state. The Electors promised that, if they were selected, they would vote for the presidential candidate of their party. Citizens voted for the candidate they preferred by voting for his Electors. The Electors were no longer free to choose a President but merely elected the man chosen by the majority of the voters.

This change in the election of the President is one of many ways in which the actual working of our government has changed without any change of the Constitution itself.

Since the President carries out, or executes, the laws of the land, he is often spoken of as the Chief Executive. He sees to it that the laws passed by Congress are put into effect. He appoints the members of his Cabinet to assist him in carrying out the laws. He also appoints many other officials to help run the government. He conducts the relations of the United States with foreign countries, appoints ambassadors and other officials to represent our country abroad, and makes treaties. The President is Commander in Chief of the armed forces.

The courts try cases under the laws. Article III of the Constitution deals with the federal courts, including the Supreme Court and any others established by Congress. The President appoints the judges and they hold office during good behavior. That usually means for life. Courts perform the judicial function of government. They decide how the law is to be applied in specific cases. If a person is accused of breaking a law of the United States, he is tried in a federal court. The federal courts decide whether a law passed by a state or by Congress is constitutional or not.

The three parts of the government depend on one another. From the first three articles of the Constitution you see that the United States government consists of three strong parts. At the same time the Constitution makes it impossible for one part of the government to seize all the power and establish a dictatorship. A system of checks and balances gives each branch some control over the others.

For example, the power to make laws is not entirely in the hands of Congress. (See Article I, Section 7). After a bill is passed by both houses, it is sent to the President. If he signs it, it becomes law. If he vetoes (refuses to approve) it, it can become law only if Congress passes it again by a two-thirds majority in each house. In that case we say the bill is passed over the President's veto.

Again, as you already know, the Supreme Court has the power to declare a law unconstitutional after it has been passed. The Constitution nowhere gives the Supreme Court this power in so many words. The Supreme Court has this power as a result of its interpretation, or explanation, of the Constitution.

The President appoints judges, ambassadors, members of the Cabinet, and many other high officials. But these appointments must be approved by the Senate. The President is the Commander in Chief of the armed forces, but only Congress can actually declare war. The President has the power to make treaties, but they must be approved by a two-thirds vote of the Senate. The President can do scarcely anything unless Congress supplies money to pay salaries and other expenses.

For a bill of rights. This scene from the film *Bill of Rights* shows Thomas Jefferson urging Virginians to adopt a bill of rights. The Virginia Declaration of Rights was made a part of the state constitution. It became a model for bills of rights in other state constitutions and for the federal Bill of Rights.

Religious liberty. Several church spires in almost every community symbolize freedom of worship, a right of all people who live in the United States.

In this way each branch of the government is kept in its place by the others and is prevented from obtaining too much power.

The Bill of Rights protects the rights of the people. You have read that many people originally opposed the Constitution because it did not contain a bill of rights. The first ten amendments were added to satisfy these people.

Why did the people of the time attach so much importance to a bill of rights? They remembered the unhappy experiences that they or their ancestors had had in Europe. European governments had punished people for attending churches of their own choice, for speaking or writing what they believed, for meeting together to discuss their problems, for sending petitions to their governments to ask for relief of their sufferings. European governments had taken property away from people without cause and had kept persons in jail for years without a trial. They had tortured people to make them confess to crimes that they might not even have committed.

The American people wanted to make sure that such things would not happen in America. That is why they wrote a bill of rights into every state constitution. That is why they added the first ten amendments to the United States Constitution.

The First Amendment guarantees the people freedom of religion, freedom of speech and of the press, freedom of assembly, or the right to get together and discuss their problems, and freedom of petition, or the right to request the government to help solve their problems.

The Fourth Amendment protects every person's property.

The Fifth Amendment protects a person accused of a crime. No person can be forced to say anything that might be used to prove him guilty of a crime.

The Sixth and Seventh Amendments

guarantee the right of trial by jury. The Eighth Amendment puts a limit on punishments.

The Bill of Rights protects every person against his government. It lists the rights that belong to him and that the government cannot take away from him. Today we do not consider as democratic any government that fails to give these rights to its people. The Bill of Rights is one of the foundations of our democracy.

The first government under the Constitution. The first Congress under the Constitution met in New York City early in April, 1789. It counted the votes cast by the Electoral College and found that George Washington, of Virginia, had received a unanimous (ū năn′ĭ mŭs) vote. He was accordingly declared first President of the United States.

As President-elect, George Washington made a triumphal journey from his home at Mount Vernon to New York, the new capital of the nation. On April 30, 1789, he stood on the balcony of Federal Hall on Wall Street and took the oath, "that I will faithfully execute the office of President of the United States, and will to the best of my ability, preserve, protect and defend the Constitution of the United States."

Summary

As soon as independence was declared, the new states wrote constitutions and established governments. The new state governments were more democratic than the colonial governments had been.

The Articles of Confederation did not give the central government the powers it needed to govern. It could not collect enough money for expenses; it could not settle quarrels between states; and it could not carry out the terms of the peace treaty with Great Britain. The Articles were, however, a first step toward forming a central government. Probably its greatest achievement was a plan for settling and governing the public domain.

The men who wrote the United States Constitution were determined to establish a central government strong enough to rule the entire nation. The most important weakness of the Confederation was that the government depended on the states. The new government was made a direct government of the people and for the people, and its

An ambassador departs. As a member of the family of nations, the new United States sent representatives to other countries. Nations carry on most of their business with each other through representatives called ambassadors.

MUSEUM OF THE CITY OF NEW YORK

First inauguration. George Washington takes the oath as President. On Wall Street, New York City, a statue now marks the place where this event occurred.

laws stood above state laws. Its activity, however, was limited to certain fields that involved all the states, such as foreign and interstate commerce, foreign affairs, national defense, coinage of money, and postal service. In all other fields the states were to keep control.

The plan for the national government included a legislature, an executive, and courts. Each branch was made dependent on the other two by a system of checks and balances. The Bill of Rights protected every individual in certain rights against the government.

For a Quick Review

1. What important powers did Congress lack under the Articles of Confederation?
2. How could territories become states according to the Northwest Ordinance?
3. Who were some important leaders of the Constitutional Convention? What experience and training had they had?
4. In what ways was the new government under the Constitution intended to be stronger than the government under the Articles of Confederation?
5. What three branches of the government are provided for in the Constitution? What are the duties of each? What checks and balances does the Constitution provide?
6. What is the Bill of Rights? What rights does it guarantee to every American? Why is the Bill of Rights essential in a democracy?

Learning to Study More Easily

MAKING A SUMMARY

Probably you have noticed that in many books, including this one, there are summaries at the ends of chapters. Perhaps you have learned to use the summary when you wish to review the main ideas in one of the chapters. Making a summary of your own sometimes helps you to organize what you have learned. It helps you to pick out the chief facts and ideas and to see how they are related. It helps you to remember the important facts. Making a summary, then, may help you study in much the same way that making an outline does. A summary includes only the main ideas, while an outline usually includes subheadings that give more detailed facts.

Many interesting books have been written about the launching of the new government of the United States. Choose one of those listed at the end of Unit 3, read a chapter or part of a chapter, and write a summary of it. Here are some tips on how to go about it.

The first step in making a summary is to read quickly through the entire section to see what main ideas the author is presenting. Then read it a second time, this time more closely, to notice how the author explains, illustrates, and proves the major ideas. You may wish to make notes of key words or phrases that will remind you of main ideas and guide you when you prepare your summary.

Now you are ready to put into your own words the ideas of the selection you are summarizing. When you have finished the first draft, ask yourself these questions about it: (*a*) Have I stated the ideas in complete sentences? (*b*) Have I used only the words that are necessary to make the meaning clear? (*c*) Have I kept to important facts and thoughts and left out all but the most necessary examples? (*d*) Have I written my summary in my own words rather than in phrases from the book?

Revise your summary after you have answered these questions, making any changes that are necessary to improve it. Then ask your teacher to check it with you.

10 *The Young Republic Wins a Place among World Nations*

From the day when our country was first winning its place in the family of nations to the present day, we Americans have always liked a good debate. Public debates help us make up our minds on important questions. Such a debate is probably going on today. Follow it on television, over the radio, and in the newspapers. Observe how people make up their minds and take sides in the debate.

If you had been reading the newspapers about the year 1790, you often would have seen the names of Jefferson and Hamilton. Thomas Jefferson and Alexander Hamilton were well known. They had given great patriotic service during the Revolution. Now in the new government they were President Washington's closest advisers. Washington must have found their advice confusing at times, however, because Jefferson and Hamilton flatly disagreed on many questions.

> Jefferson said, "The many!"
> Hamilton said, "The few!"
> Like opposite sides of a penny
> Were those exalted two.
>
> If Jefferson said, "It's black, sir!"
> Hamilton cried, "It's white!"
> But 'twixt the two, our
> Constitution started working right.
>
> Hamilton liked the courtly,
> Jefferson liked the plain,
> They'd bow for a while, but shortly
> The fight would break out again.

As you read Chapter 10, you will see how both Jefferson and Hamilton, even though they disagreed sharply, helped in establishing the new United States among the older nations of the world.

1 *The Federal Government Adopts Hamilton's Program*

BROWN BROS.

George Washington
1789–1797

As we look back now, we take it for granted that the new United States government would be strong and successful. But in 1789 President Washington and the other leaders were not so sure of its success. They had to work hard and carefully to get the new government started right.

The President and Congress had three great tasks to accomplish. They had to set up the parts of the new government and start them working. They had to decide what policies the new government would follow at home. And they had to win for the new nation a respected place among the nations of the world.

The new government is organized. When the first Congress met, it began setting up the machinery of the new government. It established the Supreme Court and other courts to enforce the laws of the new government. It organized an army and a navy. It created the first departments of the President's Cabinet. To obtain money to pay the expenses of government, it laid a tariff (tax) on imports.

President Washington appointed Thomas Jefferson Secretary of State, Alexander Hamilton Secretary of the Treasury, and General Henry Knox Secretary of War. He selected the judges of the new courts. He appointed many other officials, including men to collect the import taxes in the various ports of the country.

The President also had to decide how he and Congress would work together so that the new government would run smoothly.

There was not much disagreement on these steps to organize the government. But when the President and Congress had to decide what policies the new government should carry out, there were sharp and bitter disagreements. Alexander Hamilton had one idea. Thomas Jefferson had a very different idea. Each man won followers and each group attacked the other bitterly.

Political parties. The two groups formed our first political parties. The followers of Hamilton were called Federalists. The followers of Jefferson were called Republicans. But do not be misled by the latter name. The Jeffersonian Republicans later became the present Democratic party, while the Federalists were the ancestors of the present Republican party. (See the chart on pages 205–206.)

We can best understand the differences between the two parties by comparing the ideas of their leaders, Hamilton and Jefferson.

Hamilton's ideas. Alexander Hamilton was born in the West Indies. As a boy, he had to earn a living as a clerk in a store. At the age of 16 he came to New York City and a year later entered Kings College, now Columbia University. He was still a student when the Revolution broke out, but he had already attracted attention by writing pamphlets for the colonial cause. During the war he served on General Washington's staff. He saw how the weakness of the Continental Congress added to Washington's difficulties. He decided that a central government had to be strong. It had to be able to govern its people directly, not through the state governments.

Hamilton married a daughter of a rich landowner of New York. From then on he was friendly with the wealthy landowners and merchants of New York and Philadelphia. He admired these men and considered them to be best fitted to govern the country. He distrusted ordinary people; he said they were selfish, ignorant, and easily misled.

Hamilton believed that, in order to grow great, the United States would have to be strong in manufacturing and commerce as well as in agriculture. Manufacturers would make cloth, tools, and other products for farmers. Farmers would produce food for factory workers. Factories and farms would turn out a surplus to sell in foreign countries, so that the United States would have a large foreign trade. The factories would also make military supplies. The country could then build a large army and navy to protect its extensive commerce.

To create such a country, Hamilton believed that the national government should help manufacturing and commerce. Therefore he proposed that the government do three things: It should pay back all the money that Congress and the states had borrowed in order to carry on the Revolutionary War. With that money businessmen would be able to expand manufacturing and commerce. The government should also establish a bank. The bank would lend money to businessmen and help them to expand. Finally, the government should collect a tariff on imported goods. Under the protection of the tariff, American manufacturers would be able to sell their products at a profit. Therefore they would produce more, and manufacturing in America would increase. (For an explanation of a protective tariff see page 231.)

Jefferson's ideas. Thomas Jefferson was born in the Virginia Piedmont. His father was a self-made man who had built up an estate on the frontier. His mother was a Randolph, one of the oldest and most aristocratic families of Virginia.

Jefferson spent most of his early years in the Piedmont (see page 68). He learned to admire the small-scale farmers who lived there. He found them to be independent, honest, reasonable men and good citizens. He believed that the best kind of country would be one made up mainly of small-scale farmers

BROWN BROS.

John Adams
1797–1801

BROWN BROS.

Thomas Jefferson
1801–1809

owning and working their farms. And with the immense stretches of land beyond the Appalachian Mountains, he thought there would be enough free land for farmers for a thousand years.

From his experience in politics and from his reading, Jefferson developed his democratic ideas. He was opposed to any effort by government to control the mind of man. That is why he believed so deeply in religious freedom. Every citizen, he said, should be free to attend any church or no church and should not be forced to help support any church. His famous Ordinance for Religious Freedom became law in Virginia in 1786. That law completely separated church and state in Virginia. Religious freedom has always been a foundation of our democracy.

Unlike Hamilton, Jefferson believed that the common people were honest and intelligent and could govern themselves. Let ordinary people learn about the problems of their country, Jefferson said. Then let them discuss the problems freely and openly, and they would choose the best solutions and the best leaders. That is why Jefferson believed that government should provide schools for all children. That is why he insisted on free speech and a free press. And that is why he wished to keep government as close as possible to the people. Let most of the governing be done in the local community, he said, where the voters are personally acquainted with the candidates. Turn over to the central government only those problems that state and local governments cannot deal with. In addition, said Jefferson, hold frequent elections to keep the people watchful over their officials.

Hamilton favored manufacturing. Hamilton encouraged the factories of his day. Why?

Jefferson was opposed to Hamilton's plans because he believed they would give special favors to businessmen, investors, and manufacturers. In a democracy, said Jefferson, the government should not give special favors to anyone. It should try to provide equal opportunity for all and then leave the people free to advance to the best of their ability.

Hamilton's ideas win. In the 1790s Hamilton's views won the support of President Washington and Congress. The federal government took over all the war debts. It also established a national bank. By so doing, it won the support of businessmen and investors. Under Hamilton's direction, the new government became strong.

To collect more money, the government put a tax on whisky. When farmers in western Pennsylvania refused to pay the tax and started riots, Hamilton led an army to put down the Whisky Rebellion. But by the time the army arrived on the scene the rioters had gone home. No one was punished, but the new government had proved that it could and would enforce its laws.

While Jefferson and Hamilton were still in Washington's Cabinet, Jefferson opposed Hamilton's proposals. He encouraged newspaper editors and others to do likewise. Although both men in 1792 helped to persuade Washington to serve a second term as President, Jefferson resigned from the Cabinet the next year. After his resignation he became the active leader of his party. As time passed, the conflict between the two parties grew more bitter. Since Washington supported the Federalists, the Republicans attacked him too.

The French Revolution divides the American people. In 1789, the same year that Washington was inaugurated President, the French Revolution broke out. For many years that revolution and its consequences divided the American people.

At the beginning of their revolution, the French people obtained for themselves a voice in making their own laws. Their motto was "Liberty, Equality, Fraternity." (Fraternity means brotherhood.) At this time nearly all Americans sympathized with the French people; they believed that the French were doing exactly what they had done in their own revolution.

But the French Revolution turned out to be very different from the American Revolution. The French king and most of the French nobles urged neighboring kings to invade France to crush the Revolution. And the kings of Austria, England, and Spain were eager to do so. They feared that the success of the French Revolution would encourage their own people to revolt. Thus from 1792 on, the French Revolutionary government had to protect itself against invading armies. It defeated the invading forces, but it continued to carry on a life-and-death struggle with England.

The Revolutionary government dealt with its enemies at home by beheading the king and queen, hundreds of the nobility, and many others who were suspected of not being sympathetic toward the Revolution. Moreover, the French Revolutionists were unable to agree among themselves. One group of leaders succeeded another, and each group beheaded its predecessors. Thus the path of the French Revolution was marked by a trail of blood.

As the French Revolution became more and more violent, some Americans lost their sympathy for it. The Federalists, especially, turned against it. Many of them were wealthy persons who did not accept the idea of equal rights for all, for which the French people were fighting. They believed that the United States should join England in her war against France.

Many Americans, on the other hand, continued to sympathize with France. They expressed their views through Jefferson's Republican party. They believed deeply in liberty and equality and felt that France was fighting for those ideals. Moreover, they could not forget that France had come to the aid of the United States in the War of Independence. Now, they said, it was the duty of the United States to go to the aid of France in her war against England.

President Washington and his Cabinet decided that the United States would be neutral, that is, stay out of the war and help neither side. The new nation required a period of peace in which to grow in strength and unity. Washington avoided war with England by making a treaty with that country. John Adams, a Federalist, was elected President in 1796. He, too, kept the United States neutral, though American and French ships fought an undeclared war for two years.

Jefferson favored farming. Jefferson favored a nation mainly of small-scale farmers. Why?

Jefferson is elected President. As the election of 1800 drew near, the Federalist leaders were worried. It looked as if most of the people would support Jefferson's Republican party. Many French, English, and Irish immigrants, who had run away from persecution in Europe, strengthened the Republican party by writing and speaking for it. The two parties attacked each other more bitterly than ever before.

In an effort to weaken the Republicans, the Federalists passed the Alien and Sedition Acts. (An alien is a person who has not yet become a citizen. Sedition means arousing people against their government.) One of the acts gave the President the power to expel from the country any alien whom he considered dangerous. As soon as this

LIBRARY OF CONGRESS

The Capitol. This is a drawing of the Capitol as it looked when Washington, D.C., became the National Capital. It was partly burned by the British in 1814.

law was passed, some aliens left the country. Another act declared that anyone who criticized the government, the President, or Congress could be punished by a fine and imprisonment. Several persons were convicted under this act and were sent to jail.

But the effect of the Alien and Sedition Acts was exactly the opposite of what the Federalists had planned. Many people turned against the Federalist party for trying to win an election by violating the Bill of Rights. The Alien Act violated the right of trial by jury and the Sedition Act violated the right of free speech and a free press. The legislatures of Virginia and Kentucky passed resolutions attacking the acts as unconstitutional.

A quarrel between President Adams and Alexander Hamilton further weakened the Federalist party. The Republican party won the election easily, and Thomas Jefferson was the first member of his party to serve as President. His two successors, James Madison and James Monroe, belonged to the same party; and all three served two terms each. Thus Jefferson's Republican party held the presidency from 1801 to 1825.

As soon as he took office, Jefferson began to work out his own policies for the government. He allowed the Alien and Sedition Acts to come to an end, thus restoring the confidence of many Americans in the Bill of Rights. He tried to carry out his idea that the federal government should govern less. He ended the whisky tax, he cut the size of the army and navy, and he reduced the number of government workers. But events soon forced him to change his policy, and he and his successors used greater powers than Washington and Adams had used.

2 *The United States Fights a Second War with England*

After their revolution the French people did not have a stable government until Napoleon Bonaparte took over control of the country in 1799. He immediately set out to conquer Europe and, especially, to destroy the power of England. War between France and England started again in 1803. Before the struggle was over, the United States was also drawn into a war with England.

European war interferes with American trade. As part of the war between them, England and France tried to ruin each other's commerce; and American ships were caught in the middle. Each side issued orders forbidding American ships to trade with the other. Both countries seized American ships. The American people blamed England more, because her navy controlled the Atlantic and therefore captured the larger number of ships.

Furthermore, British naval captains frequently stopped American ships at sea, took off members of the crew, and forced them to work on British ships. Seizing sailors in this way was called impressment. The British said that they had the right to seize Englishmen who had deserted and signed up on American vessels. The United States government denied that the British had the right to stop American ships to search for deserters. Moreover, some of the men who were seized had become American citizens.

In June, 1807, the British man-of-war *Leopard* attacked the American warship *Chesapeake* to make its captain give up some sailors. The British claimed that these men were deserters from the Royal Navy. The American people were so angry that they were ready to go to war. But President Jefferson would not lead them into war. He tried to continue Washington's policy of neutrality. He believed that neutrality was the wisest policy for a young and growing nation.

Jefferson thought that he had a way to make England and France stop seizing American ships and sailors. On December 22, 1807, he declared an embargo; in other words, he ordered all commerce stopped. No ship was permitted to leave any American port for any foreign port. Jefferson believed that England would be unable to get along without food from the United States

NATIONAL GALLERY OF ART, INDEX OF AMERICAN DESIGN

Eagle, 1808. This eagle was painted on a wooden tavern sign. (See page 158.)

and that, to obtain food, she would promise not to seize any more American ships. But England, although hurt by the embargo, was able to carry on. The real sufferers from the embargo were the American people, especially those in the New England states where so many earned a living by trade.

In March, 1809, the embargo was ended. American ships began to sail to foreign countries again. The British navy began to seize American ships again. The question between the two countries became: did the ships of a neutral country have the right to trade with other countries in wartime as in peacetime? England said "no"; the United States said "yes." When the United States declared war on England in 1812, it fought to defend what it believed to be its right as a neutral to carry on trade with countries at war.

Other causes of the War of 1812. There were also other causes of the war. Americans in the West blamed the English for Indian attacks along the frontier. They accused the Canadian fur traders of selling guns and ammunition to the Indians and even of encouraging the Indians to attack the white settlements. An Indian leader named Tecumseh united the various Indian tribes to stop the westward advance of American settlement. But William Henry Harrison defeated Tecumseh's forces in 1811 in the Battle of Tippecanoe.

American settlers in the Northwest believed that the only way to end the Indian raids was for the United States to take Canada. Canada attracted the westerners for another reason. Pioneers always wanted more land even when the nation still had unsettled territory. Canada was close at hand, and much of the soil was fertile. Similarly, in the South the people wished to seize Florida for the same reasons. Hostile Indians who lived in Florida made life dangerous for the white settlers living near its border.

All along the frontier, from New Hampshire to Georgia, the people were eager to go to war in order to end the Indian danger and to expand the territory of the United States. The desire for war was expressed by a group of young congressmen from the frontier sections. They became known as war hawks. The leaders of the war hawks were Henry Clay, of Kentucky, and John C. Calhoun, of South Carolina. The war hawks helped push the United States into war with Great Britain in 1812.

New Englanders oppose the war. While the West and the South favored war, New England was mainly opposed to war. Merchants still made good money from foreign trade in spite of losing many ships to England and France. War would destroy this trade. During the war New Englanders did not cooperate with the federal government. They even sold supplies to the enemy. Two-thirds of the British forces in Canada ate meat that came from New England and New York.

In 1814 the Federalist leaders of New England met at the Hartford Convention to discuss the war. Many people expected the Convention to vote in favor of the withdrawal of the New England states from the Union. But the delegates did not go that far. They merely expressed their opposition to the embargo, the war, and most of the other actions of Presidents Jefferson and Madison. Thus the American people were not united in support of the War of 1812.

"The war nobody won." When the war began, the American Army and Navy were unprepared. The Army consisted of exactly 6,744 men and the Navy had 16 ships. Each state had a militia, it is true; but, as in the American Revolution, the militia was made up of men who had had little military training. They usually did not fight well in battle. The militia of the New England states and of New York refused to fight outside the boundaries of their own states. Furthermore, no one made any plans for carrying on the war against the British. As you read about the campaigns and battles of the War of 1812, you will understand why it has been called "the war nobody won."

The War of 1812. As you read about the War of 1812, follow the military and naval actions on this map. What event (or events) does each number refer to? How successful was the British blockade of the American coast? Notice how important Lake Erie and Lake Ontario were in the war. Which issues remained unsettled after the war?

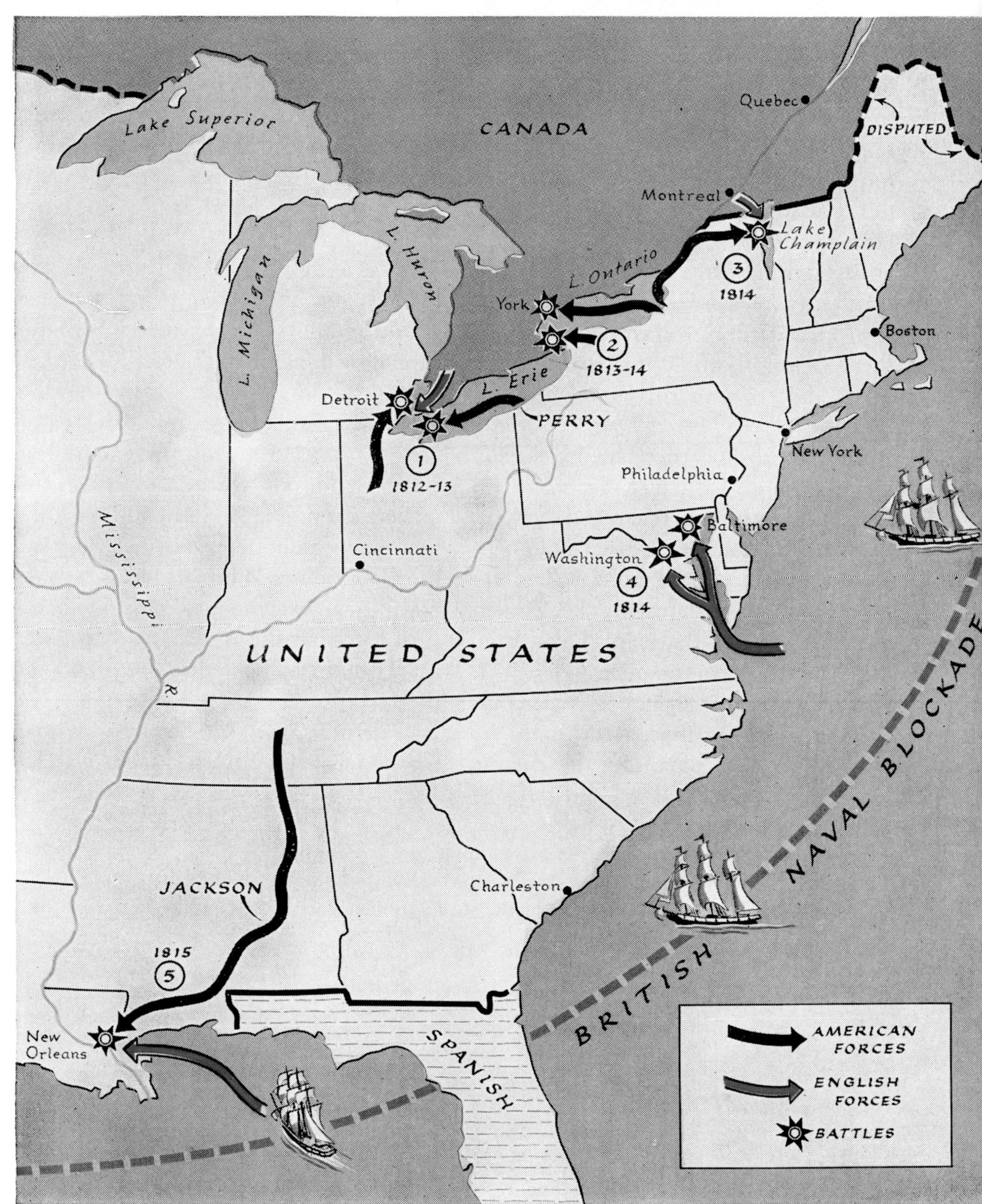

Events of the War of 1812. The Americans failed in their efforts to invade Canada. They failed near Detroit, and they failed again along the Niagara River. (See the map on page 197.) The battles in which the Canadians turned back the attempted invasions from the United States are important to the Canadian people, just as Lexington and Concord are to us. In those battles Canadians were defending their land against a foreign invader. In 1813 an American force raided the Canadian city of Toronto, then called York, and burned the government buildings there. Naturally the Canadians remembered and resented this act of destruction.

The British and the Canadians were strong enough to defeat American invasions. On the other hand, they were unable to invade the United States. In 1813 the Americans built a fleet on Lake Erie that defeated the British there. After the Battle of Lake Erie, the American commander, Oliver H. Perry, sent a message to the commander of all American forces in the Northwest, "We have met the enemy, and they are ours." With this victory the danger of British invasion of the United States in the West ended.

The next year, in 1814, the British made their strongest effort to win the war by invading New York State along Lake Champlain. They used the same route that Burgoyne followed during the Revolution. (See page 197.) Again, as in 1777, the British were defeated, this time in a naval battle on Lake Champlain.

In August, 1814, a British army landed on the Atlantic coast near Washington, D.C., to march on the capital of the United States. The Americans had done nothing to fortify the capital against attack. A hastily gathered army tried to stop the enemy but turned and ran when the British attacked. President Madison and his Cabinet fled inland. The British burned the Capitol, the White House, and several other government buildings in return for what the Americans had done in Toronto. Then they returned to their ships.

"The Star-Spangled Banner." Three weeks later the British attacked Balti-

Building a western fort. Fort Meigs was built in 1813 to protect settlers in Ohio against the English and the Indians. Soldiers first formed a stockade by standing logs upright in ditches. Then, at various points along the stockade, they erected blockhouses from which to fire upon attackers.

PUBLIC BUILDINGS ADMINISTRATION

OFFICIAL DEPARTMENT OF DEFENSE PHOTO

"Old Ironsides." These are models of the American warship *Constitution* (*left*) and the British *Guerrière*. They took part in a famous battle of the War of 1812. The *Constitution*, later known as "Old Ironsides," defeated the British ship.

more. They failed to capture the city, principally because they were unable to pound Fort McHenry into surrender. After watching the successful defense of Fort McHenry, Francis Scott Key wrote "The Star-Spangled Banner." (See pages 252–253.)

War at sea. At sea the British navy had more than a hundred large warships while the large American vessels could be counted on the fingers of one hand. Nevertheless, the American Navy won some exciting sea battles. The few American vessels met British ships in individual combat and defeated them. But after the British navy blockaded the Atlantic ports, American victories ceased. In one battle the British ship *Shannon* defeated the American ship *Chesapeake*. As he lay dying, the American captain, James Lawrence, said, "Don't give up the ship." Those words became a motto of the United States Navy.

In spite of the blockade, American privateers captured many British merchant ships, not only on the open sea, but even in the waters around the British Isles. The American privateers were schooners, the fastest sailers on the seven seas, built by skillful American shipbuilders.

The Battle of New Orleans. After the failure at Fort McHenry, the British army and navy left Chesapeake Bay to attack New Orleans. Most of the fighting in the South had been done by Andrew Jackson and his Tennessee militia. In December, 1814, he gathered his forces in New Orleans to defend that city against the British. After several skirmishes the main battle was fought on January 8, 1815. The British charged the American position but ran into a deadly fire that mowed them down and completely defeated them. The British lost more than 2,000 men; the Americans lost 71.

The Battle of New Orleans was fought after the peace had been signed in Europe and therefore had no effect on the peace terms. But it aroused the pride of the American people, and it made Andrew Jackson a popular hero.

LIBRARY OF CONGRESS

Washington burned. An artist of the time pictured the burning of the capital in 1814. The flaming building on the right is the President's Palace, as the White House was called.

The treaty settles no issues. The treaty of peace was signed in Ghent (gĕnt), Belgium, on December 24, 1814. It ended the war, but it settled none of the issues that had caused the war. The questions of impressment and the rights of neutral vessels in time of war were not even mentioned. Problems such as the boundary with Canada were left to be settled in the future. It was fortunate that these matters were postponed because in later years the United States and Great Britain were able to settle them by compromise (kŏm′prō mīz). In so doing, the two nations were to show the world that disputes between countries can be settled without going to war.

3 *The Country Shows a New Spirit of National Unity*

As a result of the War of 1812, the people of the United States showed a new pride in their country. The war gave them a national anthem (see page 253), popular heroes like Andrew Jackson and Oliver H. Perry, and patriotic slogans like "We have met the enemy and they are ours" and "Don't give up the ship." The people looked up to the federal government with a new loyalty and devotion. As a result of the war also, other countries respected the United States and treated her as an independent nation.

Political leaders propose a national program. After the final defeat of Napoleon in 1815, Europe had no big wars for a hundred years. Americans no longer needed to worry about embargoes and neutral rights. The people soon lost interest in foreign affairs and devoted themselves to problems at home. It almost seemed that the country had stopped facing east across the Atlantic and had turned around and faced west. It was an era, or period of years, when the leaders agreed on most questions. Let us solve the problem of money, they said. Now each local bank issues its own money, and the value of money changes from one place to the other. Therefore it is difficult to carry on business. Let us establish a new national bank. It will keep the value of money from changing and will help business.

Let us look after our new industries, the leaders said. American manufacturers cannot sell their products so

BROWN BROS.

James Madison
1809–1817

BROWN BROS.

James Monroe
1817–1825

cheaply as products imported from England are sold. Let us set up a tariff so that our new industries will prosper, and we shall no longer depend on other countries for manufactured goods.

Let us help the West, the leaders said. Let us move the Indians farther west and open up their lands for settlement. Let us build roads and canals to make it easier for settlers to go west and for western farmers to trade with the East.

Jefferson's party changes its views. These were the plans of the political leaders in 1815. The Republican party then in power, with James Madison as President, was the same one that had elected Jefferson in 1800 and in 1804. But it had changed its point of view. In the earlier years it had favored a weak central government. Yet what had the leaders of that party done while they were in power? They had purchased Louisiana (see page 214); they had declared an embargo; they had fought a war. Events had forced them to take one step after another to make the central government stronger. As for the future, President Madison expressed the views of the party in his annual message to Congress in 1815. He called for a larger army and navy, a tariff to protect manufacturing, and a new national bank. In short, by 1815 the Republicans had taken over the entire program of Alexander Hamilton. The aim of that program was to build a strong, united nation under the leadership of the federal government.

Federalist party disappears. What had happened to the Federalist party? Its opponents had taken over its program. Its aristocratic ideas had become

BANCROFT LIBRARY, UNIVERSITY OF CALIFORNIA

Liberators of South America. San Martín (*right*) and Bolivar (*left*) led the movement for independence from Spain. What countries did each help to free?

unpopular. Furthermore, national feeling was so strong that the people laughed at the Federalist leaders who had opposed the War of 1812 and who had talked about New England breaking away from the Union. The Federalists soon ceased to exist as a national party. In 1820 Monroe had no serious opposition for the presidency and got all but one of the Electoral votes. (One Elector voted for someone else so that Washington would remain the only President who received all the votes.) Since there was only one national party, the years of Monroe's presidency are known as the Era of Good Feeling.

John Marshall. During the years from 1800 to 1825, the Supreme Court made decisions that increased the power of the federal government. John Marshall, the Chief Justice, favored a strong government, and he persuaded a majority of the other justices to agree with him. Marshall established the fact that the Supreme Court could declare a law unconstitutional. While deciding a number of important cases, he explained the Constitution in such a way as to give the federal government the power to run a strong, expanding nation.

The Monroe Doctrine strengthens Latin-American independence. Another great expression of the spirit of nationalism after the War of 1812 was the Monroe Doctrine. The story takes us back to the Spanish colonies in America and to Napoleon. In 1808 Napoleon invaded Spain, drove out the king, and placed his brother on the Spanish throne. The Spanish colonists set up governments that pretended to be loyal to the exiled Spanish king, but they really desired independence. After the Spanish king was restored to his throne in 1814, the revolutionists had to fight for independence.

San Martín and Bolivar. Independence was won for South America by two great generals, José de San Martín (sän mär tēn′) from Argentina and Simon Bolivar (bŏl′ĭ vẽr) from Venezuela. Both were Creoles, having been born in South America. Both had served in the Spanish army and had spent many years in Europe. Both were inspired by the American Revolution and the French Revolution to win liberty for all South America.

By 1816 Argentina had an independent government. San Martín organized an army of about 3,500 men to free the rest of South America. The army made a heroic march across the Andes, hauling its cannon over mountain crags.

Latin-American neighbors gain independence. Today's boundaries are shown on this map of the Latin-American nations. Panama (6) became independent in 1903.

On the Pacific side it surprised the king's army in Chile and soon set that country free. From Chile, San Martín went on to Peru. After some fighting he entered Lima, the capital, and in 1821 Peru became independent.

In the meantime, Bolivar had liberated the northern part of South America, including the territory that is today Venezuela (vĕn ĕ zwē′lȧ), Colombia, and Ecuador (ĕk′wȧ dôr). Finally, Bolivar's army defeated the last large army of the Spanish king, and Bolivia became an independent country in 1825.

Mexico declared its independence in 1821. By 1824 Spain had lost all its empire in America except for Cuba. Brazil broke away from Portugal in 1822.

The people of the United States naturally sympathized with the Spanish Americans in their struggle for liberty. The United States government recognized the former Spanish colonies as independent nations.

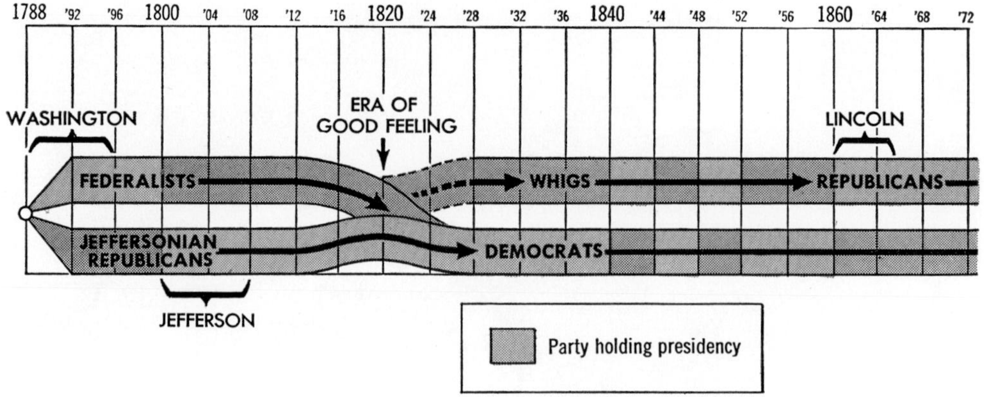

Political parties in power. This chart shows how our present political parties grew out of ear-

England supports Latin-American independence. At the same time several of the great countries of Europe agreed among themselves to help Spain win back her colonies. England was opposed to any such action. As soon as the former colonies had thrown off Spanish control, they had opened their ports to all nations. English merchants took advantage of their opportunity and built up a large trade with them. The English desired to keep that trade. The British government suggested that England and the United States announce to the world that they would not permit any country to attack the former Spanish colonies and return them to Spain.

As soon as he received the British proposal, President Monroe asked Jefferson and Madison for their opinions. Both former Presidents approved an alliance with England to keep European powers out of America. But John Quincy Adams, the Secretary of State, argued that, if our country cooperated with Great Britain, American influence would be small; the United States would look like a little rowboat being pulled along by a huge warship. He said that the United States should stand alone in its warning to the world. Great Britain would support the warning, but it would be an American policy and the United States would have the honor of stating it. Monroe followed the advice of his Secretary of State, John Quincy Adams.

The Monroe Doctrine. On December 2, 1823, in his annual message to Congress, President Monroe announced a new foreign policy of the United States. It included these points: No European government is to establish any new colonies on the American continents. The United States will take no part in European politics and European wars except when its rights are in danger. The United States will not interfere with existing European colonies in America. But it will not permit any European country to attack a former colony that has won independence.

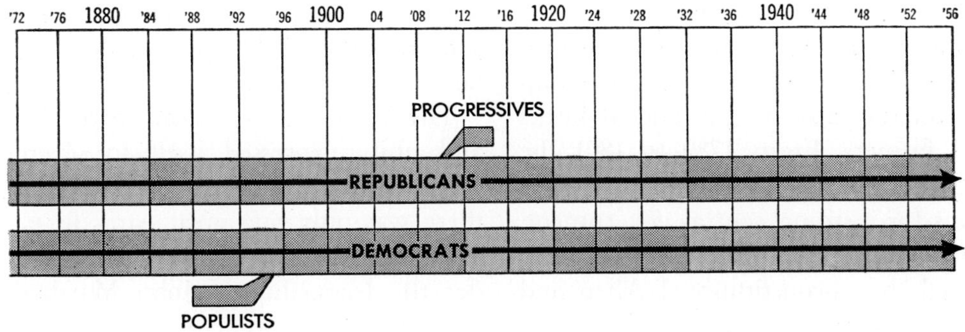

lier ones. It also shows the years in which each party controlled the presidency.

The foreign policy stated by Monroe is known as the Monroe Doctrine. The United States could not have enforced this policy in 1823 if England had supported the other European countries. But England stood back of the United States, and as a result the Monroe Doctrine was rarely challenged.

The American people turn their back upon Europe. The Monroe Doctrine expressed a policy of independence for the Americas. In effect it built a fence around the New World (except for existing colonies) and said to the Old World: "Keep out! America is no longer an unsettled wilderness in which to plant colonies. America is free and independent. You have your own system of kings and emperors and eternal wars. We want none of it. We have our own system of free republics that wish to live together in peace. The two systems cannot mix. We shall keep out of European affairs unless you deny us the right to trade. You, in turn, will keep out of American affairs."

Now the United States stood on its own feet. It had won an equal place among the nations of the world. There were no wars in Europe to disturb and divide the American people. Now they could devote themselves to their problems at home. They could turn their energies to the tremendous task of settling the West.

Summary

In the first 30 years under the Constitution, the United States established itself as a nation that could manage its own affairs. Its leaders set up a new government. The new government won the support of the American people, and it earned the respect of other nations.

Soon after the new government was put into operation, the American people divided into two political parties. The Federalists, led by Hamilton, wanted a strong central government controlled by men of property. They wanted to build a country in which manufacturing and commerce would be important. The Republicans, led by

Jefferson, wanted to keep most of the power in the state and local governments. They wished to keep the country, for the most part, a land of farms and farmers. From 1789 to 1801 the Federalists carried out many of their plans for a strong central government. To weaken the Republicans, they passed the unconstitutional Alien and Sedition Acts. By not renewing those laws, President Jefferson preserved the Bill of Rights.

The Republicans were in power from 1801 to 1825. They adopted many of the policies of the Federalists, who soon disappeared as a national party.

The major European nations, led by France on one side and Great Britain on the other, were at war during much of the time from 1789 to 1815. The Federalists favored Great Britain, while the Republicans favored France. Each President in turn, from Washington to Madison, tried to keep the United States neutral, though both sides interfered with American trade.

Finally in 1812 Congress declared war on Great Britain. The United States went into the war partly because its rights as a neutral had been attacked, partly because people in the West and the South thought they saw a chance to take Canada and Florida. Neither side was able to defeat the other decisively, and the peace treaty settled none of the disputes that had led to the war. Just the same, the War of 1812 had an important effect on the United States. The people felt more strongly than ever that they belonged together as one nation. Their country proved to the world that it could maintain its independence.

The spirit of American patriotism and unity expressed itself in several ways. While Monroe was President, there was only one great party in national politics. The Supreme Court, under the leadership of John Marshall, enlarged the powers of the national government. In the Monroe Doctrine, the United States government ordered Europe to keep hands off the Americas. European countries listened more carefully because the Doctrine was backed up by the British navy, but in announcing it, the United States had acted as an equal among nations. The new country had won its place as a member of the family of nations.

For a Quick Review

1. What opinions did Jefferson hold about government and about what would make a strong nation? What were Hamilton's opinions on these same points?

2. What events led to the entrance of the United States into the War of 1812?

3. What success did the United States have in fighting the War of 1812 and in gaining what the war hawks had said they were fighting for?

4. What conditions and leaders brought independence to the countries of Latin America?

5. Why was the Monroe Doctrine issued? It is considered an important landmark in the history of the United States. Why?

Learning to Study More Easily

USING ENCYCLOPEDIAS

When you need to find quickly information about an event, an important person, or any other subject, you can usually get help from an encyclopedia. Most encyclopedias consist of several volumes, although there are a few that are in one volume. Whatever the number of volumes, the articles are placed in alphabetical order according to their titles. To find a particular subject, look at the backs of the volumes. If you are looking up the War of 1812 in the *World Book Encyclopedia,* for example, you will find it in the volume labeled *W-X-Y-Z*. If you are looking for information about the Embargo Act, you can find it in *Compton's Pictured Encyclopedia,* for example, in the volume labeled *D-E*.

There may be other information in the encyclopedia about your topic in addition to that in the main article. One way that you can find it is by using the index to the encyclopedia. In most encyclopedias a complete index is found in the last volume. In some, however, each volume contains an index to the articles included in it. This index also gives references to related articles in other volumes. For example, if you use an encyclopedia that is indexed in this way, in reading about the Embargo Act you would consult the index in the *E* volume to find other material on the embargo.

No matter how the index is arranged, most encyclopedia articles give you cross references to other articles that will help you on the general subject you are investigating. At the end of the main article you will probably find the words *"See also"* or *"Related subjects"* followed by titles of other articles you should consult. In one encyclopedia at the end of the article on the Embargo Act you will find this note: *"See also* Blockade, International Law, Neutrality Policy of the U.S." You can also help yourself, as you read the article, by looking for important points that might be discussed in separate articles.

Sometimes students get the encyclopedia habit—that is, they find the encyclopedia so useful and so easy to use that they never learn to look in other books and magazines when they are investigating a subject. They forget that the article in an encyclopedia is a summary, and usually a brief one. (You will frequently need to find information in other books.) They forget, too, that it is one author's opinion as to which facts, of the many that are available about the topic, should go into the summary. (You will want to compare the accounts of several authors.)

Sometimes students neglect to look at the copyright date of the encyclopedia, so that they may be using information that is 15 or 20 years old. (You can check the copyright date on the title page of the volume you are using.) Sometimes they neglect to consult the yearly supplements that are published by several of the encyclopedias to bring the regular volumes up to date on many topics. (You will want to check whether the supplement contains more recent information on your topic.)

Three important encyclopedias prepared especially for students of your age are the *Britannica Junior, Compton's Pictured Encyclopedia,* and the *World Book Encyclopedia.* Two widely used encyclopedias for adults are the *Encyclopedia Americana* and the *Encyclopaedia Britannica.* Which are in your school library? Your classroom?

11 *Americans Move West*

Almost every American family has moved at least once. Some have moved many times since the first member of the family came to America, like the family of President Abraham Lincoln, for example.

In 1637 Samuel Lincoln became part of the American adventure as he made the long voyage from England to Massachusetts. His son and grandson lived all their lives in New England. But his great-grandson, whose name was John Lincoln, left New England. First he moved to Pennsylvania. From there, he followed the Shenandoah Valley into western Virginia. Here his son Abraham (the grandfather of the President) grew up, married, and had a family of his own.

Grandfather Lincoln and his family found life hard on their Virginia farm. Daniel Boone and others were spreading stories about the rich black soil and the bluegrass of Kentucky. Many Virginians were going there. Grandfather Lincoln decided to go, too. After the fighting of the Revolutionary War was over, he and his wife and their five children followed the Wilderness Road into Kentucky.

Kentucky then was just being settled by white pioneers. Life there was hard and dangerous. Three or four years after he had moved to Kentucky, while working on his farm, Grandfather Lincoln was killed by an Indian.

Grandfather Lincoln's children grew up in Kentucky. His son Thomas became a carpenter and farmer. In 1806 Thomas Lincoln married Nancy Hanks, who had also been brought from Virginia as a child. They settled on a farm near Hodgenville, Kentucky. When their first son was born on February 12, 1809, they named him Abraham after his grandfather.

When Thomas Lincoln did not prosper in Kentucky, he became interested in reports about the rich black soil in Indiana. In 1816 he sold his land in

Kentucky and moved with his family across the Ohio River into Indiana.

When they reached the spot chosen for the new home, the father built a cabin out of poles and brush, leaving one side open. In this open-faced cabin in the woods, the Lincoln family lived through the winter of 1816–1817. The next year they were able to move into a log cabin, 18 by 20 feet, that they had built. There were no doors and no windows. The floor was the bare earth, and the roof was of brush held down by poles. The father cleared a few acres and grew vegetables and a little corn, but he spent most of his time hunting. The family lived almost entirely on bread and meat, with whatever else they could find in the woods, such as wild berries, nuts, and honey.

As Abraham Lincoln grew up, he helped to support the family by working for neighboring farmers, hoeing, splitting rails for fences, and doing other jobs. Because he had to help support his family, Abraham had time for only one year of schooling.

In 1830 Lincoln's father sold his land and livestock, bought a big wagon and several oxen, and the family moved farther west, this time to Illinois. Again the Lincolns had sought out the frontier, to start anew with the hope of making a better living.

The story of the Lincoln family is like the story of thousands of other American families who moved north or south or west—mainly west—during the many years of our history. As one frontier was settled, pioneers moved on to the next unsettled region to open a new frontier. The story of the Lincolns and of all the other pioneer families is the story of the expanding frontier. It is an important part of the American adventure.

Frontier houses. A log cabin with a chimney at one end was the typical frontier home. On its own land the pioneer family produced almost everything it needed.

LIBRARY OF CONGRESS

WESTERN RESERVE HISTORICAL SOCIETY

Boom town. Cincinnati grew with the Old Northwest. By 1826 it had many miles of paved streets and sidewalks. Compare this picture with the one on page 176.

1 *Settlers Push the Frontier to the Mississippi River*

The early colonists, as you read on pages 37–38, built their homes on the coast and along the rivers. Gradually they made settlements inland. In the colonial period the expansion of the frontier was slowed up by the forests and by the continual fighting with the French and Indians. Yet by 1776 settlements had been made west of the Appalachians. During the Revolutionary War, British and Indians attacked frontier settlements. Many pioneers, fearing such attacks, went back to the older settlements to wait until the war ended.

Victory in the Revolution ended most of the danger. As early as 1781 New England pioneers whose frontier homes had been burned by the enemy began to return to their charred and weed-covered fields. After the Revolution there were still unsettled areas in some of the states, in western New York and Pennsylvania, for example. People from farms and towns along the coast filled in these areas.

At the same time large numbers of easterners moved west of the Appalachian Mountains. Many of them followed Daniel Boone's Wilderness Road. Others went overland to some river port like Pittsburgh. From there they floated down the Ohio River on flatboats to Kentucky. Planters from Virginia and Maryland bought land in Kentucky and Tennessee, brought their slaves with them, and established the plantation system on the frontier. So many people settled in Kentucky that it was separated from Virginia and became a state in 1792. Tennessee grew a little more slowly. It was separated from North Carolina and became a state in 1796.

The frontier in the Old Northwest. Before 1795 not many people went to the Old Northwest, that is, to the territory north of the Ohio River. The Indians who lived there were determined to keep out white settlers in order to preserve their hunting grounds. Some pioneers, however, insisted on settling on the land in spite of the Indians. As a result blood was shed by both Indians and whites. The settlers demanded that the federal government protect them. The government sent soldiers to defeat the Indians, but the first two armies were themselves defeated. Finally, in 1794, a third army defeated the Indians at the Battle of Fallen Timbers. Then the Indians moved farther west, giving up most of the present state of Ohio.

At once settlers began pouring into the Old Northwest. Some came down the Ohio River; others traveled across New York State and up Lake Erie. Within 10 years Ohio was admitted as a state. Ohio was the first state carved out of the public domain. The steps required by the Ordinance of 1787 for establishing states was now carried out for the first time. (See page 174.) As you read of other states being admitted to the Union, you will know that they went through these same steps.

The War of 1812 again discouraged people from going west because of the warfare between Indians and whites on the frontier. During the war the Indians were decisively defeated and thereafter were forced to give up their lands piece by piece. As soon as the war was over, thousands upon thousands of emigrants crowded the several routes to the West. Many Virginians who had settled in Kentucky crossed the Ohio River into southern Indiana and Illinois.

Cincinnati—a western town. As the population of the Old Northwest increased, cities grew up. Most of the cities were situated on rivers, for the pioneers, like the early settlers, used the rivers as highways. Many a river city became the market and supply center for farms scattered over a large area. Cincinnati, Ohio, is an example of how such a city grew.

When peace was made with the Indians of the Northwest, Cincinnati was a muddy hamlet of 94 log cabins and 10 frame houses. It had a total population of 500. Thirty years later it was a hustling, bustling city of more than 16,000 people. It had 2,500 buildings, most of them two-story frame or brick houses.

Cincinnati grew so fast because it stood where several branches of the Ohio River entered the main stream. Down these rivers came the produce of farms in Ohio, Indiana, and Kentucky. The mills of Cincinnati made flour. Its packing plants packed 40,000 hogs in three months. Cincinnati was jokingly called Porkopolis, the "city of pork." Merchants sent food products down the Mississippi. Part was sold in the South. The rest was shipped from New Orleans to eastern cities and to Europe. From eastern cities came cloth, coffee, tea, spices, china, and furniture. Cincinnati merchants distributed these manufactured goods to country stores.

It cost so much to transport manufactured goods from the East that people in Cincinnati soon began to make cloth, boots and shoes, hats, furniture, and many other things on the spot. From local iron foundries came machinery, plows, and pots and pans. Out of every three steamboats plying the Mississippi River system in 1826, one had been built in Cincinnati.

The Old Southwest. So far we have been reading about settlement of the Old Northwest. In the Old Southwest—mainly the present states of Alabama and Mississippi—settlement took a different turn. Settlers came as fast as they did farther north, and the pioneers were small-scale farmers as in the North. But in the South slavery was soon introduced into the newly settled region. Cotton growing in the seaboard states wore out the soil so fast that planters had to go west for fresh lands. They bought up the clearings made by pioneer farmers and established large cotton plantations worked by gangs of slaves. Some of the pioneers who sold out went farther west to make new clearings. Others settled in the hill country of Alabama, where the land was not bought by planters because the soil was unfit for large-scale cotton growing. Thus the New South, like the Old South, became a region of large plantations with some small farms and very few big cities.

Democracy on the frontier. Who were the people who settled in the frontier West? Some were young persons who were just starting out in life. Some settlers were Revolutionary War veterans who received their farms as a war bonus. Others were older people, with families, who had not succeeded in the East and had gone to the West for another chance. Perhaps it was their second or third move to new territory. As soon as towns grew up, lawyers, doctors, ministers, and other professional people came to serve the communities.

The pioneers who cleared land, built houses, and established communities worked hard. They lived in much the same way as the pioneers of earlier days had lived on earlier frontiers. (See pages 68–69.) From his experience the typical pioneer learned to take care of himself. The nearest neighbor might be miles away through the woods. If a job had to be done, he found a way or invented a gadget to do it. When the job was too big for one man and his family, like raising the frame of a house or husking a crop of corn, neighbors cooperated.

The pioneer respected others for what they accomplished. He looked up to the man with the largest house or the most prosperous farm or the biggest business. At the same time he believed himself to be the equal of any other man. When a constitution was written for his state, he demanded the right to vote.

Americans repeated this experience of the frontier over and over again during the entire colonial period and for a hundred years after the Constitution was adopted. This experience helped to make the American people self-reliant and independent as individuals. It strengthened their faith in democracy. It taught them to look for practical solutions to problems. As they saw a great nation growing up before their eyes, they learned to believe in progress, especially in the future growth of the United States in wealth and power.

2 *The Louisiana Purchase Doubles the Nation's Size*

While the West between the Appalachians and the Mississippi was being settled, the United States was acquiring a new West beyond the Mississippi. In 1803 the United States bought Louisiana from France. Louisiana then included all the land between the Mississippi and the Rocky Mountains and between Mexico and Canada, as you can see from the map on page 218. At one stroke the country doubled its area.

The right of deposit and the purchase of Louisiana. Farmers west of the Appalachian Mountains could not transport their products overland to sell in eastern cities because the mountains blocked the way. Think of the time, work, and expense required to carry wheat, meat, and lumber in wagons over rough mountain roads. The

Routes to the West, 1800–1820. What were the four main routes by which settlers moved west in the early 1800s? What were the geographic features of each route?

farmers could, however, load their products on river flatboats; and with a little steering, the flatboats floated down the Ohio and Mississippi rivers to New Orleans. There the products were unloaded and reloaded on ocean-going vessels that carried their cargoes to eastern cities and to the markets of Europe.

The key to this transportation route was the right to unload and reload goods at New Orleans (this right was called the right of deposit). Western farmers did not let the federal government forget that they had to have the right of deposit. New Orleans was Spanish territory, and Spain had granted the Americans the right of deposit in a treaty. But then Napoleon entered the story.

You read on page 202 of Napoleon's rise to power as the ruler of France. About the year 1800 Napoleon was planning to re-establish a great French empire in America. As a first step he persuaded the king of Spain to turn Louisiana over to him, but the transfer was kept secret. President Jefferson heard news that made him suspect the change of ownership and was worried. Having a strong country like France at one's back door was different from having a weak country like Spain there. France might not allow western farmers the right of deposit.

In 1802 the governor of New Orleans dropped a bombshell on the West by announcing that Americans would no longer have the right of deposit. The westerners were ready to go to war and capture New Orleans. Jefferson, as always, desired to avoid war. He decided to try to buy New Orleans. He directed Robert R. Livingston, American minister to France, to offer Napoleon as much as 10 million dollars for New Orleans, and he sent James Monroe to France to help with the negotiations.

By this time Napoleon had given up the idea of an empire in America. He decided instead to renew the war against England. He realized that he would be unable to defend Louisiana from the British and, besides, he needed money. He offered to sell the entire territory to the United States. Livingston and Monroe were surprised by this offer. They had no authority to buy that vast territory, but they took the responsibility upon themselves and signed a treaty, agreeing to pay 15 million dollars for Louisiana.

Flatboat. As it floated down the Mississippi to New Orleans, a flatboat was the temporary home of its crew. The boat was usually sold in New Orleans. Can you explain what power moved the boat and how the oars were used?

LIBRARY OF CONGRESS

Buying Louisiana. In this scene from the film *Romance of Louisiana,* Monroe and Livingston discuss Louisiana with French officials. Why did the United States purchase the vast Louisiana territory?

At home, President Jefferson believed that the Constitution did not give the government power to buy territory. But he was afraid to wait until the necessary amendment could be adopted; the offer might be withdrawn. He sent the treaty to the Senate without delay, and the Senate approved it. Most Americans were so happy over the purchase that they did not stop to discuss whether or not it was constitutional.

Exploring the Louisiana territory. The people knew almost nothing about most of the great territory that they had added to their nation. Within a few years several expeditions explored the Louisiana Purchase. One, sent by President Jefferson, was led by two young army officers, Captain Meriwether Lewis and Lieutenant William Clark, brother of George Rogers Clark. The Lewis and Clark expedition started from St. Louis in May, 1804. It pushed up the Missouri River to what is now North Dakota and there spent the winter among the Indians. When the expedition set out again in the spring, it included a French guide with his Indian wife and child. The Indian woman's name was Sacajawea (săk *ȧ* g*ȧ*-wē′*ȧ*), which means "bird woman." She had been taken prisoner in a battle with Indians farther west. She carried her papoose on her back and shared in all the hardships of the journey to the Pacific and back.

Journey to the Pacific. Crossing the Rocky Mountains, the party found the going rough. The Indians in what is now Idaho, never having seen white men before, suspected that the strangers were enemies. But Sacajawea recognized the Indians as her own people and acted as interpreter. The Indians became friendly and sold the white men horses, without which they would have been unable to cross the mountains. Here an old Indian described to Lewis and Clark the trail that lay between them and the Pacific coast. He said:

> You will travel seven sleeps over steep and rocky mountains. Here you will live on roots and your horses' feet will be cut by rocks. Then you will travel ten sleeps across a desert. Here there is no food and no water. Then you will travel three sleeps more. Then if any of you are still alive you will come to my people. What is farther on I know not, but it is still a long, long journey to the great lake that you seek.

The party suffered as much as the Indian had warned them they would. Finally, in October, 1805, they began to descend the Columbia River. They reached the Pacific coast and wintered there. The next spring they started back, reaching St. Louis in September, 1806. Lewis and Clark brought back many interesting and important facts. Most important, they proved that there was no water route by way of the Missouri River to the Pacific Ocean. You can read more about the adventures of the expedition in the book listed on page 263.

Pike's explorations. While Lewis and Clark were exploring the Pacific Northwest, Zebulon M. Pike made two trips into other parts of the Louisiana Purchase. In 1805 he explored the area around the source of the Mississippi River. The following year, miles to the south, he went up the Arkansas River to what is now Colorado. Here he tried and failed to reach the summit of a mountain later named Pike's Peak in his honor. From the Arkansas River,

Trail blazers. Lewis and Clark and their companions were the first white men to travel much of the route they followed to the Pacific. In this painting, which is in the Oregon state capitol, the party is shown on the Columbia River. Notice the men's buckskin suits and their weapons. Why are they carrying the boats?

OREGON STATE HIGHWAY COMMISSION

International bridge. The Rainbow Bridge connects the United States and Canada at Niagara Falls. Tourists visiting the neighboring country have only to make a brief pause at the customs office before they drive across the bridge. The United States–Canadian boundary continues to teach the lesson of peace between neighbors.

Pike cut across country to the south and reached Spanish territory. (See the map on page 218.) Spanish soldiers took him prisoner, led him across Texas, and turned him over to the Americans at the border. Although his reports were not so detailed as those of Lewis and Clark, from both of his expeditions Pike brought valuable information about the regions he had explored.

New states from the Louisiana Purchase. Some parts of the Louisiana territory, in contrast to the areas explored by Lewis, Clark, and Pike, were already occupied by white men. By 1803 there was a large French and Spanish population in and around New Orleans. In 1812 the state of Louisiana was admitted into the Union.

Even before the purchase there were American as well as French settlers in other parts of the Louisiana territory, particularly in the region now the state of Missouri. Daniel Boone, for example, came to Missouri in 1798. The Spanish authorities gave him a large farm, on which he lived the rest of his life. After the War of 1812 many Americans crossed the Mississippi into Missouri, most of them coming from Kentucky and Virginia. By 1819 Missouri had applied for statehood.

Settling boundaries. In spite of the explorations and the settlements, however, no one knew exactly how much territory the Louisiana Purchase included. It was understood to extend to Canada on the north and New Spain (Mexico) on the south, but exactly where Louisiana ended and those countries began had never been determined. After the War of 1812 the United States agreed with Great Britain and Spain on exact boundaries. The final agreements were reached by compromise.

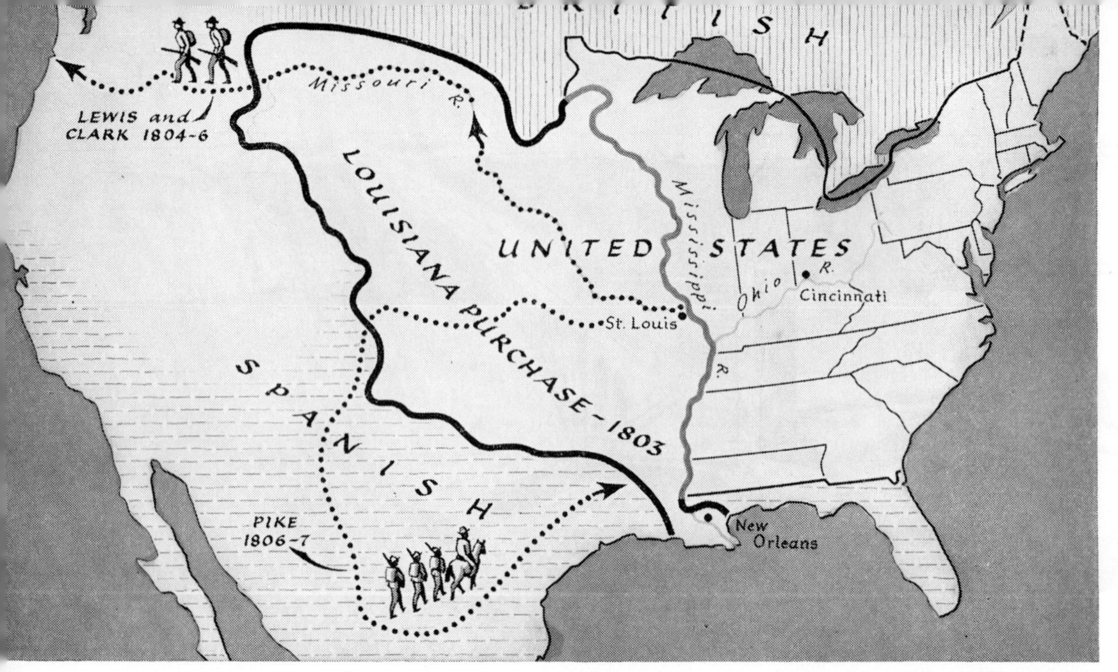

Louisiana Purchase. The territory of the United States was more than doubled by the purchase of Louisiana. Which parts of the new territory contained settlements in 1803? When was the disputed Maine boundary, shown here by a broken line, settled?

The boundary on the north. The boundary with Canada was one of the problems that were left unsettled by the treaty at the end of the War of 1812. In 1818 the United States and Great Britain agreed upon the 49th parallel as the northern boundary of Louisiana. Later the two countries agreed to keep the entire boundary between the United States and Canada unfortified, and the agreement has been in force ever since. This unfortified boundary of more than 3,000 miles is a lesson to the world, teaching that it is possible for neighboring nations to live together free from fear of one another.

When they set the northern boundary of Louisiana, the United States and Britain failed to agree on a boundary in Maine and beyond the Rocky Mountains. The Maine boundary was settled in 1842.

Oregon. The area on the Pacific coast north of San Francisco and west of the Rockies was called Oregon. Four nations had claims on it. Spain claimed the land as far north as the 42nd parallel, the present northern boundary of California. Russia claimed the land as far south as 54°40′, the present southern boundary of Alaska. The United States and Great Britain both claimed the land between these two lines.

Businessmen of the two countries were interested in Oregon because of its valuable fur trade. The two nations agreed in 1818 not to draw a boundary in Oregon. Instead, there was to be joint occupation; in other words, citizens of both countries were to be free to settle anywhere in the region.

Florida. The southern boundary of Louisiana had to be settled with Spain. It was tied up with the problem of Florida. President Madison claimed West Florida as part of the Louisiana

Purchase and in 1810 annexed it to the United States. Spain was too weak to keep order in East Florida. Seminole (sĕm′ĭ nōl) Indians, who lived there, often crossed the border into Georgia and attacked American settlers. In 1817 the War Department sent Andrew Jackson to subdue the Indians. Although his orders gave him no authority to go outside the United States, he followed the Indians into Spanish territory and defeated them. Florida was soon under his control.

Spain protested against this invasion of her territory, but the United States blamed Spain for not keeping the Indians under control. The dispute was settled in 1819 when Spain sold Florida to the United States for 5 million dollars. At the same time the two countries agreed on a boundary between Louisiana and Mexico. The boundary left Texas as part of Mexico, which was still Spanish territory.

Thus, in the years between 1803 and 1819, the United States more than doubled its territory by acquiring the Louisiana Purchase and Florida. In the North a permanent, peaceful boundary was fixed with Canada in the west to the Rockies. The Oregon boundary and the Maine boundary were not set until later. The boundary that was drawn in the Southwest turned out to be temporary, as you can see by comparing the maps on pages 292 and 293.

As it expanded, the United States simplified its boundaries. The purchase of Florida eliminated the Spanish boundary there. After the United States acquired Oregon and the Southwest, we had only peaceful boundaries with Canada and Mexico.

3 *Improved Transportation Speeds Up the Growth of the West*

While the United States was doubling its territory, the settled sections of the country were being brought closer together by improved means of transportation. Just as today, so in the early 1800s it was important to people to be able to send goods, to exchange messages, and to travel from one part of the country to another. It was important to have fast and inexpensive transportation.

Farmers need cheaper transportation. Do you remember why the western farmers were determined to have the right of deposit in New Orleans? The purchase of Louisiana made certain that they would have that right. But it did not solve the whole problem of getting their crops to market and of obtaining the things they could not make or grow themselves. There was no question, now, that they could float their produce down the Mississippi in flatboats. But the flatboats could not float back up the river. The men had to go home by land, traveling 700 or 800 miles on foot through a wilderness; they could hardly carry the manufactured goods their families needed. And the round trip between Cincinnati and New Orleans took six months.

Some manufactured goods were brought into the Northwest up the Mississippi and Ohio rivers in keelboats like the one shown on page 220. It was a slow job. Carrying goods by keelboat cost as much as hauling by wagon over the mountains. The problem of cheaper transportation remained unsolved.

The farmers of the West were eager for cheaper transportation to the East. If the cost of carrying goods were reduced, they would cultivate more land, grow bigger crops, raise more livestock, and sell the larger surplus in eastern cities. They would have more money with which to pay their debts and buy manufactured goods to make their lives more comfortable.

Turnpikes cut the cost of transportation by land. The only way to give western farmers better transportation in the early 1800s was to build better roads. Farmers in the West had no money to pay for road building. Fortunately, merchants in the eastern cities also wanted better roads to increase their trade with the back country. They invested money in companies that built toll roads, called turnpikes. Most of the turnpikes were covered with broken stones and gravel; some were dirt roads that had been scraped level. Gates were erected about every 10 miles, and travelers had to pay a fee, called a toll, to pass each gate. The money helped pay for the building and upkeep of the roads.

The Lancaster Pike. The first of these improved roads was the Philadelphia and Lancaster Turnpike, opened in 1794. It was 62 miles long. The Lancaster Pike, as the road was called, was marked off by nine tollgates. At each one a printed list of tolls was tacked up. One of these is copied on page 221. The list tells us something about the kind of traffic as well as what it cost to travel on a turnpike.

The National Road. The Lancaster Pike and other improved roads brought more and more of the western trade to Philadelphia. The merchants of New

Keelboat. The keelboat was long and narrow. One man steered while others used long poles to push the boat upstream.

BUREAU OF PUBLIC ROADS

Toll gate. This is a toll gate on a turnpike. The long pole was usually down, barring the way to travelers until they had paid the toll. The stagecoach driver did not pay a toll. The stagecoach company settled its account with the turnpike company every few months or so.

Toll Rates on the Lancaster Pike

KIND OF TRAFFIC	PRICE (*cents*)
20 sheep or hogs	12½
20 cattle	25
Horse and rider	6½
2-wheel buggy and one horse	12½
4-wheel buggy and 4 horses	37½
Wagon, with wheels less than 4 inches wide, each horse	12½
Wagon, with wheels from 4 to 7 inches wide, each horse	6½
Wagon, with wheels from 10 to 12 inches wide, each horse	3

¶ In the 1800s coins worth a half cent were in circulation. Wagons with wider wheels paid lower tolls because the wide iron tires served as rollers to pack the stone and gravel hard.

York City and Baltimore also wanted to increase their share of western trade. Therefore turnpikes were built across New York and Maryland. Two were built across New York State. Across Maryland the federal government built the Cumberland, or National, Road. The first section of this road connected Cumberland on the Potomac River with Wheeling on the Ohio River. Additional sections were later built until the road reached across Ohio, Indiana, and Illinois to the Mississippi. By joining these states to one another and to the East, this road became a powerful bond of national unity. Like the other turnpikes, the National Road increased trade, made it easier to travel, and improved communication between the cities and settlements along its route. Study the map on page 224 to see the

PUBLIC BUILDINGS ADMINISTRATION

Stagecoach station. A stagecoach stops to change horses and to discharge and take on passengers. Stagecoach travel was rough. Notice how tired the woman and child seem to be. Stagecoach passengers usually stayed in the better taverns, where they enjoyed private rooms and beds.

routes of the principal turnpikes, including the National Road.

Turnpikes carry a large and varied traffic. The turnpikes carried much of the traffic between the East and the West. Heavy freight was transported in huge Conestoga wagons with boat-shaped bodies and broad canvas tops. (See the drawing on page 264.) Going east, they carried flour, whisky, tobacco, hams, lard, and wool. Going west, they carried cloth, clothing, hardware, and other manufactured products, some of which were imported from Europe. Transportation on the turnpikes cost half as much as on the old unimproved roads.

To a person living in the 1950s, the strangest sight on the turnpike would be the large droves of cattle, hogs, and sheep being slowly driven from the West to eastern cities. Although ice was used in some cities, a method of refrigeration for shipping food had not been invented. The only way to supply the cities with fresh meat was to transport it on the hoof. At night the animals were kept in pens around the taverns where the drovers, the men in charge of the herds and flocks, ate and slept. The animals moved so slowly on the road that they often blocked traffic, especially while passing through a tollgate. Therefore drovers and their flocks were not at all popular with stagecoach drivers and wagoners, as the drivers of freight wagons were called.

Stagecoaches carried passengers and the drivers prided themselves on their speed. Everyone else on the road moved aside to give a stagecoach the right of way. Like today's railroads, the stagecoach lines were operated by large companies. Wealthy people traveled over the turnpikes in private coaches.

Travelers put up in taverns along the roads. On the main turnpikes there was a tavern about every mile. Many taverns specialized in customers of one kind—drovers, wagoners, or stagecoach passengers. People seeking homes in the West made up a large part of the westward traffic.

The steamboat improves river travel. At the same time that land travel was improved by better roads, the steam-

LIBRARY OF CONGRESS

Mississippi steamboats. Notice the paddle wheel on the boat at the right. Steamboats and flatboats were used to carry grain, tobacco, and other farm products to New Orleans. Only steamboats, however, could make the return trip carrying passengers and manufactured goods.

boat was invented for travel by water. As long as boats were moved by human muscle, rivers would remain primarily one-way roads. The steamboat was able to travel against the current and go up the river as well as downstream.

Robert Fulton is generally spoken of as the inventor of the steamboat. He was not the first person to build a boat driven by steam, for as early as 1788 John Fitch ran such a boat up and down the Delaware River. But Fulton was the first to make a regular, paying business out of the steamboat. You have probably read stories about his first steamboat, the *Clermont,* and how in August, 1807, it puffed up the Hudson River 150 miles in 32 hours and then puffed back down in 30 hours. Fulton soon had several boats steaming up and down the Hudson, making much better time than the *Clermont* on its first trip.

In March, 1811, the first steamboat on western waters was launched at Pittsburgh and was soon traveling up and down the Mississippi. In the downriver traffic the steamboat did not entirely replace the flatboat for a long time. For upriver transportation the steamboat reigned supreme, carrying dry goods and clothing, hardware, cotton, coffee, sugar, and other products to the settlements up the rivers. As fares were reduced, steamboats carried more and more passengers.

The Erie Canal provides cheap transportation. Once improvements in transportation were started, they kept on coming one right after the other. Long before the country had derived the full benefit from the turnpike and the steamboat, canals came into use. New York State led in canal building because its Mohawk Valley was the only straight and level pass through the Appalachian Mountains, as you can see on the map on page 224. The Erie Canal, completed in 1825, was dug through this valley and across the state to Buffalo. It joined the Hudson River and the Great Lakes. Thus, although it was entirely within New York State, it created a direct all-water route between East and West.

Turnpikes, steamboats, and canals tie the nation together. This map shows the major transportation routes about 1830. By 1832 steamboats had gone up the Missouri River as far as the Yellowstone River. In 1850 there were more than 3,200 miles of canals.

The Erie Canal reduced transportation costs over its route by 90 per cent. Previously it had cost $100 to move a ton of freight from Buffalo to New York. On the canal it cost $10. Farmers in western New York were now able to sell their produce in the eastern cities and could afford to buy manufactured goods. Many people from eastern New York and from New England emigrated to central and western New York. In a few years tiny settlements on the canal, like Buffalo, Rochester, and Syracuse, grew to be thriving centers of trade and industry. Traffic was so heavy that within 10 years the canal had to be made larger to keep the endless line of boats moving along.

The Erie Canal speeded up the growth of the Northwest. Emigrants traveled west on the canal. At Buffalo they transferred to lake boats that carried them to Ohio, Indiana, Illinois, and Michigan. Farmers in the Northwest sent their farm products to the East and imported manufactured goods from the East on the Erie Canal.

The Erie water route provided the cheapest transportation between the East and the West. Merchants in Philadelphia, Baltimore, and Boston found it profitable to send their merchandise to the West by the Erie Canal. Thus New York City, rather than Philadelphia or Baltimore, became the great ocean port for the trade of the Northwest.

Summary

The story of pioneer families pushing on to ever-new frontiers is the story of the settlement of our country. Many families moved three or four times, from one frontier to another. From time to time, war and the danger of Indian attack slowed up the advance. But after each of these periods, the pioneers moved to new frontiers in larger numbers than before. After the War of 1812 the stream of settlers pushed west over improved roads, on steamboats, and finally on newly dug canals.

In the Old Northwest most of the settlers were independent farmers. River settlements like Cincinnati grew into busy towns, buying surplus crops from farm families and selling manufactured goods to them. In the Old Southwest many pioneer farmers sold their clearings to planters from the seacoast, who needed fresh lands to grow cotton. The planters established plantations worked by slaves, and the New South became much like the Old South.

While the lands east of the Mississippi were being settled, our country

THE BEALE COLLECTION, MODERN ENTERPRISES, PHILADELPHIA, PA.

On the Erie Canal. This is a passenger boat hauled by horses. Passenger boats were called "packets." Compare advantages of transportation by canal and by turnpike.

Low Bridge on the Erie Canal

Low bridge! Everybody down!
Low bridge! We're coming to a town!
You'll always know your neighbor,
You'll always know your pal,
If you've ever navigated on the Erie Canal!

¶ In good weather the passengers on a canalboat sat on the flat top deck and enjoyed the scenery. When the boat approached a low bridge—and there were many over the canal—a deck hand would shout: "Low bridge! Everybody down!" Then passengers on deck would lie flat while the boat passed under the bridge. You can find other verses of this song in books of folk songs.

acquired the vast area of the Louisiana Purchase and Florida for future settlement. Exploring parties were sent to find out what the unknown parts of Louisiana were like. Soon American pioneers, passing through the hardships of one frontier after another, were crossing the Mississippi to join the earliest settlers in the Louisiana territory and push the settlement line farther west.

For a Quick Review

1. Describe the settlement of the Old Northwest and the Old Southwest.

2. Why did the United States purchase the Louisiana territory? Describe the events that led to the purchase.

3. What contributions to the growth of their country were made by Meriwether Lewis, William Clark, and Zebulon M. Pike?

4. What were the important boundary agreements signed by the United States in the decade after the War of 1812?

5. Explain why the building of turnpikes was important to (*a*) westerners and (*b*) eastern merchants.

6. Why and in what ways did the opening of the Erie Canal mark the beginning of a new period in the development of the West?

Learning to Study More Easily

UNDERSTANDING HISTORY THROUGH DRAMATIZATION

Sometimes it is hard to remember that history is about people. Perhaps you forget that people of the past lived day by day, were happy and sad, made plans and worked to carry them out—in short, that they were people like you. Studying pictures and films about the people of earlier days and reading stories about them usually help you realize that history is about real people. But perhaps the best way to understand, for example, how Americans felt about moving west after the War of 1812 is to imagine yourself in the shoes of a person who was making the trip to the frontier or who was deciding whether or not to go. Have you tried to dramatize any of the events or ways of living that you have studied in your history or social studies classes? You may find it an interesting way to understand history.

In order to imagine yourself into an earlier and different way of living, you will need information about the period in which your dramatization is laid. If a class committee is presenting scenes from a family's trip down the Ohio River to settle on the frontier, its members will have to know such things as these:

Why many people wanted to go west
How they got from their old home to the Ohio River
What kind of boat they used on the river
What kind of clothes they wore
What things they probably took with them
What kind of place they wanted for their new home
What duties each member of the family was expected to perform on the trip

You can see that the first step in preparing

a dramatization is finding background information.

The next step is planning the scenes and the stage equipment so that your play will help other members of the class to imagine themselves into the lives of people who lived over a century ago. Occasionally you may decide to write out a script for your dramatization, but many times you may wish to rehearse and give the play from an outline in which you have noted the main points you are trying to put across to the rest of the class. Plan only a few scenes, each of which "carries a punch." In this way you will have a better play than if you try to present too many scenes.

You will need little scenery and a minimum of costumes if the actors know exactly what they are trying to tell the audience. They must choose their words carefully to set the scene and make the play move quickly. An announcer can describe the scene before each act is presented. A handkerchief, a belt, a hat, or some other small property can be used to suggest the appropriate costume, and the announcer can help by giving a description of how the original characters were dressed. Signs can be put on chairs or against the blackboard to help the audience remember what properties the actors are pretending to use.

In order to plan and give a successful dramatization, members of a class must learn to work together in small committees. Each person must accept his or her share of the work and be willing to do things in the way the group decides is best. The committee chairman must see that each person's ideas are heard and that the final decisions are made by the group. Each member has a responsibility for helping the chairman to keep committee meetings moving in an orderly fashion, without any one person trying to "run things" his way.

Sometimes you may invite another class to attend your dramatization, or you may give it as an assembly program for the school. Members of one junior high school class decided, about the middle of the year, to keep all the notes from which class dramatizations had been given and prepare a pageant at the end of the year. For the pageant, which was their summary of important happenings in United States history, the students did a bit more by way of costumes and scenery than they had done for the classroom presentations. Perhaps your class will consider such a pageant as an activity for the end of the year.

You can get ideas for dramatizations by leafing through Chapter 11 to pick out important events, like the Louisiana Purchase, and major trends that affected many people, like the westward movement into the Ohio Valley. Here are some suggestions you can use as a beginning:

Cincinnati grows up
Discoveries of the Lewis and Clark expedition
The Lincolns move west
Ohio becomes a state
The purchase of Louisiana
Why the West wanted New Orleans

12 *Americans Earn a Living: Factories, Ships, and Farms*

Samuel Slater grew up in England. When he was a little older than most seventh- and eighth-graders today, he was apprenticed to the owner of a textile mill. It was one of the best mills in England, with the most modern machinery of that time. Spinning and weaving machines had been invented in England. When Sam went to work, English manufacturers were ahead of all others. The government of England tried to help them keep ahead by passing laws against sending machines or plans of machines to foreign countries. The government kept a strict watch to enforce these laws. Even the skilled workmen who knew about the machines were forbidden to leave England.

One day Sam Slater read in a newspaper that manufacturers in the United States were offering prizes to anyone who could build weaving and spinning machines like the ones used in England. If he worked hard in England, he would always make a living, Sam thought, but how much better life would be if he could go to America and win some of these prizes. Maybe he would have a factory of his own someday instead of working all his life in somebody else's factory. But, he wondered, could he build machines? He knew how to run them, but it would be more difficult to build them. And how could he get to America? He could save money to pay for his passage, but men who understood the textile machines were not supposed to leave England.

Sam Slater found answers to both his questions. As he worked, he carefully studied the machines that he used. He noticed how each part was formed and how the parts fitted together. He tried to memorize the outlines of each part and of each machine as a whole. He was learning to build machines.

To get out of England, he planned to disguise himself so that no one would recognize him as a skilled craftsman from a textile mill. Finally, he decided the time had come. At the seaport his disguise was successful. He reached the United States in November, 1789, and became part of the American adventure.

Once in America, Sam Slater wasted no time. He heard that a Mr. Moses Brown, of Pawtucket, Rhode Island, wanted to put new spinning machines in his hand-loom mill. Sam wrote to Mr. Brown that he could build the machinery for him. In fact, Sam said, if the machines he built did not prove to be as good as the English machines, Mr. Brown need not pay him for his work. The two men reached an agreement very quickly and Sam went to work. Within a year he had finished the machines. They were the first spinning machines to be run by water power in the United States.

A big change began in America when Sam Slater completed his first power-driven machines. It was the beginning of the growth of our factories, in which power-driven machinery does most of the work. It was one of many changes in the ways the people of the young republic earned a living. The story of these changes is the story of Chapter 12.

1 *The North Begins Manufacturing by Machine*

The business that Slater built prospered. He erected mills and became a wealthy man. Other skilled English workers, encouraged by his success, came to this country, built machines, and went into manufacturing. In 1800 there were 8 mills with power-driven machines; in 1810 there were 269. Some of the mills were in New York, Pennsylvania, and other states, but the large majority were in New England.

Textile mills use machines. The early mills spun cotton yarn, but the weaving was still done on hand looms. The next great forward step in the manufacture of cloth was taken by Francis Cabot Lowell, a Boston merchant. In a factory at Waltham, Massachusetts, he set up the first loom in America to be driven by water power. Now weaving as well as spinning was done by power-driven machinery.

In the Waltham factory, for the first time in America—and probably in the world—all the steps in textile manufacture, from combing the raw cotton to finishing the cloth, were completed in a single mill. Not only were there power looms as well as spinning machines; there was even a shop to make the machines. This way of bringing all the steps of manufacture together under one ownership started American industry off on a new path. The Waltham factory made large profits, and soon other mills were built on the same plan.

The early American cotton mills made only one kind of product—a

NEW YORK STATE HISTORICAL ASSOCIATION, COOPERSTOWN, N.Y.

Factory village. This is an early manufacturing village in New England. The small size of the buildings suggests how small the first American factories were.

coarse, heavy white cloth. It was cheap and strong, and the American people used it in many ways to improve their daily living. Early American mills were unable to make finer grades of cloth like those imported from England. The English factories had better machinery and more skilled operators.

Most of the workers in cotton mills were women and children. They worked from sunrise to sunset. The work was not hard; but the long hours indoors in a stuffy room full of whirring machines and spinning threads and flying lint harmed their health. Lack of a balanced diet combined with these conditions to make tuberculosis a common disease among the workers. Children suffered most; they had little chance to play outdoors, to go to school, or to grow up to be healthy men and women.

Many girls from New England farms came to the mill towns to work. The companies built dormitories for them. As a rule a girl worked three or four years and then went back home to be married.

The larger mills employed entire families. They paid women from $2 to $3 a week; men, 80 cents to $1 a day. Children eight years old received 75 cents a week; older ones, a little more. At these wages, all the members of a family had to work the whole year round in order to make ends meet.

The tariff protects American industries. The War of 1812 gave American textile manufacturers a tremendous boost. While the war was going on, it was impossible to import English goods. Therefore Americans had to buy American products. When customers demanded it, our mill operators soon learned to make finer cloth to take the place of English textiles.

Other industries also prospered during the war. Iron forges turned out farm tools, hardware, and tinware. Even the towns of the West began to manufacture iron products for the new settlements. Factories were expanded to produce enough hats, shoes, window glass, and paper to fill the home need for these products.

But soon after the war was over, there came a sudden change. Throughout the war years British manufacturers had piled up their products in storehouses at home. After the war they "dumped" this surplus into the United States; that is, they sold their goods at very low prices. They preferred to dump the goods rather than to have them rot in storage. People were able to buy British goods so cheaply that American manufacturers could not sell their products and make a living. Factories were closed and workers lost their jobs. Manufacturers and others appealed to the federal government for protection. The government helped by passing a new tariff law.

A tariff (tax on imports) can serve two purposes. First, it can provide money for the government. Second, it can protect the home manufacturer from imported goods, since the amount of the tariff is added to the price of the goods. If the tariff rate raises the price of imported goods higher than the price of similar homemade goods, the foreign goods are no longer imported. A tariff law that keeps out foreign goods is called a protective tariff.

When the first Congress met in 1789, it passed a tariff law to obtain money to pay the expenses of government. The duties (import taxes) were so low that they did not protect American manufacturers. The new law passed in 1816 raised duties in order to keep out foreign goods. It increased duties on cotton and woolen goods, hats, and paper from 50 to 100 per cent above prewar rates. Duties on iron were also raised.

These high rates protected American manufacturers by keeping out some foreign goods. After 1816 the duty on cheap cotton cloth was so high that merchants stopped importing it. As a result American manufacturers had no foreign competition in selling coarse cotton cloth. The duties on other goods were not high enough to keep foreign producers from sending them here. Since English goods were still imported in large quantities, American manufacturers demanded higher duties. In 1824 Congress passed a new tariff law that placed higher duties on products made from wool, iron, and glass. In 1828 many rates were increased still further, especially on woolen goods.

As the tariff provided greater protection by raising the prices of imported goods, manufacturing became a good way to make profits. Wealthy persons invested their money in factories, and American manufacturing expanded. More and more people in the United States made a living from manufacturing.

2 *American Commerce Reaches around the World*

Just as manufacturing grew after the War of 1812, so also did commerce. In both cases most of the expansion took place in New England. Under Jefferson's embargo and during the war, most New England ships remained tied up at their wharves. (See pages 195 and 196.) But as soon as peace was announced in 1815, they set sail again.

New England ships carry goods of many countries. As before the war, the China trade was important. You can trace its route on the map on page 234. The ships sailed around South America and to the coast of Oregon. There they remained for 18 months or 2 years. The merchants traded with the Indians, bartering pieces of bright-colored cloth, buttons, nails, and iron bracelets for the skins of sea otters and seals. Chinese aristocrats would pay high prices for these thick, glossy furs. With their cargoes of skins, the vessels set out across the Pacific. On the way they stopped at the Hawaiian Islands to get the fresh food necessary to prevent scurvy.

Factory workers. In the early 1800s many American boys and girls worked in factories from dawn until dark.

The China trade. Canton was the only port in China at which foreigners were allowed to trade. Twelve Cantonese merchants controlled the entire foreign trade. The Americans sold them the skins of sea otters and seals and bought tea, silk, and china. Although foreigners were not permitted to enter the city of Canton proper, the American sailors did catch glimpses of Chinese life. When they returned home, they had interesting stories to tell.

The way home led past the East Indies. At Java the vessels generally stopped for fresh food. There the sailors bought coconuts, mangoes (măng′-gōz), parrots, monkeys, and other things unknown in New England to take home as trophies of their adventures.

Leaving Java, the ships crossed the Indian Ocean to Africa, rounded the Cape of Good Hope, and crossed the Atlantic Ocean to home. The three-year voyage was a hard test for men and ships. It meant sailing around the globe. It involved exchanging one cargo for another twice or even three times. It demanded good seamanship and good business ability. But the rewards were great. The tea, silk, and china were so valuable in America and Europe that on a single voyage a shipowner often made 500 per cent profit on his entire investment in ship and cargo. The captain and the officers of a ship usually shared in the profits and even traded on their own. Many New England families became wealthy from the China trade.

World trade. New England commerce was not limited to the China trade. New England merchants bought and sold goods wherever opportunity offered. They bought spices, sugar, coffee, and various kinds of cotton cloth in India and sold them in Europe and America. They traded with the Mediterranean countries—Spain, France, Italy, Greece and Turkey. They carried Cuban sugar to Russia and brought back iron, hemp, and sailcloth. They took the products of China and India to South America and brought back hides and coffee. Most of the hides they sold to New England shoe factories. Most of the coffee they sold in Europe. American ships were the world's carriers by water.

By 1824 a Salem vessel brought from Brazil the first rubbers seen in New England. They were heavy and fitted badly, but they proved to be very useful in the slushy streets of Salem. Shoe lasts (models on which shoes are shaped) made in New England were sent to Brazil, and thereafter the rubbers fitted better. That exchange marked the beginning of a large rubber trade with Brazil.

New York replaces Boston as the greatest commercial center. In this varied and world-wide trade a large number of New Englanders earned a living. After the War of 1812 most New England commerce was concentrated in Boston and Salem. The people of Boston called their city "the hub of the universe." Soon, however, New York became more important than Boston as a commercial center. Many Boston merchants moved their businesses to New York. New York became the greatest commercial center in the United States.

Children in school. Modern laws require children to go to school. In many schools children learn by playing.

Why did New York become so important? The reasons are much the same as those that explain the growth of any large city, although most cities did not have all of New York's advantages. It had a good location on the Atlantic coast. It became a center of transportation by land. Its businessmen had money to invest; therefore they could attract more business to the city. New York had an excellent harbor. When the British dumped manufactured goods in the United States after the War of 1812, they chose New York as the most convenient place to sell

Foreign traders in China. This is the harbor of Canton, China, about 1800, showing the foreign trading stations. The flags show the various countries that were permitted to carry on trade with the Chinese merchants.

BETTMANN

their goods at auction. Businessmen from every part of the country came to the auction sales and became accustomed to going to New York to buy.

Packet boats. New York won another advantage for itself in 1818 when the first line of packet boats was started between New York and Liverpool, England. Before that time a ship did not sail until it had collected a full cargo. Shippers often lost money because their goods were delayed, and passengers lost time. Packet boats, on the other hand, sailed regularly once a month each way no matter how much cargo they had. Furthermore, they were fast sailers. The cost of travel on them was greater, but since they could be counted on to sail on schedule, they were soon carrying all passengers who could afford to pay for regular service. They also were used to transport the mails and the more valuable kinds of freight. The packet service brought more and more trade and travel to New York.

The cotton triangle. New York also enjoyed a large share of the cotton trade. That trade was carried on by a system known as the cotton triangle. Northern merchants sent agents to Savannah, Mobile, and New Orleans. The agents lent money to planters to pay the expenses of planting and harvesting the cotton crop. When the crop was ready for shipment, the northern firms transported the cotton to Europe and to New England and made large profits. Boston, Philadelphia, and Baltimore shared in this valuable cotton trade. But New York merchants shipped more cotton than those of all the other cities combined.

The Erie Canal. New York was the leading commercial port even before the Erie Canal was opened. The canal added another tremendous advantage. It made New York the port for a large

The world of the Yankee skipper. The China trade route, shown here, was one of the many sailed by Yankee sea captains of the 1820s. What parts of the world had been explored since the time of Drake? (See page 13.)

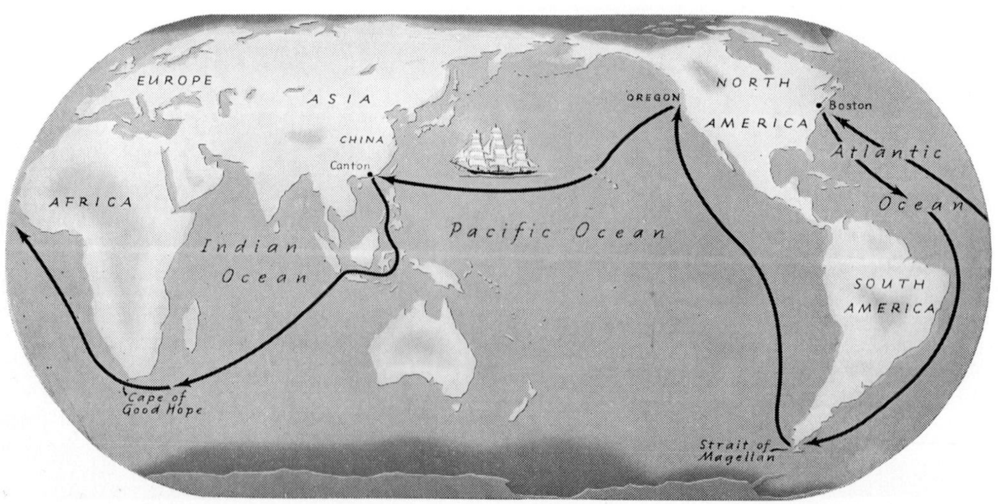

BROWN BROS.

Commerce in New York City. This is one of the streets along New York Harbor in the early 1830s. The ships crowd the wharves and the street is full of the hustle and bustle of commerce. Why did New York become the nation's largest port?

part of the West. Down the canal came western flour, meat, whisky, and lumber to be shipped out from New York. Up the canal went home manufactures and imported goods for the West. The Erie Canal put New York so far ahead that the other ports have not been able to catch up in more than a hundred years. New York also became the country's greatest center for wholesale and retail trade.

3 *"King Cotton" Rules the South*

In spite of the growth of manufacturing and commerce in the early 1800s, more than 80 per cent of the American people earned a living by farming. Most farmers continued subsistence farming, producing on their own farms almost everything their families needed. Some farmers, who lived near northern cities, sold some of their produce in the city markets and bought manufactured goods with the money. They became commercial farmers. But by 1824 only a beginning was made in the change-over from subsistence farming to commercial farming.

Southern crops. Southern farmers continued to grow staples (see pages 67–68). During the early 1800s, two of the old staple crops of the South—indigo and rice—became less important than formerly. A new staple, cotton, became the crop on which most Southerners depended for a living.

Indigo had been a profitable crop in colonial times because the British government had paid extra money for it. After the Revolution those payments stopped. At the same time, a destruc-

MORE COTTON CLOTH FOR BETTER LIVING

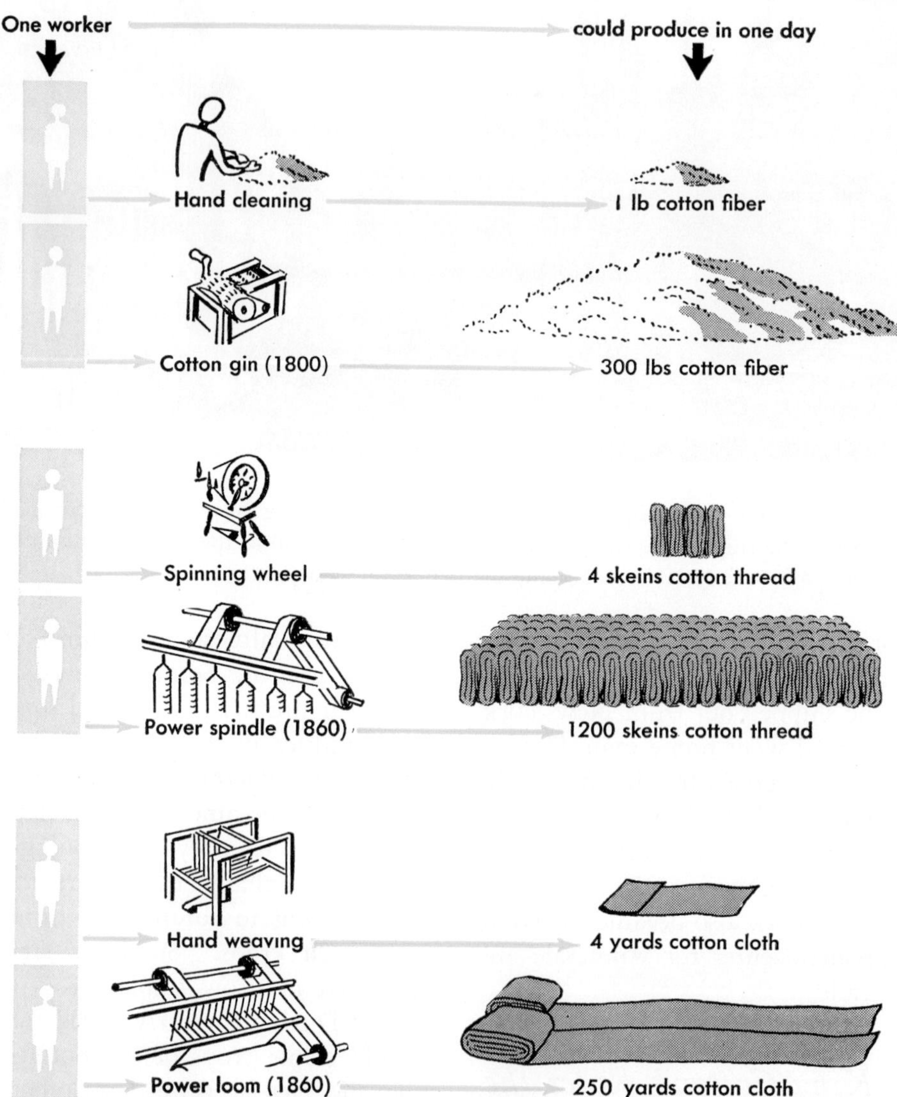

This chart shows how, by 1860, three inventions speeded up the production of cotton cloth. With the cotton gin, each worker could clean 300 times as much cotton as he could by hand. With power spindles, each worker could produce 300 times as much cotton thread as with a spinning wheel. With power looms, each worker could produce more than 60 times as much cotton cloth as with a hand loom. The charts on the opposite page show how fast the cotton crop increased in size and how rapidly the price of cotton cloth dropped. How did these advances make for better living for the American people?

U.S. COTTON PRODUCTION AND EXPORTS

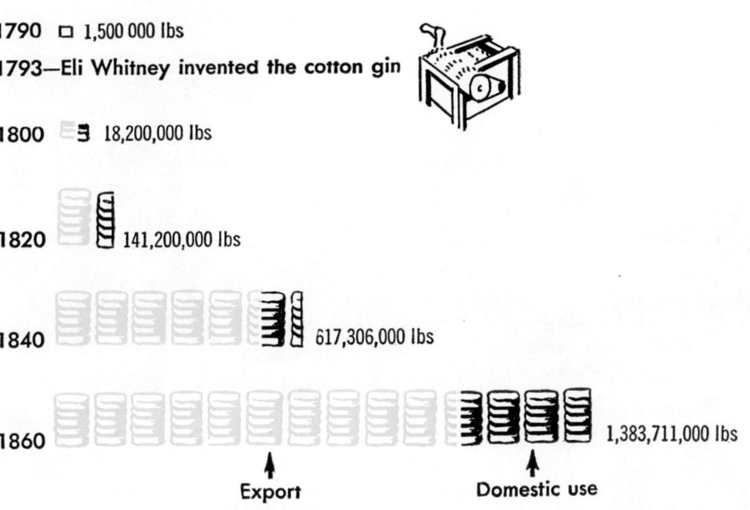

To feed the spindles of the cotton mills of Europe as well as of the United States, the South grew more and more cotton. Long before 1860 cotton was the largest single American export. Cotton was king.

DECLINE IN THE PRICE OF COTTON CLOTH

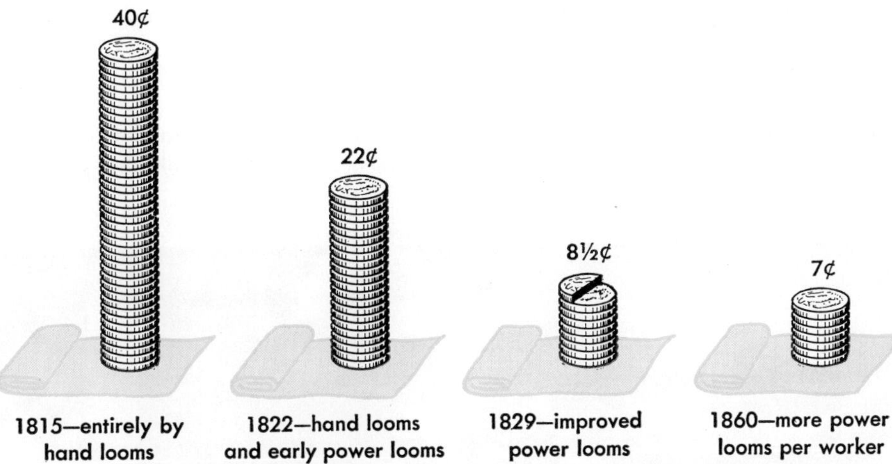

1815—entirely by hand looms

1822—hand looms and early power looms

1829—improved power looms

1860—more power looms per worker

As the price dropped, more and more people could afford to buy cotton cloth. They used cotton cloth to make shirts, stockings, dresses, and other clothing to replace the rough homespun products of earlier days. They made sheets, pillow cases, towels, and other articles for greater comfort in the home. They dressed up their homes with curtains for the windows. So more and cheaper cotton cloth made for better living for the American people.

THE CORCORAN GALLERY OF ART

Country fair. At agricultural fairs farmers saw prize livestock and produce and were encouraged to improve the products of their own farms. The first fair was held in Pittsfield, Massachusetts, in 1810. This painting was made in 1824 by John A. Woodside, an American artist.

Country peddler. In the 1800s most farmers lived too far away from town to do their shopping in stores. The peddler, with his well-stocked wagon, brought his store to the farmer.

JOHN HANCOCK MUTUAL LIFE INSURANCE COMPANY

tive caterpillar attacked the plants. Therefore southern farmers stopped growing indigo.

Farmers continued to grow rice near the coast, especially in South Carolina. Mills to grind, pound, and polish the rice were invented, so that fewer slaves were needed on rice plantations. But rice growing was limited to low, swampy land in the Tidewater Region, where the rivers rise and fall with the tides. Only there could the land be flooded and drained as necessary. Therefore rice growing could not spread far.

Tobacco remained an important staple, although much less important than cotton. From Virginia and Maryland tobacco farmers spread south and west. They produced more tobacco, but there were no new markets in which to sell the larger crops. Therefore prices dropped and tobacco growers had a hard time making a living. Gradually southern planters learned the danger of growing only tobacco. They began to grow corn and wheat as well. Then when the price of tobacco fell, they would have other crops to sell for a living.

Problems of cotton growing. In the early 1800s cotton became the most important southern crop. Small amounts of it had been grown in the South even during colonial days. There were two kinds of cotton. In one kind the seed could easily be separated from the white fiber. It was called sea-island cotton because it could be grown only on the coast close to the sea and on the islands off the coast. In the 1790s quite large crops were grown, and most of the cotton was exported to Europe. But

INTERNATIONAL HARVESTER COMPANY

Easier harvesting. The cradle, a wooden frame attached to a scythe, was first used about the time of the Revolution. As he cut the grain, the farmer caught it on the cradle and tossed it into rows. Then it was raked up and tied into sheaves, or bundles.

it was impossible to increase the size of the sea-island cotton crop very much because it could be grown only in a small area.

The other kind was called upland cotton. Since it could be grown almost anywhere in the South, larger and larger crops could be produced. But cotton could be used only after it was separated from the seed. In the upland variety the seed stuck to the cotton, and it was a long, slow job to separate the two. An experienced woman, working steadily, could clean one pound of cotton a day. It did not pay the southern farmer to grow upland cotton to sell.

Meanwhile, as you have read on page 228, machines to spin and weave cotton had been invented in England. The

Picking cotton. Slaves picked cotton on southern plantations. It was a monotonous, backbreaking job. The pickers entertained themselves by talking and singing.

machines manufactured cotton goods many times faster than the hand spinners and weavers had been able to do. English manufacturers called for more and more cotton. It seemed that cotton growers could never produce as much cotton as the machines could spin and weave.

Planters in the southern states were naturally interested in this greater demand for cotton. Now they could sell all the cotton they could grow. If someone would only find a way to separate the cotton from the seed with less labor! The cotton gin solved the problem, and cotton became the greatest crop of the South.

Whitney's cotton gin changes the South. In 1792 Eli Whitney, of Massachusetts, was visiting friends in Georgia. One evening he heard a group of southern planters talk about their need of a machine to separate the seed from the cotton. Eli Whitney had been interested in mechanical things since childhood. As a boy he had made violins. Once he took his father's watch apart, then put it together again, and the watch ran as well as ever. Now he set his mind to this new problem, and in 10 days he had the kind of machine the planters needed.

The cotton gin. Whitney's invention was a very simple machine. It was a box, one side of which consisted of bars with narrow openings between them. The cotton was fed into this side. Inside there was a roller with wire teeth. The wire teeth fitted into the openings between the bars. As the roller was turned by a handle, the teeth pulled the cotton into the box. The seeds fell outside because they were too large to pass through the openings. The idea was so simple that every crossroads blacksmith could make a cotton gin. Many persons copied Whitney's idea without paying him for the right to do so. As a result Eli Whitney did not make much money out of his invention.

Cotton and slaves in the Piedmont. If Whitney was disappointed with the returns from his invention, the South was not. His machine made it profitable to grow upland cotton, which soon became the main crop of the South. Cotton growing spread into the Piedmont and beyond the mountains into the Southwest, as the map on page 242 shows.

We have seen that during the colonial period the southern Piedmont was very different from the Tidewater. The Tidewater was a region of large plantations that produced staple crops. The planters exported them to Europe and imported manufactured goods in return. The Piedmont was an area of small farms, mainly self-sufficient. The farmers bought only a few necessities like salt, ammunition, and iron. Tidewater planters had many slaves; Piedmont farmers had very few slaves.

After the invention of the cotton gin, the farmers of the Piedmont took to growing cotton. And to do the work, they bought slaves. Cotton prices were high, and the big profits tempted the upland farmer to buy more land and more slaves and to grow nothing but cotton. To feed and clothe his slaves, he imported corn and meat from other states and bought coarse cloth from New England. Many Piedmont farms remained small, but the region became, like the Tidewater, a cotton-growing area with slaves doing the work.

Cotton plantations spread over the Old Southwest. Cotton growing did not stop at the Appalachians. It leaped the mountain wall and spread over the fertile lands of the Southwest. Planters whose land in Virginia or the Carolinas had worn out sought the fertile lands of the present states of Alabama and Mississippi. Men who had needed to sell their land to pay their debts went there for another chance. Many a rich planter's son or overseer set out with a dozen slaves to establish a kind of branch plantation farther west. This rush into the Southwest paralleled the settlement of the Northwest, and a new southern state was ready for admission every time a new northern state entered the Union.

The Southwest had many advantages over the Old South in growing cotton. Land was plentiful and cheap. The soil was fertile and required less work than the worn-out fields of the Old South. More land could be cultivated and a larger crop grown with an equal number of slaves.

DEPARTMENT OF AGRICULTURE

Modern cotton gin. More than 150 years after Whitney's invention, methods of ginning cotton are still being improved. These men in a laboratory in Mississippi are experimenting with a modern gin.

Furthermore, the planter of the Southwest had the Mississippi River and its tributaries for cheap transportation. Not only did the river boats carry his cotton down to the New Orleans market at a small cost; they also conveniently brought him corn and meat from Kentucky and Ohio. Therefore he was able to use nearly all his land and labor to grow cotton. You can understand why the planter in the Southwest made larger profits than the planter in the Old South.

With land plentiful and profits high, the southwestern planter was eager to buy more acres and more slaves so that he could grow more cotton. Thus the Southwest became a region of large plantations. The little farmer did not

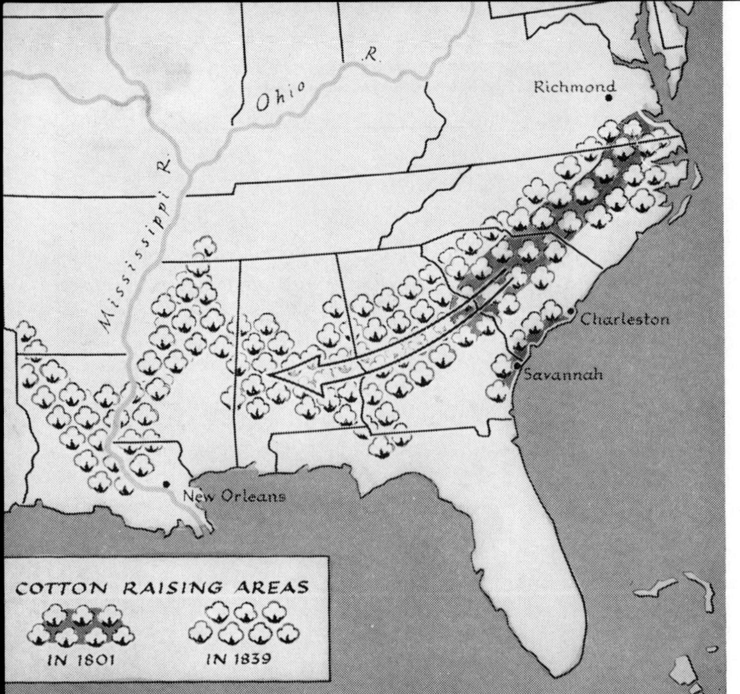

"King Cotton" in the South. Notice how the growing of cotton spread over the South. How many reasons can you give for its rapid spread?

disappear, however. The farmer with one horse and a slave or two was able to raise two or three bales of cotton each year and make a living. But the big planters controlled politics and set the pace socially.

"Cotton is king." Cotton growing became by far the greatest industry in the South. As fast as the cotton crop grew, the demand for cotton grew even faster. Cotton played an ever greater part in the economic life of the American people, in the North as well as in the South. Many thousands of people earned a living by growing it, transporting it, buying and selling it, and manufacturing it. American commerce depended largely on southern cotton. By 1830 it was the most important single item of export. (See the chart on page 237.) Textile manufacturers and workers in Europe and in the United States depended on it. The South adopted as its motto "Cotton is king" and believed that the world could not get along without southern cotton.

Because it specialized in cotton, the South remained an agricultural region. It continued to grow staple crops for export, and it continued to import manufactured goods and even a large part of its food supply. At the same time cotton growing fastened slavery on the South. Southern planters believed that they could grow large amounts of cotton only by using slave labor.

Cotton and slavery. In the years when the Constitution was being written and the new government was being organized, it had looked as if slavery was dying out. The northern states ended slavery one by one. Not only did many people believe that slavery was wrong, but northern farmers and manufacturers found it more profitable to hire immigrants and free white workers to do the labor on their farms and in their factories.

Even in the South slavery seemed to be declining. During the Revolution many southerners felt that people who were fighting for liberty and equality should not enslave other human beings. Southern leaders, including Washington and Jefferson, favored setting the slaves free. Southerners formed antislavery societies, which made plans to free the Negroes and send them back to Africa.

In the South, as in the North, it was easy to oppose slavery at that time, because owning slaves was not very profitable. Tobacco wore out the soil in Virginia and Maryland. On the exhausted fields, slaves could hardly produce enough to pay for their own keep, let alone make a profit for their masters.

The spread of cotton growing made slavery profitable again. Cotton, like tobacco, required a great deal of hand labor. If you will look at the picture on page 240, you will get some idea of the time-consuming, backbreaking labor that the growing of cotton required. Slaves could easily learn to do the work. No long training was required for it, and one overseer could supervise many slaves.

But cotton, like tobacco, wore out the soil when it was raised year after year in the same fields. Planters were always seeking more fertile lands. Thus the area of cotton growing, or the "cotton kingdom," as it was called, was continually expanding into new regions. You can follow this spread of the "cotton kingdom" by studying the map on page 242.

As the "cotton kingdom" spread, it planted slavery along with cotton. In 1790 the South Carolina Piedmont had about 90,000 white people and about 20,000 slaves, so that there were more than four times as many white people as there were Negroes. In the same region in 1830, there were 100,000 slaves to 115,000 whites. The number of Negroes then almost equaled the number of white people. Similarly, in the newer states like Alabama and Mississippi, in 1830 Negroes made up nearly half the population. By this time most southern whites thought of slavery as a permanent part of the life of the South.

Summary

In the years from 1790 to 1824, northern manufacturers began using machines to make textiles. Cities grew up around the new mills. Many women and children were employed. After the War of 1812, Congress raised the tariff to protect the new industries.

After the war, commerce increased rapidly. Northern skippers traded in every part of the world.

Northern farmers began to do commercial farming. In the South, indigo, rice, and tobacco became less important than they had been. The invention of the cotton gin and the European demand for cotton made cotton the staple crop of the South. As cotton raising spread, slavery also spread.

For the years ahead the most important changes were the beginnings of the factory system in the North and the rise of "King Cotton" in the South. With the spread of cotton growing the South remained entirely agricultural while the North turned more to manufacturing and trade. In the North slavery was dying out while it took on a new and stronger life in the South. Thus the contrast between the two sections became ever sharper.

For a Quick Review

1. What conditions and events encouraged the growth of factories in New England during the War of 1812 and after it?

2. What trade routes did New England skippers follow after the War of 1812?

3. When did New York surpass other eastern cities as a commercial center? Why?

4. What change in farming methods began in the North in the early 1800s? How was it related to the growth of cities?

5. Why did cotton growing become more important in the southern United States after 1800?

Learning to Study More Easily

TAKING NOTES FOR VARIOUS PURPOSES

When you take notes, just as when you read, the purpose you have in mind will determine the method you will use. Perhaps you are taking notes on a reading assignment in order to review it easily before discussion or before a test. A good way to take notes for this purpose is to outline the material or to make a summary of it. (See pages 258 and 186–187.) When you make an outline or a summary for your own use —perhaps for a quick review—you will probably not rework your notes as you do when you are preparing them to hand in.

When you gather information for an oral report or a paper on a special topic, you will take notes in a different way because you have a different purpose in mind. You must find material in addition to that which is given in your text. Perhaps you will go to the encyclopedia first. Then you may look for books that contain additional information. As you read, you will need to take notes in order to remember the important facts.

You will find it convenient, when gathering facts for a special report, to use half sheets of paper for note taking. On each note sheet write facts about only one particular point or part of your topic. If you follow this plan, you can put the notes first in one order and then in another as you organize the facts for your report.

On each sheet remember to write the source of the notes that you are putting on it—that is, the name of the book and the author and the page number. Otherwise you may have to spend time hunting for the reference if you need to find it again. When you write down numbers, names of persons or places, dates, and so on, be sure to write them exactly as they are in your source. If you copy exact words, put them in quotation marks so that you will know that they are borrowed words. If you use them in your report, you must keep them in quotation marks to show that they belong to the author of the reference book, not to you. Usually it is better to state ideas in your own words than to depend upon the words of someone else.

It is sometimes hard to know how full your notes should be. You must judge that by the purpose for which you expect to use them. Usually you will be wasting time if you copy complete sentences, write out detailed examples, or take notes on parts of an article that are not directly concerned with your topic. Sometimes you can save time by using abbreviations in note taking. You will have wasted time, however, if, when you start to write your paper, you cannot read your notes because of abbreviations you do not remember or because of careless handwriting.

13 *Americans Develop the Arts and Sciences*

Imagine yourself attending a reception at the home of President George Washington. Being there is a great compliment to you, for only socially prominent people are invited.

It is Tuesday afternoon at three o'clock.

As you enter the reception room, you see Washington standing before the fireplace. He is dressed in a black velvet suit with a white vest, white silk stockings, and yellow gloves. He carries a cocked hat in his hand, and at his side hangs a long sword in a white leather scabbard.

As you approach the President, your name is called out by an attendant. You stop before the President and bow. He returns the bow. Then you move on and talk with the people standing in the room.

At a quarter past three the doors are closed. You and the other guests form a circle, and the President moves from one to the other, exchanging a few words with each. When he comes to you, he asks you politely how you are. After he completes the rounds, the President goes back to his position before the fireplace. The guests come up to him one by one, bow, and leave. You take your turn to bow yourself out. The reception is over.

1 *Social Customs Become More Democratic*

The reception you just read about is an example of the way George and Martha Washington received visitors. It was like the receptions given by the

BROOKLYN MUSEUM

Martha Washington, hostess. Mrs. Washington held receptions like those of her husband (see page 245). On these occasions the President mingled with her guests. Can you find Washington in the picture? Why did Jefferson object to such social affairs?

king of England in those days. Thomas Jefferson and the Republicans did not like such aristocratic customs. They preferred the social customs adopted by the French during their revolution. (You will remember that the Republicans had sympathized with the democratic ideas of the French Revolution. See page 193.) In France all titles of nobility had been wiped out. Everyone was called "citizen" or "citizeness." In the United States many people took up this practice because they thought that titles were undemocratic. They called one another "citizen" and demanded that all titles—even "Sir" and "Mr."—be abolished. That they placed so much importance on titles showed that they were thinking about democracy and were eager to make their new nation democratic.

President Jefferson ends ceremony in the White House. Thomas Jefferson, when he became President, tried to do away with aristocratic customs. (You read on pages 190–192 about his democratic views on a number of subjects.) Believing that all men were equal as citizens, he agreed with those who thought that differences in titles and dress were undemocratic. Like most officials in Washington, D.C., about 1800, he had lived in a boardinghouse while he was Vice-President. He believed that being a high official did not entitle him to special privileges. Therefore he insisted on sitting at the foot of the table, farthest away from the place of honor. Even on the day of his inauguration as President, Jefferson refused to move to the head of the table and took his old seat. When the time came, he walked from the boardinghouse to the Capitol to take the oath of office.

As President, Jefferson decided to do away with the aristocratic receptions. The ladies of Washington, D.C., however, were unwilling to give up the most important event of their social life. At the regular time—Tuesday afternoon at three o'clock—they gathered in the White House. But President Jefferson was off on his daily horseback ride. When he returned, he came into the room in his dusty riding clothes and was very courteous and friendly. Just the same, the ladies saw that they had to give up the fight for formal receptions.

President and Mrs. Madison gave gay, informal parties at the White House. The Marine Band in scarlet uniforms played light music. Guests moved about freely, talking and meeting people. Dolly Madison was a warmhearted, considerate hostess. She remembered the names of her guests and put everyone at ease.

Mrs. Madison introduced ice cream as dessert in the White House. To please her son, she started the custom of inviting children to roll Easter eggs on the lawn of the White House.

When the Monroes came to the White House, they brought back the old formal receptions of Washington's time. Interestingly enough, the Monroes wore old-style clothes as well.

Democracy in clothes. In the early years of the nineteenth century, the style of clothes worn by men and women changed. In Paris during the French Revolution, gentlemen began wearing trousers, the dress of ordinary people, instead of knee breeches and stockings. American men soon adopted the new style. In the same spirit, women wore simple dresses and hairdos. But President and Mrs. Monroe, along with other elder people, would have none of the new fashions. President Monroe wore knee breeches, silk stockings, and cocked hats. He was the last President to wear such old-style clothes and has therefore been called "the last of the Cocked Hats."

NATIONAL PARK SERVICE

The Easter egg roll. Children were first invited to roll Easter eggs on the White House lawn almost 150 years ago. Discontinued during World War II, the custom was revived by President Eisenhower in 1953.

Later Presidents, however, returned to the simpler manners of Jefferson and wore the clothes of their own time. In so doing, they doubtless responded to the feeling of democracy and equality that was spreading and growing among the American people. It is true that the Presidents had elaborate ceremonies for special occasions, like receptions for ambassadors from foreign countries. On the other hand, they started the custom of admitting all comers to the White House, and at certain times like New Year's Day the President shook hands with every visitor.

NATIONAL GALLERY OF ART, INDEX OF AMERICAN DESIGN

History in toys. Children's toys often copy the clothes, buildings, and customs of the time when they are made. The toys shown above are: a man doll, about 1820, wearing a homespun suit; a toy house, early 1800s; a toy merry-go-round, early 1800s. Study each toy to see what it shows about its day.

2 *In the Arts and Sciences, Americans Learn from Europeans*

Perhaps, as you read about the changes in manners and clothes in the early republic, you noticed how much the Americans borrowed from Europe. Both the aristocratic and the democratic customs came from Europe, and the American people finally chose the democratic ones because they fitted in best with American ideas.

The literature and art of our country developed in the same way—but more slowly. Our early artists and writers learned by imitating European artists and writers. The first ones even painted and wrote about European subjects. Later ones began to find subjects at home and to develop an American style. American artists, however, did not stop learning from the artists of other countries. There are no national boundaries in art. Artists always learn from one another.

Jefferson's contributions. Thomas Jefferson was not an artist, but he was deeply interested in art. While he was in France after the American Revolution, he enjoyed European art and architecture. When he returned to America, he wanted to share his enjoyment with his fellow countrymen.

For example, Jefferson considered American buildings of his day to be ugly. Americans, he said, thought of a building only as a shelter to be made by piling logs or bricks one on top of the other without any idea of beauty. He wanted to teach the American people to build attractive buildings.

Influence on American architecture. Jefferson knew that the best way to teach is by example. In Europe he had admired the old Roman buildings with their huge columns and domes. While he was still in France, he sent to friends in Virginia the plans of an old Roman temple; and the Virginia state capitol was built according to those plans. After he came home, Jefferson rebuilt his house, Monticello, in the same style. Later he planned the original buildings of the University of Virginia. He also had a large part in planning our National Capitol. In that grand building, with its rows of columns and huge central dome, we can see some of the beauty that Jefferson found in the old Roman structures in Europe.

As we can see all around us today, Jefferson in large part succeeded in his purpose of making the old Roman style of architecture popular in America. Many of our state capitols, county courthouses, banks, and other buildings are built in Jefferson's favorite style. For a long period it was the most popular architectural style in the United States.

Study of science. Jefferson frequently urged his young American friends to study science. He himself described the natural resources of Virginia in his book *Notes on Virginia,* one of the earliest books written about one of our states.

The study of science in the United States really began with doctors who

NATIONAL GALLERY OF ART, INDEX OF AMERICAN DESIGN

Eagle, 1800s. This eagle was designed on a quilt by a German-American housewife in Pennsylvania. (See page 158.)

Capitol of the state of Washington. The style of architecture introduced by Jefferson into Virginia spread across the continent. Does the capitol of your state show the influence of Jefferson's ideas?

WASHINGTON STATE ADVERTISING COMMISSION

AMERICAN MUSEUM OF NATURAL HISTORY

Audubon, the naturalist. With his dog and horse, Audubon traveled around the country, studying and painting birds. Perhaps copies of his paintings are in your library.

had been educated in Europe. There they had studied minerals, plants, and animals as part of their medical education. When they were settled in their American homes, they studied the same things here. They organized societies for the study of nature. They made collections of different kinds of rocks, plants, birds, insects, fish, and so on. Thus began our modern museums of science.

Audubon, the painter of birds. One of the most important of our early students of nature was John James Audubon (ô′do͞o bŏn). He was born in the West Indies and lived his early years in France. As a boy he was interested in nature, especially birds. When he was 15 years old, he already had a large collection of bird drawings he had made. In 1803, at the age of 18, he came to the United States, living first in Pennsylvania and then in Kentucky. Wherever he went he studied and painted birds. He was not satisfied with dead birds as models. He had to study them alive, in flight, resting in the trees, or hopping in the grass; and he painted them the same way.

In Kentucky, Audubon kept a store, but he failed in business. Birds took too much of his time. He was known to leave his store for days to watch a bird he had not seen before. After his business days were over, he traveled around, studying and painting birds and paying his way by drawing portraits. In 1826 Audubon went to Europe. The next year, in England, he began publishing his bird paintings in

METROPOLITAN MUSEUM OF ART

American artists in London. This is a picture by Matthew Pratt, an American who studied with Benjamin West in London in the 1760s. West (*left*) is criticizing Pratt's work.

books. He soon became famous. Today bird lovers call their organizations Audubon societies in honor of America's great painter of birds. His bird paintings are today treasured as works of art as well as of science.

Early American painters. The first American artists were sign painters. Signs in colonial days had not only words on them but also pictures. Because many people could not read, pictures were used to tell the story. Often the pictures were of an animal or an imaginary person. It was easy, therefore, for a sign painter to turn from painting signs to painting portraits, as pictures of persons are called. Since there were no cameras in those days, many persons wanted their portraits painted.

The next step in the development of American painting occurred when European artists came to America. They painted more skillfully than the sign painters, and they brought with them copies of great European works of art. From them the Americans learned to paint in the European style. Then American artists began to go to Europe to study. Some remained in Europe; others returned to their native land.

Among the first American artists to go to Europe were Benjamin West and John S. Copley (kŏp′lĭ). They settled in London before the Revolution, became successful, and remained in Europe permanently. Many younger American artists studied with Benjamin West in London. They included Charles Willson Peale, Gilbert Stuart,

John Trumbull, Robert Fulton, and Samuel F. B. Morse. These men all returned home to paint American subjects. Fulton and Morse also won fame with inventions: Fulton with the steamboat and Morse with the telegraph. (See pages 223 and 317.)

Peale painted portraits of most of the Revolutionary heroes and early leaders of the Republic. He is famous for his series of portraits of George Washington. Stuart, like Peale, painted many of the early leaders of our nation. The best known portrait of Washington—the one that appears on our dollar bill—was painted by Gilbert Stuart. It is probably true that the "father of his country" was really not so handsome as Stuart made him out to be!

John Trumbull is famous for his great paintings on themes from American history. In his "Signing of the Declaration of Independence," 36 of the faces were painted from life. Four of Trumbull's paintings of Revolutionary War events, copied on a large scale by the artist himself, cover part of the wall space in the rotunda (rō tŭn′dȧ) of the National Capitol.

Store sign. This wooden sign hung over the door of a butcher shop. Many people could not read, but this kind of sign could be understood by everyone.

NATIONAL GALLERY OF ART, INDEX OF AMERICAN DESIGN

American music includes patriotic songs. Music in America began with the singing of hymns in churches. Soon musicians came from Europe and settled in American cities. They earned a living by playing church organs, giving lessons, and keeping music stores. Their stores became meeting places for people interested in music. These people organized singing societies and small orchestras to give concerts for the public. The music they sang and played was almost all European since little or no American music had been written.

Two great American patriotic songs were, however, written in this period. In 1798 Joseph Hopkinson wrote "Hail Columbia" to be sung as part of a program in a Philadelphia theater. You will remember that people in the United States were at that time divided between those who favored France and those who favored England in the war between those two countries. The purpose of the song was to unite all Americans in the love of their country:

> Firm, united let us be,
> Rallying around our Liberty.

You have already learned that "The Star-Spangled Banner" was written in 1814 (see page 199). On September 13 of that year, Francis Scott Key, under a flag of truce, had gone to the British fleet anchored off Baltimore to try to free a friend who had been taken prisoner. The British were planning to attack Fort McHenry that very night. Afraid that Key might warn the Amer-

"The Star-Spangled Banner." British warships bombard Fort McHenry. When the fort held out, Francis Scott Key was inspired to write the words of our national anthem.

icans, they did not let him return until the attack was over. Key stayed up all night, anxiously watching the fighting. Several times, when the firing stopped, he feared the fort had surrendered. When dawn broke, he strained his eyes looking for the fort. When he saw the flag still flying, he was inspired by the American victory. On an old envelope he wrote out the patriotic words of a poem that he called "The Bombardment of Fort McHenry." Key had his poem printed and distributed in Baltimore. Its exciting words appealed to the people. Soon, in Baltimore and elsewhere, the words were being sung to a popular tune of the day. The song came to be known as "The Star-Spangled Banner." Although the American people adopted it as their national song almost immediately, it was not until 1931 that an act of Congress, signed by President Herbert Hoover, made "The Star-Spangled Banner" the official national anthem of the United States.

The people of the countryside had their own music: religious hymns, old songs brought from homes across the sea, and the music that fiddlers played at country dances. Wagoners on the turnpikes had their songs. Boatmen on the rivers had their songs:

> Some rows up, but we rows down,
> All the way to Shawnee town,
> Pull away—pull away!

Plays and actors. The theater had a difficult time getting started in the American colonies. In New England the Puritan leaders prohibited it by law. In New York the Dutch and in Philadelphia the Quakers were opposed to it. The theater was very popular, however, in southern cities like Williamsburg, Virginia, and Charleston, South Carolina. Do you remember that, as you read on page 92, George Washington enjoyed going to see plays in Williamsburg?

In the colonial theaters the plays and the players were English. When the Revolution started, the English actors left the colonies. After the war they returned and again put on plays in the eastern cities. By 1800 theaters were al-

THE NEW-YORK HISTORICAL SOCIETY, NEW YORK CITY

An early theater. A comedy is being played at the Park Theater in New York City in 1822. On the stage are Charles Mathews, a British actor newly arrived in this country, and Ellen Johnson, a popular American actress of the time.

lowed in Boston and other New England towns.

The plays imported from England both before and after the Revolution included new ones and many old favorites. Shakespeare's plays were especially popular. The greatest English actors were brought over to attract larger audiences.

Gradually American plays and American actors became popular. Some of the early American plays celebrated heroes and battles, like Jackson at New Orleans. Others presented typical American characters like Indians or frontiersmen. One of the first great American actors was Edwin Forrest, who was born in Philadelphia in 1806, the son of a Scotch immigrant. After Forrest had become successful in America, he took part in plays in England. He was one of the first American actors to win success in Europe.

A theatergoer in the early 1800s got his money's worth. A performance started about six o'clock in the evening and lasted far into the night. A typical program consisted of a serious play of five acts, a humorous play of two or three acts, a dance between the plays, and popular songs at the end. The double feature, you can see, did not begin with the movies.

American authors. Like the artists and the actors, most writers in the young United States imitated European authors, especially the British. In the early 1800s most of the books that Americans read were written by English authors. Naturally, therefore, when

Americans wrote stories or poems, they almost always imitated English authors in the way they wrote and in what they wrote about. A few Americans, however, wrote about life in America. Of these the three best known today are Washington Irving, James Fenimore Cooper, and William Cullen Bryant.

Irving writes stories about the Hudson Valley. Irving was born in New York City in 1783. His first book was a humorous history of New York when it was a Dutch colony. In 1815 Irving went to Europe and remained there for 17 years. In England he wrote *The Sketch Book,* the most popular of all his works. It was translated into several languages and was highly praised by European critics. The parts that are best remembered are two stories about the Hudson Valley, *Rip Van Winkle* and *The Legend of Sleepy Hollow.* If you have not read these stories, try them. You will find them interesting.

When Irving returned to the United States, he was a famous author. The American people were proud of him as their first great writer. At home he wrote more books about America. But none of them was as popular as his two earlier stories—one about the man who slept for 20 years, the other about the teacher who ran away from a headless horseman.

Cooper writes about the frontier. One day in 1820 James Fenimore Cooper was reading an English novel to his wife. He got tired of the story. "I could write a better one myself," he is supposed to have said. His wife dared him to try, and he did. His first book was not very successful, perhaps because it was about life in England, where Cooper had never lived. But almost before he had finished it, he began another book, *The Spy.* It is a story about a man who served as a spy for George Washington during the Revolution. The hero, Harvey Birch, risks his life in the service of his country without hope of praise or reward. The story is exciting and full of adventure,

Headless horseman. Ichabod Crane flees in terror from a strange being. This is Walt Disney's way of picturing an incident that you can read about in Washington Irving's *The Legend of Sleepy Hollow.*

To a Waterfowl

Whither, midst falling dew,
While glow the heavens with the last steps of day,
Far, through their rosy depths, dost thou pursue
Thy solitary way?

* * *

Thou'rt gone, the abyss of heaven
Hath swallowed up thy form; yet, on my heart
Deeply has sunk the lesson thou hast given,
And shall not soon depart.

He who, from zone to zone,
Guides through the boundless sky thy certain flight,
In the long way that I must tread alone,
Will lead my steps aright.

¶ "To a Waterfowl" was first published in 1818. Since then it has been memorized by many, many school children. It is said to have been William Cullen Bryant's favorite among his early poems. What moral does he preach in it?

one which Americans enjoyed reading. The fact that they liked to read about such a hero shows how much national patriotism had grown in the half century since the United States had been formed.

Cooper's next book, *The Pioneers,* dealt with early life in Cooperstown, New York. It described the hard work of building a new settlement and also the recreations of the settlers, including sleigh riding and skating, hunting and fishing. The hero of the book is Leatherstocking, the perfect frontiersman. He learned from the Indians how to live alone in the woods and could not be happy in a settled community. Life in the forest taught Leatherstocking to be kind, gentle, honest, upright, and independent.

Cooper wrote four more novels with Leatherstocking as the hero. The stories are mainly about the struggles between whites and Indians in central New York when that region was the frontier.

The Leatherstocking Tales were very popular. They were translated into several languages and were read widely in Europe. Europeans enjoyed the stories because they were about two things in American life that made it different from their own life: Indians and the frontier. Moreover, Cooper was able to tell an exciting story that kept the reader in suspense to the end. For a hundred years European, as well as American, boys were thrilled by these stories of the struggles between white men and Indians on the wild American frontier. You may enjoy reading parts of the Leatherstocking Tales, although you will probably like them better when you are a few years older.

Bryant writes about nature. William Cullen Bryant began writing poetry at a very early age. In 1807, when he was 13, he wrote "The Embargo." In this poem he expressed the bitter opposition of New England to Jefferson's embargo. Do you remember why New England opposed the embargo? (See page 196.) When he was 17, Bryant wrote "Thanatopsis" (thăn *ȧ* tŏp′sĭs), which was highly praised. Through a long life as the editor of a New York City newspaper, he continued to write poems on American scenery, American birds, bees, and flowers, and American historical events. In most of his poems about nature, Bryant sought to teach the reader a moral lesson.

Summary

In the early days of the republic the American people copied European social manners and customs. In many of the countries of Europe, as well as in the United States, people were becoming more democratic. Americans adopted European manners and customs that emphasized equality.

American artists learned a great deal from those of Europe, where the arts had been practiced for centuries. For example, Jefferson brought from Europe the style of architecture in which many of our public buildings, such as capitols and courthouses, were built. In the early republic, musicians from Europe played and taught European music and English actors put on English plays. Gradually American musicians and actors made a place for themselves.

Before they had a chance to study European art, early American artists painted simple portraits. They improved their skill when they had a chance to learn from European artists who had come to this country. Almost all the outstanding American artists studied in Europe, and a few remained there to work. Those who came back, like Peale, Stuart, and Trumbull, painted the portraits of leaders of the Revolution and pictures of the great events of the Revolutionary period.

Similarly, American writers learned by imitating English authors. They not only copied their style; they also wrote on the same kinds of subjects. The result was that Americans frequently wrote about English subjects that they knew little about. Three outstanding writers of the early 1800s, however, wrote about American people and places. Washington Irving is best remembered for his story about Rip Van Winkle falling asleep in the Catskill Mountains and his story about the headless horseman in the Hudson Valley. Cooper's books about Indians and pioneers were enjoyed by people in Europe as well as in America. William Cullen Bryant wrote poems about the things he saw in nature around him.

You can see that European influence on American work in the arts and sciences continued to be strong in the early days of our nation. At the same time there were American artists and writers who presented themes reflecting the growth of national patriotism.

For a Quick Review

1. Contrast the social customs of Washington, Jefferson, and Monroe.

2. What were some of the things Jefferson did that influenced the arts and sciences in America?

3. Why and in what ways did American artists and writers feel European influences?

4. What did each of these men contribute to our American heritage: John James Audubon, Charles Willson Peale, Gilbert Stuart, John Trumbull?

5. What kinds of music were popular in the United States of the early 1800s?

6. How did the writings of each of these men show that he was an American, not a European: Washington Irving, James Fenimore Cooper, William Cullen Bryant?

Learning to Study More Easily

MAKING AN OUTLINE TO ORGANIZE A REPORT

Have you ever listened to a speaker who seemed to talk in circles, touching on the same subject several times without ever seeming to say what he intended? That speaker had not organized his remarks very well. As a result you and other listeners found it difficult to follow what he said. When you are giving a report or writing a paper, you will save your own time and that of your listeners or readers if you organize your information. One way to do this is to make an outline of your report before you begin writing it.

In Chapter 8 you read about how to outline a reading assignment. Perhaps you would find it helpful to review pages 162–163. As you do so, remember that making an outline to organize your own report is the reverse of outlining what someone else has written.

When you choose a subject to report on, you may know enough about it to list the major topics that you wish to investigate further and treat in your speech or paper. Probably there will be three or four of them. As you read and take notes, you may find other important topics related to your subject. You will have to decide whether or not you should include them, too.

If you do not know enough about your subject to list the major headings under which your report will be organized, you may have to do some reading in order to discover what headings are needed. In either case you will eventually find considerable information and be ready to organize it.

You begin with a few major topics or headings and then fit each fact under the topic where it belongs. One way to organize your facts under the major headings is to write each heading at the top of a slip of paper. Arrange the slips in the order you wish to follow in your report and number them.

Now go through your notes and decide which information belongs under each heading. As you decide, write opposite each note the number of the heading under which you will use it. If your notes are on separate slips of paper, arrange them in the order in which you will use them.

Next, go through the notes to be included under your first major heading and decide what subheadings the notes fall under. Write the subheads down under the main heading and arrange the notes under them. Do the same for the other major headings. You may find that some of your notes do not fit anywhere. These you can discard when you are certain they do not belong in your report.

When you have finished arranging subtopics under each major heading, examine the entire outline. Do you have all the information you need? You may have to fill in some gaps. Is there repetition of any of the major topics? Can you give this report in the time you have for it? If not, decide which parts you can leave out and still have a good report.

When you have finished these steps, ask your teacher to check over your outline with you. If you have done the job well, you will be ready to start writing your report.

MAIN EVENTS OF UNIT 3, 1780–1824

Building and governing the nation	*Earning a living*	*Science, arts, and the people*	*The nation and its neighbors*
1781 Articles of Confederation			**1781** Yorktown
			1783 Independence
1787 Northwest Ordinance			
1787 U.S. Constitution			
1789–1797 George Washington, Pres.			**1789** French Revolution
		1790 First census 3,929,214	
1791 Bill of Rights (first 10 amendments)	**1791** Textile machines		
	1793 Cotton gin		**1793** Neutrality proclamation
	1794 Lancaster Pike		
1797–1801 John Adams, Pres. (Federalist)			
1798 Alien and Sedition Acts			**1798** Undeclared war with France
1801–1809 Thomas Jefferson, Pres. (Republican)			
			1803 Louisiana Purchase
		1804–1806 Lewis and Clark expedition	
		1806 Pike expeditions	
	1807 The *Clermont*		**1807** Embargo Act
1809–1817 James Madison, Pres. (Republican)			
			1812 War of 1812
1817–1825 James Monroe, Pres. (Republican)	**1817** Cumberland Road	**1817** Bryant's "To a Waterfowl"	
			1819 Florida
1820 Missouri Compromise		**1820** Census 9,638,453	
		1821 First free public high school	**1821** Peru independent
			1823 Monroe Doctrine

Unit Roundup

HIGH POINTS OF THE UNIT

Review the suggestions on page 187 for making summaries. Skim through Unit 3, using the major headings in each chapter and reading the summaries at the end of each chapter. Write in your own words a summary of the important facts you have learned about the establishment and early growth of the United States. Then write a summary of the relations of this country with other nations from 1783 to 1824.

EXPAND YOUR VOCABULARY

1. During the first 40 years of the republic, the words and phrases listed below were used often with particular meanings. Work through the list, giving the meaning of each. If necessary, skim through Unit 3 to see how the word or phrase is used.

cotton kingdom	joint occupation
Era of Good Feeling	Republican
Federalist	right of deposit
impressment	war hawks

2. During the rest of your study of American history, you will frequently use the words listed below. Now is the time to learn what they mean if you do not already know. Skim through Unit 3 to find each word and read the paragraph in which it is used. Then define it in your own words. Check your definition in the dictionary.

Cabinet	protective tariff
constitution	staple crop
crop rotation	subsistence farming
interstate commerce	suffrage
legislature	unconstitutionality

HISTORY IN THE MOVIES

1. The new Constitution was to be the "servant of the people." Thus a film about the writing of the Constitution is given this name. You may wish to study *Servant of the People* more than once, for it presents interesting pictures of leaders and many important facts. Compare the story of the film with the account given in Chapter 9.

2. The script of *Our Monroe Doctrine,* like the scripts of *Our Declaration of Independence* and *Our Constitution,* includes many quotations from the speeches and writings of the men who are portrayed in the film. Study *Our Monroe Doctrine* to

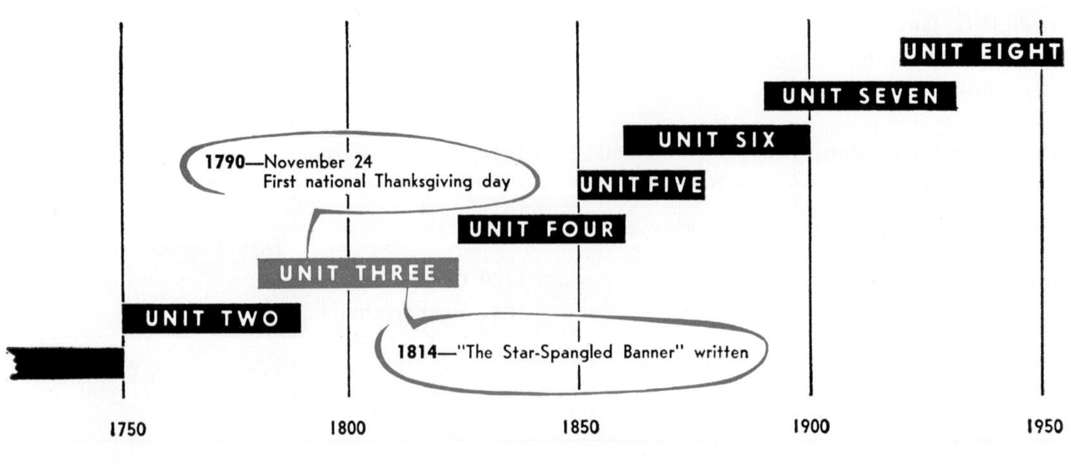

see what men had a part (and what part each took) in forming the policy that bears President Monroe's name.

3. Study *Kentucky Pioneers.* Compare the conditions of life of these pioneers with those of the earliest settlers in Virginia, New England, and so on.

4. *Flatboatmen of the Frontier* tells the story of pioneer farmers in the Ohio Valley and how they found a market for their surplus crops. What light does this film throw on the reasons for the purchase of Louisiana by the United States?

WITH CRAYON, RULER, AND PASTE

1. Make a summary chart showing the weaknesses of the government under the Articles of Confederation and how those weaknesses were remedied in the Constitution. Use these headings: Problem, Provision in the Articles, Provision in the Constitution. Give your chart a suitable title.

2. Make a chart entitled "The Branches of Our Federal Government." Organize your information under these headings: Branch of Government, Duties, Chief Officials, How Chosen, Term.

3. Draw a set of cartoons to show the difference between the views of Jefferson and Hamilton on the value of industry to the new nation, the amount of power the central government should have, and the amount of control the common people should have over the government.

4. Through class discussion decide which events studied in Unit 3 should be recorded on the large class time line. Have a committee bring it up to date.

5. Prepare a set of cartoons to show what the Monroe Doctrine meant to the Americans, the English, and the Spanish.

6. Draw sketches or find and mount pictures to show the different kinds of vehicles used for land and water transportation in the early nineteenth century. Display the pictures on the bulletin board.

7. Make a summary chart showing how the provisions of the Ordinance of 1787 were applied in Ohio's march to statehood.

8. Skim through Chapter 13, making a list of artists mentioned. Prepare a chart with the following headings to summarize information about them: Name, Period of Work, Type of Work, Special Characteristics.

PUT ON A PLAY

1. As a class, choose four or five important scenes from the Constitutional Convention and dramatize them as you think they may have happened. Each member of your class can take the part of one of the signers.

2. Plan a radio or television program laid in the United States of 1808, with a roving reporter asking these questions of people of various occupations who live in different parts of the country: In your opinion is the embargo a good thing? Should it be continued? Why or why not?

3. At the end of Chapter 12 you read a list of suggested skits. Here are some other possibilities for you to consider in planning a play:

A series of brief scenes to contrast the formality or informality of social affairs in the President's residence during the administrations of Washington, Jefferson, Madison, and Monroe

Episodes in the life of Samuel Slater, Eli Whitney, James Fenimore Cooper, or one of the other persons mentioned in Unit 3

STORIES THERE WAS NO ROOM TO TELL

1. Prepare a report on one of these topics, including material to supplement that given in Unit 3:

Military campaigns of the War of 1812
The China trade
Toll roads of the early 1800s
The *Leopard* and the *Chesapeake*
The Battle of New Orleans
Making the Peace of Ghent

2. Many colorful and important persons are mentioned in Unit 3. There was space to give only a few facts about most of them. You will find it interesting to prepare a biography (to be written or given orally, as you and your teacher decide) of one of these men:

John James Audubon
Simon Bolivar
William Cullen Bryant
Francis Scott Key
John Marshall
Charles Willson Peale
Oliver Hazard Perry
José de San Martín

USE YOUR IMAGINATION

1. Write a letter to an editor, speaking as a citizen of Virginia in 1788, urging that the new Constitution be ratified (or not be ratified) and giving your reasons.

2. Assume that you are either a western farmer or a New England businessman living in 1812. Write a letter to your congressman expressing your opinion about United States policies that have recently taken the nation into the War of 1812. Why must you decide from which section the letter is to be written?

3. Write a description of life on the Erie Canal that a reporter traveling west by way of the canal might have prepared for an eastern newspaper.

4. Prepare a series of diary entries that might have been kept by a cabin boy on a New England ship engaged in the China trade.

5. Choose one of the persons mentioned in Unit 3 and write a radio or television script in which you present some of his important achievements.

SHOW IT ON A MAP

1. On an outline map of the United States show the following and give the map a title:

The name of each of the original 13 states with the date when it ratified the Constitution
The Northwest Territory, the region dealt with by the Ordinance of 1787
The name of the river that marked the western boundary of the United States in 1787
The Louisiana Purchase
The territory purchased from Spain in 1819

2. On an outline map of the world, draw a picture map showing the chief trade routes followed by Americans trading abroad during the early 1800s. Indicate the most important articles of trade along each route. Give the map an appropriate title.

FURTHER READING

Many of the activities suggested for Unit 3 require that you find more information than could be included in this book. Use the list of books given below, as well as the ones in the appendix, to help locate the necessary facts.

Books about Interesting People

Abe Lincoln of Pigeon Creek by William E. Wilson. McGraw-Hill, 1949. Lincoln as a boy.

Alexander Hamilton: Nation Builder by Nathan Schachner. McGraw-Hill, 1952.

Fighting Frontiersman: The Life of Daniel Boone by John E. Bakeless. Morrow, 1948.††

Glamorous Dolly Madison by Alice Curtis Desmond. Dodd, Mead, 1946.††

Jefferson's Daughter by Mildred Criss. Dodd, Mead, 1948.

Liberators and Heroes of South America by Marion F. Lansing. Page, 1940. Biographies of San Martín, Bolivar, and other Spanish-American leaders.

Martha, Daughter of Virginia: The Story of Martha Washington by Marguerite Vance. Dutton, 1947.

Noah Webster by Isabel Proudfit. Messner, 1942. Father of the dictionary.

Quicksilver Bob: A Story of Robert Fulton by Corinne Lowe. Harcourt, Brace, 1946.

Thomas Jefferson by Gene Lisitzky. Viking, 1933.

Thomas Jefferson by Hendrik William Van Loon. Dodd, Mead, 1943.

Young Hickory by Stanley Young. Rinehart, 1940. Boyhood and youth of Andrew Jackson.

STORIES OF ADVENTURE AND EVERYDAY LIFE

Cap'n Ezra, Privateer by James D. Adams. Harcourt, Brace, 1940. Privateering during the War of 1812.

Clear for Action! by Stephen W. Meader. Harcourt, Brace, 1940. Impressment of a young American sailor; his adventures in gaining freedom.

Hello, the Boat! by Phyllis Crawford. Holt, 1938. From Pittsburgh to Cincinnati on a store boat in 1817.

Jemima, Daughter of Daniel Boone by Margaret Sutton. Scribner, 1942. Jemima's life, from 6 to 16, on the frontier.

Joe Mason, Apprentice to Audubon by C. M. Simon. Dutton, 1946. A boy's experiences with Audubon on the Mississippi in the 1820s.

Storm Canvas by Armstrong Sperry. Winston, 1944. Naval action in the War of 1812.

Tree of Freedom by Rebecca Caudill. Viking, 1949. Moving from North Carolina to the Kentucky frontier in the 1780s.

Two Logs Crossing: John Haskell's Story by Walter D. Edmonds. Dodd, Mead, 1943. Boy fur trapper in upper New York in the 1830s.

Westward the Course: A Story of the Lewis and Clark Expedition by Hildegarde Hawthorne. Longmans, 1946. Adventures of two boys who went with Lewis and Clark.††

OTHER INTERESTING ACCOUNTS

How Congress Makes Laws by C. C. Dill. Ransdell, 1939.

Our Freedoms Series by Chester S. Williams. Row, Peterson, 1940–1941. Fine pamphlets on rights of citizens under the Bill of Rights: *The Right of Free Speech, The Rights We Defend, Fair Trial, Liberty of the Press, Religious Liberty.*

Our Independence and the Constitution by Dorothy Canfield Fisher. Random House, 1950.

Two Oceans to Canton: The Story of the Old China Trade by Agnes Hewes. Knopf, 1944.

You and the Constitution of the United States by Paul A. Witty and Julilly Kohler. Childrens Press, 1948.

Unit 4 *The Growing Nation Divides into Sections 1824–1860*

THE UNITED STATES continued to expand and prosper after 1824 as before. In the 1840s the nation added to its territory Oregon and the great Southwest from Texas to California. Pioneers pushed their settlements farther and farther west and added more states to the Union.

With new machines the farmers of the country were able to till more land

and raise larger crops. Spurred by new inventions, more men went into manufacturing and produced more goods. Railroads carried food to the cities and manufactured products to the farms.

The democratic spirit became stronger. More men obtained the right to vote. Penny newspapers kept large numbers of people informed about the problems of the day. Free public schools began to provide the education that a free, self-governing people must have.

Yet in these years after 1824 the nation lost the strong sense of national unity that had prevailed immediately after the War of 1812. The country seemed to be breaking up into three parts—North, South, and West. It was as if the United States was growing so fast it could not hold together unless some new and stronger bonds of unity were forged.

Each section of the country wanted something different from the national government. The West wanted improved transportation and low prices to settlers for western land. Northern manufacturers wanted a high tariff. Southern planters regarded the tariff as unfair to them. South Carolina won a reduction of the tariff by threatening to secede.

In the thirties and forties the problem of slavery divided North and South more and more sharply. The abolitionists called slavery a sin and demanded that all slaves be freed immediately. Southerners demanded that Congress cease discussing the matter, that the North stop all abolitionist propaganda, and that northerners return all fugitive slaves. Many northerners were willing to permit slavery to continue in the states where it already existed but did not like to see it spread into new territories. The slavery issue finally split the nation in two.

In Unit 4 you will read how the United States grew larger, wealthier, and more democratic. At the same time it faced the danger of losing its national unity and breaking up into two parts. The West joined with the North to oppose the South.

14 *The Sections of the Country Disagree*

Do you recall reading about Dr. Ramsay, of South Carolina, who wrote that the Revolutionary War had taught the people from the different states to get along together? Do you remember the Era of Good Feeling, when there was only one political party? In those years westerners, southerners, and northerners agreed on what the United States should do about the tariff and other problems.

After 1820 the feeling of national unity was weakened. The country split into three sections—North, South, and West. Each section wanted the national government to pass laws for its benefit. Unfortunately, the laws that would help one section might harm the others. Each section had leaders who were ambitious to be President. As the leaders tried to pass laws that would favor their sections, they clashed.

If you had lived during the years 1824–1860, you might have read in the newspapers headlines like the following:

JACKSON CHARGES CHEATING IN PRESIDENTIAL ELECTION: CLAY AND ADAMS ACCUSED

SOUTH CAROLINA THREATENS TO LEAVE UNION OVER TARIFF

SOUTHERN LEADERS DENOUNCE NORTHERN ABOLITIONISTS

What had happened to the Era of Good Feeling? Why were the leaders of the North, the South, and the West so bitterly opposed to one another? What were the important problems on which the sections disagreed? To find the answers to these questions, we must look behind the headlines to the story that follows.

1 *Sectional Leaders Compete for the Presidency*

President Monroe was the last of the leaders of the Revolution to occupy the White House. There was no one candidate for President behind whom the country could unite. Instead, there were several candidates, each one representing his own section and all quarreling with one another. In fact, the period beginning about 1824 is known as the era of hard feelings.

The candidates of 1824 continued to take a leading part in national politics for many years. Let us begin with a short biography of each of the four men.

Calhoun. The candidate of the South was William H. Crawford. But John C. Calhoun, who was elected Vice-President, soon became the leader of the South. Calhoun's Scotch-Irish ancestors had emigrated from Ireland to Pennsylvania. From Pennsylvania they followed the well-worn route through the Shenandoah Valley to the Virginia frontier. From there the Calhouns moved again, this time to South Carolina. In South Carolina they settled on the very edge of the wilderness, pushing a few miles farther west than any earlier settlers.

On this frontier Calhoun spent his boyhood and youth, except for his college years in the North. After attending Yale and a law school in Connecticut, he opened a law office near his childhood home in South Carolina. There he was elected to Congress in 1810, at the age of 28. Before long Calhoun made a name for himself in Congress as one of the war hawks (see page 196). He served as Secretary of War in President Monroe's Cabinet.

Clay. In the election of 1824 Henry Clay was one of the candidates of the West. He was born in 1777 in Virginia, where his ancestors had lived for a long time. At the age of 20 he settled in Lexington, Kentucky, which was already a busy trade center. Within a few years the hard-working Clay was recognized as the best lawyer in Kentucky. In 1810 he was elected to the House of Representatives. Because of his eagerness to seize Canada, he became the leader of the war hawks. After the war he was

A frontier arrest. As a judge, Andrew Jackson once captured a criminal by beating him to the draw. Enforcing the law at the point of a gun was not unusual on the frontier.

LIBRARY OF CONGRESS

BROWN BROS.

John Quincy Adams
1825–1829

BROWN BROS.

Andrew Jackson
1829–1837

a champion of national unity in Congress. Although he was a popular leader, Clay in 1824 was not the strongest presidential candidate because there was another westerner more popular than he.

Jackson. Andrew Jackson was the other candidate from the West. He was very popular as a military hero. His experience in military affairs started early. During the Revolutionary War, at the age of 14, he fought with a small band of Patriots that attacked the British on the North Carolina frontier. After the Revolution, Jackson went to Nashville, Tennessee. There he became successful as a lawyer, planter, and politician. In the War of 1812, we remember, he commanded the Americans in the Battle of New Orleans. That victory won him his greatest popularity. In 1817, when he was ordered to punish the Seminole Indians for attacking American settlers, he chased the Indians into Florida and seized the Spanish colony (see pages 196 and 219). That rash act made Spain angry and might have led to war. But it made Jackson even more popular in the West because most westerners felt that settlers must be protected from Indian raids at any cost.

John Quincy Adams and Jackson. The candidate of the North was John Quincy Adams. He was the son of John Adams, second President of the United States. In 1778, at the age of 11, he accompanied his father to France, and he later spent many years of his life as United States minister to European nations. This experience prepared him well to serve as Secretary of State under President Monroe. He was one of the outstanding Secretaries of State in our history. Do you remember the

THE BOATMEN'S NATIONAL BANK OF ST. LOUIS

Political speech. As more people obtained the right to vote, candidates traveled around making speeches to win support. Campaign rallies, like the one Bingham has shown in this painting, were attended by people from miles around and were social as well as political occasions.

part he took in forming the Monroe Doctrine? If not, you can review it on page 204. Adams was a lonely man, never popular with the people as were Jackson and Clay. As presidential candidate in 1824, he had the advantage of being the only candidate from the North.

The two strongest candidates in the presidential campaign of 1824 were Adams and Jackson. The election was so close that it had to be decided by the House of Representatives. Clay's supporters in the House of Representatives voted for Adams and helped to elect him. Jackson and his friends charged that Adams and Clay had struck an unfair bargain. Clay, they said, had helped elect Adams to the presidency. In return, Adams had promised to appoint Clay as his Secretary of State. Adams did appoint Clay to that office. Jackson burned with anger against Adams. He spent the next four years preparing for the election of 1828.

Jackson's election a victory for democracy. In the 1828 campaign Jackson's followers sang:

Let auld acquaintance be forgot
And never brought to mind,
May Jackson be our President
And Adams left behind.

Jackson won the election easily. Thousands of people gathered in Washington, D.C., on March 4, 1829, to see Jackson inaugurated President. The crowds were so large that they blocked the main streets.

After the inauguration at the Capitol, the people followed Jackson into the White House. Pushing to see the President, they broke glasses and upset pails of punch. Men wearing muddy

CITY ART MUSEUM, ST. LOUIS

County election. This painting by George Caleb Bingham shows how voting was carried on in the mid-1800s. The voters are lining up to vote. They vote orally, so that anyone can hear for whom they vote. Politicans are campaigning right around the voting place. One tips his hat to the voter second in line and offers him a list of candidates to vote for. How has voting been changed to enable voters to express their true choices?

boots stood on satin-covered chairs to catch a glimpse of Jackson. To draw the crowd away, servants carried tubs of punch out into the garden and served refreshments there.

The people rejoiced at the election of Jackson. He was their hero who had beaten the British at New Orleans and who had seized Florida. He was one of them. All previous Presidents had come from well-to-do eastern families of high social position. He came from a pioneering family, and he had made his own way in the West.

Jackson's election was a victory for the ordinary people of the country. Remember that in their first constitutions the original 13 states had given the franchise, or the right to vote, only to men who owned property. In the early years of the republic many more people won this right. The new states of the West, as they entered the Union, gave the franchise to all white men 21 years old and over. The older states, following the lead of the new ones, soon changed their constitutions to give the franchise to all white men. So it was that small businessmen, farm laborers, and city workers obtained the right to vote. And the first chance they got, they voted for Andy Jackson.

The ordinary people believed that, as President, Jackson would help them. They felt that the United States government up to that time had helped mainly the wealthy manufacturers, landowners, and merchants by following the policies of Alexander Hamilton (see pages 192 and 201). Many people were opposed to the United States Bank and to the high tariff. They wanted the government to give away farms to settlers on the western lands. Some of them wanted jobs in the government.

As soon as he became President, Andrew Jackson placed many of his friends in offices of government. He regarded this step as a democratic reform. Any citizen, he said, should be capable of filling any government position, and changes in office gave more citizens a chance to serve. Thereafter, when control of the government passed from one party to the other, the party

BROWN BROS.

Martin Van Buren
1837–1841

BROWN BROS.

William H. Harrison
1841

coming into power swept out the old officeholders and rewarded its own workers by appointing them to the jobs. This practice is called the spoils system. It got its name from the argument by a Senator that "To the victor belong the spoils of office."

Jackson destroys the bank. After the election of Jackson, the old Republican party—the party of Jefferson, Madison, and Monroe—was split into two groups. One group, led by Jackson, was called the Democratic party. The other group, led by Henry Clay, came to be called the Whig party. (See chart on pages 204–205.) The first disagreement between the two parties was over the second Bank of the United States. Jackson strengthened his popularity with the ordinary people of the country by destroying the bank.

The first Bank of the United States, we remember, was proposed by Hamilton and approved by Congress (see page 192). Its charter ran out in 1811 and was not renewed because the Jeffersonian Republicans were opposed to the bank. But the money troubles of the government during the War of 1812 made Madison decide that a bank was necessary. The second Bank of the United States was chartered in 1816 for 20 years.

The bank was supported mainly by the businessmen of the East. Many people, especially in the West and the South, were strongly opposed to the bank. They feared that the men who ran the bank had too much power over the government and the business of the country.

Henry Clay believed he could win the election for President in 1832 as the champion of the bank. Before the elec-

NATIONAL GALLERY OF ART, INDEX OF AMERICAN DESIGN

Harrison's log cabin. The log cabin was a Whig symbol in 1840. This one was pictured on cloth. People wore miniature log cabins as charms or earrings. Are such symbols worn during political campaigns today?

tion that year, he pushed through Congress a bill renewing the bank's charter. Jackson vetoed the bill, and so the bank became the main issue, or subject for debate, in the election of 1832.

Clay and the Whigs aimed their campaign principally at winning the votes of the wealthy and the educated people. But the Democrats aimed their campaign at the many thousands of people who had recently won the right to vote. They staged torchlight parades, with the marchers singing campaign songs. They held mass meetings addressed by fiery speakers who attacked the bank. Jackson and his running mate Martin Van Buren won an overwhelming victory.

To Jackson the victory meant that the people approved his stand against the Bank of the United States. But the bank still had four years to go, and in that time it might regain its strength and win a new charter. To prevent that, Jackson decided to destroy it at once. He weakened it by withdrawing all government money from the bank; and the bank soon went out of business. Jackson's victory was complete.

Van Buren's one term. When the election of 1836 came, Jackson used his influence to have Vice-President Martin Van Buren elected President. Van Buren won over several opponents. The victory was really another triumph for Andrew Jackson. He was so popular with the people that he was able to name his successor.

Two months after Van Buren was inaugurated as President, the country was hit by hard times that lasted several years. Though the fault was not Van Buren's, the people blamed him because he was President when the hard times came. By 1840 they were ready to vote him and his party out of office.

"Tippecanoe and Tyler too." In 1840 the Whigs nominated General William Henry Harrison, of Ohio, for President. Harrison had never fully expressed his views on the problems of the time. And he had the further advantage of resembling Jackson in several ways. He was a westerner. He had been an Indian fighter and had held his own against the Indians in the Battle of Tippecanoe almost 30 years before. As his running mate the Whigs picked John Tyler, of Virginia, who was expected to attract southern votes.

In the campaign the Whigs appealed to the mass of voters but did not discuss the problems of the day. Harrison

Debate over the tariff. Our artist shows the sectional views on the tariff. Mr. North and Mr. West are building a tariff wall to protect the American factory. Mr. South is opposed to building the wall. Why?

was a retired old gentleman, living in a large, comfortable house on his Ohio estate. A Democratic editor suggested that Harrison really did not want to be President, that he would be happier with a log cabin, a barrel of hard cider, and his pension (salary paid to retired persons). The Whigs jumped to cash in on this slur. It is true, they said, we are the party of log cabins and hard cider. Those are the marks of the plain people, and we are the party of the plain people. The Whigs made the log cabin their campaign symbol. They described Harrison as a man of the people, dressed in homespun and a coonskin cap, living in a humble log cabin, and drinking cider. They sang songs and repeated slogans. "Tippecanoe and Tyler too." "Van, Van is a used-up man."

Farewell, dear Van,
You're not our man;
To guide the ship,
We'll try old Tip.

This kind of campaign was effective, especially since the people were already blaming the Democrats for the hard times they were suffering. Harrison won. The Whigs eagerly gathered to share in the spoils of office. They overran Washington, looking for jobs.

But the Whigs did not enjoy their victory for long. President Harrison, 69 years old, died one month after taking office. John Tyler succeeded him as President. Tyler had been elected by the Whig party, but he refused to support Whig policies. Though they had won the election, the Whigs no longer controlled the presidency and could

BROWN BROS.

John Tyler
1841–1845

BROWN BROS.

James K. Polk
1845–1849

not pass the laws they had planned. Having run on the Whig ticket, Tyler was no longer trusted by the Democrats and was left a man without a party. In 1844 James K. Polk, the Democratic candidate, was elected President.

2 *The Tariff Becomes a Leading Issue*

Behind the candidates and the campaigns were the important problems of the time on which the sections differed. Besides the bank, these were the tariff, the building of roads and canals by the federal government, and the sale of land from the public domain. The people of the North, the South, and the West disagreed on these questions. We can imagine a spokesman for each section expressing his views on each issue.

Disagreement on the tariff

MR. NORTH: We must have a high tariff so that our manufacturing will prosper and grow. Then factory workers will buy farm products and farmers will buy manufactured goods, and the whole country will benefit.

MR. WEST: The tariff raises the cost of manufactured goods that western farmers must buy. But we shall more than make up for it by selling our farm products to city workers. Therefore I favor a high tariff.

MR. SOUTH: I am absolutely opposed to a high tariff. It makes us planters pay more for the manufactured goods we buy. Because of the high tariff England cannot sell us as much manufactured goods as she used to. England buys most of our cotton. If she sells us less manufactured goods, she will buy less cotton from us. The tariff is a way to take money away from southern

MARYLAND HISTORICAL SOCIETY

On the National Road. Notice the heavy traffic. Other main turnpikes were equally congested with stagecoaches, freight wagons, and livestock. The benefits to the North and the West were so great that those sections wanted more improved roads.

planters and give it to northern manufacturers.

Disagreement on internal improvements

MR. NORTH: We need faster and cheaper transportation so that manufactured goods can be shipped to farmers and farm products can be brought to the cities. I believe that the government should build roads and canals.

MR. WEST: Our section of the country is new. We need roads and canals to ship our products to market and to help more settlers come to the West. Since we cannot afford to pay for internal improvements, the federal government must build them for us.

MR. SOUTH: Internal improvements may help the other sections, but we do not need them. We have enough rivers to float our cotton down to seaports. We pay taxes to the federal government. It is unfair for the government to build roads and canals in the North and the West with our money. Let each state pay for its own internal improvements.

Disagreement over public lands

MR. NORTH: The federal government should charge high prices for its western land. If it sells the land for low prices, too many people will emigrate to the West. Not enough workers will be left in the East to man the factories. Manufacturers will have to pay high wages, which will reduce their profits. Some owners may have to close their factories.

MR. WEST: We need new settlers. The more and the sooner they come, the better. A growing West will be of greater benefit to the nation than a few million dollars from land sales. The land belongs to the people, and they should be encouraged to settle on it. I favor low prices for public lands.

MR. SOUTH: We favor high prices for public lands. By charging high prices, the government will obtain a large income and will be able to reduce taxes. Besides, we are not eager to have the Northwest settled rapidly and more free states added to the Union.

North and West vote together. Not all the people in each section supported the same point of view. In the case of the tariff, for example, the people of the North who earned a living from foreign trade (importers, shipowners, sailors, and so on) were opposed to a high tariff because it would cut down the amount of imports. Yet the opinions expressed by Mr. North, Mr. South, and Mr. West were held by most of the people in each section.

No one section had enough votes in Congress to pass the bills it wanted. But the members from the North and the West generally voted together. In that way a law was passed in 1820, under which a person could purchase 80 acres of public land at $1.25 an acre. Thus for $100 a settler could buy a farm. No law was passed for internal improvements, mainly because Presidents Madison, Monroe, and Jackson believed that the federal government had no authority under the Constitution to build internal improvements. Higher tariff laws were passed in 1824 and 1828 (see page 231). The controversy between North and South over the higher tariff threatened to break up the Union.

Eagle, 1830s. This eagle design was printed on cotton cloth made in New England.

NATIONAL GALLERY OF ART, INDEX OF AMERICAN DESIGN

Calhoun proposes nullification. Opposition of the South to the tariff reached a crisis while Jackson was President. Southerners protested against the high rates of the tariff of 1828. Their leader was John C. Calhoun. He called the tariff a sectional law, taxing the South for the benefit of the North. The South did not need to accept such a law, said Calhoun, because it had the right of nullification (nŭl *ĭ* fĭ kā′sh*ŭ*n), which he explained as follows:

The Constitution was an agreement among independent states. They set up a central government with powers that were listed in the Constitution. Each state had the right to decide whether a law passed by Congress came under these powers; in other words, whether it was constitutional. If a state considered a law unconstitutional, it had the right to nullify the law, that is, refuse to allow the law to be enforced within its borders. If the central government tried to enforce the law, the state had the right to secede (sē sēd′), that is, leave the Union.

Calhoun's spokesman in Congress was Senator Robert Y. Hayne, of South Carolina. In a speech in the Senate in January, 1830, he stated the doctrine of nullification. His speech started a famous debate with Daniel Webster, who defended the Union.

Jackson's toast. Calhoun and his friends, in favor of nullification, are at the banquet table. President Jackson, at the head of the table, gets up and offers his toast: "Our Federal Union! It must and shall be preserved!"

Webster appeals for the Union. Webster ranks with Clay and Calhoun as a great statesman of his time. Frail and sickly as a boy, Webster had been excused from doing his share of the hard work on his father's farm. Instead, he was given an education. When he first went to Phillips Exeter Academy in New Hampshire, he was shy and self-conscious because of his country clothes and awkward manners. But by the time he entered Dartmouth College, he had acquired good manners, had learned to wear fashionable clothes, and was quite self-confident. His black hair, flashing black eyes, and dark complexion won him the nickname "Black Dan."

After being graduated from Dartmouth, Webster studied law and opened a law office in Portsmouth, New Hampshire. Later he moved to Boston. He was elected to Congress; and there, representing the interests of New England, he voted for bills favoring shipping and manufacturing. Throughout his life Webster was a strong defender of the Union; and he attacked the doctrine of nullification because it threatened to destroy the Union.

Webster's debate with Hayne continued for two days. Hayne explained and defended the doctrine of nullification. He argued that the federal government was an agreement between the states and could be broken by the states. Webster replied that the federal government was a government of the people, not of states. "It is the people's Constitution," he said, "the people's government, made for the people, made by the people, and answerable to the people." He made a stirring appeal for the Union. He said that the Union was the cause of national prosperity, that every citizen had benefited from living under the Union. Webster ended with a phrase that became a motto for those who opposed nullification: "Liberty

LIBRARY OF CONGRESS

The old Senate. This was the meeting place of the United States Senate until 1860, when the present Senate Chamber was completed. In this room Webster, Hayne, Clay, and Calhoun made their historic speeches on national affairs.

and Union, now and forever, one and inseparable!"*

Webster's speech was reprinted and circulated all over the country. It put into eloquent words the feelings of loyalty and love for the Union that many Americans had in their hearts. In those days children in school spent much of their time memorizing poems and speeches. For many years boys and girls learned by heart the closing paragraphs of Webster's speech and recited them again and again.

Jackson for the Union. Calhoun and his followers did not know how President Jackson stood on nullification, but they believed that he agreed with them. To find out his views, they arranged a grand dinner on April 13, 1830, as a celebration of Jefferson's birthday. Many toasts were given, all of them approving nullification. Finally Jackson arose and, looking Calhoun straight in the eye, gave his toast: "Our Federal Union! It must and shall be preserved!" There was no mistaking where Jackson stood. He was against nullification and for the Union. And thus the question of the tariff and nullification stood for two years.

* Years later this famous statement was adopted by North Dakota as its state motto.

Compromise on the tariff. In 1832 another tariff was passed. It lowered some of the duties imposed by the law of 1828, but it was still a protective tariff. Leaders in South Carolina took action. They met in a convention, which declared that the tariff laws of 1828 and 1832 should not be enforced within the borders of the state. They warned that, if the federal government attempted to collect duties by force, South Carolina would secede from the Union.

The doctrine of nullification and the right of secession (sē sĕsh′ŭn) were not brought to the final test at this time. South Carolina stood alone. The other states condemned its action. President Jackson announced that he would enforce the laws of the United States in every state. At the same time he pleaded with the people of South Carolina not to rebel against their government. Meanwhile Henry Clay was busy drawing up a compromise tariff bill, under which the rates were to be gradually reduced. It was accepted by leaders of both sides and was passed. South Carolina withdrew the nullification statement. It had won a lower tariff but at the same time had in effect admitted that the tariff was constitutional. Most important, the use of force had been avoided through compromise.

3 *The Problem of Slavery Drives North and South Apart*

At the same time that the political leaders were arguing about the bank, the tariff, and other matters, the people of the North and the South were drifting further and further apart over the issue of slavery. While Monroe was President (see page 217), the problem of slavery came up when Missouri asked to be admitted into the Union as a state. Missouri's application brought up the question: is slavery to be permitted in all parts of the Louisiana Purchase?

The Missouri Compromise. By 1819 the North had a much larger population than the South. In the House of Representatives there were 105 members from the North as against 85 from the South. (Do you remember how the number of Representatives from each state is determined? See Article I of the Constitution, pages 680–681.) Southerners feared that, if the northerners also won control of the Senate, they would pass laws harmful to the South. They might even abolish slavery. To protect itself, the South insisted on having as many Senators as the North. Since each state has two Senators, there had to be as many states permitting slavery as there were states forbidding slavery; in other words, as many slave states as free states.

Until 1819 the balance was kept. Each time a free state was admitted, a slave state was also admitted. For the future, if the Louisiana Purchase were opened to slavery, the South might have more votes in the Senate; if it were closed to slavery, the North would surely have more votes in the Senate. Some southerners threatened that, unless part of the territory west of the Mississippi were opened to slavery, their states would secede.

The dispute was settled by a compromise. Maine was admitted as a free state; Missouri, as a slave state. In the rest of the Louisiana Purchase, slavery was to be permitted only south of the southern boundary (36°30′) of Missouri. (See the map on page 693.) All territory north of that line was to remain free. That agreement was the Missouri Compromise.

Both sides were grateful that the Missouri Compromise had settled the slavery question for the time being. Some people even thought that the dispute would remain settled forever. But not everyone was so hopeful. Thomas Jefferson, now an old man watching events from his Virginia estate, wrote that the dispute over slavery frightened him "like a fire bell in the night." He predicted that the quarrel over slavery might destroy the Union.

The abolitionists. In the 1830s and 1840s the slavery issue pushed the North and the South further apart. A group of northern church leaders began to speak of slavery as a sin and to call upon the nation to wipe it out. These people were called abolitionists (ăb ȯ lĭsh′*ŭ*n ĭsts) because they wanted to end, or abolish, slavery. The abolitionists did not rest from their war against slavery. They preached against it. They printed newspapers and pamphlets urging its abolition and sent copies to all parts of the country, including the South.

Most people in the South, of course, feared and hated the abolitionists. They were afraid that abolitionist newspapers and pamphlets would get into the hands of slaves and would encourage them to rise up against their masters. Southern leaders demanded that such publications be kept out of the mails. They called upon the northern states to pass laws against antislavery propaganda of any kind.

In the North the abolitionists were a small minority. Many northerners did not like slavery but were willing to let the southern states keep it. They were satisfied to prevent it from spreading further, believing that if this were done it would gradually die out. Most northerners regarded the abolitionists as radicals whose activities might bring on war within the Union. Northern mobs broke up abolitionist meetings. They threw mud and stones at abolitionist speakers. In 1837 mobs in Illinois destroyed, one after the other, four new presses bought by Elijah Lovejoy, abolitionist editor, and finally killed him. In Philadelphia a hall built for abolitionist meetings was burned down.

Sectional bitterness increases. Bitterness between the North and the South was increased by the success of some northerners in helping runaway slaves gain their freedom. The Constitution required that such fugitives (fū′j*ĭ* tĭvz) be returned to their masters. There was a federal law, called the Fugitive Slave Law, under which anyone who was found guilty of aiding a runaway slave to escape could be fined as much as $500.

The Underground Railroad. But some northerners persisted in aiding the fugitive slaves. Because of the law they had to act secretly. They had se-

The Capitol, 1840. The building shown is the central part of our present Capitol. It was enlarged in the 1850s, and the great dome we know today was built in the 1860s.

LIBRARY OF CONGRESS

cret signals and passwords. Their organization was called the Underground Railroad. Houses where the Negroes were concealed were called stations, and the men who moved them from place to place were called conductors.

A fugitive usually arrived at a station at night. He was fed and was given new clothes if necessary. Then he was hidden in the cellar, in the hayloft, or in the woods until the time came to move him on to the next station. Conductors transported the runaways in closed carriages or in farm wagons covered with hay or other produce. Once 28 fugitives were carried across Ohio in broad daylight in a line of carriages moving like a funeral procession.

The routes of the Underground Railroad zigzagged across the northern states, but they always pointed north. Some of the Negroes settled in the northern states, but most of them crossed the border into Canada where they were absolutely safe in their freedom. Some Negroes who had thus escaped from slavery risked recapture and even death by going back to the South to help other slaves escape.

Bitterness increases. Southern slaveholders were bitter against the Underground Railroad. Their rights under the law were being violated. They were losing large sums of money. The success of some fugitives in winning freedom encouraged other slaves to run away. The southerners demanded that the Fugitive Slave Law be made more severe and that it be enforced. But enforcement of the law turned more people against slavery and against the South. Many northerners thought little about slavery because they had never seen an actual slave. But they were shocked when, as sometimes happened, they saw a man who had lived among them turned over to an owner like a piece of property. After seeing such incidents, they were opposed to slavery ever after. Many times a crowd in a northern city rescued a runaway Negro from the sheriff and sent him off to freedom on the Underground Railroad. Thus efforts to enforce the Fugitive Slave Law strengthened the bad feeling between North and South.

Tense moment. An unwelcome visitor calls at a home where two runaway slaves are being hidden between trips on the Underground Railroad. What would happen to the slaves if they were discovered? What would happen to the owner of the home?

Parties take no stand. In the 1830s and 1840s the two big political parties, the Democrats and the Whigs, avoided taking sides on the slavery issue. Both had followers in the North and in the South. If they opposed slavery, they would lose votes in the South. If they favored slavery, they would lose votes in the North. Therefore they took no stand on the issue.

Leaders who were concerned for the Union had a deeper reason for avoiding the issue. As long as the parties were national parties, drawing their strength from both sections, North and South, they helped tie the country together. But if the parties split on the slavery issue and one became the northern party and the other the southern party, the Union would be further weakened.

Summary

The spirit of national unity that came out of the War of 1812 soon disappeared. The sections wanted different laws, and many political leaders represented their sections first and the nation second. In the contests between Democrats and Whigs, the two new political parties, the Democrats generally won. The outstanding leader in the 1830s was Andrew Jackson.

Each section—North, South, and West—wanted something different from the government, usually at the expense of the other sections. These clashing interests were due mainly to the different ways the people earned a living.

In the North, manufacturing was becoming important; therefore the North favored a high tariff. Southerners imported their manufactured goods; therefore the South wanted a low tariff.

The West needed roads and canals to ship its produce and therefore favored internal improvements. The South had plenty of rivers for transportation and opposed internal improvements.

The West desired more settlers and therefore wanted the public domain sold at low prices. The North wanted people to stay east and work in the factories; therefore the North opposed low prices for public lands.

The disagreement over slavery, too, pushed the North and the South wider and wider apart. The abolitionists demanded that slavery be wiped out at once. The South insisted that the northern states must put a stop to abolitionist propaganda. Southerners also demanded the return of all fugitive slaves. When the South tried to tell the North what to do, more northerners turned against the South and slavery.

Many of the disputes between the sections, including those over tariff and slavery, were settled for the time being by compromises that gave something to each section.

For a Quick Review

1. Compare the four great sectional leaders—Jackson, Clay, Webster, and Calhoun—as to background, education, abilities, and ambitions.

2. What was the attitude of Americans in the North and in the South toward slavery in 1820? What did Jefferson mean by saying that debates over the Missouri Compromise were like "a fire bell in the night"?

3. How did sectionalism show itself in the elections of 1824 and 1828?

4. What were the steps through which an argument over tariff turned into an argument over nullification and secession?

5. On what important questions, besides the tariff, did the sections disagree in the period from 1820 to 1850? What view did each section take on each question?

6. How and why were the campaign methods of 1840 different from those of 1800?

Learning to Study More Easily

LEARNING THE MEANING OF NEW WORDS

In this chapter as well as in earlier ones, you have found words that are new to you or words that you do not clearly understand—for example, franchise, suffrage, nullification, and secession. Some of these words you can find easily in the dictionary, as you know. Sometimes, however, you will find that the authors of this book have defined a word for you the first time they use it. Their definition is made full enough to help you understand the discussion without stopping to consult the dictionary. You will find such definitions in many of the books you read.

Sometimes you can understand the meaning of a word by the way it is used. When you find a new word, read through the entire paragraph in which it is used, looking for a clue to its meaning. This is called getting the meaning from context. You will save time when you can get the meaning of new words by this method.

When you look in a dictionary for the meaning of a word, you often find that two or more meanings are given. In order to choose the one that applies, you must notice the way the word is used in the paragraph you are reading. For example, in this chapter you read that Andrew Jackson rose and "gave his toast." Look up the word "toast" in the dictionary. Why must you know how the word was used in order to choose the right meaning?

Sometimes, as you read, you find a phrase that you cannot locate easily—states' rights or sectional law, for example. Many phrases of this sort are not in the dictionary because they are not single words and because they have come to have a special meaning for one subject and are used only in connection with that subject. You may be able to find articles about them in an encyclopedia and obtain a definition that way. Often you can get the meaning from the sense of the passage in which the phrase appears.

Test your understanding of some important words and phrases by working out the following exercises, writing your answers on an answer sheet in your notebook. Give your answers first without consulting dictionary or textbook, then look up any word about which you are uncertain.

1. Which means the opposite of "to secede": (*a*) to leave, (*b*) to join, (*c*) to remain, (*d*) to move ahead?
2. A tariff is (*a*) a tax on imported goods, (*b*) an income tax, (*c*) the price of admission to a movie, (*d*) a kind of cart used to transport cotton.
3. A controversy is (*a*) a panel discussion, (*b*) a meeting of a debating society, (*c*) a disagreement or argument, (*d*) a speech of approval.
4. The opposite of "to veto" is (*a*) to disagree, (*b*) to stay at home, (*c*) to approve, (*d*) to go away.
5. A fugitive is a person who (*a*) is trying to escape, (*b*) refuses to talk with his friends, (*c*) helps an innocent person escape arrest, (*d*) leaves his country.
6. When we speak of the public domain, we mean (*a*) the government buildings in Washington, (*b*) the money collected through taxes, (*c*) the land owned by the government, (*d*) the region affected by the Missouri Compromise.

15 *West to the Pacific*

Once a man who had spent many years studying the history of our nation was asked if he could give one word that would describe the period between the election of John Quincy Adams (1824) and the election of Abraham Lincoln (1860). He thought, and then said, "Of course no single word can really describe all the events that happened in the United States during those 36 years, but if I must use just one word, that word will be *expansion.*" As you read the following chapter, you will easily see why he chose that word. The period from John Quincy Adams to Lincoln was the period of the Texas Revolution, the Oregon Trail, the California gold rush. It was a time when the restless, hopeful pioneers pushed west across the plains, long labeled the great American desert, to seek their fortune on the Pacific coast. Some of them sang to the tune of "Oh, Susanna":

California,
You're the land for me;
There's plenty of gold, so I been told,
In Cali-for-ny-ee.

Europeans, too, traveled west across the Atlantic to seek their fortune in the United States. Some of them stopped in eastern states, where they worked in factories or helped build canals and railroads. Some of them continued their journey until they found land in the West where they could settle. Many immigrants worked hard and lived happily. They were building our nation, whether they settled new lands or helped develop the older sections. They helped make the years from John Quincy Adams to Lincoln a period of expansion.

1 *The Frontier Reaches Arkansas and Iowa*

There was one group in the United States that had little share in the hope of the Oregon settler, the eagerness of the California gold seeker, or the ambition of the immigrant from Europe. The problem of this group can be seen in an old story about the Indians and the whites.

An Indian once sat down on a log next to a white man and pushed up against him. The white man, feeling crowded, moved over and the Indian moved with him. When the white man moved a second time, the Indian crowded up to him again. When the white man reached the end of the log with the Indian beside him, he asked the Indian, "Why are you pushing me off the log?" The Indian replied, "Just so, white man and Indian. White man take more and more Indian land, push Indian out. Pretty soon no more land. What poor Indian do then?"

The Indians are moved west of the Mississippi. The Indian in the story had good reason for complaining. Pioneers continually settled on Indian land. You read on page 210 of the conflict between whites and Indians in the Old Northwest. That was one example of the clashes between the settlers and the Indians. To prevent bloodshed, the federal government stepped in and bought the land from the Indians. But the settlers moved so fast that the government was unable to keep up with them. Finally the government decided to clear all Indians out of the territory east of the Mississippi and settle them on the so-called great American desert. The Indians were unwilling, but the government forced them to give up their lands and accept new ones west of Missouri and Arkansas. Since these new lands were to be reserved for the Indians forever, they came to be called reservations. The Indians were assured that the reservations would be their permanent homes. By 1845 almost all Indians had been removed from the territory east of the Mississippi.

Settlers east and west of the Mississippi. As fast as the Indians moved out, white settlers moved in. Remember how rapidly the Old Northwest and the Old Southwest were being settled in the early 1800s? (See pages 210–212.) Settlement continued in the 1830s and the 1840s on a larger scale.

In the South cotton planters filled in the open spaces in Georgia, Alabama, and Mississippi. From Mississippi many crossed over into Arkansas and established plantations. Thus Arkansas became a cotton-planting, slave-owning territory. It was admitted as a state in 1836, making a pair with the free state of Michigan, which was admitted to the Union at the same time.

Settlers streamed into the Northwest from New England and the middle

Indian educator. Sequoyah, a Cherokee Indian, created an alphabet for the Cherokee language, making it possible for many Indians to learn to read and write. He also taught his people better ways of farming.

LIBRARY OF CONGRESS

PUBLIC BUILDINGS ADMINISTRATION

Moving west in Arkansas. A family moving west in a Conestoga wagon is about to cross the river on a ferry. Notice the steamboats on the river and the homes and stores in the town. Many pioneers of the 1830s and 1840s had an easier time of it than pioneers of the 1790s.

states. They were joined by restless pioneers who left their new homes in western New York, western Pennsylvania, and Ohio for another chance to achieve success farther west.

Most of the early settlers in Indiana and Illinois came, as we have seen, from the South. They had crossed the Ohio River and settled in the southern parts of the two states. Now the northern and central parts were settled by people from the North. Soon there were more northerners than southerners in these states.

Roads across Illinois led to the Mississippi River. In the 1830s, after the Indians had begun giving up their lands just west of the river, emigrants moved into Iowa in large numbers. Some of the settlers came in large groups. From 10 to 30 families formed one company. They traveled in farm carts and in Conestoga wagons. The pace was set by the livestock that was being driven to the new home.

Most of the settlers, however, came as single families. As on earlier frontiers, many a young man came alone to make a clearing, build a cabin, and grow a crop. Then, with a living assured, he went east again to marry and bring his wife back to the new home.

Frontier conditions disappear rapidly. The pioneers of the Mississippi Valley suffered the same hardships that earlier pioneers had suffered. However, they were better off than those of earlier decades, chiefly because of improved transportation. They traveled to their new homes on canalboats and steamboats or over improved roads. They could take with them more of the necessities and comforts of life, like clothing, furniture, and farm tools, than the first settlers in Kentucky and Ohio had been able to bring. And when they had settled down, merchants soon brought more of the same things to them.

Furthermore, better transportation made travel easier, so that settlers came in large numbers and settled new areas more rapidly. Pioneers in the 1830s and 1840s were not isolated for long. The

LIBRARY OF CONGRESS

Chicago in 1833. Chicago was a small settlement in 1833. However, when steamboats and, later, railroads brought settlers and industries, the city grew by leaps and bounds. Within thirty years it was a leading transportation center in the West. How does Chicago rank among the cities of the United States today?

land was settled so rapidly that the early frontier conditions lasted but a few years.

2 *The United States Acquires the Great Southwest*

You will remember that Spanish missionaries built missions in Texas to teach Christianity and the Spanish way of life to the Indians (see page 19). Soldiers were stationed in camps near the missions to protect them from hostile Indians, and around these camps villages grew up. The total Spanish population of Texas was very small.

In the treaty by which the United States acquired Florida in 1819, it had given up the claim that Texas was part of the Louisiana Purchase (see page 219). But the westward push of the restless, hopeful American pioneers could not be stopped by an imaginary line fixed in a treaty. The treaty of 1819 was hardly signed before plans were under way for settlers from the United States to go into Texas.

American settlers in Texas. In 1821 a Missourian named Moses Austin signed a contract with the Spanish rulers of Mexico. He agreed to settle 300 families in Texas, and in return was to receive large grants of land. Moses Austin died, and his son Stephen took over the contract. By this time Mexico had won its independence from Spain. Its leaders set up a federal government, so that Mexico, somewhat like the United States, was made up of states. Texas became part of a state that included what is now northern Mexico.

The new Mexican government proved to be very unstable. One general after another overthrew his predecessor and seized control of the country. With each government Stephen Austin had to go through the trouble of having his contract renewed. One government kept him in prison in Mexico City for a year and a half.

Many Americans came to Texas, attracted by generous offers of land. Each settler was entitled to more than 4,000 acres of land practically free. By

Republic of Texas. The territory between the Nueces River and the Rio Grande was disputed between Mexico and Texas. How long did the Lone-Star Republic remain independent?

1830 there were about 20,000 people in Texas, more than had settled there in 300 years of Spanish rule. Most of the settlers came from the southern states. They raised food crops and cotton. Some brought slaves with them. The principal settlements were in East Texas, close to the United States border.

When Mexican leaders found time between revolutions to see what was happening in Texas, they were afraid that Mexico was in danger of losing that region to the United States. The United States government strengthened that fear by offering to buy Texas. In an effort to save Texas, Mexico passed a law in 1830 prohibiting any more Americans from settling there. Another law prohibited the importation of slaves, and another put a high tariff on goods imported into Texas.

These laws made the American settlers angry, even though the Mexican government was too weak to enforce them. But the Texans probably would have clashed with the Mexican government even if these laws had not been passed. It is true that all settlers promised to be loyal to Mexico. But their ideas of government were so different that it would have been difficult for them to keep that promise. The settlers from the United States were accustomed to the personal rights guaranteed by the Bill of Rights, such as religious liberty and trial by jury. The Mexican government did not recognize all these rights. The Texans were used to criticizing their government and standing up for what they believed to be their rights. In Mexico, as a rule, a few persons ran the government and ordinary people were expected to obey without question.

Texas wins independence. In 1833 a Mexican general named Santa Anna became president of Mexico. The Texans asked him to repeal the law keeping out American settlers and to make

Texas a separate Mexican state. Instead, Santa Anna did away with all state governments and sent soldiers into Texas to enforce the laws. In the last three months of 1835 groups of Texans took up arms and drove the Mexican soldiers out of Texas. They said that they were fighting for their rights as citizens of Mexico and against the dictator Santa Anna. With an army of more than 6,000 men, Santa Anna set out to crush this rebellion against him.

The Alamo. Santa Anna led his army first to occupy San Antonio. In that city there were about 150 Texan soldiers commanded by Colonel W. B. Travis. They had plenty of time to retreat, but they believed that, if San Antonio fell, all Texas would fall. Instead of retreating, they shut themselves up in the ruins of an old mission called the Alamo, determined to defend Texas with their lives.

The Mexican army occupied San Antonio on February 23, 1836, and surrounded the Alamo. Colonel Travis managed to send out several messages appealing for help. You can read the most famous of these messages on page 290. Though it meant almost certain death, 32 Texans made their way through the Mexican lines on March 1 to join the defenders of the Alamo.

With an army of more than 5,000, Santa Anna made the final attack on the Alamo in the early morning of March 6. After ten days of siege, the small band of Texans were weary from constant fighting. Yet three times they drove back the solid columns of Mexican soldiers. On the fourth try the Mexicans scaled the walls of the Alamo and overran the courtyard. The Texans retreated into the small buildings and kept on fighting. They fell back from room to room, each man fighting for himself with rifle, pistol, club—with bare hands. There were fewer than 200 Texans, but before they died they had killed or wounded about 1,500 Mexicans. Ever since that day Texans have revered the Alamo as the shrine of Texan liberty.

Among those who fell in that memorable battle were James Bowie and David Crockett. Bowie was a famous frontiersman. The story is told that, as a young man in Louisiana, he used to rope alligators and ride them. He was especially famous for his hunting knife with a curved point. Crockett was another famous backwoodsman. He was popular for his humor and his good common sense. After only six months of schooling, he had educated himself; but he admitted that he never let grammar and spelling get in his way when he wanted to say something. Before coming to Texas he had served as congressman from Tennessee.

Texas independent. After Santa Anna invaded Texas, the Texans decided that they could no longer remain a part of Mexico. On March 2 their representatives wrote a declaration of independence. They announced to the world that Texas was a free and independent nation. They also wrote a constitution and appointed Sam Houston commander in chief of the Texan army.

After the fall of the Alamo, Houston led his small army in a long retreat. Finally his army met the Mexicans in the Battle of San Jacinto, April 21, 1836. Houston attacked in the afternoon when the Mexicans were taking their siesta. He rallied his men with the cry, "Remember the Alamo!" In 20 minutes 800 Texans defeated twice as many Mexicans. Santa Anna was taken prisoner. Before he was released, he ordered the remaining Mexican forces to return to Mexico.

By that one battle Texas won its independence, though Mexico did not admit it for several years. Six months after San Jacinto, Sam Houston was inaugurated as President of the Republic of Texas. Later the Texan congress approved a flag: a single white star on a red, white, and blue banner. Texas was called the "Lone-Star Republic."

Annexation of Texas brings war with Mexico. During the Texas Revolution the United States government was officially neutral, not helping either side. But many individual citizens of the United States sent money to help Texas win independence, and hundreds of volunteers joined the fighting.

After they had won independence from Mexico, the people of Texas wanted to join the United States. The South was eager to admit them. But many people in the North opposed annexation because it would mean more territory in which slavery could expand. If Texas were admitted to the Union as one or more states, it would increase the power of the South in Congress. Furthermore, since Mexico had not recognized the independence of Texas, the United States could annex Texas only at the cost of a war with Mexico. Not until December 29, 1845, was Texas admitted into the Union.

As soon as Texas was annexed, both the United States and Mexico began

Commandancy of the Alamo,
Bexar, Feby. 24th, 1836.

To the people of Texas and All Americans in the world—

Fellow Citizens and Compatriots: I am besieged with a thousand or more of the Mexicans under Santa Anna. I have sustained a continual Bombardment and cannonade for 24 hours and have not lost a man. The enemy has demanded a surrender at discretion, otherwise, the garrison are to be put to the sword, if the fort is taken. I have answered this demand with a cannon shot, and our flag still waves proudly from the walls. I shall never surrender or retreat. Then, I call upon you in the name of Liberty, of patriotism, and every thing dear to the American character, to come to our aid with all dispatch. The enemy is receiving reinforcements daily and will no doubt increase to three or four thousand in four or five days. If this call is neglected, I am determined to sustain myself as long as possible and die like a soldier who never forgets what is due his own honor and that of his country. VICTORY or DEATH.

William Barret Travis
Lt. Col. Comdt.

P.S.

The Lord is on our side. When the enemy appeared in sight we had not three bushels of corn. We have since found in deserted houses 80 to 90 bushels and got into the walls 20 or 30 head of Beeves.

Travis

¶ This is the famous message that Colonel Travis sent from the Alamo, pleading for help and announcing his determination to hold the Alamo at any cost. Bexar was the Mexican name for San Antonio.

PUBLIC BUILDINGS ADMINISTRATION

Texas wealth. This mural suggests the variety of resources that have made Texas one of the wealthiest states in the Union. How has each of the resources shown here been important in the development of Texas?

preparing for war. The war started as a result of a border incident. Mexico insisted that the Nueces (nū̇ ā′sĕs) River was the boundary of Texas, while the United States supported the Texan claim that the Rio Grande (rē′ō grănd′) was the border. By finding these rivers on the map on page 288, you can see the territory that was claimed by both countries.

On April 25, 1846, a Mexican force crossed the Rio Grande and attacked an American patrol. As soon as he received the news of this clash, President Polk sent a message to Congress announcing that Mexico had "shed American blood upon American soil" and asking Congress to declare that war with Mexico existed. The declaration was made over serious opposition. In the eyes of New England and of most members of the Whig party, it was an unnecessary and unjust war waged against a weak neighbor to conquer its territory and turn the land over to slaveowners.

The United States annexes the Southwest and California. Although many people expected a close contest, it turned out to be not much of a war. California was taken with almost no opposition. (See the map on page 292.) In northern Mexico an army commanded by General Zachary Taylor defeated a Mexican army in the Battle of Buena Vista (bwā′nä vēs′tä). A month later General Winfield Scott and his army landed at Veracruz and in two weeks occupied Mexico City.

The Mexican Cession. The United States and Mexico signed a treaty and the war was over. Mexico ceded (sēd′ĕd)—that is, gave up, or transferred—Texas, California, Arizona, and New Mexico to the United States. In return the United States paid Mexico 15 million dollars for this territory, which was called the Mexican Cession.

The Gadsden Purchase. A few years later the United States paid Mexico 10 million dollars for another strip of land, now the southern part of New Mexico and Arizona. The land was needed for the route of a southern transcontinental railroad. It was called the Gadsden Purchase after the man

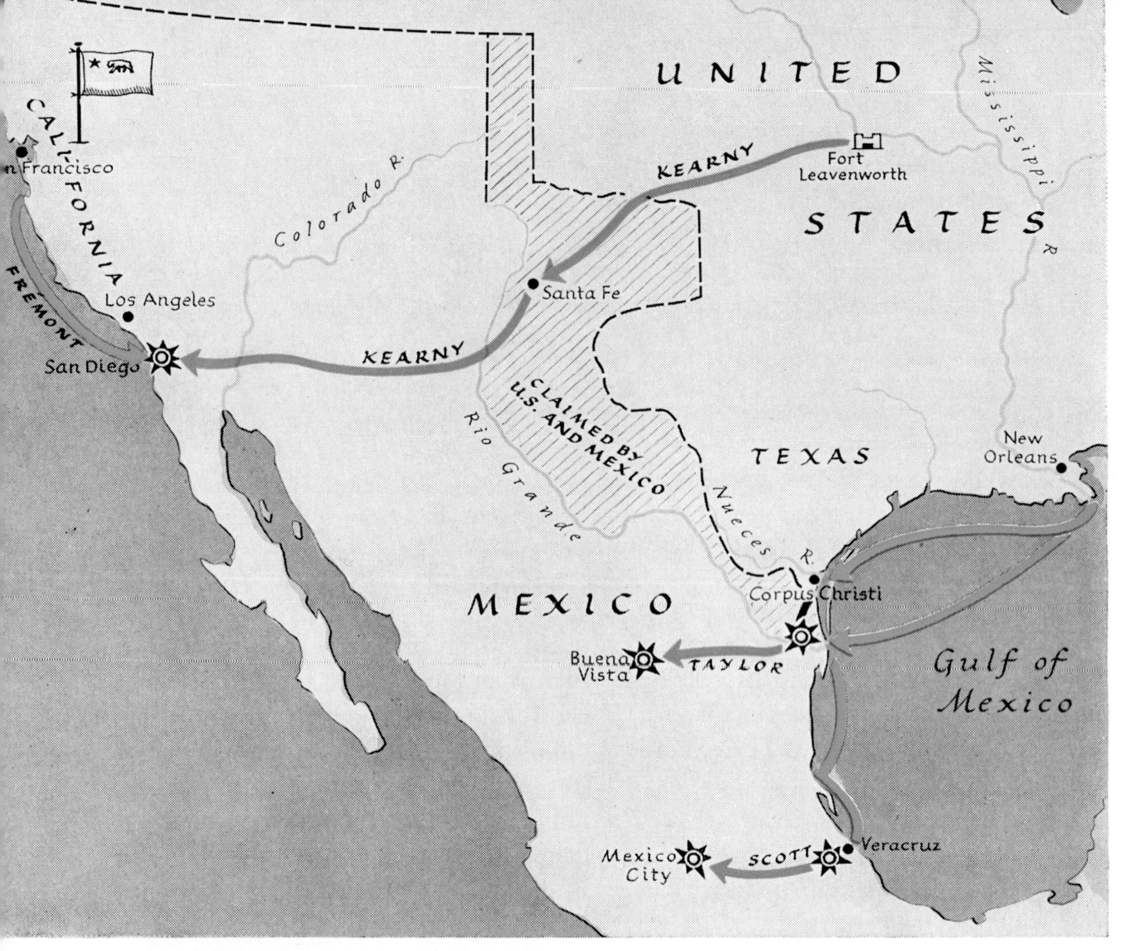

War with Mexico. This map shows the three principal campaigns of the Mexican War. Two were led by Generals Zachary Taylor and Winfield Scott. Colonel Stephen Kearny captured Santa Fe and pushed on to California. He and Captain John C. Frémont soon controlled California.

who arranged the treaty. With this purchase the United States reached its present continental boundaries. Using the map on page 293, review the story of our country's territorial growth.

The annexation of the huge territory from Texas to California aroused bitterness toward the United States in all the Spanish-American countries. They were afraid that the United States would use its growing strength to control their affairs—and even to take their land. This suspicion and distrust of the United States has continued until our own time, as you will see in later chapters.

3 *American Pioneers Settle Oregon*

While some pioneers settled in Texas, others crossed the great American desert to Oregon. Oregon was the name of the region extending from California to Alaska and from the Rocky Mountains to the Pacific Ocean. Both Great Britain and the United

States claimed the area. A New Englander, Captain Robert Gray, discovered the Columbia River in 1792, and Lewis and Clark explored the land in 1804–1805. In the early years British and American businessmen competed for the valuable fur trade of Oregon. The British won control of the trade and of the Indians. In 1818, as we have seen, the two governments agreed to keep the region open to settlers from both countries. (See page 218.)

Trappers and missionaries open a trail to Oregon. During the 1820s few people in the United States were interested in Oregon. They thought of the Rocky Mountains as the western boundary of their country. They believed that the Rocky Mountains were impassable. But fur traders and trappers proved that the mountains could be crossed. Traders, starting from St. Louis, went farther and farther into the mountains. One of them discovered South Pass in southwestern Wyoming. With an easy and gradual approach, South Pass crosses the continental divide that separates the rivers that flow to the Atlantic by way of the Gulf of Mexico from those that flow to the Pacific. At first only trappers on foot traveled over South Pass, but in 1832 a wagon train carrying supplies for the traders was driven over it.

In 1833 an American religious magazine published a story about four Indians from Oregon who came to the home of General William Clark in St. Louis and asked for a Bible. According to the story, they said that they wanted to learn the right way to worship the Great Spirit. The story inspired several young men to go out to Oregon and establish missions among the Indians. In 1836 a missionary named Marcus Whitman and his wife Narcissa made the long trip with a company of fur traders. Narcissa Whitman was the first white woman to go over South Pass.

So it was that fur traders and missionaries proved that the great American desert and the Rocky Mountains could be crossed. They opened up a route, more than 2,000 miles long, from Missouri to Oregon. We call that route the Oregon Trail. You can follow it on the map on page 295.

Settlers follow the long trail to Oregon. Reports brought back by the fur

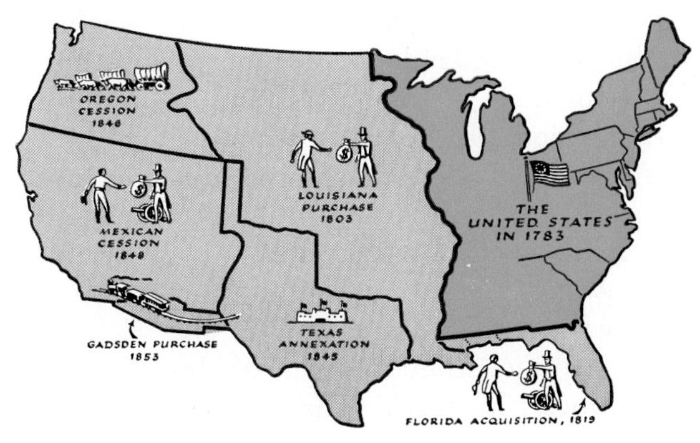

The United States reaches its continental limits. Review the steps in the territorial growth of our nation, explaining the circumstances under which each addition was made. The figures on the map furnish clues about the events in each case.

OREGON STATE HIGHWAY COMMISSION

Welcome to Oregon. Mrs. Marcus Whitman and Mrs. Henry H. Spalding, the first white women to go through South Pass, are welcomed by Dr. John McLaughlin. Though head of the British fur traders in Oregon, McLaughlin helped early American settlers.

On the Road to Oregon

August 3. Came to Fort Hall this morning. Was much cheered with a view of the fort. Anything that looks like a house makes us glad. Were hospitably entertained by Captain Wyeth from Boston, whom we saw at the Rendezvous, on his way to the East. Our dinner consisted of dry buffalo meat, turnips, and fried bread, which was a luxury. Mountain bread is simply coarse flour mixed with water and fried or roasted in buffalo grease. To one who has had nothing but meat for a long time, this relishes very well.

¶ Narcissa Whitman accompanied her missionary husband to Oregon in 1836. This is one of the entries describing the difficult journey that she wrote in her journal.

traders and the missionaries described Oregon as a land of fertile soil and mild climate, of inexhaustible furs and fish and timber. These reports aroused the interest of people all over the United States. Many farmers in the Mississippi Valley who were struggling for a living decided to try again in Oregon. They sold their farms, gathered up their families and furniture in big wagons, herded the livestock, and set out on a 2,300-mile journey to find new homes.

Emigration to Oregon began on a small scale. In 1841, 70 people emigrated; in 1842, 120. In 1843, 1,000 persons followed the Oregon Trail.

Organizing the caravan. Emigrants gathered for the journey early in the spring at the frontier town of Independence, Missouri. The caravan started out when the grass on the prairie was tall enough for the livestock to eat. Horses and oxen hauled the wagons, the oxen setting the 15-mile-a-day pace for the entire train. After a few days the travelers chose a captain, and he appointed assistants to command sections of the caravan. The captain set the time to get rolling in the morning, to stop at noon, and to camp for the night.

After supper came the time for visiting and a bit of fun. Young people danced lively square dances to the music of a fiddle or an accordion. When there were not enough girls to provide partners for all the men, some of the men tied handkerchiefs around their left arms as a sign that they were taking the place of girls in the dance.

Wherever there seemed to be any

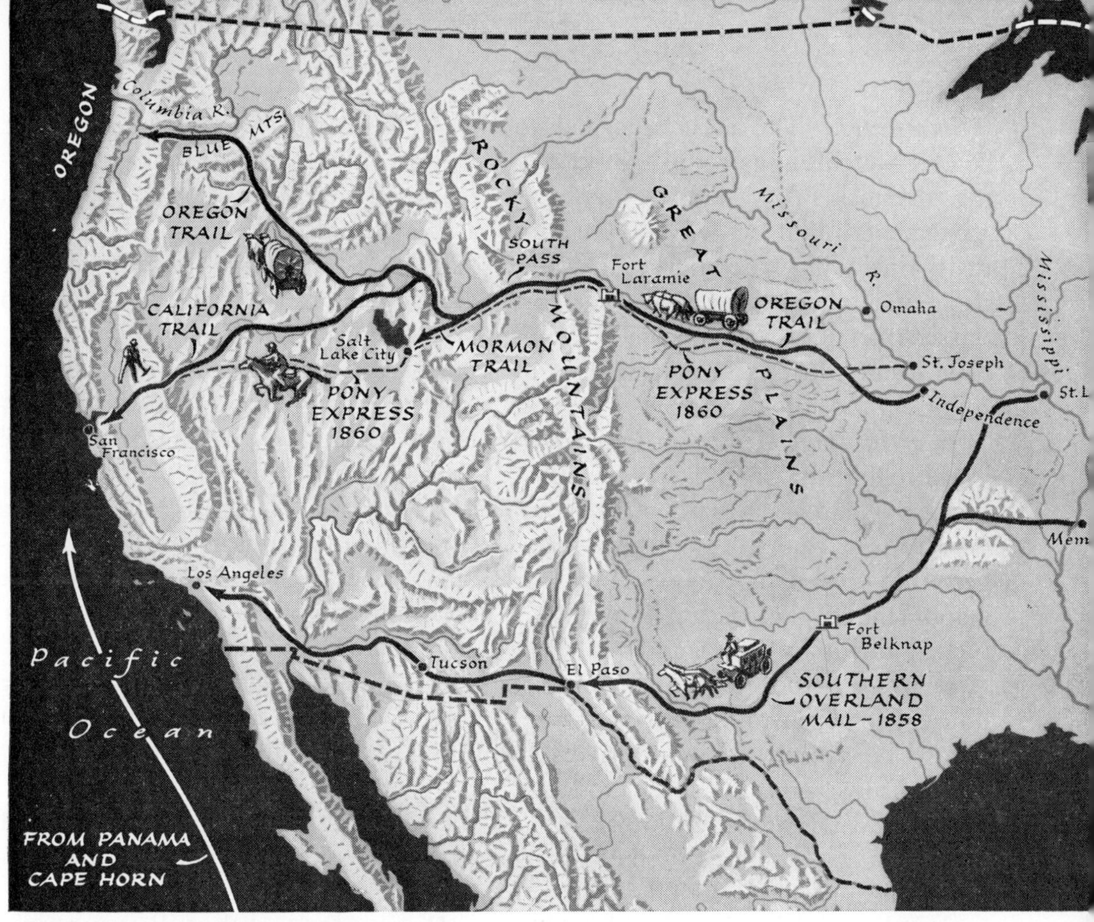

Moving west across the Great Plains. On this map you can follow the story of the Oregon migration, the California gold rush, the overland mail, and the pony express. How did the geography of western United States affect each of these?

danger of Indian attack, the captain ordered the wagons placed close together in a circle for night camp. Sometimes the travelers drove the cattle inside the circle for safety. They put out all campfires, except one for the men who stood guard.

Breaking camp. At dawn there was a general scurrying around to get the wagons ready for travel and to hitch up the oxen. At a signal the train started, each wagon falling into its place in line. Every morning the leading wagon of the day before fell back to the rear. In this way each family got its share of the dust.

Dangers and hardships of the trail. The trail brought many annoyances and dangers. Even friendly Indians could be nuisances, hanging around the wagons for days on end, begging for food, clothing, and trinkets. Afraid to offend them lest they steal the horses, the emigrants gave the Indians presents. The Indians sometimes did not understand the uses of the white man's inventions. The story is told of one Indian who was entranced by the beauty and magic of an umbrella. He carried it about with him all the time, opening it in the sun but carefully covering it with his blanket in the rain.

Stampedes. The emigrants had to be ever watchful against a stampede of the livestock. Any sudden noise or movement might set off all the animals, including the normally calm oxen, on a wild, bellowing chase across the countryside. When such a stampede occurred, it took several days to round up the animals.

River fording. River fording (driving through a river in a fairly shallow part) was another hazard of the journey. Some rivers were especially dangerous to cross. If a wagon stopped for a moment in the water, it might be sucked down by quicksand or swept away by the strong current. It was not unusual for oxen to be drowned, wagons to be overturned, and drivers to lose their lives on some of the crossings.

Disease. Disease often attacked the emigrants en route. In some years many died of cholera. The survivors buried the dead by the wayside. After a hundred years some of the graves still mark the trail.

Prairie storms. For about 450 miles through parts of Kansas and Nebraska the trail crossed the treeless prairie. The wagons rode over the rolling hillocks, up and down, up and down, without a change in the landscape. Only sudden prairie storms broke the monotony, sending down torrents of rain and hail and streaks of lightning and leaving the entire train wet and cold.

Sandy plains. After the prairie came the flat plains, where the going was tough. On sandy stretches wheels might sink in the sand to the hubs; feet might sink to the ankles. Here the emigrants began to lighten their loads by throwing out the heaviest pieces like stoves, plows, and furniture. The remains of these discards can still be seen along the old trail.

It was a relief to get to Fort Laramie (lăr′*ȧ* mĭ), a fur-trading station in present-day Wyoming. Here the emigrants enjoyed a layover for a day or two, repairing wagons and shoeing animals, sewing and baking, resting and visiting one another.

Mountains. West of Fort Laramie the emigrants came to the first mountains. The oxen strained to pull the creaking wagons up the steep slopes. For the downgrades the drivers chained the rear wheels of wagons to brake them. Where the mountainsides went straight down, they lowered the wagons with ropes. To lighten the loads, the emigrants threw away more of their possessions—blankets, dishes, bags of food.

Desert. Beyond the hills came long, long stretches of desert with scorching sand that blistered the feet. Dust covered everything and filled mouths and noses. Animals that drank the water of the alkali (ăl′k*ȧ* lī) lakes were poisoned and died. Fortunately, creeks and springs provided fresh water, and between the clumps of sagebrush was the short buffalo grass on which the livestock could feed.

Half way. By a gradual but continuous climb the trail reached South Pass. Here the wagons crossed from the Atlantic to the Pacific watershed. To the emigrants the entire region beyond the pass was Oregon. But they still had to cover one-half the total distance to their destination. And it was the harder half.

OREGON STATE HIGHWAY COMMISSION

Night camp. The wagon train to Oregon has stopped for the night. The men gather in groups to make plans for tomorrow. The women get water as the first step in preparing the evening meal for their families.

In Idaho the trail crossed the worst desert of the journey—a dreary, barren, rocky waste. The emigrants were already tired, and their equipment was worn. Wagons fell apart; animals died in their harness. Some of the weaker caravans broke up altogether, and the stronger ones made room for the people who would otherwise have been left stranded.

Oregon at last! The barren waste reached into present-day Oregon. Beyond stood the formidable Blue Mountains. Here the early wagon trains had to cut a path for themselves up and down the mountain slopes.

On the other side of the mountains was the Columbia River. After five months of hard and dangerous travel the goal was at hand. Some emigrants floated down the river; others continued overland. Most of them made for the Willamette (wĭ lăm′ĕt) Valley, where they found fertile soil for farming.

The Oregon boundary. The number of settlers in Oregon increased rapidly. In 1846 the population was 8,000. The time had come to settle the boundary question with Great Britain. Some Americans insisted we should have all of Oregon to Alaska. Their slogan was "Fifty-four forty or fight!" (54°40′ is the southern boundary of Alaska.) But you will remember that at this time President Polk was concerned about the danger of war with Mexico (see page 290), and he did not want two quarrels on his hands at the same time. In 1846 the governments of Great Britain and the United States agreed that they would divide Oregon between them at the 49th parallel. You can trace this boundary on the map on page 295. In 1848 Congress set up a territorial government for the entire region, which included today's states of Oregon, Washington, Idaho, and Montana. Later, as more settlers came in, this huge Oregon Territory was divided into smaller territories, which still later became states.

The Mormons settle at the Great Salt Lake. Not all the people who traveled the overland trail went all the way to Oregon. The Mormons went as far as Great Salt Lake and settled there. They were members of a new church that had been organized by Joseph Smith in central New York State. People who did not like the beliefs of the new church treated the Mormons harshly. From New York, Smith led his followers west to the Mississippi Valley. Looking for a home where they could live peacefully, they settled first in Missouri and then moved to Illinois. In Illinois, Smith was killed by an angry mob. Brigham Young, the new leader, decided to move his people far away from all existing settlements. He led them to the remote desert region of Utah and established the Mormon home on the shore of the Great Salt Lake. In 1847 and 1848, 12,000 Mormons in well-organized parties made the long journey on the overland trail to Salt Lake City.

For the first year in the new settlement the crops were poor, and the Mormon settlers faced the danger of starvation. But the next year there was a different story. Brigham Young taught his people to dig ditches and irrigate their fields with the water that flowed down from the surrounding mountains. The Mormons produced more than enough food for their own needs. Situated on the trail to Oregon and California, they made money from later emigrants, ferrying them across the larger streams and selling them food and other supplies. By hard work and careful planning, the Mormons built up a prosperous community in what had been a desert.

4 *The Gold Rush Brings Settlers to California*

On January 24, 1848, a week before the treaty ending the Mexican War was signed, James W. Marshall discovered gold in California. That discovery set off the biggest migration in American history. Marshall tried to keep his discovery secret, but it soon leaked out. Within six months California was caught in a mad gold rush. Businessmen deserted their stores, doctors their patients, lawyers their clients, printers their newspapers, farmers their fields, factory workers their jobs, sailors their ships—all dashed to the hills to mine gold and get rich quick. Before the end of the year reports of the discovery, along with fabulous stories of riches obtained by miners, had spread over the land; and thousands of people from every section of the country set out for California. These were the forty-niners—the men who went to California in the memorable year of 1849.

The forty-niners follow three routes to California. The first big problem of the forty-niners was to get to California. There were three main routes. One was by sea around Cape Horn, but that long voyage took from six to nine months and was entirely too long for most of the eager gold seekers.

Another way was by boat to Panama, across the isthmus to the Pacific, and by another boat to San Francisco. But there were not enough boats on the

Pacific side. Emigrants who took this route suffered from heat and risked disease and robbery on the journey across Panama. Then they often had to wait many long months for a ship.

The third way was the overland route already marked by earlier emigrants to Oregon and California. In the spring of 1849, 33,000 people from every part of the country gathered along the Missouri River from Independence, Missouri, to Council Bluffs, Iowa. In late April and early May they started the long westward journey. For two months an unbroken stream of moving wagons, livestock, and emigrants extended from the Missouri frontier to Fort Laramie.

Thus many forty-niners followed the Oregon Trail. They enjoyed the few pleasures and suffered all the hardships of overland travel. They sang:

Oh, Susanna! Don't you cry for me,
I'm off to California with my washbowl
on my knee.

Some turned off the Oregon Trail in southwestern Wyoming and went on by way of Salt Lake City. (See the map on page 295.) Others turned off in Idaho. All had to cross Nevada. On the last 40 miles of the Nevada desert they suffered more than on the other 2,000 miles of the journey. Heat, blinding dust, and lack of water took a heavy

Life of a forty-niner. First he made the long, hard journey across the plains. Then he arrived at the diggings. Next he mined for gold, digging and washing the metal out of the soil. He did his own housework, including cooking, laundry, and mending.

LIBRARY OF CONGRESS

toll. Late travelers in 1849 could not miss the trail across the desert, for it was marked by the wrecks of a thousand wagons. One man counted 750 dead animals within a distance of 15 miles.

After crossing this killing desert, the emigrants had to climb the high Sierra Nevada. (In Spanish, sierra means "mountain" and nevada means "snow-clad.") The travelers could not loiter. If they did, they might be caught in the early fall snowstorms in the mountains. The snow would block the trail, and they might die of hunger and cold. Many who came late in the autumn were saved by relief parties sent back by those already in the gold fields.

Hard life in mining camps. As soon as they had recovered from the hardships of the journey, the newcomers scattered in search of gold. But their hardships had only begun. Life in the mining camps lacked the comforts of home. The miners lived in tents or shanties. They cooked their own meals, living on a monotonous diet of beans, salt pork, biscuit, and coffee. They worked and slept in the same clothes and let their hair grow wild. They had to work hard. First they had to dig up the earth with pick and shovel. Then, standing knee-deep in a cold mountain stream, they had to wash the gold dust out of the mud and gravel.

Rumor of a rich strike in a particular place would bring a rush to the spot. A place that was one day a lonely valley might become within a few months a bustling camp of 2,000 or more people with hotels, saloons, dance halls, gambling houses, a newspaper, and express offices where the miners kept their gold dust. With rough humor the miners gave these camps such names as "Ground Hog's Glory," "Mad Mule Gulch," "Sailor's Slide," "Chicken Thief Flat," and "Git-up-and-Git." When the gold gave out, such a mining camp disappeared as fast as it had sprung up, leaving only a so-called ghost town behind.

Each community defended itself against lawbreakers. When a suspected criminal was caught, the miners acted as a jury and dealt out a rough-and-ready justice. The decision was carried out immediately, whether it was expelling the offender from camp, whipping him, or hanging him.

Miners did not gather wealth as fast as they had expected. Some struck it rich, and the stories of their exceptional luck kept alive the hopes of thousands. Most of them averaged about $50 a day in gold. That sounds like a large amount, but it often cost them nearly that much to live. With almost everyone busy mining, there was a shortage of food, clothing, and mining tools. Flour was imported from Chile and Australia; tea, from China; picks, shovels, and other manufactured goods were brought from the Atlantic coast. Sugar cost $3 a pound, flour $1.50 a pound, onions $1 a pound, sardines $4 a can, candles 50 cents apiece, pork $210 a barrel. A tin pan cost $9, a shirt $40, a miner's knife $30. Many of the merchants who sold the miners the things they needed made large fortunes.

Fast transportation to California. The people of California (by 1850 there were 90,000 of them) demanded more rapid transportation to and from

Northern California. In northern California, in the early days, lumbering was an important industry.

the East. The first steamships between New York and San Francisco began running in the early days of the gold rush. The fastest sailing vessels, called clipper ships (see page 314), made the long voyage around Cape Horn in three months.

In 1858 overland mail coaches began carrying passengers and mail from St. Louis through El Paso, Tucson, and Los Angeles to San Francisco. They traveled day and night, changing horses every 10 miles. Armed guards accompanied them through the territory of hostile Indians. The coaches covered the 2,700 miles in 25 days. Travel in coaches was very different from the journey of the forty-niners!

In 1860 the pony express began carrying mail between San Francisco and St. Joseph, Missouri, at the rate of $5 a letter. Traveling on racing ponies, the carriers covered the distance in relays. Each carrier rode 100 miles in less than 11 hours and passed the sack of mail to the next carrier. The relay was continued night and day. The pony express riders covered the entire distance of 1,900 miles in 8 days. When the people in California could send letters to the East and get mail from there so quickly, they felt closer to the rest of the United States.

California grows. The amount of gold produced in California in any one year began to decrease as early as 1853, though for another decade more Californians were engaged in mining than in any other activity. From the beginning, however, many Californians found other ways to earn a living. As early as 1850 San Francisco was manufacturing boats, mining tools, flour, cloth, and leather. Farmers settled in the valleys and produced cattle, sheep, wheat, and lumber to supply the mining camps.

In the early years of statehood the people of southern California raised cattle and sheep on the broad ranges. Beginning about 1875, big changes occurred. Engineers brought water to the land from the mountains, from rivers, and from artesian wells. The ranges were broken up into farms. The farmers irrigated their lands and developed the citrus fruit industry. Railroads connected Los Angeles first with San Francisco and then with New Orleans and Kansas City. The railroads carried

LIBRARY OF CONGRESS

Post Office, San Francisco. People standing in long lines for their mail was typical of San Francisco's rapid growth in gold-rush days. Ordinary services were hard to get. Some men actually sent their laundry to Canton, China.

California oranges, lemons, limes, walnuts, figs, grapes, and wine to other parts of the country. This new farming industry and the mild climate attracted large numbers of new settlers to southern California.

5 *Immigrants Take Part in American Expansion*

Where did all the people come from to settle these vast new territories in the West? Some came from the eastern and midwestern states. But many came from Europe, especially from Ireland and Germany. (See chart on page 349.) In the early 1840s, 100,000 Europeans entered the United States each year; by the early 1850s, 400,000 a year. What drove so many people away from their European homes, and what attracted them to the United States?

The Irish run away from poverty at home. The Irish had been a very poor people ever since English armies had conquered Ireland and the English government had given a large part of the land to Englishmen. Most of the Irish cultivated small plots of land and paid high rents to landlords living in England. The staff of life for the Irish farmer was the potato. It was the family's principal food, and the peelings helped feed the pig, the chickens, and the cow.

In the 1840s a catastrophe (kȧ tăs′-trō̍ fē̇) struck Ireland. A disease attacked the potato crop, and half the potatoes rotted in the ground. This disaster happened in 1845, again in 1846, and again in 1848. The result was famine—not enough to eat, and actual starvation in many cases. The United States sent shiploads of corn and wheat to feed the starving people.

In the years of famine Irish farmers were unable to pay their rent, and many were forced to give up their farms. A large number of them decided to go to the United States. To raise money for the voyage, they sold what few belongings they had. Some received money from friends and relatives already in the United States or from well-to-do persons in Ireland. In one way or another many Irishmen collected enough money to pay for passage across the Atlantic.

The Irish in the United States. As we shall see, almost every group of newcomers to the United States had to start earning a living by doing the hardest kinds of labor. Almost every group at first had to face some unfriendliness from their neighbors.

Although they had been farmers in Ireland, only a small number of Irish immigrants took to farming in the United States. Many of them were so poor that they could not afford to buy land. Besides, they felt strange in a new country. Rather than spread out on farms, they preferred to settle close together in cities. By 1850 New York City had 200,000 Irish residents.

Most Irish immigrants earned a living by digging canals, building turnpikes, and working on railroads. In the growing cities they dug ditches for water and gas mains, paved streets, and built stores and factories. Later some of them found jobs in factories, especially in New England, where they replaced the girls who had come from the farms.

The Irish as a group rapidly took on American customs and habits. But the process of Americanization was not altogether one-sided. While the Irish adopted American ways, they made important contributions to American life. Irish songs and Irish singers became popular in the United States, and Irish actors achieved success in the American theater. With their wit and gaiety, the Irish had a knack for getting along with people and soon took to politics. They followed their leaders into the Democratic party. They believed it to be the party of the ordinary people. By voting solidly for Democratic candidates, they helped that party win many elections. As a reward Irish leaders were appointed to political offices. Many Irishmen became policemen and firemen in the cities. Some went into business. Later their children became doctors, lawyers, teachers, judges, and governors.

Germans in the United States. The Germans, like the Irish, came in small numbers in the 1820s. After 1830 their numbers increased. From 1845 to 1860, 1¼ million Germans entered the United States.

Educated Germans, who had learned from the American and French revolutions to love liberty, led a rebellion in Germany in 1830. They hoped to win a more democratic government. The revolt failed, and many of the leaders escaped to the United States. In 1848 another revolution against autocratic government in Germany failed, and more educated Germans came to this country.

The great body of German immigrants, however, were poor people who left their European homes because of hard times. They came to America to make a better living. Some were skilled craftsmen, such as cabinetmakers, bakers, brewers, and lens grinders. Most were farmers. Many, although poor, had enough money to buy farm land in the United States. German immigrant farmers carefully selected the most fertile land for their farms. They settled mainly in the East and in Illinois, Wisconsin, Missouri, and other states in the upper Mississippi Valley.

German craftsmen, businessmen, and professional people settled in cities. Cincinnati, St. Louis, Chicago, and Milwaukee soon had large numbers of German residents. Germans were leaders in developing the brewing industry, the chemical industry, the glass industry, and the clothing industry in the United States. They made musical instruments, watches, and other delicate machines. Others went into journal-

Southern California. In southern California, in the early days, ranching was an important industry.

ism, publishing German as well as English newspapers. Some established successful bakeries, restaurants, and other kinds of business.

The Germans, like the Irish, made contributions to American life while they were becoming part of it. From the German immigrants the American people acquired much of their interest in flowers, in music, and in physical training. In the late 1800s German bands and orchestras played throughout the United States. The Germans also taught Americans to enjoy many of their favorite foods, like sauerbraten (zou′ẽr brä tĕn), frankfurters, and sauerkraut. The custom of decorating a tree for Christmas was brought to this country by German immigrants.

Smaller immigrant groups. During the years from 1824 to 1860 smaller groups of immigrants came from other countries of western Europe. Like the Germans and the Irish, they helped to build our nation. People from England, Scotland, and Wales settled in every part of the United States. They did not form separate communities as the Irish and Germans did, but merged with the rest of the people. French immigrants came from France and from across the Canadian border.

Summary

Now you can see why "expansion" is a good word to use in describing what happened to our nation between 1824 and 1860. People were moving west to make homes on new farms and to build new cities. Southerners filled in the empty spaces in Georgia, Alabama, and Mississippi and settled Arkansas. Northerners filled in the north and central parts of Illinois and Indiana and expanded into Michigan, Wisconsin, and Iowa. With improved transportation the hardships on these frontiers did not last so long as on earlier frontiers.

From 1821 to 1830 about 20,000 Americans settled in Texas, then a part of Mexico. Unhappy under Mexican rule, they won their independence in 1836 and established the "Lone-Star Republic." Ten years later Texas was admitted into the Union as a state. A war with Mexico followed. The United States won and annexed a huge territory reaching from Texas to California.

Other pioneers, eager for another chance to make a better living, crossed the great American desert and the Rocky Mountains to Oregon. On the 2,300-mile journey they went through every kind of hardship. In spite of the difficulties they had to face to get there, by 1846 there were enough American settlers in Oregon to make it necessary to agree with Great Britain on a boundary. The 49th parallel was made the boundary.

Just about the time that California became part of the United States, gold was discovered there. In 1849 thousands of eager gold seekers made their way to California by land and water. Only a small number struck it rich. As gold mining declined, Californians turned to farming, lumbering, and manufacturing.

Immigrants from Europe came to the United States in large numbers between 1840 and 1860 to take part in the rapid expansion of the nation. The largest groups were the Irish and the Germans. Many of them settled in cities and did the hard manual labor needed in a growing country. They learned American ways and made important contributions to American life. Many immigrants—or their children—won success in business, politics, and the professions.

By 1860 the United States had extended its boundaries from the Atlantic to the Pacific. Its people, including those born here and those newly arrived from other lands, had settled a vast area. (See the map on page 348.)

For a Quick Review

1. In what ways was pioneering in the Mississippi Valley from 1830 to 1860 like the pioneering of colonial days? In what ways was it different?

2. Through what events did the Texans win their independence from Mexico?

3. What were the causes and results of the Mexican War?

4. Why and when did Americans go in large numbers to settle Oregon? Tell how they reached Oregon.

5. Where in the West did the Mormons settle? How did they help later emigrants?

6. What were the immediate and the lasting results of the discovery of gold in California?

7. Why did the Irish, Germans, and other groups of Europeans migrate to the United States during the mid-1800s? What contributions did the immigrants make to our nation's growth?

Learning to Study More Easily

UNDERSTANDING HISTORY THROUGH SONGS

The songs people sing usually tell something about their daily lives. One way to "think yourself back" into an earlier day is to listen to or sing some of the songs of the people who lived then. Perhaps you will derive more enjoyment from old songs and, through them, get more understanding of the people of other times if you look carefully at one or two as examples of history through music.

As the pioneers moved west, they took with them the songs of their old homes. They sang the songs around campfires, then at parties in their new homes, and often when they gathered to work together. Sometimes they put new words to an old tune. "Red River Valley," for example, is a song about the Red River, which flows through Texas and Oklahoma, but the tune was first used for a song about the Mohawk Valley in New York. (See Luther, *Americans and Their Songs,* pages 196–198.) The forty-niners made up many different verses to sing to the tune of Stephen Foster's song "Oh, Susanna," which had been the hit tune of 1848. Some of the new verses went like this:

I came from Quakerdelphia with my washbowl on my knee;
I'm going to California the gold dust for to see.
It rained all night the day I left, the weather, it was dry,
The sun so hot I froze to death;
Oh, Anna, don't you cry.

Chorus: Oh, Ann Eliza! Don't you cry for me;
I'm going to California with my washbowl on my knee.

I soon shall be in Frisco, and then I'll look around,
And when I see the gold lumps there, I'll pick them off the ground.
I'll scrape the mountains clean, old girl, I'll drain the rivers dry;
A pocketful of rocks bring back, so, Anna, don't you cry. (*Chorus*)

What do these verses tell you about the experiences of the forty-niners?

The pioneers made up new songs, too. In some of these songs the people poked fun at themselves and at their hardships. In others you have almost a diary of the route the pioneers followed, the hardships they endured, and their feelings about their experiences. Can you follow Betsy and Ike across the country in these verses of "Sweet Betsy from Pike"? Where had they come from? Why were they moving? Where were they going? What hardships did they have to endure?

Oh, don't you remember sweet Betsy from Pike?
She crossed the broad prairies with her husband, Ike,
With two yoke of oxen, an old yellow dog,
A tall Shanghai rooster, and one spotted hog.

Chorus: Say'n': "Goodbye, Pike County,
Farewell for a while,

We'll come back again when
we've pann'd out our pile."

One evening quite early they
camped on the Platte,
'Twas near by the road on a
green shady flat,
And Betsy, quite tired, lay down
in repose.
With wonder Ike gazed on his
Pike County rose. (*Chorus*)

They soon reached the desert,
where Betsy gave out,
And down on the sand she lay
rolling about,
While Ike, in great tears, looked
on in surprise;
Said, "Betsy, get up, you'll get
sand in your eyes." (*Chorus*)

The rooster ran off and the oxen
all died;
The last piece of bacon that
morning was fried.
Poor Ike got discouraged and
Betsy got mad;
The dog wagged his tail and
looked awfully sad. (*Chorus*)

The alkali desert was burning
and hot,
And Ike, he decided to leave on
the spot;
"My dear old Pike County, I'll
go back to you."
Said Betsy, "You'll go by yourself if you do." (*Chorus*)

They swam the wide rivers, they
crossed the tall peaks,
They camped out on prairies for
weeks and for weeks,
Fought hunger and Injuns and
big storms of dust,
Determined to reach California
or bust. (*Chorus*)

Can you find the music for this song in one of your music books and arrange for your class to sing it?

How does the following song fit into the story of the forty-niners and the gold rush? It was called "Sailing for San Francisco."

You get aboard a leaky boat,
And sail for San Francisco.
You got to pump to keep afloat,
Or you *don't* float, by jingo.

The engine soon begins to squeak,
And not a thing to oil 'er;
Impossible to stop the leak,
And rip! goes the boiler!

What other songs can you find that give pictures of life in the days of the settlement of Texas, the Oregon Trail, and the gold rush?

16 *Americans Earn a Living: North, South, and West*

Expansion, the key word for the years from 1824 to 1860, meant moving west for many Americans. But it also meant new ways, new opportunities for those who remained in the East. It meant new inventions, new factories, new jobs, new ways of doing things.

Expansion did not always come easily, for expansion usually means change, and people often don't understand change and are slow to accept it. In 1827, when plans were being made to build the first railroad from Baltimore, Maryland, to the headwaters of the Ohio River, a newspaper in Washington, D.C., carried an editorial making fun of that idea. The people who are thinking about putting money into such a plan, ran the editorial, had much better put it into a canal than into a scheme for a "railway *three hundred miles long*. We cannot conceive of the practicability of such work, as a regular everyday line of transportation." But, the editorial continued, if it were practical to build such a railway, great benefits would come from having better transportation to the Ohio and the newspaper would certainly not oppose it.

On the other hand, Americans had a knack for inventing ways of doing their work more quickly and living more comfortably. That, at least, was the opinion of Alexander Mackay, a Scotsman who visited the United States in the 1840s. He wrote that Americans seemed to have a talent for making new inventions. "The Patent Office in Washington is a most creditable monument to their inventive powers. They are also quick in the adoption of an improvement, no matter from what source it proceeds." If Alexander Mackay had studied the people of the different sections carefully, he would have seen differences in the improvements they adopted. These differences resulted from the different ways of earning a living in the different sections. He would have seen, too, that some of the most important improvements were those made in transportation.

1 *Railroads Bring Improved Transportation*

Canals were a great help in the growth of the North and the West, as you read in Chapters 11 and 12. But canals had faults as means of transportation. They could not be built to reach every community. The boats moved slowly. In the winter months the canals were closed. Railroads did not have these faults. Therefore they replaced canals.

Early railroads. The first railroads were short lines joining nearby cities. These lines were gradually linked together to form railroad systems that connected the different sections of the country, especially the North and the West. At the same time engineers had to solve many problems in order to make railroads safe, comfortable, and fast. As these problems were solved, railroads became the most important means of transportation. The story of the beginnings of the New York Central Railroad will give you an idea of what the early American railroads were like.

The first unit of what is now the New York Central System was the Mohawk and Hudson Railroad, built in 1831. It was 18 miles long, joining Albany and Schenectady, New York, by a route much shorter than the Erie Canal. This early railroad was not very efficient or comfortable. The small locomotive had so little power that at each end of the road the train had to be pulled up a hill by means of a cable. The rails were of wood covered with a flat iron strip and were laid on granite blocks. The passengers were continually jolted, for such rails did not provide a smooth track. You can see from the picture on this page that the cars were stagecoaches set on special wheels. They were tied to one another with chains. As the slack was taken up when the locomotive started, the coaches were jerked into motion and the passengers were likely to be thrown off their seats. The wood-burning locomotive sent out a stream of smoke and

First passenger train in the United States. Travel on this early train had its disadvantages. Passengers were shaken up every time it stopped or started. Smoke from the locomotive covered them with soot, and sparks often burned holes in their clothing.

NEW YORK CENTRAL SYSTEM

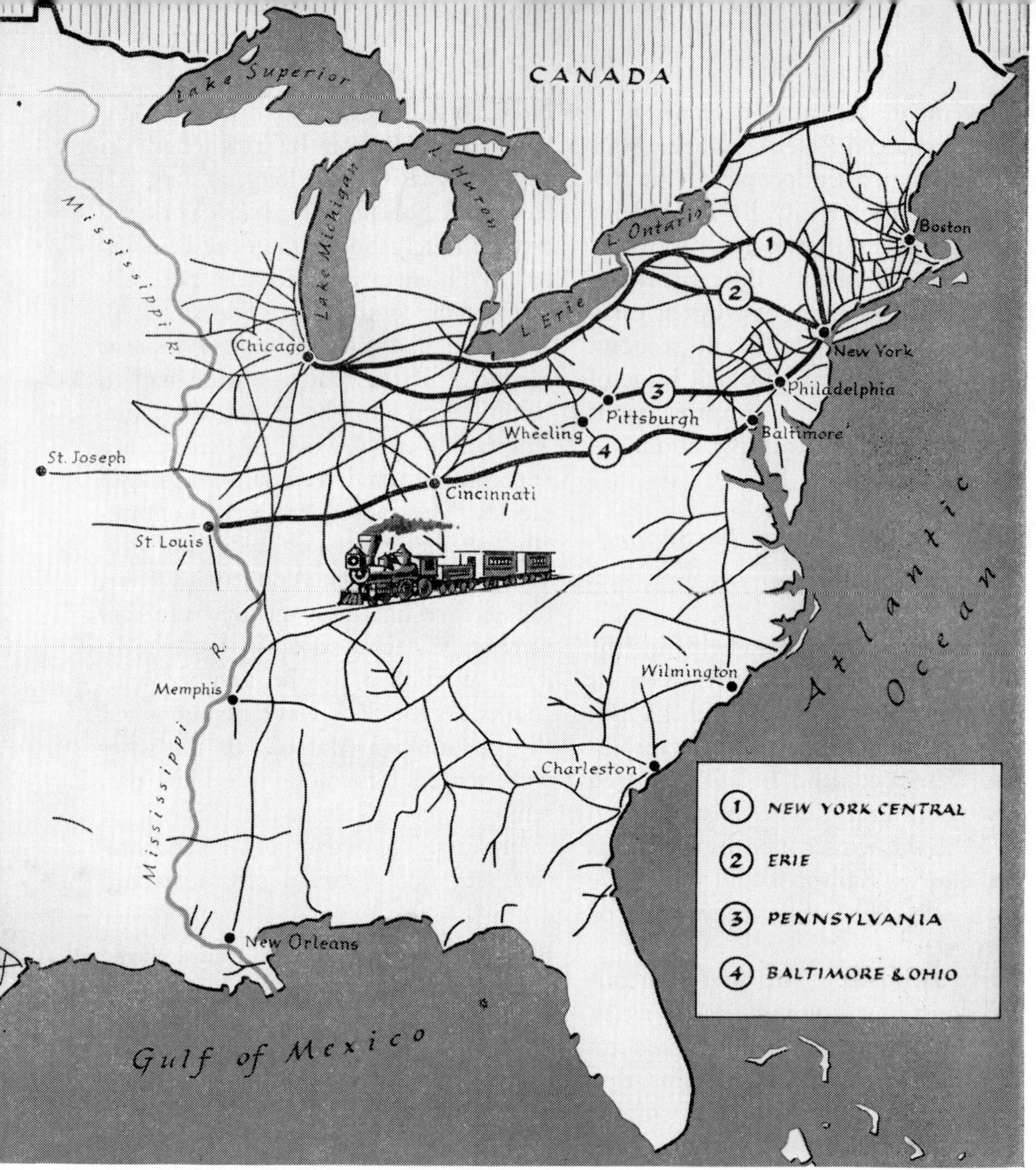

Railroads join eastern ports to the West. This map shows the major railroads in 1860. What cities stand out as railroad centers? Through what parts of the country did the major trunk lines run? How did railroads change relationships among the sections?

sparks that covered the passengers with soot and often burned holes in their clothes. When the locomotive stopped, each coach came to a halt by bumping the one ahead—jarring the passengers.

In the years that followed, engineers made improvements. They laid heavy steel rails on wooden ties. They made heavier and more powerful locomotives that used coal for fuel. They designed larger railroad cars. In 1864 George M. Pullman added to comfort by building the sleeping car. One of the most serious problems was that of stopping trains. So long as a train could not be stopped instantly, it could not travel at a high speed without danger of accident. For many years a brakeman on each coach stopped the car with a hand brake. Then in 1869 George Westinghouse made railroads safer by inventing the air brake.

Through routes. The second unit of the New York Central was built west of Rochester, New York, 200 miles away from the first. Other short lines were built until by the end of 1842 a person could go by train from Albany to Buffalo by traveling on seven different railroads. He changed trains at least three times. He had to travel half a mile through the streets of Rochester from one station to the other. If he were lucky and the trains were on time, he could cover the 300 miles in 25 hours. In 1853 the seven little roads were united into one, and passengers could travel between Albany and Buffalo without changing trains.

Two years earlier a railroad had been completed between New York City and Albany. Beginning in 1851, therefore, railroads transported passengers and freight between New York and Buffalo. The East and the West were connected by rail.

The railroad map on page 310 shows how rapidly the railroads expanded. It shows that New York did not keep for long the advantage of having the only railroad to the West. By 1853 four lines joined Atlantic ports with the West.

In the West, as in the East, railroads were built as short lines and then were connected to form through lines. Then the western lines were joined to the eastern lines. As the railroad map shows, by 1860 all the four great eastern railroads had connections to Chicago and the Mississippi River.

In 1860 the United States had 30,000 miles of railroad, of which one-third were in the Old Northwest. You can see on the map that only a small part of the mileage was in the South.

Chicago, in competition with Cincinnati, St. Louis, and Cleveland, won the honor of becoming the chief railroad center, and therefore the metropolis, of the West. In 1856, 13 railroads led to the city. More than 100 trains arrived and departed every day. Some brought the grain and the livestock of the Middle West to feed the milling and meat-packing industries. Trains going east carried the products of these industries. Trains coming from the East brought manufactured goods to be distributed throughout the West.

Effects of railroad transportation. The railroads brought rapid, cheap, reliable transportation. They speeded up the changes that canals had begun, the changes you read about on pages 224–225. These changes began before 1860, but they continued over a long period of time. Most of them occurred earlier in the East than in the West and in the South. To some extent these changes are still going on today.

Commercial farming. Railroads had an important effect on farming. Farmers who lived near a railroad could ship their products to cities hundreds of miles away. Because they could sell their surplus, they gave up self-sufficient farming and raised crops and livestock for sale. With the money they bought shoes, clothing, furniture, and other necessities.

LIBRARY OF CONGRESS

James River Canal. Railroads had many advantages over canals. Why, then, did canals continue to be used? Like others, this Virginia canal was used mainly for shipping bulky goods such as tobacco.

Bigger cities. Railroads speeded up the growth of cities. As farmers bought more manufactured goods, more and bigger factories were built in cities. Since railroads could bring in from long distances enough food for a large population, cities grew larger and larger.

Smaller villages. Railroads changed life in the villages. Before the coming of the railroad, each village tended to be self-sufficient. A village might have a blacksmith to make farm tools; a shoemaker, who not only repaired but actually made shoes to order; a cabinetmaker, who made furniture; a tinsmith, who made pots and pans; a tailor, who made clothes for men, and a dressmaker, who made dresses for women; a harness maker; a cooper; a wagonmaker; and so on. Factories could make these products in larger quantities to sell at lower prices than craftsmen could. As the railroads brought the factory products to the villages, the craftsmen had to shut up shop. Many of them went to the cities to work in factories. (See page 321.) Villages ceased to be self-sufficient and many of them became smaller.

Tie between East and West. The railroads changed the relations between the sections of the nation. As long as the Mississippi River was the principal means of transportation, the Middle West was tied to the South. It shipped its products south by way of New Orleans. (Remember the right of deposit?) After steamboats appeared on the Mississippi, the Middle West also imported most of its manufactured goods by way of New Orleans (see page 223). But the railroads, completing the East-West link that the Erie Canal had begun, changed the direction of most of that trade. The railroads carried western farm products directly to the East and brought eastern manufactured goods directly to the West. Thus the Middle West became tied to the East. As a result, when the South decided to break away from the Union, the Middle West sided with the East.

Canal and river boats continue to transport much freight. By 1860 railroads had proved to be a better means of transportation than canals. They were faster. They gave year-round service. Their service was more reliable and met regular schedules. They reached places that could not be reached by canal. They carried passengers and freight at reasonable rates.

Although some canals were abandoned, railroads did not do away with the canals entirely. An increasing amount of freight was carried on the Erie Canal. In 1860, in fact, the Erie Canal carried more freight than all the four main railroads combined. It carried the bulkiest freight, like grain and lumber, because canalboat rates were lower and these products did not require speedy transportation.

In this same period the Mississippi River steamboat trade was at its greatest. In the 1850s the Mississippi carried more products to the sea than even the Erie Canal. The largest part of its freight was cotton. The total output of the Middle West, the North, and the South increased so fast that there was enough freight for all the routes.

Clipper ships carry a large foreign trade. Still another means of transportation reached a new high in the period ending in 1860—the clipper ship. The foreign trade of the United States was three times as large in 1860 as it had been 20 years earlier. The countries of Europe, especially England, were rapidly expanding their factories, and the

"S-t-e-a-m-boat a-comin' "

¶ Mark Twain, in *Life on the Mississippi,* tells of the excitement that the arrival of a steamboat aroused in villages along the Mississippi. When the cry "S-t-e-a-m-boat a-comin' " was heard, the wharf became a center of activity.

Assembled there, the people fasten their eyes upon the coming boat as upon a wonder they are seeing for the first time. And the boat *is* rather a handsome sight, too. She is long and sharp and trim and pretty; she has two tall, fancy-topped chimneys, with a gilded device of some kind swung between them; a fanciful pilot-house, all glass and "ginger-bread," perched on top of the "texas" deck behind them; the paddle-boxes are gorgeous with a picture or with gilded rays above the boat's name . . . there is a flag gallantly flying from the jack-staff; the furnace doors are open and the fires glaring bravely; the upper decks are black with passengers; the captain stands by the big bell, calm, imposing, the envy of all; great volumes of the blackest smoke are rolling and tumbling out of the chimneys . . . created with a bit of pitch-pine just before arriving at a town; the crew are grouped on the forecastle . . . the captain lifts his hand, a bell rings, the wheels stop; then they turn back, churning the water to foam, and the steamer is at rest. Then such a scramble as there is to get aboard, and to get ashore, and to take in freight and to discharge freight, all at one and the same time. . . . Ten minutes later the steamer is under way again, with no flag on the jack-staff and no black smoke issuing from the chimneys. After ten more minutes the town is dead. . . .

JOHN HANCOCK MUTUAL LIFE INSURANCE COMPANY

Flying Cloud. Donald McKay built this famous clipper ship. The clippers were long, slender vessels with many sails to catch every breeze.

United States benefited. American grain and meat fed the European workers, and American cotton fed the spindles of European textile mills. Americans also traded with China and other parts of the world. The United States imported manufactured cloth, iron products—especially rails for railroads—and foodstuffs such as tea, cocoa, and coffee.

The *Sirius* in New York Harbor, 1838. Atlantic steamboat service began when the *Sirius* arrived from London. Early steamboats used sails in part.

BETTMANN

Most of the trade was carried on in American vessels. As foreign trade grew, more ships were needed. Beginning in the 1830s New England and New York shipbuilders built clipper ships, which were bought by American and British merchants as fast as they were turned out. The clippers were built for speed. The greatest builder of clipper ships was Donald McKay, who had his shipyard in Boston. His clipper *Flying Cloud* made a record run from New York to San Francisco in 89 days, a record never before or since equaled by a sailing vessel.

The steamship ended the era of the clipper ship. Though steamships had crossed the Atlantic earlier, regular transatlantic service began in 1838. In building and sailing steamships, Great Britain took the lead; and the American merchant marine, as the trading ships owned by Americans are called, declined rapidly after 1860.

Mail is carried faster and for less postage. As the country grew larger, the government opened many new post offices. Railroad trains and steamships carried the mail much faster than horse-drawn wagons or sailing vessels. To encourage people to use the postal service, the government reduced postal rates. In the 1830s to send a letter consisting of one sheet of paper 100 miles cost 6 cents; to send it more than 400 miles cost 25 cents. The fee for a letter consisting of two sheets was twice as much, and so on. At these high rates people usually sent only the most important letters. As rates were lowered, more letters were sent. After 1851 a letter could be sent 3,000 miles for only 3 cents.

2 *Machines Help Western Farmers Produce Larger Crops*

With canals and railroads to carry his products to eastern cities, the western farmer was encouraged to grow larger crops. Around him stretched fertile prairie soil, untouched. (Where was the West in this period? Review the maps of the frontier on pages 295 and 348.) But in spite of the fertile soil, the farmer could not increase his output as fast as he wished because he was unable to harvest bigger crops of grain. Harvesting grain was a slow job performed by hand, and farm labor was almost always scarce. Grain frequently rotted in the fields because there was no one to harvest it.

Farmers use new machinery. For many years various men tried to invent machines that would do the harvesting work faster than it could be done by hand. The first practical reaper (a machine that cuts grain) was invented by Cyrus H. McCormick, who lived in Virginia. He patented his machine in 1834 and continued to improve it. He opened a factory in Chicago in 1847 and was soon selling 1,000 reapers a year. The reaper, drawn by horses, cut the grain and deposited it on the ground. Men followed the machine and tied the grain into bundles called sheaves.

Farmers on the prairies found that they could not turn the thick prairie soil because the soil stuck to their iron plows. John Deere, a Vermont blacksmith who had settled in Illinois, made a plow with steel shares (a share is the cutting part of a plow). The prairie soil did not stick to Deere's plows. Deere established his factory in Moline (mō lēn′), Illinois, to be near his greatest market. By 1860 he was manufacturing more than 10,000 plows a year. These plows hastened the settlement of the prairies.

In the period before 1860 farmers, especially in the Middle West, also began to use other laborsaving machinery, such as horse-drawn hayrakes to pile up the hay in the fields, threshing machines to separate the grain from the straw, and grain drills to plant seeds. These early machines were not so good as the modern mechanical marvels. But with them western farmers grow larger crops with less farm labor.

The main crops of the Middle West were wheat and corn. The farmers fed much of the corn to cattle and hogs and shipped the animals to Chicago and other meat-packing centers. The farm family still produced most of its own food. Every farm had a vegetable garden, and it supplied its own milk, butter, and cheese as well as meat and fruit.

With the money they received for their cash crops, farmers bought furniture, rugs and carpets, stoves, kitchenware, cloth, and other manufactured products. Hence the farmers of 1860 enjoyed more comfort in their lives than did their fathers.

Eastern farmers turn to new cash crops. Western farmers could raise grain and livestock more cheaply than eastern farmers could. Western soil was more fertile. On their large, flat prairie farms, western farmers could use more

INTERNATIONAL HARVESTER COMPANY

McCormick reaper of the 1850s. Standing on the moving machine, one worker raked the cut grain. Others followed, piling up the grain and binding it into bundles. This reaper saved one-third of the manpower formerly used in harvesting.

machinery than eastern farmers on their small, hilly farms. As canals and railroads brought western wheat, corn, pork, and beef to be sold in eastern cities, eastern farmers gradually turned to raising other crops. They supplied hay for the many horses in the cities and firewood for city stoves. They produced vegetables, fruit, milk, butter, and cheese to sell in the cities. In the days before refrigeration and pasteurization, these products would spoil if transported long distances. Thus the eastern farmers found cash markets in nearby cities.

3 *New Inventions and New Methods Help Manufacturing Expand*

In the years from 1824 to 1860 manufacturing grew by leaps and bounds in the United States, especially in the Northeast. More and more people were drawn into factory work as a way of earning a living.

Mills and mines increase their output. Cotton mills in this period grew bigger. In 1860 the country's mills were using a hundred times as much cotton as they had used in 1790. (See chart on pages 236–237.) The early mills had made only coarse grades of cloth. Now the larger mills produced finer fabrics. With improved machines they printed attractive patterns on cloth and wove patterns into the cloth. But mills in the United States still were better at making strong, practical cloth for everyday home use. In this period New England was far ahead of the other sections in cotton manufacture, as it had been in the days of the first mills.

The manufacture of iron also expanded, and the quality of the metal was improved rapidly. The iron was used to make new products, such as coal stoves, steam engines, railroad equipment, and farm machinery.

Beginning about 1830 coal replaced

wood as fuel in smelting iron, and more coal was used for heating city homes. As we have seen, railroads began to use coal instead of wood as fuel for their engines. As a result coal mining became an important industry. The country's coal output increased from less than 50,000 tons in 1830 to more than 14 million tons in 1860. Can you show this increase in a bar graph?

This period of industrial development is important also for its many new inventions. You have already learned about farm machines and improved textile machines. Other inventions started new industries or helped old ones to grow larger.

The telegraph speeds up communication. Until 1844, except for flags and other means of signaling, one man could send a message to another only as fast as a train could carry it. It was in that year Samuel F. B. Morse sent a message from Washington to Baltimore over a wire. For the first time men communicated with one another over a long distance in almost no time.

During the first half of his life Morse was known as an artist. While on his way home from Europe on a sailing vessel, he thought of the idea for a telegraph. It was to consist of a sender to send signals by opening and closing an electric circuit and a receiver to record the signals. For signals he used dots and dashes, which stood for letters and numbers. That system of signals is known as the Morse code.

Morse worked hard and suffered poverty for many years before he completed his invention. Then he had to prove that it would work. Congress voted a sum of money for him to build an experimental line from Washington to Baltimore. The great day in Morse's life was May 24, 1844, when he sent over that line the words "What hath God wrought!"

LIBRARY OF CONGRESS

Boston Harbor, 1840s. Like other eastern seaports, Boston Harbor was crowded with ships carrying passengers and goods. What goods were exported? Which were brought in? Notice that both sail and steam were used.

Use of the telegraph spread rapidly. Lines were strung between the major cities of the country. Within 10 years the country was tied together by a network of telegraph lines. With the telegraph, news could be spread rapidly. Men were able to do business more quickly than before. Like the railroads, the improved roads, the canals, and the faster postal system, the telegraph made the nation seem smaller, its parts closer together.

Goodyear discovers a way to cure rubber. Rubber was used to make

GOODYEAR TIRE & RUBBER COMPANY

Goodyear cures rubber. While working over a hot stove, Charles Goodyear discovers how to cure rubber by mixing it with sulfur. Compare this "laboratory" with a modern industrial research laboratory.

boots and overshoes and rainproof clothing. Do you remember where the rubber came from? (See page 232.) People wanted waterproof overshoes and raincoats, but they found that the early rubberized articles were not really satisfactory. In warm weather the rubber became sticky or even melted. In cold weather it became hard and brittle. Charles Goodyear, of New Haven, Connecticut, tackled the problem of curing rubber. He was one of many inventors working on the problem. Goodyear patiently experimented to find a way to overcome these defects. He struggled, not only with rubber, but also with poverty.

Goodyear made hundreds of experiments, mixing various chemicals with rubber, but none was really successful. Then he learned from another inventor that sulfur improved rubber. Goodyear began mixing sulfur with rubber. One day he accidentally dropped some of the mixture on a hot stove. Instead of melting, as he expected, the rubber charred. From that time on he tried heating rubber mixed with sulfur in different proportions. After months of work he discovered the correct proportion and obtained a product that remained solid, elastic, and waterproof even when it was very warm or very cold.

Charles Goodyear had founded a great new industry with a product that is now used in hundreds of kinds of articles. Can you name a dozen that you use regularly? You might begin with the eraser on your pencil.

Elias Howe invents the sewing machine. In the 1830s dresses, suits, and other clothes were made entirely by hand. It was slow, tedious work. Most people wore clothes that were made at home or were made to order for them. Even ready-made clothes bought in stores were all made by hand. Therefore their cost was high. No wonder a young man working in a machine shop heard a visitor say something like this to his employer one day, "You know, clothes could be made a lot more cheaply if there were a machine to do the sewing faster. You've got a good shop here. Why don't you invent a sewing machine? You would make a fortune."

The young employee was Elias Howe. He thought about the visitor's remark. He had always been interested in machinery. Soon he was at work trying to make a machine that would stitch. Howe worked hard for six years and in 1846 patented his sewing machine. At first people were not much interested. Maybe it was because the machine did not work so easily nor so well as the sewing machines we have today. Or maybe it was because people had to get used to a new idea. At any rate, the sewing machine did not become important in industry until after 1860.

Standardized parts change industry. We have read the stories of some outstanding inventions of the years from 1824 to 1860. But the most important change in manufacturing in this period was the use of machines to produce interchangeable, or standardized, parts for other machines.

In 1798 Eli Whitney, who had invented the cotton gin, made a contract with the United States government to manufacture 15,000 guns in two years. In those days a skilled workman manufactured one gun at a time by hand, making the parts fit as he went along. It was a slow way to make guns. Moreover, each gun differed a little from all others. When a part of one gun broke, it could not be replaced by a part from another gun. The whole gun had to be sent to a gunsmith to be repaired.

Whitney did not hire skilled workers to make guns. Instead, he went to work to make machines that would turn out parts that were exactly alike. Then, in his factory in Hartford, Connecticut, he taught workers how to use the machines.

One day he brought a collection of parts into the office of the Secretary of War and divided them into 10 piles. Taking a part from each pile in turn, he fitted it together with the others. The result was a perfect gun. He had built the gun out of standardized parts. The Secretary of War saw at once the great advantage of this new method. Now a gun would not have to be sent to a skilled gunsmith to be repaired. A supply of parts could be kept on hand. When a part of a gun broke, it could be replaced by a duplicate part and the gun could be kept in use.

Whitney's achievement won him fame, but it was not until 40 years later that manufacturers began to use the method widely. In the meantime Whitney and others invented new machines, such as lathes (lāt͟hz), to make standardized parts. These machines were driven by power and were in large part automatic. Once a machine was adjusted to do a job, it could be kept going by a worker with little skill. Such machines are called machine tools.

The growth of the brass industry in Connecticut shows what could be done with machine tools. In the early 1800s clocks were made of wood by skilled workers. But when machines were used to cut out the wooden wheels and other parts, the price of a clock was reduced from $25 to $5. A man named Chauncey Jerome began making clocks out of brass, turning out the parts with machine tools. The brass clocks proved to be better than the wooden ones. He sold them at 50 cents apiece and flooded the market. (Remember that prices were much lower then than now.) Soon Connecticut factories were turning out machine-made clocks and watches, buttons, pins, kettles, lamps, locks, firearms, and many other kinds of hardware.

NEW YORK STATE HISTORICAL ASSOCIATION, COOPERSTOWN, N.Y.

Making cider. Another wagonload of apples is on its way to the cider mill. The picture, painted in 1863, shows the quiet, somewhat isolated farm life of that day.

Most people still earn a living by farming. This discussion of manufacturing must not mislead us into thinking of manufacturing as the principal way of earning a living before 1860. In that year in New England only 12 of every 100 persons worked in factories. In the other sections of the country the number was much smaller. Most Americans still earned a living by farming.

The lives of craftsmen are changed. Industry advanced far enough in this period to change the lives of workers. In earlier days the craftsman, or skilled worker, served his local community. A shoemaker, for example, made shoes to order for his neighbors. Besides making shoes, he raised most of the food for his family. He cultivated a garden and had chickens, a cow, and a pig. When orders for shoes fell off, he did not have to worry where the next meal was coming from.

The craftsman was his own boss. He set his own pace of work. He was sure that he could always earn a living for himself and his family. He could take time off to discuss questions of the day with his neighbors. He was a respected member of the community. But the improvement of transportation and the growth of machine production lessened the craftsman's independence.

You have learned that, as canals and railroads reduced the cost of transportation, products could be shipped longer distances to be sold (see page 312). In other words, because the region in which goods could be sold was larger, markets were expanded. Shoes, clothing, and other goods could be made in one community in larger quantities and sold in other communities miles away. Lynn, Massachusetts, for example, early became a shoe-manufacturing center. Shoes made there were sold in the North, the South, and the West.

The merchant hires the craftsman. Now to produce shoes in large quantities and sell them at a distance required a special skill—the skill of the merchant. The merchant had to know when and where to buy leather in large amounts. He had to distribute the leather among the skilled workers who were to make the shoes either in their homes or in a factory. After the shoes were made, the merchant had to sell the shoes in distant places. He had to raise money to pay for the raw materials and the work while the shoes were being made and transported. The merchant organized the business of making and selling shoes, and the craftsman made the shoes at his order and from materials that he furnished. In other words, the merchant became the employer; the craftsman became his employee.

The merchant sought ways to increase his profits. One way was to reduce the cost of making shoes. Women would work for lower wages than men. Therefore he divided the work. Instead of having the entire shoe made by the shoemaker, he had certain parts of the job done by women.

The craftsman becomes a wage earner. In the meantime the small town had become a city. The shoemaker had to give up his chickens, his cow, his pig, and, finally, even his garden. He had to buy food for his family with the money he earned by making shoes. Thus he became more and more dependent on the merchant who gave him work to do. When the merchant paid him less for his part in making a pair of shoes, the shoemaker had to work harder to earn a living, and even then he might not live so well as before. Many shoemakers gave up their little shops and took jobs in factories.

The result of these changes was that the shoemaker ceased to be an independent craftsman and became a wage earner. He no longer worked for himself. He could not set his own pace, nor stop to rest or chat with his neighbors.

Craftsman. Here is a shoemaker craftsman, making shoes and boots by hand.

Factory worker. Here is a shoe factory, with workers tending machines. How did the coming of factories and mass production change the worker's life?

LIBRARY OF CONGRESS

Plantation home. In the 1840s and 1850s plantations spread across the Lower South and that section took the lead in growing cotton. Many planters' homes were stately mansions. This is the Hermitage, Andrew Jackson's home near Nashville, Tennessee.

Even though he worked longer hours, often he worried about earning enough to support his family.

Wage earners try to improve their condition of life. What happened to shoemakers also happened to other skilled workers—tailors, hatters, printers, and so on. To better their condition, these skilled workers organized craft unions. The two principal changes they demanded were a 10-hour working day and free public education. With a shorter working day they believed they would have the leisure, as formerly, to take part in community affairs. They wanted free public schools for their children because they believed that education would help them when they were grown up to earn a better living.

Later, as more and more craftsmen became factory workers earning wages, they formed unions that demanded higher wages, shorter hours, and better working conditions. To secure these demands, they sometimes went on strike; that is, they left their jobs. But they won their demands very slowly.

It is true that American workers received higher wages and lived more comfortably than European workers. But when hard times came, many of them lost their jobs and had to depend on charity to live. Some of them moved to the frontier and became farmers. But for most workers frontier farming was no way out of their difficulty. Either they lacked the few hundred dollars needed to buy land and move west, or they knew nothing about farming, or they were unwilling to give up city life for life in the woods. For many Americans there was a long struggle ahead before they could realize the American dream of a prosperous life for all.

KNOX COLLEGE, GALESBURG, ILL.

Cotton port. As more and more cotton was grown in the Lower South, New Orleans became the leading port for shipping it. The main wharf was a beehive of activity, with cotton being unloaded from river boats and loaded on ocean vessels.

4 *Southerners Produce More Cotton*

People in the North and the West changed their ways of earning a living by using machines in the factory and on the farm. Manufacturing was carried on mainly in the East. As the population of the West increased, factories were built there, in which many products of everyday need, such as clothing, harness, soap, and paper, were made. Most of the factories were small and were bunched together in the rapidly growing towns.

The South remains an agricultural region. The South, on the other hand, remained an agricultural region. No more than a beginning was made before 1860 in the manufacture of cotton cloth. Cotton, tobacco, sugar, and rice were shipped from a handful of coast and river ports. Of these New Orleans was by far the biggest. Inland there were few towns of any size.

The South produced more and more cotton every year. Cotton became the country's most important article of export. The chart on page 237 shows how rapidly the amount of cotton exports grew.

By 1860 three-fourths of all American cotton was grown in the Lower South (Alabama, Mississippi, Louisiana, Arkansas, and western Tennessee). Here was the "black belt," so called because of its rich black soil. As settlement increased, wealthy planters bought the small farms of early settlers and combined them into plantations. Most of the early settlers moved farther west. As a result the free population grew smaller and the number of slaves, most of whom worked on the large plantations, grew larger. In many counties there were more slaves than white people.

Slave life. On the large plantations, slaves under the control of overseers did all the work in the fields. The slaves began their day early. A horn was blown an hour before daylight to awaken them. They had an hour to dress, wash, and prepare and eat breakfast. At daylight they went out to the fields to work. At noon they were given an hour for dinner. In very hot weather the dinner hour was stretched to two or three hours. After dinner the slaves went back to work. At sunset they returned to their cabins for supper and rest. At half past nine the curfew signal was blown. The rules required the slaves to be in bed by that time.

Most slaves were not treated so badly as northern abolitionists said. Some overseers were cruel. They were judged by the size of the profit they made for the planters who employed them. Therefore they were likely to drive the slaves hard. And some planters were harsh. But most slaveowners took pride in living up to a code that required them to treat their people kindly. And usually the slaves were protected somewhat by their value as property. If they were weakened by hunger or cold or severe punishment, they could not work. Though slaves had to work long hours, they generally did not work very hard. Since they had nothing to gain, they had little reason to do their best. Most of them did as little as they possibly could. The result was that slaves probably did not do so much work as persons working for wages. Slavery was, therefore, an inefficient system of labor.

Even where slaves were not cruelly treated, the fact remained that they were not free to live as they pleased. Today it is an American ideal, or goal, that every human being shall be respected as an individual, that everyone shall have the right to live his own life so long as he does not harm others. The slave did not have that right. Thus one of the saddest features of slavery was the selling of slaves, especially when families had to be broken up. Many slaveowners tried never to sell their slaves. But when the owner died, his slaves frequently had to be sold. Slaves from Virginia, Maryland, and the Carolinas were sold in New Orleans to planters of the Southwest. They were worth more in the Southwest than elsewhere because on its rich soil they could produce larger crops.

A minority of southern farmers own slaves. When we discuss slavery, we must remember that most southerners did not own slaves and that most slaveholders owned but a few. The small slaveholders usually could not afford overseers. They and their sons worked side by side with their slaves in the field. The large-scale planters who owned large numbers of slaves made up only a small group. But this group had a strong influence upon state and local governments and led southern social life. The rest of the population looked up to them and accepted their views.

Three-fourths of the white people of the South did not own any slaves at all. They were small farmers who tilled the soil with the aid of their families and without slave labor. They raised cotton, corn, fruits, vegetables, and live-

Southern farm. Most southern farmers lived modestly on small farms, which they cultivated themselves since they owned no slaves.

stock. They rarely used farm machinery, partly because their fields were small and often rough and partly because they seldom had enough money to pay for a machine. They had to work hard to earn a bare living.

Most southerners favor slavery. An outstanding fact about the South before 1860 is that, though only a minority owned slaves, most of the free population favored slavery. Even men who did not own slaves believed that slavery was necessary for the prosperity of the South. Many of them hoped to own slaves someday. Furthermore, they said that the question of slavery was one to be decided by the people of each state for themselves. They denied that Congress had any right to interfere in the matter. Even those who disliked slavery joined with the slaveholders in agreeing that other sections of the country should not be permitted to say whether or not slavery should exist in the southern states.

Summary

Between 1824 and 1860 important changes occurred in the way the people of the North and the West earned a living. In the South there were fewer changes, since cotton raising continued to be the most important occupation.

Improved transportation, especially the building of railroads, helped bring many of the changes. The railroad brought the East and the West closer together. It encouraged each section to specialize in what it produced: the West, farm products; the East, manufactured goods. The railroads carried the products of each section to the other.

Beginning in the 1830s many farm machines were invented. With these machines western farmers produced much larger crops, especially corn and wheat. Eastern farmers turned to producing milk, vegetables, and fruit, which they could deliver fresh to the city markets nearby.

In the Northeast manufacturing expanded rapidly. Better and more attractive kinds of cotton and woolen cloth were made. Iron production expanded as iron was needed for railroads, machinery, and other uses. Much more coal was mined. Inventions like the telegraph, cured rubber, and the sewing machine stimulated old industries and started new ones. The manufacture of interchangeable parts with machine tools made possible a much larger production of many kinds of goods. As manufacturing expanded, many craftsmen became wage earners.

The South lagged behind the North in railroad building and in manufacturing. It remained agricultural, growing larger cotton crops with slave labor. Only a small proportion of southern whites owned slaves, but all were united in defending slavery as a system of labor.

As ways of earning a living in the North changed and in the South remained the same, the two parts of the country drifted apart. The differences in the ways of earning a living made it more difficult for the people of one section to understand the people of the other.

For a Quick Review

1. Why did railroads eventually win out over canals as a means of transportation?
2. What changes in midwestern farming and crops took place after railroads and farm machinery were introduced?
3. How did each of these change American life: the telegraph, the sewing machine, Goodyear's treatment of rubber, Whitney's plan for interchangeable parts?
4. How was the worker's life affected by the new machines and the new transportation of the mid-1800s?
5. Why, since so many southern farmers owned no slaves, was slavery as important in southern life as it was?

Learning to Study More Easily

GETTING INFORMATION FROM GRAPHS

Graphs tell some stories very well; others, not at all. Two kinds of graphs that are frequently used are line and bar graphs. Turn to page 434 for an example of a line graph and to page 237 to see a bar graph. These types of graphs help you make comparisons of figures that tell how much, how fast, and so on. A line graph or a bar graph can show how much goods a factory has produced during each year of its existence; by studying such a graph, you could see which were the factory's best years and which years it fell behind. Line or bar graphs can show how many miles of railroad tracks were put down from 1830 to 1840 and from 1840 to 1850. But it would be impossible to show on a line graph or a bar graph the changes that came in women's styles from 1840 to 1860.

To tell its story, a graph should have (1) a title that tells what the graph is about, (2) a scale along one side, telling what quantity or amount each space unit stands for, and (3) a scale along another side, at right angle to the first scale, giving years or whatever labels are needed to make the facts clear. Many graphs also have a legend, or a statement explaining the facts shown on the graph.

Study the graphs on pages 619 and 623. Do they meet the requirements listed above? What information do the graphs give you? Do the graphs provide the information more effectively than words?

Now that you have studied how to read line and bar graphs, try making one. Show the following information, which is taken from *Historical Statistics of the United States,* in either a bar graph or a line graph: In 1830 there were 23 miles of railroad in the United States. In the years that followed the mileage increased, so that in 1835 it was 1,098, in 1840 it was 2,818, in 1845 it was 4,633, in 1850 it was 9,021, in 1855 it was 18,374, and in 1860 it was 30,626. When you finish the graph, check to see whether it meets the requirements suggested above.

17 *Democratic Ways Grow in the Nation*

Scene: A printer's shop in Whitehall, New York; a counter in the front of the shop, a big printing press at one side and to the rear of the room.

Time: 1822.

Characters: An 11-year-old boy, thin and pale but with an eager expression on his face, and a printer, a large kindly-looking man.

PRINTER: What do you want, son?

BOY (rather timidly): I want to learn to be a printer, mister. My name is Horace Greeley, and I wondered—would you take me as an apprentice? I'd work hard, and I know I could do a good job. I like books—I've read lots—Shakespeare's plays, and poems by Lord Byron, and . . .

PRINTER (interrupting, after looking at the boy and then glancing back at the big printing press): No, it wouldn't work, boy. I don't think you're strong enough to manage that heavy press over there. It has to be run by hand, you know.

BOY (intensely): I'm sure I could do the work. I'm really much stronger than I look . . .

PRINTER (kindly but firmly): Sorry, son. You're just not big enough yet. The thing for you to do is go back home and grow up.

Horace had no choice but to take the printer's advice and go back to his home in the nearby countryside in Vermont. The Greeleys were poor. There were four children besides Horace to be cared for. His only chance of learning the trade that he was determined to follow was to bind himself out (become an apprentice) to an established printer. He waited a while.

Four years later Horace Greeley tried again, going to a printer in another town. This time he succeeded in making a contract. In return for the boy's work, the printer agreed to feed and clothe him and pay him $40 a year. Horace worked with his first employer for four years, learning all he could about printing. When he was 19, he decided to strike out on his own. For a year he traveled from town to town in upper New York State and in Pennsylvania, working as a printer. Finally, in 1831, he came to New York City. He owned the clothes he was wearing and the $10 he had in his pocket—that was all. He decided to stay in the city. Someday, he thought, he would have his own newspaper right there. And he did.

As a matter of fact, Horace Greeley ran several newspapers, one after the other, until 1841. Then he started a paper that became one of the most important in the entire United States. It was called the *New York Tribune,* and it sold for a penny a copy. Horace Greeley wanted everybody, even poor people, to be able to buy his paper. He insisted he was going to make it a paper everybody would want to read because it was interesting and worth while. "Newspapers are, or ought to be, printed for the information and entertainment of the whole community," said Greeley. He continued to publish the *Tribune* as long as he lived, and by 1860 he was selling 200,000 copies of the weekly edition.

OFFICE OF THE CHIEF SIGNAL OFFICER

Horace Greeley. Greeley founded the *New York Tribune* and was one of our greatest newspaper editors for more than 30 years. During that time he worked for many reforms. In 1872 he ran for President but was defeated.

Maybe you are wondering what Horace Greeley's *New York Tribune* has to do with democratic ways in the United States. For one thing, it was written so that ordinary people would read it, not just those who were highly educated. For another, it was sold at a price most people could afford to pay. It favored reforms that were expected to help many people, reforms like free public schools and better working conditions. Copies of the *Tribune* were read in every northern state, in cities and on farms. What Horace Greeley wrote, his readers took seriously. Thus through his paper he was able to win the support of many people for important democratic reforms.

Toys of the 1850s. The lady doll, which belonged to a little girl in Boston, shows how women dressed in the 1850s. The man doll, back and front views shown, is dressed in buckskin clothes like those worn by Indians and pioneers about 1850. The omnibus toy shows the kind of horse-drawn bus that transported people on Broadway, New York City, in the 1850s.

NATIONAL GALLERY OF ART, INDEX OF AMERICAN DESIGN

1 *Penny Papers and Public Schools Make Better Citizens*

Before 1833 newspapers were read mainly by business and professional men. The papers printed the kind of news that would interest their readers, such as accounts of political events, news from Europe, lists of ships coming and going, and other business items. There were no interesting stories, no news about what was happening on the street or what the neighbors were doing. Papers were not sold on newsstands. The only way to get a paper was to subscribe. A subscription cost $8 or $10 a year, a large sum in those days, when many workers received no more than that for a whole week's work. No paper had a circulation of more than a few thousand. Judging from this description, how did the newspapers of the early 1800s compare with those of the 1700s? You may wish to reread the information about earlier newspapers on pages 154–155.

Penny papers. On September 3, 1833, there appeared the first number of the *New York Sun,* published by

Benjamin H. Day. The *Sun* was the first successful newspaper to be sold for a penny. It was the first paper to be sold by newsboys on the street. The boys paid 67 cents for 100 papers and sold them for a penny apiece.

The *Sun* did not print political and business news only. It also printed short, entertaining paragraphs about what individuals had done. When a murder trial occurred, it printed everything the witnesses said word for word. It published ghost stories, stories about animals in the zoo, and stories about fires. A great many people enjoyed these human-interest stories and bought the paper.

The circulation of the *Sun* soon jumped to 20,000 a day, then the largest in the world. The biggest problem of the publisher was to print as many copies as could be sold. Fortunately, the cylinder press, and later the rotary press, enabled Day to publish large enough daily issues. In a cylinder press the paper came in on a roller and was pressed against the flat type. In the rotary press the type as well as the papers turned on cylinders. The rotary press turned out thousands of newspapers an hour.

Horace Greeley's *Tribune,* about which you have just read, was another penny paper published in New York. Before long, penny papers were started in other cities as well. Some of the papers improved on the *Sun*. They did not limit their news to local items and sensational events. They printed accounts of discoveries, inventions, wars, elections, and revolutions in every part of the world. They discussed state and national questions.

The penny papers created a new reading public. They were read by thousands of people who had never read a newspaper before. By encouraging their readers to learn and think about public matters, the penny papers helped make democracy stronger in the United States.

The need for public schools. Of course, persons unable to read could not benefit from newspapers, and persons without some education could not understand the questions of the time as discussed in the papers. Today very few people in the United States cannot read, but a century and a half ago there were many who could not. You can judge how many from the fact that, in the early 1800s, in the country as a whole one-third of the children—in some states one-half of the children—never went to school. There was no public school system.

Today we take it for granted that our governments should provide free schools. We call them public schools, because the public—that is, the taxpayers—pays for them. We also take it for granted that our governments should pass laws requiring children to go to school. In the early 1800s, however, most schools were private; that is, they were run by persons who charged a fee, called tuition, for each student. People took it for granted that the education of children was the responsibility of parents and of no one else. (Was this similar to, or different from, the attitude of parents in colonial times? See page 94.) Parents could send their children to school or not as they chose. If they sent their children to school, they had to pay the tuition fees. And

NATIONAL LIFE INSURANCE COMPANY, MONTPELIER, VT.

Country school. Most rural schools had one room and one teacher. While some pupils recited, the others were assigned study lessons. Studying usually meant memorizing. In reciting, a pupil tried to repeat the words of the textbook from memory.

many of them did not think the education worth the money. Only if the parents were too poor to pay the fees and asked for help, could the children go to school free. But many poor families were too proud to ask for free education or did not care whether the children went to school.

The debate over public schools. There was a long, long fight before free public schools were accepted. Many people were strongly opposed to them. Persons of various groups argued something like this:

A property owner: "I pay most of the taxes. If schools are paid for out of taxes, I shall be paying for the schools. Why should I be forced to pay for the education of other people's children?"

A father of working children: "I earn very low wages. If my children stop working to go to school, my family will not earn enough to get along. Education is a luxury, and we cannot afford it."

A farmer: "My taxes are already so high that I can hardly pay them. I'm opposed to anything that means more taxes, especially public schools. I can't see how educating my children would make any better farmers out of them."

Many persons in the same groups

were in favor of public schools. They presented arguments like these:

A property owner: "We are giving more and more people the right to vote. Yet many of them cannot read or write. By their votes they will help decide such questions as the tariff and internal improvements. Yet they have had little chance to learn anything about these questions. Don't you see that in a democracy the people settle the problems of government? And if they are to solve them wisely, they must learn about them.

A father of working children: "I have been working hard all my life, barely earning a living. I want something better for my children. I see that, to get ahead in the world today, a person needs an education. Therefore I want my children to go to public school. We'll scrimp and save and manage to get along without the little money they earn."

A farmer: "It'll be hard to pay the additional taxes for public schools, but I'll find the money somehow. I want my children to have as good an education as any city children. I don't want their knowledge to be limited to the farm. I want them to know something about the world around them so that they will lead happier lives and be better citizens."

You know of course that the people who favored free public schools won the argument. But they did not win all at once. They reached their goal one step at a time. The first public schools were not entirely free. Each parent had to pay a certain amount, except for poor parents who declared that they could not afford to pay. Only after many years were the public schools made free of tuition fees. It took even longer to pass compulsory attendance laws, by which children were required to go to school until they had reached a certain age.

Two leaders in public education. The first public schools were called district schools. Neighbors got together, organized a school district, raised money by taxes, built a school, and hired a teacher. The term was short—usually from two to four months. One teacher taught all the pupils, who might range in age from 6 to 20. He taught little except the three Rs—reading, 'riting, and 'rithmetic.

The outstanding leaders in the movement to improve the early schools were Horace Mann and Henry Barnard. Both of them were lawyers. Both were successful in law and politics and seemed on their way toward great careers that would bring them fame and fortune. Both gave up their promising careers and took up the unpopular and unrewarding work of improving the public schools. They saw boys and girls working in factories from dawn to dusk; and they realized how important it was, for the children as well as for the country, that such boys and girls be required to go to school before they began to earn a living. They saw other children, whose parents were at work all day, roaming the streets where they were likely to learn to fight, steal, and lie. They pointed out how bad such a way of growing up was and how much better it would be, for the children and for the country, to require such children to go to school and learn to become good citizens.

JOHN HANCOCK MUTUAL LIFE INSURANCE COMPANY

For better schools. The artist shows Horace Mann speaking before the Massachusetts legislature, urging it to improve the schools. Improvements made in Massachusetts were adopted in other states.

Mann served as secretary of the board of education in Massachusetts. Barnard held the same office in Connecticut and then in Rhode Island. In the 1840s both men did a great deal of speaking and writing. They tried to persuade people to set up improved schools. They also tried to provide a better education for teachers. Both men achieved success in their states. For example, when Horace Mann gave up his office after 12 years, Massachusetts had a much improved educational system. There were larger schoolhouses with better textbooks, maps, and other equipment. Children went to school six months, instead of three, and they learned additional subjects like geography and history. Teachers were being educated in three normal schools—the first in the United States.

What Horace Mann and Henry Barnard accomplished in New England, other leaders repeated in other states. Education was gradually improved in the entire country, though the South advanced more slowly than the other sections. In many cities there were larger schoolhouses in which children were divided into grades, and each grade met in its own room. Trained teachers were hired to teach the separate grades, and schools were open for longer terms. Better schools and better education for all made a stronger democracy.

Teaching in Frontier Michigan

When I was fifteen years old, I was offered a situation as schoolteacher. By this time the community was growing around us with the rapidity characteristic of these western settlements, and we had nearer neighbors whose children needed instruction. I passed an examination before a school board consisting of three nervous and self-conscious men whose certificate I still hold, and at once began my professional career on the modest salary of two dollars a week and my board. The school was four miles from my home, so I "boarded round" with the families of my pupils, staying two weeks in each place, and often walking from three to six miles a day to and from my little log schoolhouse in every kind of weather. During the first year I had about fourteen pupils, of varying ages, sizes, and temperaments, and there was hardly a book in the schoolroom except those I owned. One little girl, I remember, read from an almanac, while a second used a hymnbook.

¶ Compare the school described by Anna Howard Shaw in *The Story of a Pioneer* with the one that you attend.

2 *More People Enjoy the Arts*

As the public school system expanded and improved, more people were educated and therefore could enjoy the works of writers and artists. Many of the writers and artists, in turn, dealt with subjects that would interest this larger audience.

American writers. Beginning about 1840, the most popular American poet for more than half a century was Henry Wadsworth Longfellow. He was almost as well known in England as at home. People enjoyed Longfellow's poems because they were musical and easy to understand. He expressed ideas that the people liked. He urged his readers to set high goals in life and to work hard to achieve them:

Not enjoyment, and not sorrow,
Is our destined end or way:
But to act, that each tomorrow
Find us farther than today.

His poems have been read by so many Americans for so many years that they have become part of our language. Almost everyone knows a line or two from such poems as "The Midnight Ride of Paul Revere," "The Village Blacksmith," and "The Courtship of Miles Standish." Have you read these poems?

John Greenleaf Whittier in his poems described New England rural life, as in "Telling the Bees," "The Barefoot Boy," and *Snow-Bound*. In his own day he was equally well known for his antislavery poems, but these are largely forgotten today.

Emerson. Ralph Waldo Emerson is considered by many people to be America's greatest writer. He was a strong believer in individualism. That is to say, he urged every American to be self-reliant, to follow his own ideas, not to imitate someone else. Similarly, he urged the American people as a whole to create their own literature and art, not to borrow any longer from Europe. His essays and poems are so packed with thought that many people find them difficult, but they are read and studied today just the same.

Thoreau. Henry David Thoreau (thôr′ō), Emerson's friend and neighbor in Concord, Massachusetts, applied the idea of self-reliance in another way. He had a special message for those Americans who were always working to earn more and raise their standard of living and, at the same time, were unhappy because they had to work all their lives. Thoreau suggested a way out of their difficulties. Why, he asked, should you work harder and harder to earn more and spend more in order to keep up with the Joneses? A person really needs very little to live on, and he can earn that little in a short time. Why not work just enough to earn money for the necessities and then have the rest of your time to enjoy life —to travel, to read books, to enjoy music and art? Needless to say, most Americans of Thoreau's day did not follow his suggestion. Nor do most Americans of our own day.

The popular theater. After about 1820 many more Americans attended the theater than ever before. English plays and English actors were still popular, as they had been in earlier years (see pages 253 and 254). But many American plays were also presented,

LIBRARY OF CONGRESS

Minstrels. The troupe of minstrels paraded in the morning to advertise the performance to come later in the day. Minstrel shows started about 1850. They remained popular until the early 1900s.

and the people were proud of American actors like Edwin Forrest and Charlotte Cushman.

In 1827 a family named Chapman built a stage on a boat on the Ohio River and moved down the river, giving performances at the little river settlements. That was the first showboat. By 1860 there were several more, sailing up and down the Mississippi and on the rivers that flow into it. These floating theaters brought the drama to small river towns that otherwise would never have seen a play. Showboats continued to grow in popularity, and their greatest days came after 1870.

The minstrel show. After 1850 the theater had a strong competitor in the minstrel show. Minstrel shows began when white actors started imitating Negro characters and the Negro music.

The Negroes had developed their own music, which was rhythmic and melodic. Their "spirituals" were the hymns they sang during religious worship. They sang other songs, both gay and sad, while at work in the fields and on the river boats. Still others they sang when they danced and made merry around their cabins. The words of the songs were simple and full of feeling; the tunes were catchy. The funny songs were usually full of nonsense humor, as:

Old Dan Tucker was a fine old man,
Washed his face in a frying pan,
Combed his hair with a wagon wheel,
Died with the toothache in his heel.

Stephen Foster. At first the white

actors in the minstrel shows sang humorous Negro songs like "Old Dan Tucker" and "Zip Coon." But before long they began writing their own songs in imitation of the Negro ones. The most popular composer of minstrel songs in the 1850s was Stephen C. Foster. His best songs, like "Old Folks at Home," "My Old Kentucky Home," and "Old Black Joe," were smash hits. Foster lived in the North and had only slight contact with the South, but he was attracted by the music of the Negroes and patterned his own simple, haunting words and melodies after it. How many of Foster's songs can you name and sing?

The big show. The minstrel show was gradually made into an elaborate performance. For the stage show the actors blackened their faces with burnt cork, except the interlocutor, or master of ceremonies. All wore colorful costumes. They sat on the stage in a semicircle with the interlocutor in the center. He carried on a rapid patter with the two end men, who provided most of the humor. He also introduced the performers as they took their turn to come forward and do their specialties—singing, dancing, reciting, or playing an instrument. The banjo and the violin were favorites. The minstrel show gave a full evening of entertainment and charged only 25 or 50 cents admission. Many people enjoyed it more than the theater. The minstrel show reached the height of its popularity in the 1870s and 1880s. Companies toured every section of the United States, and some performed in Europe as well.

Classical music. Minstrel songs were only one part of the musical activity of the country from 1824 to 1860. Some people preferred more classical music. Outstanding European musicians came to this country to give recitals. In the cities people who were interested in music got together and played at concerts. In 1842 the New York Philharmonic Orchestra was established. In the 1830s the Boston public schools, under the leadership of Lowell Mason, became the first in this country to teach music to their pupils.

NEW YORK PUBLIC LIBRARY

A beautiful scene. This picture, called "Kindred Spirits," was painted by Asher B. Durand, a leader of the Hudson River School of painters. The men are William Cullen Bryant, the poet, and Thomas Cole, the painter.

American artists. As in earlier years, most American artists devoted their time to painting portraits. One group of artists, however, painted pictures of American scenery. Another group painted scenes in the everyday life of the American people.

THE NEW-YORK HISTORICAL SOCIETY, NEW YORK CITY

"Bargaining for a Horse." This is a painting by William S. Mount. Judging from the dress of the farmers, on what day of the week did this horse trading take place?

The group that painted landscapes is known as the Hudson River School because the artists painted many scenes in the Hudson Valley. The paintings of the Hudson River School helped the American people to learn to appreciate the beauty of their country's natural scenery. To regard nature as beautiful was a new experience for most Americans. To the pioneers the woods and the mountains were obstacles that hindered their efforts to till the soil and to move westward. Now the children of the pioneers began to admire woods and mountains as things of beauty.

The artists who were interested in everyday life painted pictures that told stories about people on the farms and in the small towns. For example, William S. Mount, who lived on Long Island, painted farmers bargaining for horses and fiddlers playing at country dances. George Caleb Bingham, called "the Missouri artist," painted the river boatmen of the West and historical events like Daniel Boone coming through Cumberland Gap.

Engravings made of these pictures of everyday life were popular and were sold in large numbers. By making their pictures about ordinary people, the artists showed that they understood the democratic idea that what ordinary people do is both interesting and important. By purchasing these pictures and hanging them on their walls, the people showed that they appreciated art when it was about subjects familiar to them.

Discovery of anesthetics. Perhaps the greatest medical advance of the period was the discovery of anesthetics (an anesthetic prevents pain). In 1842 Dr. Crawford W. Long, in a small town in

Georgia, performed a minor operation on a patient, and the patient felt no pain because Dr. Long had given him ether to inhale. Dr. Long did not make his discovery public. In 1846 Dr. William T. G. Morton, a Boston dentist, saved patients from pain by putting them under ether. In the same year, in the Massachusetts General Hospital in Boston, the first major operation was performed on a patient under ether. The use of anesthetics made possible many delicate operations that could not have been attempted without it.

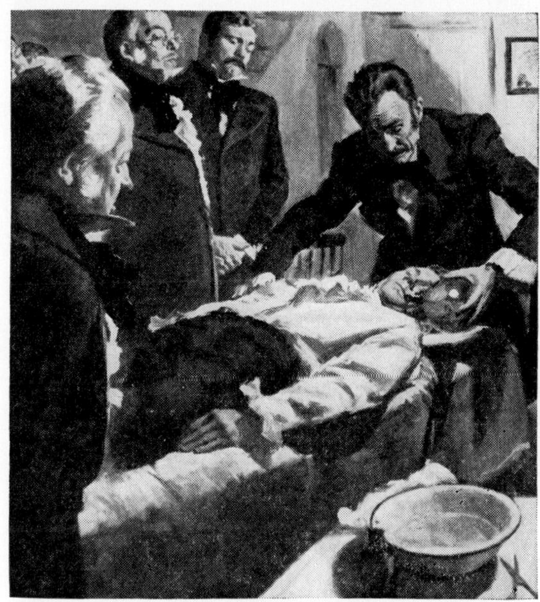

JOHN HANCOCK MUTUAL LIFE INSURANCE COMPANY

Anesthetic. Ether is being administered to a patient who is about to undergo an operation. When and where was ether first used in a major operation?

3 *Americans Work for Peace and Equality*

There is something about the democratic way of living that makes people want to help others, to make them better citizens, to relieve their suffering, to help them become free and equal.

In the 1800s there were many reform movements in the United States with a variety of aims: to send missionaries to the West and to foreign countries, to encourage the reading of the Bible, to establish Sunday schools, to enforce observance of the Sabbath, to persuade people to give up using tobacco and liquor, and to bring about universal peace.

Elihu Burritt: worker for peace. The early peace movement in the United States began in New England, where the first American peace society was organized in 1815. Elihu Burritt (bûr′ĭt) was one of the many men who devoted themselves to the cause of peace in the 1800s. Burritt was a blacksmith who had educated himself and taught himself 30 languages. About 1840 he decided that one of the greatest evils in the world was war, and he spent the remaining 40 years of his life working for peace among nations. Burritt believed there should be a congress of nations where countries would work together to solve their problems, and a court of nations where disputes between countries would be settled peacefully. To what parts of the United Nations (UN) could Burritt's congress and court be compared? If you are not familiar with the main parts of the UN, you can read about them on pages 584–590.

Burritt traveled widely. He became famous as "the learned blacksmith." Wherever he traveled, in Europe as well as in America, he found other men and women who agreed with him and worked with him for the ideals of

OBERLIN COLLEGE

Coeducation at Oberlin. Women students were admitted on an equal basis with men at Oberlin College from its founding in 1833. This drawing of the college dining hall was made about 1870.

peace and the brotherhood of man. When there was danger of war between Great Britain and the United States, he and other peace leaders organized a system of Friendly Addresses. These were messages that groups of Americans and Englishmen sent to one another, pledging friendship and peace.

The woman's rights movement. Like the movement for world peace, the movement for woman's rights began before 1860. In 1830 the law still regarded a woman as an inferior person. Until her marriage she was under the control of her father. Afterward she was under the control of her husband. If she owned property, it was taken over by her husband. If she earned money, it belonged to her husband. The husband had complete control over the children.

Almost everybody believed that woman's place was in the home. The education of most girls was limited to the three Rs and after that to homemaking, dancing, music, and good manners. There were no colleges for women—though here and there an exceptional woman managed to obtain a good education privately. A woman could not enter any profession (a vocation, such as that of doctor or lawyer, that requires special training) except teaching; and even when she taught school, she was thought to lower her social standing. When she was compelled by poverty to work for a living, she was paid about one-third of what a man received for the same work.

It was considered unladylike for a woman to show an interest in politics. She did not have the right to vote. It was almost unheard of for a woman to take an active part in public affairs or to speak in public.

In 1840 Elizabeth Cady Stanton, of Seneca Falls, New York, traveled to Europe with her husband. In London, England, she was aroused when eight American women were denied seats as delegates to an antislavery convention because they were women. Then and there she and Mrs. Lucretia C. Mott, one of the rejected delegates, determined to call a woman's rights convention and demand equal rights for women.

The convention was held in Seneca Falls in 1848. This meeting marked the beginning of the organized struggle for rights for women that would be equal to those of men—such as voting, going to school, owning property, and holding jobs on the same basis as men.

In 1850 Mrs. Stanton met Susan B. Anthony, of Rochester, New York. These two women, aided by other leading men and women of the time, led the fight for the next 50 years. They did not want to "take women out of the home," as their critics charged. They believed women could make better homes, and do other things too, if they had a chance to be educated and achieve some independence. They believed that women, like men, were people who could help build a better nation and a better world if each had a chance to develop her own particular abilities.

The right of women to vote was not completely won until 1920. But many advances were made in the years before 1860. By that year seven states had granted married women the right to own property. More women became teachers. Colleges were open to them. Oberlin College in Ohio, founded in 1833, admitted women as well as men. By 1860 there were several colleges for women alone. In 1849 Elizabeth Blackwell was graduated from Geneva Medical College in New York. She was the first woman doctor in the United States. Medical colleges for women were later opened in Boston and Philadelphia.

Temperance. The temperance movement was a growing reform that had as one of its aims the relief of poverty. It began in New England and soon spread into every state. Reformers saw that, when a worker drank heavily, both he and his family were harmed. Convinced that drinking caused much poverty and suffering, they tried to persuade people to give up liquor voluntarily. Later the temperance leaders, as these reformers were called, tried to have prohibition laws passed. They won their first great victory in 1851, when Maine passed a law prohibiting the manufacture and sale of intoxicating liquor in the state. Other states followed with laws of various kinds. Most of these provided for local option. That is, each community in the state could decide for itself whether it would permit the sale of liquor within its borders.

The antislavery movement. People of the northern states who were interested in helping their fellow human beings soon found that one reform movement attracted most of their time and attention. It was the antislavery movement, which spread rapidly through the North in the period from 1824 to 1860. You have already read something of the abolitionist movement on page 280. Opposition to slavery in the North and defense of slavery in the South drove the people of the two sections so far apart that many churches, including the Baptist and the Methodist, split into separate northern and southern branches.

Many northern writers wrote essays and poems attacking slavery. But the book that did most to strengthen northern opposition to slavery was Harriet Beecher Stowe's *Uncle Tom's Cabin*. Mrs. Stowe described slavery as brutal and inhuman. The play that was made out of the book was one of the most popular in all the history of the American theater. People who had never attended a theater before went to see it. Many a northern audience wept over the sufferings of Uncle Tom and Little Eva.

VANDAMM

Harriet. This is a scene from a play about Harriet Beecher Stowe, the author of *Uncle Tom's Cabin.* Harriet, seated at the table, is played by Helen Hayes.

After reading or seeing *Uncle Tom's Cabin,* many northerners who had disapproved of abolitionists no longer opposed them. They could not remain indifferent to slavery. By 1860, in the North, the antislavery movement had swallowed up all other reform movements for the time being. The antislavery movement held the center of attention in the nation—unfavorable attention, of course, from the South.

Summary

Several chapters in this book tell about reforms at various times in the history of our country. The purposes of these reforms included: to win the right to vote for more people, to free the enslaved, to give the people control over their government, to protect workers against unemployment, and to relieve suffering. The specific purposes were to some extent different in each period. But the aim was always to make our country more democratic. For democracy does not mean just the right to vote. It means giving every person an equal chance to be prosperous and happy.

You can easily see how the reforms begun in the period from 1824 to 1860 had this democratic aim. Penny papers and free public schools helped prepare people to carry on the responsibilities of citizenship in a democracy. The antislavery and woman's rights movements were efforts to win freedom and greater opportunity for large numbers of Americans. The aim of the peace movement was to end the suffering caused by war.

Thus the reforms of this period are episodes in a long story that runs all the way through United States history. That story makes the American adventure exciting and worth while.

Democracy means a happier life for all the people. In a democracy ordinary persons are as important as the great and wealthy. Therefore in a democracy artists take a deep interest in ordinary people. Authors write stories, plays, and essays about them. Painters paint pictures of their daily lives. Musicians write songs for them. The people enjoy these works of art and find more pleasure in life. Thus the poetry of Longfellow and Whittier, the writings of Emerson and Thoreau, the paintings of Mount and Bingham, the songs of Stephen Foster, showboats and minstrel shows—all prove that democracy in America was steadily growing stronger in the three decades before 1860.

For a Quick Review

1. How did inexpensive newspapers promote democracy in American life?

2. What were the arguments for and against free public schools in the mid-1800s? Which ones still apply today?

3. How did the work of American writers and artists of 1824 to 1860 reflect the life of their day?

4. In what ways can Elihu Burritt be compared with leaders of the United Nations, who live about a century later than Burritt?

5. What were some of the ways in which woman's rights were unequal to those of men in the mid-1800s?

6. In what forms did the theater reach the people in the mid-1800s? What part did Stephen Foster play in the popular theater? Can you sing any of his songs?

Learning to Study More Easily

GIVING AN ORAL REPORT

Would you agree that an oral report can be either one of the most interesting parts of a social studies class or a complete waste of time? If so, what makes the difference? One class discussed this question and came up with something like this list of "Things That Make a Good Report":

1. The subject is interesting to the class, not just to the speaker.
2. The reporter has new information to give the class, probably collected from several sources. He knows his material well enough so that he can talk to the class instead of reading from a paper.
3. The speaker chooses his words carefully, so that he expresses his ideas clearly; he stands straight instead of leaning on a desk or table; he looks at his audience and helps them be interested because he is obviously interested.
4. The reporter has organized his talk, so that the class can follow it easily.
5. The report is long enough to give important and interesting facts about the topic, but it does not drag on too long.
6. The report is likely to be more interesting if the reporter illustrates it with pictures, blackboard drawings, a musical record, or whatever kind of illustration is appropriate.
7. The reporter has his talk ready to give when the class is ready for it, not three days after the topic has been discussed by the rest of the class.

On pages 207, 244, and 258, you will find suggestions about collecting and organizing material for reports. On page 344 you will find a list of report topics for Unit 4; if you choose to prepare a report on one of them, apply the same suggestions.

The class that made the list given above also worked out the following scoring sheet for oral reports:

CHART FOR JUDGING ORAL REPORTS

Material will count two-thirds of the total. The following points will be considered:

1. The extent and value of the sources from which information has been taken
2. How well the material is organized
3. How well the speaker knows his or her material

Presentation will count one-third of the

total. The following points will be considered:

1. Posture
2. The use of cards or small sheets of paper for notes
3. The use of the speaker's own words
4. The interest shown by the class

Perhaps your class will think this chart a good one, or perhaps you will find ways to improve it. Other classes have worked out much more detailed scoring sheets than this one. If you decide to prepare one, your English teacher and your speech teacher would undoubtedly have good suggestions to make.

Unit Roundup

HIGH POINTS OF THE UNIT

For Unit 4 your class might plan a review session consisting of short summary speeches by various students, each speech to be followed by questions and discussion by the entire class. The questions listed below might serve as subjects for the summarizing speeches. If you are preparing one of them, use the suggestions given on page 186 about making summaries. While you are in the audience, you can be reviewing Unit 4 by taking notes on the main points presented in the oral summaries and by listing any related points that you wish to have the class discuss and clarify for you. Before the class begins its review, look through these questions and consider whether there are others you think should be added.

1. Why did sectionalism grow stronger after 1824?
2. How did increased sectionalism affect American territorial expansion and politics between 1824 and 1850?
3. What forces worked against sectionalism, toward national unity, in the period from 1824 to 1860?
4. What were the major developments and changes in ways of making a living from 1824 to 1860?
5. In what ways did democracy grow from the day of John Quincy Adams to that of Abraham Lincoln? (Consider social and economic democracy as well as political.)
6. How was the broader democracy of the period reflected in literature, art, and reform movements between 1824 and 1860? (Take into account the various sides of democracy.)
7. How did the expansion of settlement from 1824 to 1860 compare with that of earlier periods? Consider rate of settlement, kinds of problems settlers had to meet, effect on older parts of the country, what groups of people settled the new territories, and reasons why people moved to new, unsettled regions.

EXPAND YOUR VOCABULARY

1. Check your understanding of these terms, some of which may have been new to you before you studied Unit 4:

compulsory school attendance	labor union
craftsman	machine tools
cylinder press	newsboy
franchise	public school
free state	river port
internal improvements	rotary press
	showboat
	tuition fee

2. You read and used the words in the list given below as you studied Unit 4. For each of them there are several related words that you have used in your study of American history this year or are frequently used in our newspapers or daily conversation. For example, "experimental" is related to the noun "experiment"; other related words that are in comon use include "to experiment" and "experimentation." Can you find others? How many related words can you find for each of these?

abolitionist	secede
anesthetic	sectional
employee	standardized
isolated	subscriber
nullify	temperance

3. You have seen, in your study of earlier events in our nation's history, how an important happening, a whole movement, or an idea is sometimes summarized in a slogan or a saying. Many of them are well known by Americans today, and have actually become a part of our language. Can you explain what each of these refers to and tell about the circumstances from which it came?

"Fifty-four forty or fight!"
"Remember the Alamo!"
"Our Federal Union! It must and shall be preserved!"
"Liberty *and* Union, now and forever, one and inseparable!"
"Cotton is king"

HISTORY IN THE MOVIES

1. The film *Territorial Expansion of the United States from 1837 to 1853* presents many facts in 22 minutes. In order to get the most from studying it, make these preparations: (*a*) In class discussion make a list of all new territories added to the United States between 1783 and 1853. (*b*) As you list each one, locate it on a map. (*c*) Go back through the list and describe briefly the geography of each territory you have named. Then study the film to see what additional information you can get about each territorial addition. After you have seen the film, discuss it in class.

2. Probably the sewing machine eventually brought as many changes in American life as any of the many inventions of the 1830s, 1840s, and 1850s. The film *Story of Elias Howe* tells how the sewing machine was invented and of the many difficulties Howe had to face. As you study the film, look for answers to these questions: (*a*) What problems did Howe have to solve? How did he try to solve each one? (*b*)

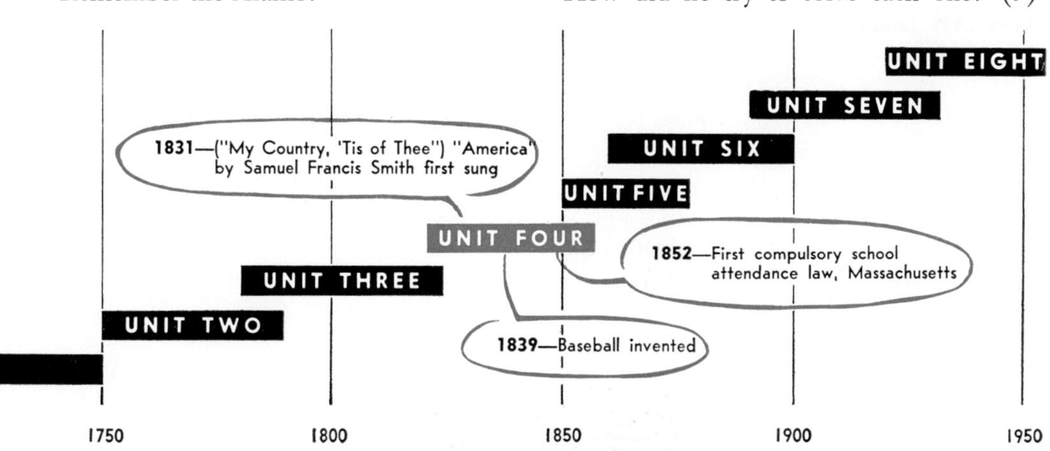

MAIN EVENTS OF UNIT 4, 1824–1860

Building and governing the nation	*Earning a living*	*Science, arts, and the people*	*The nation and its neighbors*
1825–1829 John Quincy Adams, Pres. (Republican)	**1825** Erie Canal opened		**1825** Bolivia independent
	1828 Baltimore and Ohio Railroad	**1828** American Peace Society founded	
1829–1837 Andrew Jackson, Pres. (Democrat)			**1829** Venezuela independent
1832 Nullification			
		1833 *New York Sun*	
1834 Rise of Whig party	**1834** McCormick's reaper	**1834** Oberlin College (coeducational)	
			1836 Texas independent
1837–1841 Martin Van Buren, Pres. (Democrat)	**1839** Goodyear vulcanizes rubber	**1839** First normal school	
1841 William Henry Harrison, Pres. (Whig)		**1841** Emerson's *Essays*	
1841–1845 John Tyler, Pres. (elected V-P by Whig party)			
		1842 Ether used in surgery	**1842** Maine boundary settled
	1843 Oregon Trail		
	1844 First telegraph		
1845–1849 James K. Polk, Pres. (Democrat)			**1845** Texas annexed
	1846 Rotary printing press	**1846** Smithsonian Institution	**1846** Oregon Treaty **1846–1848** Mexican War
		1848 Woman's Rights Convention	**1848** Treaty with Mexico
1849–1850 Zachary Taylor, Pres. (Whig)	**1849** California gold rush		
1850–1853 Millard Fillmore, Pres. (Whig)		**1850** Population 23,191,876	
(See also Main Events of Unit 5, page 394.)			**1853** Gadsden Purchase

What changes came in women's work and in the clothing industry as a result of the invention of the sewing machine?

WITH CRAYON, RULER, AND PASTE

1. Choose one of the persons from the list below and gather information about his or her life and contributions to America. Then draw a true comic-strip biography.

Susan B. Anthony	Crawford W. Long
Moses and Stephen Austin	Cyrus H. McCormick
Henry Barnard	Donald McKay
John C. Calhoun	Lucretia C. Mott
Charlotte Cushman	Henry Thoreau
John Deere	Marcus and Narcissa Whitman
Ralph Waldo Emerson	John Greenleaf Whittier
Sam Houston	Brigham Young
Elias Howe	

2. Perhaps you would prefer to center a true comic-strip history on an event rather than on the life of a person. If so, choose one from those listed below or from the other events described in Unit 4.

The Bear Flag Republic
The development of the reaper
The gold rush
How the Texans won their independence
Military campaigns of the Mexican War
The Mormons move west
The pony express
The settlement of Oregon

3. Draw two cartoons that might have appeared in newspapers of 1840, one supporting Harrison and the other supporting Van Buren for President.

4. Make a set of cartoons to illustrate the discomforts of early railroad travel and what has been done to remove them. A brief explanatory legend may be needed.

5. Make a multiple line graph to show the growth of population in Wisconsin, Iowa, and Illinois from 1840 to 1860. Use a different color or symbol for each state. The official census figures, as reported in *The World Alamanac,* are:

	1840	1850	1860
Wisconsin	130,945	305,391	775,881
Iowa	43,112	192,214	674,913
Illinois	476,183	851,470	1,711,951

What title should you give this graph? Show the graph to the class and explain the significance of these population figures.

6. In class discussion decide what events of the years from 1824 to 1860 are important enough to be recorded on your wall time line. Choose a committee to place them in the proper places.

PUT ON A PLAY

1. From the list of persons given on this page, select one to study in detail. Plan and present to the class a series of skits telling about that leader's life and accomplishments.

2. Many of the events listed on this page would make good subjects for a dramatization. Select one of them, or any that is mentioned in Unit 4, and plan scenes that a small committee can present to the class.

3. Work out two scenes of family life to illustrate how the industrial revolution changed the daily life of a worker who was first an independent craftsman and then went to work in a factory.

4. You can work out an especially interesting biographical play based on the life of one of the composers or writers mentioned in Unit 4 by using some of his music or writing in the play.

PEOPLING THE LAND 1790-1860

From 1790 to 1860 the population of the United States doubled every 20 years.

By 1860 Americans had settled the eastern half of the country up to the Great Plains. Hardy pioneers had begun the settlement of the Far West.

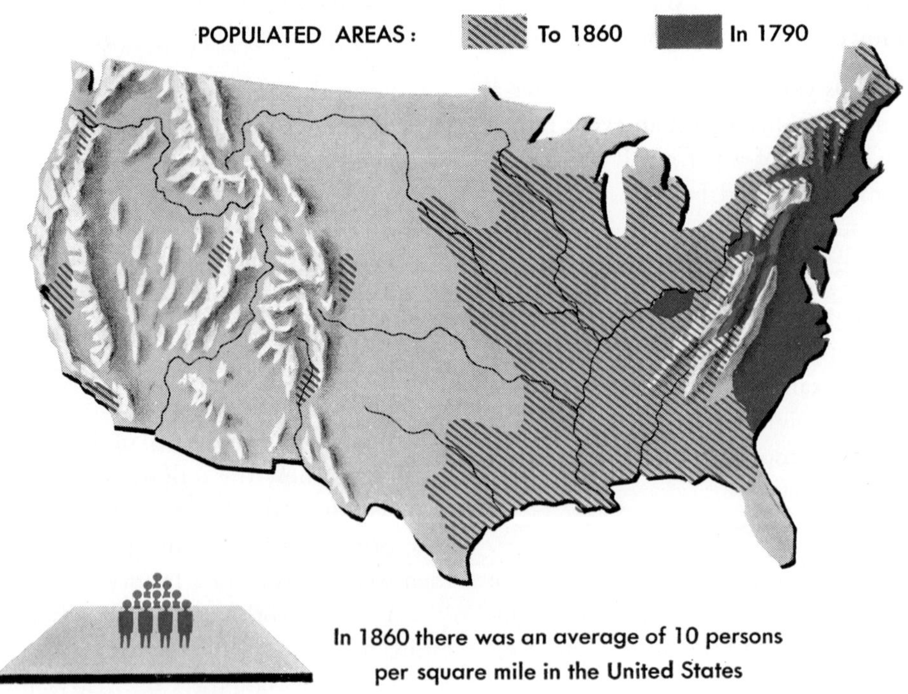

In 1860 there was an average of 10 persons per square mile in the United States

One square mile

From 1820 to 1860 most of the immigrants to the United States came from the British Isles and other countries of western Europe.

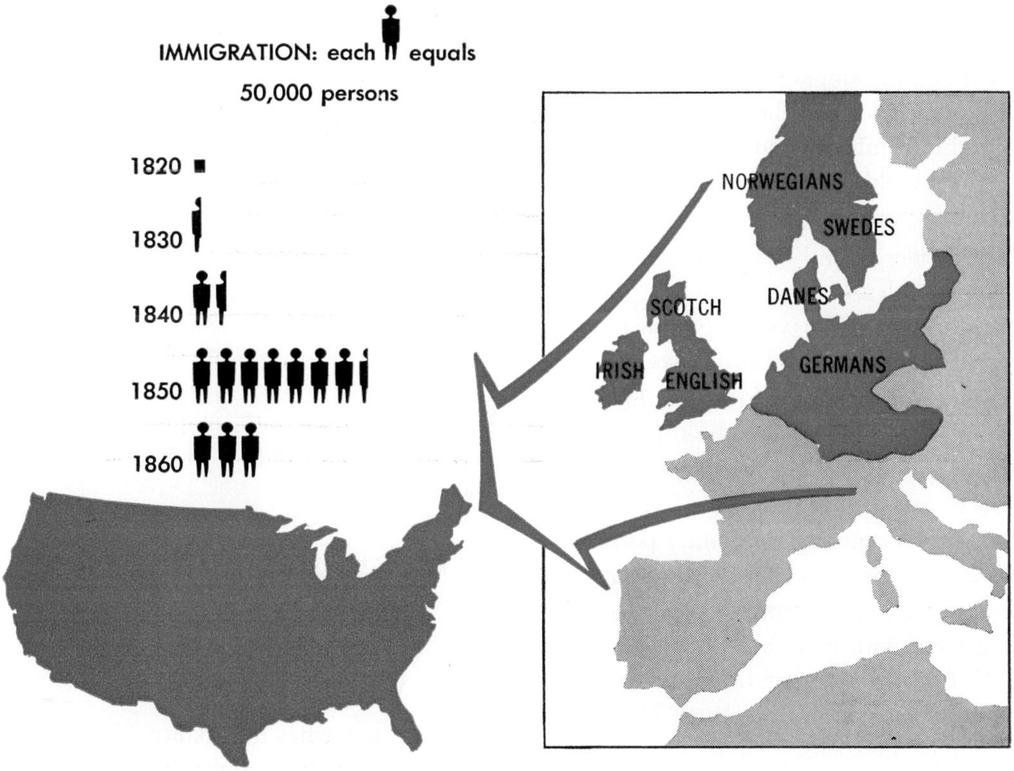

IMMIGRATION: each equals 50,000 persons
1820
1830
1840
1850
1860
NORWEGIANS
SWEDES
SCOTCH
DANES
IRISH
ENGLISH
GERMANS

In the 1800s cities grew as Americans moved from farms and villages to take jobs in city factories and many immigrants settled in cities.

City dwellers
6%
94%
1800
9%
91%
1830
20%
80%
1860
Country dwellers

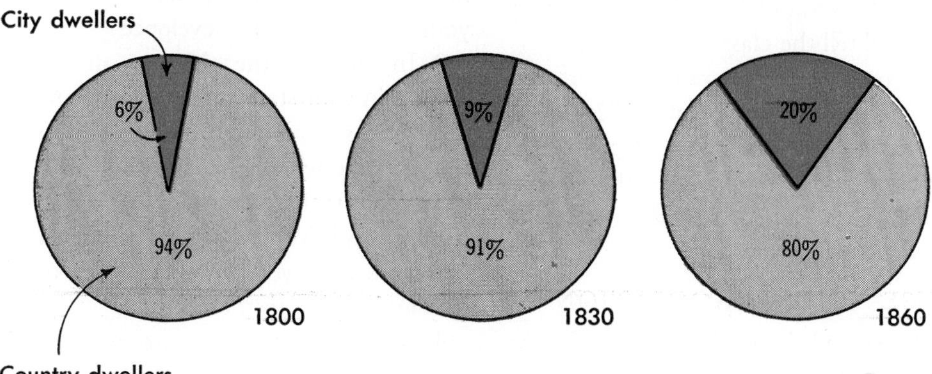

STORIES THERE WAS NO ROOM TO TELL

1. Campaign songs are among the most interesting footnotes to our nation's history. In collections of American songs, study the words and music of songs used in the political campaigns from 1824 to 1860. Tell the class about them.

2. Find information on one of these topics, in addition to what is given in Unit 4, and report on it to the class:

The Underground Railroad
The Gadsden Purchase
California in the days of Spanish rule
San Francisco in gold-rush days

3. School textbooks used in the period from 1824 to 1860 were very different from those you use today. See if you can find one or two in your public library, historical museum, or among the family possessions of one of the members of your class. Examine them and prepare a report comparing them with today's textbooks.

4. Prepare a report or participate in a panel discussion on the topic "The significance of inexpensive newspapers in the 1840s and today." As a basis for your comparison, gather facts about circulation, contents, and make-up of modern newspapers and those of the 1840s and 1850s.

5. Read several of Whittier's antislavery poems and tell the class about them.

6. Prepare an illustrated report on "Painting in the United States, 1824–1860." Find reproductions of paintings done in this period and show them to the class as you tell about them and the artists who painted them.

USE YOUR IMAGINATION

1. Prepare a brief booklet "Helps for the Oregon Settler," a guidebook to the Oregon Trail and conditions of settlement. Give the prospective settler advice about how to prepare for his journey and what to expect on the trip and during the first year in Oregon.

2. Write two news stories about the overland mail. In one the reporter tells about covering the opening of the service. The other, written a year or so later, tells of its development.

3. Write a short story about the adventures of a teen-age boy who went with his father to dig for gold in California.

SHOW IT ON A MAP

1. Make a picture map of the United States entitled "How Americans Moved West." Show each of the major routes from 1824 to 1860 and the kinds of transportation used.

2. Show on an illustrated map the ways that people in the different sections made a living from 1824 to 1860.

YOUR COMMUNITY GROWS WITH THE NATION

1. Find out what nationality groups are represented in the population (or by the ancestors of the population) of your community or state. What is the size of each group in proportion to the total? What influence has each group had on the way your community has developed?

2. Investigate the history of public schools in your state and your town. When were free schools established? What were the first free schools like?

3. What is the oldest newspaper in your community? When was it begun? Find out as much as you can about its early history and report to the class.

4. Investigate the part women play in public life in your city and your state today. Present your information to the class.

FURTHER READING

Books about Interesting People

Andrew Jackson by Jeannette Nolan. Messner, 1949.

Donald McKay: Designer of Clipper Ships by Clara Judson. Scribner, 1943.

First Woman Doctor: The Story of Elizabeth Blackwell, M.D. by Rachel Baker. Messner, 1944.

Gentle Warrior: A Story of Dorothea Dix by Corinne Lowe. Harcourt, Brace, 1948.

He Heard America Sing: The Story of Stephen Foster by Claire L. Purdy. Messner, 1940.

Narcissa Whitman: Pioneer of Oregon by Jeanette Eaton. Harcourt, Brace, 1941.††

Susan B. Anthony: Champion of Women's Rights by Florence Horn Bryan. Messner, 1947.

Western Star: A Story of Jim Bridger by Merritt Parmelee Allen. Longmans, 1941.

Yankee Thunder: The Legendary Life of Davy Crockett by Irwin Shapiro. Messner, 1944.

Stories of Adventure and Everyday Life

Boy with a Pack by Stephen W. Meader. Harcourt, Brace, 1939. A boy's trip as a peddler from New Hampshire to Ohio in 1837.

Children of the Covered Wagon by Mary Jane Carr. Crowell, 1943. The trip from Missouri to Oregon.

Gay Melody by Martha Gwinn Kiser. Longmans, 1949. Could a woman teach? Life in Concord, Massachusetts, in the mid-1800s.

Hills of Gold by Katherine Grey. Little, Brown, 1933. Gold-rush experiences show a boy that farming is more profitable than hunting gold. The author has told of earlier adventures of the same boy in *Rolling Wheels,* Little, Brown, 1932.

Keep the Wagons Moving! by West Lathrop. Random House, 1949. Adventures on the Oregon Trail.

Moccasin Trail by Eloise J. McGraw. Coward-McCann, 1952. After 11 years with the Crow Indians, a boy must decide whether to return to his family.

On to Oregon! by Honoré Morrow. Morrow, 1946. Seven children go "on to Oregon" after their parents die on the way.

Prairie Printer by Marjorie Medary. Longmans, 1949. Adventures of Tom Kenyon in Iowa in the 1850s. The author tells of Tom's earlier experiences on canals and as a printer's apprentice in Ohio in *Buckeye Boy,* Longmans, 1944.

Summer under Sail by Elizabeth Howard. Morrow, 1947. A girl's summer in Cleveland, Ohio, and on the Great Lakes in the 1850s.

Wild Waters by Lewis S. Miner. Messner, 1946. Earning a river pilot's license on the Mississippi.

Young Mac of Fort Vancouver by Mary Jane Carr. Crowell, 1940. The Pacific Northwest in the early 1800s.

Other Interesting Accounts

California Pageant: The Story of Four Centuries by Robert Glass Cleland. Knopf, 1946. A history of California.

Pony Express Goes Through: An American Saga Told by Its Heroes by Howard R. Driggs. Lippincott, 1936. Stories of the pony express told by station agents and riders.

The California Gold Rush by May McNeer. Random House, 1950.

The Pony Express by Samuel Hopkins Adams. Random House, 1950.

Unit 5 *The Union Is Broken and Restored 1850—1877*

IN THE 1830s and 1840s the United States Military Academy at West Point was training young Americans to be officers of the United States Army, just as it does today. Ulysses S. Grant entered West Point in 1839. He became friendly with other cadets, including James Longstreet, William T. Sherman, George B. McClellan, Thomas J. Jackson, and George E. Pickett. In Grant's time the cadets were still talking about Robert E. Lee of the class of 1829. Lee had gone through his four years at West Point without a single demerit for bad conduct.

After graduating, the young officers were assigned to army posts in various parts of the country. The Mexican War gave them a chance to practice the theories they had learned at West Point. Dozens of captains and lieutenants who were later to be generals in the Union and Confederate armies fought the common enemy under General Winfield Scott from Veracruz to Mexico City. (See the map on page 292.) Lee and Grant were there. Grant was in charge of supplies for his regiment. Lee helped plan the battles. George B. McClellan worked closely with Lee. A few months after the war was over, Longstreet was best man at Grant's wedding.

After the war many officers resigned from the Army to become business or professional men. But events were happening that would force them to take sides in a war between the North and the South. West Point graduates chose one side or the other, usually as their states went. Lee became commander in chief of the southern forces. Outstanding generals under him were Jackson, Longstreet, and Pickett. McClellan, Burnside, Hooker, and Grant in turn commanded the northern army facing Lee in Virginia. The friends of earlier days became enemies in war.

Officers and men in the ranks did not always act like enemies. The Confederates had plenty of tobacco but lacked coffee. The Federals had coffee but lacked tobacco. Whenever the pickets of the two sides were close enough, they exchanged news and swapped tobacco and coffee. In the early months of 1863 the two armies were encamped on opposite sides of the Rappahannock River in Virginia. Confederates on the southern bank of the river hollowed out a two-foot log, put a rudder and a sail on it, loaded it with tobacco, pointed it across the river, and gave it a push. It arrived safely on the other bank with its cargo. The Federals loaded it with coffee and sent it on its return voyage. The boat made many round trips. Sometimes groups of men crossed the river to visit on the other side.

Then on May 2–5, 1863, the northern army under Hooker and a smaller Confederate army under Lee fought savagely at Chancellorsville. The two sides left 20,000 dead and wounded on the battlefield. A few days later the northern army was back on its side of the Rappahannock. The soldiers again swapped coffee and tobacco across the river and exchanged comments about the battle.

As we look back on the stories of friendship between the soldiers of the North and the South, we wonder why the two sections went to war. This unit will help to explain the reasons for the War Between the States—"the war between brothers."

18 The Nation Divides

One evening in 1852 Samuel Jones and his wife Mary were sitting by the fireplace talking. It was almost bedtime.

"Yes, Mary," Samuel was saying, "we've been doing our share this winter. I guess we've helped send at least 35 slaves on to Canada since harvesttime. Of course, we're on one of the main routes of the railroad, living here in Indiana."

Just then a triple knock sounded on the side door.

"I wasn't expecting Jim to come through with a group tonight," said Samuel, already on his way to the door. "Is the hiding room ready, Mary?"

"Yes, I put fresh water and some cheese and bread in the cupboard down there this afternoon." Mary waited a moment to see how many were in the party and to be sure there were no unfriendly pursuers coming to seize the runaway slaves. Her husband, on the doorstep, turned back toward her. "One wagon; all seems quiet," he reported.

Mary went to the kitchen to heat some milk. She knew the travelers would be cold and hungry. When she came back to the big fireplace, her cousin Jim was warming his hands at the fire and talking quietly to a young Negro boy and his mother. Beside them, soaking up the heat of the fire, were three other Negroes, two young men and an older woman.

"We'll lay over here tomorrow," Jim decided. "Everything's been quiet along the road this trip, but they'd better stay in the cellar room out of sight. We'll go on tomorrow night, soon as it's dark."

After that night, Samuel Jones and his wife Mary could speak of 40 fugitive slaves they had helped on toward Canada since harvesttime.

The story of Samuel and Mary Jones is an imaginary story. It is based on true facts about the Underground Railroad. People who helped slaves to freedom, like Samuel and Mary, believed they were doing their duty. Slaveowners in the South naturally objected to any help that was given to runaway slaves. Thus the work of the Underground Railroad added to the bitterness between the North and the South. However, it was only a part of the disagreement, as we read in Chapter 14. From 1850 to 1860 one event after the other drove the people of the North and the South further and further apart, until finally war came, war between the northern and the southern states.

1 *The Compromise of 1850 Postpones the Final Crisis*

Even before the Mexican War was over, the United States was faced with the question: Shall slavery be allowed in the new lands obtained from Mexico? In 1820, as you learned on page 279, the nation had faced a similar question. Then it was whether slavery was to be permitted in the Louisiana Purchase. That question had been settled by the Missouri Compromise. Would the country's statesmen again be able to find a solution that would satisfy both sides?

Disagreements over slavery. The views of some northerners and southerners were very far apart. There were people in the North who insisted that slavery must not be permitted in any of the newly obtained territory. Since they wished to keep the territory free of slavery, they were called free-soilers. On the other hand, there were people in the South who insisted that slaveowning must be permitted in all the new territory. Otherwise, the South would leave the Union—it would secede.

Southerners had talked about secession before. (See pages 278 and 279. Secession meant withdrawing from the Union and making themselves independent of the United States government.) But now they were more serious about it. They realized that the North had gone far ahead of the South in population and wealth. It controlled the House of Representatives. (Why could the section with the larger population control the House? See page 182.) The South had managed to keep control of the Senate. (How could this happen? See page 182.) But if the new territory were kept free, soon several free states would be added to the Union. There would be no new slave states to keep the balance. Then, the southerners feared, the North would gain full control of the federal government. If this happened, northerners would be able to pass any laws they wanted—even a law to free all slaves. If the South was to protect itself, it had to do so now while it still had some power. Later would be too late, for the North would be in complete control. So ran the reasoning of many southerners.

California. The country could not put off deciding the difficult question of slavery or no slavery in the newly added lands. California had grown so fast in population that by 1850 it was demanding admission as a state. Its citizens had already written a constitution forbidding slavery. Southern members of Congress refused to admit California into the Union as a free state.

LIBRARY OF CONGRESS

Henry Clay addresses the Senate. This painting shows the Senate in 1848. Vice-President Fillmore presides. Webster (*left*) supports his head on his left hand. Calhoun is standing on Fillmore's left.

The slave trade in the District of Columbia. Two other questions connected with slavery were before Congress at this time. Many people in the North were urging that slavery be abolished in the District of Columbia. They did not want slavery in the National Capital. Washington had become a center of the slave trade, and slaves were bought and sold in the shadow of the Capitol and the White House.

Southerners refused to do away with slavery in the District. They believed that a free Washington would become a refuge for runaway slaves from the nearby southern states. (Look at the map on page 363 to see what states those were.)

Fugitive Slave Law. On the other question the South called for action. Slaveholders demanded that Congress pass a stronger fugitive slave law. They were losing large sums of money as people in the North helped runaway slaves to gain their freedom. Southerners wanted a new law that would enable them to get their slaves back. Many northerners sympathized with the slaves who were fleeing to Canada for liberty, and they opposed such a law.

Congress debates proposals for compromise. In the Senate, Henry Clay proposed a plan to settle all these issues at one time. The plan was called the Compromise of 1850. It included four main parts. First, California was to be admitted as a free state. This would give the North a majority in the Senate. Second, the rest of the land obtained from Mexico would be made into territories. When these territories would be admitted as states, the people who lived in them would decide whether they wanted slavery or not. This gave the South the hope that new slave states

BROWN BROS.

Zachary Taylor
1849–1850

BROWN BROS.

Millard Fillmore
1850–1853

might be admitted in the future. These states would restore the balance in the Senate. Third, the selling of slaves, but not slavery, would be ended in the District of Columbia. This would satisfy the people who believed that the sale of slaves in the capital was a blot on the nation's honor. Finally, a stronger fugitive slave law would be passed to satisfy slaveowners. Under the new law a runaway slave would have no chance to defend himself in court. Anyone who tried to prevent his return to slavery would be fined and put in prison.

The Compromise was debated in Congress for more than six months. The American people followed the debate anxiously. Most of them, north and south, hoped that the Compromise would be accepted and the Union would be preserved.

In the debate Clay, Calhoun, and Webster, the three outstanding American statesmen of this period, played their last great part on the stage of history. In 1820, as young men, they had stood together to help pass the Missouri Compromise. In 1850, as leaders soon to retire, they disagreed.

Clay said that the Compromise was fair to both sides. Calhoun represented those in the South who opposed the Compromise. He expressed their views in the last speech he ever wrote. He was so old and feeble that he had to sit quietly at his place in the Senate while a friend read his speech. He demanded that the North yield on every point. Otherwise the South would secede. Calhoun died before the debate was over.

On March 7 Daniel Webster spoke. He made one of the best speeches of his life. It is called the Seventh of March speech. "I wish to speak today," he began, "not as a Massachusetts man, not as a northern man, but as an American.

. . . I speak today for the preservation of the Union." He appealed to the country to avoid secession and war. The people of both sections, he said, should stop criticizing each other. Their disagreements could be settled by the Compromise.

The point of view of northern free-soilers was expressed by a new political leader, Senator William H. Seward, of New York. He demanded that the South yield on every point.

The Compromise of 1850 is passed. After the debate was over and these various views had been expressed, Congress passed the compromise bills. Most Americans were happy that the Compromise had succeeded. They celebrated with parades and bonfires. The joyful slogan was, "The Union is saved!"

Eagle, 1853. This eagle design on a quilt was made by a woman in Virginia. (See page 158.)

NATIONAL GALLERY OF ART, INDEX OF AMERICAN DESIGN

2 *Differences over Slavery Drive North and South Further Apart*

With the crisis of 1850 past, the American people settled down to enjoy what they hoped would be a long period of quiet and prosperity. But the quiet did not last long. New questions arose that kept the people of the two sections arguing, especially over slavery. Northerners and southerners drifted further apart in bitterness.

Bitter conflicts over slavery. In January, 1854, Senator Stephen A. Douglas, of Illinois, introduced a bill to create the territories of Kansas and Nebraska. The area was part of the Louisiana Purchase and was north of 36° 30′. Therefore, as you read on page 279, it was closed to slavery under the Missouri Compromise. Yet the new bill left it to the people of each territory to decide whether to admit slavery or not. The plan of leaving the decision to the people was called popular sovereignty.

The bill was passed and became law. People in the North stormed in anger. The North, they said, had been faithful to the Missouri Compromise. Now, they charged, the South was breaking the agreement in order to obtain more territory in which slavery could spread. As a result of the Kansas-Nebraska Act, many more northerners joined the free-soil movement.

Bleeding Kansas. Nebraska was not expected to become slave territory. But southerners hoped to establish slavery in Kansas. Northerners, on the other hand, were determined to keep Kansas free. Kansas became a battleground. So-

PUBLIC BUILDINGS ADMINISTRATION

On to Kansas! Settlers streamed into Kansas when it became a territory, searching for a better living on the new frontier. Many came for another reason, too. Southerners wanted to establish slavery in the territory of Kansas. Northerners wanted to keep slavery out. Which side won?

cieties were organized in the North to raise money to help free-soilers settle in Kansas. Societies were organized in the South to raise money to help proslavery people settle in Kansas. More northerners emigrated than southerners. It was easier for a farmer and his family to move than for a slaveowner with his slaves. Then, too, the climate and soil of Kansas were more suitable for the varied crops of the northern farms than for cotton raising.

It looked as if Kansas would become free soil. But the proslavery people in western Missouri were determined to make Kansas slave. On election day hundreds of them marched into Kansas and voted, though they did not live there and were not entitled to vote. A proslavery government was elected. But the free-soil settlers refused to recognize it and set up a government of their own. Then Kansas had two governments, one slave and one free. The supporters of the two sides clashed violently. Blood was spilled.

The struggle in Kansas increased the bitterness between the North and the South. There were violent articles in newspapers and furious speeches in Congress. One northern Senator made an especially violent speech against the South. A southern congressman beat him over the head with a cane. People on each side became more and more bitter in their feelings toward the other side.

Fugitive slaves. The Fugitive Slave Law caused hatred between the sections. Northern people saw runaways being arrested and sent back into slavery. They pitied the fleeing slaves, and many of them realized for the first time the horror of slavery. Many persons who thought slavery to be wrong considered it their duty to violate the Fugitive Slave Law. Increasing numbers of people, like the imaginary couple described at the beginning of this chapter, helped fugitives on the Underground Railroad. Sometimes crowds even rescued runaway slaves who had been

BROWN BROS.

Franklin Pierce
1853–1857

BROWN BROS.

James Buchanan
1857–1861

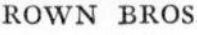

caught and arrested. Southern slaveowners protested in vain.

The Supreme Court opens all territories to slavery. The Supreme Court increased sectional bitterness by its decision in the Dred Scott case. Dred Scott had been a slave in Missouri. His master had taken him to Wisconsin Territory and then brought him back to Missouri. Wisconsin was free soil under the Missouri Compromise. In his trial Dred Scott claimed to be a free man because he had lived in a free territory.

The Supreme Court said that Dred Scott was still a slave. A citizen, it said, had the right to take his property anywhere in the territories of the United States. A slave was a man's property. Any law that said a person could not take his slaves into any territory was unconstitutional. Therefore the Missouri Compromise was unconstitutional. The federal government could not stop the spread of slavery.

The decision appeared to be a great victory for the South. Southerners would be able to take their slaves into any territory. If slavery was once established, there was little chance that it would be prohibited when the territory became a state. The way seemed to be open for slavery to spread.

But the antislavery groups in the North refused to give up the fight. They were more determined than ever to stop the spread of slavery. Many people in the North agreed with Abraham Lincoln when he said, "A house divided against itself cannot stand. I believe this government cannot endure permanently half slave and half free." More and more northerners were resolved to make it all free.

John Brown tries to free the slaves by force. Partly as a result of the Dred Scott decision, an antislavery worker named John Brown went into action. He had already taken part in the civil war in Kansas. Now he decided that he would free the slaves. His plan was to establish a headquarters in the Virginia mountains. From there his followers would swoop down on plantations in the region, kidnap the slaves, and set them free. First he had to have guns and ammunition. To get them, he decided to raid an arsenal (a supply center where arms are stored). On the night of October 16, 1859, John Brown and 18 others seized the United States arsenal at Harpers Ferry (then in Virginia, now in West Virginia). Armed troops soon poured into the little village and captured Brown and his men. Brown was quickly tried, found guilty of treason against the United States, and hanged by federal officers. (Treason is defined in the Constitution; see Article III, Section 3.)

Some abolitionists praised Brown, saying that he had died in the cause of freedom. They made up a song about him, and it was widely sung in the North. But most people in the North believed he had been wrong in using force. Southerners boiled over with rage and fear. They pictured themselves and their families being murdered by rebellious slaves. This, they said, is what happens when the leaders of one section make violent speeches against another section. Many people in the South who had remained faithful to the Union now changed their minds. They said that, if northerners were going to arouse the slaves to rebel, the South for its own safety must separate from the North.

Thus it was that, from 1850 to 1860, one event after another caused bitterness and even hatred between North and South. The people of the two sections grew further and further apart until they could no longer talk reasonably to one another. In 1860 the break came.

3 *After Lincoln Is Elected President, the South Secedes*

As the events of the 1850s turned northerners and southerners into enemies, a new party was begun—the Republican party. It started with meetings

John Brown. The artist shows John Brown going to his execution after his attempt to raid the government arsenal at Harper's Ferry. Why did the artist show him stopping to pet a Negro baby?

METROPOLITAN MUSEUM OF ART

RKO RADIO PICTURES, INC.

Lincoln debates with Douglas. The film *Abe Lincoln in Illinois* shows Lincoln speaking during the 1858 campaign for Senator. Douglas (*left*) listens. Who was elected? Why were the debates important?

held in Wisconsin and Michigan. It first nominated national candidates in the election of 1856. Its principal aim was to prevent the spread of slavery. It also worked for other laws, such as a high tariff, that were demanded by the North and the West.

The Republicans oppose slavery in the territories. The two old parties—the Democrats and the Whigs—had followers in both the North and the South. They were national parties and tied the two parts of the nation together. In order not to lose votes in either section, they took a halfway stand on the question of slavery in the territories. The new party had no followers in the South. It was a sectional party. It took a clear-cut stand on the big issue of the day. Its purpose was to keep slavery out of the territories. If the Republican party won control of the federal government, the southern struggle to extend slavery would be lost.

The events of the 1850s divided the American people into a proslavery group and an antislavery group. More and more northerners turned against slavery and joined the Republican party. In the South almost everyone joined the Democratic party. In 1856 the election went to the Democratic candidate for President, James Buchanan. The Republicans showed surprising strength for a new party.

The Lincoln-Douglas debates. In 1858, a year for congressional elections, the whole country was interested in the campaign for the office of United States Senator in Illinois. The Democratic candidate was Stephen A. Douglas, the author of the Kansas-Nebraska Act. The Republican candidate was Abraham Lincoln.

You have already followed the Lincoln family westward from Kentucky to Illinois (see pages 208–209). In Illinois, Abraham Lincoln grew up. As a young fellow he earned a living doing farm work and keeping a store, but he studied all the while. Finally he became a lawyer and settled down in Springfield, the state capital. After a few years he turned to politics. He served in the state legislature and for one term in the House of Representatives. Then he gave up politics and devoted all his time to his law practice. He became a successful lawyer.

When Douglas introduced the Kansas-Nebraska bill in Congress, Lincoln again became active in politics. He traveled around Illinois, making speeches criticizing Douglas. Lincoln believed that Congress had no power to abolish slavery in the southern states. But he hoped that slavery would gradually be ended somehow. Like the free-soilers, he believed the first step in that direction was to prevent it from spreading in the territories.

In the campaign for Senator the two candidates met in a series of debates. Large crowds gathered to hear them. Douglas was an experienced speaker and campaigner. In these meetings Lincoln proved that he, too, was a skillful debater.

Lincoln asks Douglas a question. The Democratic party was divided. According to the Dred Scott decision, the federal government must protect slavery in all the territories. According to the Kansas-Nebraska Act, the people in a territory were to decide whether to permit slavery or not. The question was: suppose the people of a territory prohibited slavery, did the federal government still have to protect slavery in that territory? In other words, which ruled—the Dred Scott decision or the Kansas-Nebraska Act? Most southern Democrats preferred the Dred Scott de-

The Confederate States of America. The first Confederate capital was Montgomery, Alabama; in July, 1861, Richmond became the capital. Which states left the Union before fighting broke out? West Virginia became a state in 1863, when a government loyal to the Union was formed in western Virginia.

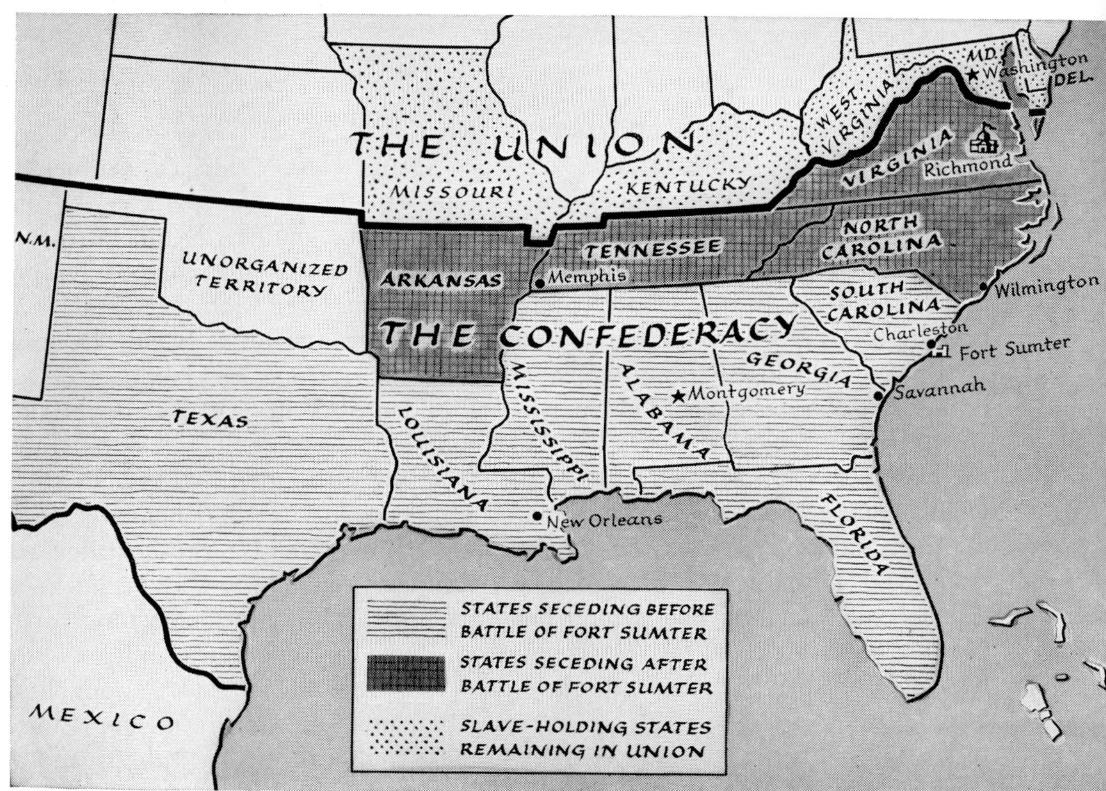

LIBRARY OF CONGRESS

Confederate President and cabinet. Jefferson Davis (*seated at the head of the table*), President of the Confederate States, meets with his cabinet to hear a report by General Robert E. Lee (*standing center*).

cision. Most northern Democrats preferred the Kansas-Nebraska Act.

In one of the Lincoln-Douglas debates, Lincoln asked Douglas a question. Under the Dred Scott decision, Lincoln asked, could the people of a territory prohibit slavery? If Douglas answered "yes," he would lose southern votes. If he answered "no," he would lose northern votes. (See page 374.)

Douglas answers Lincoln's question. Douglas answered that, in practice, it made no difference what the Supreme Court said. If the people in a territory did not want slavery, they would not pass local laws to protect it. Slaveowners would not risk bringing their slaves into that territory. As a result the territory would remain free.

Thus Douglas gave the people of a territory the final power to decide for or against slavery. His answer helped him win the election as Senator from Illinois. But southern Democrats never forgave him for not completely supporting the Dred Scott decision.

Republican victory. In 1860 Douglas won the Democratic nomination for President, but he was not accepted by southern Democrats. The delegates from several southern states held a separate convention. They named as their candidate John C. Breckenridge, of Kentucky, who was Vice-President at the time. Thus the Democratic party, with two candidates, was split.

The Republican party nominated Abraham Lincoln. In their platform the Republicans opposed the spread of slavery. They promised to pass a protective tariff to aid the manufacturers of the North. They promised to pass a homestead law that would give a farm to every settler in the West. And they promised federal aid for building a railroad to the Pacific. From 1850 to 1860 all of these measures to help the North and the West had been defeated or delayed by the South. Now, if it won, the Republican party promised to carry out these policies.

Election day came. Lincoln, the Republican, was elected although nobody voted for him in 10 southern states. The result of the election meant that the federal government would be controlled by a party opposed to slavery. What would the South do?

Southern states organize the Confederacy. During the campaign many southerners had threatened to secede if Lincoln were elected. After the election South Carolina seceded and was followed by Mississippi, Florida, Alabama, Georgia, Louisiana, and Texas. In February, 1861, these states organized themselves as the Confederate States of America. They elected Jefferson Davis President of the Confederacy.

When Abraham Lincoln was inaugurated President on March 4, 1861, he faced a divided country. In his inaugural address he stated his views. He assured the South that he would not interfere with slavery in the states. But he insisted that no state had the right to secede from the Union. As President he would enforce the laws in every part of the country. He made a strong plea for a peaceful agreement. In one part of his speech he talked directly to the South:

In your hands, my dissatisfied fellow

Northern supply depot. This is a picture of a supply depot for the Union armies. What were the principal supplies stored? How were they transported?

countrymen, and not in mine, is the momentous issue of civil war. The government will not assail you. You can have no conflict without being yourselves the aggressors [the ones who begin the conflict]. You have no oath registered in heaven to destroy the government, while I shall have the most solemn one to "preserve, protect, and defend" it.

I am loath to close. We are not enemies but friends. We must not be enemies.

Fighting begins at Fort Sumter. President Lincoln did not act hastily. Several southern states had not yet seceded. Perhaps he could keep them in the Union. Then the Confederacy would be too weak to stand alone for long. But in April, Lincoln had to act.

When the southern states seceded, they seized the forts of the United States within their borders. Fort Sumter in the harbor of Charleston, South Carolina, refused to surrender. But the soldiers in the fort were running out of food. They had to be supplied with food by April 15 or they would have to surrender.

What could Lincoln do? If he withdrew the soldiers from the fort, he would be recognizing the independence of South Carolina. If he sent food to the fort, the southerners would fire on it and war would start. Lincoln finally decided to send food. Jefferson Davis ordered an attack on Fort Sumter. On April 12 the cannon in Charleston Harbor were fired on the fort, over which the American flag was flying. The next day the fort was surrendered.

The attack on Fort Sumter was the beginning of the War Between the States. Lincoln called upon the northern states for 75,000 soldiers. Now that the fighting had begun, Virginia seceded, followed by Arkansas, Tennessee, and North Carolina. A total of 11 states withdrew from the Union and joined the Confederacy.

4 *Both North and South Have Advantages and Problems*

How did the two sides compare in strength when the war began? (See the chart on page 368.)

The North consisted of 23 states with a population of 22 million. The South had 11 states with 9 million people, including 3½ million slaves. The slaves counted in the war because they produced food and did other important work on the southern home front. But the North had much the larger manpower. Throughout the war northern armies were bigger than southern armies.

The North is strong industrially. The North, as you have read, was the industrial section. The war caused an industrial boom in the North. More iron ore was mined than ever before. Factories turned out guns, railroad rails, locomotives and freight cars, machinery, and other products. The North kept its railroads in good condition throughout the war and so was able to supply its armies with food, clothing, and munitions. Textile mills made immense amounts of cloth. With sewing machines, workers turned out army uniforms and pairs of shoes by the thousands. On northern farms there were no slaves, but there were machines, and machines were better. Many farmers were in the army. But with reapers drawn by horses, women, boys, and older men were able to harvest the crops. The North produced such large crops during the war that it continued to export wheat to feed England's factory workers. The northern victory in the war was largely a triumph of free workers and machines over slaves and hand labor.

The South suffers for lack of industries. The South was far behind in manufacturing. Its people had spent most of their time raising cotton. Southern leaders hoped to sell cotton in Europe and buy war supplies. But the northern navy blockaded the entire southern coast. Only England was strong enough to break the blockade, and England decided not to do so. (See page 378.)

To keep up the war, the southern people had to start almost from scratch to produce uniforms, munitions, and railroad supplies. They achieved wonders. At no time during the four years of war was a southern army without guns, powder, or bullets. But the pinch was felt in other ways. As the war stretched out, the South was unable to keep its army well supplied. Some Confederate soldiers had to march barefooted because there were not enough shoes. They had to sleep on the bare ground because there were not enough blankets. They wore tattered uniforms. Many had no overcoats or warm clothing. In the winter they padded their clothes with newspapers to keep warm. They were urged to grow beards as a protection against the winter cold. The southern armies lacked medicines and

LIBRARY OF CONGRESS

"Stonewall" Jackson. General Thomas J. Jackson was one of the many outstanding officers who resigned from the United States Army to fight for the South. How did he earn his nickname?

medical supplies for the sick and wounded. The soldiers seldom had enough food. There was no tea, and coffee was very scarce.

The South did not have the iron products with which to keep up its railroads. Toward the end of the war the railroads were in very poor condition. It was all they could do to transport troops and war supplies. They could not take care of civilian needs. As a result it happened that people in some sections of the South suffered from hunger while food was piled up a few hundred miles away.

Southerners at home suffered a great deal. Southern women accepted their full share of the hardships. Most of them had no new clothes during the war and made the old ones do. They cut up the carpets in their homes to make blankets for the soldiers. They

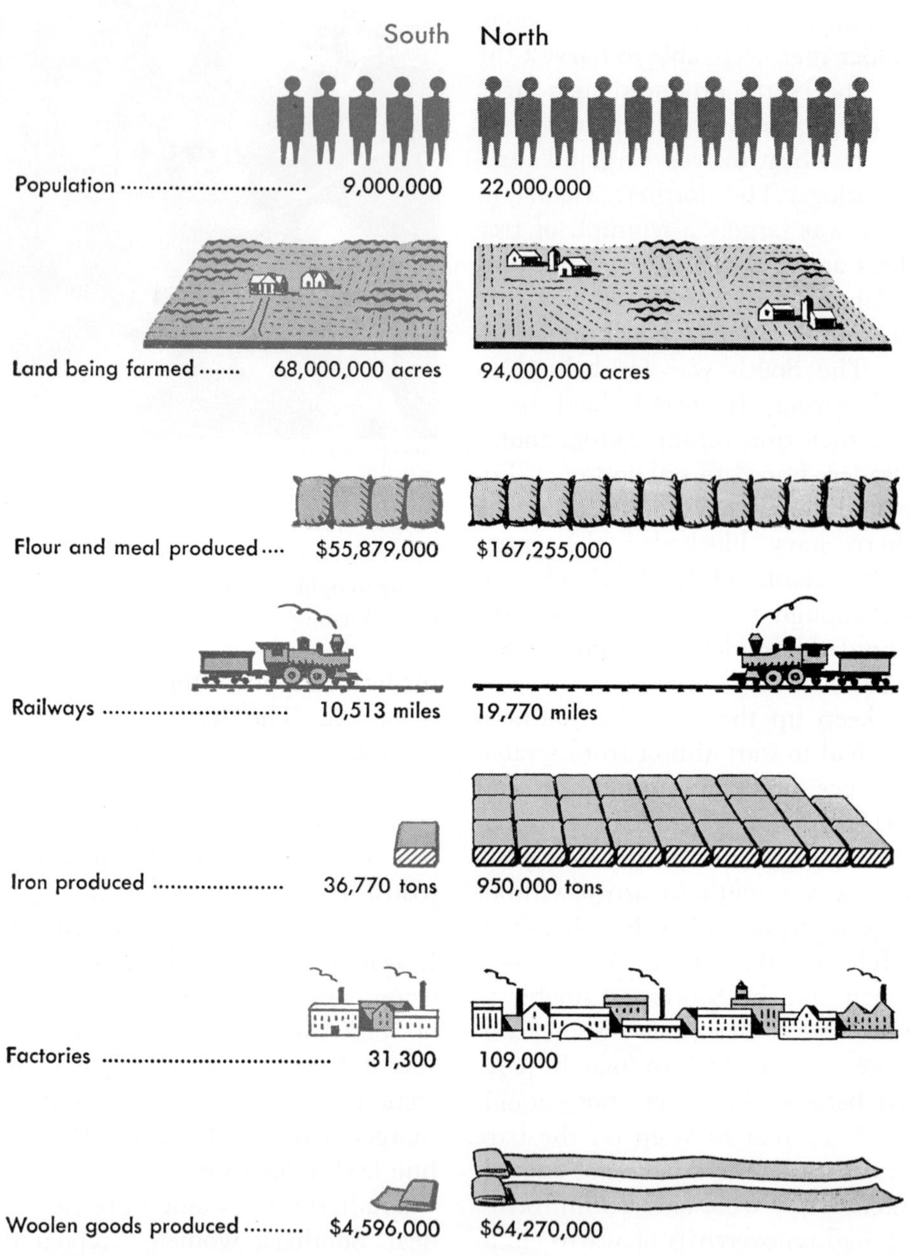

In the War Between the States, the North was ahead of the South in many important ways. With a larger population, the North could raise larger armies. It produced bigger crops and more manufactured goods. And it had more railways to transport food and other products. What effect did these advantages have on the outcome of the war?

Southern Life in Wartime

We women formed into a sewing society —resting not on Sundays. Sewing machines were put into the churches, which became depots for flannel, muslin, strong linen, and even uniform cloth. When the hour for meeting arrived, the sewing class would be summoned by the ringing of the church bell.

It had not been many years since every Virginia farm owned a house for a great cumbrous loom, with beams supported against the ceiling. The door of the loom house was again opened, and the weaver installed upon her bench. Cotton cloth was woven and dyed yellow with butternut, black with walnut bark, gray with willow. . . . Every atom of black silk was a treasure. It was shredded to mix with the cotton before carding. . . . Pins became scarce. People walked about with downcast eyes; they were looking for pins! Thorns were gathered and dried to use as pins. Dentists' gold soon disappeared. The generation succeeding the war period had not good teeth.

¶ This description of life in Petersburg, Virginia, during the War Between the States is from *Reminiscences of Peace and War* by Mrs. Roger A. Pryor.

Southern women in war. Southern women nursed wounded Confederate soldiers back to health in southern hospitals. What other sacrifices did southern women make to supply food and blankets for the Confederate armies?

THE NEW-YORK HISTORICAL SOCIETY, NEW YORK CITY

The Lincolns. This painting shows the Lincoln family in 1861. The boys are Willie, Bob, and Tad. Willie's death in 1862 was a great sorrow for the Lincolns. Bob was a student at Harvard at this time, while Tad lived in the White House.

took out old looms that had been stored away and wove cloth. They went hungry and cold themselves in order to send packages of food and warm clothing to the men at the front. They nursed the wounded and sick soldiers in hospitals. They kept up their own spirits by giving parties at which no refreshments were served. Jokingly they called such gatherings "starvation parties."

The South fights on the defensive. The South had definite advantages on its side. It would be on the defensive in the war; that is, it had only to defend itself. It did not have to invade the North. On the other hand, in order to bring the seceded states back into the Union, the North had to take the offensive. That is, it had to invade the Confederacy, defeat its armies, and seize and hold its territory. A smaller army acting on the defensive could defeat a larger army acting on the offensive, especially if the smaller army were better led.

The South has better generals. Another advantage of the South was in its superior military leaders. Several hundred of the best trained officers of the United States Army resigned and joined the Army of the Confederacy. Outstanding among them was Robert E. Lee. In 1861 Lee was offered command of the Union Army, but he could not fight against Virginia. He resigned from the United States Army, and later was appointed to command the Confederate Army in Virginia.

The secession of Virginia brought two more great generals to the southern side: Joseph E. Johnston and Thomas J.

(Stonewall) Jackson. It was in the first Battle of Bull Run that another southern general, seeing Jackson's men standing solid against a northern attack, said: "There is Jackson, standing like a stone wall." In 1862 Jackson kept the northern army divided so that it could not attack Lee in full strength. Jackson was wounded in the Battle of Chancellorsville and died. His death was a great loss to the South.

Southern generals won a series of brilliant victories in the early campaigns of the war. Again and again Lee outgeneraled his northern opponents. Though commanding a smaller army, he defeated them in battle. Lincoln, meanwhile, searched in vain for a northern general who could win battles.

Lincoln leads the North. On the northern side Lincoln stood out as the greatest leader in the national crisis and the strongest supporter of the Union. In the beginning many people doubted Lincoln's ability to lead the country in war. He was awkward in appearance. He had had no experience as an executive, and he often seemed to hesitate about making up his mind. In time, however, he proved his leadership. Lincoln did not let himself be turned aside from the main issue. The Union had to be saved. To him the question of putting an end to slavery took second place, for the time at least. Lincoln wrote, "If I could save the Union without freeing any slave, I would do it; and if I could do it by freeing all the slaves, I would do it."

As a war leader President Lincoln found it necessary to exercise a great deal of power. Some individuals called him a dictator (a man who takes all the power of government into his own hands and runs everything his way), but most of the people of the North trusted him. Lincoln's greatest strength lay in the fact that the people always had faith in him. He grew up as one of them, and he remained one of them. His education came partly from reading good books and from studying law. But it came also from his close contact with people, learning how they thought and felt.

Out of his varied experience Lincoln gained an understanding of the minds and hearts of the people. He was full of stories about ordinary people. He was able to express their thoughts in simple

Robert E. Lee. Lee commanded the Confederate Army in Virginia. This picture shows him when, after the war, he served as president of Washington University, known today as Washington and Lee.

BETTMANN

THE NEW-YORK HISTORICAL SOCIETY, NEW YORK CITY

Draft riot. When the North began to draft men for the Army, riots occurred. The picture shows one of the outbreaks in New York.

language that everyone understood. No wonder that the people confided in him and followed him. Lincoln never lost touch with the common people of his country. Even when the burdens of war were heaviest, he set aside time to receive in the White House any person who wished to talk to him.

Both sides face the problems of wartime. As the fighting went on, both sides were faced with serious problems —problems that every government at war has to face. Many people in the North and the South soon lost their enthusiasm for the war. As a result both sides had to draft men for their armies. On both sides the laws allowed men to send substitutes. In many cases a rich man paid someone to serve his term in the army while he stayed at home living his usual life. Some people in the South complained that the war was "a rich man's war and a poor man's fight"; in other words, that it was being fought to protect rich men's property, but the fighting was being done by the poor. In many places in the North, men started riots to protest against the draft.

Lack of money. Both governments had a hard time obtaining enough money to pay for the war. The Confederacy had a bigger problem since its people had little wealth except for slaves and land. In the last years of the war, instead of collecting taxes in money, the Confederate government took one-tenth of all farm products. Otherwise it supported itself by printing paper money. The more money it printed, the less value the money had.

The North had greater resources to carry on war than the South, and it spent more. The federal government raised money by selling bonds and raising taxes. It also printed large sums of paper money, called greenbacks. But northern paper money totaled less than half the amount printed in the South.

Profiteering. Both North and South had their share of men who made big profits by dishonest practices. Some northern merchants sold to the army uniforms and blankets of the cheapest material, called shoddy, which soon wore out. Some delivered spoiled food that was not fit to eat. Perhaps one-fourth of the money spent by the Union government during the war would have been saved if there had been no dishonesty.

In the South profiteers bought up supplies of salt, coffee, sugar, leather, and other scarce goods. They hoarded these products until prices went away up. Then they sold them, making huge profits. Desperate people sometimes took matters into their own hands. In Mobile, Alabama, for example, a group of women broke open the stores of businessmen who were hoarding goods. Then they helped themselves to the food and clothing they needed.

Opposition groups. Both governments had to deal with groups that opposed their war efforts. The people who lived in the mountain regions of western North Carolina, eastern Tennessee, and northern Alabama were strong Unionists, and thousands of them fought on the Union side. Sympathy for the North was especially strong in mountainous western Virginia. There the Confederate forces were driven out in the early months of the war. A separate state was formed, and West Virginia was admitted into the Union in 1863.

In the North many Democrats opposed Lincoln and the war. As a rule they were left free to express their opinions so long as they did not interfere with carrying on the war. They were called Copperheads, because they used to cut out the copper heads from pennies and wear them as pins or clasps.

Summary

At various times between 1850 and 1860 northerners and southerners argued, became angry, and actually fought with one another. Not all the disagreements were over slavery, but the ones that aroused the greatest anger on both sides were. In 1850 a difficult question arose. Would slavery be permitted in the new lands annexed from Mexico? That question, along with other related problems, seemed to be settled by the Compromise of 1850. But

Hoarding food. During the War Between the States, as during other wars, some individuals selfishly hoarded food and other scarce goods.

it soon came up again as a result of the Kansas-Nebraska Act and the Dred Scott decision.

A large group of northerners organized the Republican party. Unlike the Whig and the Democratic parties, all its members were northerners. When the Republicans elected a northern President in 1860, many southerners felt sure their views would always be defeated in a government headed by a Republican. They were ready, therefore, to secede. Although Lincoln tried to reassure the southerners in his inaugural speech, secession had already begun and war soon followed.

As the North and the South faced each other at the beginning of the war, each side had certain advantages. The North had more people, more factories, a greater variety of agricultural products, and more adequate transportation than the South. The South had many excellent leaders and the advantage of fighting on the defensive. In a long war the advantages of the North were sure to count heavily. Each side faced the problems of enlisting soldiers, raising money to pay for the war, and uniting the people in support of the war effort.

For a Quick Review

1. What parts of the Compromise of 1850 were favorable to the North, and what parts were favorable to the South?

2. Why did so much argument and violence arise over the Kansas-Nebraska Act?

3. Why were the Lincoln-Douglas debates of 1858 of national importance although they were part of a state campaign?

4. Was the Republican party a sectional party? Give evidence to support your answer.

5. Why did the southern states secede after the election of 1860?

6. What decision did Lincoln have to make about Fort Sumter? Why was it important?

7. What were the advantages and problems of each side in the War Between the States?

The Lincoln-Douglas Debates

Lincoln asked Douglas this question: "Can the people of a United States territory, in any lawful way, against the wish of any citizen of the United States, exclude slavery from its limits prior to the formation of a state constitution?"

Douglas replied: "I answer emphatically . . . that in my opinion the people of a territory can, by lawful means, exclude slavery from their limits prior to the formation of a state constitution. . . . It matters not what the Supreme Court may hereafter decide as to the abstract question whether slavery may or may not go into a territory under the Constitution. The people have the lawful means to introduce it or exclude it as they please, for the reason that slavery cannot exist a day or an hour anywhere, unless it is supported by local police regulations. Those police regulations can only be established by the local legislature; and if the people are opposed to slavery, they will elect representatives to that body who will by unfriendly legislation effectually prevent the introduction of it into their midst."

Lincoln objected: "I will ask you, my friends, if you were elected members of the legislature, what would be the first thing you would have to do before entering upon your duties? Swear to support the Constitution of the United States. Suppose you believe, as Judge Douglas does, that the Constitution of the United States guarantees to your neighbor the right to hold slaves in that territory; that they are his property: how can you clear your oaths unless you give him such legislation as is necessary to enable him to enjoy that property?"

Douglas answered: "I say to you that there is but one hope, one safety for this country, and that is to stand immovably by that principle which declares the right of each state and each territory to decide these questions themselves."

Learning to Study More Easily

REVIEWING AND TESTING YOUR SKILL IN FINDING INFORMATION

In the first part of this book, you were introduced to various kinds of reference materials and to various ways of finding information. How much of an impression have these introductions made on you? Find out by giving yourself the quiz that follows, writing your answers on a sheet in your notebook. Perhaps your whole class will take the quiz, and you can discuss the questions together afterward—or you may decide to work them out together.

1. What parts of this book would you use to find quickly information on the Compromise of 1850?
2. On what pages is the Dred Scott decision mentioned?
3. Where would you look, outside of this textbook, to find information about the founding of the Republican party?
4. Where would you look, besides in this textbook, to find the meaning of free-soilers? What is the meaning?
5. Where would you look to find the meanings of these words: rally, ultimately, secede, extension, fugitive, arsenal? What does each mean?
6. Where would you look, outside of this text, to find information about the abolitionists?
7. On what pages in this text is abolition discussed? What relation was there between the abolitionists and the events described in Chapter 18?
8. On what pages in this text is nullification discussed? States' rights? What relation was there between nullification, states' rights, and the secession of the southern states in 1860 and 1861?
9. If you were preparing a floor talk on or a dramatization of the life of Stephen A. Douglas, where would you look for information?
10. John C. Calhoun is mentioned in Chapter 18. Is he mentioned elsewhere in this book?
11. List headings, other than "Secession," under which you might look for information about the beginning of the war between the northern and the southern states. Test your list by seeing how many of the headings can be found in (*a*) the index of this book, (*b*) an encyclopedia, (*c*) the card catalog of your school or public library.

19 *The Union Is Restored*

For months the country had waited in suspense to learn what would happen at Fort Sumter. When the news of the attack and the surrender was flashed across the nation, the uncertainty was ended. The people of the North and the South celebrated. Those on each side believed they were sure to win a quick victory. They read warlike editorials in their newspapers. "Washington is the weak point with our enemies," declared a Richmond paper. It urged the Confederacy to capture the Union capital at once. "Forward to Richmond! Forward to Richmond!" ran an editorial in a New York City paper. It urged the northern army to capture the Confederate capital at once. In North and South the people rang church bells, waved flags, and attended mass meetings where they cheered fiery orators. Today we know they had little reason to celebrate, with four long years of war and suffering ahead. But in April, 1861, they could not see into the future.

The people of the South were joyful over the fall of Fort Sumter. As they saw it, a single state had humbled the federal government. The surrender proved to them what they already eagerly believed: that the Yankees would not fight to preserve the Union. The war would be a short and easy one. Southerners flocked to join the Confederate Army. So many came that some had to be sent home to wait until guns could be provided for them. A southern woman wrote that the women of the South "were all enthusiastically in favor of secession . . . if the southern men had not been willing to go [to war], I reckon they would have been made to go by the women."

In the North the fall of Sumter helped unite the people. The great majority were determined to preserve the Union. Leaders of the Democratic party, like Stephen A. Douglas, announced their support of President Lincoln. Workers, lawyers, businessmen, and clerks enlisted. In the beginning more men volunteered than the Army could take care of. In far-off Wisconsin one enthusiastic volunteer wrote, "We thought the rebellion would be over before our chance [to fight] would come."

1 *North and South Fight a Bitter War*

By June, 1861, North and South had each collected an army of 25,000 partially trained volunteers. People in the North expected their army to capture Richmond immediately and smash the Confederacy. In July the northern army met the southern army in the first Battle of Bull Run (see map on page 381). The northern army was defeated and fled in retreat. Strangely enough, the untrained Confederate Army was equally confused by victory and failed to pursue the fleeing Union troops.

The blockade. After the Battle of Bull Run it became clear that the war would be long and hard-fought. To fight a long war, the South had to import guns, clothing, shoes, blankets, and other products needed by its armies and its people at home. To pay for these goods, the South had its large cotton crops, which England and other countries needed.

But northern leaders were determined to keep the South from getting help from other countries. The northern navy blockaded the entire southern coast and cut the South off from Europe. (See the map on page 380.) Some

The *Monitor* and the *Merrimac*. Here are the Confederate and Union ironclads in bitter battle. What advantages did each possess? How did the battle end?

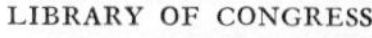

LIBRARY OF CONGRESS

ships got through the blockade, but not enough to supply the needs of the South.

The *Merrimac* versus the *Monitor*. Southern leaders were determined to break the blockade. Their "secret weapon" was the *Merrimac,* an old wooden warship covered with iron. The *Merrimac* entered Chesapeake Bay on March 8, 1862, and destroyed two northern warships. But when it returned the next day to complete the destruction of the northern navy, it was met by the *Monitor*. The *Monitor* was a northern ironclad that looked like "a cheesebox on a raft." It fought off the *Merrimac* and saved the northern navy. (See figure 1 on the map on page 380.)

England refuses to break the blockade. The southern people hoped that England would break the blockade. For lack of southern cotton, English mills were closed down. Thousands of English workers were unemployed. Because the English needed cotton to run their mills, the British government was tempted to support the South. But for many years England had led the world in abolishing slavery, and the South stood for slavery. The very English workers who were unemployed because of the lack of cotton urged President Lincoln not to make peace until the slaves were freed. The English government decided not to break the blockade.

War in the East. On land the war was fought in two main areas, as you can see from the map on page 380. One was in the West. The other was in the East, in northern Virginia between the two capitals, Washington and Richmond.

In Virginia the purpose of the Union forces was to capture Richmond, the southern capital. Lincoln hoped that the loss of their capital would dishearten the southern people and so shorten the war. In three years of bitter fighting the northern armies failed to take the city, thanks mainly to the brilliant generalship of Lee and Stonewall Jackson.

At the end of August, 1862, Lee won a great victory in the second Battle of Bull Run. Then he decided to invade the North. If the invasion would be successful he might capture a large city like Harrisburg or Baltimore. After such a victory England might decide to recognize the Confederacy as an independent nation and break the blockade. But the Union army, commanded by General George B. McClellan, defeated Lee's forces at Antietam (ăn tē′*tă*m), Maryland. Lee led his army back across the Potomac River into Virginia.

The Emancipation Proclamation. In September, 1862, five days after the northern victory at Antietam, President Lincoln made an announcement. He said that on January 1, 1863, he would issue a proclamation freeing all the slaves in the Confederacy. Accordingly, on the first day of 1863, Lincoln issued the Emancipation (ḗ măn *sĭ* pā′ sh*ŭ*n) Proclamation.

Actually no slaves were freed immediately. They were set free only as northern armies gained control of the areas in which they lived. Slavery was abolished in the United States by the Thirteenth Amendment to the Constitution, which was adopted after the war was over.

The Emancipation Proclamation was

LIBRARY OF CONGRESS

The *Kearsarge* sinks the *Alabama* in 1864. While officially neutral, Great Britain permitted the Confederacy to build warships in British shipyards. The best known, the *Alabama,* captured more than 60 northern merchant vessels before it was sunk. Later, Great Britain paid the United States for the destruction caused by the *Alabama*.

a war measure. Its purpose was to weaken the South and strengthen the North. It encouraged northern abolitionists to support the war more enthusiastically. It announced to Europe that the North would abolish slavery in the United States if it won the war. Thus the Proclamation made certain that England would not support the South.

Gettysburg. In December, 1862, Lee won a victory over the northern army under General Ambrose Burnside at Fredericksburg. In May, 1863, he won another great victory over the Union army under General Joseph Hooker at Chancellorsville. Encouraged by his success, Lee decided to invade the North again. He planned to march into Pennsylvania. Perhaps he would defeat the northern army and capture Baltimore or Philadelphia. Some people in the North were talking of peace. Such a blow might discourage enough people so that Lincoln would have to make peace even if it meant letting the South go. Whatever the future might bring, Lee had an immediate reason for marching north. There was not enough food in Virginia to feed his army. On the fertile farms of Pennsylvania there was plenty of food.

The Union army followed Lee's army northward. The two armies clashed in the Battle of Gettysburg on the first three days of July, 1863. The northern army was commanded by General George G. Meade.

On the first day the southern forces attacked with some success. The northern army took up a position along a high ridge called Cemetery Ridge. On the second day the southern forces attacked both ends of the northern line. Again the South won only partial success. Overnight the North strengthened its position along Cemetery Ridge.

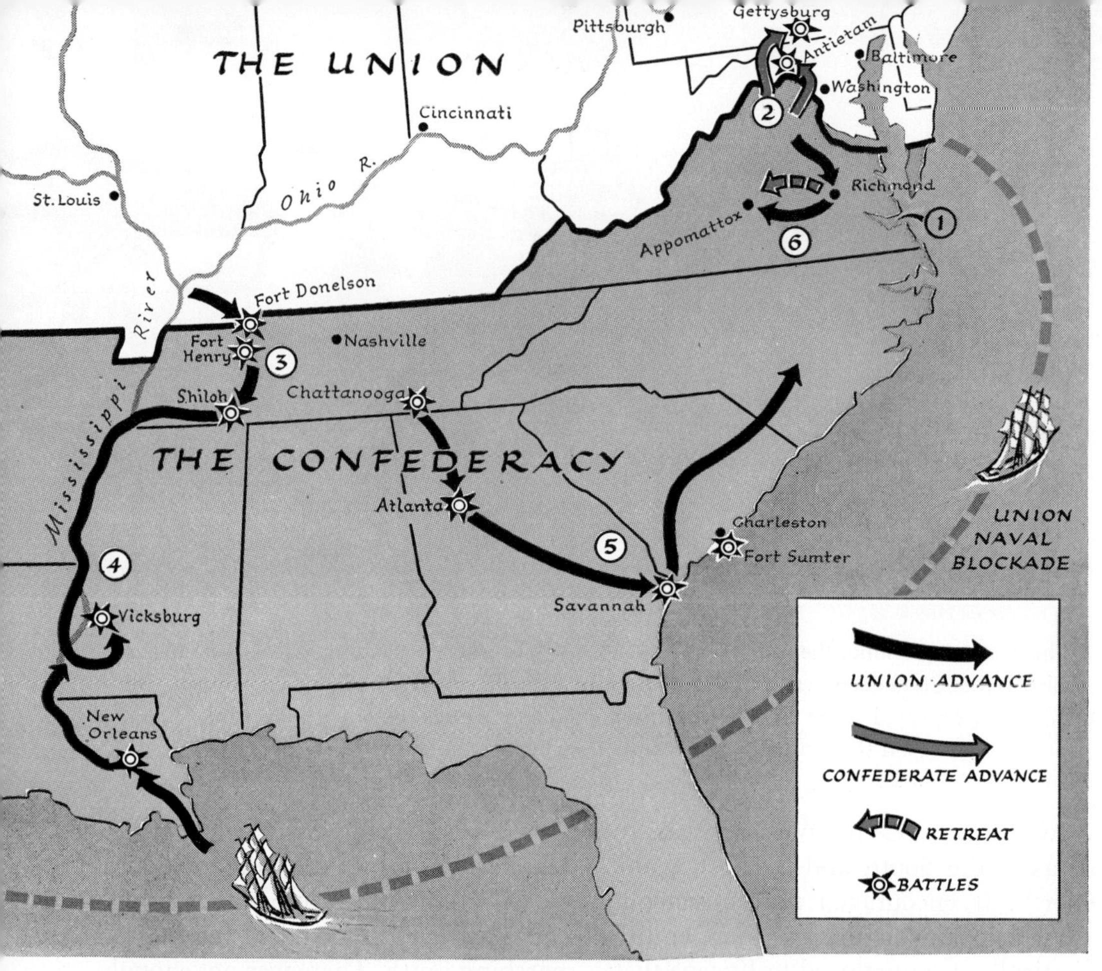

The War Between the States. As you read on pages 377–384 about military events in the war, follow the action on this map. Why did the North set up a naval blockade of the South? Why was control of the Mississippi important to both sides? What was the military purpose of Sherman's march through Georgia? What were the aims of the fighting in Virginia, Maryland, and Pennsylvania?

On the afternoon of the third day, 15,000 southern soldiers came across the fields straight toward the center of Cemetery Ridge. Their commander was General George E. Pickett. They marched as if on parade, in straight ranks, on a line a mile and a half across. Their battle flags were flying. Their officers led them with drawn swords. As Union cannon shot holes through the ranks, more men came up and filled the gaps. The line moved across the fields and up the slope. At the brow of the hill the two sides fought bitterly around a stone wall. Some Confederates got across the wall and into the Union line. But there were not enough men to support them and hold the position they had won. Those who did not fall had to retreat. Pickett's charge had failed. Just when it was close to success, the strength of the Confederacy had given out.

After the battle, Lee led his army back into Virginia. The losses on both sides in the Battle of Gettysburg were about the same. Each army lost about 20,000 men in killed, wounded, and missing. But the North could replace the losses. The South could not. Lee could never again hope to take the offensive. He could not with one great victory win independence for the Confederacy. Thereafter he remained on the defensive. He tried to keep the war going until the North would grow tired of fighting and make a compromise peace.

War in the West. In the western campaigns the aim of the northern armies was to weaken the South so that it would be unable to continue fighting. The plan was to split up the South into parts and to seize or destroy its rail-

The war in Virginia and the North. Some of the bitterest fighting in the War Between the States took place in Virginia. What city were the northern armies trying to capture? What was Lee's purpose in invading Maryland and Pennsylvania?

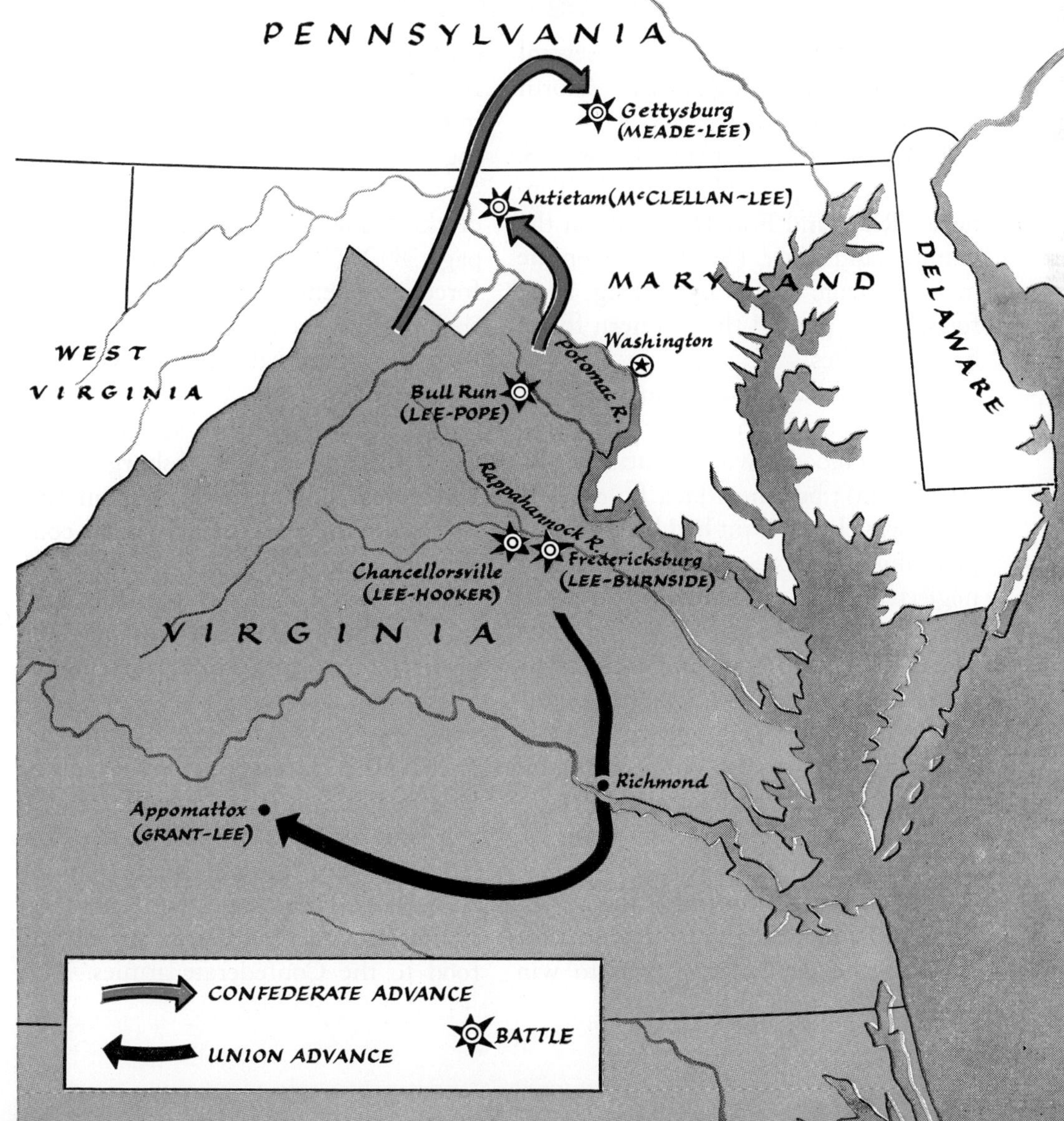

Battle of Shiloh. The Confederates caught Grant off guard at Shiloh and almost won back Tennessee. Locate Shiloh on the map on page 380.

LIBRARY OF CONGRESS

roads and its supplies. After several hard-fought campaigns the North achieved its aim.

Early in 1862 General Ulysses S. Grant captured Fort Henry on the Tennessee River and Fort Donelson on the Cumberland River. (See figure 3 on the map on page 380.) By taking these forts, Grant pushed the southern forces back 200 miles.

The Confederates tried to win back this important territory by attacking Grant in a bloody two-day battle at Shiloh (shī′lō); but the attack failed. The battle was close. Grant had been so busy planning his next attack that he had neglected to set up outposts to warn him of an approach by the enemy. Moreover, he had gone nine miles away from the army without appointing anyone to command in his place. Lincoln was urged to remove Grant from his command for this carelessness. But Lincoln said, "I can't spare this man; he fights."

The North wins control of the Mississippi. The main plan of the North for splitting the Confederacy was to win control of the Mississippi River. In April, 1862, Admiral David G. Farragut ran his ships past the forts defending the mouth of the Mississippi. He captured New Orleans, the biggest city of the Confederacy. (See the map on page 380.) This victory gave the Union forces an opening to work up the Mississippi from the south at the same time that they pushed down the river from the north.

The last Confederate stronghold on the Mississippi was Vicksburg. For a whole year Union forces tried in vain to capture the place. Where other commanders had failed, Grant succeeded. On July 4, 1863, the day after the battle at Gettysburg had ended in northern victory, the Confederates surrendered Vicksburg to Grant.

A few days later the North controlled the Mississippi in its entire length. Texas, Louisiana, and Arkansas were cut off from the rest of the Confederacy. (See figure 4 on the map on page 380.) These states had sent large numbers of men and large amounts of food to the Confederate armies. Now this aid was almost altogether stopped.

Though much bitter fighting was yet to come, Gettysburg and Vicksburg marked the beginning of the end for the South. After Gettysburg, as you have read, Lee remained on the defensive. With the control of the Mississippi, the Union armies began the process of cutting the Confederacy into pieces. That process was continued, weakening the South until Lee was unable to keep up even his defensive fighting.

Sherman's march. In March, 1864, Grant was placed at the head of all the Union armies. He went to Washington, leaving General William T. Sherman in command at Chattanooga, Tennessee. Sherman now planned to drive across the very middle of the Confederacy and so cut it into smaller pieces. In continuous fighting from May to September he pushed the Confederate Army farther and farther south until he occupied Atlanta, Georgia.

From Atlanta, with 60,000 men, Sherman marched through Georgia to Savannah. On the way, on a path 60 miles wide, the Union Army destroyed everything useful. It tore up railroads. It burned barns and food supplies. It looted houses and drove off livestock. When he reached Savannah, Sherman had again split the South. He had cut the states from Florida to Mississippi out of the war. (See figure 5 on the map on page 380.) Only the Carolinas and part of Virginia were left to fight the North.

From Savannah, Sherman turned north into South Carolina, continuing to destroy southern property. General Philip H. Sheridan carried out the

LIBRARY OF CONGRESS

Friendly enemies. Confederate soldiers had tobacco but were short of coffee. Union soldiers had coffee but little tobacco. Between battles, soldiers on the front lines often traded such items.

Army kitchen. This Union Army kitchen in Virginia was photographed by Mathew Brady, whose camera recorded many important events of the war.

OFFICE OF THE CHIEF SIGNAL OFFICER

Confederate homecoming. After the war Confederate soldiers returned home to find their houses and farms in ruins.

same kind of destruction in the Shenandoah Valley in western Virginia.

The war ends at Appomattox. Meanwhile, in eastern Virginia, Grant was hammering away at Lee. (See figure 6 on the map on page 380.) He had a much larger force, but he had to attack while Lee remained on the defensive. In the daily battles the northern army suffered the greater losses. Finally, on April 2, 1865, after a siege of nine months, Lee gave up Richmond.

Grant and his staff. After victories in the West, General Grant was chosen by Lincoln to command all the Union armies.

LIBRARY OF CONGRESS

To save his men from further unnecessary suffering, Lee decided to surrender. On Sunday, April 9, the two generals met near Appomattox Courthouse, Virginia. Lee, tall and erect, was in a bright new uniform with a jeweled sword. Grant, short and stoop-shouldered, wore a dusty private's blouse, only the stars on his shoulder straps showing his rank. They agreed on the terms of the surrender, and Grant wrote them out in pencil. At Lee's suggestion, Grant permitted the Confederate men to take their horses home with them to plow their farms. He ordered food to be given to the half-starved southerners. When the Union men began to cheer, Grant ordered that there were to be no cheers and no celebrations. "The war is over," he said.

The Gettysburg Address

Fourscore and seven years ago our fathers brought forth on this continent a new nation, conceived in liberty and dedicated to the proposition that all men are created equal.

Now we are engaged in a great civil war, testing whether that nation or any nation so conceived and so dedicated can long endure. We are met on a great battlefield of that war. We have come to dedicate a portion of that field, as a final resting place for those who here gave their lives that that nation might live. It is altogether fitting and proper that we should do this.

But, in a larger sense, we cannot dedicate —we cannot consecrate—we cannot hallow —this ground. The brave men, living and dead, who struggled here, have consecrated it, far above our poor power to add or detract. The world will little note, nor long remember, what we say here, but it can never forget what they did here. It is for us the living, rather, to be dedicated here to the unfinished work which they who fought here have thus far so nobly advanced. It is rather for us to be here dedicated to the great task remaining before us —that from these honored dead we take increased devotion to that cause for which they gave the last full measure of devotion —that we here highly resolve that these dead shall not have died in vain—that this nation, under God, shall have a new birth of freedom—and that government of the people, by the people, for the people, shall not perish from the earth.

LIBRARY OF CONGRESS

Home! An artist shows a soldier of the War Between the States arriving home. What details express the joy that his family feels? Why was the soldier permitted to go home?

The next day a crowd with a band gathered around the White House to serenade Lincoln. The President appeared at a window and asked the band to play "Dixie." The war was over; the Confederate war song was now a national song; and the people of the North and the South were fellow countrymen.

2 *Congressional Reconstruction Increases Bitterness in the South*

The cost of a war cannot be given entirely in figures. We can say that in the northern armies about 360,000 men died and in the southern armies about 260,000. We can say that the war cost the North about $3\frac{1}{2}$ billion dollars; the

BROWN BROS.

Abraham Lincoln
1861–1865

BROWN BROS.

Andrew Johnson
1865–1869

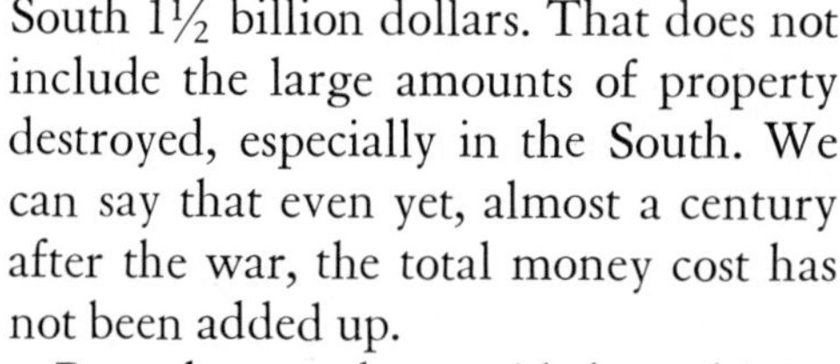

South $1\frac{1}{2}$ billion dollars. That does not include the large amounts of property destroyed, especially in the South. We can say that even yet, almost a century after the war, the total money cost has not been added up.

But when we have said these things, we have told only one part of the story. There was all the human suffering—the anguish, the sacrifices, and the broken lives. There have been continuing sectional misunderstandings that have sometimes kept Americans from working together on common problems.

Bitterness continues after the war. During the war and for many years afterward, southerners were bitter toward Yankees because of the suffering they had endured. Bitterness that lasted a long time was caused on both sides by the treatment of prisoners. Sanitary conditions in both northern and southern military prisons were bad, and thousands of men died from preventable diseases.

The bitterness after the war was made greater by the tragic assassination of President Lincoln. John Wilkes Booth, a young actor, was devoted to the South. He was crazed with grief over the defeat of the Confederacy, and he blamed Lincoln for it. On the evening of April 14, 1865, Lincoln went to see a play in Ford's Theater, Washington. Booth entered the President's box and shot him through the head. Abraham Lincoln died the next day. It has been said that with the death of Lincoln the southern people lost their best friend in the North. As you read about events of the next decade, see if you agree.

Radical reconstruction. After the war there were many problems. The principal ones were to restore the Union and to rebuild the South. We call the years after the war the reconstruction period.

To national leaders, the first problem of reconstruction was how to get the former Confederate states back into good standing in the Union. President Lincoln said that the states had never really left the Union. He was ready to restore a state to good standing on three conditions. Ten per cent of its citizens had to take an oath to support the Union. These citizens had to elect a government that was loyal to the Union. The new government had to free the slaves in the state. Lincoln's successor was Andrew Johnson. He also wished to make it as easy as possible to readmit the southern states.

But a group of Republican leaders in Congress were determined that Congress rather than the President should decide how the Union should be restored. They rejected the views of Lincoln and Johnson. They held that the southern states had left the Union. Now these states were to be treated as a foreign nation that had been defeated in war. Because of their extreme views these leaders were known as Radicals.

When President Johnson opposed their program, the Radicals impeached him; that is, they brought him to trial with the purpose of removing him from office. Under the Constitution a President is removed from office if he is convicted of wrongdoing by a two-thirds vote of the Senate. (See the Constitution, Article I, Sections 2 and 3, and Article II, Section 4.) When the vote on Johnson was taken, it was one vote less than the two-thirds required to remove him. Thus the Radicals failed to get rid of President Johnson. But they controlled enough votes in Congress to put their program through over his veto.

One reason why the Radicals were able to carry out their program was that there was no strong President to oppose them. Andrew Johnson had never been elected to the office. He had become President upon the death of Lincoln. Since he came from Tennessee, Johnson was suspected of being in sympathy with the South. Ulysses S. Grant was elected in 1868 and 1872. He

Andrew Johnson appeals to the people. During his struggle with the Radical Republicans, President Johnson made a long trip to explain his reconstruction program to the people. He often spoke from the rear platform of the train.

was much less successful as President than he had been as a general. He knew little about politics and did not understand the duties of the office. He appointed friends to important positions, and some of his friends used their positions to make money for themselves dishonestly. Rutherford B. Hayes, who was elected President in 1876, brought the Radical reconstruction program to an end.

Reconstruction governments. The Radicals wanted to punish the southern states before readmitting them to the Union. They also wished to keep the Republican party in power in the nation for a long, long time. They wanted to make sure that, when the southern states did come back, they would send Republican congressmen to Washington.

Under the Radical program, the South was put under military government. It was divided into five military districts. Each of the districts was governed by a major general. Congress made the rules for readmission of the states, and the Army enforced the rules.

To be readmitted, a state had to write a new constitution. The constitution had to deny the right to vote or hold office to the leaders of the Confederacy. Thus the men with the most experience in public affairs could take no part in the new state governments. Furthermore, the new constitution had to give the right to vote and hold office to Negroes. Having been slaves, very few Negroes had the education or experience needed to run a government or even to vote.

Because the Negroes were given full political rights, many southern whites who could have voted refused to do so. They also refused to take any part in the new governments. Some southern whites did vote and hold office. Their white neighbors considered them no better than traitors and called them scalawags. Many northerners came to the South to participate in the new governments. They were called carpetbaggers. Carpetbags were traveling bags made of carpet, which were widely used in those days. The northerners came south in such a hurry, said the southerners, that they brought only such belongings as could be crammed into carpetbags.

Thus the reconstruction governments consisted mainly of scalawags, carpetbaggers, and Negroes. Clearly they did not represent all the people of the South. Yet the new governments made some forward-looking plans. The right to vote and hold office was given to all men (except leaders of the Confederacy). There was to be free education for all, to be paid for out of taxes. Also, the governments were to help rebuild roads and railroads.

Unfortunately, however, the new state governments generally failed to accomplish these good purposes. They failed partly because many southerners refused to cooperate. More important, officials who wanted to do right were inexperienced and did not know how. Many of those who had experience were interested mainly in graft (dishonest gain) for themselves. A large part of the money provided for the service of the people was either wasted or stolen.

The end of the reconstruction governments. Under the reconstruction

BROWN BROS.

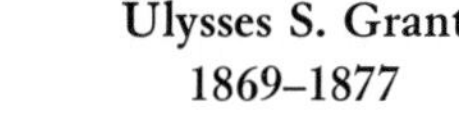

Ulysses S. Grant
1869–1877

BROWN BROS.

Rutherford B. Hayes
1877–1881

governments the southern states generally sent Republican representatives to Congress. They also supported Republican candidates for President. But gradually the large majority of southern whites regained control of their state governments. They took advantage of quarrels in the reconstruction governments to elect their own men. They acted through secret societies like the Ku-Klux Klan. Members of the Klan, clad in white sheets, rode out at midnight and frightened Negroes into staying away from the polls. Sometimes they threatened white supporters of the reconstruction governments from both the North and the South. They punished their victims with tar and feathers and with whippings.

By 1876 the reconstruction governments had disappeared except in South Carolina, Florida, and Louisiana. The next year, after Rutherford B. Hayes became President, federal troops were withdrawn from those states; and the last three reconstruction governments were replaced by governments elected by southern whites. Thus the reconstruction plan of Congress came to an end.

The "solid South." The southern people did not forgive the Republican party for its reconstruction program. They all supported the Democratic party. The southern states became the "solid South," united in support of the Democratic party. Most of the southern states have supported the Democratic party ever since.

Amendments. Three amendments to the Constitution were made part of the reconstruction program. The Thirteenth Amendment abolished slavery. The Fourteenth Amendment protected

Sharecropper's cabin. Many free Negroes settled down as sharecroppers on the old plantations.

the rights of Negroes as citizens. The purpose of the Fifteenth Amendment was to assure Negroes of the right to vote. But southern leaders found ways to prevent the Negroes from voting. These methods also kept many poor white men from voting.

Congressional reconstruction fails. Looking back at the congressional plan of reconstruction, we can see that it did not work out well for the nation as a whole or for the South. By causing quarrels between Congress and the President, it kept the government from operating smoothly and efficiently. It made the southern people hate the North, perhaps even more than the war had done, and so prevented national unity. Congressional reconstruction also failed to obtain full rights for the Negro. It tried to force on the South immediate equality for Negroes. It did not provide time and opportunity for the Negroes to learn the responsibilities as well as the rights of free citizens. It made the relations between whites and Negroes much worse than they otherwise might have been. Finally, all the strife and hatred of the reconstruction period slowed down the rebuilding of the South itself—its cities and its farms.

Rebuilding the South. The South faced an enormous task of rebuilding. In the cities many homes, stores, wharves, and warehouses had to be rebuilt. Railroads had to be rebuilt and supplied with new locomotives and cars. Businessmen had to begin all over again to build up trade.

Many a farmer and plantation owner returned home from the war to find his land overrun with weeds. He had to rebuild from the ground up: clear and plow the land; obtain seed for a crop and tools to cultivate it; build fences and barns; stock his farm with horses, mules, and cattle; and gradually work his way back to normal. Rebuilding the South was a long, hard pull and took many years.

The freedmen. One of the most difficult problems was that of the former slaves. How were the freed Negroes to fit into postwar southern life? There were no jobs for Negroes, since the southern white people could hardly take care of themselves. To many freedmen, as the former slaves were called, freedom at first meant freedom to come and go as they pleased. They wandered over the countryside looking for food. Thousands crowded into the southern cities where they were fed by northern officials.

As might be expected, many of the wandering freedmen finally returned to their old homes. Since they had no money with which to start out in farming or business, many of them settled down as sharecroppers. Under the sharecrop system a plantation owner gave a Negro the use of a piece of land and a cabin. He also supplied him with food, seed, and tools. After harvest the two divided the cotton. The sharecropper's part of the crop usually hardly paid for his family's basic needs of food and clothes.

Other freedmen paid rent for their small farms. Having no money, they obtained tools, food, seed, and other supplies on credit. They promised to pay the debt with the cotton they would grow. At the end of the year the crop often was not worth enough to pay all that a tenant owed. In such a case the law required the tenant to work on the land until the debt was paid. In many cases the tenants were tied to the land by debts that grew larger year after year. Freedmen improved their way of life slowly over a long period of time.

Summary

The War Between the States was fought almost a century ago. After so many years we can look at the war coolly and clearly as Americans, not as northerners and southerners.

We can agree today that it is too bad the war had to be fought at all. The leaders of the two sections might have agreed to settle their differences peacefully. If the war had been avoided, how different our history would have been! But what a big "if"!

We can see now that, once war came, the North was almost sure to win. It had so many more people, factories, farms, and ships. The Confederates hoped to sell their cotton and obtain from England the manufactured goods they needed. But the northern blockade prevented them from doing so. Southerners bravely endured great hardships in order to carry on the war.

Considering the advantages of the North, it is a tribute to the courage of the South's armies, the skill of its leaders, and the sacrifice of its people that the war lasted as long as it did. Confederate forces invaded the North twice. They were turned back at Antietam in 1862 and at Gettysburg in 1863. In the West the Union forces won full control of the Mississippi in 1863, thus splitting the Confederacy. Then from Tennessee they cut across Georgia to the coast, again splitting the South. In the East, Lee successfully defended Richmond for four years. Finally in 1865 he had to surrender to Grant. The terms of surrender were easy, as was fitting between fellow Americans. The southerners went home to rebuild plantations and cities that had been damaged or destroyed in the war.

The northern victory meant that the Union was preserved and the slaves were free. If the war had to be fought, we can all be thankful for these results. On the other hand, we can regret that the reconstruction policy of Lincoln and Johnson was not adopted. Today the reconstruction laws that were passed by Congress seem extreme and unfair. We can see that they caused perhaps more bitterness in the South than did the war itself. Under these laws the South was ruled for a while by military commanders. When governments were set up, many southern leaders were forbidden to take part—or even to vote. Most southern whites refused to cooperate with the reconstruction governments. As the federal soldiers were withdrawn, the southern people took charge of their state governments again. Only then did the South begin the long, hard task of rebuilding its life under new conditions.

For a Quick Review

1. What was the over-all military plan of each side in the War Between the States? (Include naval as well as land operations.)

2. How did the attitude of Great Britain help decide the outcome of the war?

3. Why has it been said that the year 1863 marked the turning point of the war?

4. What were the main problems of the reconstruction period from the point of view of a white plantation owner, a freed Negro, and a southern businessman?

5. In what ways did the Radical plan of reconstruction make it hard for the South to start rebuilding?

Learning to Study More Easily

IMPROVING CLASS DISCUSSION

Can you remember a social studies class discussion that you thought was interesting and another that seemed dull? What made the difference? Was the subject under discussion more interesting one time than the other? Did you know something about the subject one time and not the other? Did you in either case take part in the discussion? These points sometimes make the difference between an interesting and an uninteresting class period.

What can you do to help make your social studies discussions more lively and interesting? Whatever you do to improve the class discussions will probably help you to increase your own understanding of the subjects being discussed.

When you are studying in preparation for a discussion, you are taking the first step—gathering information. As you read, however, you can be taking a second step—raising questions about the subject. You can talk over these questions with your classmates and teacher when the discussion is on. You will remember your questions if you make brief notes on them as you study.

Remember that being interested is catching. You can raise the interest of others if you show that you are really thinking about the topic and want to talk with others about it. You can show your interest by volunteering to answer questions and by answering them clearly and directly. A good discussion moves along quickly, without people repeating statements already made by others or stopping to "uh" or "er" while they hunt for words. You can show your interest by asking some of the questions you thought of while you were studying or by giving your opinion on points that come up. Sometimes you will want to disagree with opinions expressed by someone else or to agree. In either case you will want to give the reason for your point of view.

It is important in any discussion to express your opinions in such a way that you advance the discussion rather than cut it off. If one member of the group bothers others by rude interruptions, scares them with sarcasm, or hurts their feelings by such tactics as name calling, the discussion will soon die. If you show that you are interested in knowing the other person's point of view and that you respect his right to his opinion, the discussion will grow in interest.

These are general suggestions that would apply in most social studies classrooms where students are working together. What are the particular problems your class needs to solve in order to improve your discussions? Can you list some things you can do to improve class discussions?

Unit Roundup

HIGH POINTS OF THE UNIT

Here is an opportunity to practice the suggestions you have just read for improving class discussions. Use the oral discussion method to summarize the major developments you have studied in Unit 5.

You can prepare by the following steps: As a class, decide on the four or five major headings around which you should plan the summary or review discussion. Decide how much time can be planned for the entire discussion. Then make a time allotment for each topic. Arrange for student leaders to preside during the discussion, one for each topic. Review the characteristics of a good discussion and the responsibilities of each person in a group discussion. Make your individual preparation for the discussion. After holding the summary discussion, ask each person (including your teacher) to make a list of good and poor features of the discussion.

Talk over the lists of comments on the discussion. In what ways can you improve future discussions?

EXPAND YOUR VOCABULARY

1. Divide a sheet of paper into three columns, one of them a narrow column along the left side. In this first column list the words that appear below. In the second column define the word. In the third tell what event or topic discussed in Unit 5 is related to the word.

aggressor	dictator
arsenal	fugitive
assassination	impeach
blockade	reconstruction
compromise	treason

2. How many meanings can you give for each of these words? How is each one used in Unit 5?

campaign	offensive
civil	preserve
draft	solution
endure	term

WITH CRAYON, RULER, AND PASTE

1. Make a picture chart of a series of cartoons to show the advantages of the North and those of the South in the military struggle of 1861–1865. What title will you give to your chart?

2. Prepare a chart to show how the North and the South faced the same wartime problems—for example, getting men for the army. Perhaps you can use three columns headed: Problem, Southern Solution, Northern Solution. What general conclusions can you draw from the information on the chart? Write them in a sentence or two at the bottom of the page.

3. Make a time line entitled "Important Events in the United States, 1850–1877."

MAIN EVENTS OF UNIT 5, 1850–1877

Building and governing the nation	*Earning a living*	*Science, arts, and the people*	*The nation and its neighbors*
1850 Compromise of 1850			
		1852 *Uncle Tom's Cabin*	
1853–1857 Franklin Pierce, Pres. (Democrat)	**1853** N.Y. Central Railroad		**1853** Gadsden Purchase
1854 Kansas-Nebraska Act			
1854 Republican party			
1857–1861 James Buchanan, Pres. (Democrat)	**1857** Railroad, New York–St. Louis	**1857** *The Atlantic Monthly*	
1857 Dred Scott decision			
1858 Lincoln-Douglas debates	**1858** Overland mail	**1858** Atlantic cable	
1860 Secession	**1860** Pony express		
1861–1865 Abraham Lincoln, Pres. (Republican)	**1861** Telegraph, New York–San Francisco		**1861** Blockade of South
1861 Fort Sumter			
1863 Emancipation Proclamation		**1863** "Gettysburg Address"	
1863 Gettysburg and Vicksburg			
1865 Appomattox			
1865–1869 Andrew Johnson, Pres. (elected V-P)			
1865 Amendment XIII			
1867 Reconstruction			**1867** Purchase of Alaska
1868 Amendment XIV			
1869–1877 Ulysses S. Grant, Pres. (Republican)	**1869** Transcontinental railroad completed	**1869** First college football game	**1869** Suez Canal opened
1870 Amendment XV			
1877–1881 Rutherford B. Hayes, Pres. (Republican)			

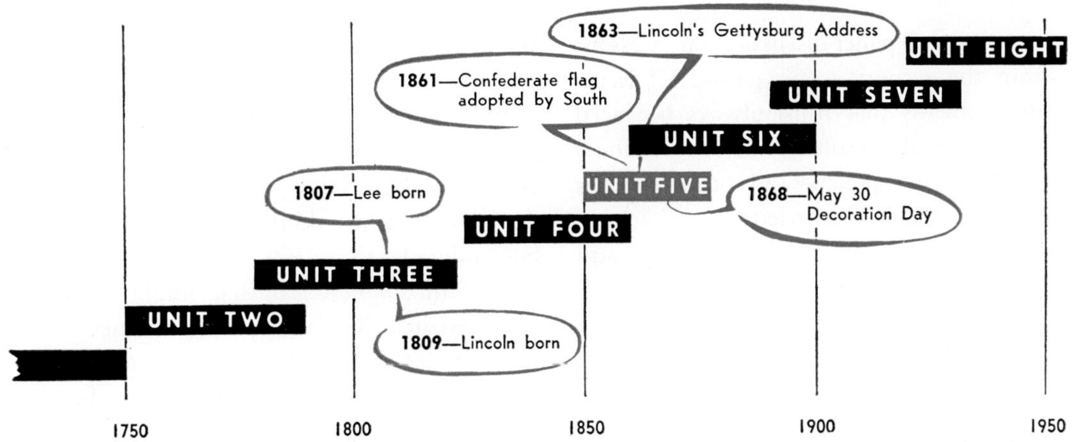

For each event that you choose to put on the time line, attach a note explaining why it was important.

4. Decide, as a class, on the important events between 1850 and 1877 that should be recorded on your large time line. Arrange to have this done.

PUT ON A PLAY

1. Write a script for a roving-reporter radio program in which the reporter interviews people in different parts of the country, getting opinions on the Fugitive Slave Law. You might give two roundups of opinion, one in 1850 when the law was discussed in Congress and the other about 1855 after it had been in operation.

2. Find additional information about one of the major battles of the War Between the States and prepare a "You Are There" radio-broadcast. Include a commentator's account of events, interviews with leaders of both sides at their field headquarters, brief "soldier in the ranks" interviews with participants on both sides, and a final news flash telling of the outcome.

3. Plan and present a series of skits showing the part women, at home behind the lines, played in the northern and the southern war efforts.

4. Plan scenes for a biographical play, presenting important events in the life of Robert E. Lee (or one of the other leaders mentioned in Unit 5). You might have a narrator set the stage for each scene by describing other important happenings in the United States at the time.

STORIES THERE WAS NO ROOM TO TELL

1. With three or four other students plan, prepare, and present a panel discussion on the topic "Was war between the sections inevitable?" Remember that in a panel discussion a speaker can present evidence on all sides of a question. Remember also that a panel does not try to prove a "yes" or "no" answer to a question but draws as many conclusions as possible from the facts that have been presented. See page 630 for other suggestions about conducting a panel discussion.

2. Prepare a report on the naval history of the War Between the States.

3. Choose one of the military campaigns of the War Between the States and prepare a report for the rest of the class. Illustrate your presentation with diagrams on the blackboard.

4. With other students, plan, prepare,

and present a panel discussion on "Lessons from the reconstruction period." Discuss the problems that must always be faced after a war, the results of the congressional reconstruction policy, and other policies that might have been tried.

5. Investigate one of these topics and prepare a report on it:

The emigrant aid societies in Kansas
John Brown's life and influence
Life on a southern plantation during wartime
Hospitals at the time of the Confederacy
Brady, photographer of the War Between the States
Life in an army camp, 1861–1865
Weapons of the War Between the States compared with modern weapons

USE YOUR IMAGINATION

1. Write a series of news stories that might have been sent to his paper by a reporter covering an important event of the period from 1850 to 1877. Here are three suggestions to start you off (remember that local color and background are important in such news stories): the debates in Congress on the Compromise of 1850, especially the speeches of Clay, Calhoun, and Webster; the inaugurations of Lincoln in 1861 and 1865; the Battle of Gettysburg.

2. What would have been your impressions if you had been present at one of the debates between Lincoln and Douglas? Record them in a letter to a friend. You will need to find more information than could be given in your text about the topics they discussed, the behavior and size of the audience, the appearance and manner of each of the two men, and other such facts.

3. Write an editorial entitled "The Question of Fort Sumter" for a newspaper that might have been published in Charleston, South Carolina, during the last week in March, 1861. Write another that might have been published the same week in New York City. Give to President Lincoln the advice that you think each editor might have offered.

4. Write an editorial that might have appeared in a Richmond, Virginia, newspaper in 1862 under the title "Cotton Still Is King." Express the southern hope for getting foreign aid, giving reasons for the hope.

5. Prepare the news stories that might have been written by a reporter who witnessed the battles in which the *Merrimac* and the *Monitor* were engaged.

6. Write two editorials, dated January 2, 1863, concerning the Emancipation Proclamation. Make one of them suitable for an abolitionist paper and the other suitable for a northern nonabolitionist paper that supported the Union cause.

SHOW IT ON A MAP

1. The maps in Chapter 19 give you an over-all view of the military and naval action of the War Between the States. Arrange with your teacher to prepare a supplementary map (or series of maps), for the class bulletin board, to show the details of one major campaign or battle.

2. On an outline map of the United States show:

The states that seceded before February, 1861
The states that seceded after February 1, 1861
The first capital city of the Confederacy
The city where the capital of the Confederacy was located after July, 1861
The slave states that did not secede
The free states in March, 1861

YOUR COMMUNITY GROWS WITH THE NATION

1. Did any of the military events of the War Between the States occur in your state? If so, investigate and report to the class.

2. Did your state furnish men for northern or southern armies in 1861–1865? Investigate and report to your class.

3. Memorial Day is celebrated as a national holiday in all parts of the country. Find out about the origin and significance of this day. How has it been celebrated in your community in recent years? Tell the class of your findings.

FURTHER READING

Books about Interesting People

Abe Lincoln and His Times by the Editors of *Look* and Enid La Monte Meadowcroft. Crowell, 1946.

Abraham Lincoln by James Henry Daugherty. Viking, 1943.††

Gray Knight: The Story of Robert E. Lee by Belle Moses. Appleton-Century-Crofts, 1936.

Robert E. Lee by Guy Emery. Messner, 1951.

Stonewall by Julia Davis. Dutton, 1931. Stonewall Jackson.

Victorian Cinderella by Phyllis Wynn Jackson. Holiday, 1947. Harriet Beecher Stowe, author of *Uncle Tom's Cabin.*

Vinnie Ream and Mr. Lincoln by Freeman H. Hubbard. Whittlesey House, 1949. At 17, Vinnie modeled Lincoln from life; later she did the statue of him that stands in the rotunda of the Capitol.

Stories of Adventure and Everyday Life

A Recruit for Abe Lincoln by Maribelle Cormack. Appleton-Century-Crofts, 1942. Wartime experiences of a crippled telegrapher who sees duty in the field.

Bittersweet by Martha Rebecca Harper. Longmans, 1948. Life in central Pennsylvania in wartime.††

By Secret Railway by Enid La Monte Meadowcroft. Crowell, 1948. Adventures of a boy helping the Underground Railroad.

Calico Ball by Emma G. Stern. Dodd, Mead, 1934. A story laid in Birmingham, Alabama, during the reconstruction period.

Gentlemen, Hush! by Jere H. Wheelwright. Scribner, 1948. Experiences of three young southerners in the war and in rebuilding after the war.

Green Peace by Marjorie Hayes. Lippincott, 1945. Growing up in Boston in the 1860s; Dr. Howe's school for the blind.

Henry's Lincoln by Louise A. Neyhart. Holiday, 1945. A farm boy hears one of the Lincoln-Douglas debates.

Mary Montgomery, Rebel by Helen Fern Daringer. Harcourt, Brace, 1948. Wartime experiences of Mary, who was 14 in 1861; a true story.

The White Feather by Merritt Parmelee Allen. Longmans, 1944. A border-state boy joins Morgan's Raiders.

Young Folks' Uncle Tom's Cabin adapted by Grace Duffie Boylan. Whitman, 1947. Based on the famous antislavery book by Harriet Beecher Stowe.

Other Interesting Accounts

Abraham Lincoln's World by Genevieve Foster. Scribner, 1944. Major events around the world during Abraham Lincoln's lifetime.

Lee and Grant at Appomattox by MacKinley Kantor. Random House, 1950.

Unit 6 The United States Becomes a Great Industrial Nation 1860–1900

BEFORE THE southern states seceded from the Union, southern congressmen prevented the passage of many laws desired by the North and the West. The South opposed laws that would speed up the settlement of the West, for that would mean the admission of more free states. The South opposed laws to encourage manufacturing and trade. The southern people made a living from agriculture, and they did not want a country of factories and of factory workers.

After the southern states seceded and southern congressmen resigned, the Republican party controlled Congress. It passed the laws that the North and the West had long wanted. It passed the Homestead Act, which gave 160 acres of land free to every settler on the public domain. It set up much higher tariffs to encourage American manufacturers. It gave large grants of land and

loans of money to build a railroad across the continent.

These laws set the stage for a great burst of expansion and industrial growth. Railroads, branching out into every section of the West, carried settlers to their new homes. First miners and cattlemen and then farmers settled the Rocky Mountain area and the Great Plains. Within 25 years after the end of the War Between the States, the frontier line disappeared. The American adventure of settling the continent had come to an end. There were still unsettled regions in the Far West, but they were mainly dry plains and desert.

At the same time manufacturing in the United States grew tremendously. With new methods, steelmakers produced steel in abundance and at low prices. Out of steel Americans made heavier rails, locomotives, and cars for railroads. Out of steel they built bridges and skyscrapers, ships, and barbed-wire fencing. Out of steel they made automatic machines that turned out products at whirling speeds. America changed from a country built of wood and iron to a country built of steel.

With the improved machines, factories produced enormous quantities of clothing, shoes, furniture, and innumerable other products for better living. New industries grew up, such as meat packing and petroleum refining. Inventors turned electricity into a source of light and power. Railroads carried goods rapidly and cheaply into every part of the country.

This industrial growth brought deep and permanent changes in American life. Big factories replaced little craftsmen's shops. Big corporations absorbed many little businesses. Since workers could no longer bargain individually with their employers, they organized unions to bargain collectively for higher wages and shorter hours. As cities became business and manufacturing centers, they grew bigger and bigger. Americans from farms and villages and immigrants from Europe flocked to the cities to seek new opportunities.

In the years from 1860 to 1900 agricultural America was becoming industrial America. Rural America was becoming urban America. America, once divided into regions and sections, was becoming a single, interdependent community. At the same time the American people were becoming more prosperous, better educated, and more proud of their country. That is the story of Unit 6.

20 The Last Frontier Is Settled

"Gold! Gold in the Rockies!"

This was the news that traveled east late in 1858, the year that Lincoln debated with Douglas and Douglas was elected Senator from Illinois.

"They found gold in Colorado! It's near Pike's Peak where the best finds have been made so far, but there's gold lots of other places in the Rockies."

"Sure. Remember California. They're still making new strikes there once in a while. But Colorado's the place to go now! There you can still get in early before all the good claims are staked."

"Well, what're we waiting for? 'Pike's Peak or bust!' That's for me. Are you in?"

So went the talk. And in the spring months of 1859 about 100,000 people started off from Missouri River towns on the long trail west. They traveled on horseback, in covered wagons, in farm wagons, and on foot. Some 50,000 "fifty-niners" reached Pike's Peak. Of these about half were disappointed in their search for gold and hit the trail back east the same year. On the way out signs on their wagons had announced, "Pike's Peak or bust!" On the way back the signs read, "Busted!"

The "busted" prospectors were doubtless discouraged and glad to get back home, but there were some who stayed in the West. During the years of sectional war and reconstruction many other Americans moved west. By 1890 they filled in the last frontier. Miners opened up the Rocky Mountain areas to settlement. Cattlemen and farmers settled the vast open spaces of the Great Plains. Railroads played an important part in the story of the last frontier.

It was in these years that the wild West appeared—the wild West of cowboy and Indian, of rancher and farmer, of outlaw and vigilante, of straight-shooting he-men. We have seen and heard it described over and over again in westerns—stories, movies, and radio and television programs.

1 *Miners Find Gold and Silver in the Rocky Mountains*

The first prospectors for gold and silver in the Rocky Mountains came from the California gold fields. Soon they were joined by seekers of wealth from eastern United States, from Europe, Australia, China, and other parts of the world. The Rocky Mountain mining frontier repeated the history of the California gold fields. (See pages 298–302.)

Gold and silver in the Rockies. As you have just read, most of the "fifty-niners" who rushed to Pike's Peak soon rushed right back home. They were disappointed because they could not pick up handfuls of gold pebbles. But the prospectors who remained were rewarded with new finds. Little mining camps rose up in the narrow hollows between the hills. The men took as little time as possible from their search for gold. When they needed to restock their supplies of bacon, beans, coffee, and flour or to buy new tools, they would make a hurried trip to Denver or some other supply center. Later, merchants sent supplies to them by mule train. The Rocky Mountain camp was a world apart, where people paid little attention to what was happening in the rest of the country.

The rush to Pike's Peak occurred in 1859. In the same year two miners discovered the Comstock lode, a rich deposit of gold and silver in what is now western Nevada. Immediately hundreds of miners from California poured over the Sierra Nevada to get their share of the wealth. The next year 20,000 people—Americans, Irishmen, Germans, Frenchmen, Mexicans, and others—crossed the mountains to the new gold fields. Supply center for the diggings was Virginia City, built halfway up the mountain slope right over the mines. By the end of 1860 Virginia City had 38 stores, 25 saloons and gambling places, 9 restaurants, 8 hotels, 8 lawyers, and a newspaper.

Other gold and silver strikes were

Denver in 1859. Notice the covered-wagon camp, Indian tepees, and wooden dwellings. The city was actually founded in 1860 when three such villages were united. In 1867 Denver became the capital of Colorado. When did Colorado become a state?

LIBRARY OF CONGRESS

BERKO-HENRY STUDIO, ASPEN

Ghost town. This is Aspen, Colorado, in 1949. Deserted after early miners had removed the surface gold, it slowly crumbled into ruins. Today Aspen is a thriving town. Can you find the story of Aspen's revival?

Old governor's mansion, Arizona. Prescott, early capital of Arizona, grew up around the governor's home. This house was built in 1864, a year after Arizona became a territory. For the frontier, it was a very grand house.

ARIZONA STATE COLLEGE

made in every part of the Rocky Mountain area from Montana and Idaho to Arizona and New Mexico. Each new discovery attracted ever-hopeful miners from the older gold fields. Many of them wandered from field to field, always hoping to strike it rich. Through the years of conflict between the North and the South and during the reconstruction period, the gold seekers continued their search. Events of the war seemed far away to them.

As the miners moved to new areas, they sometimes left behind empty, uninhabited towns. Some of these ghost towns have become famous. Among the best known are Deadwood, South Dakota, and Tombstone, Arizona.

Lawbreakers and lawmen. In the frontier mining towns, there was plenty of gold and silver in circulation and law enforcement was weak. Naturally these towns attracted lawbreakers of every description. No man's property or life was safe. Respectable citizens organized vigilance committees, just as they had done in California during the early days of the gold rush there (see page 300). The vigilantes (vĭj ĭ lăn′tēz) rode out at night, mounted and armed. They seized wrongdoers and punished them with or without a trial. In many cases the vigilantes maintained order in their communities until government officials were appointed or elected. But, as is likely to happen when men take the law into their own hands, the vigilante bands sometimes punished innocent men. Sometimes the vigilantes themselves were controlled by lawbreakers and helped enforce lawlessness rather than justice.

These wild West conditions did not

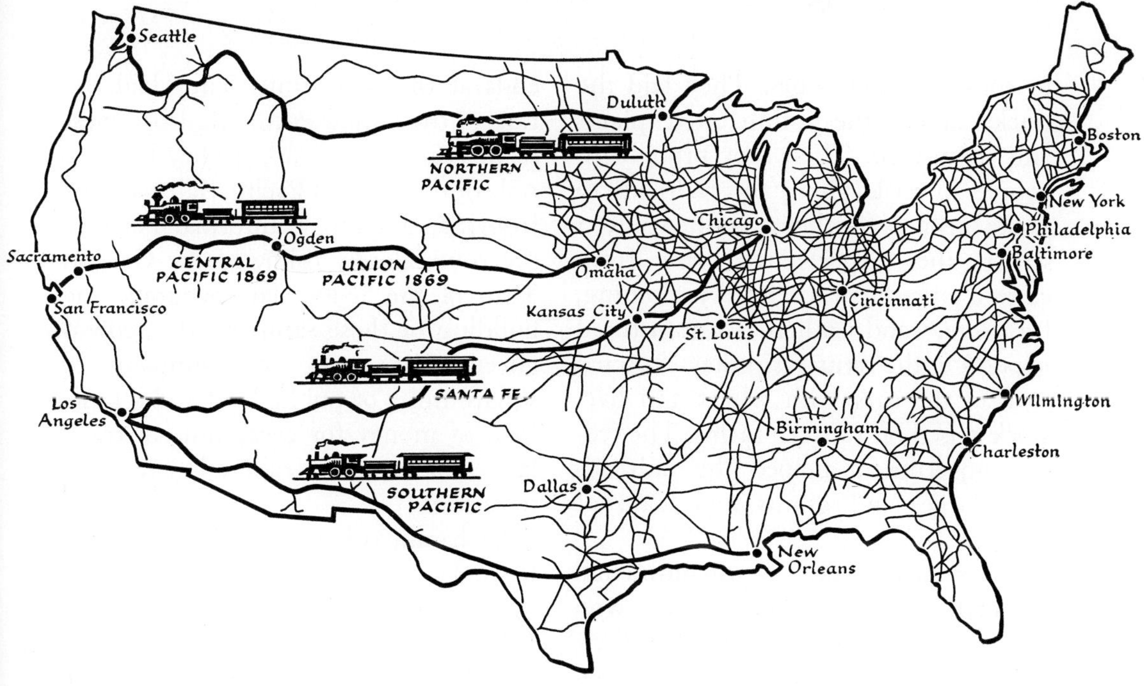

Railroads bind the nation together. This map shows the major railroads of the 1890s. What cities stand out as railroad centers? Compare the main routes of the western railroads with the routes followed by western emigrants of gold rush times. (See map, page 295.)

last long in the mining camps. Even during the years of sectional war, Congress set up territorial governments for Colorado, Nevada, Arizona, Idaho, and Montana. As soon as these governments were organized, they established law and order.

Large-scale mining. The early prospectors and miners searched for gold only at or near the surface of the earth. As a rule the surface gold gave out in two or three years, and the early miners moved on to new fields.

They left behind the richest part of the mines, the deposits of precious metals embedded deep in the earth. Large mining companies with headquarters in San Francisco or New York took over. They brought in machinery and operated large-scale mines. For many years, however, there were solitary prospectors who continued to follow their dream of golden wealth.

The large mining companies used scientific methods of prospecting as well as of mining. Their men discovered rich deposits of copper, lead, and other metals. Mining became a basic industry in many of the Rocky Mountain states. Farmers and cattlemen moved in to supply food for the miners. Cities grew up and became centers of trade and manufacture.

2 *Railroads Speed Up Settlement on the Last Frontier*

The railroads speeded up the settlement of the last frontier. Railroadmen did not wait until the Great Plains and the Rocky Mountain area were settled to construct their lines. They laid the tracks across the uninhabited plains and mountains. Then they brought in people to settle along the railroads to make business for them. To the western settlers they expected to bring from eastern cities farm machinery, clothing, furniture, and other manufactured goods. On the return trip they expected to load the cars with wheat and livestock raised on western farms. The federal government helped the railroads with large land grants and loans of money.

Americans build transcontinental railroads. The railroad builders won the admiration of the world by their spectacular feat of spanning the continent. They built railroads from both ends at the same time. They laid the rails of the Union Pacific Railroad west from Omaha, Nebraska. They laid the rails of the Central Pacific Railroad east from Sacramento, California. Parts of the route closely followed the Oregon Trail of the 1840s. To encourage the building of these railroads, the federal government gave each company 20 square miles of public land and a large loan of money for every mile of track laid. The land the railroads later sold to settlers.

Driving the last spike. This is how a modern movie pictured the completion of the first transcontinental railroad in 1869. Where did the event take place? Why was it important in American history?

PARAMOUNT PICTURES INC.

Each railroad company had its problems. To build the Union Pacific across the plains, the builders had to bring in from the East, not only rails but even rock for the roadbed and wood for the ties. Workers were chiefly Irish immigrants and veterans of the War Between the States. The railroad workers had to be housed and fed as they laid the track through the uninhabited plains. They lived in a movable city of tents and frame shanties. Life in this movable railroad town was much like that in the mining and cattle towns of the wild West.

For the Central Pacific, rails and other necessary supplies came from the Atlantic coast in ships that went around Cape Horn. The company had to build its road over the high mountains—the Sierra Nevada—on the eastern border of California. Labor was so scarce that the construction company imported thousands of Chinese coolies (laborers) to help build the railroad.

The two roads finally met on the shore of Great Salt Lake, several miles out of Ogden, Utah. In a ceremony at Promontory Point famous citizens gathered on May 10, 1869, to celebrate

LIBRARY OF CONGRESS

Steamboat in the Northwest. Many early settlers traveled to the Northwest by steamboat. Here is a steamboat at Fargo, North Dakota, which was as far up the Red River as steamboats could go. How did the settlers continue their journey?

the joining of the two railroads. As a part of the ceremony California's governor, Leland Stanford, drove a final spike of gold into the last tie. Then, as two locomotives touched cowcatchers, a telegrapher tapped out the news:

> The last rail is laid.
> The last spike is driven.
> The Pacific railroad is finished.

The American people celebrated. Completion of the transcontinental railroad symbolized the final conquest of the continent. Soon the frontier would come to an end. Settlement would be unbroken from the Atlantic to the Pacific.

By 1871 three more transcontinental railroads were chartered by Congress and were given generous land grants. By 1883 they were completed: the Southern Pacific, the Santa Fe, and the Northern Pacific. (Trace the routes of these lines on the map on page 403.)

The railroads bring settlers to the plains. The railroads sold or rented most of their land in farm-size plots to actual settlers. They took people who were thinking of buying farms on trips to the land free of charge. The railroads sent hundreds of agents to the East and to Europe to persuade people to buy and settle on railroad land. Whole colonies of immigrants were transported to the plains in special immigrant trains.

It was good business for the railroads to get the land settled. They would make money hauling crops out and bringing in manufactured goods. Towns on the railroad lines grew rapidly and increased the freight and passenger traffic.

Thus the last frontier was settled at a new tempo. In earlier days emigrants depended on horses, oxen, and canalboats and river boats to take them west. Then a well-located and fertile region took 20 years or more to develop from raw frontier to settled community. In the days of the railroad, similar western areas passed out of the frontier stage much more rapidly. In 1890 the population of Kansas was 4 times what it was in 1870; that of Nebraska, 8 times what it was in 1870; that of the Dakotas, 40 times what it was in 1870.

3 *Cattlemen and Farmers Occupy the Great Plains*

By 1865 the settled area of the United States included much of Minnesota and Iowa and reached into Nebraska and Kansas. West of this settled area were the Great Plains. The Great Plains make up a vast, level region, the "wide open spaces" of the West. They begin at about the 98th meridian and rise gently to the foothills of the Rocky Mountains.

Early explorers like Lewis and Clark reported that farming would be impossible on the Great Plains. The soil, they said, was mainly sand. No trees grew on it. There was not enough water. Rain did not fall for years at a time. Temperatures were extreme—very hot in the summer, very cold in the winter. High winds blew across the vast open spaces, carrying everything before them. The entire area was called the "great American desert." Daniel Webster described it as "a region of savages, wild beasts, shifting sands, whirlwinds of dust, cactus, and prairie dogs."

The description of the climate was accurate. Yet the idea that farming was impossible on the Great Plains was

On the way to their American adventure. Immigrants from Europe had to endure a long and often uncomfortable ocean voyage to reach their new homes in the United States.

Refrigerator Cars

The Davis Refrigerator Cars . . . are again employed this season for transporting fish, fruits, etc., over long distances. These cars are made thirty feet in length, and are about seven feet wide . . .

Ice boxes of galvanized iron are placed at each end of the car. Two and a half tons of ice last ten days. On the roof are placed two boxes of salt, one barrel of which lasts ten days. The ice boxes are filled from the top once every twenty-four hours. . . . It is stated in the Detroit *Post* that strawberries have been kept sixty days in these cars; and other fruits and different kinds of meats are equally well preserved.

If this is the case, there are few products raised in any part of the United States that need fail to find a market, however perishable they may be. We shall expect to see grapes, raised in California and brought over the Pacific railroad, for sale in the New York market this season.

¶ The editorial was published in the *Scientific American* on July 17, 1869. How long after the completion of the first transcontinental railroad did the editorial appear? Was its author a good prophet? How are perishable products transported today?

gradually disproved. Pioneers on their way to Oregon and California discovered that their livestock found enough forage and water. Soldiers stationed in forts on the Great Plains planted trees and raised vegetables. In 1864 a trader with a wagon train of supplies for western forts was caught in Wyoming by a heavy snowstorm. He turned his oxen loose, expecting them to perish. They

NATIONAL GALLERY OF ART, INDEX OF AMERICAN DESIGN

Old-time log hauling. Lumbering attracted many Scandinavian settlers to the upper Mississippi Valley in the late 1800s. This model of oxen and sled was carved by a Norwegian-American lumberjack.

surprised him by returning to him well-fed. They had grazed on wild grass.

The Indians settle down. The United States government had given the Great Plains to the Indians as a permanent home. But white men invaded this Indian home over and over again without asking permission. Pioneers on the long trails to Oregon and California crossed the Great Plains. The coaches of the Overland Mail crossed the Plains. Miners and cattlemen settled on the Indians' land. The United States government built forts and stationed soldiers in Indian territory.

The government took care of the Indians by placing the various tribes on reservations. (A reservation is an area of land owned by an Indian tribe for the use of all its people.) But many Indians refused to be restricted to reservations, or, as they said, "to walk the white man's road." They ran away and organized warring bands. They made a last desperate effort to save their old way of living. They attacked covered

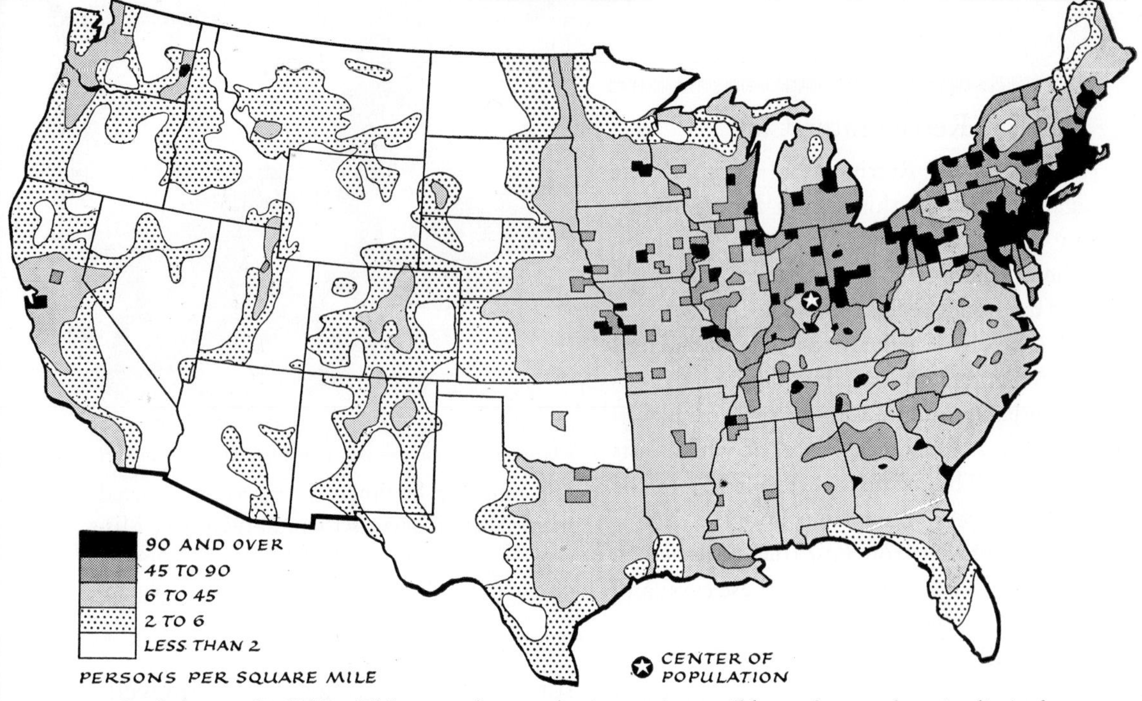

Settled areas in 1890. This map shows why it was impossible to draw a frontier line after 1890. What was the importance of that fact in American history?

wagon trains, stations of the Overland Mail, mining camps, ranches, railroad crews, and the isolated homes of settlers. The United States Army fought the hostile Indians for more than 20 years. Finally the Army defeated them and forced them to stay on reservations. The end of the Indian wars removed one obstacle to the settlement of the Great Plains.

The Homestead Act. The Great Plains were settled by cattlemen and farmers. The two frontiers overlapped, but we shall take them up one after the other.

But first, how did pioneers on the Great Plains obtain land to settle on? One way was under the Homestead Act of 1862. By that law a person 21 years old or over could become the owner of 160 acres of public domain. All he had to do was to build a house on the land, live on it for five years, and pay a fee of $18. The homesteader selected his land and filed his claim in the nearest land office. After five years he came back to the land office and brought witnesses to prove that he had built a house on the land and lived in it. Thereupon he was given a deed and became the owner of his homestead.

By 1890 more than 370,000 homesteaders had taken title to their land. Counting 5 persons to a family, that meant that almost 2,000,000 people lived on homestead farms.

The Homestead Act, however, did not fit conditions on the Great Plains. In the eastern states and the Middle West 160 acres were enough for a farm family to make a living. But on the Great Plains conditions were different (see pages 413–414), and a farmer had to have much more than 160 acres to run a paying farm.

Settlers on the Great Plains could obtain land from other sources besides the federal government. The government gave the railroads about 130 million acres of land, or more than twice as much as was homesteaded between 1862 and 1890. It also gave the states large amounts of land for education and other purposes. Speculators bought up large tracts of land. The land taken up by railroads and speculators was usually the best land. It was for sale, but usually only settlers who had some cash could afford to buy it. The homesteaders had to be satisfied with the poorer land.

The cattlemen's frontier. Texas was cattle country far back in Mexican days. In the early years of the War Between the States, Texan beef fed Confederate armies. But in 1863 the Union forces

BUREAU OF INDIAN AFFAIRS

Indian farmers. On the Santa Clara Indian Reservation in New Mexico, Indians build a pipe line to bring irrigation water to their lands. This project is an example of the federal government's efforts to help the Indians help themselves.

Canadian pioneer. Our neighbor nation on the north went through a frontier period that paralleled our own. What details of this Canadian homestead of the 1880s remind you of frontier life in the United States?

PUBLIC ARCHIVES OF CANADA

closed the Mississippi River (see page 382). Then there was no market for Texan cattle, and the huge herds ran wild.

In the prosperous years after the war, the people of the industrial East ate more beef. Texan cattle would be worth money if they could be brought to market. All a cattleman had to do was to brand the wild animals and deliver them to a railroad.

In the late 1860s and early 1870s the railroads had reached into Missouri and Kansas. Texan cattlemen started the "long drive" from Texas to cattle towns on the railroads. The first cattle town was Sedalia, Missouri. The herds on their way to Sedalia were diverted to Abilene, Kansas. Abilene became the most important cattle town. As the railroad was extended westward, Abilene was succeeded by other towns, like Wichita and Dodge City, Kansas.

Cowboy on the long drive. To look after the cattle on the long drive came the cowboy on his horse, carrying his six-shooter and his rope. He wore leather chaps to protect his legs from thorns and briers. He wore leather cuffs to protect his wrists from rope burns while roping a calf. His tight boots had high heels to prevent his feet from slipping forward in the stirrups, so that if he fell from his horse, he could pull his feet out fast. The high heels also helped him to dig in his heels when throwing a roped steer. He wore a broad, heavy felt hat that shed the rain and repelled the blazing rays of the sun. When necessary, the hat was a wash basin or a scoop for water to drink. The cowboy's kerchief protected the back of his neck from hot winds. Pulled over his face, it kept out the dust, raised by thousands of cattle. The cowboy saddled his horse with a big, heavy, roomy saddle. In it he spent the 10 or 12 hours of his working day. In that time he usually wore out two horses. To us the cowboy's outfit appears picturesque. To him every part of it was highly useful.

A dozen cowboys could drive 10,000 cattle 1,000 miles. Six or eight horses were taken along for each cowboy, and two boys called wranglers looked after the horses day and night. A cook with his chuck wagon completed the outfit. The cattle plodded along day after day in a narrow line a mile or two long. The cowpunchers hovered on every side to keep them moving peacefully. At night when the herd was bedded down, the cowpokes took turns riding around the bed ground, singing to the cattle in a low tone, soothingly, to prevent them from stampeding at a sudden noise. Over the hot, dry, dusty plains, through long stretches without water, across swollen rivers, and past many other dangers, the cowboys brought the bulk of the herd safely to the railroad. Upon reaching their destination, the cowboys were paid off and had a good time in the cattle town.

The cattle industry spreads northward. Cattle lost a great deal of weight on the long drive. The Texan range (grazing land) was overcrowded. Cattlemen learned that the northern range was better than the southern because it had longer grass and more water. Soon the cattle industry spread over the entire Great Plains. Attracted by the promise of profits, wealthy easterners and even members of the British nobility invested their money in ranches.

The roundup. In the vast expanse of the Great Plains there was plenty of grassland for grazing but too little water. Grassland without water was useless, for the cattle would die of thirst. Whoever owned a stream or a spring controlled the grass for a long distance in every direction. That was the rule accepted by cattlemen among themselves. A cattleman who owned 180 acres along a stream grazed his cattle on perhaps a million acres of public land that he did not own at all.

Boundaries were indefinite and there were no fences. Left to shift for themselves the year round on the open range, the cattle of neighboring herds mingled. Ownership was shown by brands. In the spring the cattlemen of each district got together and organized the calf roundup. Cowboys rounded up all the cattle in the area and brought them to one place. Soon there would be several thousand cattle milling around. A cowboy would ride straight into this moving mass, pick a mother and her calf, and drive them out to the edge of the mass of cattle. This was called cutting out. Next the cowboy lassoed the calf with his rope and dragged it to a nearby fire, where it was branded with the same brand that the mother carried. Thus each rancher kept track of his herd and established his ownership of new calves. Later in the year came the beef roundup, when the older cattle were cut out for the drive to the railroad.

This was the "cattle kingdom." Soon it was to be invaded by farmers, who broke up the open range with their little homesteads and their plowed fields.

The farmers' frontier. At the eastern edge of the Great Plains, pioneer farmers found an area of tall grass. The soil was fertile. When the rainfall was 20 inches or more a year, there was enough for farming. This area extended

Branding. On the spring roundup, cowboys branded calves with their owners' brands. How could they tell which calves belonged to each owner?

NEBRASKA STATE HISTORICAL SOCIETY

Prairie home. This housewife used curtains and flowers to make her sod house homelike. It was hard to keep the house clean, with dust dripping constantly from walls and roof. Life was lonely on the sod-house frontier, with the nearest neighbor miles away.

into the Dakotas and central Nebraska and Kansas. This was the area of the sod-house frontier.

In the 1860s and 1870s pioneers made homes for themselves in the tall grass region of the Great Plains. Many of them came from the states of the Middle West. Large numbers were immigrants, especially Scandinavians, Czechs, and Hungarians. With hard work and patience, these immigrants helped conquer the empty spaces of the plains. They built the foundations of new states. Respectful of the law and eager to learn, they became good and progressive citizens.

With no trees out of which to build log cabins, settlers on the eastern plains built sod houses. They cut out squares of sod and piled them up to make the walls. They laid a sod roof on poles. The furnishings were as crude as the house. Empty boxes served for chairs and tables. The pioneer made a bed out of boards and covered it with a mattress stuffed with cornhusks or wheat straw. He used twisted straw and corncobs as fuel.

The settlers on the open plains suffered many hardships. Sometimes floods drowned their crops; sometimes drought (dry weather) burned up the growing wheat and corn. Grass, or prairie, fires frequently threatened to destroy all they had. Winter blizzards isolated individual families for weeks, and occasionally the unsheltered cattle froze to death. In 1874 and for several years thereafter, plagues of grasshoppers descended upon the plains during the summertime and ate up the standing crops. The hardships of the sod-house frontier were not the same as those of earlier frontiers, but perhaps they were as difficult to bear. (See pages 68–69, 210–212, 284–287.)

Many people who started out to be homesteaders on the eastern plains gave up the struggle and went back east. Of those who remained, some never rose out of their poverty. Others were luckier. Their land increased in value. Railroads reached their neighborhood and brought many more settlers. The railroads carried away the crops and brought in lumber and manufactured goods. The homesteader could now buy lumber and build a frame dwelling. He turned the sod house into a stable. He borrowed money to make improvements on his farm, purchase machinery, and buy more land.

Barbed wire and dry farming. In the rush for land, farmers pushed their

My Government Claim

Hurrah for Greer County, the land of the free,
The home of the bedbug, grasshopper, and flea,
I'll sing of its praises, I'll tell of its fame,
While starving to death on my government claim.

My house it is built out of national soil,
Its walls are erected according to Hoyle,
Its roof has no pitch, it's as flat as the plain,
I always get wet when it happens to rain.

How happy am I as I crawl into bed,
A rattlesnake hisses a tune at my head,
A gay little centipede, all without fear,
Crawls over my pillow and into my ear.

Now all you claim holders you're welcome to stay,
To chew your hard tack 'til you're toothless and gray,
But as for myself, I will not remain,
To starve like a dog on my government claim.

¶ You can see from this song of the sod-house frontier that the pioneers of the plains, like earlier pioneers, could joke about their hardships. There is a recording of "My Government Claim" in the album "Who Built America."

NATIONAL GALLERY OF ART, INDEX OF AMERICAN DESIGN

Eagle, 1860s. This eagle is on a bedspread woven about 1860 by a pioneer woman in Minnesota. (See page 158.)

frontier farther west into the semiarid (half-dry) plains. Rainfall comes to these plains in cycles—several years of adequate rain, then several years of drought. The late 1870s and early 1880s were a rainy cycle. Pioneer farmers believed that the climate of the great American desert had changed. They moved the farming frontier into western Kansas and Nebraska, into central Dakota, into Wyoming, Colorado, and New Mexico.

Then the years of rain came to an end and a period of drought followed. The soil turned to dust and the winds blew it away. The farmers were unable to raise crops. Many of them gave up and returned east. Then a few years later a rainy cycle began again and farmers came back to the high plains.

In time the farmers, with the aid of industry and science, established themselves permanently on the Great Plains. Barbed wire, invented in 1874, solved the fence problem. Industry supplied well-drilling machinery for digging deep wells to tap the underground water for livestock and home use. Industry also supplied windmills. In this level land of high winds, windmills pulled

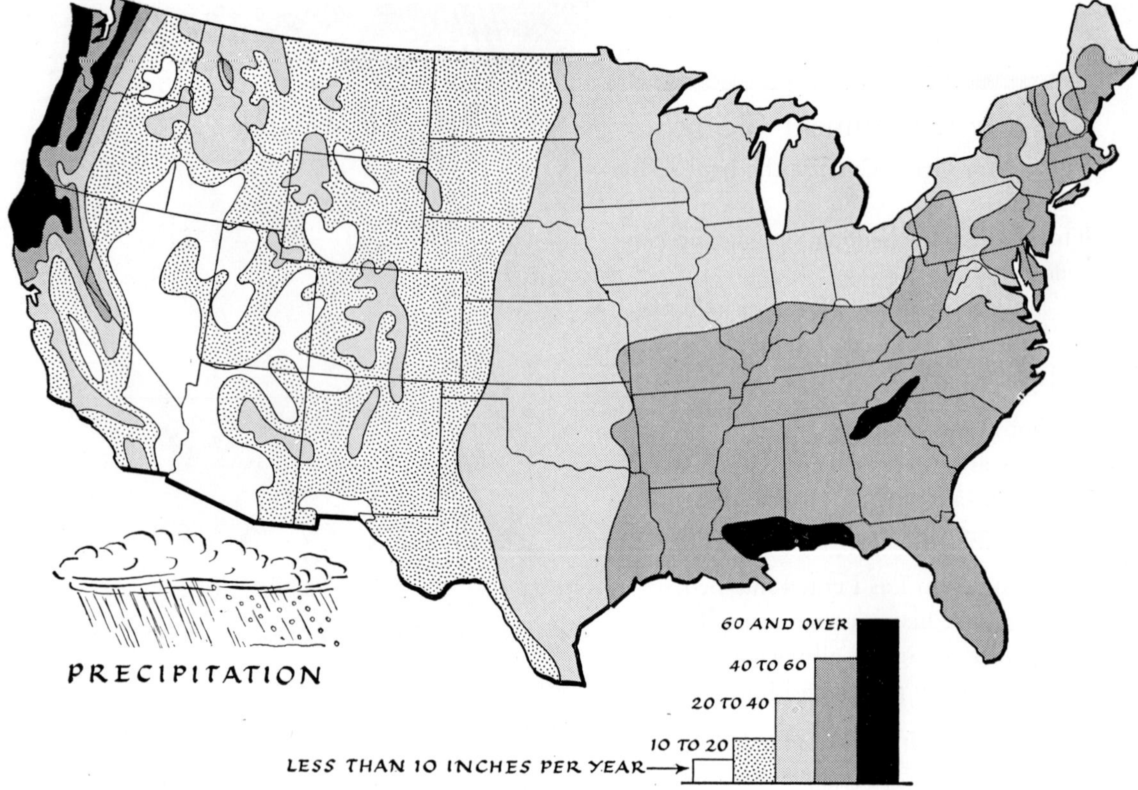

Annual precipitation in the United States. Consult your dictionary to learn what is included in precipitation besides rainfall. Where are the regions with the heaviest rainfall? What can this map tell you about farming in our nation? What is the annual precipitation in your state?

the water to the surface. Industry supplied farm machinery with which one man could do the work of many on the broad fields of the Great Plains. To make a living on the Great Plains, a man had to cultivate a much larger farm than farther west. With machinery he was able to do the job.

Agricultural scientists taught the plains farmers the methods of dry farming. The purpose of dry farming is to keep the water in the soil to nourish the plant roots. Moisture evaporates through pores on the surface of the soil. By frequently turning the soil with a harrow, the farmers kept it like a powder, which filled the pores and cut down the evaporation. The farmers often raised only one crop in two years. By these methods they were able to raise crops of wheat during the years of average rainfall.

Finally, the farmers on the Great Plains used new varieties of wheat and other crops that would grow well in the soil and climate of the Great Plains. There is an interesting story about the introduction of "Turkey Red" wheat into the plains. The Mennonites were a German religious group who were opposed to war. From Germany they had moved to Russia to escape military service. They settled in the Crimea, an area much like our Great Plains. After a number of years the Mennonites decided to settle in America. Their agents bought land from the railroads in Kansas and Nebraska. Before leaving the Crimea, the elder folks put the children to work picking out the fattest kernels of wheat to use for seed in the United States. Thus "Turkey Red" hard wheat was introduced into America. With this variety of wheat, farmers were able to settle down permanently and grow crops on the Great Plains.

The "battle of the fences." As soon as farmers settled on the plains, they came into conflict with the cattlemen. The farmers put barbed-wire fences around their fields to protect their crops from cattle roaming the range. Then the "battle of the fences" began. When cattle tried to get to fenced-in water holes or to the growing crops, they tore their flesh on the fence barbs. Angry cattlemen had their cowboys cut the wire and shoot at the farmers when they came to repair it.

As more and more farmers fenced their farms, in order to protect their cattle, the cattlemen fenced in the range. Frequently they enclosed hundreds of square miles of land. Sometimes they fenced in large areas of the public domain, including water holes and long-established roads. Then the farmers, in turn, cut the cattlemen's fences. They settled on the fenced-in government land, traveled on the roads, and used the water. The cattlemen tried to keep them off, and blood was shed on both sides.

The government was usually on the side of the farmers, and the cattlemen finally gave in. Other troubles helped defeat them. Too many people went into the business of cattle raising. A series of unusually severe winters in the late 1880s killed off many cattle on the range. The cattlemen gave up the old system of raising livestock on the open range and turned to a more careful type of stock farming. They bought or leased from the government enough land for their needs and fenced it in. Most of it they used for pasture. They obtained water by drilling wells and erecting windmills. On part of the land they grew hay to feed the cattle in the winter. They even built sheds to shelter them from blizzards. The railroad ran close by—in many cases right through the ranch—so that cowboys no longer had to drive cattle hundreds of miles to the railhead. The old-time cowboy disappeared. He was replaced by a hired hand whose principal duties were to grease windmills and repair fences.

The last frontier. Part of Oklahoma made up the last region that had been reserved for Indians. On April 22, 1889, it was opened to settlement. On that day land speculators and settlers, called boomers, gathered along the boundaries of the territory. They were waiting to

Battle of the fences. Ranchers and farmers fought the "battle of the fences." Why? Who won?

RKO RADIO PICTURES, INC.

Oklahoma land rush. Thousands of "boomers" massed on the border of Oklahoma. On April 22, 1889, at a signal, they dashed across the border to stake out their claims. As this movie scene shows, they went on horseback, on bicycles, on foot, and in covered wagons.

dash in and stake their claims. When noon came, a spectacular land rush took place. By sunset boom cities had sprung up at Guthrie and Oklahoma City. Eighteen years after the boomers' land rush, Oklahoma became a state. The story of Oklahoma is one of the exciting chapters in the history of the western frontier.

The Great Plains region was the last frontier. In 1889 and 1890 six new states were admitted to the Union: North Dakota, South Dakota, Washington, Montana, Idaho, and Wyoming. By 1890 the frontier line had disappeared. That does not mean that no free land was left. More land was taken up as homesteads after 1890 than before. The map on page 408 shows what we mean when we say that the frontier line had disappeared. Settled areas so filled in the map with their irregular lines that it was no longer possible to say, "Here is where settlement ends and frontier begins."

The disappearance of the frontier line in 1890 meant that the day would soon come when there would be no more free land suitable for agriculture. The great task of settling the continent would be completed.

Summary

Prospectors, digging for gold in the Rocky Mountains, and cowboys, driving cattle north from Texas to the railroads in Kansas, led the way in the conquest of the last frontier. Even while the War Between the States held the attention of most Americans, the gold seekers were establishing new communities. These were scattered through the Rockies from the northern to the southern boundaries of the United States. Meanwhile the cattle industry was started on the Great Plains. Soon after the war was over and railroads were built west to the plains, the long drive began. Cowboys drove the cattle over the dusty plains from the Texan ranches to the northern railheads. Later the cattle industry spread over the Great Plains. This was the wild West period in the history of the frontier.

The Homestead Act, which offered 160 acres of public land to every settler, encouraged farmers to invade the Great Plains. Those who settled on the sod-house frontier suffered many hardships. Gradually farmers moved into the semi-arid regions. There they established themselves with the aid of barbed wire, windmills, dry farming, "Turkey Red" wheat and other hardy varieties of grain. Barbed-wire fences brought the open range to an end, and cattlemen developed fenced-in ranches.

Settlement of the last frontier was speeded up by the construction of transcontinental railroads, the first of which was completed in 1869. Soon there were shorter lines that reached into every section of the Great Plains. The railroad companies brought in more settlers from the East and from Europe. The western states became another melting pot, as Germans, Scandinavians, Czechs, Hungarians, and others learned American ways and brought their contributions to American life.

By 1890 an unbroken frontier line separating settled from unsettled land could no longer be drawn. There was still some free land that settlers could homestead, but the days of Daniel Boone's "elbowroom" were gone.

For a Quick Review

1. Describe the gold and silver rushes of the early 1860s.

2. When and where were the early transcontinental railroads built? What effect did they have on the frontier?

3. How did the railroads start the "cattle kingdom" and then destroy it?

4. From which European countries did settlers on the Great Plains come during the period 1865–1900?

5. What was the effect on the Indians of the settlement of the Great Plains?

Boom town. By nightfall of the first day of settlement, Oklahoma City had a population of 10,000. This movie scene shows how rapidly the city was built up.

RKO RADIO PICTURES, INC.

Learning to Study More Easily

USING PICTURES TO UNDERSTAND HISTORY

Perhaps you have noticed that the pictures in this book give you additional information about topics discussed. By studying both the text and the picture with its caption, you can get a clearer understanding of the specific topic than you could from either alone. Pictures are often better than words to help you understand the shape, size, and appearance of objects—a house, for example, or a stagecoach. From studying a picture of a crowd that had come together in a city, you may be able to learn many facts: *what* the weather was like—people's clothes may show the season of the year, whether it was hot or cold, rainy or clear; *when* the crowd had collected—the costumes may show whether the people were living in colonial times, about the time of the War Between the States, or in the 1950s; *why* the crowd had gathered—for games, a play, a speech, a protest meeting; *where* the people lived—the kind of landscape, trees, flowers, houses, and so on, might show in what part of the country the scene took place.

To learn from a picture, of course, a person must study it. Just as you look first for the main idea in a paragraph, try to look first for the important fact or idea the picture gives you. Perhaps it will help to ask yourself, "Why did the authors put this picture here? What were they trying to tell me? How does it explain the ideas in this section of the book?" Read the caption. It will help you answer your questions.

After you have decided what the main idea of the picture is, then study the details. How are the people dressed? What are they doing? What relation do the people in the picture have to one another? What can you learn about the climate from the people or houses or other objects in the picture? Each picture will need different questions, of course, depending on its subject, but these suggest the kind of question you will need to ask yourself.

21 *Manufacturing Expands in the United States*

One of the biggest birthday parties our country has ever seen took place in Philadelphia in 1876. The birthday celebrated there was the hundredth anniversary of the Declaration of Independence of the United States of America. The birthday party was the Centennial Exposition. The invited guests were the people of the United States and of the world. Over 8 million of them came to see the sights during the year the Exposition was open. Let us join the Johnsons (an imaginary family) for a moment as they enter Machinery Hall. Mr. Johnson, who has visited the Exposition before, is explaining something to Jim, Martha, and Mrs. Johnson as they go in.

"Just look at this building. It covers 14 acres of ground. And look at all these machines in operation. One big steam engine is furnishing the power for all the machinery in this hall."

"I want to see the printing press, Dad, the one you said turns out 20,000 newspapers an hour," said Jack.

"It's down this way. We'll come to it," Mr. Johnson replied. "You're right on the number of copies. The machine actually prints, cuts, and folds the papers, so that they're all ready to be delivered. But first let's watch this loom operate. How would you like to have a dress made of the cloth that's being woven there, Martha?"

"Oh, I'd like it. Isn't it a pretty shade of blue? But, Daddy, the machine seems to be running by itself."

"There are the men who are in charge of it, just to the right," Mr. Johnson told Martha. "It is an automatic machine, like most of the others here. The men just have to keep an eye on it to be sure that it's operating correctly and that it's supplied with thread."

"Come on," urged Jack. "Let's go find the printing press."

REMINGTON RAND, INC.

Typewriters, then and now. Above is an early typewriter of the 1870s. The typist moved the carriage by pressing on a foot pedal. Below is a modern typewriter, compact and easy to handle.

REMINGTON RAND, INC.

1 *With New Machines and New Industries, the American People Produce More Goods*

As they toured Machinery Hall, visitors such as our Johnson family saw many automatic machines at work. The printing press and the other machinery mentioned above were actually there. In addition there were machines turning out paper, rubber shoes, watches, carpets, and sugar. A huge steel furnace made steel. One mechanical wonder cut, folded, and counted envelopes at the rate of 120 a minute. Another made 40,000 bricks a day.

Visitors at the fair were entertained by a new invention called the telephone. Many of them thought of it only as a toy. Another new invention, called the typewriter, attracted little attention. Representatives of one company explained how the telegraph worked. Others showed how glassware, paint, and stoves were made.

Foreign visitors were astonished at American progress. Machines were exhibited that made parts for railroad cars and for many kinds of machinery. Others stamped out forks and spoons, buttons, parts of watches, clocks, and locks. Woodworking machines turned out parts for houses and furniture in every kind of design. They made molded trimmings, paneled doors, carved mantels, turned banisters, and so on—all in large quantities and at low cost. Americans could afford to make their homes more attractive with these machine-made products.

Progress in inventions. The Centennial Exposition in 1876 proved that the United States was making remarkable progress in industry and invention. But it showed only the beginning of that progress. In the years following, old machines were improved and new ones were added more rapidly than before. The United States granted more patents than any two other countries combined. By 1890 the Patent Office was granting 25,000 patents a year.

The many inventions kept the older industries changing. Thousands of patents were taken out on improvements in farm machinery and machinery for making textiles, shoes, clothing, and other products. The refrigerator car changed the meat-packing industry. Now meat could be sent to every part of the country and to foreign lands.

The printing and publishing industry of today was made possible by three advances that came about the same time. First, the Linotype was invented by Ottmar Mergenthaler (mĕr′gĕn tä-lẽr) in 1884. A printer no longer had to set type by hand. The Linotype machine turned out lines of type as fast as the operator pressed the letters on a keyboard, much as if he were operating a typewriter. Second, new methods and machines for making paper out of wood pulp reduced the cost of paper. Third, huge printing presses were built that could print, cut, fold, and count 1,600 newspapers a minute. (Compare this output with that of the machine exhibited at the Centennial Exposition.)

"THE POUGHKEEPSIE NEW YORKER"

Linotype. This drawing shows the inventor operating his Linotype. He works a keyboard like that of a typewriter, and the machine turns out a whole line of type at once. How was type set previously?

Railroads are made safer and more comfortable. As you have read (pages 310–311), important improvements had already been made in railroading. This progress continued. From 1880 to 1890, 65,000 miles of new railway were laid in the United States, and the older railroad companies put down much new track and improved their equipment.

New inventions cut down accidents and reduced the danger of travel and work on the railroads. The T-shaped steel rail and the flanged (flănjd) wheel kept trains more securely on the track. The automatic coupler, invented in 1873, was another safety device. Previously a workman had to step between two cars and link them together by hand. Since at least one car was moving, many serious accidents occurred. The automatic coupler joined cars automatically. It was made required equipment for all trains by law.

In 1869 George Westinghouse took out the first patent on his air brake for trains. Before that time brakemen had

WESTINGHOUSE

The air brake worked! A real test of the air brake occurred when a train with George Westinghouse and many railroad officials on board was leaving Pittsburgh. Suddenly a horse and wagon appeared on the track. The engineer put on the brake and the train stopped with a jolt a few feet from the horse and wagon. The air brake was indeed a success!

to put on the brakes by turning a wheel on each car separately. With the air brake the engineer in the locomotive could apply the brakes on all cars in the train at the same time, smoothly and at once.

In signaling, the block system was introduced. A railroad line was divided into sections, or blocks, and signal lights in each block showed whether or not there was a train in that section. If there was, a train that was following would wait until the one ahead left the block. At first the signals were set by hand. Therefore there was danger of error. The next improvement was the automatic block signal. Today the train itself, by means of an electric current, throws the danger signal as it enters the block. This system reduces greatly the danger of wrecks from collisions. Fast trains can follow one another safely at short intervals.

Many other additions to train equipment, like steam heat, more comfortable seats, and better sleeping cars (the first one was used in 1864) made railroad travel more attractive.

The steel industry. One of the most important inventions of the 1800s made it possible to make steel in large quantities and at a low price. Steel is iron with most of the impurities removed. Iron is hard and brittle; it breaks under pressure. Steel is hard but resilient (rē̍-zĭl′ĭ ĕnt); that is, it may bend under pressure but it holds. Steel lasts much longer than iron and can be used for many purposes for which iron is useless.

The main problem in making steel is to remove most of the carbon from the iron ore. For centuries steel had been made in small batches, from 25 to 50 pounds at a time, by heating iron for a period of two weeks in order to drive out the carbon. Steel was so expensive that it was used only for special tools that required a sharp cutting edge. In the 1850s William Kelly in the United States and Henry Bessemer (bĕs′ĕ mẽr) in England discovered how to make tons of steel in a few minutes. They forced a stream of air through iron that was heated to the melting point. The oxygen in the air combined with the carbon in the iron to form a gas (carbon dioxide), which escaped from the furnace. As the carbon left the ore, the iron turned into steel.

The United States had plenty of iron ore for making steel. There were large ore beds in northern Michigan and in Minnesota. After the ore was mined, it was hauled by rail to ports on Lake Superior. From the railroad cars it was loaded on lake boats and carried by water to points on Lake Erie. From Lake Erie ports a short haul brought it to Pittsburgh, the center of iron and steel manufacture. The map on this page shows the routes. The ore in the Lake Superior region was richer in iron than any other then known. It helped make the United States the industrial leader of the world.

By 1900 this country was producing more steel than the rest of the world combined. The use of steel brought great changes in industry. It made possible more complicated machine tools and better machinery for farm and factory. Out of steel, manufacturers made heavier rails, safer railroad equipment, and longer and stronger bridges. New products like typewriters and bicycles were made of steel. The United States began building a navy of steel ships. Architects began building skyscrapers with steel frames. The United States

Iron and coal resources of the United States. In what states are there important deposits of iron ore? Of coal? The arrows show major routes over which these resources are carried to steel-manufacturing centers.

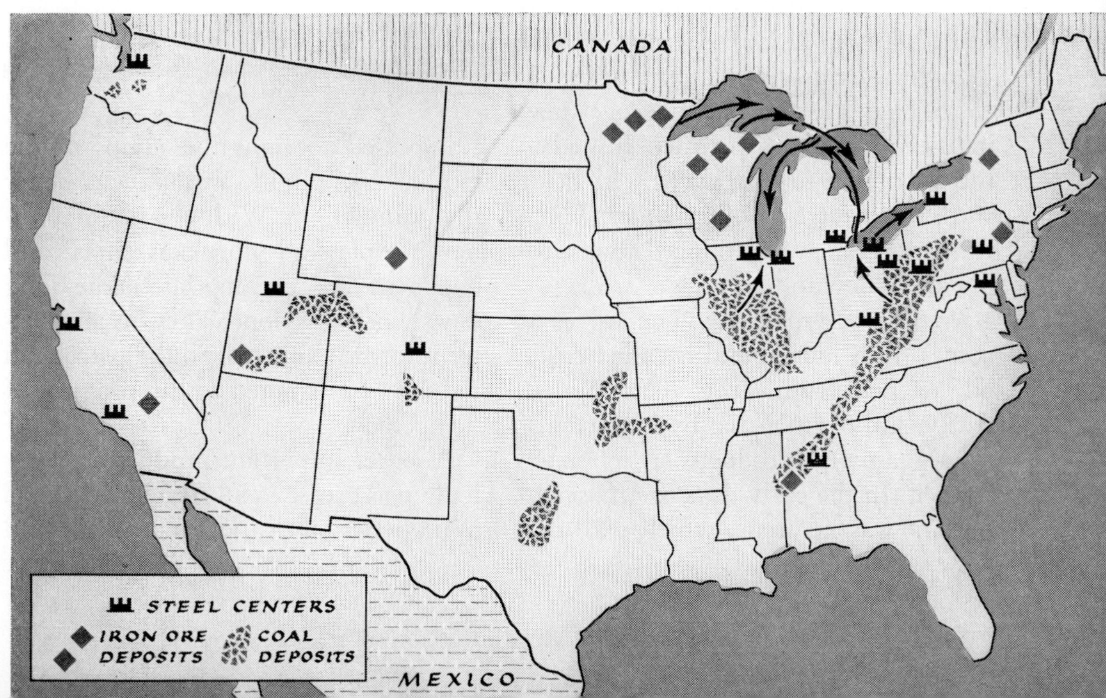

U.S. STEEL

Iron mine. An electric shovel loads iron ore on a truck. Because ore in Michigan and Minnesota lies close to the surface, it can be mined in this way from open-pit mines. How does an open-pit mine differ from a shaft mine?

was changed from a country of wood and iron to a country of steel. The story of steelmaking in the United States is part of the story of American business that you will read about later in this chapter.

New sources of light and power. While the steel industry was bringing about these great changes in American life, the first successful oil well was drilled. Edwin L. Drake struck oil near Titusville, Pennsylvania, on August 28, 1859. That was the birthday of a new industry. Thousands of men rushed to the oil region to drill wells. Oil fields were discovered in other states. For a time more oil was produced than people knew how to use.

Petroleum products. The oil as it comes from the ground is called crude oil, or petroleum. It is dark-colored, sticky, and of little use. By a process of refining, many products are obtained from it. In the early days the most important was kerosene, which was soon

John Henry

John Henry said to his captain,
"A man ain't nothing but a man.
An' before I'll let your steam drill beat me down,
I'll die with the hammer in my hand, Lawd, Lawd!
Die with the hammer in my hand."

John Henry got a thirty-pound hammer,
Beside the steam drill he did stand.
He beat that steam drill three inches down,
An' died with his hammer in his hand, Lawd, Lawd!
Died with his hammer in his hand.

They took John Henry to the graveyard,
An' they buried him in the sand,
An' ev'ry locomotive come roarin' by
Says, "Dere lays a steel-drivin' man, Lawd, Lawd!
Dere lays a steel-drivin' man."

¶ There are many versions of this folk song about John Henry, famous Negro steel driller who worked on the railroad in West Virginia about 1870. Even a man as strong as he could not compete with power-driven machinery.

being used to light the lamps of the world. Lamplight was much better than candlelight. With good light, ordinary people read more newspapers and books in the evening after the long day's work was done. They became better informed citizens. So the petroleum industry contributed to the progress of democracy.

Another important product of petroleum was grease to lubricate machinery. With better lubrication, machines could

LIBRARY OF CONGRESS

Pittsburgh in the 1870s. Pittsburgh grew up where the Allegheny and Monongahela rivers join to form the Ohio. The rivers provided inexpensive transportation. Iron ore could be brought in at a low cost. Nearby were coal and limestone, both necessary for manufacturing steel. With such advantages Pittsburgh became a great steel center. Can you name other cities that have become steel centers?

run longer and at greater speeds without stopping. So the petroleum industry helped produce more goods at lower cost.

In the 1870s and 1880s oil men had no use for gasoline, another product obtained in refining petroleum. They threw it away. You will learn more about the growth of the oil industry on page 430, when you read about the rise of large businesses.

Electricity. Before 1876 electricity was already used in the operation of the telegraph and the telephone. After 1876 it became a source of light to see by, a source of power to do work, and a source of heat to produce new wonders in chemistry. As in the case of steel, the use of electricity produced many important changes in American industry and American life.

The most famous American inventor in the field of electricity was Thomas A. Edison. But he was not alone. Others invented the dynamo, which generates

Edison and Steinmetz. Thomas A. Edison was a great inventor in the field of electricity. Charles P. Steinmetz won fame by creating man-made lightning. Here, in Steinmetz's laboratory, Edison is examining the effects of artificial lightning. Who discovered that lightning is electricity?

GENERAL ELECTRIC COMPANY

LIBRARY OF CONGRESS

Large-scale harvesting in the Dakotas. On the big wheat ranches in the 1890s, wheat was cut by long lines of harvesting machines. The foreman on horseback directed the work. The large ranches, farmed with machinery, were profitable, but neighboring small-scale farmers found it difficult to break even.

(produces) electricity; the electric motor, by which electricity is made to turn wheels and do work; the storage battery, in which electricity is stored to be used as needed; and so on.

In 1880 Edison patented his electric lamp. He and others kept on improving it. Edison combined his own inventions and the inventions of others to harness electricity so that it could be used to provide light, heat, and power. The entire system by which electricity is supplied to home, farm, and factory is largely his work.

Electric power was soon being used to drive streetcars, locomotives, passenger elevators, printing presses, and many other machines. With its aid the cost of making aluminum was reduced from $4 to a few cents a pound. With electricity new substances like Carborundum (kär bō rŭn′dŭm) were manufactured. Carborundum is a hard material used for polishing and grinding. With electricity, dyes, perfumes, and medicines were extracted from coal tar.

Farmers use more machinery. In the years after the War Between the States, just as manufacturers produced more goods, so farmers raised larger crops. As the Great Plains were settled, more land was cultivated. And farmers did more of their work with machinery.

Plows, harrows, and seed drills were improved. Machines to load hay and plant corn were invented and improved. Farmers used multiple horse- or mule-drawn units, such as gang plows, riding cultivators, and four-horse harrows. With these machines one farmer could do the work formerly done by two or more farmers.

One of the greatest savers of manpower was the automatic binder, invented in the 1870s. Two or more men had to follow the old reaper to gather the grain and tie it into bundles. The automatic binder tied the grain into bundles and deposited them in neat rows on the ground.

The American people produce more goods. By means of these marvelous machines, new inventions, and new sources of power, the American people were able to produce more goods than ever before. Machines turned out products at an unheard-of speed and at low cost. In 1900, compared with 1860, the United States produced 6 times as much cotton textiles, 3 times as much woolen goods, 20 times as much coal, 30 times as much iron and steel.

In 1900 one man, using farm machinery, could do as much work as 20 men had been able to do in 1830. From 1830 to 1900 the worktime required to produce an acre of wheat was reduced from 60 hours to 3 hours, an acre of corn from 38 to 15 hours, an acre of hay from 21 to 3 hours. By using machinery, fewer people working on farms could produce larger crops at a lower cost. (See chart on page 539.)

The population of the country increased rapidly from 1860 to 1900. But the production of goods increased much more rapidly. (See charts on pages 446–447, 634–635.) As a result the level of living went up. In other words, the American people used and enjoyed many more products in much greater quantities in 1900 than in 1860.

LIBRARY OF CONGRESS

Mining coal. In the 1800s coal mining became an important industry. Why? These pictures show the principal steps in mining coal. (1) The miner digs at the wall of coal with his pick. (2) He drills a hole to insert dynamite. (3) The dynamite explodes, breaking up the coal. (4) The miner shovels the coal into cars. (5) The coal is hauled to the surface.

2 *American Businessmen Build Large Corporations*

We have seen how rapidly the American people settled the West. We have seen how new machines and new in-

BUREAU OF MINES

Open-hearth steel. Molten steel flows from an open-hearth furnace into ladles. It is made into many products. Can you name six articles in everyday use that contain steel?

ventions created new industries and made it possible to produce more goods than ever before. Railroads were ready to carry manufactured products to every section of the nation. The next step was to build factories with many machines. The factories would produce goods in large quantities to be sold all over the country. Only big companies with a great deal of money could take this step. Businessmen organized such companies.

A big company, or corporation, obtains money to carry on its business by selling shares of stock. A person who buys one or more shares of stock is called a stockholder. He becomes a part owner of the company and receives part of the profits. The stockholders elect a board of directors to run the company.

The American people gained many advantages from the rise of big corporations. But they soon found that big business also created new problems. Let us see how big corporations grew by following the lives of Andrew Carnegie and John D. Rockefeller. They started two of the biggest corporations in the world.

Carnegie enters the steel business. Andrew Carnegie belonged to a poor family that had come from Scotland to live near Pittsburgh, Pennsylvania. At the age of 13 he worked in a cotton mill from six o'clock in the morning to six o'clock at night for $1.20 a week. The next year he became a telegraph messenger. He learned the Morse code and at the age of 16 earned $4 a week as a telegraph operator. He became telegrapher for the Pennsylvania Railroad. His employers rapidly gave him more and more important jobs in that company.

Meanwhile Carnegie borrowed money and made several good investments. At 28 he was a rich man. Soon he resigned from the Pennsylvania Railroad and organized companies to manufacture iron rails, iron bridges, and locomotives.

In 1870 he was 35 years old and was thinking of retiring from business. But on a visit to England he saw steel being manufactured in large quantities at low cost by the Bessemer process. He knew that steel, if it could be made so cheaply, would soon replace iron for most purposes. As a railroad telegrapher Carnegie had received many a message that an iron bridge or an iron rail had crumpled under the heavy load of a train. Steel bridges and steel rails would make railroads safer. Carnegie returned to the United States and put all his money into a plant for the manufacture of steel.

His company grew rapidly. By 1880 it was manufacturing more steel than any other company in the world. The main reason for its success was Carnegie's efficiency in running his business. He expanded his company to include everything necessary to make steel. He mined his own ore, shipped it on his own boats and railroads, smelted it with his own coke, and made the steel in his own plants. He reduced the cost of manufacture at each step because he did not pay a profit to another business. Also, Carnegie kept his mills up to date. In the 1890s he rebuilt them almost completely at a tremendous cost. He did it in order to change to a new and better process for making steel, called the open-hearth process.

Because Carnegie was more efficient, he was able to make steel at a lower cost than his competitors could make it. To get more business, he could sell steel at a lower price than his competitors sold theirs and still make more money than they did.

Carnegie's company did not make many finished products ready to be used by people. It did make rails for railroads and steel frames for buildings. But it sold most of its steel to other companies. These companies used the steel to make products like wire, nails, hoops, and steel pipe.

In 1901 John P. Morgan, the New York banker, organized the United States Steel Corporation. In it he combined the Carnegie company, which made steel, with nine other companies that made steel products like wire and nails. This huge new corporation performed all the stages of steel manufacturing. It took the iron ore from the mine and turned it into the finished product in the hardware store. The United States Steel Corporation was so big that few other steel companies were able to compete with it.

When the Carnegie company was sold to the United States Steel Corporation, Andrew Carnegie received about 250 million dollars. In the years that followed, he gave away most of his fortune for educational projects of various kinds.

Rockefeller in the oil business. The

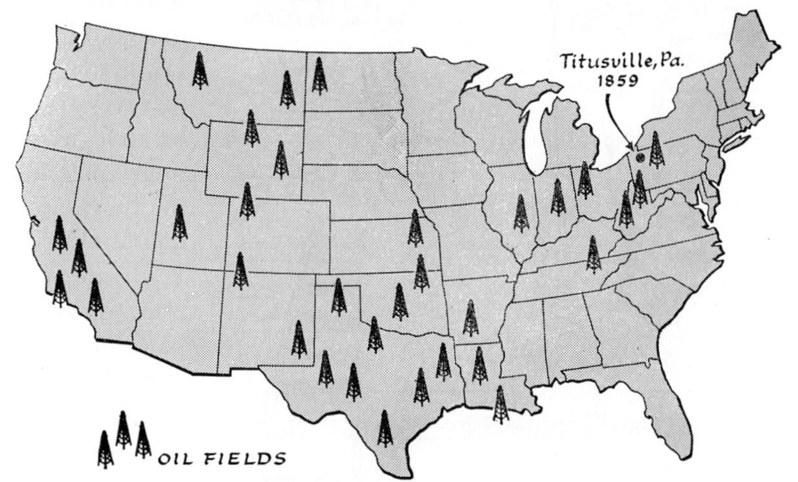

Oil fields of the United States. When Rockefeller built his first large corporation, the oil came from Pennsylvania and Ohio. Name the states in which there are important oil fields today.

career of John D. Rockefeller in the oil industry was in many ways like that of Andrew Carnegie in the steel industry. Rockefeller was born in a New York village in 1839 and lived the first 14 years of his life in that state. Then he moved with his family to Cleveland, Ohio. There, after a course in a business school, he took a job as bookkeeper at $25 a month. Later he and a friend went into business for themselves as commission merchants. They sold grain, meat, and other products from midwestern farms to eastern traders. They received a certain per cent of the sale price as payment for their services. During the War Between the States the partners made a great deal of money. In 1863, just four years after Drake's discovery of oil in Pennsylvania, they invested their extra money in an oil refinery.

Railroad telegrapher. As a telegraph operator on a railroad, young Andrew Carnegie worked on an exciting frontier of his day—building the transportation system that helped make the United States an industrial nation.

Oil refining was then a new business, and no one knew what its future would be. When a new oil field was opened up, the price of oil would drop fast. When the supply in the oil fields was low, the price would shoot up. The refineries hardly knew from day to day how much they would have to pay for crude oil.

The way to stabilize the industry, Rockefeller decided, was for one company to control the refining of oil. Then oil producers would have to sell their oil to it at a regular price.

Soon after Rockefeller entered the business, there were 50 refineries in Cleveland and more in other cities. They waged price wars against one another. One refinery, in order to sell more products, would cut its prices. Another, in turn, would cut its prices still more. Prices were reduced until almost no one made a profit. The smaller plants had to close down.

Rockefeller saw that, in order to stand up under the competition, he had to make his company efficient and big. He made it efficient by reducing costs in every possible way. To make it big, he took in rich partners who invested their money in the business. He used the money to expand his plant. Soon he had the largest refinery in the world. With the cooperation of other refineries, he was able to set the price to be paid for crude oil.

Rockefeller continued to enlarge his business by buying up refineries. They had to sell out to him because they could not meet his competition. He

Early oil field. Where oil was discovered, oil derricks and shacks sprang up almost overnight. In the early days there was a lot of waste in the oil industry.

forced railways to transport his oil at lower rates than those his competitors paid. By 1880 his Standard Oil Company owned most of the refining industry in the nation.

Standard Oil expands. Rockefeller continued to expand his business. He transported oil in his own pipe lines, tank cars, and ships. He built factories to make chemicals, pumps, oil cans, and tank cars. In special plants he manufactured 300 by-products. He built up a large export business, selling Standard products in every part of the world. In short, like the United States Steel Corporation in the steel industry, the Standard Oil Company expanded until it was engaged in every step in the oil industry from the mineral in the ground to the can of kerosene on the store shelf.

As kerosene was replaced first by gas and then by electricity, it ceased to rank first among the products made from oil. With the coming of the automobile, gasoline became the most important product. By that time Rockefeller had retired from the active management of the business.

Standard Oil made enormous profits. John D. Rockefeller, the principal stockholder, became known as the richest man in the world. Like Carnegie, he gave away hundreds of millions of dollars to improve the life of people in the United States and in many other parts of the world.

The age of big business. The United States Steel Corporation and the Standard Oil Company are but two examples of the growth of large business organizations in the 1880s and 1890s. Similar corporations grew up in other industries. They refined sugar and packed meat. They manufactured rubber and farm machinery and ran railroad, telephone, and telegraph systems.

Our study of two companies helps us

understand why large corporations were formed. Men in the same industry combined their companies to avoid competition that might drive many of them out of business. At the same time, under one management they could make better products at lower costs. A big company could afford expensive laborsaving machinery. It could supply much of its raw material for itself. The raw materials that it bought could be purchased in large quantities at lower prices. It could make use of the by-products of its factories to manufacture other products. It could carry on scientific search for improved and less costly ways of manufacturing. Such a big business made profits for its owners. It also provided the public with better goods at lower prices.

Fear of monopoly. Yet a large number of Americans feared big business. They were afraid that big corporations would be able to set prices for their products as high as they wished. In some industries one huge corporation actually did control prices to a great extent. A small company in the same industry had to follow the lead of the big company, or it would be forced out of business. In other industries, where there were several large corporations, the directors of the companies could get together and agree on the prices they would charge.

When one company or a group of companies controls prices in an industry, it is called a monopoly (mȯ nŏp′ȯ lĭ). The American people were strongly opposed to monopoly. A monopoly could easily raise the prices of its products and so make very high profits at the expense of consumers.

Some persons opposed big business for other reasons as well. They believed that a large business could prevent anyone from organizing a new competing company. As a result there would be less opportunity for Americans to become independent businessmen. Again, many persons were afraid that businesses might become so powerful that they could influence government in city, state, and nation. They feared that laws might be passed to favor big business, not to promote the welfare of all the people.

For these and other reasons many Americans complained about big business. In spite of these complaints big business became bigger. It became an important part of American life. Almost every subject that we shall discuss from now on will be connected in one way or another with big business. At the same time we must keep in mind that small business continued to exist, even in industries with big corporations.

3 *Many American Workers Join Labor Unions*

We have already seen in Chapter 16 how craftsmen became wage earners and how they moved to the cities and depended entirely on their wages for a living. They found working for a large corporation very different from working for a small company owned by one or two persons.

Workers lack bargaining power. In a small business the employer knew the worker personally. He usually knew the worker's family and its needs. He felt responsible for paying the worker enough for a living.

In asking for an increase in wages, the worker of earlier days had certain advantages. As a rule he was doing skilled work. If he left the job, the owner would have trouble finding someone to take his place. Besides, with a few hundred dollars the worker could open up his own business and go into competition with his employer. Thus the worker was rather independent and usually could obtain wages high enough to give him a good living.

After the growth of big business, the worker employed by a large corporation was in a different position. The owners of the business were thousands of stockholders. They did not know the worker and did not feel any responsibility for him. They were interested only in making large profits. To increase profits, the manager of the factory looked for ways to reduce costs. A large part of the cost was the wages paid to workers. Therefore the manager would try to keep wages as low as possible.

Furthermore, the workers had lost most of their independence. In many industries they no longer used their handicraft skills but instead tended machines. Many jobs that once required skilled labor could now be done by unskilled workers. If one worker left his job at a machine, another could be trained to do the work in a day or two. And there were plenty of unemployed workers to be trained. Again, as the machinery used in producing goods became more expensive, it became more difficult for an individual worker to start a successful business of his own.

In short, the worker now depended entirely on employment for a living. Therefore he was almost helpless. He could not bargain with the employer, but had to work for the wages that were offered him.

Workers organize labor unions. Workers, however, found a way to increase their bargaining power with their employers. If one worker threatened to leave unless his wages were increased, the company simply hired someone else to take his place. But suppose all the workers in a factory threatened to leave their jobs at the same time. And suppose they threatened to march around the factory to prevent others from replacing them. Then the employer would have to pay serious attention to their demands.

In order to bargain with their employers, not one at a time, but all together, workers organized labor unions. A union would ask an employer for higher wages and shorter hours. If it could not reach an agreement with the employer, all the union members were likely to leave their jobs—that is, they went on strike. The strikers guarded the factory gates in order to prevent other workers from taking their places. In other words, they picketed the factory.

Some employers oppose labor unions. Employers naturally were opposed to labor unions. They refused to recognize unions and insisted on dealing with workers individually. Many employers tried to prevent their employees from organizing unions. When a new worker was hired, he often had to sign an agreement that he would not join a union. Such an agreement was called a

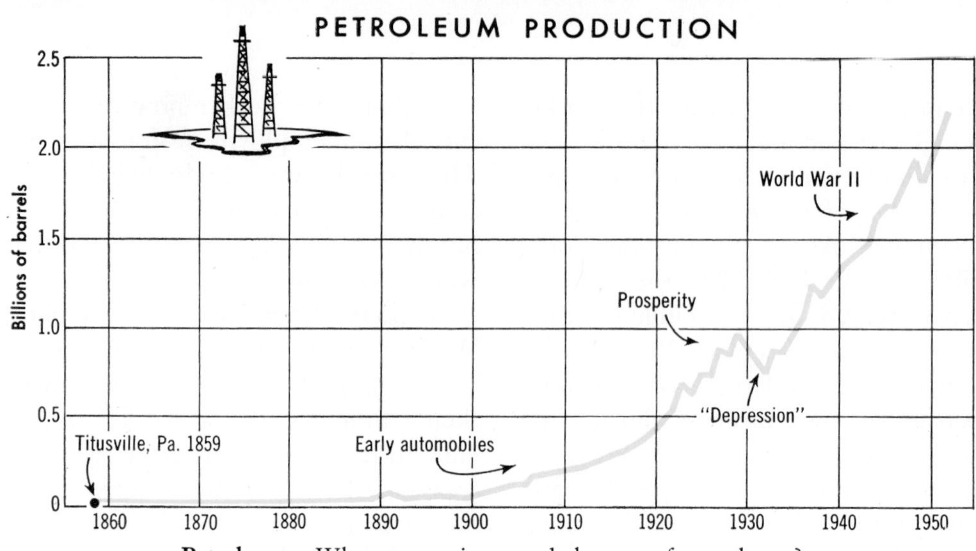

Petroleum. What events increased the use of petroleum?

yellow-dog contract. A worker who encouraged others to join a union was fired and black-listed. That is, his name would be sent to other employers so that they would not give him a job.

If his employees picketed his plant as part of a strike, an employer frequently hired people to enter the factory and begin working. These people were known as strikebreakers. The strikers called the strikebreakers scabs. When the scabs tried to go through the picket line to enter the factory, fighting was likely to break out. Then police, or in some cases soldiers, would be sent to put down the violence. That often meant the end of the picket line and of the strike.

In spite of these obstacles, workers continued to form unions. During the War Between the States and the years immediately following, many large unions were organized. But from 1873 to 1880 the entire country suffered from hard times. Many people were thrown out of work. Wages were reduced. If the workers went on strike rather than accept lower wages, they usually had to give up their strike or lose their jobs to the unemployed. Workers in the coal mines and on the railroads went on strike. Violence occurred and people lost their lives. In none of the strikes did the union workers gain their objectives. Since the unions could not help them, most workers left the unions. Thus, as often happened during a depression, the unions became weak and almost disappeared.

Two kinds of unions. After the depression was over, labor unions began to grow again. In the 1880s the strongest union was the Knights of Labor. The plan of the Knights of Labor was to include all workers in all industries in one big union. That idea proved to be the weak point of the organization. It was impossible to get skilled and unskilled workers in the various industries to cooperate in the union's plans. If the union called a strike in an industry, the employers often could hire plenty of unskilled workers to take the place of those on strike. Naturally, employees who lost jobs in this way blamed the union. When the Knights of Labor began losing strikes, it dwindled away.

The next strong labor organization was the American Federation of Labor (AFL). It was set up in a different way. It consisted of a number of unions. Each union took in only skilled workers of one trade or craft, like cigarmakers, printers, machinists, or carpenters. Hence the unions were called craft unions. They were organized into a federation, as the name of the AFL shows. Unskilled workers were not included.

The purpose of the American Federation of Labor was to obtain higher wages and shorter hours for its members. It tried to make employers bargain with the local union as the representative of the workers. That is called collective bargaining. The AFL moved slowly toward its goal. For 50 years after its beginning in 1886, it was the most important labor organization in the country.

Samuel Gompers, leader of the AFL. One of the men who did the most to make the American Federation of Labor successful was Samuel Gompers. He was one of the leaders in organizing the AFL in the beginning. He served as its national president every year but one from the year it was founded until his death in 1924.

Gompers was born in London in 1850, one of nine children of an English workingman. When he was 10 years old, his father apprenticed him to a cigarmaker and he learned that trade. When the family came to America in 1863 to live in New York City, Sam got a job as a cigarmaker. He joined the Cigarmakers' Union in 1864. How old was he then?

In the cigar workroom where Sam was employed, men were paid at piecework rates—that is, a certain amount for each cigar they made. Often one worker would read aloud to the others for a while. When he stopped, the others would hand over to him enough finished cigars so that he would not be short in his day's pay. Sam had gone to school only four years before he started work. But he could read well, he had a loud voice that could be heard in all parts of the large workroom, and he liked to read. Therefore he frequently

Violent strikes. In the 1870s and 1880s serious strikes took place among railroad workers and coal miners. Companies often hired private police for protection. This picture shows a battle between striking miners and company police. After such violence the Army was sometimes called in to keep the peace.

DEPARTMENT OF LABOR

did. He read newspapers to the other workers. He read to them sections from books and pamphlets in which the problems of workingmen were discussed. Probably he taught his fellow workers a good deal, and he must have learned a lot himself.

The Cigarmakers' Union to which Sam belonged went to pieces when hard times came to the country in the 1870s. Sam was one of the leaders who started to work at once to reorganize it. He believed that workers had to join together in unions if they were to gain better working and living conditions. He insisted that members must pay dues. The money would carry the union through any future depression. Eventually the union would pay sickness and unemployment benefits to its members. Within a few years the Cigarmakers' Union was considered one of the strongest and best organized in the country. Its success was one reason why Gompers was a leader in the American Federation of Labor from the beginning.

Summary

From 1860 to 1900, by the use of new and improved machines, the American people tremendously increased the amount of goods they produced. New inventions made possible modern large-scale industries like meat packing and printing and publishing. Railroad travel was made fast, safe, and comfortable. The steel and petroleum industries were developed. Edison and others harnessed electricity and made it a source of light, heat, and power. Farmers used new and better machines and produced larger crops.

After the War Between the States, large corporations grew up. Big business was usually more efficient than small-scale business and reduced the cost of producing goods. But many Americans distrusted big business. They were afraid it would control prices and charge consumers too much for its products in order to make bigger profits. They were afraid big business would lessen the opportunity of Americans to go into business for themselves. They were afraid that big business might become so powerful that it would influence the government.

Workers employed in factories and big businesses did not have much bargaining power when each one separately asked the employer for more money. They formed unions to bargain collectively with their employers for higher wages and shorter hours. If their demands were not met, they sometimes went on strike. There were two important labor organizations in this period. The Knights of Labor included all workers in one big union. It disappeared before 1900. The American Federation of Labor was made up of unions of skilled workers. It was the leading labor organization after 1900.

As you review the changes that came between 1860 and 1900 in the way Americans made a living, you can see that new machines influenced the life of most groups. Increased production meant a higher standard of living for the people as a whole. At the same time, the increased use of machines created problems for businessmen, factory workers, and farmers. These problems became the problems of the nation.

For a Quick Review

1. What were some of the steps by which railroads were made safer, faster, and more comfortable during the late 1800s?

2. Describe the methods used by Carnegie and Rockefeller to build up their businesses.

3. What methods did employers use to oppose labor unions? What methods did workers use to secure acceptance of their demands?

4. How did the use of farm machinery affect farming and farm crops in the later 1800s?

Learning to Study More Easily

READING PICTORIAL GRAPHS

Many of the graphs in this book, and many of those you find elsewhere, are pictorial graphs. A pictorial graph is one in which amounts are shown by the use of picture symbols instead of by the use of bars. The symbols represent the subject of the graph, and each stands for a certain quantity. For example, a pictorial graph may show how many American children were in school in various years. It may use as a symbol a picture of a boy or a girl walking along with a book under one arm. Each picture stands for perhaps 100,000 children.

To read a pictorial graph, first look at the title to learn what the graph is about. Next examine the key and any explanatory legend. Now you are ready to compare the number of symbols shown for each year. If you wish to learn the number in school in a particular year, check the key to see how many students each symbol represents and multiply by the number of symbols shown for that year. Finally, you are ready to draw conclusions as to the meaning and importance of the statistics shown.

Examine the pictorial graph on page 446. What is the subject of the graph? What symbols are used? Why were they chosen? For what does each symbol stand?

22 *Americans Learn to Live in Cities*

About 1850 a big, slow-moving fellow named Walt Whitman lived with his family on Long Island. He helped his father in carpentry work, but most of the time he seemed to be doing nothing. He liked to ride on the ferry from Brooklyn to Manhattan (New York City) and mix with the crowds on the streets. He had traveled across the country as far as New Orleans and Chicago and had seen cities and farms and rivers. He liked to watch people, to think about what they were doing and what they were like.

Walt Whitman began to write poems, and he put all he had seen and felt into his poems. He included the people of America, the fields and rivers, the cities and farms. He wrote in a new style, free from the strict rules followed by European poets. Whitman wrote poetry like this:

See, steamers steaming through my poems,
See, in my poems immigrants
  continually coming and landing . . .
See, pastures and forests in my poems--
  see, animals wild and tame—
  see, beyond the Kaw, countless
  herds of buffalo feeding on short
  curly grass,
See, in my poems, cities, solid,
  vast, inland, with paved
  streets, with iron and stone
  edifices, ceaseless vehicles,
  and commerce,
See, the many-cylinder'd steam
  printing press—see, the
  electric telegraph stretching
  across the continent . . .
See, the strong and quick locomotive
  as it departs, panting,
  blowing the steam whistle,
See, ploughmen ploughing farms—
  see, miners digging mines—
  see, the numberless factories,
See mechanics busy at their benches with
  tools . . .

You can find all of America of the 1860s and 1870s in the poetry that Whitman wrote in those years. He described the growing crowded cities with their slums, the quiet small towns, the farms on the prairies and plains where Americans lived hard and lonely lives.

1 *More People Come to Live in Cities*

The United States government has counted the American people every 10 years since 1790. The census figures of the past give us much important information about the development of the American way of life.

The census bureau divides the American people into city and country dwellers. It calls city dwellers urban (from the Latin *urbs,* "a city"). It calls country dwellers rural (from the Latin *rus,* "the country"). It considers as a city any place with a population of 2,500 or more.

The census figures show that in the late 1800s the American people were rapidly becoming a nation of city dwellers. (See the chart on page 447.) From 1860 to 1900 the rural population increased from 25 million to 45 million. In the same period the urban population increased from 6 million to 30 million. In 1860 there were 400 urban communities; in 1900 there were 1,700.

We can think of at least two impor-

City hotel. As cities grew, large hotels were built. A traveler of the 1880s staying at the Palmer House in Chicago, shown below, was much more comfortable than a traveler of the 1820s could have been in the best inn of his day.

PALMER HOUSE

WHITNEY MUSEUM OF AMERICAN ART

Threshers' dinner. Grant Wood, a twentieth-century American artist, painted this picture of farm women serving dinner for the threshing crew. Threshers came only at harvesttime, but all year round farm women worked hard at cooking, cleaning, sewing, gardening, and many other tasks. In what ways and by what inventions has the housework of farm women been made easier and more pleasant in recent years?

tant reasons for this rapid growth of cities. As more and bigger factories were built in the cities, large numbers of people came from the farms and villages to work in the factories. These workers in turn attracted many other people to provide services—doctors, lawyers, teachers, clergymen, storekeepers, construction workers, streetcar conductors, government workers, and so on. The second reason was the rapid increase of immigration after the War Between the States. (See the graph on page 447.) Many immigrants settled in cities. There they could find jobs and there they could live close to others who spoke their language.

We must not jump to the conclusion that the United States was a nation of city dwellers by 1900. Most Americans still lived on farms and in villages that were close to the land. Yet cities were growing fast, and more and more Americans were changing to a new way of life—life in the city.

Hard life on farms. Farm life in the 1870s and 1880s, especially on the prairies and the plains, was hard. Men—and boys—worked on the crops until their backs ached and their hands were sore. Women and girls worked just as hard at never-ending tasks: cooking, baking, washing, sewing, churning butter, preserving fruits and vegetables. Farmhouses were far apart, and there was little recreation. The loneliness of farm life was relieved only by church on Sunday and by holiday celebrations that were few and far between. In the winter a blizzard might cut off a family from the rest of the world for two or three days at a time.

The experience of the Garlands was typical of thousands of farm families. The Garlands moved from Wisconsin to Minnesota to Iowa to South Dakota.

Hamlin Garland, the son, later went to Boston, became a well-known writer, and wrote books about his boyhood life. The family home in Iowa, he wrote, was like a dry-goods box standing on the treeless prairie. One unpleasant boyhood incident he remembered was a blizzard that lasted two days and three nights. In writing about it, he told how the wind howled and roared and whistled around the rickety house. Twice each day his father fought his way through the drifted snow to the stable to feed the imprisoned cows and horses or to fetch more fuel. On the third morning the sun appeared. Then, wrote Garland, "We met our schoolmates that day, like survivors of shipwreck, and for many days we listened to gruesome stories of disaster. . . . It was long before we shook off the awe with which this tempest filled our hearts."

Villagers have an easier life. Life in a village or a small town was in many ways little different from life on a farm. Many villagers owned cows, chickens, pigs, and a horse or two and cultivated a fruit and vegetable garden. They drew water from a well in the yard, got light from a kerosene lamp, and warmed themselves with a wood or coal stove in the kitchen. On winter mornings the children jumped out of bed in the cold upstairs bedrooms, grabbed their clothes, and dashed down to the warm kitchen to dress. On Saturday night the washtub was placed in the middle of the kitchen floor, pails of water were heated, and the members of the family took a bath one after the other. In such ways as these, life in town and life on the farm were alike.

But town life was easier and more enjoyable. Townspeople did not have to get up so early in the morning. Men

Kitchen in town house, 1870s. This kitchen was much easier to work in than the farm kitchen shown on page 440. There was running water instead of a pump. The stove burned coal instead of wood and heated the water in the boiler next to it.

LIBRARY OF CONGRESS

LIBRARY OF CONGRESS

Fire fighting. Volunteer fire departments and hand pumps were still the rule in most cities in the 1870s. Why were steam engines and a paid staff of trained firemen important advances?

and boys were free of the backbreaking labor connected with growing field crops. With less housework to do, women visited more with neighbors and took part in church socials, sewing bees, and various clubs. With less farm chores to do, boys had more time for swimming, fishing, and hunting in the woods. They played baseball and other games. Once a year they watched the circus arrive in town. Some of them carried water for the elephants to earn free tickets to the show. In contrast to the isolation of the farm, townspeople enjoyed the advantage of living where they could enjoy the companionship of others. Yet they were near enough to the country to enjoy it, too.

City governments provide many services. In the large cities everyday life was quite different. City dwellers had to buy all of their food and most of their clothes in stores. Many city families could not afford to own houses. Instead, they rented apartments. Many city workers had to travel long distances to their jobs. Some cities were so crowded that there were no open spaces for recreation. Children, then as now, often had to play in the streets.

City people could hardly get along unless their city government furnished such services as a supply of pure water, care of the streets, and fire protection. The cities grew so rapidly that the city governments were unable to keep up with the need for these services. Many cities took their water from the same nearby lakes and rivers into which their sewers emptied. Therefore drinking water was not pure. Sewers were not built so fast as new streets were laid out. Therefore some residents lived on streets that had no drainage. Many city people lived in homes that had no plumbing. In that respect they were no better off than people living in the country. In fact, their situation was worse because the cities were so crowded.

Sanitation. In the 1870s and 1880s scientists were finding out that diseases like typhoid fever, diphtheria, and cholera are caused by germs. They learned that germs flourish in dirt. They knew that insanitary conditions may lead to epidemics in which many people suffer from rapidly spreading disease. The danger was greatest in cities, where masses of people lived close together.

City governments started the long campaign for sanitation. They began to supply pure water to their people. They enlarged and improved sewerage systems. Either the city hired men to collect garbage or residents had to pay private companies to remove it. Cities established street-cleaning departments. They began to require plumbers to pass examinations before receiving licenses. City officials inspected the plumbing in buildings. Inspectors checked foods like meat, milk, and fish for freshness. Children entering school had to be vaccinated against smallpox. City health departments quarantined persons ill with certain diseases like measles and scarlet fever. These are called contagious diseases, because well people can catch them easily from those who are ill. The sick person was kept separate from other people until there was no danger that someone else might catch the disease. Frequently the entire family of the sick person was quarantined.

Other city services. Cities also improved their protection against fire and crime. Fire-alarm boxes and steam fire engines were added to equipment for fighting fires. Police departments introduced patrol wagons, mounted police, and detectives.

In other ways city life was made more convenient and more attractive. Streets were lighted, first by gas, then by electricity, which came into use in the 1880s. Streetcars made it possible for cities to spread out more, since people could travel to and from work at a low cost. At first the cars were drawn by horses. Later they were moved by electricity.

Recreation in cities. Cities set aside areas of trees and grass as parks and built boulevards to connect them. The

LIBRARY OF CONGRESS

Popular sports in the 1880s. Tennis was popular among wealthier city residents. Women players, as you see, wore long street dresses that slowed them up. Bicycling clubs demanded smoother roads and started road-improvement programs.

LIBRARY OF CONGRESS

NATIONAL GALLERY OF ART, INDEX OF AMERICAN DESIGN

Toys of the 1870s and 1880s. The toy fire engine, the steamboat model, and the stove with its miniature pots and pans are all copied after things that were used in everyday life. How do they compare with fire engines, kitchen stoves, and steamboats you have seen in use today?

parks provided breathing spaces for city dwellers. Flower gardens and lakes, museums and zoos made the parks more attractive and more interesting places for people to visit.

Unlike the country, the cities did not provide enough space for people to play games. As cities grew, many persons enjoyed spectator sports. That is, they sat and watched teams of experts play the games instead of playing themselves. Our three greatest spectator sports—baseball, football, and basketball—were developed in this period. Before 1900 there were crowds of 10,000 persons attending baseball games and 50,000 watching football games.

The circus. The circus reached its greatest popularity after 1870. The circus grew by combining various shows in one—clowns, acrobats, equestrians (skillful horseback riders), collections of human freaks and strange animals. The greatest organizer of the circus was P. T. Barnum. Barnum's circus was the first to have two (and later three) rings, so that the audience could watch more than one show at once. He was always adding new attractions: midgets, giants, bearded ladies, the biggest elephant. And when he failed to find new freaks, he made them up. After he and James A. Bailey combined their circuses, Barnum and Bailey's circus was "the greatest show on earth."

The circus was made complete when in the 1880s William F. Cody, Buffalo Bill, put his wild West show on the road. In the circus ring cowboys and Indians acted out bronco bustings, stagecoach holdups, and Indian attacks on frontiersmen. Folks in the East and in Europe were entertained by imitations of the real dangers that western plainsmen were going through at the very same time.

The circus provided entertainment for millions of Americans. Its arrival in a town was one of the big events of the year. Some people would travel 50 or 75 miles to see the show—a much longer trip in 1890 than now. The circus was more than just entertainment. Its colorful performers and strange animals brought to its audience a hint of far-off countries in a wide, wide world.

2 *Progress Is Made in Reform and Education*

Visitors to American cities in the 1880s were shocked by the great contrast between the life of the well to do and the life of the poor people in the slums. Every large city had its crowded slum area. New York City's was the largest and the worst.

The curse of the slum was the tenement house, three, four, or five floors high. These houses were dirty, dark buildings. Each floor was cut up into long, narrow apartments. Many bedrooms had no windows to the outside air. The typical slum home consisted of three rooms, one for cooking, eating, and living and two dark bedrooms. In such a home there often lived as many as a dozen people—men, women, and children. In the yards behind the houses there were rear tenements, even darker and more crowded.

Reformers try to help slum dwellers. Many persons felt sympathy for the families that lived in the slums and tried to help them. In many cities they formed charitable organizations to provide food, fuel, and clothing for those in need. Some groups of citizens looked

Wild West Show. Buffalo Bill's Wild West Show was very popular with children and adults in the East and in Europe. It presented exciting and dangerous moments in the lives of western cowboys, Indians, and settlers.

LIBRARY OF CONGRESS

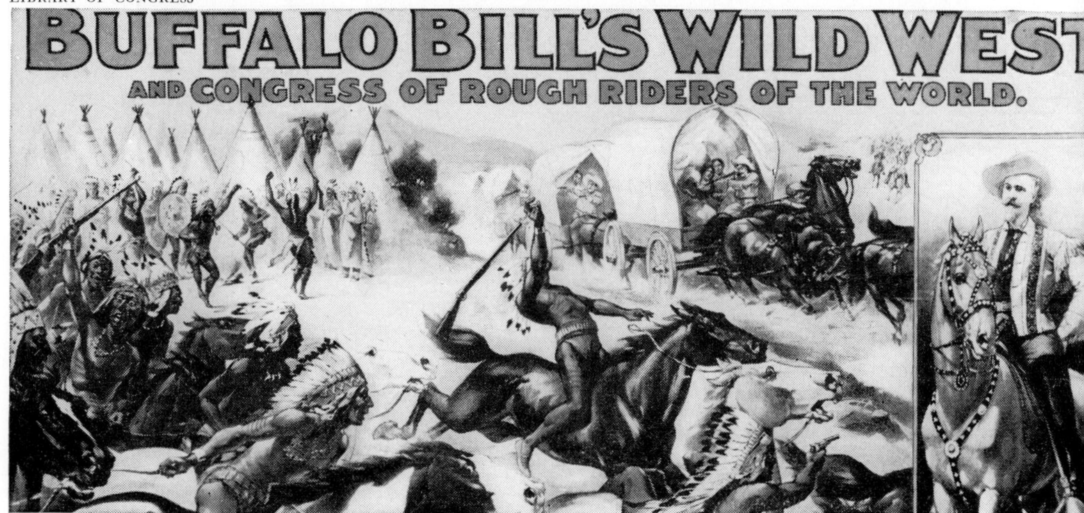

PEOPLING THE LAND 1860-1920

After 1860 the number of Americans just about doubled every 30 years.

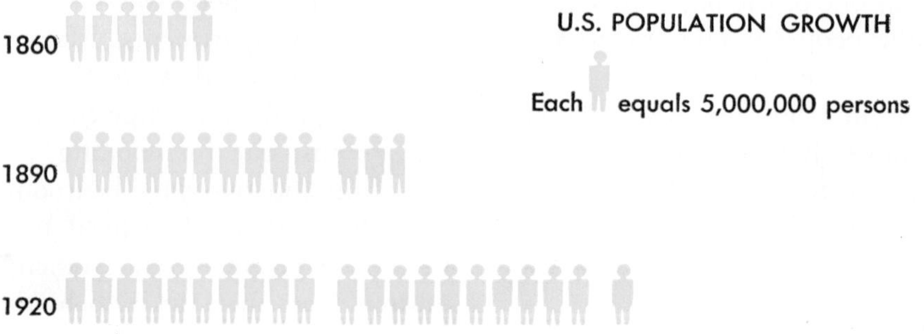

By 1890 it was no longer possible to draw a frontier line between settled and unsettled parts of the country. The American adventure in settling the land was coming to an end.

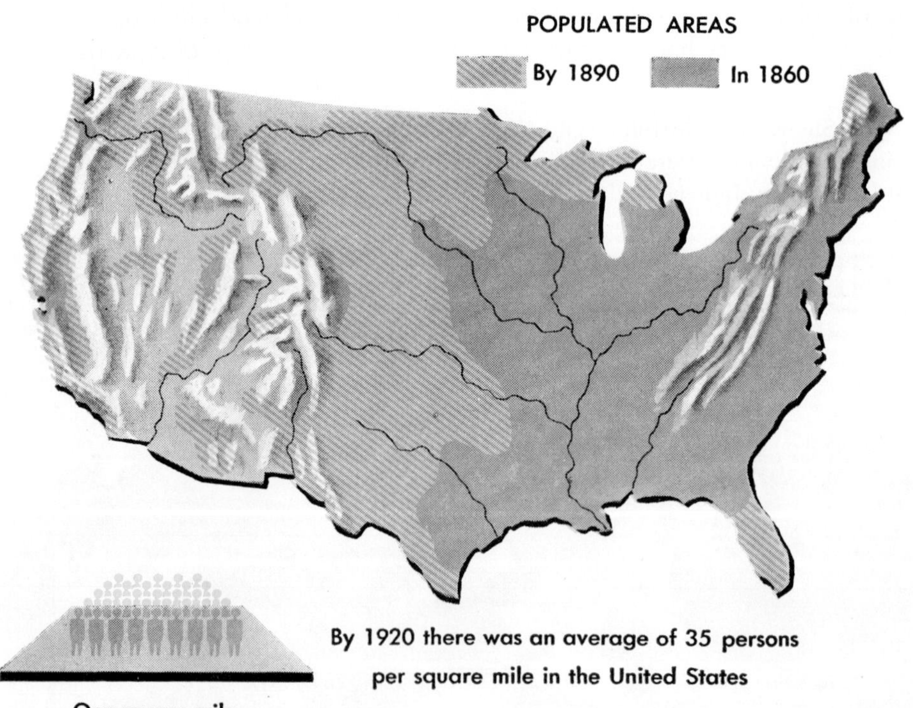

By 1920 there was an average of 35 persons per square mile in the United States

While some immigrants continued to come from western Europe, after about 1890 most immigrants came from southern and eastern Europe.

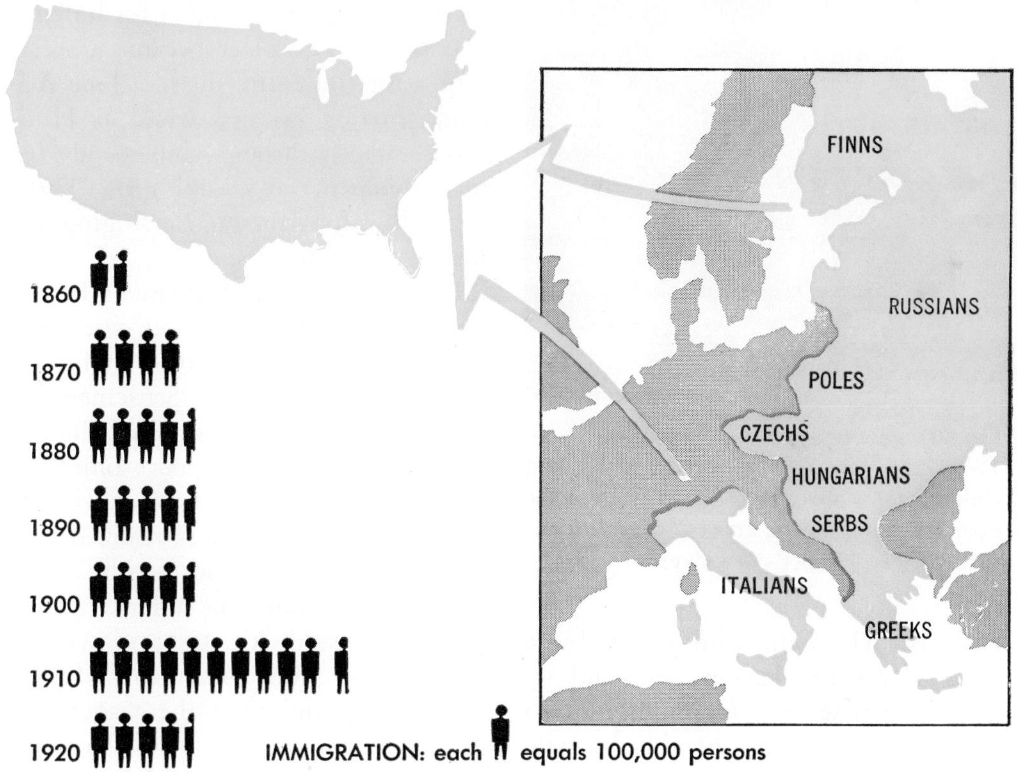

FINNS
RUSSIANS
POLES
CZECHS
HUNGARIANS
SERBS
ITALIANS
GREEKS
1860
1870
1880
1890
1900
1910
1920
IMMIGRATION: each equals 100,000 persons

Between 1860 and 1920 American cities grew rapidly. Opportunities in factories, business, and the professions drew more people to the cities.

City dwellers
20%
80%
1860
Country dwellers
35%
65%
1890
51%
49%
1920

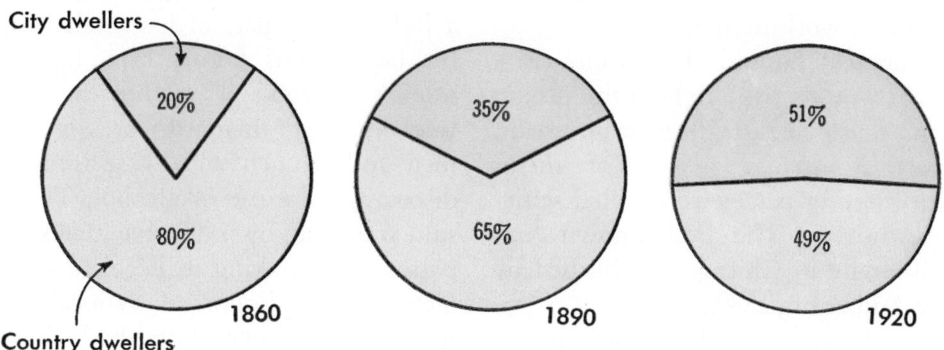

"CHRISTIAN HERALD"

Country vacation. A social worker of the 1870s in a New York slum area is selecting children for a short vacation away from the hot city streets. Do you know of organizations that carry on this activity today?

after the children, who suffered the most. For example, children's aid societies ran newsboys' lodginghouses. In these, newsboys and bootblacks who had no homes could obtain a meal or a night's lodging for six cents. (Remember that six cents bought much more then than it buys today.) Day nurseries took care of children of working mothers during working hours.

Settlement houses. In various cities certain women tried to help the people in the slums by providing clean, warm, attractive meeting places for them. Such meeting places were called settlement houses. The best known was Hull-House in Chicago, established by Jane Addams in 1889.

Jane Addams bought a house in the slums and moved into it. She furnished it neatly and invited her new neighbors to call on her. At first they were shy, but soon as many as 2,000 people were coming to Hull-House each week. One evening was set aside to receive German neighbors, another for Italians, and so on. The place became a social center for the entire district. Jane Addams carried on her work at Hull-House mainly through clubs—clubs for men, women, boys, and girls. There were clubs for dancing, for singing, for many other activities.

Reform by law. Settlement houses were opened in many other cities—for example, South End House in Boston and the Henry Street Settlement in New York. The services of these houses made the life of the poor somewhat easier and happier. But Jane Addams and other social workers realized that the way to help the poor was by doing away with the causes of suffering. They urged states and cities to pass laws that would end slum tenements, forbid child labor, and raise the wages and lower the work hours of working women. Gradually, after 1900, many such laws were passed. (See page 481.)

Social workers saw that the saloon sometimes added to the poverty of the people they were trying to help. Often a father spent part of his small wages for liquor. His family then had less money for food. Therefore the social workers gave their support to other men and women who were trying to discourage the use of alcohol. The result was that by 1900 five states had passed laws making it illegal to manufacture or sell liquor. Many local communities in other states had similar laws.

Clara Barton founds the American Red Cross. Of the social workers we have mentioned, many were women. During the middle and late 1800s other women became active in helping persons who had met with misfortune. One of the most famous of such women was Clara Barton. Her work was not in the slums but on the battlefield.

Up to the time of the War Between the States, soldiers who were wounded on the battlefield were usually left to suffer and die there. There was no one who had the responsibility of bringing all the wounded to hospitals. Even those who were removed from the battlefield had little chance to recover. There were not enough doctors, hospitals, and medical supplies. During the War Between the States, Clara Barton was living in Washington, D.C. She collected food and other supplies and brought them to the wounded on the battlefields.

In 1869 Clara Barton went to Europe and there learned about the Red Cross. In the preceding few years several European countries had formed national Red Cross societies. They had signed a treaty recognizing the Red Cross as a symbol of mercy. They agreed that in time of war all doctors, nurses, ambulances, and hospitals under the Red Cross would not be shot at but would be given full protection. Clara Barton returned to the United States. After much hard work, she succeeded in organizing the American National Red Cross in 1881. The next year the United States signed the international treaty recognizing the Red Cross.

The American Red Cross is closely connected with the government, but it obtains all its money from contributions by the people. Under Clara Barton's leadership the American Red Cross was the first to serve in peacetime by relieving victims of floods, fires, and other disasters. It did such work in foreign countries as well as at home. Later it went into other fields, such as training nurses, teaching first aid and accident prevention, and setting up first-aid stations along our roads. It organized the Junior Red Cross in our schools. The Junior Red Cross teaches American children health care, service to the community, and friendship for children in all countries. Is there a Junior Red Cross chapter in your school?

New opportunities and rights for women. Jane Addams and Clara Bar-

Junior Red Cross workers. Red Cross workers help victims of floods and other such emergencies. Junior Red Cross members also help others. Here a group is packing books and food for children overseas.

HULL-HOUSE ASSOCIATION

Basketball at Hull-House. From its early days Hull-House gave young people a chance to play games and enjoy other recreation. Today it continues to offer varied activities for young and old.

ton are but two out of a large number of women who performed important services for the American people in the late 1800s. They serve as examples to show that, after the War Between the States, women played a larger part in American life outside the home. Many women became bookkeepers, typists, stenographers, store clerks, nurses, and telephone operators. Larger numbers of women earned a living as factory workers and teachers. As a rule they were paid about half as much as men for the same kind of work.

More colleges admitted women. Some women became lawyers and doctors, but they had a very hard time making a living. Most people were still prejudiced against women in the learned professions.

As women entered more fields of work, they gained rights more nearly equal with men. In almost all states by 1900 a woman had the right to own property and carry on business in her own name. In more than half of the states women had the right to vote in local school elections. But only in Wyoming did women have the same right

After the Battle

The ground, for acres, was a thinly wooded slope—and among the trees, on the leaves and grass, were laid the wounded. . . . Bales of hay were broken open and scattered over the ground like littering for cattle, and the sore, famishing men were laid upon it . . . the most fearful scene was reserved for the night. I have said that the ground was littered with dry hay and that we had only two lanterns, but there were plenty of candles. The wounded were laid so close that it was impossible to move about in the dark. The slightest misstep brought a torrent of groans from some poor mangled fellow in your path. . . . The slightest accident, the mere dropping of a light, could have enveloped in flames this whole mass of helpless men.

¶ This description is taken from a letter by Clara Barton. In it she also told of the equipment that she had for feeding 3,000 wounded soldiers. There were 2 buckets, 5 tin cups, 2 kettles, 4 bread knives, 3 plates, and 1 tin dish. Compare such provisions for the care of wounded servicemen with those of today.

to vote in all elections as men had. Compare the rights and activities of women in 1900 with their rights and activities in the 1850s. (See page 341.)

Public schools are improved and expanded. From 1860 to 1900 the public schools of our country were improved, a great deal in some sections, less in others. The cities led the way. More boys and girls went to school as the schools became open to them without fee. (See graph on page 635.) To make room for the growing number of pupils, the cities built larger schoolhouses. Students were divided into classes, or grades. Instead of having pupils from 6 to 16 years old in one class, a teacher taught a single grade. Beginning in the 1870s, many city schools added a kindergarten. Some schools charged tuition fees for this extra year of school and some offered it free.

Town and village schools slowly made the same improvements. Rural schools lagged far behind. Improvements required higher taxes, and most farmers earned so little cash money the year round that taxes were hard to pay. The typical rural school still had only one room, with students of all ages enrolled. But in many cases several small school districts were combined to establish one large school, in which children were divided into grades.

State governments helped to improve education, especially in the rural schools. The states encouraged local schools to make improvements, such as keeping open for longer terms and hiring trained teachers. Schools that made improvements received money from the state to pay part of the cost. Schools that made no improvements received

"LADIES' HOME JOURNAL" © C.P. CO.

Women at work. One of the many new ways in which women began to earn a living in the 1870s and 1880s was clerking in city stores.

Adventure! Tom Sawyer and Huckleberry Finn are fishing in the Mississippi River. Almost every American knows the story of these two imaginary boys.

JOHN HANCOCK MUTUAL LIFE INSURANCE COMPANY

History in Rhyme—The Constitution

The thirteen States had through the war
Preserved confederation;
They met at Philadelphia now
To form themselves a nation.

In seventeen hundred eighty-seven
They framed the Constitution,
Which came in force in eighty-nine
By general resolution.

Electors of the United States
In unity arose;
George Washington for President,
With glad acclaim they chose.

¶ Grade school students in the 1800s were taught to memorize assignments. The authors of *Story of the Union in Rhyme,* from which this quotation is taken, believed that students would save time by learning history in rhyme.

no state money. Thus the states encouraged higher standards of education.

Many states passed laws requiring boys and girls to attend school. In the beginning the number of years of schooling required by law was small. Children from 8 or 9 years to 12 or 13 were required to attend school no more than 10 or 12 weeks a year. Even such limited laws were not fully enforced. Step by step, however, older children were included and enforcement was tightened up. The truant officer, the official who enforced school attendance laws, became an important person in the lives of many children.

High schools grow. The elementary schools continued to grow after 1860. They enrolled an ever-larger per cent of the boys and girls of school age. A new development in public education between 1860 and 1900 was the tremendous growth of high schools.

In the early 1800s boys and girls who wished to continue their education beyond elementary school had to go to an academy. Academies were private schools, where pupils had to pay tuition. Many towns had no academies. Children in those towns had to leave home to go to school and had to pay for room and board. Attending an academy, therefore, meant a rather large expense, more than many people could afford.

As education in elementary schools became free of charge, people began to demand that the kind of education offered by academies also be made free. That was done in the public high school. The first high school was opened in Boston in 1821, but before 1860 high schools did not spread rapidly. In that year there were about 300 of them. At about the same time there were 6,000 academies.

After the War Between the States, the number of high schools increased rapidly. Some people objected, using the same arguments that had been used against free elementary schools. (See page 332.) More people saw that it was important to the nation that children be educated for citizenship. They saw, too, that a person needed more than an elementary education to get ahead in the age of the machine and of big business. By 1900 there were about 6,000 high schools and about 1,500 academies.

3 *American Artists Describe the American Land and People*

In the late 1800s American artists in every field of art used as their subjects their own country and their own people more and more.

The poet who stood out was Walt Whitman. You read one of his poems at the beginning of the chapter. Whitman began to write his unusual poetry before the War Between the States. During the war he worked in army hospitals, trying to relieve the suffering of the wounded. He wrote a number of war poems and two great poems about Abraham Lincoln. In his poetry after the war he emphasized how great America was in his own day and how much greater she was to be in the future.

Local-color writers. The greatest storyteller of the late 1800s was Samuel L. Clemens, who wrote under the name of Mark Twain. He wrote entertaining, humorous stories about the people and places he knew. *The Adventures of Tom Sawyer* and *Adventures of Huckleberry Finn* are his two greatest books. In them Mark Twain relived in his imagination his own boyhood years on the banks of the Mississippi River. Perhaps you have read them; if so, you will agree that they are interesting and full of humor and adventure.

Many other writers told stories about the parts of the country they knew well. They wrote about New England,

Academy students in class. Many academies gave a thorough education. Why did public high schools eventually take their place?

the Appalachian Mountain area, the South, and other regions. They were called local-color writers because they presented interesting word pictures of the people in the various parts of the country. They described the daily lives of the people and their clothes, their customs, their peculiar ways of talking.

It is interesting that the writings of authors like Walt Whitman and Mark Twain were extremely popular in Europe. "This is what we want from the United States," European critics seemed to say. "We are not interested in American writers who merely imitate our writers. We admire and enjoy writers like these, who tell us in their own way what America and its people really are like."

Music for Americans of the late 1800s. In music we have to distinguish between serious, or classical, music and popular music. The man who did most to teach Americans to enjoy serious music was Theodore Thomas. He organized an orchestra of his own and traveled across the country with it, giving concerts. In Boston, Chicago, and other places, symphony orchestras were organized as a direct result of concerts by Thomas. He encouraged American composers by playing the music that they wrote.

One of the Americans whose compositions were frequently played by Thomas was Edward MacDowell. In his music MacDowell was able to express the pleasure he found in the forest, the fields, and the ocean. Many people enjoyed hearing his works. His best known pieces were the "Woodland Sketches." If your school has a record collection, you will probably find some of MacDowell's music in it. MacDowell's farm at Peterboro, New Hampshire, is now the site of the MacDowell Colony. There, in summer, poets, musicians, painters, and sculptors live, finding it a quiet and pleasant place to do their work.

Popular music. The story of popular music in this period begins with the songs of the War Between the States. It is also closely connected with the minstrel shows described on page 337. In 1859 a northern member of a minstrel show named Dan Emmett wrote "Dixie." The South soon adopted the song as its own. Southern soldiers used it as a marching song during the war. After the war it became a national song. Many other war songs were sung long after the war was over, and some are still sung today. Such songs as the "Battle Hymn of the Republic" and "Maryland, My Maryland," which you know well, were first sung by northern and southern soldiers.

Negro spirituals, another type of music, became more and more popular. In 1871 a chorus of Negro students began touring the country to raise money for their school, Fisk University in Nashville, Tennessee. They called themselves the Fisk Jubilee Singers. The spirituals they sang formed the most popular part of their program. Musical composers later used the melodies of some of the Negro spirituals in composing concert music.

Lumberjacks, cowboys, mountain folk, and other groups had their own songs. Lumberjacks usually sang their songs in camp in the evening when the day's work was over. Cowboys, riding around the sleeping cattle at night, sang so that the cattle would not be frightened by any sudden noise. People living in the southern Appalachians sang the same ballads that their grandfathers and great-grandfathers had brought over from England and Scotland, songs such as "Sweet Barbara Allen," for example.

In the late 1800s Americans heard and played more music than ever before, though not nearly so much as we do today. After all, they did not have phonographs, movies, radios, and television. Yet even in those days American composers of popular songs were busy, and there was a new hit song almost every year. Most school children learned to read musical notes and to sing. Many children took lessons on some musical instrument, the favorite being the piano. They were taught by private music teachers.

THE NEW-YORK HISTORICAL SOCIETY, NEW YORK CITY

"Fetching the Doctor." This sculpture by John Rogers shows a farm boy on horseback rushing a doctor to someone who is sick. Can you write (or tell) a good story suggested by this sculpture?

Painters and sculptors. As in earlier years, most American painters learned their art in Europe. Some made their homes in Europe. Others returned to this country but continued to imitate their European masters. On the other hand, as in the first half of the 1800s, a number of American painters described their own country and its people in their paintings. One of these was Winslow Homer. He painted pictures of the life of soldiers in the War Between the States, of Negro life, of farm and village life, of the life of children. One of his best known pictures, "Snap the Whip," shows a line of schoolboys running down a hill, playing the game for which the picture is named. Another shows the inside of a country schoolhouse, with one small boy being kept in after school. Perhaps Homer's most famous paintings are his pictures of the sea.

Painters like Homer were popular with the American people. Perhaps it was because each of their pictures told a story. People could understand and enjoy the story without having studied the fine points of painting.

Architects follow a variety of styles. American architecture went through a period of confusion in the late 1800s. It began when architects designed large homes for wealthy Americans, imitating the style of old European castles. These mansions, usually of stone, had many towers and balconies. Then carpenters began building houses of wood in the same style. You read on page 420 that factories turned out cheap carved ornaments of wood and iron. These were tacked on to the houses wherever there was space. People seemed to believe that the more ornament there was, the more beautiful the house would be.

MUSEUM OF ART, RHODE ISLAND SCHOOL OF DESIGN

Baseball players practicing, 1875. Thomas Eakins, who painted this picture, made many paintings of American sports of his day. Notice that the catcher wears none of the modern catcher's equipment. What other changes in baseball since 1875 do you know of?

Other American architects began designing buildings in the styles then in use in France and Italy. These were simpler in plan, more like the buildings of ancient Greece and Rome. Still other architects copied the American colonial style. Builders soon had many styles to choose from. American homes and other buildings were designed in many styles and combinations of styles.

At the same time American architects started to develop the skyscraper, a kind of building that originated in this country. The first skyscrapers were erected in Chicago in the 1880s. The skyscraper was made possible when builders learned to use structural steel beams to hold up the floors in buildings. One other feature was necessary—the elevator to take people up and down. Elisha G. Otis had invented the elevator in the 1850s, and now it came into wide use as taller buildings became common in cities.

Summary

American life in the period after the War Between the States showed great contrasts. People living on the Great Plains, for example, had to struggle hard against nature. Americans living in small towns had more comforts, though they still lived close to the countryside. The cities grew rapidly and began to provide the many services that city residents enjoy today, such as paved and lighted streets, sanitation, police and fire protection, parks and playgrounds. Many city people found recreation by watching games instead of playing them. The circus became very popular with most Americans.

The growth of cities brought new problems to those Americans who wanted to make the democratic idea of equality and happiness apply to everybody. People living in the city slums, for example, did not have opportunities equal to those of many Americans. Private charities, such as Jane Addams's Hull-House and other settlement houses, tried to help the slum dwellers. Laws were passed to improve slum conditions. Some people worked to relieve suffering from other causes. For example, Clara Barton founded the American Red Cross.

In addition to the efforts of reformers, during the period from 1860 to 1900 the democratic forces that were at work in the previous 30 years (see Chapter 17) expanded and grew stronger. The public elementary school system was improved, and in most states the public high school system was added. Women had a chance to fill many kinds of jobs in business, and they gradually obtained more rights.

Writers and artists responded to the feeling of democracy and gave more importance than formerly to the lives of ordinary people. Music that became popular among the American people included Negro spirituals and the songs of cowboys and lumberjacks. Walt Whitman put all of America into his poems and foretold the future greatness of his country. Mark Twain wrote about his boyhood on the Mississippi and about the mining camps of the West. In their paintings artists showed Americans at their daily jobs and recreations. American architects still mainly copied the Europeans. But those Americans who built the early skyscrapers started a new style that was purely American.

American life in the later 1800s showed great contrasts, as we have seen. It also showed an increasingly democratic spirit as the needs and interests of ordinary people were considered more and more. Many of the problems that appeared resulted from the industrialization of our nation. Many of them were to become more serious as the nation moved into today's machine age.

For a Quick Review

1. In what ways was village life like farm life in the 1870s and 1880s? In what ways was it different? How did village life compare with life in the cities?

2. What new duties did city governments accept as cities grew larger?

3. What means did social workers use to try to help poor people in the cities?

4. What improvements were made in schools in the late 1800s? Why did city schools improve more rapidly than rural schools?

5. What kinds of recreation and entertainment were popular after the War Between the States? Can you explain why each one you mention became important in American life?

Learning to Study More Easily

UNDERSTANDING HISTORY THROUGH FILMS AND RECORDINGS

While studying the growth of our nation this year, you have probably seen a number of films about American history. Here are some general rules for studying films and other audio-visual materials.

Often students think of a film or a recording as something for amusement rather than for learning. Of course, you will enjoy a good film or recording that is used in class. But your enjoyment will be different from the kind you get from watching commercial movies or television or listening to the radio. The films and recordings you have in class, while interesting, are intended primarily to present important information. They provide additional details that will help you understand better the facts you already know. You must learn how to "study" a film or recording most efficiently, just as you try to study a book in order to get the most out of it.

The first step in studying a film or recording is to know what you are looking for as you see or hear it. Usually it is better to have two or three questions in mind than to try to find answers to eight or ten. Many students find it helpful actually to write down beforehand the questions for which they want answers. For example, one class that was to hear the recording "Jane Addams" in the Cavalcade of America Series looked for answers to these questions: What was Jane Addams's major purpose in her settlement-house work? What were the big problems she ran into? How did she try to solve them?

A second step in studying films and records is to make brief notes as you see or hear the material. As you jot down the major questions, leave some space between them on your sheet of paper. As you study the film or record, write down key words that will help you remember the information that was given. Your first note taking on films and recordings may seem hard. But when you become used to making your notes brief and doing them quickly, you will find this method helpful.

A third step in learning from films and records is to discuss with the class what you have seen and heard. Often there will be surprising differences among students as to what was in the film or record or as to the way events were interpreted. Talking it over will help you get the facts straight and remember the important ones.

Frequently you may need to repeat the film or record to clear up some point on which students have disagreed or to look for more details. Sometimes it is a good idea to look at a film first for the high spots and then study it for such details as how the people were dressed, how they spoke, what the houses looked like, and so forth.

Unit Roundup

HIGH POINTS OF THE UNIT

Often, when you wish to summarize important developments that took place over a period of years, you will find it helpful to make a review time line. Try doing so now. Make a summary of the facts showing the growth of the United States in the last part of the nineteenth century.

On a full-page sheet of paper, draw three parallel time lines that show the decades from 1860 to 1900. Label the lines Settlement, Making a Living, and Everyday Life. Next, skim Chapters 20, 21, and 22, selecting events. (Can you make use of headings and summaries in doing this?) Place each of the events that you select on the appropriate line of your review time line.

When you have finished your selection, check each line to make sure you understand why each date was important. Prepare to explain and defend your selections to the class. Read across the three lines decade by decade. Can you see cases where events listed on one line affected those you have placed on another? Draw arrows between events on different lines that are

MAIN EVENTS OF UNIT 6, 1860–1900

Building and governing the nation	*Earning a living*	*Science, arts, and the people*	*The nation and its neighbors*
(See Main Events of Unit 5, page 394)	**1862** Homestead Act	**1862** Morrill Act, land grant colleges	
	1867 Typewriter		**1867** Alaska
	1869 Transcontinental railroad	**1869** First college football game	**1869** Suez Canal
	1869 Knights of Labor		
	1876 Bell's telephone		
1877–1881 **Rutherford B. Hayes, Pres.** (Republican)	**1877** Selden's automobile	**1877** Phonograph	
1877 Reconstruction ends			
		1879 Edison's electric light	
		1880 Population 50,155,783	
1881 James A. Garfield, Pres. (Republican)		**1881** American Red Cross founded	
1881–1885 Chester A. Arthur, Pres. (Republican)			
1883 Civil Service Act			
1885–1889 Grover Cleveland, Pres. (Democrat)	**1886** American Federation of Labor		
1889–1893 Benjamin Harrison, Pres. (Republican)	**1889** Dept. of Agriculture in Cabinet	**1889** General Federation of Women's Clubs	**1889** Pan American Union founded
	1890 Frontier line declared ended		
	1890 Sherman Antitrust Act		
1892 Populist party			
1893–1897 Grover Cleveland, Pres. (Democrat)	**1893** First Ford auto		**1893** Chicago World's Fair
		1894 Moving pictures	
1896 Bryan-McKinley campaign	**1896** Rural free delivery of mail		
1897–1901 William McKinley, Pres. (Republican)			**1898** Spanish-American War
			1898 Hawaii annexed

closely connected. Be ready to explain to the rest of the class the relationships that the arrows indicate.

Finally, write a one-paragraph summary of main developments in the growth of the United States during the last part of the nineteenth century.

EXPAND YOUR VOCABULARY

1. The following phrases from Unit 6 may be found frequently in newspapers today. Do you understand each one? Make a list of any about which you are uncertain and arrange to have them discussed by the class.

automatic block signal	dry farming
collective bargaining	interchangeable parts
compulsory school laws	settlement house
craft union	spectator sports
	strikebreaker
	structural steel

2. Working with three or four other students, present brief skits to illustrate each of the following terms. Write all the terms on the board before your presentation begins and let the class guess which term each skit is meant to illustrate.

competition	quarantine
contagious	roundup
epidemic	sewing bee
monopoly	spectator
picket	tenant

HISTORY IN THE MOVIES

1. *Pioneers of the Plains* tells about a family's journey from Illinois to settle on the Great Plains about 1870. Prepare to study the film by reviewing what you have learned about American frontiers before 1870. Then you will be able to compare life on the plains frontier with life on the earlier frontiers.

2. Use the film *Westward Movement* to review the story of the settlement of the Mississippi Valley, the Great Plains, and the Far West. The film uses animated maps to show much of the story. Because the film moves rapidly, you will need to give it close attention.

3. In the film *The Great Meddler* the beginning of the Society for the Prevention of Cruelty to Animals (SPCA) is described. Henry Bergh, founder of the SPCA, is the "great meddler." To what extent did the growth of cities bring about the conditions that Henry Bergh was trying to correct?

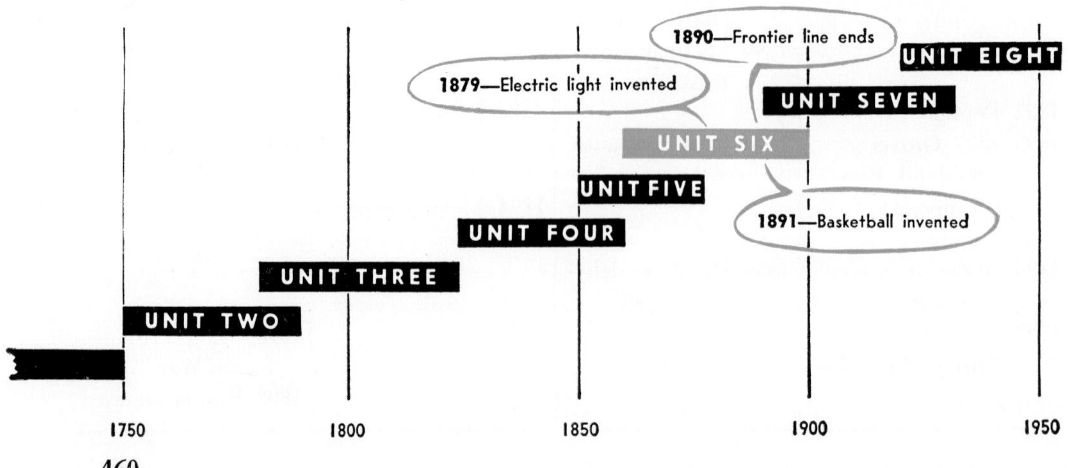

WITH CRAYON, RULER, AND PASTE

1. Using the title "How to Homestead," prepare a picture strip showing the steps necessary to earn a homestead.

2. Make a picture chart showing a number of the products that are made today from petroleum.

3. Prepare a true comic-strip biography of one of these persons or another about whom you have read in Unit 6:

Jane Addams	Thomas A. Edison
P. T. Barnum	George M. Pullman
Clara Barton	Mark Twain

4. Make a set of graphs that show comparison of each of the following in the United States in 1860 and 1900: population, production of cotton textiles, production of coal, production of iron and steel.

5. Review Unit 6 and make a list of important events, major laws, and so forth, to recommend to the class for inclusion on the large class time line. After the class has decided which ones to use, place them on the time line.

6. Prepare a set of costume plates to show how Americans dressed about 1860 and about 1890. You may draw them or find pictures to mount.

PUT ON A PLAY

1. Plan and present one or more skits showing the causes of conflict between cattlemen and farmers on the Great Plains in the later nineteenth century and the kinds of incidents that took place.

2. Three girls might present a one-act play entitled "Things Were Different in My Day" with a cast including a grandmother, mother, and teen-age daughter living in a frontier town in Nebraska in the 1880s. The play should bring out the differences between the grandmother's experiences on the Wisconsin frontier in the 1830s and the conditions existing in the Nebraska town, which is on a railroad line.

3. Arrange a musical show with dramatic episodes to illustrate the development of popular music during the last half of the nineteenth century. You might use some records and have the group sing some of the songs.

STORIES THERE WAS NO ROOM TO TELL

1. Prepare a report on the topic "Mining for gold, then and now." Find out where and how gold is mined in the West today and compare with the places and methods of gold mining in the 1860s and 1870s.

2. "Life on the sod-house frontier" would make an interesting report topic. As you gather information and organize your report, look for opportunities to compare the sod-house frontier with earlier frontiers. Use pictures and diagrams to illustrate your report.

3. Investigate dry farming and irrigation farming as used on the Great Plains today. Report to the class.

4. Prepare a report dealing with one of the immigrant groups that were important in American life in the 1870s and 1880s. "Scandinavian Pioneers in America" (or German or Irish) might be your title. Include information as to where they settled, the kind of work they were likely to do, evidence of their influences on American life today, and so on.

5. Choose one of these report topics, adapting it to your particular interest:

The development of baseball in America (or football or basketball or another spectator sport)

Farm machinery in America—yesterday and today (Obtain pictures from farm machinery companies to illustrate the report; make comparisons with the farm machinery of the 1880s and 1890s.)

The history and present work of the American Red Cross and the International Red Cross (Be sure to include information about the Junior Red Cross.)

The importance of the steel industry to modern America (Show through such points as the processes used, sources of raw materials, uses made of products, and number of employees.)

The modern printing industry (If possible, supplement your research in books by visiting a printing company and interviewing officials there. See page 651 for suggestions about preparing for your visit and interview.)

Safety in railroading—the development of accident-prevention techniques and devices for safety

The work of the Patent Office

6. Choose one of the writers, composers, or artists mentioned in Chapter 22. Prepare a biographical report, building it around examples from the person's writings (read parts), music (play records), or pictures (show reproductions).

USE YOUR IMAGINATION

1. "The Good and Bad of the Vigilantes" could have been the title of an editorial in a mining-town newspaper during the period of the wild West. Write the editorial.

2. If you had been an easterner visiting a cattle ranch in the 1880s, you would have found the dress, customs, and duties of the cowboys of great interest. Write letters that such a visitor might have sent to friends in the East, describing ranch life.

3. Find out more about the activities carried on at Hull-House. Prepare a series of diary entries that might have been written by one of Jane Addams's assistants, describing the work of the settlement house and the people whom it served.

SHOW IT ON A MAP

1. Make a map entitled "New States, 1860–1900." Show by a color or other symbol the states that were in the Union in 1860. Print within its boundaries the name of each state that was admitted between 1860 and 1900 and the date of admission.

2. The population center of the United States has moved steadily westward. Show this westward movement on an outline map. Write a paragraph explaining the major reasons why the center of population continued to move west both before and after the closing of the frontier.

YOUR COMMUNITY GROWS WITH THE NATION

How much information you can discover about these topics will depend on the community in which you live—its size, when it was first settled, and so forth.

1. Investigate your community's better health program. Include such topics as water supply, sewerage system, garbage disposal, street cleaning, food inspection, quarantine laws, vaccination laws.

2. What is the history of fire fighting in your community? How does the fire department operate today?

3. Investigate the parks and other public recreational facilities in your community. Include state parks and recreational areas that you may visit.

4. Is there a settlement house or community center in your city? If so, find out

when, why, how, and by whom it was founded. What is its present program?

5. Does your community or a city near you have a symphony orchestra, an opera or concert season, or an active theater? Find out about its history and its program.

6. Did any of the events described in Unit 6 take place in your community or state? Choose one, investigate it in detail, and report to the class.

FURTHER READING

Books about Interesting People

Buffalo Bill by Doris Shannon Garst. Messner, 1948. William Cody.†

Clara Barton by Mildred Mastin Pace. Scribner, 1941.

Cochise, Apache Warrior and Statesman by Edgar Wyatt. McGraw-Hill, 1953.

Custer's Last Stand by Quentin Reynolds. Random House, 1951.

Have You Seen Tom Thumb? by Mabel L. Hunt. Lippincott, 1942. The midget made famous by P. T. Barnum.

River Boy: The Story of Mark Twain by Isabel Proudfit. Messner, 1940.

Sitting Bull, Champion of His People by Doris Shannon Garst. Messner, 1946.

Sounding Trumpet: Julia Ward Howe and the Battle Hymn of the Republic by Louise Hall Tharp. McBride, 1944.

Stories of Adventure and Everyday Life

Caddie Woodlawn by Carol R. Brink. Macmillan, 1935. Living on the Wisconsin frontier in the 1860s.

Jonathan Goes West by Stephen W. Meader. Harcourt, Brace, 1946. From Maine to Illinois by schooner, railroad, steamboat, foot, and bookseller's caravan in the late 1800s.

Let the Hurricane Roar by Rose Wilder Lane. Longmans, 1933. Homesteading on the sod-house frontier.†

Middle Button by Kathryn Worth. Doubleday, 1941. A girl of the 1880s who wanted to be a doctor.

Nikoline's Choice by Margaret Maw. Oxford, 1947. A Danish family stakes a land claim in Utah in the 1880s.

Powder and Hides by Val Gendron. Longmans, 1954. One of the last great buffalo hunts.

Shadow over Wide Ruin by Florence Crannell Means. Houghton Mifflin, 1942. A Denver girl's year (1886) at a trading post in the Navajo country.

Song of the Pines by Walter Havighurst and Marion Havighurst. Winston, 1949. Adventures of a 15-year-old Norwegian boy in a northwestern logging camp.

Stocky: Boy of West Texas by Elizabeth Whitemore Baker. Winston, 1945. A 12-year-old boy's adventures in the 1870s.

These Happy Golden Years by Laura Ingalls Wilder. Harper, 1943. Life in Dakota in the 1880s. This book is the last of an interesting series on frontier life.

Wind Blows Free by Loula G. Erdman. Dodd, 1952. Establishing a home on the Texas Panhandle in the 1890s.

Winter on the Johnny Smoker by Mildred Houghton Comfort. Morrow, 1943. Living on the Mississippi in Minnesota in the 1870s.

Other Interesting Accounts

Story of the Great Plains by May Yonge McNeer. Harper, 1943. The settlement and development of the plains region.††

The Building of the First Transcontinental Railroad by Adele Nathan. Random House, 1950.

Unit 7 *Americans Face New Problems 1890–1932*

BY USING machines on farms and in factories, as described in the preceding unit, Americans produced more goods. But those machines at the same time created new problems for Americans to solve.

With their machines and on their newly settled lands, American farmers raised larger crops and more livestock. But farm prices fell so low that it did not pay farmers to sell their corn. They burned it as fuel in their stoves. Farmers earned so little money that they were forced to sell their mortgaged farms. The farm problem became a problem for all Americans. How could farm prices be kept up so that hard-working farmers would be able to make a living?

Big business organizations, called corporations, provided most of the money and leadership that brought about the industrial expansion of the late 1800s. Corporations built railroads, refined oil, made and distributed electrical power, started new industries,

and produced goods of many kinds and in huge quantities. In the process the corporations grew enormously powerful. In many cases they, rather than the voters, decided who was to be elected to office and what laws were to be passed. The American people faced the problem of regaining and preserving control over their own government.

The American people faced new problems, not only at home, but also in their relations with other nations.

Like the United States, other countries expanded their factories in the late 1800s and produced more goods. The other governments sought colonies in the undeveloped parts of the world. From the colonies they would obtain raw materials for their factories, and to the colonies they would sell manufactured goods. The other countries made it difficult for Americans to trade in their colonies. The other countries threatened to seize islands close to the United States. From those islands they might one day attack the United States.

The American people faced a very difficult problem. In a world of machine production, the industrial nations competed and fought for raw materials and markets. How could the United States protect itself in such a world?

The United States acquired islands in the Pacific and the Atlantic. Americans faced the problems of governing colonial peoples. They soon decided that they did not want to build an empire.

In 1917 Americans found themselves fighting in a world war. After the war, try as they would, they could not separate themselves from the rest of the world.

As we look back on the period from 1890 to 1932, we see now that the United States was continually growing more powerful while the world was continually becoming smaller. The American people had to answer the question: What was to be the role in world affairs of the nation that was growing stronger and stronger in a world that was becoming smaller and smaller? The whole world waited for their answer.

23 The American People Carry Out Reforms at Home

Bill Barnes was a farm boy in western Kansas in the 1880s. He was unhappy. He did not understand all that was going on, but he knew that his father and most of the neighboring farmers were in trouble. The prices for wheat and corn were so low that it did not pay to haul the crops to the railroad. Bill himself had stuffed corn into the stove and burned it for fuel.

One day he went with his father and mother to a farmers' meeting. All the men and women looked tired and worried. They talked about the "wicked railroads" and the "bad monopolies" and the "selfish politicians." They spoke in favor of income tax, initiative (ĭ nĭsh′ĭ ā tĭv), referendum (rĕf ẽr ĕn′-dŭm), and free silver. Bill did not understand all that was said. But after that he disliked monopolies and the railroads, and he was in favor of free silver.

A few days after the meeting a man came to Bill's home. Bill's father and mother signed some papers and the man left. Later the boy found his mother crying. When he asked her why, she told him that they no longer owned the farm. It now belonged to the person who had lent them money when hard times had forced them into debt. Conditions had not improved. They could not repay what they had borrowed. They had lost their farm. They would still live on it, but they would be tenants and pay rent. All his father's work had gone for nothing. Bill felt like crying, too, but did not. Instead, he went out to the field to help his father.

Bill Barnes is imaginary, but there were thousands of farm families like his in the West in the late 1800s.

BROWN BROS.

James A. Garfield
1881

BROWN BROS.

Chester A. Arthur
1881–1885

1 *Western Farmers Demand Help from the Government*

In the 1880s and early 1890s our farmers produced larger crops. But they did not earn a better living. The prices of farm products fell rapidly. The larger crops of 1890 brought hardly any more money than the smaller crops of 1860.

Low prices and high costs. Farmers in the West, especially the recent settlers on the Great Plains, suffered the most. They had to ship their grain long distances to market, and the railroads charged them very high freight rates. Some farmers in the Dakotas had to pay more to ship their wheat to Minneapolis than it cost to transport the same wheat from Chicago to Liverpool, England.

Other expenses were also high for the farmers. Many of them had come to settle in the West with little money. In the beginning they borrowed money to build homes, barns, and fences. Then they borrowed more money to buy machinery and make other improvements. About half of the farmers of the West had mortgages on their farms. That is, they had borrowed money on the condition that, if they did not repay it in time, their farms would be sold to pay the debt. Eastern loan companies were glad to lend money at interest rates from 8 to 20 per cent. The farmers had to pay the interest in bad years as well as good or lose their farms. In many cases the company that had lent the money took over the farm when the farmer could not pay.

Farmers in the South had many of the same troubles. They grew more cotton, but the price went down from about 15 cents in the 1870s to about 6 cents in the 1890s. Sharecroppers fell deeper and deeper into debt. Many independent farmers had to mortgage their farms.

Tenant farmers. It is no wonder that farmers had to work early and late to make ends meet. Many of them lived in dread of losing their farms to the banks or the loan companies that held the mortgages. One bad year was often enough to sink them. Many a farmer had to give up his land to others and continue to live on it as a tenant, paying rent for it. The number of tenant farmers mounted steadily until by 1900 about 25 per cent of the nation's farmers did not own the land they plowed.

In earlier years, when American farmers found it difficult to make a living in one place, they packed up and went west. There they could try again on a new frontier. But now there was no longer a new frontier farther west for them to go to. They had to find a way to keep the homes they had. They organized political parties to get laws passed to help them.

Drought. The worst times started about 1887. In that year a period of drought began on the western plains. The region had been settled during a cycle of wet years. The settlers were unprepared for a cycle of dry years. Their crops, already dry because of lack of rain, were burned by the hot sun and the hot winds. Thousands of settlers deserted their land and moved back east. Many more would have gone, but they had borrowed money on their horses and wagons and therefore could not use them to move away.

The world market. The farmers' troubles were caused only in part by conditions at home. About a third of the wheat grown by our farmers was sold in Europe. In the 1880s farmers in faraway countries, such as India and Argentina, were growing more wheat than before. They were exporting large amounts to Europe. So much wheat came to Europe that the price dropped. Therefore our farmers received less for their wheat than they used to. They were part of a great international business. The price they received went up and down with the world market.

Farmers blame their troubles on monopolies. Our farmers, however, did not understand this. They did not see the shiploads of wheat from India and Argentina landing in Europe. They did know, however, that they were paying high freight rates to ship their crops. They knew that they were paying high prices for manufactured goods.

Imagine yourself attending a farmers' meeting in one of the wheat-growing states—Kansas, for example—in the 1880s. A farmer gets up and makes a speech as follows:

How long can we go on like this? We get 10 cents a bushel for our grain. We have no choice but to ship our grain on the railroad. The railroad knows that and charges us very high freight rates. We do the hard work and the owners of the railroads get the profits.

At the same time, while we get less and less for what we sell, we pay more and more for what we buy. Many of us have lost our farms to the loan companies.

What shall we do? Let us demand help from the federal government. The government is helping the railroads by giving them millions of acres of land. With the

Over the fence. You can imagine one farmer saying to the other: "I tell you, it's the railroads and other monopolies that keep us from making a good living."

tariff the government is helping the manufacturers keep their prices high. Now the time has come for the government to help us. In a democracy a government should keep opportunity equal for everyone.

We demand that the government regulate the railroads and other monopolies so that they will charge us reasonable prices. We demand that the government issue more money. If the government will act, we will be able to pay our debts and live.

Thus the farmers blamed their troubles mainly on the railroads and other monopolies. They demanded aid from the government. At the same time many businessmen were complaining that the railroads were being unfair by charging some companies lower rates than others. They also complained that large corporations were using unfair methods to destroy small businesses and prevent competition. (See pages 430–432.) In answer to these protests Congress passed two laws.

Interstate Commerce Act. In 1887 Congress passed the Interstate Commerce Act. This law ordered the railroads to charge reasonable rates and not to favor some shippers over others. The Interstate Commerce Commission was set up to enforce the law. But it found that it did not have enough power to make the railroads obey the law.

Sherman Antitrust Act. To prevent other monopolies, Congress passed the Sherman Antitrust Act in 1890. (In those days a company or association of companies large enough to be thought of as a monopoly was usually called a trust.) The law prohibited any kind of monopoly. But it was very difficult to prove in court that one company or a group of companies actually prevented competition. Therefore the law did not stop monopoly.

The Populist party. These laws brought the farmers no relief. Unable to get the Republican party or the Democratic party to favor the laws they wanted, the farmers organized the Populist party. They were joined by other

BROWN BROS.

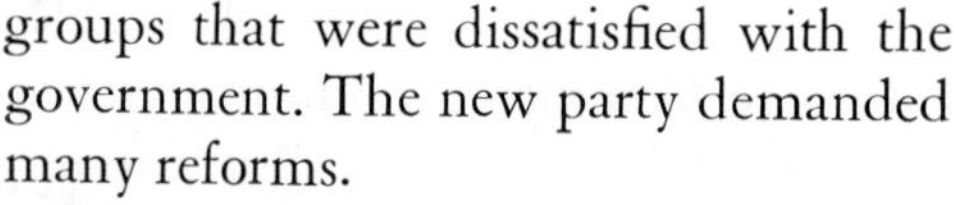

Grover Cleveland
1885–1889 1893–1897

BROWN BROS.

Benjamin Harrison
1889–1893

groups that were dissatisfied with the government. The new party demanded many reforms.

The farmers felt that businessmen had too much control over political parties and government officials. They wanted reforms that would put parties and officials directly under the control of all the people. (See pages 472–475.)

The farmers also wanted the government to help them directly by issuing more money. Imagine a farmer who had borrowed $100 when wheat was $1 a bushel. The debt represented 100 bushels of wheat. A few years later, when he had to pay the debt, wheat sold for 50 cents a bushel. To pay the debt, he would have to raise 200 bushels of wheat. As the farmer saw it, he would have to pay back twice as much as he had borrowed.

Now, said the farmers, if the government issued more money, people would have more dollars in their pockets. They would buy more flour and wheat and other farm products. The price of wheat would go back up to $1. Our imaginary farmer would be able to pay his debt with 100 bushels of wheat.

Election of 1892. Thus the Populists demanded political reforms and more money issued by the government. In the election of 1892, James B. Weaver, the Populist candidate for President, made a good showing. But he did not come close to being elected. Grover Cleveland, the Democratic candidate, was elected. It looked as if, in order to win, the Populists would have to combine with one of the two old parties. They would not do so unless one of the old parties accepted at least some of their demands.

In the years after 1892 the people of the West and the South came to feel that the main difficulty was the shortage of money. The Populists insisted that the government should buy all the silver that was being mined and turn it into money. In other words, they demanded the free coinage of silver. On the other hand, most businessmen were opposed to the free coinage of silver. They said that free silver would be bad for business.

Free silver and Bryan. Free silver became the leading issue in the 1896 presidential campaign. The Republicans opposed it and nominated William McKinley, of Ohio, as their candidate for President.

At the Democratic convention the silver question was hotly debated. The last speaker for free silver was William Jennings Bryan, of Nebraska. In the first few sentences his confident manner and his strong, musical voice quieted the huge assemblage. Before he was through, he had the audience of 20,000 people roaring applause after every sentence. He made a stirring plea for free silver. When he had finished, the convention went wild with approval. After order was restored, the convention voted to include a demand for free silver in the Democratic platform.

Today we can see that Bryan's speech was the voice of farmers protesting against the low prices they received for their crops and the high rates they had to pay for money they borrowed. Bryan and the farmers blamed the businessmen and bankers for all of their troubles. The farms of the nation, said Bryan, are the foundation of its prosperity:

> Burn down your cities and leave our farms, and your cities will spring up again as if by magic; but destroy our farms and the grass will grow in the streets of every city in the country.

Bryan's speech was also the voice of the mass of the people, demanding that the government aid all the people and not just special interests. If ordinary people are prosperous, he said, then the entire country will be prosperous.

Bryan's speech not only captured the Democratic party for free silver; it won Bryan the Democratic nomination for President. The Populist party also nominated him. Thus the two parties fought for free silver together.

When he was nominated, Bryan was 36 years old. He was a young lawyer and newspaper editor who had served four years in Congress. Bryan was to remain a national leader for more than 20 years. He was the first presidential candidate to tour the country by train to speak to the people. He made as many as 30 speeches a day. He covered 18,000 miles and spoke to more than 5 million people. In the West he was hailed as a great leader. In the East he was called a dangerous radical.

During the campaign the Republicans told the people that, if Bryan were elected, stores would close, crops would rot in the fields, families would starve to death. Some manufacturers announced to their workers that they need not return to work the day after election if Bryan were elected. McKinley won.

The end of the Populist party. After the defeat of Bryan the Populist party disappeared. The Democratic party was older, bigger, and better organized than the Populist party. Most voters thought of Bryan as the Democratic rather than as the Populist candidate. The Democrats had, so to speak, swallowed the Populist party by taking over its best candidate and its main idea.

Furthermore, free silver ceased to be a popular issue even with the farmers. This happened partly because crops in foreign countries were small in 1896 and farm prices went up in Europe. Our western farmers had big crops that year and were prosperous for a while. From 1896 until 1920 farmers generally enjoyed prosperity. In times of prosperity American voters, farmers as well as others, are usually satisfied with things as they are and want few changes.

2 *Reforms Are Made to Improve the Government*

Though the Populist party did not last long, it had an important influence on our national progress. It showed that many Americans were dissatisfied with the way government was being run, and it suggested ways to reform, or improve, it. After the Populist party disappeared, the two older parties carried out most of the changes it proposed.

The need for reform in government. One reason why many people were dissatisfied was that too often the government, especially in states and cities, was under the control of political bosses. A strong political boss was the real head of his party in city or state, although he might not hold any office nor be known to the voters. He picked the party's candidates for office. If they were elected, they usually obeyed his orders.

Because of his control of the government, the boss was able to do favors for people. They, in return, gave him money to pay party expenses and even to buy votes. As a result in many states and cities the government was run by political bosses and their wealthy supporters. Elected officials often did what the bosses wanted, not what the people wanted. In such cases, of course, democracy was not working successfully.

Public-spirited citizens desired to make democracy stronger. They fought for reforms that would make officials do what the majority of the people wanted done.

Civil service reform. One of these changes was the reform of the civil service. (All the employees of a government taken as a whole are called its civil service.) Government workers were appointed, as a rule, not because they were qualified for their jobs, but because they had helped the successful candidate to be elected. They often did more work for their party than for the government. You will remember that this way of appointing government workers was called the spoils system. (See pages 270–271.)

In the time of Andrew Jackson the weaknesses of the spoils system might not have been too serious. But by the 1880s the federal government had grown much larger. Many of its employees did work that required special training. When an employee had learned to do his job well, he might be fired just because a new party had come into power.

Under the spoils system the President of the United States made thousands of appointments to government positions.

After a new President took office, he was pestered for months by persons applying for jobs. He had hardly any time to take up the important problems of the nation. Many people realized that this was wrong. But nothing was done until after one day in 1881 when President James A. Garfield was shot by a disappointed office seeker. After that tragedy Congress took action.

The merit system. In 1883 Congress passed the Pendleton Act, the first law to make the civil service more efficient. The law placed about 14,000 government positions under the merit system. Persons who applied for these jobs had to take examinations. Appointments were made from a list of those who received the highest grades. After a period of trial, a person appointed to one of these positions was to hold it permanently. He could not be dismissed just because another party came into power. The Civil Service Commission was set up to carry out the law. The President was given the right to place other positions under the merit system, and every President did so.

Many state and local governments also established the merit system. In some cases, however, politicians found ways to get around the law, especially in state and local governments. Members of the local civil service commissions belonged to political parties and appointed party workers to jobs under the merit system.

The secret ballot. Another effort to improve the operation of government was the adoption of the secret ballot. Previously the voter voted in public, and anyone watching could tell how he voted. Sometimes voters were threatened with loss of their jobs, or with physical violence, unless they voted a certain way. In such cases a voter was often afraid to vote as he believed.

LIBRARY OF CONGRESS

Office seekers in the White House. A newly inaugurated President was kept so busy interviewing job seekers that he hardly had time for more important duties. How has this problem been reduced?

The secret ballot was introduced into this country from Australia in the 1880s and was rapidly adopted by the states. The ballots, containing the names of the candidates of all parties, were printed by the state or local government. The voter took his ballot into a booth to mark it. The secret ballot made it possible for citizens to vote as they believed and therefore made it more difficult for any one group to control the government. If citizens used the secret ballot to express their will, democracy would be strengthened.

Direct election of United States Senators. One change suggested by the Populists was the direct election of

DEPARTMENT OF AGRICULTURE

Secret ballot. A farmer and his wife come to vote. Each one will take a ballot into a booth and mark it secretly. Compare this method of voting with that shown in the picture on page 270.

United States Senators. You read on page 182 that, under the Constitution as originally adopted, Senators were elected by the state legislatures. Big corporations and party bosses, working together, were often able to pick the men whom the legislatures would elect as Senators. Then the Senators would often vote as the political bosses and the men who paid their bills ordered, not as the people wanted. As a result the United States Senate sometimes refused to pass laws that probably a majority of the people desired.

If the Senators were elected directly by the people, the reformers said, they would have to listen to the people. It took a long time to bring about the necessary change in the Constitution. Not until 1913 was the Seventeenth Amendment adopted. Under that amendment Senators are elected by the people of the states. Turn to the Constitution now and read the Seventeenth Amendment (page 691).

Initiative, referendum, recall. Sometimes a state or local government would not pass a law that the people wanted passed. Sometimes the people were dissatisfied with a law passed by the government. The reformers suggested two ways for the people to take over the job of making and unmaking laws. These two ways are called the initiative and the referendum. Under the initiative a small number of citizens can, by signing a petition, propose a bill to be voted on. If a majority of the voters vote for it at the next election, the bill becomes a law. The legislature has nothing to do

Arguing for woman's rights. In the 50 years before 1920 women continued to battle for the right to vote. Here a group of women present their arguments for woman suffrage to a congressional committee.

LIBRARY OF CONGRESS

with it. Under the referendum, by signing a petition, a small number of citizens can request a vote on a law already passed by the legislature. If a majority of the voters vote against it, it ceases to be a law.

The reformers also suggested the recall, a way for the people to put an unworthy official out of office before his term ends. If a petition is signed by a certain percentage of the voters, a special election is held immediately. Other candidates may be nominated, and the official must run against them as he would in a regular election. If he is defeated, he loses his office, of course.

The direct primary. The purpose of the direct primary was to give the members of each political party the power to select their party's candidates for office. Under the old system the candidates were picked by party conventions. Often it was easy for the political boss to control the convention, so that he really chose the candidates. Then on election day, no matter which candidate the voters elected, they were electing a man chosen by a party boss. As a new way to pick candidates for office, the reformers proposed the direct primary election. First there would be a primary election in which the party members would select the candidates of the party. Then in the regular election the people would vote for the candidate they preferred.

Many cities and about half the states adopted the initiative, the referendum, and the recall. Nearly all the states adopted the direct primary. By these laws the citizens were trying to bring their governments and their political parties under their own control.

Woman suffrage. Another change in the later years of this period was national woman suffrage (suffrage is the right to vote). For many years the suffragettes (sŭf rȧ jĕts′), as the women who worked for this right were called, had carried on campaigns in the separate states. By 1914 they had won equal suffrage in 11 states. About that time they changed their plan. They began to work for an amendment to the Consti-

LEAGUE OF WOMEN VOTERS OF THE UNITED STATES

Learn how to vote! In many communities the League of Women Voters provides information for voters. The purpose is to persuade all citizens, regardless of party, to vote.

tution, which would give them suffrage in all the states. The Nineteenth Amendment became part of the Constitution in 1920. Having won the vote nationally, women began to play a more active part in politics. Eventually women were serving as members of Congress, as governors and mayors, and in other offices.

The problem of reform. But these reforms did not produce all the benefits that their supporters had hoped for. The trouble was that many people, men and women, would not take enough interest in politics. Many of them would not even bother to vote, and voting is only one small part of a citizen's duties in a democracy. In order to vote intelligently, a citizen must take time to study his government. He must know the qualifications of candidates for office. He must know how well officials are performing their duties. He should join a political party. He should help make his party an organization that carries out the plans and ideas of the people rather than those of party bosses. And he must be willing, when called upon, to run for office himself. If he is elected, he must serve his community to the best of his ability.

Since many people would not carry out these duties of citizenship, any organized small group could control the government. The various reforms seemed to make very little difference. For example, so few party members took the trouble to vote at primaries that usually the persons picked by party bosses won the nominations without any trouble. In a few states the direct primary was done away with. As time passed, the initiative, the referendum, and the recall were used less and less.

It is clear that our democratic government will not operate to carry out the wishes of the people if the people will not show a real interest in the government and take part in it.

3 *The Government Begins to Regulate Business*

An important part of the program of the Populist party was its attack on monopoly. According to the Populists, the farmers had to pay very high prices for manufactured goods because the large businesses could avoid competition and so raise prices. The Populists demanded that the government compel the big companies to break up into small ones. The small companies would compete with one another, and prices would go down. The Populists also demanded that the government either run the railroads or make them charge reasonable rates.

Small businessmen joined in the attack on monopoly because some of them found it hard to continue in business by the side of big companies. Working people opposed monopoly because they, too, had to pay high prices for goods. Trusts were formed to control the prices of many of the necessities of life, such as sugar, meat, flour, and the oil people burned in their lamps. There was even a trust to keep the price of candy high.

Many other Americans joined the fight against monopoly because they feared the big companies would become so powerful that they could gain control of the federal government itself. Since, as you read on page 469, the early laws had failed to stop monopoly, all these people demanded stronger laws.

With so many people aroused, both the Republican and the Democratic parties favored new laws to regulate business. Before we discuss the laws that were passed, let us get acquainted with the Presidents who were leaders during this period.

William McKinley. William McKinley, who was elected President in 1896, had little interest in trying to enforce the Sherman Antitrust Act. During his first term the Spanish-American War, which you will read about in the next chapter, held the center of attention. The easy victory of the United States made McKinley popular. Besides, the people as a whole were prosperous in those years. Therefore in 1900 McKinley had no trouble defeating Bryan for President the second time.

In September, 1901, six months after the beginning of his second term, President McKinley was visiting the Pan-American Exposition in Buffalo, New York. One afternoon he was standing and shaking hands with people as they came up to him one by one. Suddenly two shots rang out. A young man, later

A Bryan campaign poster. Notice the many appeals to the voters on this poster. The octopus represents the trusts. It is being attacked by "Democracy." Note the slogans. Why was each one used?

LIBRARY OF CONGRESS

LIBRARY OF CONGRESS

"T.R." This photograph of Theodore Roosevelt talking with a train crew shows one reason for his popularity as President. "T.R." was friendly and had many interests.

discovered to be insane, had shot the President.

Theodore Roosevelt. McKinley was succeeded by Vice-President Theodore Roosevelt. Roosevelt belonged to a wealthy old New York family. He had been sickly as a boy but had toughened himself up, partly by living the life of a cowboy for a while on a cattle ranch in Dakota Territory. He had held a number of political offices, including that of police commissioner in New York City. In these offices he had defied the political bosses. As Assistant Secretary of the Navy in 1897, he prepared the Navy for the coming war with Spain. When the war started, he joined the Army and led his regiment of Roughriders into battle in Cuba. He came home a hero. He was elected governor of New York and later Vice-President. When McKinley died, he became President.

Theodore Roosevelt was the youngest of our Presidents and one of the most popular. He bubbled over with energy. He was always doing or saying something to get his name in newspaper headlines. In 1905 Japan and Russia were at war, and he made peace between them. He sent the American fleet around the world to show the strength of the United States. He won the affection and respect of most of the American people—even of many who did not always agree with him.

Theodore Roosevelt did just about everything most American boys dream of doing. He punched cattle and hunted buffalo in the West, was a chief of police, led his men in battle, shot lions in Africa, and was President of the United States.

His six children were the first young children to live in the White House since Lincoln's day. The two youngest boys, Archibald and Quentin, made it a place of noisy fun. They walked around in the White House on their stilts and took their pony up and down in the elevator. At one time or another they kept in the White House guinea (gĭn′ĭ) pigs, turtles, a badger, a parrot, squirrels, white rats, and snakes. Their father did not allow his presidential dignity to keep him out of the fun.

Roosevelt and Taft. "I stand for the square deal," said Theodore Roosevelt as President. He made many Americans understand how important it was to conserve our natural resources and to control big corporations. (This he called trust busting.) He was elected for a full term as President in 1904. He was so popular that he probably could have been the Republican candidate for

President again in 1908. But he refused the honor. He used his influence within the Republican party to have his good friend William Howard Taft, the Secretary of War, nominated.

Taft was elected. He was a big, friendly man. As President he tried to continue Roosevelt's policies, but he failed to inherit Roosevelt's popularity. When he refused to follow Roosevelt's advice in some things, the close friendship between the two was broken. In 1912 Roosevelt tried to win the Republican nomination away from Taft but failed.

While Taft was President, many political leaders interested in reform became dissatisfied with the old parties. They wanted all the reforms you have been reading about in this chapter carried out at once. These leaders organized a new party, called the Progressive party. In 1912 they chose Theodore Roosevelt as candidate for President.

Woodrow Wilson. As their candidate in 1912 the Democrats nominated Woodrow Wilson, who was then Governor of New Jersey. In New Jersey, Wilson put through a number of reforms such as progressive leaders in many parts of the country were demanding. He became popular, especially because he stood up against the political bosses. As candidate for President he promised to push similar reforms for the entire country. He called his program the New Freedom.

Woodrow Wilson was a stern-looking man, and indeed it was hard for him to make friends easily. But within his own family he showed deep affection. He and his wife and daughters were all close to one another and would go to a great deal of trouble to celebrate birthdays and holidays together.

Wilson was a very serious person. His purpose in life was to serve the people of his country and of the world by giving them a better chance for happiness. In fighting for this goal, he would not

¶ In public Woodrow Wilson appeared very stern and cold. But he had a lively sense of humor, which he often used against himself. Here is a limerick he wrote about himself and often repeated:

For beauty I am not a star,
There are others more handsome by far,
  But my face—I don't mind it;
  You see I'm behind it;
It's the fellow in front that I jar.

Two Presidents. President William H. Taft (*left*) and President-elect Woodrow Wilson ride together to the inauguration of Wilson in March, 1913.

LIBRARY OF CONGRESS

compromise. You will see an example of his firmness when you read about his battle for the League of Nations. (See page 515.) Some people called him stubborn. He believed it was his duty to stick to what he thought was right and for the good of the people of the world.

Government, business, and consumers. After 1900 most Americans agreed that the federal government should have stronger control over the railroads. Laws were passed giving the Interstate Commerce Commission authority to decide how much railroads could charge for passengers and freight. At the same time the regular workday of railroad employees was reduced to eight hours.

Theodore Roosevelt's administration won a popular victory over a railroad company. A number of bankers organized one huge company to control all the railroads of the Northwest. Roosevelt had the company brought to court as a monopoly. The Supreme Court decided that the company had violated the Sherman Antitrust Act and ordered that it be broken into small companies. This action tremendously increased Roosevelt's popularity. Many people felt he had proved that the federal government could control business for the public good.

Roosevelt and Taft brought a large number of trusts to trial, and the courts ordered many of them to break up into smaller units. The officials of some trusts broke up their companies without going to trial. But as fast as the old trusts were broken up, new monopolies were formed in new ways. Sometimes the directors of one corporation became directors of other corporations. In that way the companies were really managed as one company although they were separate corporations. As a result a few men were able to control a large part of American industry. Under President Wilson a law (the Clayton Act) was passed prohibiting such exchange of directors and other ways of creating monopoly. But some businessmen succeeded in getting around the new law. The federal government still failed to solve entirely the problem of controlling big business.

The Food and Drugs Act of 1906 was another kind of regulation of business for the protection of the consumer. Investigators had found that food-packing companies were using dyes and other chemicals, some of which were harmful, to make stale foods look and taste fresh. The foods included candy, preserved fruits, butter, eggs, and meat. Consumers did not know what they were buying and eating. The new law prohibited the sale of food that was likely to injure anyone's health. On the label of every package the manufacturer had to list everything that went into the making of the food.

Other reforms. One of the reforms demanded by the Populists had been a tax on incomes. They complained that, while farmers paid taxes on their lands, manufacturers, businessmen, and others did not pay taxes on their earnings. Congress passed an income tax law in 1894. But the Supreme Court ruled that it was unconstitutional because it was a direct tax. (See the Constitution, Article 1, Section 9.) Therefore the Sixteenth Amendment was added to the Constitution in 1913, and an income tax law was passed in the same year. At first the tax rate was fairly low. In later years, however, as the costs of government increased, income tax rates were made much higher. Though it was opposed at first, the income tax is now considered to be a just tax. It is collected from the taxpayers in proportion to their ability to pay.

The reformers had also demanded a new banking system. In 1913 the Federal Reserve System was set up. The country was divided into 12 districts with a Federal reserve bank in each district. Over all was placed the Federal Reserve Board. Federal reserve banks are not like ordinary banks. They do not have individuals as customers. Their customers are member banks. When a local member bank needs more money, it is able to borrow the money from its Federal reserve bank. When the emergency is over, it returns the money. The Federal Reserve System keeps money moving to where it is needed.

State laws protect workers. So far we have been considering control of business by the federal government. In the early 1900s a large number of states also regulated business within their borders. Laws were passed limiting child labor. In some states children below a certain age—usually 14, 15, or 16—were forbidden to work in factories or business except by special permission. Children who did work could do so for only a certain number of hours—usually 48 hours a week. Laws were passed limiting the number of hours women might work. Workmen's compensation laws required employers to pay employees who were injured while working. In these and other ways the state govern-

TREASURY DEPARTMENT

Income tax. Each year, in April, millions of Americans figure how much they owe the federal government in income taxes. Some states also collect income taxes. Does yours?

Child labor, 1908. When this picture was taken, some states had laws limiting child labor. Today most states have such laws. Federal laws forbid the employment of children in some industries.

NATIONAL CHILD LABOR COMMITTEE

STANDARD OIL CO. (N.J.)

Training for safety. Today many factories carry on safety campaigns and train their workers to observe safety measures. Here workers are learning how to avoid accidents.

ments looked out for the welfare of the working people.

If we add up the changes brought about by the reform movement from 1880 to 1920, we find that it accomplished a great deal. It set up new ways to make government more responsive to the will of the people. It made some progress in regulating business and in protecting consumers. On the state level it protected workers, including men, women, and children. The reform movement was democracy's response to the problems of the machine age.

Summary

The reforms of the period from 1880 to 1920 began with protests from the farmers of the West. The farmers were suffering from hard times. They formed their own Populist party. In 1896 the Democrats took over the Populist demand for free silver. The Populist party soon disappeared. Many of the reforms it had sponsored, however, were later made into law.

A great change was taking place. Our country was changing from one that was mainly agricultural to one that was mainly industrial and commercial. That change brought two fundamental problems.

First, some state and local governments, and even parts of the federal government, were under the influence of a few people. These people worked hand in hand with political bosses. The problem here was to place the control of government in the hands of the people. Reformers proposed such reforms as the direct election of United States Senators, initiative, referendum, recall, and direct primary. These reforms were only partly successful. Too many Americans neglected to do their full duty as citizens of a democracy.

Secondly, as large corporations grew up in many industries, the danger of monopoly arose. Companies making the same product could set its price very high. They could make unfair profits at the expense of the people who bought the product. The problem here was to protect the people by using the power of government to prevent monopoly. Theodore Roosevelt and Woodrow Wilson gained much of their popularity by opposing political bosses and the unfair practices of some big businesses.

The first laws passed by Congress to regulate railroads and prevent the growth of monopolies were not effective. Later, under the leadership of Roosevelt and Wilson, stronger laws were passed. These laws helped, but they were not entirely adequate. After 1920 the problem of protecting the country against the bad effects of monopoly still faced the government.

For a Quick Review

1. What kinds of help did the western farmers demand from the federal government in the 1890s?

2. The Populist party grew up quickly and then quickly disappeared. Tell why. In what ways did it contribute to the development of the United States?

3. What condition was each of the following expected to correct: merit system in civil service, secret ballot, direct election of Senators, initiative, referendum, recall, direct primary, woman suffrage?

4. What groups of Americans demanded that the government regulate big business? What reasons did each group give?

5. What measures to regulate business were taken by the federal government under these Presidents: Theodore Roosevelt, Taft, Wilson?

6. What is each of the following: income tax, Federal Reserve System, pure food law? What was the purpose of each?

Learning to Study More Easily

UNDERSTANDING HISTORY THROUGH CARTOONS

You have undoubtedly read comic books or comic strips in the newspapers. Would you agree that they are stories in pictures? Of course, the pictures often seem to be roughly drawn sketches, but they carry the ideas of the story with only a few written words. In the same way the cartoons that we find on the editorial pages of our newspapers express opinions in pictures. Often a cartoon catches the eye of more readers and expresses a point of view more strongly than a long article.

If you will examine the cartoons in your daily newspapers, you will find that certain symbols are often used to carry certain ideas. Here are some of them: money bags, for wealth; a dove, to suggest peace; skull and crossbones, for death; a pair of scales, for justice or a court; a rainbow, to express a feeling of hope; the Statue of Liberty, to mean freedom or liberty; an oak tree, for strength; an octopus, to represent greediness or grasping selfishness; a fox, to show slyness or underhandedness; a lamb, to represent innocence.

Political parties and countries are represented by particular symbols, too. The elephant is used for the Republican party; often it has GOP written on it, standing for "Grand Old Party." The Democratic party is represented by a mule. The United States may be represented by an eagle, by Uncle Sam, or by Miss Columbia. England is often symbolized by a lion, by John Bull, or by Britannia, a goddess-like figure that is dressed in a long flowing gown and wears a helmet.

When you first see a cartoon, look for the title. It tells you the subject of the cartoon and helps you to interpret the symbols the cartoonist has used. Next, look at the figures and any labels the artist has put on them. If there is a subtitle or a caption, read it. It may give additional ideas that the cartoonist could not express in his pictures.

Clip the cartoons from your daily newspaper for one week and list the symbols used in them. In one sentence for each, state the ideas expressed in the cartoons.

24 *The United States Expands Overseas*

Do you know where, in United States territory, only a few generations ago people recorded their history on totem poles? (Imagine what a job it would be to learn from totem poles all the history you have studied this year!)

Do you know where, in United States territory, it is the custom to welcome a traveler or say good-by to him by placing leis (lā′ēz)—garlands of flowers—around his neck?

Do you know where, in United States territory, over 2 million people are living on an island that is about 100 miles long and 35 miles wide? About the same number of people live in Oklahoma or the state of Washington today. The area of the island is 3,435 square miles. In Oklahoma there are 69,919 square miles; in Washington there are 68,192 square miles.

If you do not know the answers to these questions now, you will find them as you read how the United States has expanded overseas. Each question applies to a part of the territory of the United States that has been added since the War Between the States. The last addition of territory before the war had come during two exciting years of our national history, from 1846 to 1848. In those years the United States had added the entire Southwest and Oregon. It obtained a long coast line on the Pacific Ocean, reaching from Puget (pū′jĕt) Sound to southern California.

Some American leaders, in the 1850s, were proud that their country had grown so fast and expected it to continue to grow. They hoped to make the United States a world power. Then came the War Between the States, and the American people were busy with the more immediate problems of waging war. Expansion was forgotten for the time, but after the war the talk about expansion started again. This time it soon brought results.

1 *The United States Obtains Alaska and Hawaii*

William H. Seward, who was Secretary of State from 1861 to 1869, was one of the American leaders who had favored expansion by the United States. When the War Between the States was over, he thought the time to acquire new territory had come. But he found that Congress would not go along with him. For example, the Senate refused to approve the purchase of the Virgin Islands for less than a third of the amount we later paid for them.

Seward buys Alaska. In 1867 Russia offered to sell Alaska to the United States. The Russian tsar (zär) was little interested in faraway Alaska. He realized too that, if Russia and Great Britain should go to war, he would lose that possession. When the Russian minister in Washington offered to sell Alaska, Seward could hardly wait to set the price and complete the deal. One evening the Russian minister came to his house and told him the Russian government had accepted the price and the treaty could be written the next day. "Why wait until tomorrow?" asked Seward. "Let's make the treaty tonight." And they did. The United States promised to pay Russia $7,200,000 for Alaska.

At first most of the members of Congress, and probably most of the American people, were opposed to the treaty. They thought of Alaska as a barren wasteland covered with ice and snow and of no possible value to the United States. They called it "Seward's icebox"

Wheat farms in Alaska. In the fertile soil of the Matanuska River Valley, near Anchorage, farmers raise fine crops of wheat and other products.

BLACK STAR

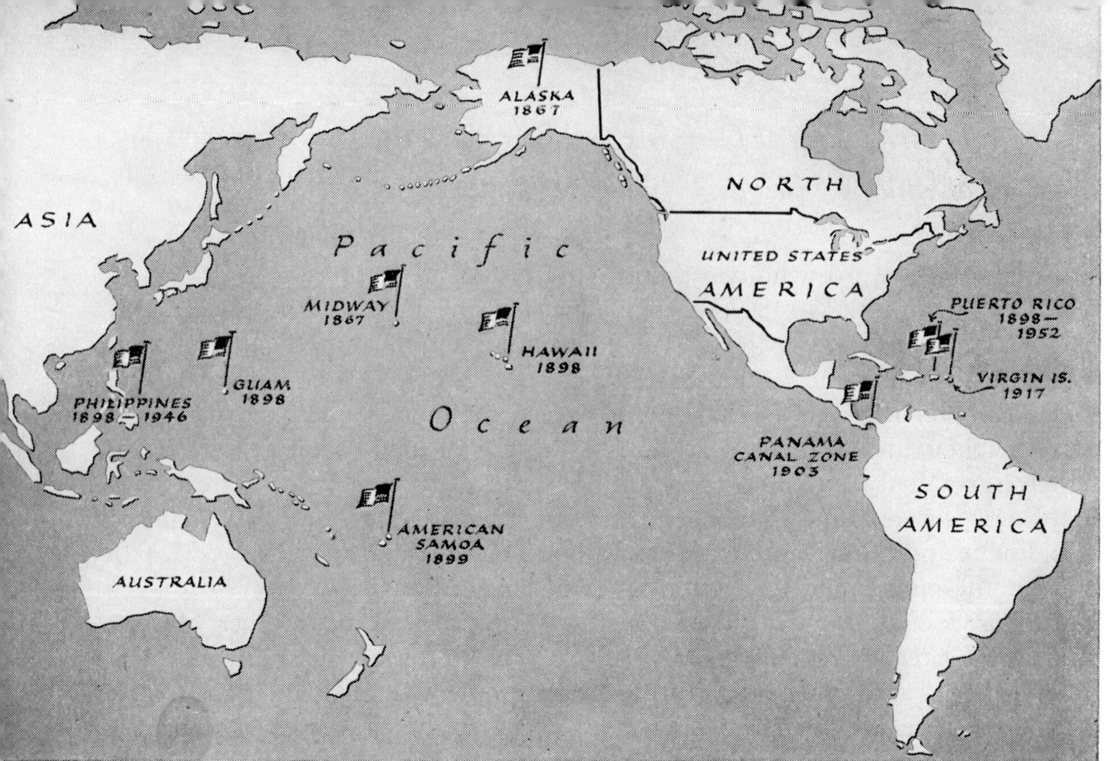

The United States expands overseas. Each possession of the United States is marked with a flag. The date below each name shows when the United States acquired the territory. Why are there two dates for the Philippine Islands and Puerto Rico?

and "Seward's folly." But Seward and the Russian minister published a great deal of information about the land and its resources in the American newspapers. They convinced the people that it was worth the price. Congress finally approved the purchase.

In gold and other minerals, in furs and fish and lumber, Alaska has repaid its purchase price many times over. It promises to be even more valuable in the future.

The land of Alaska. The picture that some people have of Alaska as a land of snow and ice fits only the part that is north of the Arctic Circle. In southeast Alaska, along the Pacific coast, the climate is much like that of the Puget Sound area of the state of Washington. Here, and around Anchorage (ăng′kẽr ĭj) and Fairbanks, people raise wheat, vegetables, and livestock.

Since Alaska is so far north, its days are long in summer and short in winter, while the nights are short in summer and long in winter. Above the Arctic Circle there is almost no night in summer and almost no day in winter, so that there are six months of day and six months of night. In Fairbanks, which is south of the Arctic Circle, a baseball game is played every year at midnight on July 4 without artificial lighting. Like the early settlers of New France, people in Alaska do most of their work in the summer and spend their time in the winter visiting friends and having a good time.

Industries. Alaskans earn a living

mainly from fishing, canning salmon, fur trapping, lumbering, and mining gold and silver. Canning salmon is the most important industry. To get furs, Alaskans not only trap the animals but also raise them on fur farms. The Pribilof (prĭb′ĭ lôf) Islands, west of the mainland, are famous for fur seals. The United States controls the hunting of the seals on these islands, limiting the number taken each season.

In 1896 gold was discovered in the Klondike region along the border between Alaska and Canada. It turned out that the larger part of the gold field was in Canada. But gold was discovered in other places in Alaska as well. In 1898–1899 Alaska had a gold rush like the one in California 50 years earlier. Silver, copper, tin, and coal also are mined in Alaska.

Transportation. Until the time of the Second World War, about the only way you could travel to Alaska was by boat from Seattle or some other Pacific coast port. During the Second World War, the United States and Canada cooperated in building the Alaska Highway, formerly called the Alcan Highway. It runs through northwestern Canada to Fairbanks, Alaska. The road was built for transporting supplies to the armed forces in Alaska, but it helps peacetime travel as well. From Fairbanks a railroad and a road provide transportation to the Alaskan coast.

In the interior, away from road and railroad, people travel by river boat in the summer and by dog sled in the winter. Since distances are so long and the means of transportation so slow, travel by air has rapidly become popular.

The people of Alaska. The population of Alaska is 90,000, about the same as the population of Fresno, California, or Harrisburg, Pennsylvania. About two-thirds of the Alaskans are white people. Most of them or their parents came from the United States. The remaining third are native Indians and Eskimos.

The Eskimos are probably descendants of Indians, but they have lived apart so long and have changed so much that they are now considered to be a separate people. In Alaska they live

Totem pole. Among some Alaskan Indians it was customary to carve tribal symbols and records of important events on a wooden pole, which was erected near the family dwelling. Today tourists in Alaska can buy small copies of totem poles as souvenirs.

SMITHSONIAN INSTITUTION

Klondike gold rush. Early mining camps in the Klondike were largely tent cities. The miners had stoves in the tents to keep them warm against the bitter cold. The miners transported their heavy supplies on sleds.

along the western and northern coast. They are very skillful in the water, especially in their one-man canoes, or kayaks (kī′ăks). They live by hunting and fishing. Whales and walruses are especially valuable to them. From these animals they get meat, fat for food and fuel, skins for clothing, and bones for making such things as dishes and spoons. To help them out when such game is scarce, the federal government has given them herds of reindeer. The Eskimos are a healthy, happy people, content with their northern homes.

Many of the Indians of southeastern Alaska work in the canneries and mines. Some also trap and fish. They are well known for their totem poles. The Indians of the interior live much as the Indians of our West lived in the 1800s. They hunt, trap, and fish, and trade their furs for manufactured goods.

Government of Alaska. Alaska is a territory of the United States. It has a government very much like the governments that our western territories had. (See page 174.) The President of the United States appoints the governor. The people elect their own legislature. They also elect a delegate who sits in Congress but has no vote. In the 1950s the people of Alaska were asking to be admitted as a state.

The Alaskan government operates schools for white children, including high schools and a college. The United States government operates schools for Indian and Eskimo children, but these go only to the eighth grade. People live so far apart, however, that only about half the children are near enough to schools to be able to attend.

Alaska's future development. Alaska is one-fifth as large as the United States. If you compare the number of people living there with the number in the United States, you will see how small the population is for the size of the land. Of course, northern Alaska can hardly be lived in. Also, much of the interior is suitable only for hunting and trapping. Alaskans could farm some areas now left wild, but they would not be able to sell their farm surpluses. They are too far from markets and transportation would be too costly. It pays them better to let the land stay wild and obtain furs from it.

There we have one of the main problems of Alaska. It is far away from the large centers of population, and the cost of transporting goods to those markets is high. As long as these centers can get the goods from places nearer to them, they will not buy Alaskan products.

New importance of Alaska. Since the Second World War, Alaska is important to the security of the United States. It is separated from Asia by Bering (bḛr′ĭng) Strait, which at its narrowest is only 56 miles across. Eskimos easily travel back and forth in their canoes. The Aleutian (*ȧ* lū′shăn) Islands of Alaska reach farther west into the Pacific than Hawaii, as you can see from the map on page 486. Finally, Alaska is on some of the most direct air routes to other continents. An enemy who would want to attack the United States from the west or the north might very well plan to establish a base on Alaska first. Consequently, for the United States, Alaska is a good place to be prepared to stop an attack and to start a counterattack.

The Alaska Highway is one of the advantages that have already come to Alaska as a result of this new importance. The United States has also built naval bases and airports in Alaska and has stationed large numbers of men there. That means more population and more business for Alaskans. It also means the greater use of some of Alaska's natural resources. Another result may be statehood for Alaska.

The United States Annexes Hawaii. Thirty years after purchasing Alaska, the United States added more territory by annexing the Hawaiian Islands. The story may remind you of the story of Texas. In Hawaii, as in Texas, settlers from the United States became dissatisfied with the existing government under a native ruler. They revolted and established a republic, hoping it would become part of the United States. Like Texas, Hawaii had to wait for several years. Finally, in 1898 our country annexed the islands. One reason for taking them at that time was that the United States had recently won a victory in the Philippines during the Span-

Alaskan port. Juneau, the capital of Alaska, is a center of the salmon-canning industry and a trading center for the mining and lumbering region around it.

EWING GALLOWAY

HAWAII VISITORS BUREAU

Scouting in Hawaii. Boy Scouts in Hawaii are like Boy Scouts in the rest of the United States. They make their camps of bamboo and sleep under coconut palms, but the spirit of self-reliance and service is the same.

ish-American War (see page 493). Hawaii would be an excellent stopover place for ships carrying men and supplies to the Philippines. Another purpose was to prevent any other country from seizing the islands. It was feared that a foreign nation with a base on the islands might be able easily to attack our west coast.

The land of Hawaii. The Hawaiian Islands include eight large islands and a number of small ones. The biggest is Hawaii. The most important is Oahu (ō ä′hōō), on which Honolulu, the capital, is situated. More than half of the 530,000 people who inhabit the islands live in Honolulu.

The Hawaiian climate is mild, averaging about 70 degrees. The winds blow in from the Pacific generally from the northeast, bringing much rain. As they strike the mountains on the islands, the winds lose their moisture. The result is that the northern sections of the islands have a great deal of rain, while the southern sections are sunny and dry.

Sugar is Hawaii's biggest and most valuable crop. Pineapples are second. Both are grown by large corporations on huge plantations. They use modern machinery and scientific methods. Mills in Hawaii make raw sugar, which is shipped to San Francisco and is there refined. Pineapples and pineapple juice are canned on the islands. Both products are sold mainly in the United States, from which Hawaii also receives most of its imports.

Next to sugar and pineapples, the biggest business in Hawaii is the tourist trade. Every year thousands of Americans visit the islands. They come to enjoy the mild climate and bathe on famous Waikiki (wī kĭ kē′) Beach. They enjoy seeing live volcanoes, coral reefs, palm groves, and sugar and pineapple plantations. The friendly Hawaiian custom of greeting visitors with leis is known around the world.

The people of Hawaii. For many years before annexation, sugar planters had not been able to obtain enough labor among native Hawaiians. They had brought in outsiders to do the work. People came from Japan, China, the Philippines, Puerto Rico, and Portugal and other European countries. As a result Hawaiian-Americans, like mainland Americans, come from ancestors of many different nationalities. In Hawaii the percentages are somewhat different from those on the mainland. About one-third of the population is of Japanese ancestry. Another third is of American and European ancestry, with smaller numbers of Filipino, Chinese, and Puerto Rican blood. Native Hawaiians and part Hawaiians make up about 14 per cent of the population.

The people of Hawaii learned American ways early, although it was an Englishman, Captain James Cook, who discovered the islands in 1778. Soon after the discovery, whaling ships, traders, and missionaries from the United States visited Hawaii. Some settled there and established plantations, banks, churches, schools, and hospitals like those at home. When annexation came, therefore, it made little difference in everyday Hawaiian life. Today life in Hawaii is very much like life in continental United States.

Government of Hawaii. In 1900 Hawaii was made a territory. The people pay taxes to the federal government. The government collects more tax money in Hawaii than in any one of a dozen states. The governor and other principal officers are appointed by the President of the United States, but the persons appointed must be residents of the islands. The people elect their own legislature. The two main parties are the Republican and the Democratic. All persons born in Hawaii since annexation are citizens of the United States. As early as 1940 the people of Hawaii voted to ask for admission as a state.

The importance of Hawaii. In the Second World War, which is covered in Chapter 28, the people of Hawaii proved their loyalty to the United States. The Hawaiian-Japanese were especially put to the test since Japan was our enemy in the Pacific. How did they

Irrigation in Hawaii. Ditches have been built to collect rain water on the windward side of the island and carry it through mountain tunnels to the southern side, where rainfall is slight. There the water is used to irrigate the fields of sugar cane.

HAWAII VISITORS BUREAU

HAWAII VISITORS BUREAU

Soldiers resting in Hawaii. During World War II thousands of wounded American servicemen were sent to camps in the Hawaiian Islands to rest and regain their strength.

respond? More than half of all Hawaiians in our armed forces were of Japanese descent; 80 per cent of all Hawaiians killed and 88 per cent of all Hawaiians wounded were of Japanese descent. Japanese-Americans, including many from Hawaii, made a record of outstanding heroism in the fighting in Italy.

Before and during the Second World War, Hawaii was an important military base. It was the Japanese attack on Pearl Harbor, the great American naval base in Hawaii, on December 7, 1941, that brought the United States into the Second World War. In Hawaii, American forces were brought together to prepare for attacks farther west in the Pacific. After the war, as the United States came to play a leading role in the Far East, Hawaii grew in importance as an American military outpost.

2 *The United States Obtains the Philippines and Puerto Rico*

The greatest overseas expansion by the United States came as a result of the Spanish-American War. For many years the United States had been interested in Cuba. That long, narrow island had belonged to Spain since Columbus had discovered it. It lay close to the American coast. Americans carried on a large trade with Cuba, exporting flour, lumber, and manufactured goods and importing sugar. Many American businessmen had invested money in sugar plantations and mills. The Cuban people had for many years been in rebellion against Spain, trying to win independence. Americans sympathized with the Cubans because of the harsh and cruel rule of Cuba by the Spanish army. Americans had not forgotten their own struggle for independence.

War with Spain. In January, 1898, the American government sent the battleship *Maine* to Havana Harbor. It was to be at hand if needed to protect the lives and property of American citizens who lived in Cuba. On February 15 the *Maine* was blown up. Two officers and 258 members of the crew were killed. How or by whom the explosion was caused, or whether it was an accident, is still in doubt. But the American people blamed the Spaniards. "Remember the *Maine!*" was the battle cry of the war that followed.

The Spanish government was weak and unprepared and did not want war. It was ready to accept the American demands, probably even to give Cuba her freedom eventually. President McKinley and his Cabinet did not want war. American public opinion, however, seemed to favor it. Our people had been aroused by sensational newspapers. These papers featured stories of Spanish cruelties and demanded revenge for the sinking of the *Maine*. On April 25, 1898, Congress declared that the United States was at war with Spain.

The war lasted a little more than a hundred days. The United States Army was unprepared for war, but Theodore Roosevelt as Assistant Secretary of the Navy had prepared the fleet. In one battle in the Philippines half the Spanish navy was destroyed by an American fleet under the command of Admiral George Dewey. In another battle off Cuba the other half of the Spanish navy was destroyed by another American fleet. In the two battles the United States Navy lost but one man. After some confusion, an army, including Theodore Roosevelt and his Roughriders, landed in Cuba and captured that island. Another force overran Puerto Rico with almost no opposition.

The fighting ended in August, 1898. The Senate approved the peace treaty the following February. Cuba became independent. The United States received Puerto Rico, Guam, and the Philippine Islands. For the Philippines the United States paid Spain 20 million dollars.

Coaling station. For many United States ships traveling to the Far East in the early 1900s, the Philippine Islands made a convenient place where the vessels could take on coal and other supplies.

Independence for the Philippines. In the Philippine Islands the United States at first found trouble. The Filipinos wanted independence immediately. They fought against Americans just as they had fought against Spaniards. Defeated in the towns, they retired to the jungles and carried on guerrilla warfare. The United States had to keep an army of 60,000 men on the islands. The fighting came to an end only after Aguinaldo (ä gē̇ näl′dō), the Filipino leader, was captured in 1901.

Even before peace was established, the United States began to improve conditions in the Philippines. Many new schools were opened, and American teachers were brought in to teach the Filipino children.

New independent republic. In Manila the American flag was lowered and the Philippine flag was raised to mark the independence of the Republic of the Philippines. The date was appropriate: July 4, 1946.

PRESS ASSOCIATION

The Filipinos continued to demand independence. The United States granted them their independence in 1946. On July 4 of that year the Republic of the Philippines became an independent nation.

The Philippines today. The Republic of the Philippines includes more than 7,000 islands about 800 miles off the coast of Asia. More than half of the islands are so small that they do not even have names. The most important islands are 11 large ones, including Luzon (lo͞o zŏn′), Mindanao (mĭn dȧ-nä′ō̇), and Cebu (sȧ̇ bo͞o′). The climate of the islands is warm, even in the winter.

The people earn a living mainly from agriculture. The largest crop is rice, but not enough is grown for the people on the islands. Some rice has to be imported. The principal imports are manufactured goods; the principal exports are sugar, coconuts, and hemp. About three-fourths of the trade is with the United States.

The Philippine government is patterned after that of the United States. It has many hard problems to solve. When the United States bought the islands, only about 10 per cent of the people could read and write. In 1950 about 50 per cent could read and write. That was a great improvement in 50 years. But the Philippine government still has the big job of providing schools for a large part of the population. In many districts the people are poor and the national government has to build

LIBRARY OF CONGRESS

Perry in Japan. In 1854 Commodore Matthew C. Perry landed in Japan and made a treaty with the Japanese emperor. After that first contact with the outside world, Japan adopted Western ways and rapidly became the strongest nation in the Far East.

schools and roads and keep them up. The government has bought many large estates and has divided them into small farms for poor families. The government has also tried to increase manufacturing in the islands.

The open-door policy in China. European nations discovered in the late 1800s that China was a weak country, helpless to defend itself. Its huge population made it a valuable market for trade. The European countries and Japan decided to divide China among themselves.

The United States took no part in the grab. But our government feared that the other countries would bar us from trade with China. It insisted, therefore, that merchants of all nations must be free to trade in every part of China. That was called the open-door policy.

The other countries respected the open-door policy for a while. But after 1915 Japan took control of large parts of China and "closed the door." In other words, the Japanese government favored its own merchants in those areas. It refused to give merchants from other countries an equal chance to trade with the Chinese.

By its open-door policy the United States opposed the Japanese plan to control China. Japan, on the other hand, objected to American traders in Asia and to American forces in the Philippines. Japan regarded the Philippines as part of Asia, which she planned to control. The Japanese, furthermore, felt insulted by laws passed in 1924 to keep Japanese immigrants out of the United States. Thus the relations between Japan and the United States, which once had been very friendly, became less and less so.

BROWN BROS.

William McKinley
1897–1901

BROWN BROS.

Theodore Roosevelt
1901–1909

3 *The United States Develops a Policy toward Latin America*

After the Spanish-American War the United States had possessions in the Atlantic and in the Pacific. In order to guard them all, our Navy had to be in both oceans. Obviously, we needed a canal across Central America so that our ships could sail quickly from one ocean to the other. The American people learned how necessary the canal was when, at the beginning of the Spanish-American War, the battleship *Oregon* had to make the 14,000-mile dash from San Francisco around Cape Horn to Cuba.

The Panama Canal. Congress voted to build the canal across the Isthmus of Panama, which was then part of Colombia. United States representatives were told to buy a strip of land across Panama for the canal. At first Colombian leaders were enthusiastic, but then they refused to sell the land. President Theodore Roosevelt was in a hurry to get the canal built. With American warships nearby, a group of Panamanians (păn *ȧ* mā′nĭ *ă*nz) staged a successful revolution. Panama became an independent country and was immediately recognized by the United States. Within two weeks Panama signed a treaty selling the present Canal Zone to the United States. The canal was opened in 1914 and has been of great value to world commerce.

In 1922 the United States government gave Colombia 25 million dollars to make up to that country for the part we played in helping Panama win her independence. But the action of our government in the Panamanian revolution increased the distrust felt by the Latin-American countries toward the United States. That distrust had begun at the time of the Mexican War (see page 292), when the United States took a large territory from Mexico. The fact that the United States had paid Mexico a large sum of money did not change the Latin-American attitude of fear and suspicion.

The Latin Americans fear our country. Many other events after 1898 increased Latin-American fear of our country. At the beginning of the Spanish-American War, the United States promised to give Cuba back to the Cuban people. Cuba was made independent. But the United States kept the right to send troops to the island whenever necessary to protect the property of Americans. Our troops were landed in Cuba several times to do so. In Panama, to protect the canal, the United States obtained the same right.

At various times after 1900 the governments of the Dominican Republic, Haiti, and Nicaragua (nĭk *ȧ* rä′gw*ȧ*) were unable to keep order and to pay their debts to American and European investors. At such times the United States sent marines into these countries to collect duties and pay off the debts. It is true that, under American control, order was restored, debts were paid, and health and education were improved. But in entering those countries, the United States did not treat them as independent and equal nations. Therefore the Latin-American peoples felt insulted, and they feared the United States.

American opinion divided. The American people were divided in their opinion about what their government was doing in Latin America. Some approved, some disapproved.

Those who approved of the government's policy had many arguments to support their position. Under the Monroe Doctrine the United States had warned European nations to keep out of America (see page 204). That meant that the United States took the responsibility for maintaining law and order in all American countries. We were therefore doing our duty by sending troops into weak countries to keep order. Furthermore, if the United States did not require Latin-American nations to pay their debts, European countries would take over those countries to collect the debts. Then, not only would the Mon-

Marine on duty. This drawing shows a United States marine patrolling a street in a Latin-American town. Although they maintained order, United States forces were not welcomed by the people of Latin America.

AMERICAN-HAWAIIAN STEAMSHIP CO.

Link between Atlantic and Pacific. This is a picture of a ship passing through the Panama Canal. About 200,000 commercial vessels have passed through the canal. When was the canal opened?

roe Doctrine be violated, but the Panama Canal would also be in danger of attack. Besides, the Latin-American countries benefited from American occupation. They obtained governments strong enough to keep order and collect taxes. Their business prospered. The health and education of the people were improved.

Those who opposed the actions of the government argued otherwise. No nation, they said, has the right to interfere in the home affairs of any other nation. If we believe in democracy, we should respect the right of every people to choose their own government. We do not show respect for the right of a Latin-American nation to self-government when we send our marines to govern it. If we wish to help a Latin-American country improve its tax collecting, business, health, and education, we ought to wait until we are invited. Then we should work together with its government. If conditions get so bad in one country that its neighbors are put in danger, then the United States ought to join with the other American nations and decide with them what is to be done. Just because the United States is stronger, she is not justified in acting as policeman over the other American countries. By so doing, she makes them her enemies. If she treated them as equals, they would be her friends.

A new American policy. The Americans who wanted their government to change its attitude toward Latin America gradually won out. Beginning about 1924, under Presidents Calvin Coolidge and Herbert Hoover, the United States began to withdraw its marines from Latin-American countries. The United States stopped trying to solve Latin-American problems by herself. She discussed them with all the American countries and cooperated with them in taking any necessary action.

The United States carried out its new policy largely through the Pan American Union. It was organized in 1890. Its purpose "is to promote understanding and friendship among its members." All 21 American republics are members. In normal times they hold a conference every five years. (For the Pan American Union today see pages 594–595.)

A good example of the new American way of dealing with our Latin-American neighbors was our government's policy toward Mexico. Beginning in 1910, that country went through a revolution that lasted 10 years. After it was over, the government of Mexico decided to take over the land, mines, and oil fields that United States citizens and other foreigners owned in Mexico. The plan raised two questions. Did the Mexican government have the right to take the properties? If it did, how much should it pay the owners for them? Throughout the long discussion that followed, the United States government respected the independence of the Mexican government. It recognized the right of the Mexican people to take over their natural resources. Our government persuaded the American property owners to reach an agreement with the Mexican government.

Puerto Rico. The United States obtained Puerto Rico as a result of the Spanish-American War. Puerto Rico is a mountainous island 100 miles from east to west and about 35 miles from north to south. The population is over

Cultivating young pineapple plants in Puerto Rico. Although industries have been started in Puerto Rico, the island depends mainly on agriculture. The principal crops are sugar, tobacco, and citrus fruits, with pineapples becoming increasingly important.

HAMILTON WRIGHT

HAMILTON WRIGHT

Modern housing in Puerto Rico. Thousands of homes like this one have been built in Puerto Rico. But many thousands more are needed to relieve the crowded conditions.

2,200,000. The island has more people per square mile than Massachusetts. But in Massachusetts most people earn a living by working in factories and live close together in cities. In Puerto Rico most of the people earn a living as farmers—and there is simply not enough land to support everyone comfortably. As a result many Puerto Ricans live under crowded, unsanitary conditions and suffer actual hunger.

Under United States control there has been a rapid improvement in health and education. In these respects Puerto Rico has one of the best records among Latin-American countries. But many Puerto Ricans still need better sanitation and housing. About 25 per cent of the people still cannot read or write. It is clear that, although there has been progress, much remains to be done.

After 400 years of Spanish rule the change to control by the United States was difficult for Puerto Rico. Its people have remained proud of their Spanish background. While English is used in business and trade, the language of the people is Spanish. Today in schools below senior high school the Spanish language is used in all teaching.

Since 1898 the Puerto Ricans have been given more and more control over their own government. In 1952 Puerto Rico became a self-governing commonwealth. The people elect their own governor and legislature. To improve the conditions of life among the people, the Puerto Rican government has tried to attract industries to the island.

The need to protect the Panama Canal has led the United States to keep military bases in the Caribbean. In 1917 we bought the Virgin Islands from Denmark.

Summary

The United States purchased Alaska in 1867. It annexed the Hawaiian Islands in 1898. It obtained Puerto Rico, Guam, and the Philippines as a result of the Spanish-American War.

When Japan and several European countries began to divide up China, the United States announced the open-door policy. By that policy our government hoped to keep China open for the merchants of all countries, including our own. That policy placed us in opposition to Japan, which wanted to control China entirely for the benefit of the Japanese.

Now that the United States had possessions in the Atlantic and in the Pacific, it needed a canal across Central America through which to move ships from one ocean to the other. The Panama Canal was built. By the way he obtained land for the canal, President Theodore Roosevelt aroused distrust of the United States among Latin Americans. In later years that distrust grew stronger as the United States again and again sent troops into Caribbean and Central American countries to keep order.

The American people, however, decided against forcing United States decisions on other peoples. Instead, a policy of cooperation was gradually worked out. The 21 American republics cooperated in peace and friendship through the Pan American Union.

The American people wanted no empire. They granted independence to the Philippines. They made Puerto Rico a self-governing commonwealth. In the 1950s Hawaii and Alaska were applying for admission as states.

HAWAII VISITORS BUREAU

Leis. With leis, or garlands of flowers, Hawaiians express friendship.

For a Quick Review

1. What are some of the contributions that Alaska and Hawaii have made to the national strength of the United States?

2. What possessions did the United States obtain as a result of the Spanish-American War?

3. What measures helped to prepare the Philippines for independence?

4. Why was the open-door policy important to the United States? Why was it important to China?

5. What policy did the United States follow in Cuba, Panama, the Dominican Republic, and Nicaragua during the early 1900s? What did people of Latin America think of it? How was that policy changed?

6. What major problems exist in Puerto Rico? What efforts are being made to solve them?

Learning to Study More Easily

UNDERSTANDING LATITUDE AND LONGITUDE

An understanding of latitude and longitude is important to you when you read a globe or a map.

Geographers and map makers have agreed on imaginary points and lines in order to have definite places from which to measure distances. The points are the North Pole and the South Pole. The imaginary lines are the equator, the parallels, and the meridians.

Find the North Pole and the South Pole on the globe in your classroom. Halfway between the poles you will see the equator, an imaginary line circling the earth. Parallel with the equator are the parallels of latitude. They measure latitude, the distance north and south of the equator.

Crossing the equator at right angles and running from pole to pole are lines called meridians. The meridians show longitude, or distance east and west from Greenwich, England.

Latitude, or distance north and south from the equator, is measured in degrees (indicated by the symbol °). Thus we say that Philadelphia, Pennsylvania, which is between the equator and the North Pole, is located at about 40° north latitude. Melbourne, Australia, which is between the equator and the South Pole, is located at about 38° south latitude. Often you will have to measure from the nearest parallel to get the latitude of a place.

The meridian running through Greenwich, England, is called the prime, or zero, meridian. Longitude, like latitude, is measured in degrees. Longitude readings are given as west longitude or east longitude, depending on whether they are in the Western or Eastern Hemisphere. Find the prime meridian on your classroom globe. What is the longitude reading for Philadelphia, Pennsylvania? For Melbourne, Australia?

25 The United States Strives for Democracy and Peace

"Bill is a leader in our school," you may say when you are talking about your class president or a student who holds some other important office. You probably mean that Bill is a person to whom other students turn when some school project is being planned. They know he will have ideas about how to get things done. He will also show the energy and ability to work with others in carrying out his ideas. His classmates admire Bill because he ranks high in his studies. They admire him also because he thinks of the other person as well as of himself. Since Bill's classmates respect him, they will work together under his leadership.

If you were to explain why the United States is a world leader, you might give some of the same reasons that you gave for Bill's leadership. To be a leader, a nation must have the respect and confidence of other nations. It must be able to cooperate with other nations. It must think of the needs and hopes of other peoples as well as of its own. Like Bill, a leader among nations must have energy and ability. In a nation, energy and ability mean natural resources, large factories, and skillful people to turn out great quantities of goods for itself and its allies to use.

Comparisons between individuals who are leaders and nations that are leaders go only so far, however. Bill is a leader in his school community. It is a community with rules that are known to students, teachers, and parents. The rules are enforced by the school authorities. Bill knows the requirements for conduct that he and other people must meet.

The United States has to be a leader in a very different kind of community —the community of nations. In this community of nations there are no rules

AUTOMOBILE CLUB OF NEW YORK

Obeying traffic laws. Because we obey laws, we lead safe and peaceful lives. Nations are still trying to work out, through agreements, rules that will bring world peace.

that all nations have to obey. The lack of rules helps to explain the problems the United States faces as a world leader. It helps to explain the actions our country took during the first half of the twentieth century. Before we study the role of the United States as a leader among nations, therefore, we need to know more about the problem of law and order among the nations of the world.

1 *Governments and Individuals Work for Peace*

When you leave for school in the morning, you take it for granted that you will come safely home again in the afternoon. You expect to obey the traffic laws so that you will not be run over. You expect car drivers also to obey the traffic laws—for example, to stop when the traffic light is red. Why do you and your fellow citizens obey laws? Because you live under a government. It makes laws and its police officers and courts enforce them. A government can make and enforce laws because you and your fellow citizens accept the authority of the government. The few who break the laws can be tried and punished because most people agree that the government should make and enforce laws.

National governments recognize no higher authority. On the other hand, nations do not need to look up to any authority higher than themselves. There is no supergovernment to make laws that nations must obey. There are no police officers that can hail a nation into court against its will and charge it with violating law, breaking the peace, or harming its neighbors. Each nation is free and equal. It is free to do as it pleases. It is equal with all other nations. And each nation needs to protect itself from harmful actions by others. This freedom of each nation is called national sovereignty.

Nations have agreed, it is true, to follow certain rules in carrying on relations with one another. Some of the rules concern peacetime affairs—for example, how far into the ocean beyond its coast line a nation can enforce its laws. Some are rules that nations promise to observe in war—for example, how prisoners shall be treated. The rules that nations have accepted are called international law.

It is important to remember, however, that no nation can be forced to accept the rules of international law. Even after a nation has agreed to a rule, it cannot be forced to obey it in the way an individual citizen can be forced to obey the laws made by his government.

How keep peace? We know that two individuals who have a serious dispute—say a dispute as to which of them owns a piece of land—can settle their difference peacefully and fairly in a government court. In fact, the law requires them to do so. But what happens when two nations get into a dispute? They may, of course, find a way of settling it peacefully. They may, on the other hand, go to war to settle it. People are killed; property is destroyed. Eventually the stronger side wins. Of course, we know that, in the case of nations as well as of individuals, being stronger is not necessarily the same as being right.

Big nations are responsible. As long as disputes between nations may lead to war, nations will continue to build up their military strength. Since small nations cannot defend themselves, they usually tie up with bigger ones for protection. The large nations—the great powers—are the ones that usually supply most of the money and material, and sometimes most of the men, for a war. Therefore they usually decide whether a war is to start or not. At least it is mainly up to them to decide whether a war that breaks out is to be permitted to spread. Indeed, if just one great power wants war, the others may have to defend themselves. It is easy to see, therefore, that every great power has a particular responsibility for helping to keep the world at peace.

Nations make progress in peaceful settlement of disputes. Men in many countries have worked long and hard to find an answer to this question: How can war be eliminated in a world of independent nations? The nations of the world have not succeeded in doing away with war. But they have been trying for a long time, and most people believe they have made some progress.

To make war less horrible, nations signed treaties in which they promised to observe certain rules. For example,

Red Cross ship. This was one of the ships used by the International Red Cross in World War II to carry supplies to prisoners in enemy countries. The nations at war had agreed not to attack anyone bearing the Red Cross symbol.

AMERICAN RED CROSS

ACME

International air mail. A transatlantic airplane is loading mail. You can mail a letter to any country in the world. You can send parcels to 23 foreign countries. To provide this easy world-wide communication, the nations work together in the Universal Postal Union.

they agreed to respect the Red Cross as an agent for helping the sick and wounded. After many nations had promised to obey such a rule, that rule was considered a part of international law.

There was no way to force nations to obey the rules. Nevertheless, the rules were important. International law became a standard of conduct that the people of the world expected nations to observe. In peacetime a government thought twice before breaking accepted international law. If it did violate one of the rules, it tried to give good reasons for doing so. In wartime, however, when victory was at stake, nations paid less attention to international law.

Mediation and arbitration. Many people insisted that the way to end war was to find peaceful ways of settling disputes—not just to make rules about how to carry on wars. Gradually governments worked out peaceful ways of settling disputes.

One way was mediation (mē dĭ ā′-shŭn). If two governments got into a dispute, a third one offered to help as a friend of both. If its offer was accepted, it tried to bring about an agreement between the quarreling countries. In many cases it was successful.

Another method of settling disputes was the international conference. Representatives of all the nations concerned in a dispute met in a conference. They discussed the problem and arrived at a solution that all accepted.

A third way to settle disputes peacefully was arbitration (är bĭ trā′shŭn). Under this method each disputing country selected two neutral persons as arbitrators. The four usually selected a fifth person, and together they settled the dispute. In arbitration, each country agreed beforehand to accept the decision of the arbitrators. In the 1800s the United States and Great Britain used arbitration to settle many of their differences.

BROWN BROS.

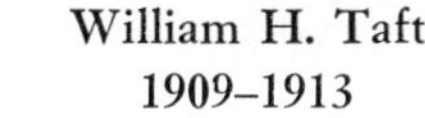

William H. Taft
1909–1913

BROWN BROS.

Woodrow Wilson
1913–1921

Limitation of armament. People in many countries believed that the danger of war would be reduced if the strongest countries would limit the size of their armed forces. These people argued this way: Nations race one another in building up their armed forces. As their armies and navies grow bigger, they become more suspicious of one another. Since they are ready to fight, the slightest quarrel can start a war. To reduce the danger of war, therefore, let the nations agree not to increase their armed forces or even to reduce them. In only a few cases did nations make such agreements, and the agreements covered only certain kinds of armaments.

The Hague conferences. During the first hundred years of our country's history, the leaders of nations tried to make rules for war and peace. They discussed ways of settling disputes peacefully. They discussed rules nations should observe if they went to war. Two important peace conferences were held at The Hague in the Netherlands in 1899 and 1907. At both, United States representatives took an important part. At the Hague conferences the nations of the world agreed to observe a number of international laws. They agreed, for example, not to use poison gas against an enemy. They also agreed not to put out floating mines in any ocean, because a ship of a nation at peace might run onto one and be sunk. The nations also agreed to set up a Permanent Court of Arbitration with headquarters at The Hague.

In their efforts to reach international agreement to prevent war, the nations of the world made little progress beyond the achievements of the Hague conferences. But they proved through other actions that they could cooperate to solve common problems. For example, in order to make it possible for citizens of the various countries to write letters to one another, the governments of the world organized the Universal Postal Union. Under its direction, mail from any one country was delivered to any other country to which it was addressed. Today the Universal Postal Union is an agency of the United Nations. There were other cases of such cooperation among nations. People interested in preventing war said, "You see, nations can work together. It is a hopeful sign."

Private individuals and groups work for peace. All the work for peace was not being done by governments. While they were slowly trying out ways to avoid war, private persons in many countries worked hard for permanent peace. Do you remember Elihu Burritt, the learned blacksmith who taught himself 30 languages and talked peace in all of them? You read about him on page 339. During his lifetime—the middle 1800s—peace societies were organized in many of the countries of Europe and in this country. They held meetings attended by large crowds to demand the end of all war. Workers for peace said that war caused much unnecessary waste and suffering. They said that all men were brothers and it was a sin for brothers to kill one another. Many persons who devoted their lives to helping others, like Jane Addams of Hull-House (see page 448), worked for peace.

The peace societies had a program for ending war. Their final aim was to organize a congress of nations to make international law and a court to settle disputes by that law. In the meantime they urged their governments to use peaceful means of settling disputes. They continued to try to get the support of people in all countries.

Many men and women were impressed by what had been accomplished by the Hague conferences and became interested in the peace movement for the first time. Beginning about 1900, the movement grew in popularity. As interest grew, more societies were formed to work for cooperation among nations. In 1914 there were 63 peace societies in the United States alone. The peace workers felt encouraged. But all the efforts for peace failed to prevent the First World War.

2 *The United States Contributes to Victory in the First World War*

The First World War started in 1914. Like earlier wars, it was caused partly by disputes over boundaries of nations in Europe and partly by disputes over colonies in other parts of the world. The principal countries on one side were Great Britain, France, Russia, and Italy. This group was known as the Allies. On the other side were Germany, Austria-Hungary, and Turkey. This group was known as the Central Powers. You can locate these countries on the map on page 509. The leader of the Central Powers was Germany, the country with the strongest army in Europe. The generals in command of the German army made the decision to start the war.

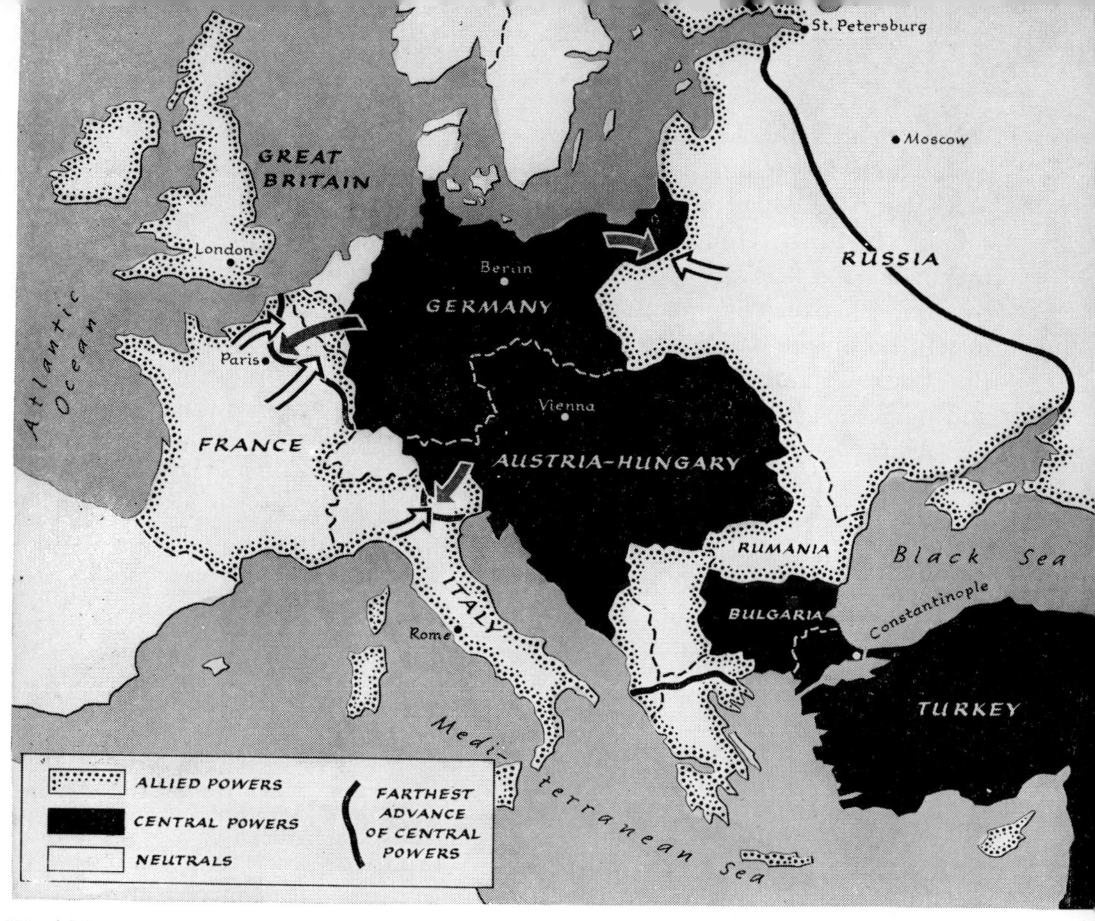

World War I in Europe: the line-up. What nations joined the Allied Powers? (Use the classroom atlas to get the names of the Balkan countries.) Name the Central Powers. Locate the eastern battle front, in Russia, and the western front in France.

The United States enters the war. As soon as the war began, President Woodrow Wilson urged the American people to be neutral—not to take sides. He urged them not to favor one side over the other even in their thoughts. In that way he hoped the United States would be able to keep out of the fighting. But President Wilson, along with most of our people, sympathized with the Allies. Most Americans felt closer to Great Britain than to any other country. In their schools they learned the English language and read English authors. As you know, many of their ideas about freedom and democracy came from England. It was true that the United States had been at war with England twice, in the Revolution and in the War of 1812, but that had been long before. Actually, for many years the United States and Great Britain had been working together as friends.

On the other hand, many Americans disliked the German government. Since Germany was not a democracy, they felt that the German rulers, and not the people, wanted war. Most Americans of German descent had little sympathy with Germany, because they had left the old country to escape military service.

As a neutral the United States permitted both sides to buy arms, ammunition, food, and other supplies in this country. Since the United States was a manufacturing and food-producing country, its citizens had many products to sell. Both sides wanted to buy here. But Great Britain controlled the seas and blockaded its enemies. As a result the Allies bought large quantities of American goods while Germany could buy and carry home almost none. Germany, in turn, sent out large numbers of submarines to sink all ships headed for Great Britain and France. The submarines did such a complete job that in 1917 Britain was almost starved into making peace.

With each side blockading the other, it was the story of the Napoleonic Wars all over again with modern improvements. (See page 194.) Both sides violated the rights of the United States. The British seized American ships and cargoes. German submarines destroyed American lives. When a submarine torpedoed a ship, it could not look out for the safety of passengers and crew, as required under international law. If it stopped to do so, the submarine could easily be destroyed by the ship. Therefore many lives were lost on Allied vessels. In several cases Americans traveling on these ships were drowned.

German submarine warfare. Thus there was an important difference in the damage done by the British and by the Germans. The British could pay for the property they seized, but money could not make up for the lives destroyed by the Germans. President Wilson warned Germany that, if her submarines continued to sink ships without providing for the safety of passengers, the United States would fight. German leaders did not want to bring the United States into the war against them. Therefore the commanders of German submarines were careful for a time. Early in 1917, however, they began again their former method of warfare. More American lives were lost, and a few American ships were sunk. The United States declared war on Germany in April, 1917.

President Wilson said that the United States was going to war in order to make the world safe for democracy and to end all war. For these purposes the American people cooperated with all their might. They made every sacrifice that their government called for to ensure victory. As a result, the strength shown by the United States in the First World War convinced the rest of the world that our country had the power to be a leader among nations.

We help win the war. The United States contributed money, munitions, food, ships, and men to the winning of the war. The government urged the American people to save so that there would be more for the war effort. To save food, Americans were asked to eat no bread or other wheat products on Mondays and no meat on Tuesdays. To save fuel, they were not to heat their homes on Mondays. To supply money for the war, they paid high taxes and bought huge amounts of United States war bonds. "Work or fight" was the slogan.

American food was important in victory, for the Allies were unable to feed themselves. Large areas of their farm lands had been turned into battlefields, and many of their farmers were serving in the armed forces. American farmers were short of help, but made up for it by using more machinery. During the war farmers turned more and more to tractors to supply the power for farm machines. Some women and children from cities spent their vacations working on farms. City residents planted war gardens in back yards and empty lots.

American factories that produced things for everyday use turned to making articles for war. For example, auto factories made airplane parts and piano factories made airplane wings. (Remember that the airplane industry was just beginning then.) To make sure that the necessary products would be manufactured, the government regulated many industries. To make sure that men and goods would be transported to where they were needed, the government took over and operated the railroads. American shipyards built ships faster than the German submarines could sink them. Thus we built a "bridge of ships" to Britain and France, on which men and supplies were carried to the war.

To raise an army quickly, the United States drafted almost 3 million young men. By the end of the war there were 1½ million American troops in France. This was the first time that the American Army had fought in Europe. The map on page 513 shows where it took part in major battles. In July, 1918, the American Army played an important part in stopping the last German attack at Château-Thierry (shä tō′ tyĕ rē′). In September, in the Meuse-Argonne (mūz′är′gŏn) Battle, more than a million Americans helped push the Germans back in the counterattack that ended the war. Within a few weeks the German armies were in retreat all along the battle line. Germany signed an armistice (an agreement to stop fighting while peace is being made) on November 11, 1918, and the war ended.

BETTMANN

Food-saving campaign, World War I. This photograph shows a women's committee driving around town reminding everyone, and especially housewives, to save food. Why are there always food shortages in time of war?

Making the peace. The American people joyfully celebrated the armistice. Students were dismissed from school. Citizens paraded up and down the main streets of their villages and cities. The people agreed with President Wilson that the peace should be a "peace without victory." In other words, the defeated countries were not to be punished so that they would have no excuse for starting another war later on. President Wilson himself went to Paris to help write such a just peace. This was the first time a President had ever gone to Europe during his term of office. Perhaps Wilson's so doing was a symbol of the new position the United States was taking as a world leader. He was unable, however, to persuade the members of the peace conference to make exactly the kind of treaty he wanted.

In Europe the victors wanted revenge —and gain. France wanted to weaken Germany so that the Germans would never be able to attack her again. Italy wanted territory from Austria. Great Britain and Japan wanted German colonies. President Wilson had to give in on some points. The treaty turned out to be partly one of revenge of the victors against the defeated nations.

But there was one point to which President Wilson clung stubbornly. He insisted upon including in the peace treaty the plan for the League of Nations. He had told the American people that the United States was entering the war to establish permanent peace. When American soldiers were sent to the European battlefields, the President told them they were going to fight in a war to end all war. Woodrow Wilson hoped to make good on those promises by persuading the countries of the world to establish the League of Nations.

3 *The Countries of the World Set Up a League of Nations*

The war that ended in 1918 taught many people a lesson. It taught them that war had become more horrible than ever before. New weapons like machine guns, submarines, and airplanes were more deadly than the old ones. In earlier wars, while armies

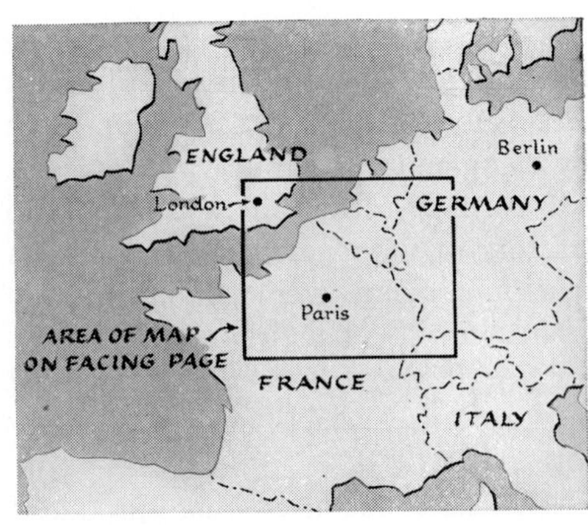

fought on the battlefields, most people at home carried on their work without danger. But in this new kind of war the people making weapons in factories were as important in carrying on the war as were the soldiers. If the enemy could get to them, he was as likely to attack them as to attack the soldiers at the front. In such all-out war, a government would be likely to ignore international law that prohibited attacks on civilians. It would use every possible means to destroy the enemy's ability to fight.

The need for cooperation. After the First World War many people were convinced that it would be harder and harder for any great power to keep out of future wars. Fast steamships and railroads had made the world smaller as measured in time, and the airplane was to make it smaller still. Cable, telegraph, and radio carried news around the globe in a matter of minutes. Manufacturing nations had to have raw materials like oil, steel, and aluminum. They had to import these products from many regions of the earth. The same nations had to sell part of their products abroad if their people were to be

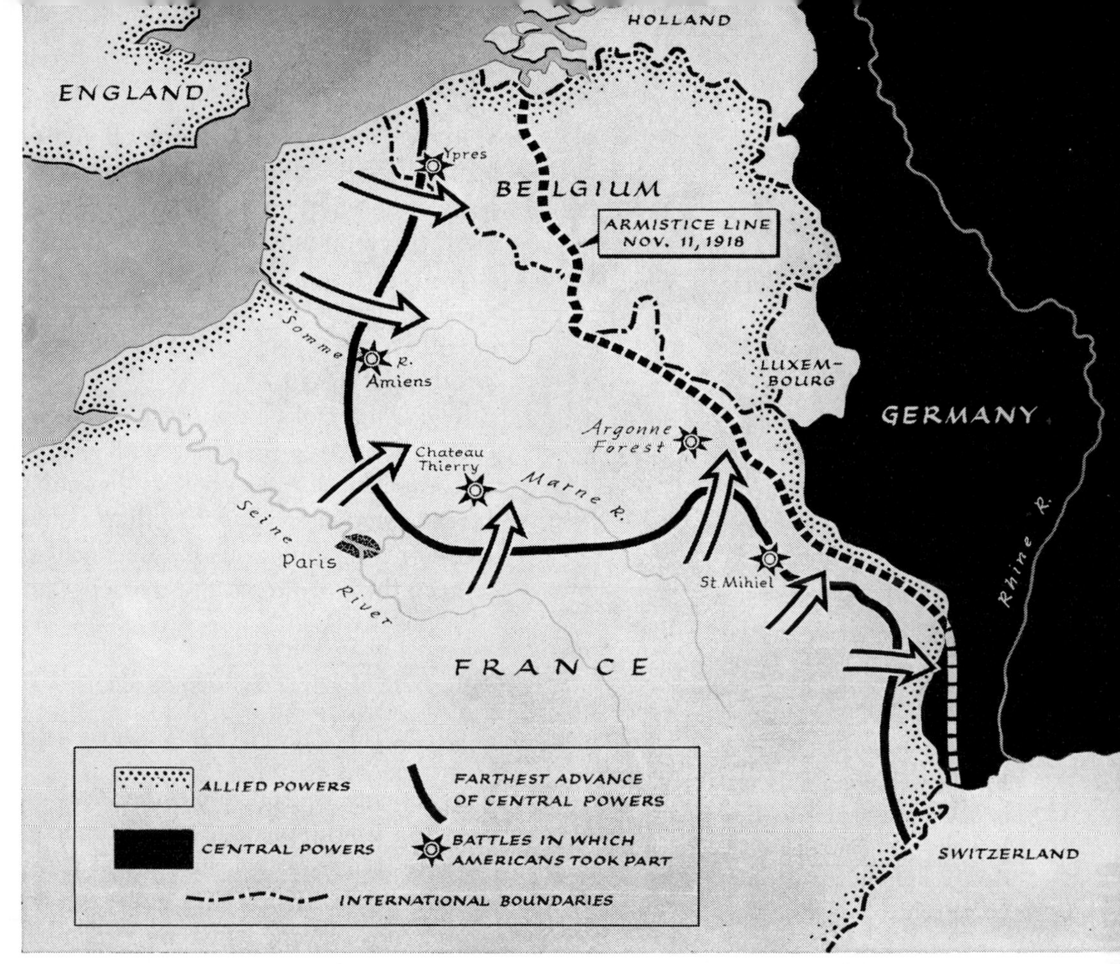

World War I in Europe: U.S. aid helps the Allies to victory. The last part of the war was fought on the western front, mostly in northeastern France. Compare the line of farthest advance of the Central Powers with the armistice line drawn when the fighting ended.

prosperous. In short, the nations of the world had become dependent on one another. If war started in one place, it would probably spread to the whole world. Unless the nations learned to cooperate as members of the world community, all peoples would suffer.

The end of the First World War—at least, so many people thought—would be a good time to organize the nations for peace. While the war was still on, leaders in many countries suggested plans for doing so.

In the United States, for example, former President William Howard Taft headed a society to work for peace. This society drew up a plan for an international organization that would settle disputes by peaceful means. Another plan was worked out by Jan Christiaan Smuts (smŭts), the Prime Minister of the Union of South Africa.

The League of Nations. The men at the peace conference studied these and other plans. The final plan borrowed ideas from the earlier plans. The peace conference set up an organization known as the League of Nations. All member nations sent representatives to the Assembly. The Assembly met once

BETTMANN

France welcomes Wilson. President Wilson is being welcomed to Europe in 1919 by a woman representing France. What did President Wilson hope to achieve by attending the peace conference in person?

a year to discuss international problems and make recommendations. The Council consisted of four permanent members (Great Britain, France, Italy, Japan) and four members elected by the Assembly. The Council had the main duty of keeping peace. All the members had to vote in favor of any action to be taken. The World Court (also called the Permanent International Court of Justice) was set up to decide disputes that nations agreed to bring before it.

The nations that joined the League promised to reduce armaments and to work for peace. They promised to try to settle disputes by arbitration or in the World Court. If these means should fail, the Council was to take charge, investigate, and give a decision. If member nations became involved in a dispute, they would not go to war for at least three months after the Council gave its decision. If war should come, all the League members would break off all contacts with the nation in the wrong.

The League of Nations was not, however, a world government with power to compel nations to obey its decisions. It was a cooperative society that would work only as long as its members chose to keep their promises and to cooperate.

4 *The United States Works Separately for Peace*

President Wilson took the lead in drawing up the plans for the League of Nations. He regarded the League as the greatest work of his life. He was very proud and happy when he presented the final plan to the peace conference. In his opinion the League represented the victory of right over might. He said, "People that were suspicious of one another can now live as friends and comrades in a single family."

The United States rejects the League of Nations. As soon as he came home from the Paris peace conference, President Wilson presented the treaty to the Senate for approval. Immediately it met strong opposition from many Senators for several reasons. Wilson had made the mistake of not taking any Senators with him to help make the treaty. A majority of the Senators were Republicans, while Wilson was a Democrat.

The main opposition was to the League of Nations. Some Senators said that, by joining the League, the United States would give up control over its own actions. We would become entangled in every European quarrel. Standing alone, the United States could keep out of European wars just as it had done for 100 years after 1816. It looked as if the Senate would not approve the treaty.

President Wilson decided to appeal to the people. He was sure that he could convince the people of the importance of the League. Then they would demand that their Senators vote for the treaty and the League. Since there were no radios in homes in 1919, the President had to go through the country to talk to the people. In 22 days he traveled more than 8,000 miles and made 37 speeches. He explained the League. Nobody claimed, he said, that the League was certain to stop war. But it was the greatest attempt ever made to do so. The American people ought to do their best to help make it succeed. The United States, as a leader in the world, had a responsibility to make the League a success.

Before he started on the tour, Wilson had been worn out by the heavy burden of leading the country in war and of making the peace. The strain of the trip was too much. He collapsed and was brought back to Washington an extremely sick man. The Senate rejected the treaty and the League along with it. The United States later made a separate peace with Germany, but it never became a member of the League of Nations.

Good work by the League. There is no doubt that the absence of the United States weakened the League. It was a serious drawback to have one of the great powers of the world outside the only world organization. How different would the history of the next 30 years have been if the United States had joined the League? That is one of the big "ifs" of history.

ACME

Jan Christiaan Smuts. South Africa's greatest statesman in peace and war, Smuts helped plan the League of Nations. In the 1940s he helped plan and organize the United Nations.

Even without the United States, the League of Nations became a strong organization with more than 50 member nations. In the 25 years of its existence it performed valuable service. It brought experts from many countries together to improve health, education, and conditions of labor in all parts of the world. For example, the League had hundreds of thousands of European men, women, boys, and girls vaccinated against typhoid and smallpox. The health organization of the League spread knowledge

BROWN BROS.

Warren G. Harding
1921–1923

BROWN BROS.

Calvin Coolidge
1923–1929

about how much and what kinds of food children need to be healthy.

Other parts of the League carried out equally useful jobs in other fields. This work contributed to peace because happy and satisfied people are less likely to go to war. Many of the persons who worked for the League later also worked for the United Nations. (See pages 583–584.)

In the beginning, under President Warren G. Harding, the United States government tried to pretend that the League of Nations did not exist. Its officials did not even answer letters from the League. But the work of the League soon became so important, and American interests became so world-wide, that our government could not ignore it. First we sent representatives to observe League meetings, but they were not to speak in them. After a time they began to express opinions. Then they took the lead in some of the League's projects, especially those in health, labor, and education. Our government signed agreements with League members on many subjects. It helped pay the cost of the conferences in which it took part.

Besides the representatives of the government, many United States citizens worked with the League as private individuals. Some served as members of the staff of men and women who ran the offices of the League. Several were elected judges of the World Court. All together, almost 300 citizens of the United States served the League in one way or another.

United States efforts for disarmament and peace. The American people were deeply interested in two of the main purposes of the League of Nations: to reduce armaments and to settle disputes peacefully. Since our government did not become a member of the League, it tried to achieve these purposes outside the League.

After the war the United States, Great Britain, and Japan found themselves in a race to build the biggest navy in the world. Here was a good place to limit armament. In 1921 the United States invited a number of countries to a disarmament conference in Washington. The conference adopted a plan for reducing the size of the five biggest navies of the world. But it limited only battleships. The building of small ships and submarines went on faster than before.

In 1928 the United States joined France in proposing that all nations sign a treaty outlawing war. This treaty is known as the Pact of Paris. It was signed by 62 nations, all of whom promised never to start a war. No way was provided however, to enforce the treaty. Peace could be preserved only as long as all the countries were willing to keep their word.

Thus our country cooperated with the League in many of its activities. It worked with members of the League to reduce armaments and promote peace.

Failure of the League. The League of Nations succeeded several times in settling disputes between small countries. For example, it settled a dispute between Greece and Bulgaria. Greek soldiers were already on Bulgarian soil when the representatives of the League arrived. But the Greek government obeyed the orders of the League and called its army back.

When a great power defied it, however, the League was not successful. In 1931 the Japanese army seized a large part of China. Japan had clearly broken its promise to settle disputes without war. But the other great powers did not cooperate to stop Japan. Japan resigned from the League and remained in China.

Japan's action encouraged others. In 1933 Germany resigned from the League and began building a big army and air force. In 1935 Italy attacked the weak and defenseless country of Ethiopia. This time the other members of the League cooperated up to a point. They stopped lending money and sending many kinds of supplies to Italy. But they did not stop selling to Italy the one commodity without which Italy could not make war: oil. The other countries continued to ship oil to Italy, and Italy conquered Ethiopia.

Such failures showed that the League of Nations could keep the peace only when all the great powers worked together. Since they did not work together, international cooperation through the League broke down. As the League became weaker, the nations of the world went back to the old way of looking for allies in preparation for the next war.

Americans hope to keep neutral in future wars. Thus the League of Nations failed to enforce peace, and the danger of war returned. The American people were deeply discouraged. They blamed Europe for the unhappy condition of the world. They did not stop to think that they themselves were partly to blame.

The majority of the American people were determined not to get mixed up

ACME

Japan invades China. In spite of promises to settle disputes peacefully, in the 1930s Japan attacked China and resigned from the League of Nations. These actions helped bring on World War II.

in any European quarrels again. Suffering from the worst depression in their history (see pages 546–549), they had troubles enough at home. From 1935 to 1937 Congress passed a number of laws intended to keep the United States neutral in any future war. For example, our citizens were forbidden to travel on ships owned by citizens of countries at war. Our own ships were to keep out of areas where war was being fought. The United States would avoid doing things that had led us into the First World War. If humanly possible, our country would keep out of the next war. That was the idea behind these neutrality laws. It was an idea that all Americans hoped would work. But it ignored the interdependence of modern nations. It ignored the fact that the United States had become a powerful nation, with many reasons for caring what happened in other parts of the world.

Summary

The First World War, which began in 1914, showed that the United States was becoming a world leader. The men and the supplies furnished by the United States gave the Allies the extra push they needed to win victory in 1918 over the Central Powers. The First World War showed, too, that in the modern world, war spreads rapidly. Although the United States had tried to stay out of the fighting, it had failed in its effort to remain neutral.

The world in which the United States was taking a leader's place was a world without laws that could be enforced among nations. Even if they promised to follow the rules of international law, nations could not be forced to do so. There was no way to keep nations from making war.

For hundreds of years, however, people had been trying to find ways to abolish war. Leaders of nations had worked out the methods of mediation, conferences, and arbitration to settle disputes. At the Hague conferences the nations set up the Permanent Court of Arbitration. Individual citizens of several countries organized peace societies to spread ideas on how to prevent war.

The end of the First World War seemed to many people—one of whom was President Woodrow Wilson—a good time to organize for lasting peace. Wilson made the plan for the League of Nations a part of the peace treaty. The United States, however, never became a member.

In its 25 years of existence the League of Nations carried out many successful projects. The United States cooperated with the League in many of its activities. Many American citizens took part in the League's work. Independently of the League, the United States called the Washington Conference to try to reduce armaments. It also joined with France to sponsor the Pact of Paris to try to outlaw war.

The League of Nations settled a number of disputes between small nations in the 1920s. But in the 1930s it failed to stop great powers like Japan, Italy, and Germany from attacking other nations. As the League grew weaker, the United States Congress passed laws to keep our nation out of future wars. But these laws could not change the position of the United States as a great power of the twentieth century. Our country had become a leader in an interdependent world.

For a Quick Review

1. Name and explain three ways in which international disputes were settled before the First World War.

2. Why did the United States finally take part in the First World War in spite of its efforts to be neutral?

3. How did the United States help the Allies to win the war?

4. What were some of the achievements and some of the failures of the League of Nations during the 1920s and 1930s?

5. Besides the formation of the League, what attempts to keep peace were made after the First World War?

Learning to Study More Easily

USING ATLASES TO FIND INFORMATION

One kind of reference book that is especially useful in studying history is an atlas. World atlases contain maps of all parts of the world as it is today. Historical atlases show on maps some of the major movements of peoples, military campaigns, and changes in boundaries of countries. Atlases usually also contain charts and tables giving figures on such subjects as population, largest cities, and so on.

An atlas contains a table of contents and an index. The table of contents usually contains a list of the titles of maps and charts. Often there are two indexes in an atlas. In one you can look up topics on which you want information. The other lists places you may wish to find.

The index of places gives a page number and two other references, a letter and a number. For example, the reference for Atlanta, Georgia, in one such index is page 56, D-3. If you turn to page 56, you find that the map is divided into squares by a network of lines. Across the top and bottom of the map the squares are labeled with letters, while down the sides they are labeled with numbers. To locate Atlanta, Georgia, look for the square labeled "D" at the top and "3" at the side. The square D-3 is small enough for you to find Atlanta.

Using the atlas in your classroom or school library, look up these places: Panama Canal; Nicaragua; Geneva, Switzerland; Honolulu; Canal Zone. Explain how each one is related to the events you have studied in Chapters 23 and 24.

Unit Roundup

HIGH POINTS OF THE UNIT

In Chapter 23 you found suggestions about drawing cartoons. As you tie together the ideas and events you have learned in Unit 7, try to summarize and emphasize them by using cartoons.

Review Chapters 23, 24, and 25. Select three or four important topics from each chapter and make brief notes on each. Compare the list you have selected with those which other members of the class have selected. After discussing them, let the class agree upon a final list.

Members of the class can then volunteer to prepare cartoons to illustrate the selected topics. There should be at least one cartoon for each item on the list. The student who prepares each cartoon should present and explain it to the class. The cartoons can then be posted on the bulletin board for two or three days so that class members may examine them closely.

EXPAND YOUR VOCABULARY

The words and phrases given below are frequently used in discussions of public affairs in newspapers and magazines and on radio and television. Review (or look up if necessary) the meaning of each one. Then divide the list among members of the class or of a committee and arrange to have each word or phrase illustrated for the class. The illustration can be a quotation, a cartoon, or a skit.

arbitration	mediation
civil service	military base
income tax	political boss
international law	raw materials
international trade	recall

HISTORY IN THE MOVIES

1. Study the film *How We Elect Our Representatives* to see how Mary Carter, who is just 21 years old, carries out her responsibilities as a voter.

2. In *Expanding World Relationships* we see some of the reasons why our world has become interdependent and some of the problems that result from interdependence. Study it with these questions in mind: (*a*) What differences are shown between life today and life in Thomas Jefferson's day? (*b*) What causes for increasing interdependence are shown? (*c*) What problems that result from interdependence are emphasized?

WITH CRAYON, RULER, AND PASTE

1. Make a set of graphs that show the area and population of Alaska and your own state, Hawaii and California, and Puerto Rico and New York. At the bottom of each graph write a sentence interpreting the facts shown.

2. Investigate one of the following topics and draw a picture strip about it:

The pineapple industry in Hawaii
The Klondike gold rush
The origin and work of the Universal Postal Union

3. Draw cartoons to show the meaning of each of the following:

"Remember the *Maine!*"
"Seward's icebox"
The open-door policy

4. Make a chart to summarize what you have learned about efforts to reform the government during the years 1880–1930. Use these headings: Name of Measure, Purpose, Date or Period Adopted. Include all reforms you have read about in Unit 7.

5. What events that you have studied in Unit 7 should be shown on the class time line? Decide through discussion and record them.

PUT ON A PLAY

1. Plan and present a roving-reporter radio program entitled "Latin-American Views of Uncle Sam." Use flash backs to show the attitude many Latin Americans held towards the United States at the following times:

When the Monroe Doctrine was announced
At the end of the Mexican War
After the signing of the treaty that provided for the building of the Panama Canal
During the presidency of Herbert Hoover

2. Prepare and give an Independence Day program that might have been given in Manila on last July 4. Your speakers should review the history of the Filipino efforts for independence, the development of the Philippines, and the problems that are now faced by the young republic. What music and other ceremonial procedures could you use?

3. Make a list of duties of a citizen in a democracy. Then plan skits to show right and wrong ways to carry them out. You could call your series "This—Not This."

STORIES THERE WAS NO ROOM TO TELL

1. Each of the topics listed below is mentioned in Unit 7. There was not enough space, however, for much of the interesting information that can be told about them. Investigate one of the topics and prepare to report on it in class.

Builders of the League of Nations
Digging the Panama Canal
Efforts to obtain child labor laws in the United States
The influence of Hawaiian music on popular music in the United States

Military and naval operations of the Spanish-American War
Military operations of the First World War
The sugar-cane industry in Hawaii
The United States naval base at Pearl Harbor
A vacation in Hawaii or Alaska
The work of peace societies in the United States

USE YOUR IMAGINATION

1. During the 1930s a number of American families went to "pioneer" in Alaska. Learn where in Alaska they settled, what conditions they found, and what problems they had to face as they built their new homes. Compare the experiences of Alaskan pioneers with those of pioneers in earlier periods of our nation's history.

2. Prepare a series of news dispatches that might have been written by a foreign correspondent stationed in Geneva, Switzerland, covering the withdrawal of Japan, Germany, and Italy from the League of Nations. The dispatches should explain why each incident occurred as well as when and how. They should quote opinions that the correspondent has obtained about the probable results of each withdrawal.

3. Write a letter to the editor of a newspaper in which you comment on problems of Puerto Rico today and suggest possible solutions for them. In preparing to write the letter, take an imaginary trip to the island by reading about conditions there. Write the letter as if you had just returned.

SHOW IT ON A MAP

1. Make a picture map of Hawaii or Alaska that shows major cities, products, and vacation attractions for tourists.

2. Make a set of maps to show the military and naval campaigns of the Spanish-American War. At the bottom of each map write a brief explanation of the campaign that you have shown.

YOUR COMMUNITY GROWS WITH THE NATION

1. Investigate the civil service laws of your state and city. When were the laws enacted? What are the good features of them? What criticisms of them are made? Which positions do they place under the merit system? Summarize your information in a written report.

2. Find out what laws of your state deal with the following and learn specifically how the laws operate:

direct primary
income tax
initiative
recall
referendum
voting qualifications

3. Investigate the voting record of citizens of your state over the last seven presidential elections by finding the answers to the following questions: How many votes were cast in each election? How does the total of votes cast compare with the population in that year? Make a graph showing the figures. Explain it to the class, calling attention to any marked increases or decreases in the number of votes cast.

4. What are the regulations in your state concerning employment of persons under the age of 18? Prepare an article for the school paper explaining the regulations.

5. Prepare a report on home-front activities in your community during the First World War. You can collect information by interviewing people who lived there during that war and by consulting the files of your local newspaper for that period. (See suggestions about conducting an interview, page 651.) If your school, or the

high school that you will attend, had a yearbook during those years, examine it to see what effect the war seemed to have on school life.

6. Investigate your community's participation in the military side of the First World War. How many men served in the armed forces? Can you find out something about where they served in France and about their experiences?

FURTHER READING

Books about Interesting People

Soldier Doctor: The Story of William Gorgas by Clara Judson. Scribner, 1942. A pioneer in the battle against yellow fever.

Theodore Roosevelt, Strenuous American by Alvin F. Harlow. Messner, 1943.

Walter Reed, Doctor in Uniform by Laura N. Wood. Messner, 1943. Another leader in conquering yellow fever.

Woodrow Wilson: A Biography for Young People by Alden Hatch. Holt, 1947.††

Stories of Adventure and Everyday Life

Falcons of France by Charles B. Nordhoff and James N. Hall. Little, Brown, 1929. A story of aviation in the First World War.

Stories of the Great West by Theodore Roosevelt. Appleton-Century-Crofts, 1940. True stories written by one of our Presidents.

Totem Casts a Shadow by Margaret E. Bell. Morrow, 1949. A sequel to *Watch for a Tall White Sail.*

Watch for a Tall White Sail by Margaret E. Bell. Morrow, 1948. Life in Alaska in the 1880s.

Other Interesting Accounts

Here Is Alaska by Evelyn Stefansson. Scribner, 1943. The development of Alaska and life there today.

Ocean Outposts by Helen T. Follett. Scribner, 1942. Information about the Pacific island possessions of the United States.

Picture Map Geography of South America by Vernon Quinn. Lippincott, 1941. Geography stories of the South American countries.†

The Philippines by Donn V. Hart and Howard E. Wilson. American Book, 1946. The history, geography, and problems of the islands.

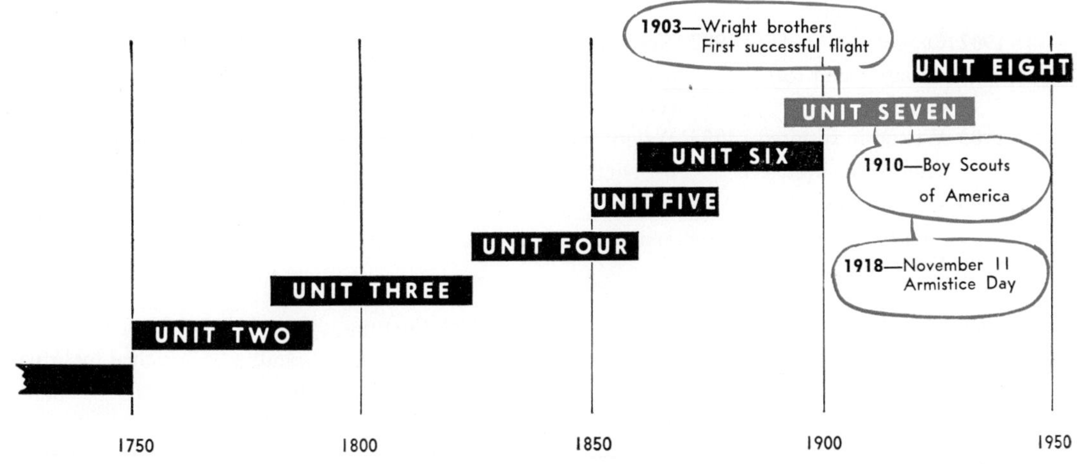

Building and governing the nation	*Earning a living*	*Science, arts, and the people*	*The nation and its neighbors*
1889–1893 Benjamin Harrison, Pres. (Republican)			
	1890 Sherman Anti-trust Act		
		1891 Basketball invented, Springfield, Mass.	
1892 Rise of Populist party			
1893–1897 Grover Cleveland, Pres. (Democrat)	**1893** First Ford automobile		**1893** Chicago World's Fair
		1894 Edison's first moving picture	
		1896 Rural free delivery of mail	
1897–1901 William McKinley, Pres. (Republican)			
			1898 Spanish-American War
			1898 Hawaii annexed
		1900 American Baseball League organized	**1900** U.S. open-door policy
1901–1909 Theodore Roosevelt, Pres. (Republican)			**1901** Marconi's wireless signal, Europe–U.S.
1902 Oregon adopted initiative and referendum	**1902** Newlands Act, irrigation projects		**1902** Cuba independent
1903 Wisconsin adopted direct primary	**1903** Wright brothers' first flight	**1903** *The Great Train Robbery*, first storytelling movie	**1903** Canal Zone obtained by U.S.
1903 Los Angeles adopted recall			
1906 Food and Drugs Act			
1909–1913 William Howard Taft, Pres. (Republican)		**1909** First night baseball game, Grand Rapids, Mich.	**1909** North Pole reached by Peary

MAIN EVENTS OF UNIT 7, 1890–1932

Building and governing the nation	*Earning a living*	*Science, arts, and the people*	*The nation and its neighbors*
	1910 Postal savings system established	**1910** Population 91,972,266	
1912 Theodore Roosevelt's Progressive party	**1912** Parcel-post service for rural areas	**1912** Girl Scouts	
1913 Amendment XVI **1913–1921 Woodrow Wilson, Pres.** (Democrat) **1913** Amendment XVII	**1913** Federal reserve banks established	**1913** Willa Cather's *O Pioneers*	
	1914 Moving assembly line introduced		**1914** First World War **1914** Panama Canal
			1917 U.S. bought Virgin Islands **1917** U.S. entered First World War
1919 Amendment XVIII			**1919** Treaty of Versailles
1920 Amendment XIX		**1920** First radiobroadcasting station, KDKA, Pittsburgh	**1920** League of Nations
1921–1923 Warren G. Harding, Pres. (Republican) **1923–1929 Calvin Coolidge, Pres.** (Republican)		**1921** Immigration limited	**1921–1922** Washington Arms Conference
		1924 Regular transcontinental airmail service **1925** Sinclair Lewis's *Arrowsmith*	
			1928 Paris Peace Pact, to outlaw war
1929–1933 Herbert Hoover, Pres. (Republican)	**1929** Depression		
			1931 Japan invaded Manchuria

Unit *8 The United States Becomes a World Leader 1920—1955*

IN UNIT 6 you read about the rapid growth of American industry up to about 1900. After 1900 American industry grew even more rapidly. Machines made close-fitting, interchangeable parts. Workers put the parts together on moving assembly lines. Products old and new came off the assembly lines in endless streams. The United States became the greatest producing nation on earth.

This increased production made our country more dependent than ever on other countries for raw materials and markets for surplus goods. With the rest of the world the United States went through a severe depression. With the rest of the world the United States went through the Second World War, the biggest war in history.

To produce for war, our country again tremendously enlarged its productive power. The American people hoped to use their production and their wealth for peace. For that purpose they cooperated with the other peoples of the world in the United Nations.

But the communists, under the lead-

ership of the Soviet Union, divided the world in two—a communist world and a free world. They grabbed the weaker countries of Europe and Asia and brought them under communist control. Their aim was to extend their power over the entire world.

Only our country was strong enough and wealthy enough to lead the free world in its defense against communism. We gave billions of dollars to the free nations of Europe and Asia. We helped them improve their industries and their agriculture so that their people would enjoy a better living. We helped strengthen their armed forces for defense against the communists.

When communist armies invaded free Korea, we joined with other members of the United Nations in sending our armed forces to stop the communists. The United States joined in an alliance with the countries of western Europe for the defense of that continent against possible communist attack. We made similar alliances for the defense of the Americas and the Pacific Ocean.

After the First World War, as you remember, the American people were doubtful about the role they would play in world affairs. After the Second World War there was no longer any doubt. If the free world were to survive, the United States had to take on the burden of leadership. Only the United States had the wealth and the power. The steps that the American people took to save freedom in the world is the story of Unit 8.

26 *The United States Leads in Mass Production*

The Washington Junior High School bus stopped outside one of the main buildings of the big automobile factory, and the students began to get out. Mr. Gray, their social studies teacher, and the factory guide were nearly the last ones out. It was a sunny spring day. Everyone was glad when Mr. Gray said to the guide, "Do you suppose that we could stand out here in the sun while you brief us on what goes on in this plant?"

"Yes, indeed," he replied. "Here you are going to see one of the most interesting parts of our factory—one of the final assembly lines. Have any of you ever seen an assembly line in operation?"

John spoke up. "I've never actually seen one in a factory, but we saw one in a movie in social studies last week."

"What are the main things you remember about it?" asked the guide.

"Men all along the line keep putting parts on the thing that's being made as it moves along."

"That's the general idea, at least," said Mr. Gray. "Why don't we go in now and see this assembly line in operation?"

As the class entered the plant, they saw the moving track that reached from one end of the building to the other. Workmen were busy on each side of it. A crane placed the frame of an automobile on the moving track. The frame moved slowly past the groups of workmen along the line.

One group added the axles. Another placed the engine in the frame. The next fitted in the steering gear. The next put on the wheels.

"Notice how everything the mechanic needs is right there. No fumbling around for the right wrench," Andy said.

Mr. Gray, just behind, added, "And notice how the job is broken down into simple operations. Some men put in the bolts and nuts, and others tighten them."

"I wonder how it feels to do the same thing over and over again all day," said Andy.

As the class followed along the assembly line, they saw other groups of workmen add the fenders, the battery, the body, the radiator, and so on one after the other. In a surprisingly short time the car reached the end of the track. A driver stepped in, started the engine, and drove the new automobile away under its own power.

Later the class went into the visitors' room to talk over what they had seen. "Here is my question," said Mr. Gray. "Why has someone called the assembly line one of the greatest timesavers of the twentieth century?"

Can you answer the question? Reading the next few pages should help you to do so.

1 *American Industries Use Mass-production Methods*

During the 1800s, you will remember, the American people made the United States a great manufacturing and agricultural nation. They rapidly increased the amount of goods they

Assembly line. High school students inspect an assembly line. Here automobile engines are being put together. Why does the use of the assembly line reduce the cost of manufactured products?

GENERAL MOTORS CORPORATION

A horseless carriage. Can you see why the early cars were called "horseless carriages"? In this picture the Studebaker brothers are about to drive off in one of their early electric automobiles.

THE STUDEBAKER CORPORATION

produced. The surprising fact is that in the 1900s our people increased their ability to produce goods even more rapidly than in the 1800s. By the 1950s this country was by far the greatest producer of goods on earth.

The story of the automobile industry illustrates one important new method that made possible this rapid progress in manufacturing after 1900. In 1895 there were 4 automobiles in the United States. In 1954 there were 48 million passenger cars alone, enough to provide a seat for every person in the country. Behind those figures is the story.

In the years around 1900 each automobile was built separately and was very expensive. Few people could afford one. About 1907 Henry Ford began to build automobiles that would be easy and inexpensive to run and would sell at a low price. In 1908 his company produced 6,000 Model T Fords. In 1923 it produced more than 2 million cars. Something had happened to enable Ford to make cars in such large numbers. For one thing, he introduced the assembly-line method of production.

The Ford assembly line. What was this assembly line and how did it work? On the final assembly line workmen put parts together to form completed automobiles. (See page 529.) This assembly line was fed by sub-assembly lines. On one sub-assembly line men put parts together to make frames. On another they made motors out of parts. On still another they made bodies, and so on. The work was carefully scheduled, so that the products of each sub-assembly line reached the main assembly line at the right place and at the right speed. A complete automobile factory might have as much as 25 miles of assembly lines.

Each assembly line moved along at just the right speed to give every worker enough time to do his special job and no more. Each worker did a simple task. He remained in one place, and his job came to him. He did not have to collect parts or even bend down to pick them up. The moving line brought them to him at the right time and at just the right height.

In a factory so efficiently organized,

an automobile could be made in much less time than formerly. In 1913 the steps in the final assembly of a car had already been divided among groups of workers. Each group did one job over and over again. But the unfinished cars stood still, and the workers brought the parts to the car. Under this system it took 12 hours and 28 minutes to put a car together on the final assembly line. Then the moving assembly line was introduced. The time on the final assembly line was reduced to 93 minutes.

By using the assembly line, Henry Ford reduced the cost of making his cars. He was able to sell them for less and still make a profit. In 1909 a Ford car sold for $950. The 1924 model, a much improved car with a self-starter, sold for $375. As the price went down, many more people bought cars and Ford's total profits grew larger.

Once Ford showed the way, other automobile manufacturers also set up assembly lines in their factories. Soon the Chevrolet, produced by the General Motors Corporation, was a successful competitor to the Ford. In 1929 the Chrysler Corporation brought out the Plymouth car to compete with the Ford and the Chevrolet. Then there were three major competitors in the low-price field.

The assembly line produces more goods per worker. The assembly-line method was not limited to the automobile industry. It was used in the manufacture of radios, vacuum cleaners, refrigerators, washing machines, and numerous other products made of standardized parts. During the Second World War even airplanes and cargo vessels were made on assembly lines.

This method of manufacture by putting standardized parts together on an

Stuck in the mud! This picture suggests some of the troubles that early motorists faced. As soon as the automobile became popular, the people demanded and obtained good roads.

LIBRARY OF CONGRESS

Southern cotton mill. In this Georgia cotton mill the machines are automatic. One man can look after a large number of them. What advantages does a cotton mill in the South have over one in the North?

assembly line was called mass production. People from foreign countries came to observe this highly efficient system of manufacture.

By using the assembly line, fewer employees could produce more goods. Other changes also made possible the production of more goods with less human labor. For example, with newly invented machines an operator could make electric light bulbs five times as fast as formerly. Furthermore, our industries used more electric power. In 1914 only 30 per cent of our manufacturing was done with electric power. By 1930, 70 per cent was done with electric power.

What were the results of this greater production per worker? Owners of industry made larger profits. Employees received higher wages and worked shorter hours. Consumers were able to buy more goods because of lower prices. (See the charts on pages 634 and 635.)

Many workers find jobs in new industries. When fewer workers produced more goods in an industry, some lost their jobs. But as long as the country was prosperous, they usually did not remain unemployed for long. Every growing industry created new jobs in other industries. The automobile industry, for example, used huge quantities of materials such as steel, glass, rubber, nickle, and copper. Those who drove automobiles used petroleum products. As the automobile industry expanded, many more persons got jobs producing and transporting these materials. Nor was that the end. Think of the many thousands who earned their living as automobile salesmen, garage mechanics, and filling-station attendants, and by providing other services that automobile users require.

So it was that the manufacture of automobiles created new work. Several other new industries sprang up in the early years of this century. Each resulted in thousands of new jobs. The development of motion pictures meant employment for actors in Hollywood. It also meant many more jobs all over the country for builders of theaters, distributors of films, cameramen, ushers, and others. Radio and television made jobs for workers who manufactured the sets, and for technicians, broadcasters, actors, musicians, salesmen, and repairmen.

The airplane industry also arose in this period. So did the electrical-appliance industry, which produces electric toasters, irons, washers, stoves, refrigerators, and so on. While the chemical industry was not new, several entirely new fields were opened in it. For example, scientists produced a group of man-made substances called plastics. The best known, called nylon, is used instead of silk to make parachutes, fine stockings, shirts and blouses, strings for tennis rackets, and many other products. Other plastics are used to make fountain pens, radio cabinets, buttons, jewelry, phonograph records, and a long list of other things. Scientists also found ways to make artificial rubber.

Southern industries expand rapidly. In the 1940s and 1950s the northeastern states, from New England to Delaware, remained the most important industrial section of the country. At the same time, industry grew in other sections of the country as well. Manufacturing expanded rapidly in the Middle West, in the Rocky Mountain states, in California and the other Pacific coast states, in Texas and in other states of the South.

Since there was plenty of labor and the raw cotton was right there, the South has long manufactured textiles. There were cotton mills in the South even before the War Between the States. After the war many more were started. By 1880 the southern states had about one-fourth of the nation's cotton mills. After 1900 the southern textile industry grew fast. By 1955 the South had more than half the spindles in the entire country. Many textile mills moved from New England and New York to the South.

Birmingham, Alabama, became the center of the southern iron industry and the largest industrial city of the South. Factories in the Birmingham district produced mostly iron and iron products. The Tennessee Valley Authority (see page 553) provided electric power for many new factories in Ten-

Steel mill. Since its founding in 1871, Birmingham, Alabama, has become one of the nation's great steel-manufacturing centers. Nearby are many natural resources, such as coal, limestone, iron, graphite, and marble.

LIBRARY OF CONGRESS

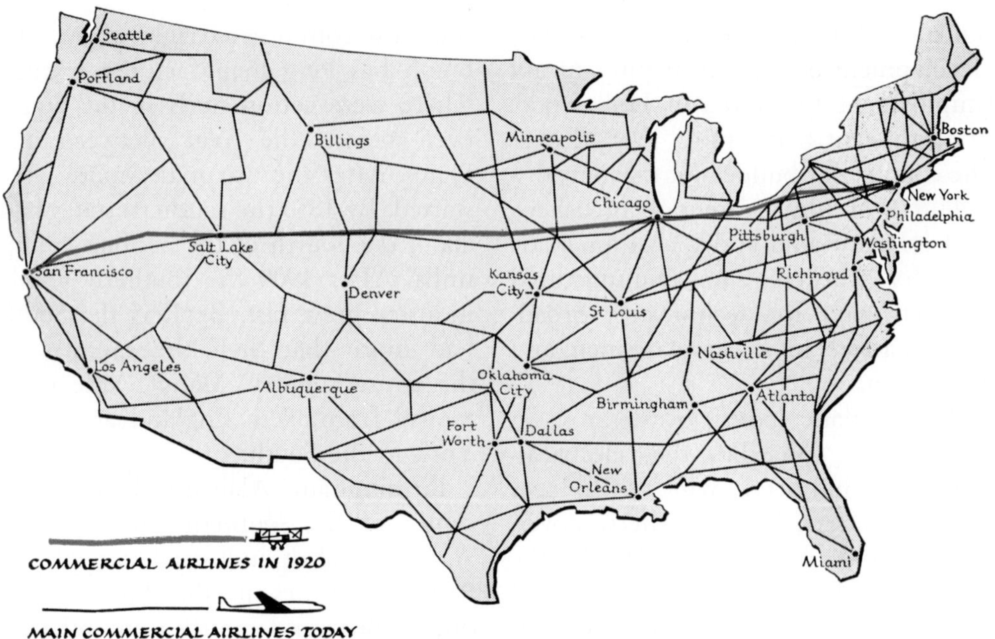

Airlines bind our nation together. From a single transcontinental route in 1920, airlines have expanded to cover all parts of the United States.

nessee. The South produced two-thirds of the nation's petroleum. Most of the oil wells were in Oklahoma and Texas. Texas was an important producer of sulfur.

The South had a variety of industries that prepared its farm crops and forest products for use. Its factories made almost all the cigarettes produced in the United States. In earlier days workers rolled cigarettes by hand, and a worker could roll about 2,500 a day. A modern machine turned out 1,000 a minute. The South produced large amounts of lumber and wood pulp for paper. It had many furniture factories. In mills, cottonseed was pressed for oil, and the hard material that was left was used for feeding livestock and for fertilizer.

A prosperous nation. Old and new industries expanded rapidly in the 1900s. They employed millions of workers. They produced more and more goods for people to enjoy. They helped make the United States a prosperous country. In 1929 the United States was the greatest producer of goods in the world. In 1955 the United States produced twice as much as in 1929. And plans were being made to increase our production more and more.

2 *American Farmers, Aided by Science and Machinery, Produce Bigger Crops*

After 1900 our farmers, like our manufacturers, rapidly increased their production. A farmer in the 1950s could produce twice as much as a farmer produced in 1900. By using more machinery, he did more work in less time. By using better seeds and better methods of caring for the soil, he raised bigger crops. (See the chart on page 539.)

American farmers use more machines and more electric power. One of the most important new machines on the farms was the tractor. The tractor was a great improvement over the horse. It saved the time of farm workers. Much of the land formerly used to raise hay could now grow other crops. In 1910 there were about 1,000 farm tractors in use. During the First World War we needed more food for our allies and ourselves. Since there were fewer workers to help them, our farmers bought tractors and raised larger crops. In 1952 there were 4,170,000 tractors in use. Other machines, like trucks and automobiles, helped farmers save time on the farm and in getting their products to market.

The improvement of machines for planting, plowing, cultivating, and harvesting continued. After the First World War the combine came into wide use. As its name suggests, it combines the processes of harvesting and threshing. It cuts, binds, and threshes grain as it moves on the field. With a combine, two men can do the work that 100 did in the old days of cutting by sickle, binding by hand, and threshing by flail. From 1910 to 1953 the number of combines in use on our farms increased from 1,000 to 918,000.

Farmers also bought in large numbers machines like corn planters and corn pickers. There were even cotton-picking machines. The first ones were built in 1930, but only large-scale farmers could afford to use them.

Electricity helped mechanize the farm. More and more farms used elec-

Nylon. This worker in a southern nylon plant is inspecting a hank of finished nylon. The nylon will be used to make bristles for tooth brushes, hair brushes, and brushes for industry.

E. I. DU PONT DE NEMOURS & CO.

DEPARTMENT OF AGRICULTURE

Farm tractor. This farmer is using his tractor to spread lime on his field to enrich the soil. In 1910, 12 million farm workers cultivated 879 million acres of land. In 1950, 10 million farm workers cultivated more than 1 billion acres and produced much larger crops. With more machinery, fewer workers cultivated more land and produced more food.

tricity. In the farm home, electricity is used mainly for the radio, iron, washing machine, and other appliances. In the work of the farm itself, electricity is used to operate brooders (heated places for raising chicks), water pumps, milking machines, and electric motors doing various jobs.

Scientists help farmers produce more. Just as farmers used more machinery and power after 1900, so they made greater use of scientific methods of agriculture. Scientific aid to farming began long before, but it has reached its highest importance in this century.

In 1862 Congress established the Department of Agriculture; its head became a member of the Cabinet in 1889. In 1862, also, Congress passed the Morrill Act. Under this law the federal government made large land grants to the states. The states were to use the money obtained from the sale of the land to establish agricultural and engineering colleges. Later the federal government made grants of money for the agricultural colleges. It also gave money for agricultural experiment stations in the states. Scientists in the Department of Agriculture, in the agricultural colleges, and in the experiment stations continually carried on experiments. They discovered ways by which farmers could increase the size and quality of their crops. Students in the colleges learned the best scientific methods and later applied them on their farms.

Farm agents. Then in 1914 Congress passed a law to establish the nationwide Agricultural Extension Service. Under this law the federal government helped pay the cost of having a farm agent in each county. The farm agent brought to the farmers information about new and improved farming methods.

Many counties set up farm home bureaus with home demonstration agents. These agents taught farm housewives the results of scientific research about healthy diets and efficient housekeeping methods. Some counties appointed club agents. They organized clubs for young people—the 4-H Clubs, the Future Farmers of America, and the Future Homemakers of America. The clubs gave farm boys and girls a chance

EXTENSION SERVICE, STATE COLLEGE OF WASHINGTON

4-H Club. Members of a 4-H Club in the state of Washington learn from one another how to make articles of leather. In their 4-H Clubs and in chapters of the Future Farmers of America, farm boys and girls enjoy many kinds of activities.

Farm agent's visit. Here a farm agent tests soil. As a result of the tests he is able to tell the farmer how to improve the soil and raise better crops. Besides visiting farms, farm agents often hold meetings to explain new methods to farmers.

DEPARTMENT OF AGRICULTURE

to get together regularly for fun—and for serious work as well. Each club member chose one or more projects to work on, such as raising livestock or canning fruit. They learned the best scientific methods by using them. Sometimes the boys and girls taught their parents the better methods they had learned.

Using the results of scientific experiment helped the farmer in his every activity. He learned to save his soil by planting different crops from year to year. He practiced scientific conservation. (See page 626.) The farmer improved his methods of planting, cultivating, and harvesting his crops. He learned how to fight insect pests like the corn borer and the boll weevil and to cure and prevent diseases of livestock.

New grains. Agricultural experts brought new varieties of grains from Asia and Africa. These varieties were suited to growing conditions in particular regions of the United States and produced larger crops. Scientists also created new, improved varieties by crossing old ones. The best known of these crossings is hybrid corn. The new varieties gave 25 per cent more corn per acre.

After the Second World War hybrid corn supplied Americans with bigger crops than ever before. After all other needs had been satisfied, there were large amounts of corn left over to send abroad to help feed starving people. In our foreign aid program (see page 594), we have sent to foreign countries seed of hybrid corn and experts to teach farmers how to produce hybrid corn. Everywhere it has yielded larger crops.

Modern farming. In recent years farms have tended to be larger. More farmers have specialized in growing

A well-run farm. A modern farm, such as the one shown here, is run like any other business. The farmer has to know how much money is being earned and how much is spent. The farmer and his wife keep careful accounts of income and expenses.

DEPARTMENT OF AGRICULTURE

INCREASED FARM PRODUCTION

1830, 1890, 1955

In 1830 one man, to produce one bushel, worked 3 hours

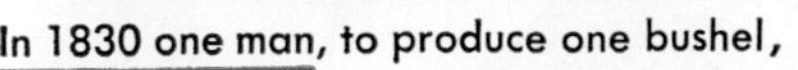

In 1890 one man, to produce one bushel, worked ½ hour

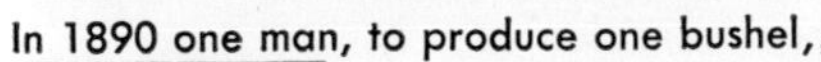

In 1955 one man, to produce one bushel, worked 10 minutes

INTERNATIONAL HARVESTER COMPANY PHOTOS

Machines on the farm. In 1830 one man cut wheat with a scythe and cradle and another tied the bundles. In 1890 one man, driving a binder that cut and tied the wheat, did the work much faster. A farmer in 1955 drove a combine that cut and threshed the wheat in one operation.

one main crop or one kind of livestock. Take a small farmer who had three or four cows and raised a few acres of corn, hay, and vegetables. He could not afford to own a milking machine, a corn picker, and a hay baler. But a farmer who specialized in one or two crops on a large farm, using scientific methods to keep the soil fertile, could make more money by using machines.

Modern specialized farming became more like a business than old-fashioned farming had been. It cost large amounts of money to buy farm machinery and keep it running. To earn something on money invested, the specialized farmer gave most of his effort to his special crop. With the money from its sale, the farm family bought what it needed just as a city family did.

LIBRARY OF CONGRESS

Science aids agriculture. Students of Tuskegee Institute, in Alabama, experiment with ways to improve crops. A greenhouse serves as laboratory.

Farming in the South. Farmers in the South shared in the improvements of agriculture. In some sections they raised rice and sugar cane with the use of tractors and machinery. George Washington Carver, a famous southern scientist, succeeded in making dozens of products out of peanuts, and peanuts became an important crop in the South. Southern farmers raised early spring vegetables to be rushed north by motor truck and refrigerator car and sold in northern cities.

Some southern farmers, however, continued their old ways without benefiting from the new methods. Such a farmer grew one crop, cotton or tobacco. Though his crops used up the soil rapidly, he did little or nothing to restore its fertility. The farmer planned to buy what he needed with his cotton or tobacco money. He grew no other crop that he could sell. Too often he did not keep livestock or raise vegetables for food for his family. Then, if the price for cotton or tobacco was low, he and his family did not have enough to eat. Even when the crop was good, the family diet lacked fresh vegetables.

Sharecroppers. One of the main reasons for the problems of southern agriculture was that about half of the farmers of the South were tenants. They worked on land and lived in homes that did not belong to them. Some tenants had their own horses or mules and bought their own seed and paid rent for the land. Then the crops they produced belonged to them. But large numbers of southern farmers were sharecroppers. For a sharecropper the landowner supplied horses or mules, seed, tools, and everything else needed for farming. The sharecropper gave only his labor and received one-third of the crop in return. A sharecropper usually stayed one or two years on one farm and then moved on to another. Naturally, he was not interested in conserving the soil or repairing the house on a farm that he intended to leave at the end of the season. His one interest was to produce a cash crop—cotton or tobacco—and sell his share for money.

But in the 1940s and the 1950s farm conditions in the South improved. Farmers received good prices for their crops. The federal government lent them money to buy farms and improve them. (See Chapter 27.) Many more southern farmers learned from county farm agents and other experts how to improve their methods. They raised less cotton or tobacco and more of a variety of crops. They conserved the soil and produced more of their own food. Southern farmers gradually improved their standard of living. From 1930 to 1950 the percentage of tenants among southern farmers was reduced from 55 to 40.

Prosperous farms. In the 1940s farmers were generally prosperous all over the country—more prosperous, perhaps, than our farmers had ever been before. They produced record crops, and they received high prices for them. During the Second World War (see Chapter 28), most Americans earned big money and ate more meat and other farm products than formerly. Farm surpluses were also needed to feed the peoples of other countries at war. After the war, as in the 1930s, the federal government helped keep up farm prices. The prosperity of the farmers showed itself in many ways. The number of tenant farmers was reduced. Many farmers paid back money they had borrowed. Many bought new machinery and improved their homes. In the 1950s the prosperity of the farmers continued.

As farmers bought more goods, they created jobs for workers who made the goods, transported the goods, and sold the goods. So the prosperity of the farmers helped make the whole country more prosperous.

Summary

In the years after 1900 the United States produced more goods than ever before. Manufacturers used mass-production methods. New machines made goods in enormous quantities. On assembly lines men turned out products at an unheard-of speed by putting standardized parts together without loss of time or motion. New inventions, such as the automobile, motion pictures, and electrical appliances, gave rise to great new industries that provided jobs for many people and products for everyday use. Manufacturing increased in every part of the country, especially the South.

Farmers produced more after 1920. They used more machinery and more electricity. Through county farm agents and agricultural colleges, they learned to use scientific methods to increase their output. Southern farmers, particularly the sharecroppers, progressed more slowly than those in other sections. But many southern farmers bought modern machinery and learned new methods. In the 1950s most farmers all over the country were prosperous.

In the 1950s the United States produced more goods than any other country in the world. The American people enjoyed a better living (see charts on pages 634–635). But before they reached that prosperity, they went through the worst depression in American history. You will learn about that depression in the following chapter.

For a Quick Review

1. How do mass-production methods reduce the cost of products?

2. How have mass-production methods changed the job of the factory worker?

3. Explain how scientific research has brought about new industries. Give examples.

4. How has scientific knowledge changed farming and farm life?

Learning to Study More Easily

MAKING PICTORIAL GRAPHS

An interesting way to report statistics to the rest of the class is to show them in a pictorial graph. You will find such a graph easy to make if you will follow the suggestions in these paragraphs.

Choose the topic on which you wish to make your graph. Decide on the title and list the exact statistics you will use. Next, create the symbols you will use. For example, you can use stick figures for people, dollar signs for money, baskets of farm products for agricultural production. The simpler the symbols are, the easier they will be to draw and the better they will be understood.

After you have selected the symbol, you must decide on a scale. You will want each symbol to represent as small an amount as possible and yet make the graph of manageable size. You need two numbers. First, what is the largest total you must show? Second, about how many of the symbols can you use in one line on your sheet of paper? Now figure out how many times the second number will go into the first. That is your scale.

With the statistics at hand and the scale decided, you are ready to start making the graph. Work through the same steps you would use if you were making a bar graph. When you have finished, check these points: Is the title clear and descriptive? Is the source of the statistics given? Is the scale clearly explained? Are the symbols neatly drawn and in proportion? Have you been accurate? Have you drawn the correct number of symbols for each number you are showing? Is the graph a suitable size for the use you expect to make of it?

27 *Americans Fight a Depression and Build Prosperity*

Born in 1882, Franklin Delano Roosevelt received his early education from private tutors. Part of the time he lived at home, on his father's estate at Hyde Park, New York. Part of the time he traveled with his family in Europe. Later he attended Groton, a private school in Connecticut; Harvard University; and Columbia Law School.

Aside from a few years in the practice of law, Franklin D. Roosevelt spent most of his life in public office. During the First World War he served as Assistant Secretary of the Navy under Secretary Josephus Daniels of North Carolina. Elected President in 1932, he led the American people through their worst depression. He used the powers of the federal government to improve the living conditions of ordinary Americans. Then he led the United States and the free world to victory in the most critical war Americans have ever faced, the Second World War.

Born in 1884, Harry S. Truman grew up as a farm boy in Missouri. He attended the local public schools. Because he had to wear glasses, he could not take part in sports. He spent much of his time reading, especially books about American history. He also took piano lessons and became a proficient musician. After his father died, Harry ran the family farm for his mother. In the First World War he was a captain in the field artillery.

Back home after the war, Harry Truman entered politics. He was elected presiding judge in Jackson County, Missouri. As such, his duty was not to preside at trials but to control county expenditures. In 1934 he was elected United States Senator and was reelected in 1940. In 1944 he was elected Vice-President. The next year, upon the death of Franklin D. Roosevelt, he became President of the United States. In 1948 he was elected for a full term.

President Truman presided over the country through victory in war and through the changeover from war to peace. He established the policy of sending American aid to free countries opposing communism. He led the American people into accepting the leadership of the free world.

Born in Denison, Texas, in 1890, Dwight David Eisenhower lived his boyhood years in Abilene, Kansas. The family was not well-to-do, and the six brothers had to help support themselves. "Ike" delivered newspapers and mowed lawns. While in high school, he worked nights in a creamery. But he found time to hunt and to play basketball and football on the Abilene High School teams.

Upon entering West Point in 1911, Eisenhower began a career in the Army that lasted 40 years. During the First World War he trained men for combat. Between the First and Second World Wars he served on various assignments. During the Second World War he was rapidly promoted from colonel to lieutenant general. He commanded the allied invasions of North Africa, Italy, and France. After the war he served as Army chief of staff. Then he retired from the Army to become president of Columbia University, New York City. In 1951 he organized the defense of western Europe (NATO, North Atlantic Treaty Organization) against communism. In 1952 General Eisenhower resigned from the Army to run for President. He was elected in 1952 and re-elected in 1956.

President Eisenhower kept the defenses of the United States and of the free world strong against possible communist attack. At the same time he sought agreement with the Soviet Union to reduce armament. At home he continued government programs to keep the country prosperous. In his administration the American people achieved the greatest prosperity in their history.

Three American boys, born within a period of eight years, grew up in far-apart homes under very different conditions. All three served through the First World War. All three found careers in the service of their country. All three were elected President of the United States. Under their leadership the United States became the prosperous and powerful leader for peace and democracy in the world.

This chapter will tell about the policies of these three Presidents at home. Chapters 28 and 29 will tell how they led the country in world affairs.

1 *We Live in an Interdependent World*

The American people have frequently suffered from hard times. (See pages 272 and 434.) In the 1930s our country had one of the worst depressions in its history.

How a depression grows. How does a depression grow? Suppose that, for some reason, automobile manufacturers in Detroit made fewer cars. Workers in auto factories would work shorter hours and earn less. With smaller incomes, the workers and their families would buy less. Perhaps they would put off

LIBRARY OF CONGRESS

Depression home. During the depression of the 1930s many fathers took their families with them as they traveled about looking for work. They often lived in tents by the roadside. In cities the unemployed sometimes stood in long lines to receive food from charitable organizations.

buying new clothing and shoes. Since they would sell less, clothing and shoe stores in Detroit would order less.

As orders declined, shoe manufacturers in St. Louis, Missouri, and Lynn, Massachusetts, and clothing manufacturers in New York City would cut production. Therefore workers in those cities would earn less and would buy fewer cars. More auto workers in Detroit would lose their jobs.

As the production of clothing went down, less wool and cotton would be used. The prices of these crops would drop. As the production of shoes went down, the price of leather and therefore of cattle would drop. Eventually families with smaller incomes would buy less food. Farmers would receive lower prices for grain, meat, milk, and vegetables. Then farmers would buy less of such things as new farm machinery, new cars, new clothing, and new shoes. The production of these goods would go down still more. Workers making them would earn still less. People earning less would not build new houses and would not repair old ones.

Since fewer autos and farm machines would be made and fewer homes would be built, there would be less need of such materials as steel, rubber, lumber, and glass. Thousands of workers in these industries would lose their jobs. Coal miners producing fuel for factories would lose their jobs. There would be less freight, so thousands of railroad workers would lose their jobs.

We began with a cut in the number of automobiles manufactured. Of course,

BLACK STAR

Abandoned mill. During the hard times of the 1930s, this mill closed and its workers were unemployed. Later its machinery was removed, much of it to be sold for scrap, while its buildings fell into ruin. Depression brings serious losses to both employers and employees.

the beginning could come in almost any industry. Beginning with such a downward movement, the country might soon find itself in a severe depression. Millions of people would be unemployed, not because they were inefficient or lazy, but because something had gone wrong somewhere and had slowed up the entire system.

An interdependent society. We live in an interdependent society. Our ways of earning a living make us depend on one another. People in different industries depend on one another. People in factories and business and people on farms depend on one another. It looks as if we shall all have to be prosperous together or poor together.

An interdependent world. Our interdependence is not limited to our own country. In the 1930s almost all the countries of the world were going through a depression at the same time. The hard times lasted longer everywhere because the peoples of the world could not trade with one another as much as they had done earlier. From 1920 to 1932 the foreign trade of the American people, for example, was reduced by 75 per cent. Countries suffering from depression could not buy goods from one another because they had no money to pay for them.

We must therefore expand our conclusion about our system of earning a living. Not only are the people within a country dependent on one another for prosperity; each nation is to some degree dependent for its prosperity upon the prosperity of other nations. In short, our whole world has become a single, interdependent community. Other countries are our customers, and we are theirs. For our own prosperity, if for no other reason, we are concerned with the prosperity of other peoples.

2 *Americans Meet the Problems of Depression*

The American people were generally prosperous in the 1920s. The Republican party was in power under Presidents Warren G. Harding, Calvin Coolidge, and Herbert Hoover. The people gave the Republicans credit for the prosperity. Then hard times struck in 1929, and the people blamed the Republicans for the depression.

A true-life story. We can understand what a depression can mean to a person by following the true-life story of Sylvia.

In 1935 it looked as if Sylvia would have to drop out of high school a year before graduation. Her father had been out of work for a long time, and there was no money for Sylvia's carfare and other school expenses. Sylvia would have to give up her plans to go to college. She would have to find a job immediately—in the midst of the depression.

One morning Sylvia's high school principal had good news for her. The federal government had appropriated money to be used to keep pupils in school. Out of this money the high school would pay Sylvia to work in the principal's office two hours a day. With the money she earned she would be able to continue her education.

World-wide depression. The troubles of Sylvia and her family were typical of those that millions of Americans faced in the hard times that began in 1929. What makes prosperity, and what brings hard times? Experts tell us that no single thing—a particular political party being in power, for example—causes prosperity or depression. Rather there are a number of causes for any period of prosperous times and for any depression.

One cause of the great depression that began in the United States in 1929 was the First World War. The war had upset business conditions all over the world. The destruction caused by the war added to the confusion. Many European countries faced reconstruction problems somewhat like those of our southern states after 1865. Europe felt the depression first. Hard times, as you know, spread easily in an interdependent world. (See pages 544–546.) Perhaps the surprising thing is that it took over 10 years for the depression, which began in Europe, to have serious effects in the United States.

Unemployed. Workers who lose their jobs during a depression find it hard to get other employment. How does the government help people who cannot find work?

BROWN BROS.

Herbert C. Hoover
1929–1933

BROWN BROS.

Franklin D. Roosevelt
1933–1945

Election of Franklin D. Roosevelt. Once under way, the depression grew steadily worse through 1932. Now the people who had given the Republican party credit for the prosperity of the 1920s blamed the same party for the hard times. They expressed their opinion with their votes. In the election of 1932 Franklin D. Roosevelt, the Democratic candidate, was elected President.

Franklin D. Roosevelt was a distant cousin of former President Theodore Roosevelt. He grew up in the state of New York and became interested in political affairs early in his life. During the First World War he served as Assistant Secretary of the Navy. In 1920 he was the Democratic candidate for Vice-President, but the Republicans won the election and Franklin Roosevelt returned to private life. The next year he suffered an attack of infantile paralysis. For seven years he struggled to regain his health. He won his health back, but his legs remained paralyzed. He was able to walk very little, and then only with steel braces to support his legs. Many of his friends believed that his personal experience with disease deepened his sympathy with others who had handicaps to overcome.

In 1928 Franklin Roosevelt re-entered politics by winning the election for governor of New York State. He was elected again two years later. Then in 1932 the Democratic party chose him as the party's candidate for President. He won the election, defeating Herbert Hoover.

In his speech accepting the nomination for President, Franklin D. Roosevelt said, "I pledge myself to a new deal for the American people." From that sentence his program for the following years took its name—the New Deal. (Do you remember that his cousin, Theodore Roosevelt, had called his program the Square Deal?)

Relief and jobs for the unemployed. When Franklin D. Roosevelt took office in March, 1933, the country was suffering severely from the depression. Many banks and other businesses had closed. Thousands of people lost their savings and investments. There were about 15 million unemployed, and there were no jobs for them. That meant that about one-third of the American people did not have money to buy food, clothing, and shelter.

The first task of the new administration was to help these needy Americans. As in previous depressions, care of the unemployed had thus far been left to local governments and to private charities. But this time the local groups had spent all their money, and the state governments had stepped in to help. As the states used up their money, the need became greater than ever. The federal government decided to give money to the states for home relief. That is, with the money the states supplied the needy with food and clothing and paid their rent and doctor bills. The federal government spent more than 3 billion dollars in this way.

Work relief. But President Roosevelt, like most of the American people, was not satisfied with such direct relief. He knew that most Americans wanted jobs, not handouts. They wanted to earn their money. Roosevelt believed the government ought to make jobs for those who were unemployed but were able to work. He started a program of work relief under which the federal government provided jobs for millions of unemployed. It was carried out through a number of agencies, the largest of which was the Works Progress Administration (WPA). The work relief program put men to work building roads, sidewalks, bridges, dams, parks, schools. It put women to work sewing garments for the needy, keeping nursery schools, and teaching in schools for adults. It put older boys to work in the forests, clearing trails, preventing soil erosion (ē rō′zhŭn), and planting trees. High school and college students who might otherwise have to leave school were paid for doing library and secretarial work. Artists painted pictures and decorated the walls of public buildings. Musicians gave concerts, which anyone could attend for a small admission price or without any fee at all. Actors put on plays, which, like the

WPA youth center. One way in which the WPA created jobs was to set up youth centers, in which men and women taught crafts to children and directed recreational activities.

WORKS PROGRESS ADMINISTRATION

PUBLIC BUILDINGS ADMINISTRATION

WPA art. Artists working for the WPA painted many pictures, called murals, on the walls of public buildings. The artists often chose subjects out of American history. Why was this scene appropriate for the walls of the post office in Livingston, Texas?

concerts, were inexpensive or free to the public. Writers wrote books, especially state guidebooks.

For and against the New Deal. Opponents of the New Deal found much to criticize in the work relief program and the way it was carried out. They said that the program was giving the federal government too much power over the states. They objected that it cost too much. They pointed out that a great deal of waste occurred in many of the projects. They said that New Deal leaders played politics with the work relief program—that is, used it to get votes at election time.

Leaders of the New Deal replied that it was better to make jobs for the unemployed than to give them food and clothing and let them remain idle. The individual and the nation as a whole benefited from the work done and the things built. The workers kept up their skills and learned new ones, so that they were ready to take private jobs when the time came. By working, they created jobs in private industry to supply the materials that they used. Thus the work relief program would help the country recover from the depression.

Aid to businessmen and farmers. Under President Herbert Hoover the government began to aid business directly. When Franklin D. Roosevelt became President, he increased this aid. The government lent money to railroads to buy new equipment and continue their services. It made loans to manufacturers so that they could keep open their factories and thus provide jobs. It made loans to banks to enable them to keep open or to reopen. The government also insured the money deposited by people in banks up to $5,000 (later $10,000) for each account. If a bank failed, its depositers would be protected.

The farmers of the nation were especially hard hit by the depression. In fact, they had been suffering from hard times since the 1920s. During the First

World War they were encouraged to buy more land to raise larger crops. To pay for the additional land, they mortgaged their farms. After the war was over, farm prices fell rapidly. Many farmers were unable to pay the interest on the money they had borrowed.

Farm conditions got worse during the depression of the 1930s. Since the American people earned less, they ate less meat, bread, and milk. Farm prices fell even lower. Farm families had to buy less at the store in town and live so far as possible on what they could raise on the farm. Thousands of farmers lost their farms and had to live as tenants on the farms they had formerly owned.

The government tried to increase the farmer's income. This was a difficult task because of the huge surplus crops, that is, crops larger than could be sold. In order to keep prices up, the government bought the surplus products. Some of the food was distributed to needy families. The rest was stored away.

For the future the government worked out a plan to encourage farmers to raise smaller crops of corn and wheat and cotton. On part of the land formerly used for these crops they would plant crops that would rebuild the soil. The result would be smaller surpluses and better soil. The farmer who cooperated not only received higher prices for his products; he also received cash payments from the government for practicing soil conservation. Many people objected to this farm aid program. To some it seemed that the government was paying farmers *not* to raise crops. To others it seemed that the government was reducing the amount of food grown while millions of persons were going hungry in this country and in other parts of the world.

Conservation of human resources. Before the depression some Americans had believed that government should help the poor and the handicapped. They said that government should protect the people against unemployment, guard them against poverty in old age, and aid those who were blind, crippled, or otherwise handicapped. Some states had made a beginning by adopting laws for these purposes. The depression of the 1930s convinced many people that there should be such laws for the whole country. As a result Congress passed the Social Security Act in 1935 and later amended it in 1939 and 1950.

Under this law the federal government helps the states to provide unemployment insurance. The states collect from employers a small percentage of the amount of wages they pay out. In some states employees also pay a small tax on their earnings. Out of this money the state governments make payments to people who are out of work. State laws differ as to the amount.

The Social Security Act also provides old-age assistance. A worker may retire at the age of 65 and receive a monthly payment from the federal government. The amount varies, depending on how much the person earned and how many dependents he has. The money for these old-age payments comes from a tax on wages paid partly by employers and partly by employees.

Under the Social Security Act the federal government also contributes large sums of money to the states to help pay for the care of blind people, crippled children, and mothers and their children who have no one to support them.

One purpose of this social security program is to help Americans in need. People out of work, people too old to work, and handicapped persons receive some money to live on. They can preserve their independence and self-respect. At the same time, this program is expected to help prevent bad depressions in the future. People out of work will have some money to buy goods, so that other workers will not lose their jobs.

Conservation of natural resources. During the depression years the federal government did more for conservation of natural resources than ever before. Through its agricultural program, federal officials taught millions of farmers practical ways to save the soil. They built flood-control dams. They developed plans to protect wild animals, birds, and fish in national preserves. Two conservation agencies set up by the New Deal were the Civilian Conservation Corps and the Tennessee Valley Authority.

CCC workers. The boys are cutting down a tree as part of their work in improving a California forest. The CCC program was so planned that many who enrolled continued their education in camp.

U.S. FOREST SERVICE

CCC. From 1933 to 1942 the Civilian Conservation Corps (CCC) provided jobs for about 300,000 young men each year. The men planted trees on millions of acres of land. They cleared roads through forests to make it easier to fight forest fires. They built check dams across gullies to stop soil erosion (the wearing away of topsoil). They drained swamps to reduce the mosquito nuisance and thus improve health conditions in many areas. They built trails and camp sites in the national parks.

TVA. The Tennessee Valley Authority (TVA) was established by Congress in 1933. Its purpose was to develop a system of flood control for the Tennessee Valley. It was also to help the people of the valley make the best use of the resources of their region. The area of the valley includes parts of seven states.

Before 1933 the region was very poor and was rapidly becoming poorer. Its natural resources were being exhausted. The thin soil was being used up by unwise farming and by yearly floods. There were few industries to give jobs to the people of the valley, and there was nothing to attract new industries.

The TVA built a series of dams on the Tennessee River and its tributaries. The dams prevent floods in the valley. The water is deep enough so that the river can be used by boats and freight barges. When water is needed, it is provided from the stored-up supply.

Electric power. At the dams, as the water drops from one level to a lower level, it is used to generate electricity. The TVA sells the electricity to private companies, which distribute it at low rates to city homes and farm homes in the valley. With electric power the farmers can do a better job on their farms. Electricity makes the work easier, both in the fields and in the kitchen.

Cheap electric power soon attracted industries, especially aluminum plants, which meant more jobs in the valley. The TVA itself used electric power to manufacture phosphate (fŏs′fāt), a valuable fertilizer. Officials of the Authority taught valley farmers to use phosphate on their land. The land became more fertile and produced larger crops.

Conservation. Acting on the suggestion of farming experts employed by the TVA, the farmers began to vary their crops. They stopped growing a single crop, like cotton or tobacco, which used up the soil rapidly. They rotated their crops so that the fertility of the soil would be renewed. They stopped farming fields that were unsuited for cultivation and planted trees on them. Thus the land was saved and human labor was saved. In time the farmers will probably receive more money for their timber than they could have earned by cultivating these fields.

The farmers learned to save and restore other land that had lost much of its topsoil. They filled gullies, built dams, and seeded the fields with varieties of grass that grew thick, matted roots. The roots held the remaining topsoil in place. When the farmers plowed, they made the furrows follow the contour, or shape, of the land instead of running them up and down the slopes. Contour plowing keeps the rain water from flowing off and carrying away the soil.

TENNESSEE VALLEY AUTHORITY

Shipping on the Tennessee. The TVA dams make the Tennessee River navigable for over 600 miles. River barges carry mainly bulky products like lumber. Water transportation saves shippers millions of dollars a year.

TVA officials work with local groups—farmers, businessmen, and others—in studying, planning, and carrying out its program. They make suggestions about possible improvements, but the suggestions are valuable only if they are accepted and carried out by the people themselves. In other words, the TVA helps, but has no power to give orders.

For and against TVA. The work of TVA has raised important questions for Americans to consider. Should the

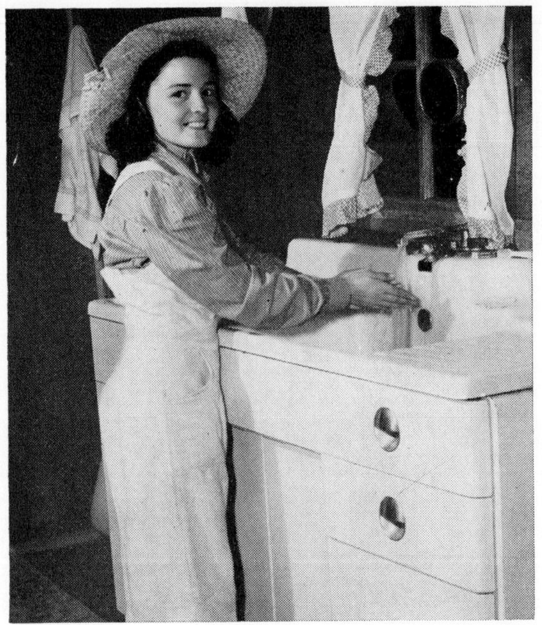

TENNESSEE VALLEY AUTHORITY

TVA improvements. There is running water in this Tennessee Valley farm kitchen because the farm has electric power. Before TVA only 1 out of 26 farms in the valley had electricity; now over 85 per cent have it.

government go into the business of making and distributing electricity? Should it lead in plans for developing a region? Critics of TVA have said that the government should not compete with private businesses like the electric-power companies in the TVA region. They have said that the competition of TVA is unfair because it does not have to pay taxes. They have said that the costs of TVA to taxpayers are too large and that the development of a region should be left to the people who live there.

On the other side, supporters of TVA have called it an example of democracy in action. They pointed out that TVA has succeeded in reducing the cost of electricity to the people in the Tennessee Valley. They have said that TVA would pay for itself over a period of years, so that the nation would get back the money it had invested there. The supporters of TVA have also said that the government must supply leadership if regional development plans are to succeed.

3 *Labor Unions Gain a New Place in American Industry*

While fighting the depression, the New Deal also started other important changes in American life. One of these made labor unions stronger than they had ever been before in the United States.

Labor unions did not gain in strength in the 1920s. Sharing in the prosperity of these years, many people kept out of labor unions. They were afraid that labor strikes might disturb business and prosperity. When the depression began in 1929, many unemployed workers gave up their membership. It was as if they thought, "What can the union do for me now, when so many people are out of work?"

The Wagner Act. As the depression continued, President Roosevelt and the other leaders of the New Deal favored making labor unions stronger. They said that the country as a whole would benefit if more workers joined together in unions to work for better conditions of labor. In 1935 Congress passed a law called the National Labor Relations Act. It is better known as the Wagner Act, after Senator Robert F. Wagner, of New York, who introduced the bill. It has been called the most important labor law in American history.

Certainly, it marked a major change in the conditions of workers in the United States.

The purpose of the Wagner Act was to encourage workers to organize unions so that they could carry on collective bargaining with their employers. In other words, the union representatives would bargain with the employer in the name of all the workers. The new law guaranteed to workers the right to organize and bargain collectively. An employer could not interfere with the employees' efforts to organize a union. He was required to meet with the union representatives to discuss such topics as working conditions and wages.

The National Labor Relations Board (NLRB) was set up to enforce the law. It could hold an election, with secret ballots, among the workers in a factory. If a majority of the workers supported one union, the employer had to accept that union as the official representative of his workers.

Two groups of labor unions. After the Wagner Act was passed, the number of workers in labor unions doubled. At the same time American unions divided into two groups, the American Federation of Labor and the Congress of Industrial Organizations (CIO).

The AFL, as we have seen, was a federation of craft unions, made up of skilled workers (see page 435). There were a few unions in it, however, that were industrial unions—the coal miners' and the clothing workers' unions, for example. An industrial union aims at including all the workers in its industry, both skilled and unskilled, in its membership.

ST. LOUIS "POST-DISPATCH"

Union members vote. Members of a labor union vote in a union meeting. Why is it important that members study the questions before them and take part in deciding the policies of their union?

The leaders of the industrial unions in the AFL believed that their kind of union was stronger than craft unions. In an industrial union skilled and unskilled workers cooperate. These leaders wanted the AFL to form industrial unions instead of craft unions. When AFL officials refused to do so, the industrial unions in the AFL withdrew and formed the Congress of Industrial Organizations.

The CIO then set out to organize unions in the mass-production industries like steel, oil, automobiles, textiles, and electrical appliances. By 1941 there were strong industrial unions in those industries. The CIO also established unions among groups of workers, like truck drivers, dock workers, store

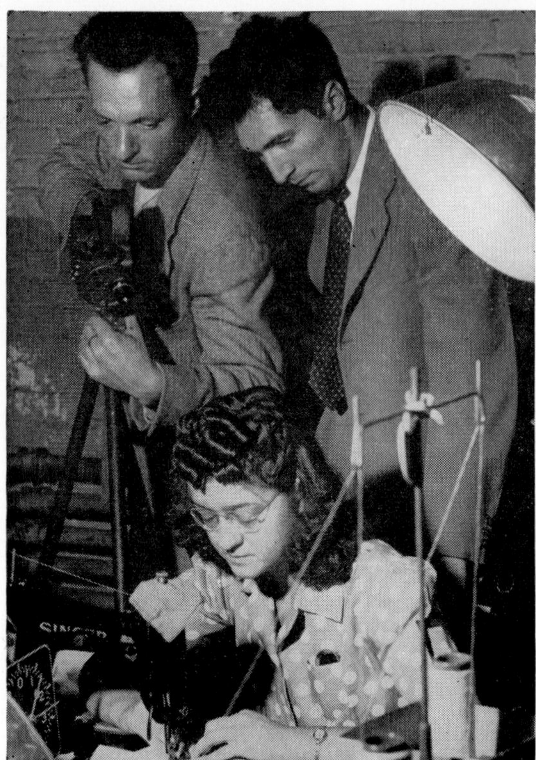

INTERNATIONAL LADIES' GARMENT WORKERS' UNION

Time study. By analyzing movies of a worker doing her job, union experts determine how long each part of a job takes. They also search for more efficient methods. This information is used in setting fair wages.

clerks, and newspapermen, who had not had unions before.

In the 1940s the CIO became almost as large as the AFL. Outside of these two groups the railroad workers had the strongest unions. In 1933 the labor unions of the United States had 2,800,000 members. In 1955 they had 16,000,000 members. In 1955 the AFL and the CIO were merged nationally into a single labor organization called the AFL-CIO. State units were merged later.

The Taft-Hartley Act. The Wagner Act required employers to bargain with union representatives, but it did not require the two sides to reach an agreement. Most of the unions, however, were strong enough to obtain higher wages, shorter hours, and better working conditions for their members. In 1947 the average factory worker earned enough to buy twice as much as the average worker in 1909. In 1947 he had 11 hours a week more leisure than in 1909. The typical workweek in 1947 was 40 hours, with a higher rate of pay for any additional hours of work.

In fact, in the late 1940s some people believed that labor unions were becoming too powerful. They demanded that a law be passed to forbid labor unions to do certain things, just as the Wagner Act forbade employers to do certain things. Such a law, called the Taft-Hartley Act, was passed in 1947. It limited the right of unions to strike. It also forbade unions to contribute money to political parties to help elect candidates for federal offices. The leaders of organized labor attacked the new law, but they were unable to have it repealed.

Methods of collective bargaining. You can see that labor unions have come to play an important part in American life. Therefore we should understand what their aims are and how they operate.

In bargaining with an employer, a union represents the wage earner. Union leaders want to obtain the best possible terms for the workers. They want those terms set down in a written agreement with the employer. By 1950 there were more than 100,000 such agreements in effect.

Labor agreement. A typical labor agreement, or contract, covers many subjects. The employer recognizes the union as the bargaining agent for his employees. The two parties agree on wages, hours of work, vacations, holidays, pensions, and other conditions of employment. The contract states the order in which workers are to be promoted or laid off if that becomes necessary. The employer agrees to maintain safe and sanitary conditions in the factory. An agreement usually lasts a year or two. Then a new one is made, after much hard bargaining.

Settling complaints. Employer and union agree on a way to deal with complaints. Usually there are shop stewards, representing the union, to whom workers can take their complaints. The shop stewards talk the matter over with representatives of the employer. Most complaints are soon settled. If an important one arises, it is discussed by higher officials on both sides. If they cannot agree, a strike may result. But the employer and the union usually try to avoid a strike because a strike is very costly to both sides. More and more contracts provide for arbitration of disputes that cannot be settled by discussion. An arbitrator is selected to serve as an impartial judge. Both sides agree to accept his decision, and both contribute to his salary. Arbitration has worked successfully in many cases.

Thus, through the collective-bargaining agreement, workers have a voice in determining the conditions under which they work. From the employer's point of view, too, collective bargaining has advantages. As a result of the labor agreement with the union, an employer is able to make his plans well in advance. He knows that for some time there will be no change in the wages he has to pay. Under the agreement, disputes are settled that might otherwise lead to strikes. In many industries, employers and labor unions cooperate fully in collective bargaining. In these industries, strikes seldom occur.

Wages and Hours Act. Another New Deal law important for workers was the Wages and Hours Act. It provided that workers were to be paid no less than 40 cents an hour and that no worker was to work more than 40 hours a week. If he worked longer, he had to receive extra pay for overtime work. In 1950 the minimum wage was raised to 75 cents an hour. In 1956 it was raised to $1 an hour. The Wages and Hours Act also prohibited the employment in most industries of children under the age of 16.

Health inspection. Modern industries often provide certain medical care for employees. This man, returning to work after illness, is having his throat inspected by a nurse.

DEPARTMENT OF LABOR

4 *Americans Enjoy a New Prosperity*

In the 1940s and the 1950s the American people enjoyed abundant prosperity. During the Second World War millions of Americans were employed at making guns, tanks, ships, airplanes, and other materials of war. After the war they made the many products that a prosperous people were eager to buy, such as radios, television sets, refrigerators, new houses, and automobiles. With more machinery and more power, factory workers and farmers turned out greater quantities of manufactured goods and farm products than ever before.

Third term. President Roosevelt was re-elected in 1936. In 1940 he again won, becoming the first President to serve three terms. Probably he will be the only President to do so, for in 1951 the Twenty-second Amendment to the Constitution set two terms as the maximum. In 1944 he was elected a fourth time, in the midst of the Second World War. He died after serving only three months of the term.

President Truman. When President Roosevelt died, he was succeeded by Vice-President Harry S. Truman. President Truman continued many features of the New Deal. He called his program the Fair Deal. Under President Truman the minimum wage was raised from 40 cents to 75 cents an hour. More workers were made eligible for old-age benefits, and the benefits were made larger. Opposition in Congress prevented Truman from carrying out more of his program.

President Eisenhower. Dwight D. Eisenhower was elected President in 1952. His opponent was Governor Adlai E. Stevenson of Illinois. In eloquent speeches salted with humor, Stevenson "talked sense" to the American people. But Eisenhower was a popular leader with a reputation earned as allied commander in the Second World War and as commander in chief of the North Atlantic Alliance (NATO). He was famous for his ability to get people from different countries to work together. Besides, many voters believed that after 20 years of Democratic rule it was "time for a change."

Middle of the road. In domestic matters President Eisenhower took a middle-of-the-road position. He favored limiting the activities of the government. For example, he wanted the government to give up, so far as possible, its program of developing water resources to produce electric power. His view was that private companies and state governments should build most water power projects. The federal government would build only those that were too big for private business or state governments to undertake.

Continuing welfare programs. At the same time Eisenhower favored expanding social security and other programs to promote the welfare of the people. Under the Eisenhower administration, 10 million more persons were brought into the social security system, and the benefits were increased. The minimum wage was raised from 75 cents to $1 an hour. The federal government continued to give financial aid for building low-cost homes for people

BROWN BROS.

**Harry S. Truman
1945–1953**

BROWN BROS.

**Dwight D. Eisenhower
1953–**

who could not afford to pay high rents. The government began a program to aid the states in constructing a network of modern interstate highways. President Eisenhower also urged that the federal government help the states and localities to build more schools.

The farm program. Under the Truman administration the federal government, by buying surplus crops, kept farm prices up to 90 per cent of what they had been immediately after the Second World War. With prices kept high, farmers raised larger crops. And the government spent huge sums of money buying the surpluses.

The Eisenhower administration sought to decrease the enormous cost of the farm program to the government. It proposed to make farm price supports "flexible." The government would fix price supports at from 75 to 90 per cent of the postwar level. If farmers continued to produce very large crops of wheat, for example, the government would buy less of the surplus. Then the price would go down to, say, 75 per cent of the postwar level. As the price went down, farmers would raise less wheat. The surplus would be reduced, and the cost of the program to the government would be less.

This Eisenhower proposal met strong opposition in Congress, not only from Democrats, but also from Republicans, especially those from midwestern farm states. Finally a compromise was reached. On the basic crops—cotton, corn, wheat, rice, peanuts, and tobacco—prices were to be supported within the range of 82½ per cent to 90 per cent of postwar levels.

In 1956 a "soil bank" feature was added to the farm program. The government would pay farmers for withdrawing some of their land from crop production and using conservation measures to improve the idle soil. This plan was much like the New Deal program of the 1930s. (See page 551.)

Eisenhower re-elected, 1956. Although President Eisenhower suffered a heart attack in September, 1955, by the summer of 1956 he had recovered his health sufficiently to be a candidate for re-election. The Democrats renominated Adlai E. Stevenson. The election results indicated the continuing popularity of President Eisenhower and the confidence the American people had in his leadership. He won re-election by a larger majority than the first time. On the other hand, the Democratic party won control of Congress.

Adlai E. Stevenson. In 1952 and 1956 Stevenson was Democratic candidate for President.

MARTIN HARRIS

Summary

Beginning in 1929, a depression spread through the nation. By 1933 there were 15 million people out of work. The unemployed and their families suffered severe hardship. Many other Americans were employed part-time and had to live on smaller incomes.

When Franklin D. Roosevelt was inaugurated as President in 1933, he immediately introduced the New Deal program. First, it provided food, clothing, shelter, and medical attention for the unemployed. Then it made jobs for them so that they could work for a living and keep their skills.

The New Deal brought important changes. By the Wagner Act, it strengthened labor unions. It established minimum wages and maximum hours for workers. It set up unemployment insurance and social security systems.

The voters re-elected President Roosevelt in 1936, 1940, and 1944. When Vice-President Truman became President after Roosevelt's death, he continued most of the New Deal program. In 1948 he was elected for a full term as President.

In 1952 General Dwight D. Eisenhower was elected President. His policy was to limit the activities of the federal government. But he continued and expanded many of the New Deal measures. He was re-elected in 1956, with a Democratic Congress.

For a Quick Review

1. Why does a depression spread more rapidly today than in George Washington's day?

2. List some of the effects of the depression of the 1930s.

3. Why did the government favor work relief instead of direct relief for the unemployed? What kinds of work relief projects were carried out?

4. How did the New Deal program aid businessmen? How did it aid farmers?

5. How did the Wagner Act of 1935 affect the legal rights and the growth of labor unions?

6. What have been some of the effects of the Social Security Act and the Wages and Hours Act upon the lives of Americans?

7. In what ways did President Eisenhower limit federal activities, and in what ways did he enlarge them?

Learning to Study More Easily

READING CURRENT HISTORY IN NEWSPAPERS

Newspapers are valuable sources of information. They can give you current facts that you cannot find in books, thus helping you keep up to date on any particular topic. Here are some suggestions for judging how accurate and how complete the news stories in a newspaper are.

The headlines on the front page attract the reader's attention to the events that the editors have chosen to emphasize. As readers we need to get the habit of going behind the headlines to find the facts on which the headlines are based.

News stories are supposed to be factual accounts of what happened, where, and when. Opinions are supposed to be printed on the editorial page or in signed columns of editorial comment. One standard by which we can judge a newspaper is how carefully its editors observe this rule.

Besides accounts of events that have taken place and editorials expressing the views of the editors, most newspapers have many special features. A newspaper usually lists its features in an index. What features does your newspaper have? Which ones do you read?

One step in evaluating a newspaper is to compare it with major newspapers like the *New York Times* or the *Christian Science Monitor*. Compare your newspaper with an outstanding paper, answering the questions: How do the stated facts about important international events compare? How do the accounts of events within the nation compare? Are all the major events included? Are the headlines accurate, or do they lead you to expect something that is not in the story? Are various sides of the story given when the subject is one on which different views exist? Are editorial opinions restricted to the editorials?

28 *The United States Helps Win the Second World War*

Sunday, December 7, 1941, was clear and sunny. "You'd never know Christmas was less than three weeks away," thought Sue.

After the Holmes family had eaten dinner and Mrs. Holmes and Sue had finished the dishes, they joined 19-year-old Sam and Mr. Holmes in the living room.

"Let's get the Philharmonic," suggested Mrs. Holmes. She was referring to the Sunday afternoon radio program broadcast by the New York Philharmonic Orchestra.

"There's a good news summary just before the Philharmonic. Let's hear that first," proposed Mr. Holmes. He reached over to turn the dial to the right station.

First came the news: "Japanese officials are in Washington conferring with the Secretary of State about the various problems that have arisen between Japan and the United States." Then came the music.

Suddenly the music was interrupted by the excited voice of the announcer: "We interrupt this program to bring you an important news flash. The White House has just announced that Pearl Harbor has been attacked by Japanese war planes." The statement was repeated. Then the music came on again.

Sue did not understand what had happened. She looked at the serious faces of her mother and father.

Sam was excited. "This is it!" he said. "This means war. I'll be in the Army in six weeks. Just see if I'm not."

"Wait, Sam," Mr. Holmes began. "Now, Mother, let's not get excited. Let's see if we can get some more news and find out what it means." He began turning the dial from station to station.

Sue asked Sam, "What is Pearl Harbor, Sam?"

"It's our big naval base in the Hawaiian Islands, Sis. And this is a sneak attack. It can't help but mean war. You'll find out."

The American people did find out. Many of them had been listening to Sunday afternoon radio programs on December 7, 1941, as had the imaginary Holmes family in the story you just read. They all heard the announcement. An hour and a half after the first announcement, an eyewitness in Honolulu was telling his radio listeners in the United States, "It is a real war; it is no joke."

Americans of 1941 were stunned by the attack on Pearl Harbor, just as Americans of 1775 had been stunned by the battles at Lexington and Concord, just as Americans of 1865 had been stunned by the fall of Fort Sumter.

The next day, December 8, at 4:10 P.M., President Roosevelt signed a joint resolution of Congress. The resolution declared that a state of war existed between the United States and Japan.

The American people were more united than perhaps ever before in their history. They were joining other democratic nations in a war against three very undemocratic governments. In order to see the situation more clearly, we must look at some of the events that happened in the 1920s and 1930s.

1 *Conflict between Dictatorships and Democracies Brings War in Europe*

After the First World War several European countries came to be governed by dictatorships. A dictatorship is a government controlled by one man or a small group of men. The laws are made by the group in power and are carried out by its party. No other party is permitted. Anyone who dares find fault with the dictator is likely to be put into prison or executed.

Dictatorship suppresses liberty. You can see how dictatorship is the direct opposite of democracy. Under a dictator there is no free speech or free press. There is no free vote. The dictator is the leader, and the people must follow him blindly.

Under a dictatorship the individual citizen has no rights. Since the dictator makes the law, he can do as he pleases with the individual. A person can be torn from his family, kept in prison, or executed without a trial, without knowing what crime he is accused of or by whom he is accused. The individual does not count; the state is supreme; and the dictator is the state. In a democracy, on the other hand, the individual comes first. His rights are protected by law even against his own government.

Dictatorship makes for war. A dictator has often gained power by promising to conquer new lands in order to make his people strong and prosperous. He usually believes that might makes right. His first aim is to make himself strong. Since he governs by

ACME

Dictator in Germany. Adolph Hitler, the man with the mustache standing behind the first bench (*left*), receives the Nazi salute. Dictators gained power by using colorful uniforms and symbols, by staging exciting meetings and parades, and by promising victories against their neighbors.

himself, he can prepare for war in secret. When he is ready, he can attack his victim without warning.

Democracy, on the other hand, makes for peace. The great mass of people in any country never want war. They want to live in peace among themselves and with their neighbors. This does not mean that the people of a democracy are not ready to defend their country if that becomes necessary. They have often done so. But where the people control the government, their desire for peace works to prevent war. Democracy is based on the belief that the weak have equal rights with the strong. It is based on the idea that the way to settle disagreements is to sit down around a table with your neighbors, discuss all differences, and agree on a reasonable compromise.

We see, then, that the difference between democracy and dictatorship is deeper than a mere difference in how government is organized. It is the difference between individual freedom and slavery. It is the difference between rule by justice and rule by force. It is the difference between peace and war. We can understand why in the 1930s, as the dictators rose to power, the democracies lived in fear.

The dictators conquer most of Europe. The most powerful dictator was Adolf Hitler of Germany. He set out to avenge his country's defeat in the First World War. In the treaty ending that war, Germany had been made to promise not to rearm. Hitler broke that promise and built up a huge army and a powerful air force. His aim was to conquer Europe—and then perhaps the rest of the world.

Allied with Germany were Italy, ruled by another dictator named Benito Mussolini, and Japan, ruled by its military leaders. Each country, in violation of many promises, attacked its neighbors. When they were criticized for their actions in the League of Nations, the three countries resigned from the League. (See page 517.)

The Second World War. For a time Great Britain and France did nothing. These countries were not so well prepared for war as Germany was. They had not been planning for it as Hitler had. They were especially afraid of Germany's great air force. Yet they realized they could not let Hitler go on conquering until he became too strong ever to be stopped. Finally, Britain and France warned Hitler that, if he attacked Poland, they would declare war on Germany. On September 1, 1939, the Germans invaded Poland. Two days later Great Britain and France declared war. The Second World War had begun.

The Germans took Poland without any trouble. In the summer of 1940 they rapidly conquered France and drove the British army off the continent. Great Britain alone stood between Hitler and victory. His air force tried to bomb Britain into submission, but the British air force defeated the German flyers. Hitler did not dare send his army across the English Channel to invade England. Instead, in June, 1941, he turned to the other end of Europe and invaded the Soviet (sō′vĭ ĕt) Union (Russia), though two years earlier he had signed a treaty not to do so. At the same time he repeated the German plan of the First World War. He tried to starve Great Britain into surrender by sending submarines to sink ships carrying supplies to that country.

"LIFE" © TIME INC.

War from the sky. Aerial bombing was first used on a large scale in World War II. Homes and factories were destroyed. This is a London street after a bombing attack.

The United States supports the democracies. What was the attitude of the United States toward the war? Of course, the people wanted to stay at peace. Many Americans seemed to believe that their country could keep out of any European conflict. In the 1930s, as you read on page 518, Congress passed neutrality laws. These laws were intended to keep the United States neutral if war should come. On the other hand, many Americans believed that the United States was so closely tied into world affairs that it would surely be drawn into any major war. The neutrality laws, they said, ignored the fact that the United States was part of an interdependent world. They said that these laws actually encouraged Hitler to start the war because he thought the United States would not help Great Britain and France.

It became obvious to the American people that the Second World War was being fought mainly between democratic countries and the enemies of democracy. The American people could not remain neutral in their thoughts. Hitler made them angry by saying that democracy was weak and helpless and by boasting that dictatorship would dominate the world. He shocked the American people by persecuting millions of people of his own country and of other countries.

Furthermore, many Americans believed that, if Hitler conquered Great Britain, he would attack the United States next. For our own protection, they reasoned, we had to help Britain. That is what we did. Congress changed

LIBRARY OF CONGRESS

War equipment for overseas. Throughout World War II the United States sent weapons and supplies to its forces overseas and to its allies. This picture shows a soldier checking the air pressure in the huge tires before this equipment is loaded for shipment.

the neutrality laws so that Great Britain could buy war supplies in the United States. When Britain had used up all her money buying supplies, Congress passed the Lend-Lease Act. This law authorized the President to send war supplies to any country fighting against the dictators. The question of payment was left to be decided in the future.

Under lend-lease the United States sent to its allies around the world supplies to the value of 50 billion dollars. We sent lend-lease materials to Europe, the Soviet Union, Turkey and other countries of the Near East, China, and the American republics. The principal items sent were foodstuffs, rails and railroad cars, trucks and jeeps, and airplanes. The United States became, in President Roosevelt's words, the "arsenal of democracy."

The United States prepares to defend itself. In the meantime, the United States was preparing at home to defend itself. Congress provided money to build a navy big enough to fight in both the Atlantic and the Pacific, a large number of warplanes, and a much bigger army. For the first time while at peace, the United States began drafting men into the Army.

Cooperation with Latin America. As part of this preparation for defense, President Roosevelt took steps to bring together all the American nations in support of democracy. In Latin America he had strengthened the policies begun by Presidents Coolidge and Hoover (see page 499). He had already gone a long way toward winning the friendship of the Latin-American countries by his good-neighbor policy. He had accepted the principle that no country has the right to interfere in the affairs of any other country. The Monroe Doctrine, he said, did not make the United States a policeman to keep order in the Western Hemisphere. Rather, he said, the Monroe Doctrine should be applied by all the nations in cooperation. If a problem arises, all the countries should decide together what is to be done. In short, President Roosevelt recognized that all the Latin-American countries—the big and the little, the strong and the weak—should help make decisions that would affect them all.

As a result the 21 American countries cooperated closely after the war broke out in Europe. They agreed to oppose dictatorship and the use of force. They agreed to help one another with money, food, and other supplies. They agreed that, if one American country should be attacked, all the others would consider it as an attack on themselves.

Canada. President Roosevelt also cemented the old friendship between the United States and Canada. In 1940 the two countries agreed that their armed forces would cooperate closely for the defense of North America. Thus the United States won the promise of solid support from all her American neighbors in case of any trouble with Europe or Asia.

The four freedoms. Finally, to unite the democracies all over the world, President Roosevelt stated what the democratic countries were fighting for. In his annual report to Congress in January, 1941, he said that the democracies wanted a peaceful world founded upon four freedoms for all people. These were freedom of speech and expression, freedom of every person to worship God in his own way, freedom from want, and freedom from fear. These four freedoms were accepted as the peace aims of the nations fighting against the dictators.

Atlantic Charter. In August, 1941, President Roosevelt and Prime Minister Winston Churchill, of Great Britain, met off Newfoundland and signed the Atlantic Charter. In the Charter they gave the aims of their two countries. These were the right of all peoples to choose their own governments, better living conditions in all countries, and permanent peace for all countries. You can see that the four freedoms were reflected in the Atlantic Charter.

2 *The American People Cooperate at Home*

While Hitler was winning victories in Europe, Japan was expanding its conquests in China. Japan depended mainly on the United States for many necessary supplies, such as scrap iron, oil, and machinery. Since Japan was using these products to conquer China, the United States gradually stopped selling such goods to Japan. In July, 1941, the United States brought all its trade with Japan to an end.

Pearl Harbor brings the United Nations alliance. On Sunday, December 7, 1941, two representatives from Japan were in Washington. They were pretending to discuss an agreement with Secretary of State Cordell Hull. At the very same time, without a previous declaration of war, Japanese airplanes

LIBRARY OF CONGRESS

Extra! War! A newsboy peddles his papers on Pearl Harbor day.

bombed Pearl Harbor, the American naval base in Hawaii. The Navy was taken by surprise. The Japanese destroyed five battleships and severely damaged three. Several other vessels were lost. It was the greatest disaster the American Navy had ever suffered.

The next day Congress declared war against Japan with only one negative vote. A few days later the United States was at war also with Germany and Italy.

On January 1, 1942, all the countries fighting Germany signed the Atlantic Charter as a statement of their aims. They agreed to fight side by side until victory. At the suggestion of President Roosevelt, the 26 countries called themselves the United Nations. This name was given to the international organization that was later set up to maintain peace.

The United States supplies a world at war. After the attack on Pearl Harbor, the American people immediately got to work to do their share toward winning the war. It was the biggest job they had ever undertaken. The dictators had won great victories before the United States entered the war. They continued to win great victories for about a year afterward. The American people had to put all their strength into the war effort in order to turn the tide.

The United States became truly the arsenal of democracy. The Second World War was largely a mechanized war. That is, it was fought with airplanes, tanks, trucks, and other machines. American workers produced these machines, as well as guns, ammunition, ships, and other supplies, for our forces and for our allies. American farmers produced food for their own country and huge surpluses for other countries. American ships and planes delivered these supplies wherever they were needed in every part of the world.

Science at war. Every war is a scientific race. Each side tries to improve old weapons and to invent new ones against which the enemy would have no defense. In the Second World War, American and British scientists cooperated and won the race in science.

The British invented radar (rā′där) and used it to defend their island against an air attack. On a radar screen a person can see an object long before it can be seen with the eye, and he can tell exactly where the object is. With radar the British spotted approaching enemy bombers. British fighters were able to go up and attack the bombers before they reached their targets. Our bombers used radar to find their targets. The Germans had radar, too, but our scientists invented ways of jamming their radar so that it did not work well.

Scientists made many existing weapons more deadly. They made fire bombs which not only exploded but also started fires. They made the magnetic mine, which exploded when a ship came close to it. They made jet propulsion engines, which enabled warplanes to fly faster. On the other hand, scientists saved the lives of many wounded by the use of the sulfa drugs, penicillin, and blood plasma for transfusions.

The Germans were far ahead of our scientists in the development of rockets. Toward the end of the war they were shooting huge rocket bombs from the French coast into London. American and British scientists more than evened the score, however, by producing the atomic bomb.

The atomic bomb. The story of the making of the atomic bomb goes back to the 1930s. During those years a number of outstanding foreign scientists came to live in the United States. They left their homes because they were persecuted by dictators. Early in the Second World War, these men joined American scientists to warn President Roosevelt that the Germans were trying to make an atomic bomb. If the German scientists were to succeed in doing so, Germany would undoubtedly win the war. The government of the United States, the scientists said, should put men to work on the problem of making an atomic bomb. President Roosevelt agreed.

The work was done in secret. After the United States entered the war, British and Canadian scientists cooperated. The democracies succeeded in making the atomic bomb first. They were helped by German, Austrian, and Italian scientists. These men and women had come to America because they could not live under the dictators of their native lands. The atomic bomb hastened the victory of the democracies. (See page 578.)

Americans cooperate to produce more goods. During the war the United States produced more goods than any other country in history. In the year of 1944 we produced about

Women in war production. These women are riveting the fuselage (body) of an airplane. During World War II, millions of women worked in factories and in shipyards. Women also replaced men in such jobs as taxicab drivers and streetcar conductors.

DEPARTMENT OF LABOR

LIBRARY OF CONGRESS

Swing-shift movies. In many towns during World War II, stores and movies kept open late at night so that workers on various shifts would be able to shop and see a show.

Citizens serve. During the war many Americans offered their special abilities to the government. Here Undersecretary of War Patterson (*right*) confers on military problems with William H. Hastie, a civilian aide.

LIBRARY OF CONGRESS

twice as much goods as Germany, Italy, and Japan combined. The world was astonished by this production miracle. How was it done? All unemployed found jobs. Older men who had retired came back to work. Women and older boys filled many kinds of jobs. Many people worked overtime. Some people held one job in the daytime and another at night. Men, women, and children spent their vacations working on farms. Increased numbers of workers from Mexico and Puerto Rico came to the United States to help with the farm work.

Three shifts. Manufacturing was organized according to the best mass-production methods. More machines were used. More goods were produced per worker than ever before. Factories were kept in operation day and night, seven days a week. Workers were employed in three eight-hour shifts; the regular day shift from 8 A.M. till 4 P.M., the swing shift from 4 P.M. till midnight, and the night shift from midnight to 8 A.M.

Housing. To fill the jobs in the war factories, people streamed into the cities from the farms and the small towns. So many came that there were not enough houses. The housing shortage remained a serious problem during the war and long after.

Transportation. Getting workers to and from their jobs was part of the difficult transportation problem during the war. The American people had become a nation on wheels. They depended mainly on their automobiles to get around. But during the war, automobiles were not made for civilians and there was not enough rubber for

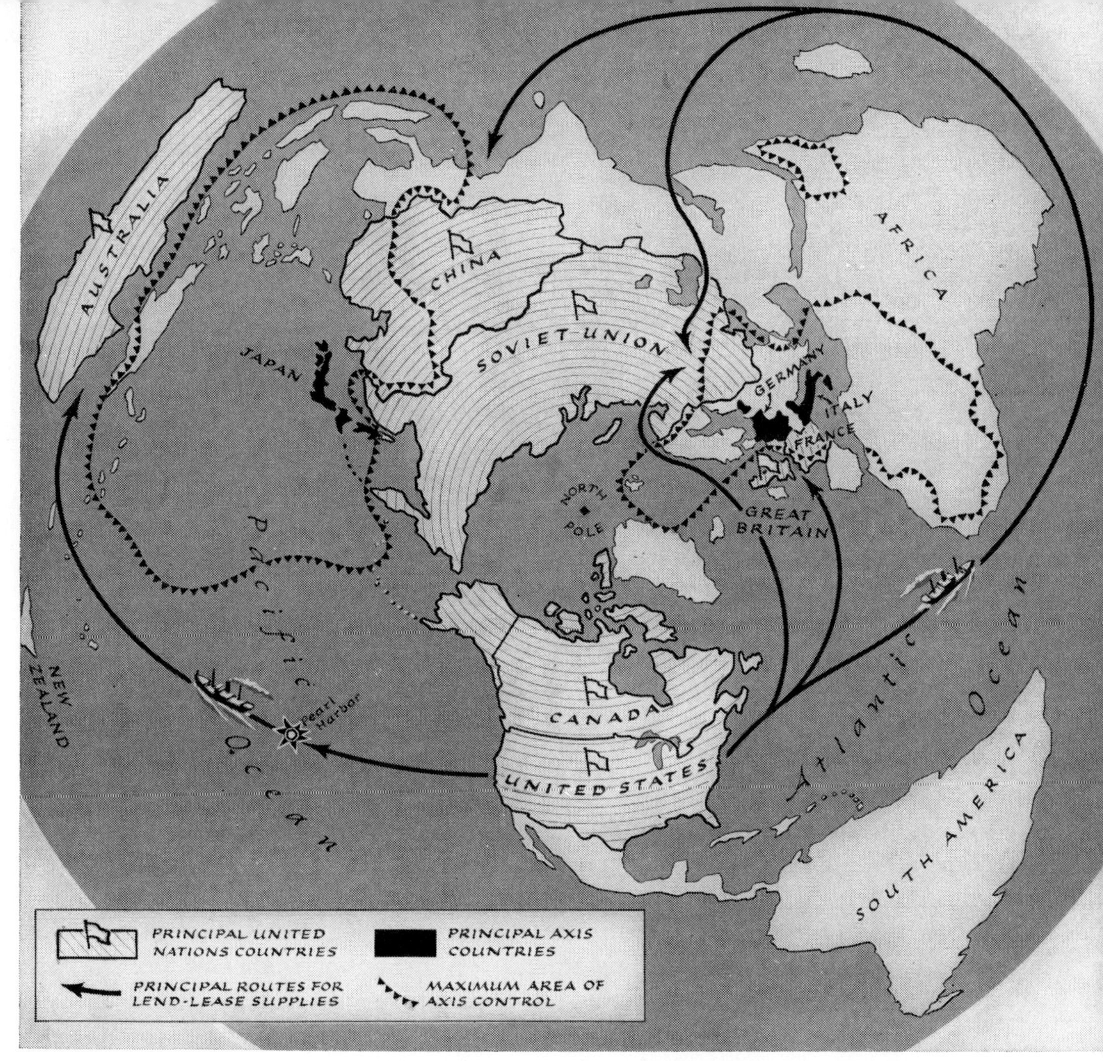

World War II was fought around the globe. Name the major United Nations. What countries were partly or wholly conquered by the Axis powers during the first part of the war?

tires. It was of utmost importance to make the existing cars and tires last through the war. War workers cooperated to "share a ride" with fellow workers who lived near them. To save wear on cars and tires, the speed limit was set at 35 miles an hour. Gasoline was rationed. Each car owner was permitted to buy only the minimum amount needed for essential driving. People were urged to use streetcars and buses as much as possible. By these means cars and tires were made to last.

Wartime controls. In this land of plenty, during the war, rationing became an accepted part of everyday life. In the case of some foods that had to be imported, like sugar and coffee, there was a definite shortage. But even the supply of butter, meat, and canned goods was limited because so much was sent to our armed forces and to our allies. At the same time the American people were earning more money and wanted to buy more food than ever before. If things had been allowed

DEPARTMENT OF AGRICULTURE

Young people helped. During World War II, thousands of boys and girls worked on the farms. They took the places of men who had joined the armed services or had obtained jobs in war industries.

to go their way, prices would have climbed sky-high. Then many people who received fixed salaries, like civil service workers, teachers, and ministers, would have been unable to buy milk, fats, and other necessary foods.

To make sure that every person would get his share, scarce foods were rationed. A family received stamps entitling it to a certain amount of each kind of food. When a person bought rationed food, he had to pay with ration stamps as well as with money. But rationing in the United States was not on the semistarvation level that other countries like Great Britain reached. As a matter of fact, because more people were earning more money than ever before, Americans as a whole ate more and better food during the war than ever before.

Rationing alone would not solve the problem. Storekeepers could still charge excessively high prices. To protect consumers, the government set the highest prices at which various commodities could be sold. Again, if workers insisted on higher wages, employers would have to charge more for their products. To keep prices from rising, the government ordered that wages could not be raised without its consent.

In the wartime emergency the people accepted many kinds of controls in their everyday lives. They were denied new cars and tires and were limited in the amount of gasoline they could use. Persons with cars shared them with neighbors. People obeyed rules that limited the amounts of certain kinds of food they could have. The prices that storekeepers could charge were controlled. Landlords were told how much rent they could charge. Wages were controlled. A few persons violated the rules, but the great majority of the people recognized that controls were necessary to meet the emergency. They knew that the government was acting for the benefit of the entire nation. For the most part, the spirit of sportsmanship and of share and share alike prevailed. Americans cooperated for victory.

Services of volunteers. A tremendous amount of work had to be done to enforce these wartime controls. Most of the work was done by volunteers without pay. Thousands of men and women served on committees that carried out rationing and price laws. The teachers of the country issued millions of books of ration stamps in the schoolhouses. Persons on local draft boards decided which men were to be drafted into the armed forces and which were to be kept at their jobs at home. Many people sold war bonds. Boys and girls performed a valuable service by collecting tin cans, waste fats, scrap paper, and scrap iron for the war effort.

The largest number of volunteers served in civilian defense, that is, the protection of the people at home. Air warfare had advanced so rapidly that there was real danger that the United States might be bombed by enemy planes. More than 5½ million volunteers were organized to prepare for such an emergency. Some kept a lookout for enemy planes. Some were trained to fight fires or to give emergency medical aid. Practice blackouts were held to test the entire organization. In a blackout, no light was to be visible from the air so that, in the unbroken darkness, enemy planes would not be able to sight their target.

As it turned out, no large-scale bombings of United States territory occurred. But that was something no one could foresee. The civilian defense organization was very important for national safety. It showed how much free citizens could accomplish by cooperating in the service of their community.

3 *American Forces Fight around the World*

The Second World War was long and hard fought. It was the most widespread war that the world had known. It was by far the largest conflict in which the United States had taken part.

Scrap drive. Girl Scouts collect scrap rubber for use in new products. During the war citizens saved tin cans, scrap rubber, and many other scarce materials.

GIRL SCOUTS OF THE U.S.A.

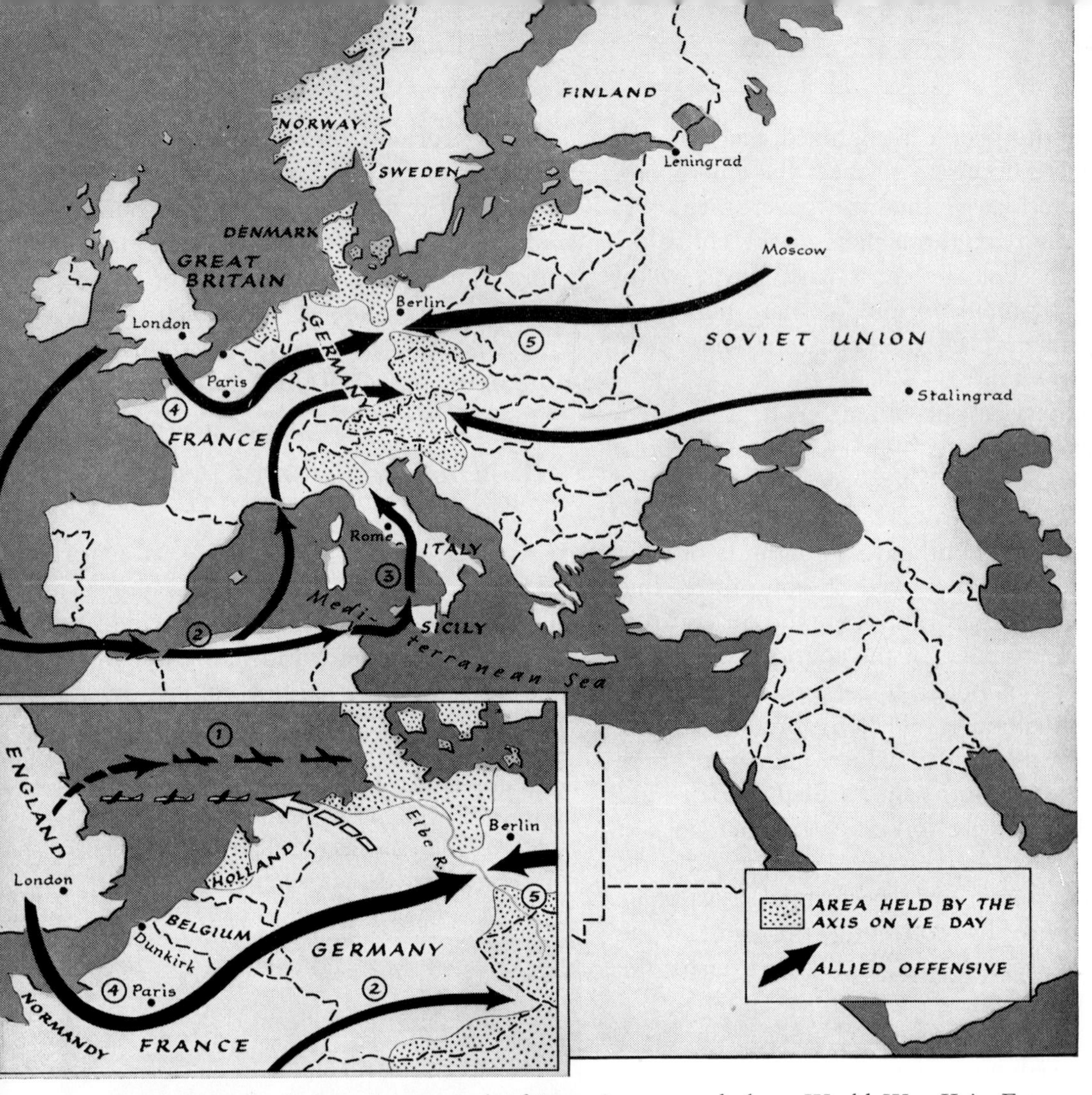

Defeating the Axis in Europe and Africa. As you read about World War II in Europe (pages 575–577), follow the action on this map. Compare the European areas held by the Axis on VE Day with the maximum area that had been controlled by Axis countries in Europe. (See page 571.)

Before it was over, more than 11 million Americans had served outside the United States, on all the seas and continents of the globe. (How does this compare with the number who served in Europe in the First World War? See page 511.)

The Japanese had been well prepared. They had weakened the American Navy at Pearl Harbor. They were able to conquer the Philippines, the Dutch East Indies, and several other island groups in the western Pacific. But the American Navy finally stopped the Japanese advance and began to prepare the counterattack. The American Navy stopped the Japanese advance in the Battle of Midway. In this battle in June, 1942, the Americans sank four large Japanese aircraft carriers. In this

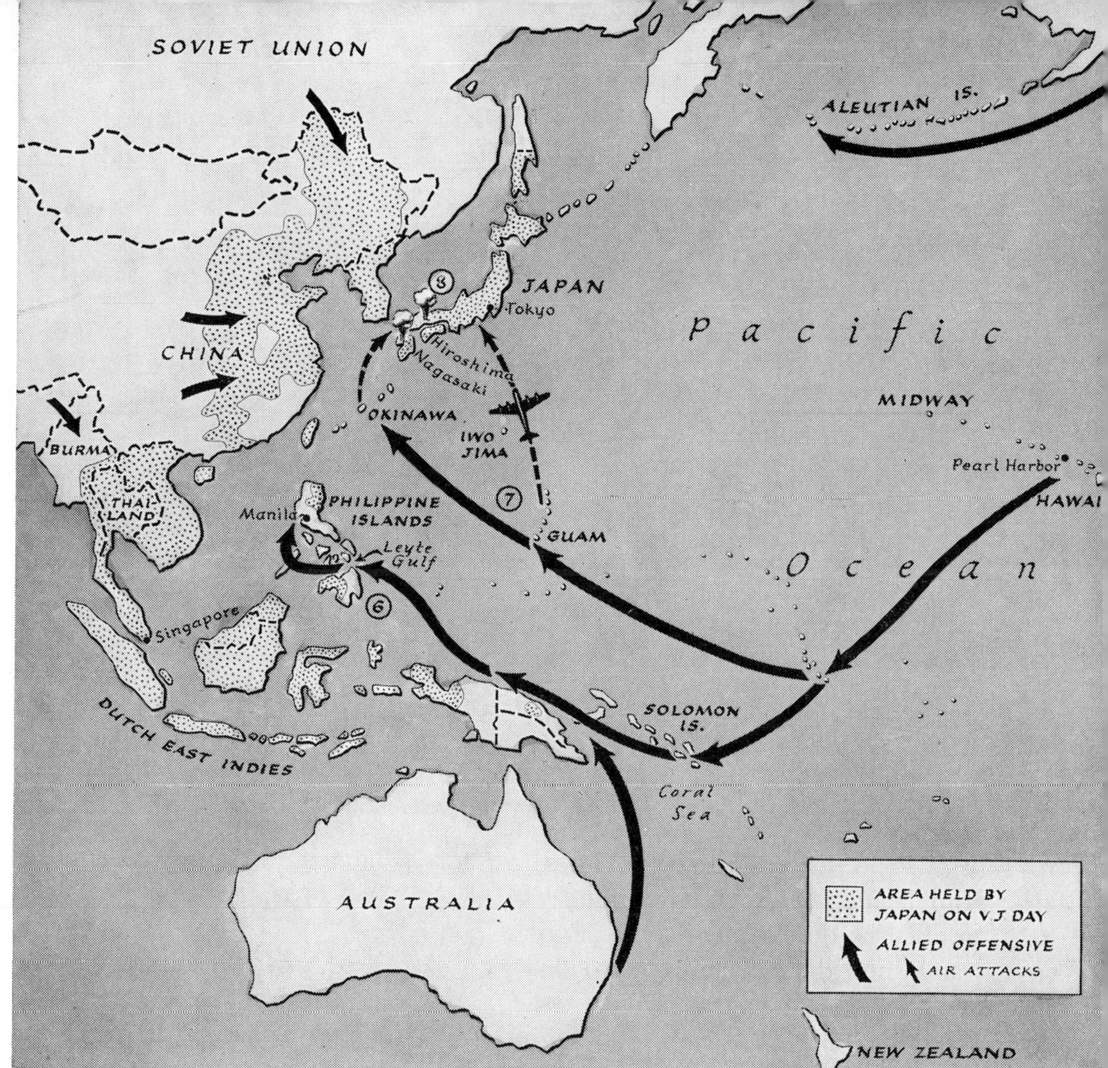

Defeating the Axis in Asia and the Pacific. Use this map to follow World War II in the Pacific as you read pages 577–578. How far had Japan been driven back by VJ Day?

battle the two opposing fleets never saw each other. All the destruction was done by aircraft.

The war in Europe and Africa. In the first year of the war, the United States used most of its power in Europe and Africa. In western Europe the war was fought from the air. German planes bombed England. American and British planes, flying from Britain as a base, bombed enemy cities, factories, and railroads. (See figure 1, inset map on page 574.) The British attacked by night; the Americans, by day. The allies fought great battles in the sky against German planes. Both sides suffered large losses. But the German air force was gradually defeated. British and American planes caused ever-greater destruction in Germany.

The Germans, however, could not be bombed into submission. To defeat the enemy, ground troops had to be landed in Europe with guns, tanks, and other

WIDE WORLD

The advance in Germany. American soldiers are marching through the ruins of a bombed German town in the final stages of World War II in Europe.

weapons. Since Hitler held almost all of Europe, the troops would have to land from the sea on a coast heavily fortified by the enemy. Such a landing was a most difficult and most dangerous military action. But it was done. While the United States was gathering its strength for the landing, the forces of the Soviet Union were successfully holding off huge German armies in a bitter struggle in Russia.

Landing in Africa. American and British forces made their first landings at Casablanca (kăs *à* blăng′k*à*), Oran (ō răn′), and Algiers (ăl jērz′) in northern Africa. (See figure 2 on the map on page 574.) Part of the troops came from Britain; part, directly from the United States. It was the first time in history that a major invasion was made from across an ocean. The landings were successful, and an important campaign followed. After defeating the Germans and Italians in Africa, our forces landed in Sicily and then invaded Italy. (See figure 3 on the map on page 574.) The Italian government surrendered, but German armies took over the country. The Americans had to fight long and hard to make their way slowly up the Italian "boot."

Landing in France. The most important and most dangerous landing was made on the Normandy coast of France on June 6, 1944. (See figure 4 on the map on page 574.) About 3 million men and millions of tons of supplies had been made ready in Britain. The Germans had fortified the coast with every possible means of defense. Yet the British and the Americans landed and established a beachhead (a base from which they could continue operations). Within a week we had more than 300,000 men, fully supplied with weapons, in France.

Three weeks later the number had risen to a million.

The Germans fought hard, and at first the going was slow. But once a break was made through the German lines, the Americans and British advanced steadily. Later the advance became a race. Allied troops entered Germany itself. At the same time the Russians were pushing the Germans back in eastern Europe. In April, 1945, the American and Russian armies came together in Germany. (See figure 5 on the map on page 574.) On May 9, 1945, Germany surrendered. By that time, Hitler had committed suicide, and Mussolini had been put to death by his own people.

The war in the Pacific. In the Pacific the American Navy inflicted several defeats on the Japanese navy. The American plan of campaign was called island hopping. It consisted of capturing one enemy-held island after the other, always getting nearer and nearer to Japan. The purpose was to obtain island bases close enough to Japan for large bombers to bomb Japanese cities. For almost three years the American Army, Navy, and Air Force cooperated in a series of amphibious (ăm fĭb'ĭ *ŭ*s), sea and land, operations. First the Japanese navy had to be beaten off. Then our soldiers had to land on the beaches. Then they had to defeat the Japanese on the islands, often in hand-to-hand fighting.

In October, 1944, the Americans began the reconquest of the Philippines. (See figure 6 on the map on page 575.) In that month, in the Battle of Leyte (lā'tē) Gulf, the American Navy won the greatest victory of the war over the Japanese navy. The Americans destroyed 27 large Japanese warships. By April, 1945, the Philippines were again free. The Americans won bases closer to Japan by seizing the islands of Iwo Jima (ē'wō jē'm*ȧ*) in March and Okinawa (ō kĭ nä'w*ȧ*) in April. (See fig-

Invasion from the sky. In modern war one method of attack is to land paratroopers behind enemy lines.

WIDE WORLD

OFFICIAL U.S. NAVY PHOTO

Smoke screen. A ship lays a smoke screen around an American battleship to protect it from Japanese torpedo planes. This is a scene from the Battle of Leyte Gulf, World War II.

ure 7 on the map on page 575.) From these bases American bombers were able to attack Japanese cities regularly.

The war ends. Yet, when the Germans surrendered in May, it looked as if the war with Japan might go on for a long time. Hundreds of thousands of American lives might still be lost in the conquest of the Japanese homeland. Then on August 6, 1945, an American plane dropped an atomic bomb on the Japanese city of Hiroshima (hē rō shē′mȧ). (See figure 8 on the map on page 575.) It destroyed a large part of the city and its people. On August 9 another bomb partly destroyed Nagasaki (nä gȧ sä′kē), another Japanese city. A few days later Japan surrendered.

Thus ended the biggest and most destructive war in all history. It was fought on most of the continents and on most of the seas. It involved more people than any other war. More persons were killed, more property was destroyed, and more money was spent than in any previous war. Like many wars of the past, it raised problems that were at least as difficult as the problems it solved.

Summary

During the 1920s and 1930s dictatorships arose in Italy and Germany. Each of these dictatorships tried to seize territories from other nations. The Second World War began when the German army, ordered by Hitler, invaded Poland. Great Britain and France led the countries that resisted the dictators. The United States remained neutral for two years. During this time it built up its military strength. The sympathy of Americans was always with the democratic nations of Europe and against the dictatorships. While still neutral, the United States gave aid to Great Britain and France.

In 1941 a Japanese attack on Pearl Harbor brought the United States into the Second World War. The democracies of western Europe were its allies. Its enemies were the autocratic governments of Japan, Germany, and Italy. A united American people plunged into work to produce the goods needed by the armed forces of the United States and its allies. They worked long hours. They accepted rationing and control of prices and wages. In the Second World War the work on the farms, in the factories, and in the scientific laboratories made possible the victories on the battlefield.

The Second World War was the most widespread and the most destructive the world had ever experienced. The United States had to fight in Europe and Africa to the east and in the Pacific to the west. In Europe and Africa it was necessary to land huge armies for invasion of German-held territories. Forces of the United Nations, as the United States and its allies were called, defeated the Germans and Italians in Africa. Then they fought their way into Italy. Finally, in 1944, a great invasion army was landed in France and the last stage of the fighting in Europe began. In May, 1945, came VE Day—victory in Europe. In the Pacific the tide was turned in June, 1942, when the Japanese were stopped in the Battle of Midway. But it was a long, hard fight before Japanese surrender in August, 1945. Before the Japanese surrender came, the United States had used two atomic bombs.

Air navy. American torpedo bombers get ready to attack Japanese aircraft carriers during the Battle of Midway. Carriers were favorite targets because their destruction weakened the enemy's power in the air as well as on the sea.

OFFICIAL U.S. NAVY PHOTO

From the beginning of American participation in the war, our nation was committed to the four freedoms and the Atlantic Charter as its peace aims. From the first days of the war, Americans were thinking about how to make a lasting peace once the war was won.

For a Quick Review

1. What are the important differences between a dictatorship and a democracy?

2. Trace the events that led to the Second World War in Europe. How did the United States become involved in the Second World War?

3. What are the four freedoms?

4. Mention some of the important ways in which the American people cooperated to meet wartime problems.

5. How did science affect the fighting and the outcome of the Second World War?

6. Name the principal military and naval events of the Second World War in Europe and in the Pacific.

Learning to Study More Easily

USING THE BULLETIN BOARD

Students learn a great deal from helping prepare displays for the class bulletin board and from studying them. Bulletin-board displays help you remember important things. They make history study more interesting if they include local-interest pictures, graphs, and other materials related to the topics you are studying. Bulletin boards should have some new materials on them almost every day. Something new keeps people looking at them.

In some classes there is a bulletin-board committee whose members plan and post displays for a designated period—one week, one month, or during the study of one unit, for example. Membership rotates, so that many students have a chance to serve during the year. In some classes individual students take responsibility for the entire bulletin-board display for a short period of time or for one part of the display for a longer period. If your class has not done so, perhaps you would like to try one of these systems.

Bulletin boards, like newspapers, can be organized by departments. A heading for each department, printed in large letters, sets off the board very well. Your class will need to decide what departments to have, of course, but here are several that have proved interesting in some schools:

It's Happening Now—including news items, editorials, and cartoons concerning events that are happening today in the United States and throughout the world

Our State Grows with the United States—including materials on the history of the town as well as the state and focusing on the period of history that you are studying at a given time

Fashion News—dress, furniture, houses, customs, and so on, of the period the class is studying

Important Events in Graphics—including pictures, maps, graphs, charts, and time lines having to do with the unit being studied

Today Grows Out of the Past—including news items, cartoons, and pictures showing a direct relationship between current happenings or conditions and past events

If you volunteer to manage a part or all of the bulletin board for a time, how will you find materials? Try these suggestions.

1. Ask your school librarian to help you find appropriate pictures in the picture file.
2. Ask your teacher whether there are materials you could use from the classroom files.
3. Ask the class whether anyone is preparing a graph, map, or other material that would fit into your bulletin board.
4. Ask the class to bring in news items. Perhaps individual persons will volunteer to read and clip for you one particular newspaper or magazine that they get at home.
5. Ask at your public library for pictures and other materials that can be used on your bulletin board.

Below is a check list of things that make an effective bulletin board. How does yours rate?

1. Is the general appearance neat and attractive?
2. Are the items shown connected with work that the class is doing?
3. Is there variety in the items shown (pictures, graphs, time lines, clippings, etc.)?
4. Is the number of items displayed small enough that each one commands attention, yet large enough that a person will feel it worth while to stop and look?
5. Is each item correctly and adequately labeled?
6. If there are departments, are they given clear, interesting titles?
7. Is some of the material changed each day?

29 *Americans Strive for Peace and Democracy*

A college student named Henry Smith became interested in the subject of world peace. He decided to see if there was something that he as an individual could do to promote peace. He chose to go to an international work camp for the summer. Henry signed up with the American Friends Service Committee, a Quaker organization that was helping to rebuild Europe after the Second World War. Henry paid $500 for his own expenses, and was sent to a work camp in the coal-mining area of Belgium. He received no pay for his work. There were 30 other young people in the camp from many of the countries of Europe. Henry, who is an actual person, told the following story of his experiences:

Our project was to rebuild a burnt-out convent and make it into an old-age home for ex-miners. The work was hard—knocking down walls, clearing away rubble, picking out good bricks and cleaning them off, mixing cement, laying bricks, and so on.

We started working at 5:30 in the morning and stopped at 8 for breakfast. Then we stopped again at 10 for tea, at 12 for lunch, at 3 for tea, and at 6 for supper. The reason that we ate so often was that we didn't eat so well. The food was always the same: bread and butter and tea, tea and bread and butter, bread and butter and soup, stew and bread and butter and water. There wasn't much money for these work camps.

After a hard day's work, almost every

night was an activity night. Monday nights we invited people from the village for tea and dancing. At first they were a little suspicious. They couldn't understand why 30 people should come from all over the world to work for them free. But soon they became friendly, helping with the work, bringing us vegetables which were very welcome, and inviting us to their homes for tea.

Wednesday nights we sang the songs of different nations. Each person taught us the songs of his country. On Friday night we carried on planned discussions within the group. Persons told about life in their countries. We talked about the problems of war and peace.

We learned to understand and respect one another's point of view.

We met the people in the village and in neighboring towns, and—more important—they met us. After knowing me, those Belgian people will no longer think that every American is a millionaire in a Cadillac smoking a big cigar. So we helped remove their prejudices.

Now that I'm home, I tell my friends about my impressions of people of other countries, about everybody's desire for peace. The home we worked on is now open, and many old miners are living there. The people in that Belgian village know the benefits of building instead of destroying, of working, not for war, but for peace and understanding among men.

1 *The UN Is Set Up to Work for Peace*

You have read that, out of the horror and suffering of the First World War, a demand for permanent peace arose. Then the leaders of the world organized the League of Nations. The Second World War had tanks, flame throwers, huge bombers and blockbuster bombs—not to mention the atomic bomb. These weapons caused much more terror and destruction than those of the First World War. The atomic bomb and the hydrogen bomb were so destructive that many people feared atomic warfare would destroy mankind. More than ever it seemed necessary for the nations of the world to organize for permanent peace.

Planning for the United Nations. President Franklin D. Roosevelt, like Woodrow Wilson earlier, was a leader in the planning of a new peace organization. The four freedoms and the Atlantic Charter were drawn up before the United States entered the Second World War. They outlined the kind of world peace-loving people hoped for. (See page 567.) During the war President Roosevelt met frequently with leaders of Great Britain and the Soviet Union. At each meeting he spent part of the time planning with them how to preserve peace after the war was won. He did not leave any doubt as to the attitude of the American people. In his fourth inaugural address in January, 1945, he said:

> We have learned that we cannot live alone, at peace; that our own well-being is dependent on the well-being of other nations, far away. We have learned that we must live as men and not as ostriches, nor as dogs in the manger.
>
> We have learned to be citizens of the world, members of the human community.

Out of the hopes and plans of peace-

UNITED NATIONS

World court meets. These are judges of the International Court of Justice meeting to hear a case. Judges in Europe usually wear wigs.

minded people was born the United Nations. President Roosevelt did not live to see it set up. He died on April 12, 1945. On April 25 President Harry S. Truman opened the conference at San Francisco that wrote the Charter of the United Nations.

As you read about the United Nations, do not be surprised to find that you are reminded in many ways of the League of Nations. Some of the people who helped plan the UN had worked in the League. They knew which parts of the League had worked well and where the weaknesses had been. They used their experience to plan the new world organization. Furthermore, the UN was much like the League because it had the same problems to solve.

The UN, like the League, is a world organization of independent states, not a world government. It will do its job well only as long as the member nations, especially the great powers, can agree on the policies to be carried out. Those who planned the UN expected it to be changed as the nations learned by experience how to improve it. Some hoped that the UN Charter, with changes as needed, might become the lasting basis of a world organization for peace. In 1957 the UN had 81 member nations.

Purposes of the UN. The United Nations has these main purposes: to help keep nations friendly and at peace; to help improve conditions of living everywhere in the world; to promote respect for human rights; to help nations cooperate for these ends.

These purposes are closely related to one another. There will always be differences and disputes among nations, just as there are always arguments among people in our country and among leaders in our Congress. But if leaders of all nations meet together to talk over their differences, they are likely to find ways of settling them without fighting. If all peoples have an opportunity to earn a decent living, a major cause of war will have been removed. If war does not destroy homes, factories, and crops, people will have more to use and enjoy. If there is no fear of war, people can enjoy their freedom in safety. If all peoples enjoy democratic rights, no dictator can mislead his country into war. On such beliefs as these, the United Nations was built.

The General Assembly at work. The diagram on page 586 shows the major parts of the United Nations that were set up to achieve these purposes. The General Assembly is the place where all the members of the UN meet to talk about the problems of the world. The

The world of the United Nations. The numbers indicate cities where UN agencies are located: (1) New York, UN Headquarters; (2) Washington, D.C., International Bank and Monetary Fund; (3) Montreal, International Civil Aviation Organization; (4) Paris, UNESCO; (5) The Hague, International Court of Justice; (6) Berne, Universal Postal Union; (7) Rome, Food and Agriculture Organization; (8) Geneva, WHO, International Telecommunication Union, International Labor Organization.

Assembly receives and discusses reports from all other parts of the UN. It sends committees to investigate and report back to it on trouble spots in the world. On the basis of the reports it recommends what should be done.

A recommendation by the Assembly is not a command; a member nation is not obliged to obey it. Yet its recommendations have very great force because they are supported by world opinion. As a rule a nation will hesitate and think twice before it stands up against the united opinion of most of the na-

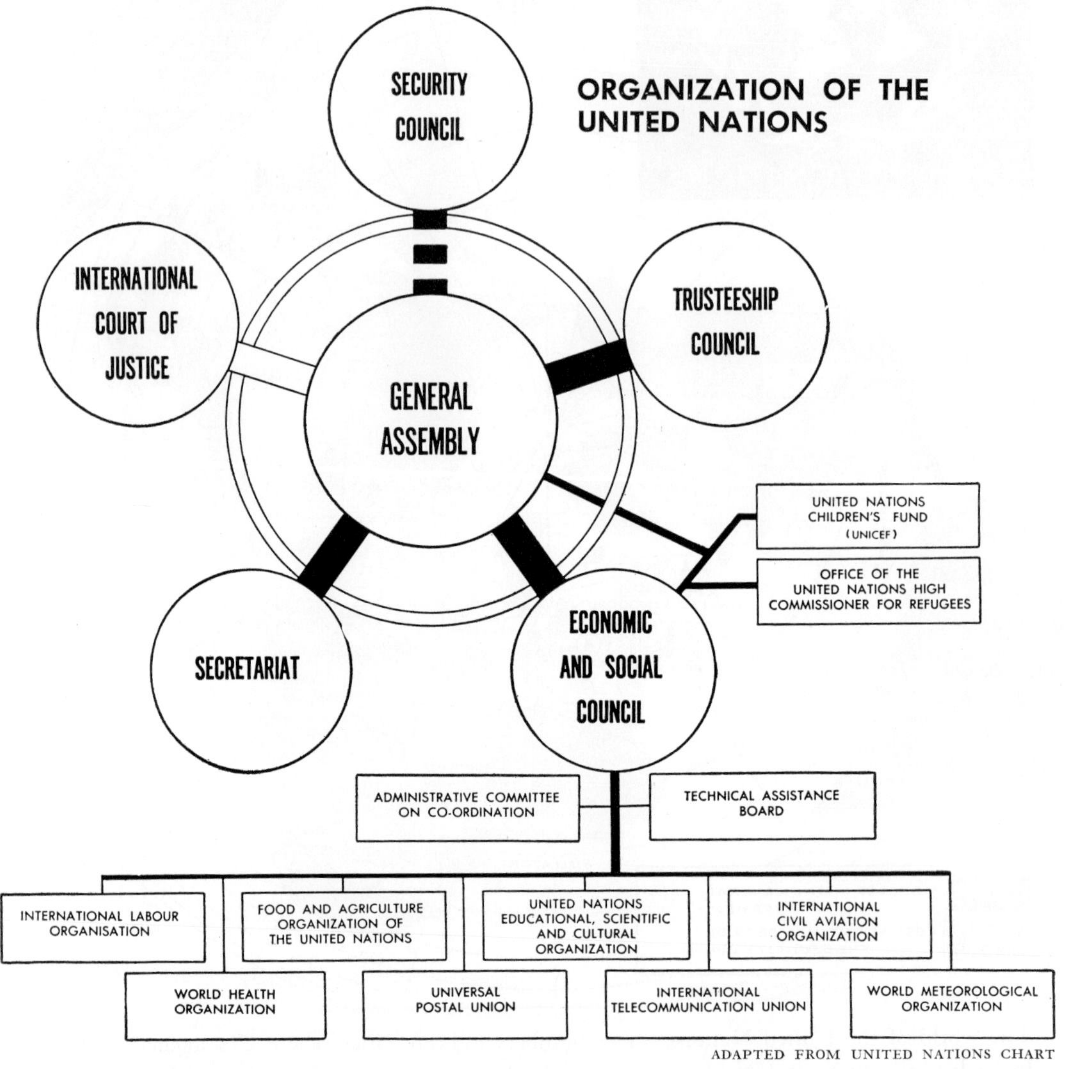

This chart shows the principal parts of the United Nations. Do you know what the main duties of each part are? Can you give the initials by which each agency is known?

tions of the world. The Assembly usually meets during the last three months of each year.

Duties of the Security Council. The Security Council meets all the time. The five great powers—China, France, the Soviet Union, the United Kingdom (Great Britain), and the United States—are its permanent members. The other six members are elected by the Assembly, each for a term of two years.

When the Security Council makes a decision, all member nations of the UN are obligated to obey it. To pass the Security Council, a proposal has to have seven votes. If the matter is important, it must receive the votes of all five permanent members. Thus, even if all other members of the Council favor an important proposal, one permanent member can keep it from passing by voting "no." This power of the permanent members is called the veto.

The Security Council is the part of the UN that is directly responsible for keeping peace. Every nation when it joins the UN agrees to practice tolerance and to live in peace with all other nations as a good neighbor. When a disagreement arises between member nations, the Security Council is expected to try every possible way to settle it peacefully. As in the case of the Assembly, the force of public opinion is strong, for the disagreement is openly discussed in Council meetings. If a nation refuses to accept a just and peaceful settlement, it stands accused before the world.

If one nation attacks another, the Security Council has power to call on (though not to require) all other members to send armed forces to help put down the aggressor. (The aggressor is the one that attacks.) In that case there would be war, but in an important way it would be different from previous wars. The law-abiding nations of the world would be punishing a nation that broke its promise and violated the law. (For an example see page 598.)

The UN Secretariat. The Secretariat is the part of the UN organization that keeps the wheels turning. It makes preparations for the meetings. It provides secretaries and translators, and it provides economic and social experts to carry on investigations. The members of the Secretariat are from many coun-

UNITED NATIONS

UN in the field. Representatives of the UN Trusteeship Council visit a West African tribal chief. The Council regularly sends committees to the various trust colonies to investigate and report on conditions.

tries of the world. At the head of the Secretariat is the Secretary-General, one of the most important officials of the UN.

The International Court. The International Court of Justice of the UN takes the place of the World Court of the League of Nations. It has 15 judges, elected by the Assembly and the Security Council. The judges may be citizens of any country, but no two are to be from the same country. In general it may be said that the International Court deals with cases that nations agree to bring to it.

The Trusteeship Council. People read and hear most about the General Assembly and the Security Council, but other parts of the UN are doing very important work for the peace and progress of the world.

One of these parts is called the Trusteeship Council. It supervises the work

UNITED NATIONS

UNICEF helps. One of the many agencies set up by the UN is UNICEF (United Nations International Children's Emergency Fund). It provides for some of the needs of helpless children. This Greek girl, receiving a pair of UNICEF shoes, signs a receipt.

UN technical assistance. Two experts, working on a UN technical assistance mission, discuss a flood-control project in Greece. The project made a large area of land useful for farming. By helping free peoples improve their ways of living, we make them stronger to resist communism.

UNITED NATIONS

of member nations who run a number of colonies. These include colonies that were taken away from Germany after the First World War and islands in the Pacific taken from Japan after the Second World War. Under the UN these colonies are called trusts. The countries in charge, called trustees, promise to help the people in these colonies improve their ways of living and become self-governing. They make annual reports to the Trusteeship Council. The Council sends committees to the colonies to investigate and report on conditions.

The Work of the Economic and Social Council. Another part of the UN is the United Nations Economic and Social Council (ECOSOC, pronounced ĕc′ō sŏc). It has the special task of helping peoples all over the world to improve their living conditions. The activities of ECOSOC are so many that we cannot even mention all that it does in a single year. It carries on its work through a number of commissions and in cooperation with special organizations. We can tell of only a few of the most important of its activities. With these discussions as examples, your class can arrange for special reports on the other organizations and other activities of ECOSOC.

Technical assistance. One important ECOSOC activity has been to help countries that have not advanced so rapidly as others in industry and agriculture. Through ECOSOC all interested groups and nations work together to help countries that need and ask for aid to improve their living standards. ECOSOC sends people from underdeveloped countries to more advanced countries to learn modern methods and special skills. Then these people return to their own countries to use their knowledge and to teach others.

ECOSOC also sends many experts to countries that need help. They teach people how to fight diseases. They teach both children and grownups how to read and write. They teach farmers how to use farm machinery and conserve the soil. In the 1950s such experts worked in more than 80 countries.

As the people in these countries learn to produce more, they are able to live better and buy more goods from the countries that helped them. Thus a nation that takes part in the UN plan to aid poorer countries is not only doing good to others; it is also increasing its own business.

Declaration of Human Rights. In the field of democratic rights, an important step taken by the UN was the adoption of the Universal Declaration of Human Rights. It was adopted by the UN in December, 1948. The Declaration lists the rights each person should have. Besides those in our Bill of Rights, it includes the right to social security, the right to work, and the right to join labor unions. It also includes the right to a good life, adequate income, education, and leisure. The Declaration also emphasizes the duties of every individual to his community—including the duty of respecting the equal rights of everyone else.

UNESCO. The United Nations Educational, Scientific, and Cultural Organization (UNESCO, pronounced ū nĕs′cō) works for lasting peace principally by getting the peoples of the world to know one another better. For that purpose it is essential that newspapers, movies, and radio everywhere in the world should be used in the service of peace and human welfare. It is also essential that all peoples be free to exchange ideas. UNESCO studies the barriers that prevent the free flow of ideas. Then it recommends international agreements to remove those barriers.

UNITED NATIONS

Studying arithmetic. This Haitian boy attends a school that was built as part of a UNESCO project in Haiti.

Education. UNESCO helps countries exchange students and teachers with one another. It arranges summer meetings that teachers from many countries attend. By living and studying together, the teachers learn the customs of other countries. By exchanging ideas on methods of teaching, they promote better education throughout the world. They discuss ways of improving school textbooks so that pupils will learn to understand and respect the

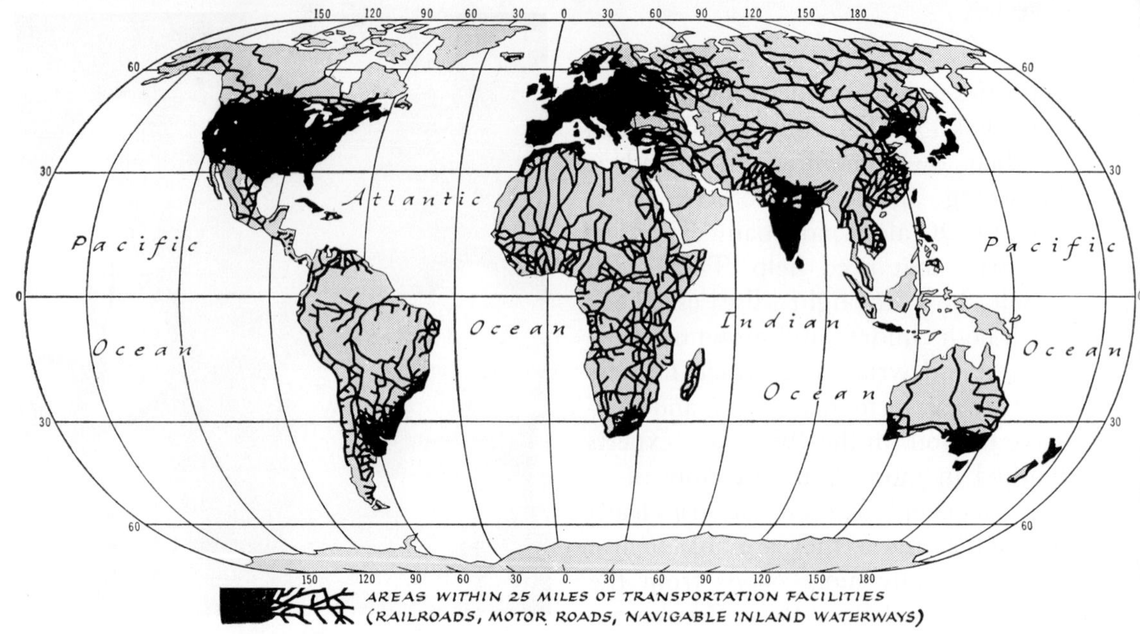

The world's transportation facilities. Adequate transportation is important for improved living conditions. What parts of the world have many transportation facilities? What parts of the world have few?

peoples of other countries. UNESCO also encourages the establishment of work camps, like the one described at the beginning of this chapter.

WHO. The World Health Organization (WHO) works to improve health all over the world. One example of its activities is its campaign against tuberculosis. In Europe alone its field workers have given skin tests to 50 million children and young people to see whether or not they had tuberculosis. (Have you ever had such a skin test? Many young Americans have.) The WHO workers followed up the skin tests by vaccinating many millions of people to help them avoid the disease. WHO has sent trained workers with the latest equipment to a number of countries to introduce new methods in preventing and treating tuberculosis.

In the 1950s WHO started an anti-yaws campaign. Yaws is a crippling tropical disease. People suffering from it cannot work for a living and have to be supported by others. In most cases just one injection of penicillin will cure it. By 1955 WHO had cured about 4 million people who had been suffering from the disease.

There are many other special agencies that work with the UN. Their names suggest the fields in which they work. For example, there are the Food and Agricultural Organization (FAO), the International Labor Organization (ILO), the Universal Postal Union, and the International Telecommunications Union.

The UN in the world community. Underlying the activities of the United Nations is the fact that the world has become a single community. Poverty, ignorance, disease, or injustice in any one part is bound to hurt every other part. Therefore, when a country co-operates with others to do away with poverty, ignorance, disease, and injustice, it is helping itself as well as other peoples.

2 *The United States Helps the Free World Against Communism*

In the past, after a war, the nations of the world divided into groups, and such groups soon meant rivalry and more war. Many people hoped that the United Nations would create "one world"; in other words, that all the countries would work together for peace.

The democracies and the communist states disagree. However, even as the organization of the United Nations was being set up, the members divided into two groups. One group was led by the Soviet Union; the other was led by the United States. People immediately began to fear a future war between the two groups. To understand the danger, we must know something of the Soviet Union, and how its way of life differs from ours.

Communist dictatorship. The government of the Soviet Union is government under a dictator. It is run by the Communist party, to which only a small proportion of the people belong. Not every citizen can join, even if he wants to, for members of the Communist party are chosen by party leaders. Even within the party, a small group of men make the important decisions. No opposition to the government is allowed, and no other party is permitted. When an election is held, the people have the choice between voting for the Communist candidates or not at all. They do not have a choice between diffent candidates for the same office. The Communist party decides what the people may read in the newspapers, hear over the radio, and learn in the schools. The rights of free speech, free press, and trial by jury have never been enjoyed by the people of Russia in the past, nor are they today. The way the people of the Soviet Union earn a living is also different from ours. The Communist party tries to provide for the needs of the Russian people by planning. It decides beforehand how much wheat is to be raised, how many houses are to be built, how much clothing is to be made, how many automobiles are to be manufactured, and so on. It also decides how many guns, tanks, warplanes, and atomic bombs are to be made. In order to carry out its plans, the Communist government must assign a certain number of workers to each industry. It forbids workers to change their jobs without permission. Thus a Russian person has no freedom either as a citizen or as a worker.

American freedom. Those who believe in democracy find many faults in the communist system. Americans are opposed to government that takes away from all persons their freedom and their equal rights. We believe that the individual should be protected by law against his government. That is why our Bill of Rights is important. We believe that the government should be responsible to the people. That is why we hold elections regularly. That is why the people must be free to speak and print what they believe and to express their opinions through opposition parties. We believe, with Thomas Jefferson, that the only safe and just government is one that has to go back regularly to the people for their approval.

With regard to earning a living, we believe that every person must be free to select his work. Since he has a free choice, he will select work he is fitted for and enjoys doing. To earn the rewards that come with success, he will do his best at his job. He will be encouraged to invent ways to do the job better.

A free people, we believe, will make greater progress in producing goods than an enslaved people. We can point to the fact that the standard of living of the American people is much higher than that of the Russian people.

Though the communist system and the American system are very different from one another, differences do not necessarily mean that war must come. In the years after the Second World War, each side was suspicious of the other. Leaders of the Soviet Union said that the aim of the United States was to destroy communism. Americans pointed to the writings of the Soviet leaders. These writings state that communists must not rest until they have established communism in all countries. But the world hoped for peace.

Action to halt the spread of communism. After the war, communists gained control of European countries bordering on Russia. Within each country a Communist party was formed. Though a minority, it seized power. It destroyed its opponents, often by executing them. By 1940 all the countries of eastern Europe except Greece were under the communist system. Their governments, except Yugoslavia, followed the Soviet Union in every way. The communists could be expected to try next to take over the governments of Greece and Turkey, Russia's southern neighbor in Asia Minor. Sure enough, armed guerrillas invaded Greece from her communist neighbors on the north, and the Soviet Union began to pick a quarrel with Turkey.

Aid to Greece and Turkey. Many Americans feared that communism would expand until it won control over all Europe. Then it might be strong enough to attack the United States. They believed that the United States could defend itself and save other democratic nations only by preventing the communists from spreading any farther in Europe.

Why had some countries fallen to the communists? The governments had been too weak to oppose communism. The people had accepted the false promises of communism because they had been suffering from want. The United States could prevent the spread of communism in two ways. It could help free governments arm against communism. It could help improve the living conditions of free peoples.

Accordingly, on March 12, 1947, President Truman asked Congress to grant money to Greece and Turkey to improve living conditions in those nations and to strengthen their armed forces. He said that the United States should help any country to protect itself against attempts of communists to take it over by force. The aid was given, and Greece and Turkey remained free of communism.

European recovery through the Marshall Plan. Greece and Turkey were not the only countries in need of help. Almost all the peoples of western Europe were suffering as a result of the world wars. Their farms had been laid waste and their factories destroyed. They were unable to produce enough food and clothing for themselves. They had no money to buy what they needed. In Italy and France there were strong Communist parties that might seize power any minute.

Communism was not so strong in Great Britain, but the British people were desperate. They had long been accustomed to importing most of their food and paying for it mainly by exporting manufactured goods. Now their industries were destroyed, and they had no money to pay for food. Right after the war the United States lent Britain 4 billion dollars, but that had been used up.

Western Europe needed help, and the United States was the only country able to give that help. The United States had already done much. It had given away 40 billion dollars' worth of war lend-lease without asking that any of it be paid back. It had spent more billions in war relief. But after the war the European countries still depended on the United States for help.

In June, 1947, General George C. Marshall, then United States Secretary of State, proposed the Marshall Plan. Let the European countries get together, he said, and prepare a program of recovery that they would be ready to follow. Then the United States would contribute money to help carry out the program. Sixteen European nations met and prepared such a program. The Soviet Union and the other communist countries did not take part. In 1948 Congress made a first grant of 5 billion dollars for European recovery. With American aid the western European countries were able to rebuild their farms and factories. Life was still far from easy, but their peoples gradually began again to earn a living. They did not adopt communism.

The technical aid program. In 1949 President Truman proposed a plan to help underdeveloped countries. It was called the Point Four program because it was the fourth in a list of points describing our future relations with the rest of the world. The plan was like the one already being carried on by the

U.S. aid. A French farmer cultivates his farm with an American tractor. Under the Marshall Plan, money and equipment have been given to free nations of Europe to rebuild their farms, factories, and armed forces.

ACME

IT'S A SMALLER WORLD

As we invent ways of traveling faster, the world becomes smaller as measured in time. People can get around more rapidly and exchange goods more easily. The representatives of nations can get together to discuss world problems.

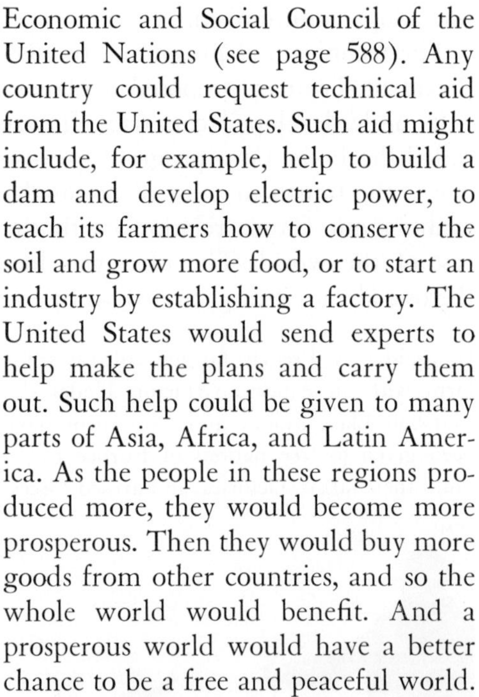

Economic and Social Council of the United Nations (see page 588). Any country could request technical aid from the United States. Such aid might include, for example, help to build a dam and develop electric power, to teach its farmers how to conserve the soil and grow more food, or to start an industry by establishing a factory. The United States would send experts to help make the plans and carry them out. Such help could be given to many parts of Asia, Africa, and Latin America. As the people in these regions produced more, they would become more prosperous. Then they would buy more goods from other countries, and so the whole world would benefit. And a prosperous world would have a better chance to be a free and peaceful world.

U.S. leadership in regional groups. The United States did not stop with money aid to Europe and the technical aid program. The noncommunist countries were too weak to defend themselves separately. They needed to cooperate in their defense against communism. The United States took the leadership in organizing the free nations in regional groups for self-defense.

This leadership meant a change in our foreign policy. In two world wars the United States had tried to remain neutral by keeping out of European affairs. Each time its world-wide interests had drawn it into the war. Many Americans, including leaders in both Republican and Democratic parties, now took a different attitude. They saw that in our interdependent world a country as important as the United States would almost surely be involved in any major war. This time, instead of keeping apart from other countries, the United States took a leading role in the UN. It worked to make the UN a successful organization through which nations might settle their differences. The United States also became a member of several regional groups.

OAS. The United States joined with the other 20 American republics in changing the Pan American Union, which you read about on page 499, into the Organization of the American

States (OAS). Its charter, drawn up in Bogotá (bō gô tä′), Colombia, in 1948, established a system much like that of the United Nations. It used the Pan American Union in Washington, D.C., as its secretariat. The purposes of the Organization are the same as those of the UN.

At the meeting in Bogotá, the American republics agreed upon ways to settle disputes among themselves peacefully. At Rio de Janeiro (rē′ô dĕ jȧ-nā′rō), Brazil, in 1947, they had already agreed that, if any American nation is attacked by another, all the other American countries will come to the aid of the country attacked.

NATO. In 1949 the United States joined with Canada and 10 nations of western Europe in signing the North Atlantic Treaty. Under this treaty the 12 nations agreed to cooperate in their common defense. One of their plans was to establish a single armed force to which all would contribute. This force would be ready to defend western Europe against possible attack. General Dwight D. Eisenhower was the first commander in chief of the united armed forces of the North Atlantic Treaty Organization (NATO).

SEATO. The United States also joined with Australia, New Zealand, and other free countries in the Pacific in the Southeast Asia Treaty Organization (SEATO). Its purpose is to stop the spread of communism in that part of the world.

3 *Striving for Peace*

The opposition between the free nations, led by the United States, and the communist countries, led by the Soviet Union, caused serious difficulties in the world. The United States sought earnestly to solve these difficulties and establish a firm peace.

The problem of controlling atomic energy. An important example of the deep differences between free and communist nations was the problem of controlling atomic energy. Atomic energy could be used for peacetime purposes with benefits to mankind that can

HOMAI VYARAWALLA, "BUSINESS WEEK"

Bhakra Dam, India. This is an example of projects made possible by financial aid from the United States. Such aid helps other countries raise their standard of living.

hardly be imagined today. Or it could be used in the atomic bomb and the hydrogen bomb to destroy mankind. It was obvious that the nations of the world had to cooperate and see to it that atomic energy was used for building, not for destroying.

The United States proposed a plan to establish international atomic control. Under this plan the UN would own and run all atomic-energy plants everywhere in the world. The Soviet Union rejected the American plan. It said that all nations should destroy their atomic bombs. Then a United Nations committee would inspect all atomic-energy plants to see that no more bombs were made.

The free world could not accept the Soviet plan. While a committee was inspecting known atomic-energy plants, some nations might be making atomic bombs in secret plants. If any nation ever got ahead in the production of atomic weapons secretly, the rest of the world would be at its mercy. The UN, therefore, must control all work in atomic energy. In the meantime President Eisenhower proposed that the nations cooperate in using atomic energy for peaceful purposes; for example, to generate electric power and to carry on research in health. (See page 636.)

"Open-sky" proposal. At the Geneva Conference in 1955, President Eisenhower proposed to the Soviet Union an "open-sky" plan as a first step toward disarmament. The Soviet Union and the United States would exchange blueprints of their military establishments, and each country would permit the other to fly planes over its territory to take photographs of its military installations. This information would prevent a surprise attack by one country on the other. In 1957 the Soviet Union offered to accept the President's suggestion in part.

The problem of aggression in Korea. The Korean (kō̇ rē′ăn) story shows how the opposition between the communist and noncommunist nations threatened to explode into a third world war.

By agreement, after the Second World War, the Soviet Union occupied the northern half of Korea and the United States the southern half. The boundary was the 38th parallel. It was also part of the agreement that Korea was to be united and become an independent nation. However, when a UN committee went to Korea to help establish a government, the Soviet Union refused to permit the committee to go into northern Korea. The UN committee then supervised an election in southern Korea. A government was set up, and the United Nations recognized it as the Republic of Korea. The United States withdrew its army from the new nation. In North Korea another government was set up under the supervision of the Soviet Union.

Now China came into the story. While the free countries had stopped communism in western Europe, they had not stopped it in Asia. After several years of fighting, Chinese Communist armies won control over all of China except the island of Formosa (fôr mō′sȧ). The old Chinese government retreated to that island. The Soviet Union demanded that the Chinese Communist government be given the seat in the UN Security Council held by China as a permanent member. (See page 586.) In January, 1950, when the Soviet demand was voted down, the Soviet representative walked out of the Security Council. Soon the Soviet representatives stopped attending the meetings of all parts of the UN. The UN carried on without the Soviet Union.

On June 24, 1950, armies from northern Korea crossed the 38th parallel and invaded southern Korea, now the Republic of Korea. It was clearly an example of aggression and a violation of the UN Charter. The whole world waited to see what the United States would do. Would it carry out its pledge under the UN Charter and oppose aggression with its armed forces?

UN action in Korea. Within a few days after the attack two things happened. With the Soviet Union absent, the UN Security Council asked the member nations to repel the attack. President Truman ordered American forces to help the Republic of Korea defend itself. Other nations sent soldiers, ships, and planes to Korea. General Douglas MacArthur was named commander of the UN forces. For the first time in history, armed forces were acting under the flag of a world organization to defend a country against attack.

The communist attack was so well prepared that for the first three months the UN forces in Korea were driven back until they held only a small beachhead. Then the tide turned. The UN forces pushed the communists back and followed them into northern Korea. In

NATO flag. General Eisenhower, Commander of the North Atlantic Treaty Organization forces when this picture was taken, looks at the new flag of SHAPE (Supreme Headquarters, Allied Powers in Europe). The swords and olive branches suggest arming to preserve peace. The Latin motto means "Vigilance is the price of liberty."

WIDE WORLD

Divided world. This is how the world is divided between communist and noncommunist countries. Yugoslavia, a communist country, is not under the control of the Soviet Union.

December, 1950, the UN forces were about to complete the liberation of Korea. Just then huge Chinese Communist armies crossed over into Korea and again drove the UN forces back. For a second time communist forces had used military power in violation of the United Nations Charter.

The war in Korea continued. In the UN, meanwhile, the member nations were trying hard to find a way to end the fighting. An armistice ending the fighting was signed in July, 1953. Korea remained divided as before.

Peace by the threat of retaliation. Besides Korea, the communists attempted to expand by force in Vietnam in southeast Asia. That country, like Korea, was divided between free and communist governments.

UNITED NATIONS

Security Council. A historic moment in the UN Security Council, July 7, 1950. The members are voting to recommend that a "unified command under the United States" be formed to oppose aggression in Korea in the name of the UN.

President Eisenhower and his Secretary of State, John Foster Dulles, decided that the United States would not wait to send its armed forces to any spot in the world where the communists decided to start trouble. The United States would help strengthen the forces of free countries to meet small-scale attacks. Most important, the United States would build a tremendous striking force of jet planes and missiles that could drop atomic and hydrogen bombs anywhere in the world. Such a threat of retaliation would prevent any possible enemy from starting another world war.

Crisis in the Middle East. The crisis in the Middle East went back to 1955 when the communists sold arms to Egypt. At the same time Egypt was seeking aid from the United States and Great Britain to build a huge dam.

In July, 1956, the United States and Great Britain decided not to provide money for the dam. A week later Egypt seized the Suez Canal. The canal had been run by an international company. It was important principally because through it came from the Middle East almost the entire oil supply of western Europe. Now Egypt could cut off that oil supply at will. Another danger was the possibility that the communists might gain a foothold in the Middle East.

Great Britain and France negotiated with Egypt through the United Nations. But Egypt refused to place the canal under international control.

Israel had many complaints against Egypt, including the charge that Egyptian guerrillas were attacking across the border. In October, 1956, first Israel and then Great Britain and France attacked Egypt. Israel seized a large part of Egyptian territory. But before British and French troops could seize the Suez Canal, the Egyptians blocked it by sinking ships in the channel.

The United Nations, with United States support, demanded that the three nations withdraw from Egypt. Presi-

MOHAMMED YOUSSEF, "BUSINESS WEEK"

Clearing the Suez Canal. Egypt blocked the Canal before the British and French seized it. Until it was cleared, oil from the Middle East to Europe had to be shipped around Africa.

dent Eisenhower said that they had violated the charter of the United Nations by using force. The three nations withdrew and United Nations troops were stationed in Egypt. But soon Egypt took over control, and the UN force was limited to policing the border between Egypt and Israel. Egypt remained in control of the Suez Canal. The Middle East remained an area of crisis.

Eisenhower's Middle East Doctrine. At one time there was danger that the Soviet Union might send troops into the Middle East. President Eisenhower, with the support of Congress, announced his Middle East Doctrine in 1957. If any country in the Middle East, in danger of communist attack, asked the United States for military aid, the United States would give that aid. Eisenhower's Middle East Doctrine was a blunt warning to the Soviet Union that open communist intervention in the Middle East would mean war.

Communist oppression in Hungary. At the same time as the crisis in the Middle East, the people of Hungary rose up against the communist government that had been imposed on them. Russian soldiers, tanks, and planes put down the revolt with a great slaughter of Hungarians. The communists paid no attention to repeated UN demands that they leave Hungary. They did not even permit Dag Hammarskjold, Secretary-General of the UN, to visit Hungary to determine the facts of the situation.

Summary

After the Second World War, as after the First World War, the nations of the world tried to build for a peaceful and prosperous world. They set up an organization, the UN, to preserve peace. In the UN General Assembly the representatives of all member nations have the opportunity to express their countries' views on world problems. The settling of disputes and the preserving of peace are the special responsibility of the Security Council. The great work of improving living conditions and strengthening democratic rights in the world is carried on by ECOSOC. It works through its many commissions and with special organizations.

The UN can be successful only if the members keep their promises and co-operate for peace. The success of the UN has been endangered by the continued disagreement between the communist and the noncommunist countries.

Many people were afraid that the Soviet leaders planned to establish their form of government all over the world. The Soviet Union, on the other hand, charged that the rest of the world was planning to attack it.

Because of its democracy and productive power, the United States became the leader of the anticommunist nations. It gave assistance to countries that wanted to defend themselves against communism. Under the technical aid program we sent aid to underdeveloped areas of the world to help their inhabitants improve their way of life. Under the Marshall Plan the United States helped the peoples of western Europe restore their factories and farms so that they could support themselves. The United States joined alliances with other countries in the North Atlantic Treaty Organization (NATO), the Organization of American States (OAS), and the Southeast Asia Treaty Organization (SEATO).

Communist aggression in Korea endangered world peace. By acting against the aggressors, UN leaders hoped to strengthen free governments everywhere. The United States provided most of the armed forces that stopped the communists in Korea.

After Korea and Vietnam were divided, the United States prepared a great military force to discourage any possible enemy from attacking the free world. It also continued to build up the strength of other free nations to resist. In the Middle East crisis it prevented Russia from openly supporting Egypt with armed forces.

At the same time the United States worked for peace. President Eisen-

(*Continued on page 604*)

The first atomic submarine. This is the *Nautilus,* the first submarine driven by power derived from atomic energy. Built for the United States Navy, it underwent its first sea tests in January, 1955. It cruised 1,000 miles, running on nuclear power for almost 150 hours. Details about its atomic power unit are closely guarded secrets.

OFFICIAL NAVY PHOTOGRAPH

MAIN EVENTS OF UNIT 8, 1920–1955

Building and governing the nation	*Earning a living*	*Science, arts, and the people*	*The nation and its neighbors*
1921–1923 Warren G. Harding, Pres. (Republican)		**1921** Immigration limited	**1921–1922** Washington Arms Conference
1923–1929 Calvin Coolidge, Pres. (Republican)			
	1924 Regular transcontinental airmail service		
		1926 First flight across North Pole	
			1928 Paris Peace Pact to outlaw war
1929–1933 Herbert Hoover, Pres. (Republican)	**1929** Depression	**1929** Byrd's first expedition to Antarctica	
			1931 Japan invaded Manchuria
1933–1945 Franklin D. Roosevelt, Pres. (Democrat)	**1933** New Deal began		**1933** Good Neighbor Policy
1933 Amendment XX	**1933** TVA		**1933** Hitler in Germany
1933 Amendment XXI			
			1935 Italy invaded Ethiopia
	1935 Wagner Act (labor relations)		**1935** First U.S. neutrality laws
	1935 Wages and Hours Act		
	1935 Social Security Act		
	1935 CIO founded		
		1936 Carl Sandburg's *The People, Yes*	
	1939 Regular air service, U.S.–Europe	**1939** John Steinbeck's *The Grapes of Wrath*	**1939** Second World War in Europe
		1940 Population 131,669,275	

MAIN EVENTS OF UNIT 8, 1920–1955

Building and governing the nation	*Earning a living*	*Science, arts, and the people*	*The nation and its neighbors*
	1941 Many industries converted for war production	**1941** First commercial television license	**1941** Lend-Lease Act **1941** Atlantic Charter **1941** Dec. 7, attack on Pearl Harbor
1945–1953 Harry S. Truman, Pres. (Democrat)	**1945** Industries reconverted for peacetime production		**1945** First atomic bomb **1945** End of Second World War **1945** United Nations **1946** Philippines independent
	1947 Taft-Hartley Act		
			1948 Marshall Plan **1948** Organization of American States **1949** Point Four program announced **1949** NATO
	1950 Minimum wage, 75 cents per hour	**1950** Population 150,697,361	**1950** Korean War began
1951 Amendment XXII **1953 Dwight D. Eisenhower, Pres.** (Republican)			**1953** Korean Armistice
			1954 SEATO

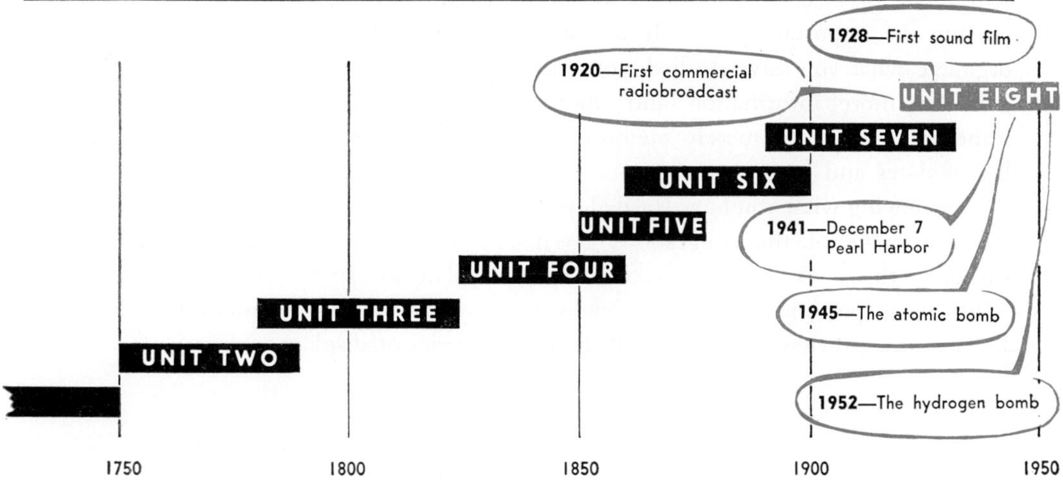

1928—First sound film
1920—First commercial radiobroadcast
UNIT EIGHT
UNIT SEVEN
UNIT SIX
UNIT FIVE
1941—December 7 Pearl Harbor
UNIT FOUR
UNIT THREE
1945—The atomic bomb
UNIT TWO
1952—The hydrogen bomb
1750
1800
1850
1900
1950

hower proposed developing the power of the atom for peaceful purposes. He proposed that, as a first step toward disarmament, the United States and the Soviet Union be permitted to photograph each other's military installations from the air.

For a Quick Review

1. What are the purposes of the United Nations? Name its main parts.

2. What are some of the things that the United Nations and its agencies have done successfully?

3. What is each of the following and why is each important: OAS, NATO, the Point Four program, the Marshall Plan?

4. What actions did the United States take to stop the spread of communism?

5. What actions did the United States take to promote disarmament and international accord?

Learning to Study More Easily

REVIEWING

The purpose of reviewing is to organize what you have learned about a subject. By organizing your knowledge, you will understand it better and remember it longer.

To organize facts is to see relationships between them. How do the facts fit together? How do they help explain one another?

To organize what you have learned, you must begin with the important points and big ideas. Follow through the connections between them. Then the smaller details will fall into place, explaining and supporting the important points. If you will organize what you studied, you will gain far more information and understanding than if you merely memorize a list of dates and facts.

In reviewing what you have learned, you can use many of the suggestions given earlier in this book. Consider each of the following as possible means of reviewing:

1. The unit previews. See page 20. Read the unit previews, thinking of them as a short short history of our nation. They will help you see the high points.
2. Perhaps your class can agree on a list of topics to cover the year's work. The students can prepare summaries of these topics. Remember the hints on preparing summaries given on pages 186 and 187.
3. Time lines. See page 458. Can you adapt those suggestions to a review of your year's study?
4. An outline. See page 162. You might use the table of contents of this book as the skeleton outline to be developed.
5. Class discussion. See page 392. How can you use these suggestions for review?
6. Panel discussions. See page 630. Plan a review through panel discussions.
7. Bulletin board. See page 580. Can you plan one review bulletin board for the year's work, or should you arrange a series of displays?

Unit Roundup

HIGH POINTS OF THE UNIT

In Unit 8 you have studied four important aspects of the continuing search by the United States for peace and prosperity in the modern world. These aspects are the development of mass production, the effort to end depression and poverty at home, the defense of democratic ideas in the Second World War, and the attempts to work toward lasting peace and prosperity after the war was won. To summarize them, your class could plan a bulletin-board review.

First, through discussion, make a list of important events during the 1930s, the 1940s, and the 1950s. You could start with the four topics suggested above as headings and place under the appropriate one each event you decide to include.

When the class has decided on the list of events to be included, decide how each one could be presented graphically—that is, in a map, cartoon, chart, or picture. Let each student be responsible for preparing a graphic presentation of one or more of the items so that each one will be covered.

Divide the bulletin board into four sections, or one for each of the major topics of the review. Decide on a suitable, interesting title for each section and post it conspicuously. Arrange the charts, maps, and other materials under the appropriate heading. By reading the entire board, a student should have a review of recent efforts in our continuing search for peace and prosperity.

EXPAND YOUR VOCABULARY

1. Can you define each of the following words or phrases? Use each of them in a sentence to show that you have made it a part of your working vocabulary.

assembly line	labor contract
bargaining agent	mass production
charter	mechanized war
craft union	old-age benefits
human rights	private charities
hybrid	shop steward
impartial	social security laws
industrial union	unemployment insurance
interdependence	

2. The terms in the following list came into wide use for the first time during the Second World War. Many of them are part of our everyday vocabulary now. Check your understanding of each one; look up any meanings that you do not know.

aircraft carrier	jet propulsion
atomic bomb	lend-lease
civilian defense	radar
draft board	rationing

3. You are likely to find the following names, made up of initial letters only, in your newspapers and magazines from time to time. What is the full name of each organization? What does it do?

AFL-CIO	OAS
ECOSOC	SEATO
NATO	UNESCO
NLRB	WHO

HISTORY IN THE MOVIES

1. The film *Despotism* will help you understand how life under a dictatorship is different from life in a democracy. (The word "despotism" means rule by one man or a small group of persons.)

2. The film *Round Trip* suggests how important foreign trade is to the United States and why foreign trade must be a two-way exchange.

WITH CRAYON, RULER, AND PASTE

1. Prepare a picture strip entitled "How the Tractor Has Changed Farm Work." Show the many uses of the tractor and the changes it has made in the farmer's work.

2. Make a picture chart showing as many as possible of the products made from peanuts. Draw sketches and use pictures. What title will you give the chart?

3. Show in a graph the number of members in labor unions in 1920, 1930, 1940, and 1950.

4. Make a picture strip to show the losses that result from strikes. Consider losses to employer, employee, and consumer.

5. What events that you have studied in Unit 8 should be recorded on the large class time line? Decide through class discussion and arrange for a committee to bring the time line up to date.

PUT ON A PLAY

1. Prepare a series of skits to illustrate one of the following:

How collective bargaining is carried on
The purposes and operation of social security laws
The organization and purpose of NATO
The meaning of the four freedoms

2. Plan and present a biographical dramatization of important events in the life of Franklin D. Roosevelt. You might use quotations from his speeches and letters in your script.

3. Choose one of the commissions or specialized agencies of the UN and plan a series of scenes to illustrate the work it has done.

STORIES THERE WAS NO ROOM TO TELL

Each of the topics listed below is mentioned in Unit 8, but its story was too long to tell. Choose one to investigate further and prepare to report on it to the class.

The CIO-AFL
The aluminum industry (you may substitute another new industry—for example, television or plastics)
Improving the world's health—the work of WHO
4-H Clubs at work (you may substitute Future Farmers of America or Future Homemakers of America)
Battles of the Second World War in the Pacific (or the European) Theater

USE YOUR IMAGINATION

1. Write a series of letters that might have been written home by one of the following:

A soldier serving in the Korean fighting
A soldier or sailor serving in the South Pacific battle area during the Second World War
A teen-age boy working in the Civilian Conservation Corps
A WAC on duty in western Europe during the Second World War
A young woman serving on the UN Secretariat staff

2. Prepare an editorial about one part of the New Deal program, such as the work relief measures or the social security laws. Remember that opinions should be stated clearly and facts given to support them.

3. Choose a recent event in international relations and write an editorial commenting on the policy the United States has fol-

lowed in it. Perhaps your editorial can be published in the school paper.

SHOW IT ON A MAP

1. Study the maps given in Chapter 28 of campaigns in the Second World War. Choose one of the major campaigns and prepare a set of more detailed maps to show the military strategy and tactics used in that campaign. Write a paragraph of explanation and post the maps and the explanatory statement on the bulletin board.

2. Make a map showing where UN technical assistance missions worked during one calendar year. Use the most recent information you can find.

3. Prepare a map of your own state showing its major industries. Use appropriate symbols.

YOUR COMMUNITY GROWS WITH THE NATION

1. Is there in your community a manufacturing plant that uses an assembly line? If there is, arrange to visit it and see how it operates.

2. Is there a farm agent in your community? If there is, arrange to interview him and report to the class.

3. What are the principal industries in your community? Have any new ones come in since 1940? Discuss the importance of its industries to the community.

4. Each state, under the social security laws, sets up its own system of unemployment insurance. What is the system in your state and how does it operate?

5. What contributions to the war effort in the Second World War did your community or state make? Include service in the armed forces and contributions on the home front. Did your school help in paper drives, scrap drives, or similar activities? Did the teachers of your school help with rationing? Prepare an illustrated floor talk for the class.

FURTHER READING

BOOKS ABOUT INTERESTING PEOPLE

Dr. George Washington Carver, Scientist by Shirley Graham and George Dewey Lipscomb. Messner, 1944.

General "Ike" Eisenhower by Delos Lovelace. Crowell, 1952.

Henry Ford by Cy Caldwell. Messner, 1947.††

Marconi, Pioneer of Radio by Douglas Coe. Messner, 1943.††

The Courage and the Glory by John J. Floherty. Lippincott, 1942. Eight great Americans of the Second World War.

Thomas Alva Edison, Builder of Civilization by H. Gordan Garbedian, Messner, 1947.††

Young Franklin Roosevelt by Rita H. Kleeman. Messner, 1946.

STORIES OF ADVENTURE AND EVERYDAY LIFE

Bomber Pilot by Philip Harkins. Harcourt, Brace, 1944. Story of the U.S. Army Air Force in the Second World War.

Boom Town Boy by Lois Lenski. Lippincott, 1948. The discovery of oil in Oklahoma.

Jonathan's Doorstep by Helen Clark Fernald. Longmans, 1943. An American girl's experiences during the Second World War.

OTHER INTERESTING ACCOUNTS

Story of Air Transport by James R. Ray. Winston, 1947.

The Bright Design by Katherine B. Shippen, Viking, 1949. The development of knowledge about electricity.††

Understanding Science by William H. Crouse. McGraw-Hill, 1948. Atomic energy and other modern scientific developments.

Unit 9 *The American People Look Ahead*

THE AMERICAN adventure changes but goes on. In the past, as you have seen, large numbers of immigrants from all parts of the world took part in the American adventure. From the first settlers at Jamestown and Plymouth (who were immigrants), about 40 million immigrants came to the United States. They and their descendants built our country and created the American way of life. In the 1920s the United States began to put a limit on immigration. Since then, only a small number of immigrants have entered our country each year. Thus, soon after the frontier of free land came to an end, America ceased to be a haven for the poor and oppressed of the world.

The land frontier has come to an end, but many other frontiers remain to challenge young Americans.

There is the frontier of conservation. In an age of mass production and global war, the United States must begin to conserve its natural resources.

There is the frontier of education

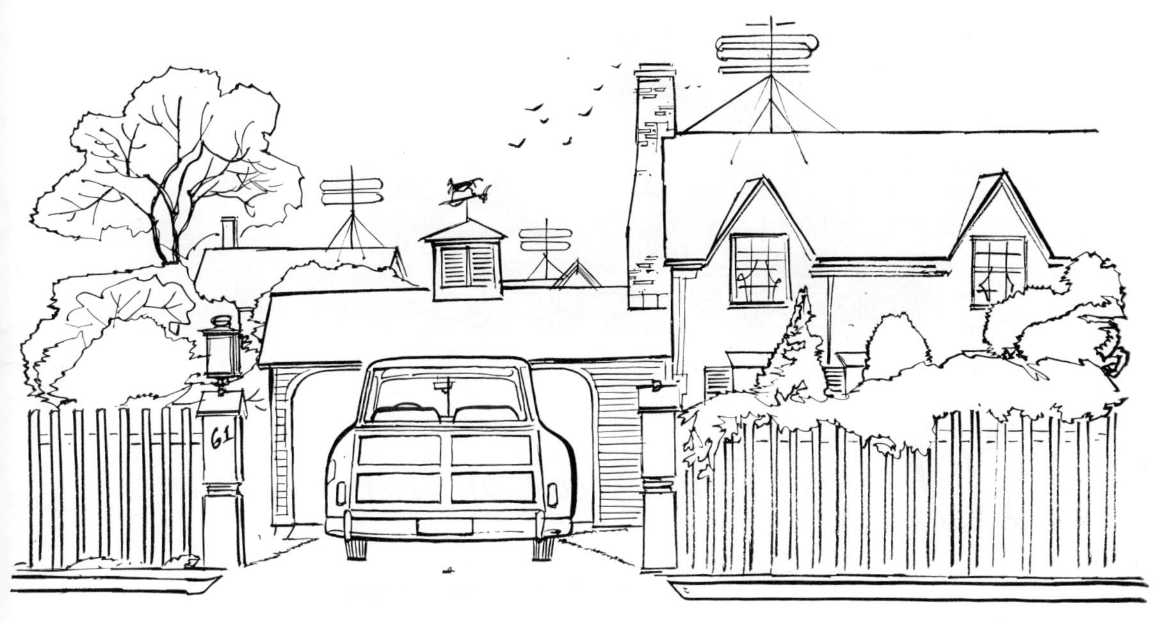

and the laboratory. From here will come the men and the methods for making life healthier and more comfortable.

There is the frontier of business management and cooperation between employers and workers. With improved business efficiency, we can produce more goods and services at lower costs. Employers and workers, by cooperating, can assure the continued flow of goods, so that all Americans may enjoy more of the comforts and conveniences of a good life.

There is the frontier of the fight against inequality. The advance of democracy is a never-ending, gradual progress toward the ideals of individual freedom and equality of opportunity.

There is the frontier of the wider appreciation of the arts and sciences. Such appreciation brings a deeper understanding and enjoyment of life.

Finally, there is the frontier of peace. A future all-out war would destroy a large part of the world. The American people must remain strong, along with the rest of the free world. We must defend the free way of life. At the same time we must cooperate with the other peoples of the world for peace.

Americans are proud of the American adventure of the past. They look forward with confidence and high hopes to the American adventure of the future. Your share in this future adventure with its new frontiers is the story of the ninth and final unit of *The American Adventure.*

30 We Take Stock of Our Human and Natural Resources

A crowd of people stood on deck as the big ocean liner pulled into Boston Harbor one day in 1894. They were people from Europe, coming to make their homes—and their fortunes, they hoped—in the land of promise. They were eager to begin their American adventure. Among them were Mrs. Antin and her four children, including little Maryashe.

Mr. Antin was waiting impatiently on the dock to welcome his family. It had been a lonely three years he had spent in America, earning the money to bring his family over from Russia. This was the day he had looked forward to, when the family would be with him in their new home. He had everything planned and ready. He had a place for his family to live. He even had food all ready for their first meal.

Mary (as she soon was called) was excited, and so were her brother and sisters. Later she remembered how strange it all seemed and how much she wanted to learn American ways. Mr. Antin bundled his family into a rickety cab, to go to their new home. "He told us," wrote Mary long afterward, "not to lean out of the windows, not to point, and explained the word 'greenhorn.' We did not want to be greenhorns and gave the strictest attention to my father's instructions."

When they got home, they soon sat down to the meal Mr. Antin had planned. There were, Mary remembered, several kinds of food, ready to eat, without any cooking, from little tin cans that had printing all over them. And there was a queer kind of fruit that Mary had never seen before.

It was long and slippery, and her father called it "banana." Mary didn't like bananas, and neither did her brother or her sisters. But they knew already that they liked America. Perhaps, as she went to sleep that first night in America, Mary thought to herself: "There's lots to learn here in America. But I'll learn fast." And she did. She tells the whole story in a book called *The Promised Land.*

1 *The United States Limits Immigration*

The Antins were immigrants. They came to the United States from Russia. To be an immigrant is the first step toward becoming an American. If you stop and think for a minute, you will realize that all of us who live in the United States today, except the Indians, are immigrants or the descendants of immigrants.

Early immigrants are mainly British. In the first 200 years of settlement the largest immigrant groups came from the British Isles (see pages 38–40 and 348–349). They—the English, Scots, and Scotch-Irish—established the English language and the English way of life in the 13 colonies.

Other early but smaller immigrant groups, like the Dutch, the Germans, and the French, tried hard to preserve their own languages and customs. Eventually, they or their children adopted the way of life of the English majority, but not in every detail. Some of their words became part of the American language. Some of their music came to be sung by other Americans. Some of their customs became part of the American way of life. Can you give examples? If not, review pages 89–90.

One large group of early immigrants were brought to America by force—the Negroes. They, like other immigrants, have made important contributions to our nation's life and culture. Like people of other groups, they helped to build America by their work. Their music and their dances became a part of the American heritage. (See pages 336 and 337.) In short, the American way of life was built up by the contributions of many immigrant groups.

Irish and German immigrants enrich American life. After 1830 immigrants continued to come to the United States from many European nations. The largest numbers between 1830 and 1890 came from Ireland and Germany (see pages 302–304 and 348–349).

By 1830 the descendants of the earlier immigrants shared an American way of life with American customs. The customs of the Irish and the Germans were different. As often happens when newcomers join a group, some Americans refused to accept the Irish and the Germans as equals. Such Americans refused to consider each immigrant as a person and judge him by what he was and what he could do. They jumbled all immigrants together under the name "greenhorns" and too often treated them unfairly.

Partly because of this feeling against newcomers, many Irish and German immigrants had to struggle hard to make a place for themselves in American life. Given time, however, the new immigrants proved that they were equal

BETTMANN

"Sweet land of liberty." Ever since it was unveiled in 1886, the Statue of Liberty has been a symbol of the promise of free America to immigrants entering New York Harbor.

to earlier Americans in all respects. At first the newcomers often formed separate communities in their own sections of American cities. There they continued their old customs. Gradually they or their children adopted American customs. But it was not a one-way process. The older Americans benefited by adopting some of the immigrants' customs and ideas. (See pages 302–304.) Throughout our history American life has been enriched by the knowledge, the skills, and the new ways of living contributed by immigrants.

The new Americans organized German-American and Irish-American societies to preserve the memory of their Old World origins. Germans, for example, organized the Steuben Society, named in honor of the German general who served with Washington in the American Revolution. The Irish organized the Society of the Friendly Sons of Saint Patrick, named for Ireland's patron saint. As the members came to feel more at home in America, their societies placed less emphasis on Old World customs and continued to serve as social groups. Such societies have become a typical part of American life.

The Scandinavians came in large numbers after the War Between the States. Most of them settled on farms in the Middle West. They went through much the same steps in becoming Americans as had the Germans and the Irish.

New immigrants from southern and eastern Europe. After 1890 the largest immigrant groups were Italian and Slavic. The Slavic groups included Poles, Czechs, Slovaks, Lithuanians (lĭth ū ā′nĭ ănz), Russians, and others who spoke the Slavic languages. They came from different parts of Russia and Austria-Hungary. Large numbers of Finns, Jews, and Hungarians also came from those countries.

Like earlier immigrants, these people had good reasons for leaving their European homes. Most of them were poor, with no hope of ever getting ahead in the Old World. Many of them belonged to minorities who were mistreated and not given equal rights in the countries in which they lived. Besides, most European governments required every young man to serve three or four years in the army, and many people emigrated to avoid that service. The immigrants all regarded the United States as a land of peace, of opportunity, and of personal freedom.

Like many earlier immigrants, these people did not come uninvited. They were urged to come by agents in Europe who represented American steamship companies, railroads, and large industries in need of workers. Special low steamship rates were made to attract immigrants to the New World.

Immigration reached a peak from 1901 to 1910. In those 10 years more than 8,000,000 immigrants came to the United States—nearly 1,000,000 a year. They settled mainly in the industrial areas north of the Ohio River and east of the Mississippi. By 1910, in many states in this region, the foreign-born made up a large proportion of the population. In Massachusetts and New York, for example, about one-third of the people were foreign-born.

New immigrants meet difficulties. The new immigrants who came in such large numbers were from parts of Europe that had not sent many immigrants in earlier years. The old immigration had come from western and northern Europe, mainly from the countries that had contributed most of the early settlers of America. The new immigration came from southern and eastern Europe. The customs of the newcomers were noticeably different from those which had grown up in the United States. These newcomers had to repeat the struggle that earlier immigrants had gone through to make a place for themselves in American life. In fact, many of them had a harder time than those who had come before. One reason was that their ways of life were so different. The other reason was that the country was more crowded than in earlier years.

In becoming part of the main stream of American life, the new immigrants went through the same stages as the earlier immigrants. Feeling strange in

Night school, 1910. Immigrants were taught the English language and citizenship duties in Americanization classes, like this one in St. Louis. Such classes were held in many cities in the early 1900s.

DEPARTMENT OF JUSTICE

Immigrant contributions: music. Some of our outstanding musicians came from other countries to become citizens of the United States. Much of the music they play we have borrowed from Europe.

a new country, the new immigrants settled close together in cities. Since they were very poor, they had to look for houses at the lowest rent. They moved into slum tenements, not because they wanted to live in the slums, but because it was the best they could pay for.

Many Americans were afraid that these separate colonies of new immigrants would never become part of American life. They feared that, if war should come, the immigrants might favor their native countries over their adopted country. Thus they would weaken the defense of the United States. Therefore Americanization programs were started. Night schools were opened to help immigrants learn the English language, the history of their new country, and the responsibilities of democratic citizenship. Various patriotic societies aided in the program.

New immigrants take their place in American life. Americans who feared that the new immigrants would not adapt themselves to the American way of life had forgotten the lesson of history. The Italians and the Slavs, like the Dutch, French, Germans, Irish, and Scandinavians before them, gradually became full-fledged Americans.

The older generation kept in close touch with their old homes and tried to preserve the old-country customs. But they valued highly the freedom and the opportunity that America offered. Like parents in America, and in other parts of the world, they were determined that their children should have a chance to "make good." Many Italian and Polish fathers worked all their lives with pick and shovel to pay for their children's education. Meanwhile they did the hard manual labor in laying our country's railroads, building our cities, and working in our coal mines, steel mills, and factories. They helped make the United States the greatest producer of goods in the world.

The younger generation of immigrant families came here as small children or were born here. They learned from their parents a feeling of kinship for the old country. But the ties were weaker for the children, and their loyalty went to their new homeland, the United States. As they started to make their way in America, they found many opportunities. They also found, as had earlier immigrants, that they were not always given an equal chance.

In spite of difficulties, however, these children of the new immigrants made long strides toward playing a full part in American life. Americans of Italian, Polish, Czech, Hungarian, or Jewish parents—they became businessmen, doctors, lawyers, druggists, teachers, civil service workers. Some of them were elected mayors and governors, judges, members of state legislatures and of Congress. Some became prominent in science, art, and literature; in the theater, the movies, and on the radio and television; in popular music, symphonic music, and opera. Others became outstanding athletes, in baseball, football, basketball, boxing, and golf. By their accomplishments they gained the respect of other Americans.

An American View

My people came to this country
In need of a land that was free,
So I think the only thing I can do,
If a decent man I would be,
Is to walk with my head held high and
  proud
For the blood that runs in me.

My people came to this country
—And the seas were a green great space—
Because the trees were kind and tall
And the fields a pleasant place,
And brave men worshipped as they would
And thought with an open face.

¶ The above stanzas from "My People Came to This Country" express love and high regard for the United States. The poem is by Struthers Burt.

Immigrant contributions: folk dancing. Polish-American folk dancers, in colorful Old World costumes, bring gaiety to the harvest festival held each autumn in a town in New York State.

Some Builders of America

NAME	DATE	COUNTRY OF BIRTH	PRINCIPAL ACTIVITY
John Roebling	1806–1869	Germany	Engineer, bridge builder
Louis Agassiz	1807–1873	Switzerland	Naturalist, botanist
Alexander T. Stewart	1803–1876	Ireland	Merchant
Henry Villard	1835–1900	Germany	Journalist, financier
Carl Schurz	1829–1906	Germany	Political leader
Joseph Pulitzer	1847–1911	Hungary	Publisher
Jacob A. Riis	1849–1914	Denmark	Journalist, social reformer
John Philip Holland	1840–1914	Ireland	Inventor
John Ireland	1838–1918	Ireland	Religious leader
Charles P. Steinmetz	1865–1923	Germany	Electrical engineer
Fannie B. Zeisler	1863–1927	Silesia	Concert pianist
Michael Pupin	1858–1935	Yugoslavia	Scientist (physicist)
Hendrik Van Loon	1882–1944	Holland	Author
Arturo Toscanini	1867–	Italy	Conductor
Fritz Kreisler	1875–	Austria	Violinist
Enrico Fermi	1901–1954	Italy	Physicist and teacher
Andre Kostelanetz	1901–	Russia	Popular orchestra leader
Anna M. Rosenberg	1901–	Hungary	Public relations expert
Lily Pons	1904–	France	Singer

¶ The lives of these men and women who came from other lands to help build our nation make interesting stories. Your class might arrange a series of talks about their careers and their contributions to America.

The grandchildren of the new immigrants are all American-born. They have few, if any, ties with the old country. Their language is American, and their way of life is American.

So the process by which, over and over again, immigrants have been turned into Americans has been repeated. Among the most recent arrivals it is still going on. As before, it is not one-sided. As the immigrants learn the ways of America, they contribute some of their customs, their ideas, and their skills to American life.

The United States sets a limit on immigration. It may be that we are now witnessing the last time that the American people will absorb any considerable number of immigrants from Europe. During the First World War immigration from Europe decreased sharply. Before it could start again on a large scale, the United States closed the doors almost completely. By laws passed in 1921, 1924, and 1927, Congress limited the number of immigrants to about 150,000 a year.

The American people had good reason for restricting immigration. In earlier years many immigrants had taken up land on the frontier. In the 1900s there was no more free land. The newcomers crowded into settled areas and competed for jobs with workers already living in the United States.

But our country lost as well as gained from immigration restriction. For in the past immigrants contributed to our national life, not only laborers and skilled workmen, but also great inventors, artists, scientists, and outstanding leaders in business and the professions. In fact, the 40 million immigrants who came here from 1607 to 1920—they and their descendants—were the people who built America.

The sharp cut in immigration speeded up the work of the "melting pot" in the United States. The number of foreign-born in the country grew smaller. The old people died, and few new immigrants came to take their place. In 1920, 12 per cent of the population was foreign-born; in 1930, 10 per cent; in 1940, 8 per cent; and in 1950, less than 7 per cent. With few recent immigrants, contacts with the old country became weaker.

In the 1940s and 1950s many immigrants came from Mexico and Puerto Rico. The limitation on immigration did not apply to them. In 1956 the United States admitted thousands of Hungarian refugees after the failure of their revolt against communism.

2 *The American People at Mid-century*

Every 10 years since 1790 the people of our nation have been counted by officials of the federal government. The original purpose was to determine how many Representatives each state would send to the House of Representatives in Congress. As they have done the counting, the officials have collected many other facts about our population. The process of counting the people and collecting this information is called taking the census.

From the census we can get a picture of the American people at the various periods of our history—how many there were, where they lived, and so on. We can learn more about our people from recent censuses than from the early ones, because more information is collected now. In 1790, for example, each of the 600 enumerators (the officials who took the census) got this information in each home: the name of the head of the family, the number of free white men and women over 16, the number of free white boys and girls under 16, and the number of slaves. In 1950 each of the 150,000 enumerators asked questions about each person's education, occupation, place of birth, citizenship, and so on, as well as his name, age, and address. From the facts collected in the 1950 census, we can form an interesting picture of the American people in the mid-twentieth century. By comparing these facts with those from earlier censuses, we can see the changes that have come about in the United States. (See chart on page 619.)

Continued increase in numbers. In 1950 the population of the United States was over 150 million. You can see from the graph on page 618 that the total population of the nation had continued to increase after 1900, though not so fast as in earlier years when the

PEOPLING THE LAND

Throughout the history of our country, its population has grown more rapidly than that of any other nation.

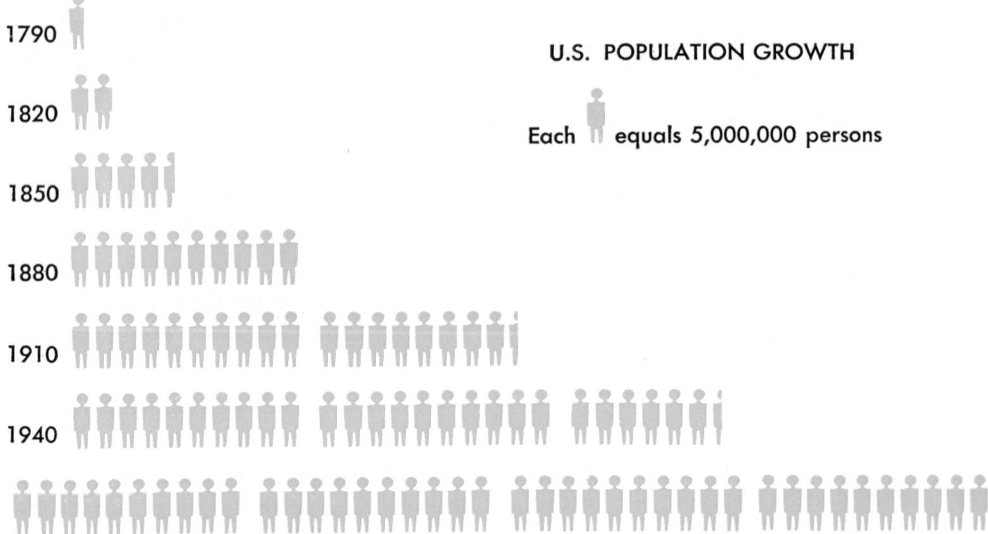

The immigration laws of the 1920s reduced European immigration to a trickle. At the same time, immigrants continued to enter the United States from neighboring countries.

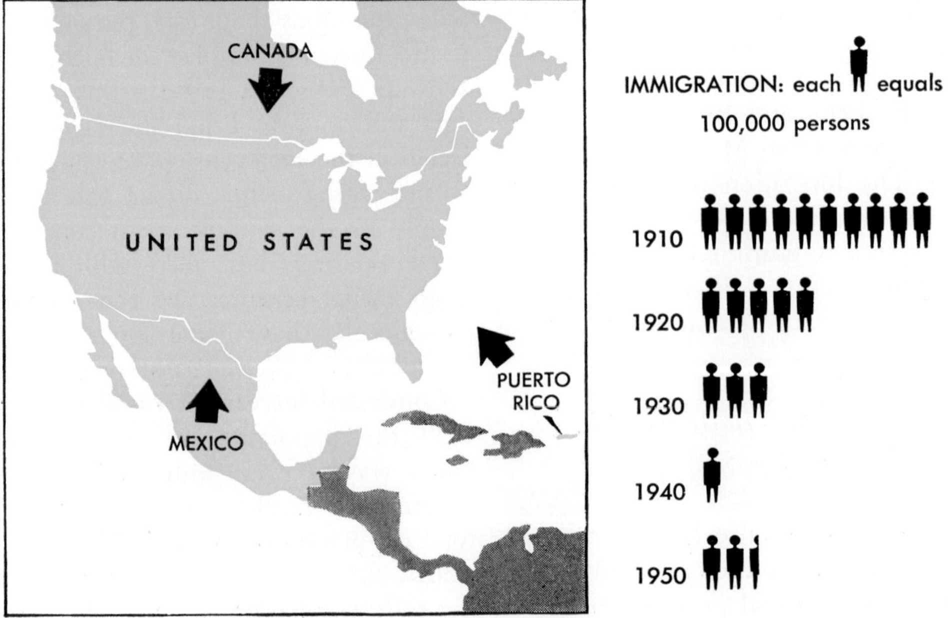

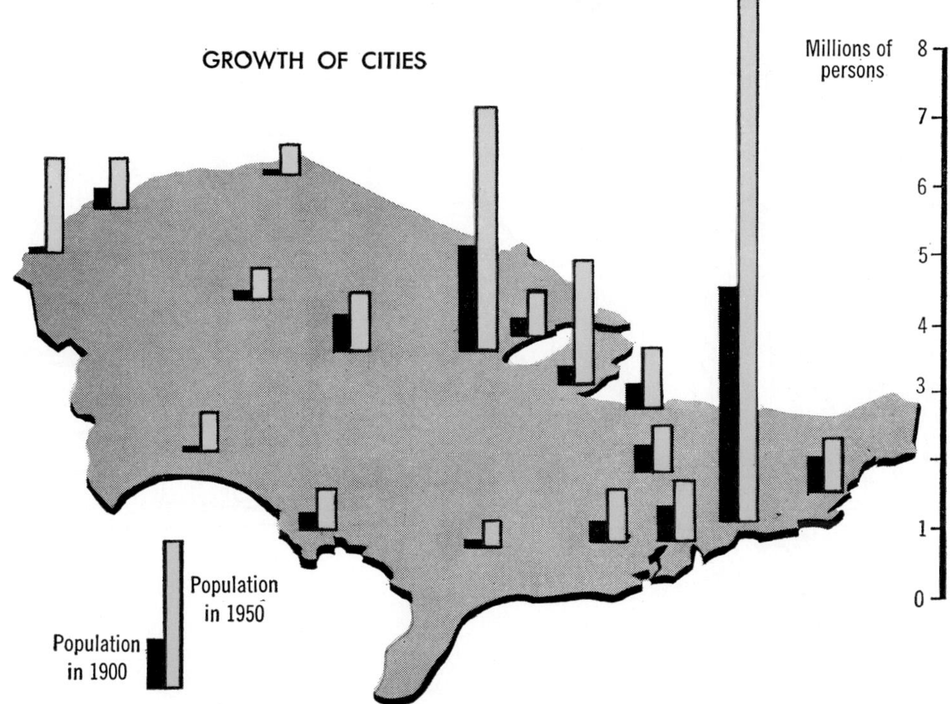

In the 1900s American cities grew by leaps and bounds. Immigrants and people from farms and villages flocked to the cities to find new opportunities in rapidly expanding business and industry.

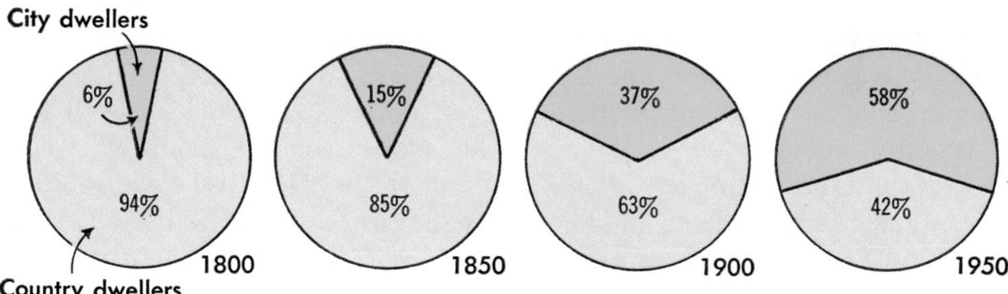

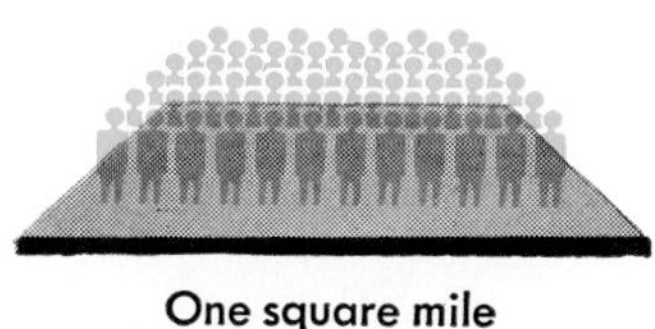

In 1970 there will be an average (est.) of 66 persons per square mile in the United States

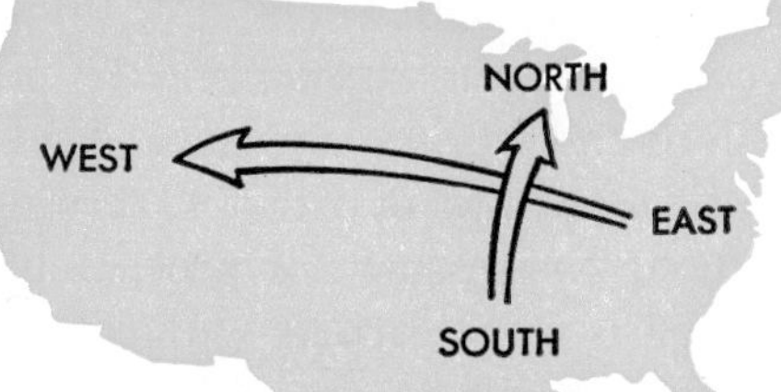

The American people are still on the move, mainly from south to north and east to west

Census taker. A census taker is collecting information from a housewife. What are some of the questions he asks her?

West was being settled. From 1880 to 1890 the population increased by 12 million, or 25 per cent. From 1930 to 1940 the increase was 9 million, or 7 per cent; and from 1940 to 1950, 19 million, or 14½ per cent. Most of this later increase was not caused by immigration. It was the result of the high birth rate and low death rate among the American people.

People continue to move. Americans continued to move from the farm to the city. (The Bureau of the Census calls every community of 2,500 people or more an urban community, or city.) In 1950 about 58 per cent of the population lived in cities. Do not think, however, that the remaining 42 per cent lived and worked on farms. About half of them lived in villages, earning a living as businessmen or professional people or as wage earners with jobs in the village or in a nearby city. Between 1920 and 1950 the number of people living on farms actually decreased. Not so many farmers were needed because of the use of farm machinery and improved methods of agriculture.

Though the frontier was a thing of the past, people continued to move west through the first half of the twentieth century. The industrial Northeast continued to be the most heavily populated area. From 1900 to 1950, however, millions of persons moved from the Northeast and Southeast to the West. In the 1930s and 1940s the three Pacific coast states, considered as a unit, grew more rapidly in population than any other part of the country. California's population actually increased 53 per cent during the 1940s.

The main attraction of the Pacific coast was no longer free land. Large numbers of people settled in the three Pacific coast states because of their mild climate. Some went to earn a living at growing vegetables and, in California, citrus fruits. People were attracted by jobs in the rapidly growing industries of the region. Petroleum fields were discovered in California, and many workers went to drill for oil. The motion-picture industry drew many people to southern California. The great fishing and lumbering industries attracted many workers to Washington and Oregon.

During the Second World War the west coast was the base for the war in the Pacific area. Many people went to the west coast to serve the increased commerce and to work at shipbuilding, airplane manufacturing, and other war industries. After the war a large proportion of the workers decided to make their homes in the West permanently.

Another important shift of population has taken place as large numbers of Negroes have left southern farms to live in cities. They have moved to southern cities like Birmingham and to northern cities like New York, Chicago, and Detroit. There they found jobs in the growing industries where their manpower was needed. In 1900 there were 60,000 Negroes in New York City; in 1950 there were about 600,000.

Strength in human resources. The strength of America has always depended on its people—on its human resources. The fertile farms, the great transportation systems, and the huge factories of the United States alone cannot produce goods. They must be used by manpower with a great variety of skills in the right amounts and at the right time. During the Second World War the need to use our human resources wisely was dramatically emphasized by the manpower shortage of the war years. There were not enough people to do many kinds of jobs in agriculture, industry, commerce, and the armed forces.

The war emergency created special needs. But it is equally important for national strength that we make the best use of human resources in peacetime as well. This is not merely a matter of assigning people to jobs. In democratic America it means that each person should have opportunity to develop his particular abilities and to find the place in life for which he is best fitted. It means that the health of the people should be protected so that our human resources will not be wasted in illness and suffering. It means that Americans, rather than waste their energies in bickering and hatred among themselves, should work together for the common good.

3 *The American People Conserve Their Natural Resources*

An active, energetic people help make a country prosperous and strong. But they cannot do so without natural resources. From the time the first white settlers landed at Jamestown and Plymouth, the American people have been searching out the natural resources of the country in order to make a better living. In the process they conquered the continent and built a great nation.

Settlers, spreading across the continent, used chiefly four natural resources: soil, water, forest, and wildlife (fish, birds, and animals). The soil, together with water, was and is today a most precious resource. From it comes almost everything necessary for life. Settlers used it recklessly, exhausting it

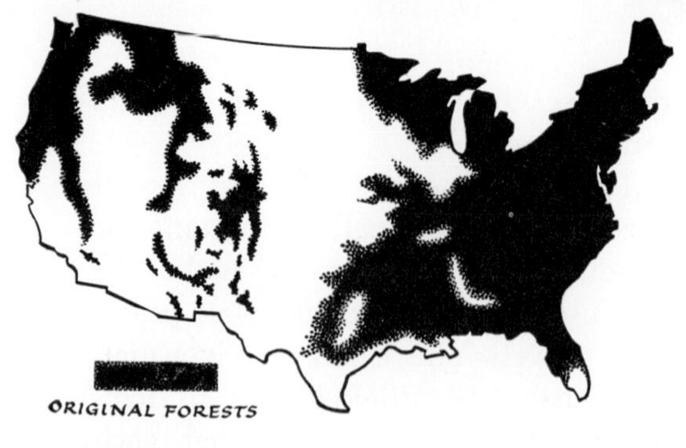

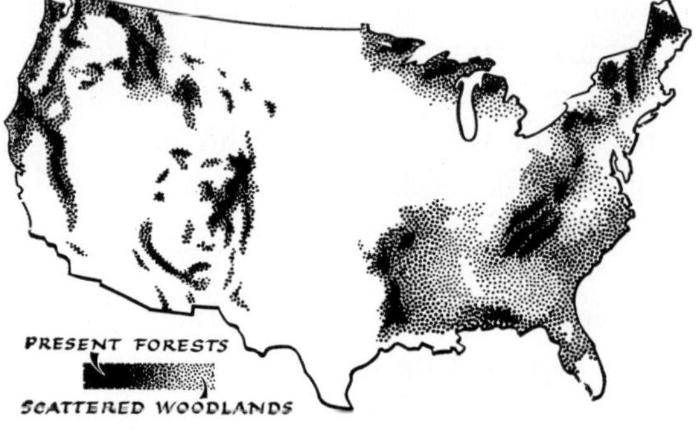

Forest lands, then and now. What sections of the United States were covered with forests in colonial times? How has the cutting of forests affected soil erosion and floods? Locate the approximate area of your own state on these maps. How has it been affected by the destruction of forests?

with their crops and making no effort to restore its fertility. (See pages 67–68 and 211.) To pioneers the forest was an obstacle in their way, something that prevented their cultivating the soil. They cut down trees impatiently, wishing they could use the time and the energy to plant crops (see page 65). They used a small part of the wood for lumber and fuel and destroyed the rest without using it at all. As larger and larger areas of the forest disappeared, the number of wild animals declined. On the plains, hunters shot buffalo for sport until that animal was all but exterminated.

Minerals. The industrial revolution gave a new importance to mineral resources, as you read on pages 310 and 423. Iron and coal became the most important minerals; iron for machines and coal for fuel. New discoveries and inventions made other minerals essential, like copper for telephone wire, petroleum for automobile engines, aluminum for airplanes, and uranium and other minerals for atomic power.

The United States like other great industrial countries, came to depend on supplies of minerals brought from all parts of the earth. It was more fortunate than other countries. It had large supplies of most of the minerals essential in modern industry. But even the United States lacked some minerals, like nickel and manganese (măng′gȧ-nēs). It had to import these from other regions of the globe.

Water. Water had always been necessary for growing crops, but the industrial revolution also made water power valuable as a natural resource. In the early years water power was used directly to turn factory wheels, with the factories built alongside the water-power dam. Later water was used to generate electricity, which could be carried to factories located within an area of several hundred miles.

Conservation begins with the forests. The United States was so big in land area and so rich in mines and forests that it seemed to the American people that the country's natural resources never could be used up. But in the 1870s scientists began to warn the country that the end of its timber supply was in sight. Most of the magnifi-

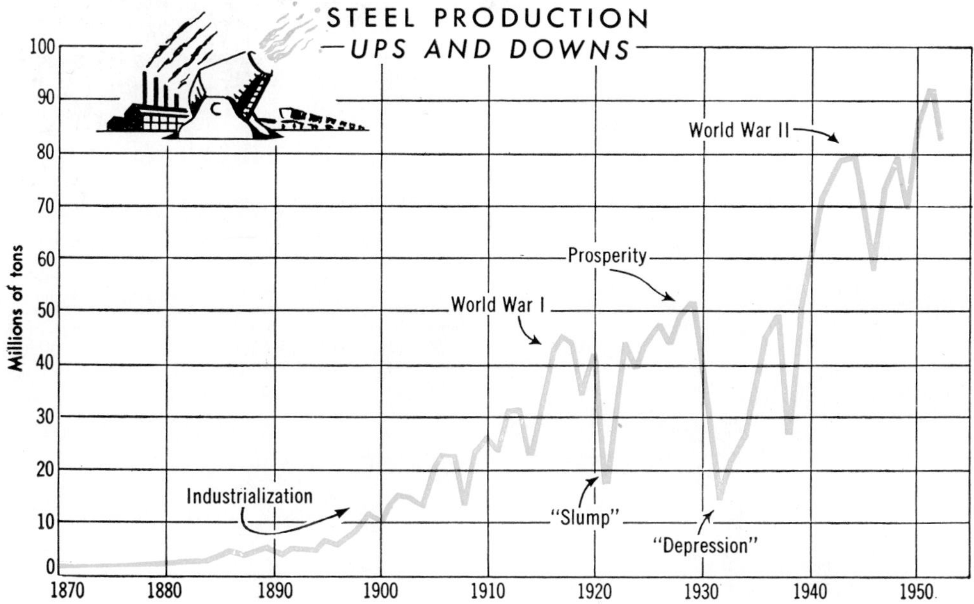

Steel. The United States produces almost as much steel as all the rest of the world.

cent forest that had once covered much of our land had disappeared. Timber was being used up faster than it could be replaced by new growth. (Remember the old proverb in *Poor Richard's Almanac?* It said, "Wood burns faster than it grows.")

Thus interest in conservation began with the problem of preserving our forests. In 1891 Congress passed a law giving the President the power to set aside timberlands. These lands were not to be sold to private persons. They were to be owned by the government, and the timber on them was to be saved.

It was President Theodore Roosevelt who first made the American people as a whole understand that our country's natural resources must be conserved. (To conserve means to use wisely, with careful plans for replacing resources that can be replaced.) Theodore Roosevelt taught us that conservation must include, not only forests, but also soil, water, and minerals. Under his leadership the country took important steps in planning for wiser use of resources. He set aside three times as much timberland as had earlier Presidents. He established national parks and wildlife preserves. In these preserves animals, birds, and fish could flourish, since hunting and fishing were limited to certain seasons. He obtained a law under which the federal government built dams to provide water for irrigating desertland in the West.

The lumberman's part in conservation. Conservation of the forests does not mean that lumbering has to stop. There are two ways to carry on lumbering. One is the way of the wasteful lumberman of the past. He regarded a forest as a one-time crop. He cut down all the healthy, grown trees and carelessly broke the young trees standing in the way. He left the land strewn with branches trimmed from the logs.

U.S. FOREST SERVICE

Cutting lumber the wrong way. Here you see wasteful lumbering. Few young trees have been left to grow a new crop. Logs and branches lie around to serve as fuel for forest fires. There will be no second crop of trees here for a long, long time, perhaps a century.

U.S. FOREST SERVICE

Cutting lumber the right way. Only selected older trees have been cut down. Enough trees have been left to provide seed for future growth. Space has been made for the young trees to grow tall and strong. Here a crop of trees can be cut about every 20 years.

Enjoying conservation. Children are enjoying the bathing in the Davy Crockett National Forest, Texas. National forests provide places where healthy forests can grow, as well as places where healthy people can find recreation.

U.S. FOREST SERVICE

The dry branches became fuel for forest fires that burned over large areas. Burned-over soil may never return to forest unless seeds or young trees are planted on it.

The lumberman who regards a forest as a crop to be harvested year after year carries on lumbering in a very different way. He cuts only part of the grown trees and carefully preserves the young ones. The trees that are left standing will provide seed for a new growth and the forest will restore itself. In 30 years the lumberman can come back and cut another crop of timber on the same land. Meanwhile, the forest has continued to protect the soil, prevent floods, and provide shelter for wildlife and a place for recreation.

Forest fires cause enormous damage every year. Many destructive forest fires are started by hunters, fishermen, and picnickers who carelessly leave campfires smoldering and by passing tourists who toss away lighted cigarettes on the dry leaves of the forest floor. Federal and state fire wardens keep watch over large forested areas to spot fires at the start and put them out.

The farmer's part in conservation. Some of the land that is being farmed in the United States should never have been cleared for cultivation. For example, during the First World War when wheat prices were high, farmers began to cultivate new areas, the grassland of the Great Plains. For a few years the rain was sufficient, and crops were good. But you will remember what had happened to pioneer farmers on the western plains in the 1880s. Many of them had to leave their homesteads and return to the East because of the drought. (See page 413.)

In the 1930s drought came again. The soil became a dry dust. Left with no grass cover and nothing else to hold it down, it was picked up by the winds and carried across the country. This happened in a large area where the prairie-grass cover had been plowed away. This area was called the Dust Bowl. It included parts of Oklahoma, Colorado, Texas, and New Mexico. Farmers in the Dust Bowl left their farms to move anywhere they could find work. These Dust Bowl farmers suffered because a great mistake had been made. The land on the Great Plains was not suitable for cultivation; it should have been kept for grazing.

DEPARTMENT OF AGRICULTURE

Water for thirsty land. A California farmer irrigates his land. Without water, this land would be desert.

Prevent forest fires! That is the message of Smokey, the fire-warden bear, as he leads young animals out of a burned-over forest.

U.S. FOREST SERVICE

Saving the soil requires the cooperation of every farmer. If a farmer has a field that has been worn down and gullied, he can begin to restore it by planting it with grass. He can build little dams in the gullies to slow up the water so that it will deposit the silt, or topsoil, it carries.

When he plows a sloping field, the farmer should make the furrows run across the slope, not up and down. An up-and-down furrow becomes a little ditch for the water to run down and carry off the soil. A crosswise furrow becomes a little dam that holds the water and saves the soil.

When land has lost nearly all its topsoil, it cannot be restored by these methods. Such land should be replanted with trees and left to restore itself over a period of many centuries.

The engineer's part in conservation. Engineers help to conserve water by building dams in rivers. Behind the dams, water is stored up in large lakes. The dams prevent floods lower down on the rivers and save the water until it is needed. The water may be used for several purposes. In dry areas, as in southern California, for example, water thus stored is used to irrigate fields. The water is also used to generate electricity. As the water drops from a higher to a lower level, it is made to turn the wheels of electric generators and make electric power.

Conserving mineral resources. Today our modern industrial world uses up minerals faster than ever before. Our country has large supplies of coal and iron, as you can see from the map on page 423. We are rapidly using up the richest deposits, however, and those which are nearest the surface. When these are gone, coal and iron may become more expensive since we shall

Abandoned farm, 1935. The sand is six feet high around these barns of an abandoned farm. It is hard to believe that anything will ever grow on this land again.

DEPARTMENT OF AGRICULTURE

The same farm, 1938. The sand was cleared away, and grass was planted to hold the remaining soil. After three years of scientific farming, the farm is livable again.

DEPARTMENT OF AGRICULTURE

DEPARTMENT OF AGRICULTURE

Contour plowing. This farmer in Texas is saving topsoil and water by plowing his land along the slope, instead of up and down it.

have to dig deeper or use low-grade deposits.

The United States is fortunate in having large reserves of petroleum. We use tremendous quantities of it in our automobiles and airplanes. So far we have been able to keep the supply up with the demand by opening up new oil fields. Because of the importance of gasoline and oil in modern life, the conservation of petroleum is necessary.

Conservation in the future. We can see that, after the start given it by Theodore Roosevelt, conservation made progress. The federal government has led the way. Many states, too, have taken steps to conserve some of the resources within their borders. Science and industry have cooperated. But the advance has not been fast enough.

What would happen if the United States used up its iron, petroleum, and other resources in the near future? It would have to import these materials over long distances from foreign regions at a great cost. Manufacturers would have to pay higher prices for materials. They, in turn, would charge more for their products. Americans would not be able to buy as much as they now do. They would live less comfortably. The United States would change from a "rich" country to a "poor" country.

An individual may see the need for conservation but may be helpless to do anything about it alone. But individuals can cooperate to work for conservation. All Americans can join organizations devoted to conservation and help in their work. Every citizen can know what the government is doing for conservation and work for wise conservation laws to be passed.

What can the government do in developing long-range conservation plans? One thing it can do is to keep under its own control forests, mineral lands, water-power sites, and other resources it now owns and see that they are developed in the most efficient way. A second thing the government can do

DEPARTMENT OF AGRICULTURE

Wasted land. Rain has carried away the topsoil. Nothing will grow on such wasteland.

Conservation through mine safety. Limestone powder is mixed with coal dust to prevent accidental explosions in coal mines.

BITUMINOUS COAL INSTITUTE

is to cooperate with the people who own the natural resources to help them put conservation methods into practice. A third way is to set up plans for private owners of natural resources to cooperate among themselves and with the government to avoid waste.

The best way of all to conserve natural resources is to prevent war. Even in a short modern war we use up for purposes of destruction and death more essential materials than we use in a century of peaceful living.

Summary

Immigrants and their descendants have built our nation. They have been the human resources of our America. During the colonial period and the early 1800s, most of the settlers in what became the United States were from the British Isles. Important exceptions were the Negroes, who were brought by force from Africa, and the Dutch, the Germans, and the French. Between 1830 and 1890 the largest groups of immigrants were from Ireland and Germany. Toward the end of this period many Scandinavians also came to settle on the farms of the Middle West. From about 1890 until the First World War, most of the newcomers to the United States were from the countries of southern and eastern Europe. After the First World War laws were passed to limit immigration.

Each new group of immigrants faced many of the same problems—poverty, new ways to learn, and sometimes prejudice. Some immigrants learned American ways more rapidly than others, but gradually the members of each new group became Americanized. As they learned, they also taught, for each immigrant group made contributions to American life.

The population of the United States has continued to increase since the limiting of immigration, though not so rapidly as before 1900. Each census has shown that we are increasingly a nation of city dwellers, with a smaller and smaller proportion of our population living on farms. Each census has shown a westward movement of our population.

From the beginning of settlement, our people have used the rich natural resources of America freely, even wastefully. Within the past half century it has become increasingly urgent that we conserve our remaining resources. We practice conservation when we use our natural resources carefully. We must remember that these resources belong to the Americans of the future as well as to us. They will need rich resources to keep America strong and free.

When the United States became concerned with conserving its natural resources, it began a new period in its history. As Americans today take stock of their human and natural resources, they see that the old frontier of free land and unlimited natural resources is past. The new frontier will be a frontier of scientific progress, of cooperation to conserve the natural resources that remain, and of finding ways for all Americans to share and to serve in the national life.

BITUMINOUS COAL INSTITUTE

Testing for safety. This inspector is testing a coal mine for poisonous gas.

For a Quick Review

1. Why did large groups of Italians and Slavs come to the United States after 1890? Compare their reasons for coming with the reasons of earlier immigrant groups.

2. How did the problems faced by the "new" immigration and the efforts made to solve them compare with the problems of earlier immigrant groups and their efforts at solution?

3. What regions of our country are most heavily populated? Why?

4. What were the main natural resources the pioneering settlers used? Do we use natural resources today that they did not use? Explain.

5. When and why did Americans first become interested in conservation of natural resources? What steps for conservation were taken at that time?

6. Why is it important that we conserve our natural resources?

Learning to Study More Easily

EXCHANGING IDEAS THROUGH PANEL DISCUSSIONS

There are several ways of learning from any panel discussion. If you are a member of the panel, you take one kind of part in the discussion and learn in one way—by collecting information and presenting it. If you are a member of the audience, you learn in another way—by listening carefully, taking notes, asking questions, and discussing points that have been raised.

A panel discussion in school is usually presented by a group of from four to eight students. They are "experts," because they have made a special investigation of the topic to be discussed. They sit around a table, facing the rest of the class. Thus they are close enough to exchange their ideas easily, and the rest of the class can follow their discussion.

In a true panel discussion, there are no set speeches. Instead, the panel members meet in advance, work out an outline of the points they wish to discuss, and then search for information on those points. When the discussion begins, each panel member is ready to give some information and perhaps an opinion on most of the points in the outline. If the discussion is to go smoothly, the panel members must speak in a conversational manner, no one speaking too long at one time and everyone having a chance to take part.

There is a chairman, who has the duty of seeing that panel members stay on the subject and carry on their discussion according to the outline. He introduces the subject of the discussion. He watches the time. If the discussion stays too long on a minor point, the chairman reminds the members that there are other topics to talk about. He may ask them to summarize the point they are on so that the panel can move on to another.

As the panel finishes its discussion of each major topic, the chairman may summarize it or call on a panel member to do so. Then he will introduce the next point for discussion. At the end of the panel discussion, the chairman or one of the panel gives a brief summary of all the points that have been presented. Usually time is set aside for the audience to raise questions and express opinions on the discussion.

31 *Americans Live a Longer and a Better Life*

Even though it was late fall, it was a hot day in Cuba. It was hot in the United States army hospital, where soldiers lay dying of yellow fever, and it was hot in the office of Major Walter Reed. Two young men came through the door of the office. As the major looked up, he saw that one was in uniform and one was in civilian clothes. They wanted to talk with Major Reed. The conversation went something like this:

MAJOR REED: Yes, gentlemen?

SOLDIER: We've come to volunteer for your experiments on yellow fever, sir.

CIVILIAN: Yes, we heard you need men to let mosquitoes bite them to see whether that's what gives the men yellow fever . . .

MAJOR REED: But gentlemen, this is dangerous business. Do you know that Dr. Lazear, who died just a few weeks ago, had been bitten by a mosquito—that we think he got yellow fever that way? Do you know you may die if you do this?

SOLDIER: Yes, we know it's dangerous. But don't you want volunteers?

CIVILIAN: We heard you had to have men . . .

MAJOR REED: Yes, we do need men for these experiments. That is the terrible thing about it. The men who volunteer are risking their lives. They are risking them to help all mankind. If we can just prove that it's the mosquito that spreads this horrible disease—well, we know how to wipe out mosquitoes. But until we know how yellow fever is spread, we can't do one thing to wipe it out.

SOLDIER: That's why we're here.

CIVILIAN: We still want to volunteer.

MAJOR REED: Gentlemen, your offer is accepted. Report back tomorrow for further instructions.

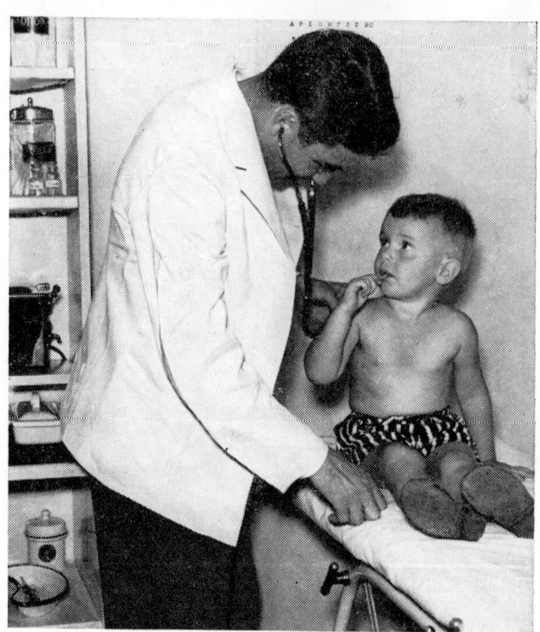

LIBRARY OF CONGRESS

Keeping healthy. In modern clinics, doctors examine healthy children to find any weaknesses that might result in ill-health. Through regular examinations, doctors can help children and adults to avoid illness. Good health means more productive lives.

Private Kissinger of the United States Army and civilian John J. Moran reported the next day. They were bitten by mosquitoes. They became ill with yellow fever, but they did not die. They risked their lives to help prove, through a scientific experiment, that yellow fever was carried by a certain kind of mosquito. Today, thanks to Private Kissinger and civilian Moran, to Dr. Walter Reed, and to the other brave men who planned and carried through the experiments, yellow fever has been conquered. A deadly disease, which for many years had taken hundreds of lives in the United States almost every summer, was brought under control. How has this affected you, living over half a century after the experiment in Cuba?

1 *The American People Continue to Gain in Health and Recreation*

When a baby was born in 1900, the year of Walter Reed's experiment, it could be predicted that he would probably live about 50 years. That was then the average length of life. But a baby born in 1950, experts say, will probably live about 69 years. This longer life has been made possible by scientific research in many fields and by the widespread use of the new knowledge gained.

Improvements in fighting disease. You have read how men learned to control yellow fever, one of the serious epidemic diseases of the 1800s. There were other epidemic diseases that had to be controlled. Typhoid fever was one of them. It was discovered that typhoid fever had been spread mainly by water and food that were contaminated, or impure. Cities spent large sums to obtain pure water. Los Angeles, for example, spent millions of dollars to bring water across the desert and the mountains from the Colorado River 350 miles away. Many cities built sewage-disposal plants and stopped disposing of sewage in rivers or lakes. Laws were enforced requiring sanitary handling of food in stores and restaurants. All milk sold in cities had to be pasteurized, that is, heated to a high temperature to destroy germs. These measures helped to control typhoid and other diseases that are easily spread through water or food.

Tuberculosis was another disease that caused many deaths. No absolute cure was discovered, but much was learned about how to treat it and how to keep it from spreading. The number of people who died from tuberculosis each year in the United States was rapidly reduced. Many states established special hospitals where tubercular patients enjoyed rest, sunshine, and good food. In some cases, where the disease had been discovered early, the patient was completely cured. In the 1950s many scientists were continuing to search for the cause and cure of tuberculosis and of other diseases like cancer and infantile paralysis. This work goes on with increasing energy.

American and foreign scientists discovered new drugs with which to fight diseases. Insulin (ĭn′sû lĭn) was developed to bring relief to persons suffering from diabetes (dī ȧ bē′tēz). Then in the 1930s and 1940s came the new "wonder drugs," including the sulfa drugs, penicillin (pĕn ĭ sĭl′ĭn), and streptomycin (strĕp tō mī′sĭn). In 1955 Dr. Jonas E. Salk introduced a promising new vaccine against polio.

Another aid to health was improvement in diet. Through continuing experiments, scientists learned that certain foods contain vitamins and minerals that are necessary for good health. Following the reports of the scientists, more and more Americans learned to balance their diet. They drank more milk and fruit juices and ate more green vegetables, eggs, and cereals. Children were fed cod-liver oil to supply them with vitamin D, the "sunshine" vitamin, which kept them strong during the years of rapid growth.

Children under the age of five benefited from medical progress more than any other age group. The lives of large numbers of them were saved as many epidemic diseases were eliminated. Anyone suffering from a contagious disease was quarantined to prevent the disease from spreading. (Do you remember that this practice was begun in the nineteenth century? See page 443.) Doctors discovered ways to inoculate children against diseases like diphtheria, scarlet fever, and whooping cough.

Better equipment for doctors. Newly invented equipment gave doctors new ways to help their patients. The X ray, for example, enabled a doctor to learn what was happening inside a patient's body. With it he took pictures of bones and various other parts. From the pictures the doctor could often tell exactly what was wrong.

Milk at school. Children learn in school to drink milk for good health. How much milk do you drink each day? What other foods do you need for a healthful diet?

DEPARTMENT OF AGRICULTURE

BETTER LIVING FOR AMERICANS

The chart (*right*) shows how Americans reached the highest level of living in history. By using more power-driven machines on farms and in factories, Americans produced ever-larger quantities of food, clothing, furniture, and other goods. The graphs and pictures (*below*) show how Americans use these products for better living.

How are the rising wages shown on the income chart related to the amount and variety of food that an American family eats? How is the drop in working hours related to the family picnic? How else do Americans use their growing leisure?

How is American prosperity related to the increase in the number of students?

How does taking chest X rays help Americans live longer and healthier lives? What other health services do Americans enjoy?

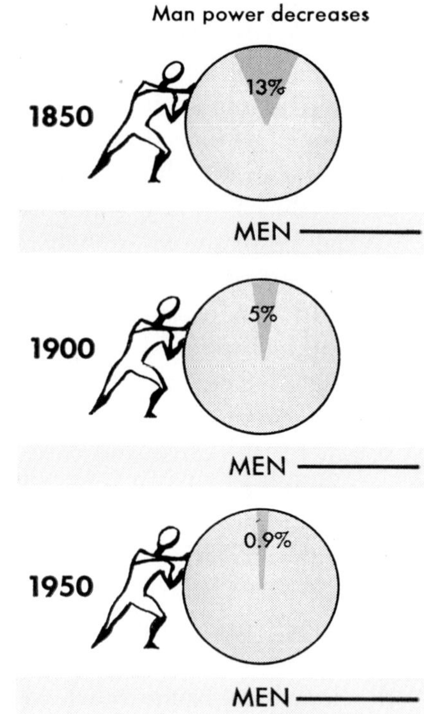

INCOME • • • • •

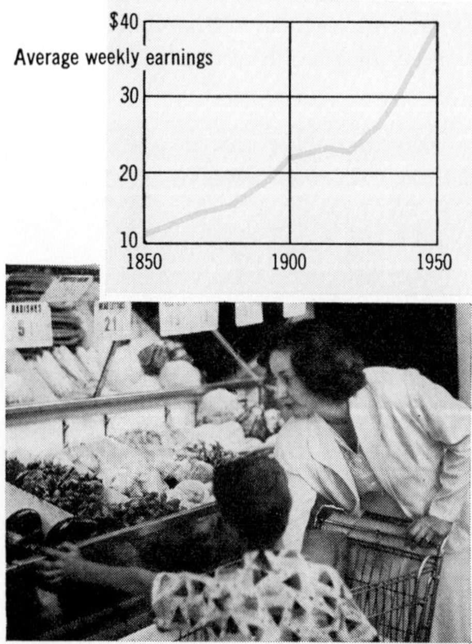

INTERNATIONAL HARVESTER COMPANY

WORKING HOURS • •

STANDARD OIL COMPANY (N.J.)

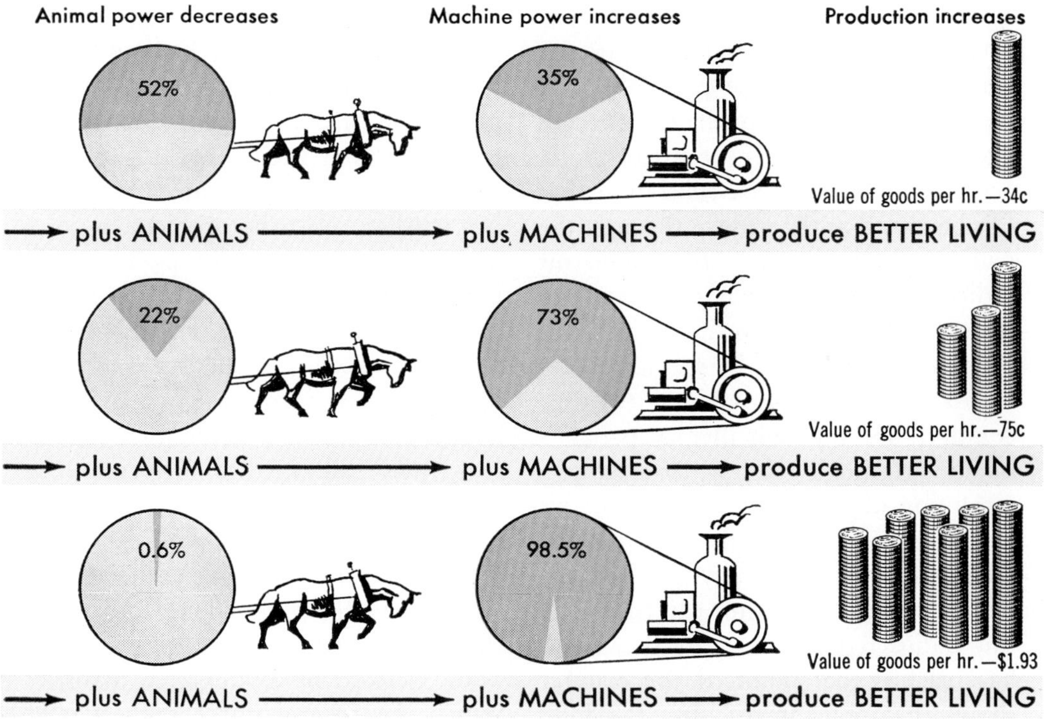

Animal power decreases
Machine power increases
Production increases
52%
35%
Value of goods per hr.—34c
plus ANIMALS
plus MACHINES
produce BETTER LIVING
22%
73%
Value of goods per hr.—75c
plus ANIMALS
plus MACHINES
produce BETTER LIVING
0.6%
98.5%
Value of goods per hr.—$1.93
plus ANIMALS
plus MACHINES
produce BETTER LIVING

EDUCATION • • •

Millions of students in public schools
30
25
20
15
10
1880
1900
1950

STOP
SCHOOL BUS
RUPERT SCHOO

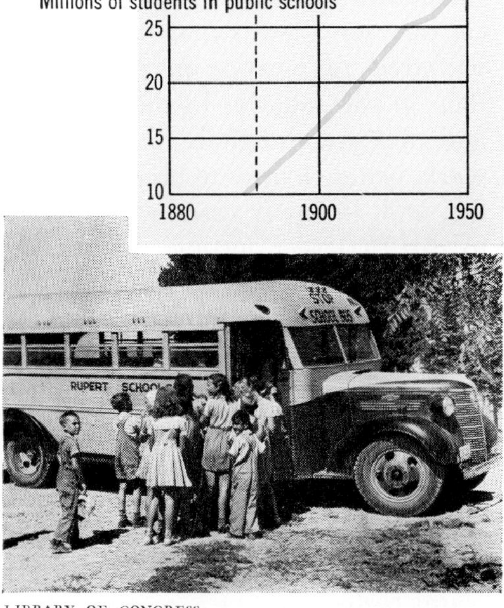

LIBRARY OF CONGRESS

HEALTH • • • • •

Average length of life
70
60
50
40
1850
1900
1950

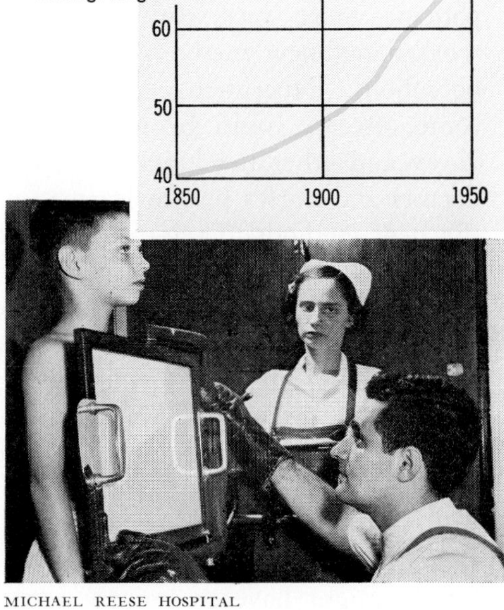

MICHAEL REESE HOSPITAL

Other means of helping the doctor study the inside of the patient's body were developed. One of the most recent and most important is the use of radioactive tracers. These are substances that can be traced as they move through the patient's body because they give off radioactive rays. These rays are not strong enough to harm the patient, but they can be measured by special instruments, such as the Geiger (gī′gẽr) counter. To test whether a patient's blood is circulating freely, for example, a solution of radioactive salt can be injected into his arm. By holding the Geiger counter near any part of the patient's body, the doctor can tell when the radioactive solution in the blood has reached that point. If the counter shows that none is reaching the foot, for example, the doctor knows that the patient's blood is not circulating normally.

With such improved means of finding out what was troubling their patients, doctors were able to treat their patients more successfully. Surgeons worked out new methods for delicate operations. Experiments showed that some diseases could be treated with X-ray and other machines. Of course, doctors and nurses had to learn to use the new methods. Their training was broadened as American schools of medicine and nursing were improved.

The problem of adequate medical care. These advances made medical service more expensive. Many families with small or medium incomes could not afford to be sick. If a member of such a family required an operation or special treatment for a long time, the family might have to borrow money for the expenses. Then it would have to deny itself some necessities, like good food or clothing, for a long time in order to pay the debt.

In the 1940s a large number of families tried to solve the problem by joining health insurance groups. A family paid a certain amount of money each month for insurance. If sickness came, part of its medical expenses were paid by the health insurance group. Some group plans, with higher membership fees, paid all medical expenses. In many cases people who needed such protection most could not afford to pay the fees of the health insurance plans. There has been much discussion of the best ways to solve this problem. Some persons have suggested plans by which the federal government would set up a health insurance system that would insure all the people. Others have argued that such a plan would not be satisfactory to doctors or their patients.

Another obstacle to adequate medical care for all was that most doctors preferred to practice in cities rather than in the country. In the cities they had modern hospitals in which to work, better chances to become specialists, and, in many cases, opportunities to earn a larger income. Many rural areas could not afford to build and keep up modern hospitals. Doctors who practiced in the country often had to work with minimum equipment. They spent time and energy traveling far to see patients. In many farm regions, as a result, there were not enough doctors or hospitals. To meet this need, the federal and state governments helped pay the cost of setting up public health services in many rural counties.

Other aids to better health. The health of the people was protected in many other ways. Children learned good health habits in the schools and in the groups to which they belonged, such as the 4-H Clubs and the Boy and Girl Scouts. Cities provided more parks and built more playgrounds where people could get sunshine and fresh air. Cities passed zoning laws, which allowed factories only in certain parts of town. Thus residential areas were kept free of smoke and heavy traffic. A beginning, at least, was made in slum clearance. Private business and the federal, state, and local governments cooperated to pull down some of the worst tenements. These were replaced by clean, light, airy apartment houses that had room for lawns and playgrounds. Unfortunately, there were not enough of the new apartments to meet the need.

The health of the American people improved also because they had more leisure time and enjoyed more recreation. Most Americans worked no more than eight hours a day and five days a week. Many received two weeks' vacation with pay every year.

Housekeeping took less time, and housewives had more leisure. Fewer families did their own baking, for example. Many kinds of healthful food could be bought frozen in cans or packages and required only short cooking to be ready for the table. More and more families could afford to buy laborsaving devices such as electric irons, washing machines, and vacuum cleaners.

GIRL SCOUTS OF THE U.S.A.

Washing up. Girl Scouts in camp keep up the habit of cleanliness learned at home. Does your community have a camp sponsored by a young people's organization or civic club?

Variety in recreation. What did Americans do with their leisure time? Much of it they spent in seeking entertainment. Several large industries grew up to provide the entertainment. The movies played to millions of customers a week. About 9 out of every 10 homes had radios. The radio offered a wide variety of entertainment. It was also important in advertising and in politics. Candidates for office could talk by radio to almost all voters.

In the 1950s more and more families enjoyed television programs in their homes. Like radio, television provided many kinds of programs, including sports, variety programs, plays, and concerts. Political candidates found television even more useful than radio. Color television was a product of the 1950s.

Christmas shopping. A busy street full of shoppers tells us of a nation that produces much, earns much, and lives well. Is this scene typical of your community at Christmastime?

Sports provided entertainment for many people. Baseball, football, basketball, boxing, and horse racing attracted larger crowds than ever before. Besides intercollegiate football, professional football teams were established and organized into leagues as in baseball. These were all spectator sports. Large numbers of people also participated in sports like golf, tennis, bowling, hunting, and fishing.

With one passenger car for every five or six people, the automobile became an important means of recreation. It was used to take evening drives, weekend trips, or long vacation tours. National and state parks attracted millions of visitors every year. Taking care of tourists and vacationists became an important industry, especially in mountain areas and along the seashore. Americans liked to keep moving, probably more so than the people of other nations.

Large numbers of Americans spent part of their leisure at hobbies like photography and stamp collecting. Some people attended school at night to add to their education. As the leisure time of American people increased, many read more books and magazines. Inexpensive paper-bound volumes, many of them reprints of literary classics, were sold in large numbers in drugstores and at newsstands. Sales of more expensive books increased, too, as did the number of books borrowed from libraries.

Changes in farm life. An important change took place as life on the farm became more like life in the city. We have observed the wide difference between rural and urban life in the earlier periods of our history (see pages

84–92 and 440–444). In the 1900s that difference was reduced.

The change occurred as people on the farms became less isolated. It began even before 1900 as railroads and telephone lines were built in the rural sections. In 1896 the United States Post Office Department began delivering daily mail to farmers. In 1912 the mail began carrying parcel post, making it easier for farmers to receive goods from mail-order companies. These were business firms that sold almost every kind of article by mail. Each company distributed a catalog containing pictures and descriptions of the goods it had for sale. Farm families did a large part of their shopping from the mail-order catalogs.

But the farmer was still unable to travel quickly and easily. A 20-mile trip by horse and buggy took all day. Then in the 1920s came the automobile. It caused an enormous change in rural life. With it neighbors could get together more easily. Farm families could do their shopping in a nearby town or in a large city farther away. The big mail-order companies, which had been serving farmers by parcel post, realized the change and opened retail stores in many shopping centers. Owners of other stores, too, were eager to do business with rural families.

With the aid of the federal government, electricity was brought to more and more farms. Electric motors made the farmer's work easier, and electric appliances made his wife's work in the home easier.

The automobile made it possible for people on the farms to go to town and enjoy the same forms of entertainment that city folk did. They attended ball games and dances and saw the movies. They read city newspapers and magazines. They bought clothes in the same styles that city people wore. The radio and television brought into the farmhouse the same entertainment, advertisements, political speeches, music, and national and world news to which city people listened. Thus farm life became less isolated and less lonely. The automobile also brought more city people into the country for vacations, short or long. The differences between farm folk and city folk became less and less.

2 *Americans Continue to Find New Ways of Learning*

More Americans were "going to school" in the 1950s than ever before. Of the boys and girls from 7 to 13 years old, 97 per cent were attending school.

Rural free delivery. With mail delivered daily, farm families are much less isolated.

DEPARTMENT OF AGRICULTURE

CLEVELAND PUBLIC SCHOOLS

Safety. The chairman of the safety committee conducts a discussion of traffic safety. By working to solve immediate problems, students are preparing to help solve other problems of their country and of the world.

Shop class. These students in a school in West Virginia are learning to operate machines. Shop machinery, like other equipment found in modern schools, adds to the cost of a good education.

LIBRARY OF CONGRESS

Of those from 14 to 17 years old, about 80 per cent were at school. College and university enrollments were the largest in our history. Men and women beyond college age were attending night classes arranged especially for them by colleges and universities. Many older people were enrolled in special adult-education classes sponsored by business, civic, or farm organizations. Young people and mature citizens, city dwellers and country folk, northerners, southerners, and westerners—Americans were going to school.

Expansion and improvement of public schools. The greatest expansion in public education took place in high schools. In 1900 only about 10 per cent of American boys and girls between the ages of 14 and 17 attended high school. By 1950 about 80 per cent were enrolled. In no other country in the world were so many young people of those ages in school. Just as in the late 1800s Americans believed that everyone should have a public school education (see page 334), so in the 1900s they regarded a high school education as necessary.

For students in the public schools, especially in the elementary grades, a new way of education spread in many parts of the country. It may not seem new to you, but it was a change from earlier methods. Pupils were now expected to learn, not only by studying textbooks, but also by engaging in many other activities. New courses were added, such as drawing, industrial arts, and homemaking. In these courses pupils became skilled in many practical and interesting arts that they could use in everyday life. It was believed that these new ways of education prepared pupils to be better citizens.

The largest number of high school students took a general course. It included such subjects as mathematics, science, literature, and social studies. In many high schools vocational courses were given—that is, courses to prepare students for earning a living immediately. Boys took business courses and courses in operating machine tools, in repairing automobiles, in electrical work, in carpentry, and in other trades. In rural areas many high schools gave courses in agriculture. All students were taught about the duties and responsibilities of a citizen.

As in earlier years these changes were made first in city schools. But rural schools also improved. One-room school districts were consolidated, and larger schools were built to serve the combined districts. In these new rural schools the pupils had the same advantages as pupils in city schools.

As more young people were graduated from high school, a demand arose for higher education in local communities. To meet the demand, several hundred junior colleges were established, many of them in the western parts of the country. In a junior college young men and women obtained two years of college education.

Paying for education. Education in the 1900s cost more than in earlier periods, and it is easy to see why. Additional schools had to be built for the larger number of pupils. It was more expensive to equip a machine shop or a practice kitchen than an ordinary classroom. Many of the new schools also had science laboratories, an auditorium, a library, a lunchroom, a gymnasium, and athletic fields. To look after the health of pupils, the schools employed nurses, doctors, and dentists. It all cost money.

LIBRARY OF CONGRESS

Home economics class. These girls in an Ohio school are learning to sew. They also study cooking. In many schools today boys as well as girls enjoy studying home economics.

To encourage local communities to improve their schools and add new services, the state governments contributed more funds for education. As formerly, the states required that local schools meet certain standards in order to obtain their share of this money.

Many of the southern states were handicapped in their efforts to improve their schools. The total income of the people was low and they could not pay heavy taxes. Therefore the states could not spend so much money on schools as wealthier states did. Furthermore, since Negro and white children were taught in separate schools, the southern states had the added expense of keeping up two sets of schools. Yet after 1900 the South improved its schools more rapidly than did other parts of the country. The school year was made longer, modern schools were built, and better trained teachers were hired. In 1954 the United States Supreme Court declared that keeping white and Negro children in separate schools was unconstitutional.

The question of how to pay for improved schools has aroused much discussion. Some persons believe that the federal government should contribute money to the states, especially to the poorer states, to enable them to improve the education of their children. These persons argue that the education of future citizens in any part of the country is the concern of the entire nation. On the other hand, some Americans believe that schools should be locally supported in order to be sure they are run the way local people want them to be run. These persons fear that, if federal money were used to improve the schools, the federal government might control education. The two sides debated the subject of federal aid to education vigorously during the 1950s.

Expansion of colleges and universities. Just as the high schools grew in the 1900s, so did the colleges. In 1920 there were 600,000 students in American colleges and universities; in 1950 there were more than 2,000,000. Can you show the increase in a graph?

In most colleges students receive a general education, studying science, social studies, and literature. In universities students obtain a general education and also special training in such fields as medicine, law, engineering, business, agriculture, and architecture. Universities also have graduate schools, in which college graduates carry on the search for new facts in science, medicine, government, and all other fields of study.

Study for adults. Many Americans continued their education after leaving school. There were night schools in almost all cities. Some of the courses were for immigrants, who learned the American language, American history, and the rights and duties of citizenship. Other people took courses that would enable them to win promotion and higher wages in their work. Still others studied subjects simply because they were interested in them and wished to increase their knowledge. Professors from many universities traveled to communities where there was no college and taught classes there. Many colleges and universities also operated correspondence schools so that men and women who lived far away could take courses by mail.

Newspapers. Education is not limited to schools and courses. People educate themselves in many ways—for example, by reading. Publishing newspapers, magazines, and books for American readers became a very large industry in the 1900s. Newspapers became bigger and livelier in style. They included a large amount of advertising,

COMMUNITY CONSOLIDATED DISTRICT NO. 10, WOODSTOCK, ILL.

Consolidated school. In this consolidated school, pupils enjoy a light, airy library. What other advantages does a consolidated school usually provide?

A Newspaper Index

	Page		Page
Art	31–33	Marine & Air	59
Books	27	Music	33–35
Business	42–43, 49	Obituaries	29
Buyers	42	Radio and TV	41
Crossword	27	Real Estate	51
Editorial	28	Screen	31–35
Events Today	28	Society	26
Fashions	32	Sports	36–40
Financial	43–48	Theatres	33–35
Food	32	Weather	59

The New York Times

¶ In addition to an index like the above, some newspapers print a full-column index of news, business and finance, sports, and advertising. By using the indexes of a newspaper, you can quickly find the items you are interested in.

which was a chief source of income. They printed material on a variety of subjects to interest different types of readers. They published the accounts of national and international events that they received from the great news agencies, such as the Associated Press and the International News Service. From other nationwide companies they obtained daily comic strips and columns on current events, household hints, fashions, teen-age activities, manners, and other subjects. As a result the papers across the country were able to give their readers more complete news and more interesting features than if each newspaper had to gather its own material.

Magazines. Magazines of many varieties were published. Most of them were primarily for entertainment. Others, like the *Atlantic Monthly* and *Harper's,* published both interesting stories and helpful articles discussing problems of the day. Business and industrial magazines, like *Business Week, Chemical Week,* and *Electrical World,* were read principally by businessmen and people interested in the specific industries.

Several new kinds of magazines became very popular. One kind, like *Life* and *Look,* told the news as far as possible in pictures. Another kind, like *Time* and *Newsweek,* covered the week's news in short, lively paragraphs. Then there was still another kind of magazine, like *The Reader's Digest,* which summarized the best articles in other magazines and even printed summaries of new books. Such magazines became popular with Americans.

Books. Book publishing also expanded greatly. Two new ideas helped increase the sale of books. One was the book club. A book club selected books for its members, usually one a month, and frequently charged less than the regular price for the books. The other idea was to reprint popular books to be sold at a low price. Many books were reprinted in pocket-size, paper-covered editions. They could be bought for 25 or 35 cents apiece at newsstands, in grocery stores, in department stores. The little books were sold by the millions. Altogether, the American people bought and read many more books than formerly. They had more leisure. Larger numbers had gone to high school and had learned to enjoy reading. The 1900s were a time of great changes in the world, and many Americans wished to keep up with events.

3 *Artists and Scientists Continue to Influence American Life*

When you go to a museum of art, you will notice that there are paintings and statues by artists from many countries of the world. Perhaps you have heard our symphony orchestras and opera companies perform music written by Italian, French, German, English, and American composers, among others. You have probably read books by authors from various countries. The painters, sculptors, musicians, and writers whose works you enjoy belong to the great international world of art.

After 1900 many American artists and writers became leaders of this in-

NATIONAL GALLERY OF ART

Enjoying art. School children visit the National Gallery of Art, Washington, D.C., to study great art masterpieces. Thousands of persons from all parts of the nation come to enjoy this museum. Has anyone in your class visited it?

ternational world of art. Their works were good, whether they dealt with American subjects or others. Because our space is limited, we shall discuss some of the American artists who portrayed American subjects.

After 1900 many more artists in all fields of art and literature described America—its land and its people. Most of the earlier artists of the 1800s had described only the charming and attractive sides of American life. They ignored the hardships and difficulties. The artists of the 1900s tended to emphasize the problems and hardships in American life as well as its attractive sides. They said they were trying to describe life as it really was. These artists were admired in foreign countries as well as at home for the very reason that they showed many sides of life in America.

American writers. Many of the outstanding novelists in the 1900s suggested through their stories ways in which they thought American life could be improved. Sinclair Lewis, for example, in many of his books blamed the American people for being so concerned with making money that they had little time for interest in art, music, and science. In *Babbitt* he told the story of an American businessman who was so absorbed in his business that nothing else counted with him. In *Arrowsmith,* Lewis followed the career of a young doctor. The hero was tempted to spend his life making money, but he finally devoted himself to scientific research. John Steinbeck in *The Grapes of Wrath* followed a poor family from the Dust Bowl in Oklahoma to California. This dramatic story reminded Americans that terrible poverty existed in the United States, often through no fault of those who suffered from it. Probably the two outstanding American writers of the middle 1900s were Ernest Hemingway and William Faulkner.

Many novelists described earlier times and outstanding events in America's growth. Willa Cather and others told about the experiences of immigrants who settled in the Middle West. Kenneth Roberts wrote exciting stories about the Revolutionary War. Walter D. Edmonds described life along the Erie Canal. Margaret Mitchell wrote a long novel about the South during and after the War Between the States.

American writers wrote very many good short stories. One of the best was *The Devil and Daniel Webster* by Stephen Vincent Benét (bĕ nā′). The story tells what a high opinion New Englanders had of Daniel Webster, who was their spokesman in Congress for many years (see page 277). They believed he could outsmart even the devil. Stephen Vincent Benét was also well known as a poet. He wrote a book-length poem about the War Between the States, called *John Brown's Body.*

Several other poets of the 1900s stand out for their pictures of American life. Robert Frost wrote simple, gentle poems about the countryside and the farmers of New England. You will find some of them in almost any collection of poetry by Americans. Carl Sandburg's poems (you can read part of one on page 648) were mainly about the prairies and the cities of the Middle West. He also wrote a long biography, in prose, of Abraham Lincoln. In his book of poetry called *The People, Yes,* Sandburg expressed his faith in the deep wisdom of the people. He

Birches

When I see birches bend to left and right
Across the lines of straighter darker trees,
I like to think some boy's been swinging them.
But swinging doesn't bend them down to stay.
Ice-storms do that. Often you must have seen them
Loaded with ice a sunny winter morning
After a rain. They click upon themselves
As the breeze rises, and turn many-colored
As the stir cracks and crazes their enamel.

From "Birches" by Robert Frost

felt that in the long run the people were always right and chose the best thing to do. He believed firmly in the democratic way of leaving the power of government in the hands of the people.

The theater. In the 1900s the theater was prosperous only in New York City. Elsewhere it could not compete with the movies. Residents of other parts of the country seldom had an opportunity to see a play by professional actors unless they went to New York or to a nearby large city. In many places persons who were interested in the theater organized "little theater" groups. They were amateurs. They put on plays and acted in them, not to earn money, but because they enjoyed acting. The little-theater movement kept many Americans interested in the theater and provided them with opportunities for relaxation and fun.

American musicians and writers were successful in cooperating to write musical comedies—that is, light, entertaining plays with music. As examples, four outstanding musical comedies were based on life and events in America. *Show Boat* was about life on river showboats, of the kind that you read about on page 336. One of its songs, "Old Man River," has remained popular for a long time. *Porgy and Bess,* with excellent music by George Gershwin, dealt with Negro life. *Oklahoma!* portrayed the American West. *South Pacific* was based on experiences of American servicemen and women during the Second World War.

The writers of musical comedies also wrote many hit songs, songs that everybody sang. George M. Cohan's "Over There" was probably the most popular during the First World War. During the Second World War, Irving Berlin's "God Bless America" and "White Christmas" were heard all over the world, wherever Americans went.

Jazz and classical music in America. The most popular form of music in America was the kind called jazz. It was heard on phonographs, in dance halls, on radio and television programs —wherever music was played. Perhaps it became so popular because it was lively and free in form. Perhaps it expressed the energy and freedom of the American people. At any rate, many people in other countries thought of this music as typically American. Jazz originated in Negro music and was first played by Negro bands in New Orleans.

For years people debated whether jazz could be considered "good" music, and the argument still goes on. But George Gershwin, by composing "Rhapsody in Blue," proved to many people that jazz could be written as serious music. Other composers also wrote serious compositions that reflected the influence of popular music. Then many persons whose taste had been limited to classical music took an interest in jazz, and many who had enjoyed only popular music became interested in the classics.

Classical music became much more important to the American people as a whole. You will remember that symphony orchestras were started in a few cities in the late 1800s. In the mid-1900s many of the large cities had excellent symphony orchestras whose concerts were well attended. After each season,

¶ In the following lines from *The People, Yes,* Carl Sandburg tells some of the folklore of the American people. There are many more such stories in the book of poems.

They have yarns
Of a skyscraper so tall they had to put hinges
On the two top stories so to let the moon go by,
Of one corn crop in Missouri when the roots
Went so deep and drew off so much water
The Mississippi riverbed that year was dry,
Of pancakes so thin they had only one side,
Of "a fog so thick we shingled the barn and six feet out on the fog,"
Of Pecos Pete straddling a cyclone in Texas and riding it to the west coast where "it rained out under him," . . .
Of the boy who climbed a cornstalk growing so fast he would have starved to death if they hadn't shot biscuits up to him, . . .
Of Paul Bunyan's big blue ox, Babe, measuring between the eyes forty-two axhandles and a plug of Star tobacco exactly,
Of John Henry's hammer and the curve of its swing and his singing of it as a "rainbow round my shoulder."

orchestras and the Metropolitan Opera Company gave performances in other cities. Outstanding musicians toured the country giving concerts. The United States continued to depend on Europe to supply many of its artists and compositions. But more American music was heard, and more American musicians won success. The works of such American composers as Deems Taylor, Ferde Grofé, and Aaron Copland were often performed. American singers, such as Marian Anderson, Lawrence Tibbett, Helen Traubel, and Gladys Swarthout, built successful careers in concerts, radio, opera, movies, and television.

American architecture. In architecture American cities tended to look more and more alike. Buildings of each kind—banks, hotels, movie theaters, and public buildings—were built in more or less the same style. The suburbs of each city, where many of the new homes were built, showed the same variety of attractive styles. There were some local differences. In New England many houses were built in the colonial style. In California and the Southwest many were built in the Spanish style.

American architects raised the skyscraper to greater heights and gave it a new beauty. The Empire State Building in New York City, 102 stories, was the tallest. It was also an example of the way skyscrapers were designed with setbacks. The building becomes narrower and narrower as it rises until it ends in a great central tower. The famous Rockefeller Center was planned as a group of skyscrapers separated by open spaces so that each building would have enough light and air. Apartment houses built in the slum-clearance programs were planned with plenty of open space between the buildings.

Practicing and enjoying the fine arts. One of the most interesting things about twentieth-century America has been the great increase in people's in-

BROOKHAVEN NATIONAL LABORATORY, UPTON, N.Y.

Atomic energy. In this huge Long Island laboratory, scientists work together to experiment with atomic energy. They use costly equipment, which most scientists could not afford to purchase for private laboratories. Cooperative research such as this is common among modern scientists.

terest in the fine arts. Men and women got together in hundreds of choral societies to enjoy the pleasure of singing together. Children studied music at home and in schools and played together in school orchestras. There were many excellent music schools for advanced students. Symphony concerts and operas were broadcast over television and radio. Large numbers of Americans bought phonograph records of musical masterpieces as well as of jazz pieces and popular songs.

Many Americans took up painting or sculpture as a hobby. Those who wished to study to become professional artists could attend one of a number of outstanding schools. Many Americans who had collected works of art gave them to museums, where artists and students of art could study them.

Outstanding contributions in science. Scientists, like artists, have many international ties. A scientist in one country makes an experiment in which he discovers something new. He writes an article in a magazine telling exactly how he did it. The magazine is read by scientists all over the world. Another scientist in another country repeats the experiment and perhaps carries it a little further, adding to the new discovery. A third scientist and a fourth do the same. Thus scientists cooperate to carry on their work.

Scientists today do not as a rule do their work by themselves in private laboratories. With the rapid development

DEPARTMENT OF AGRICULTURE

Tobogganing in Vermont. Healthier Americans enjoy more outdoor sports, in winter as well as in summer. Skiing and tobogganing have become popular winter sports. Which summer and winter sports are your favorites?

of modern science, a great change has come in the way that research is carried on and inventions are made. In the 1800s an individual, usually working alone, tackled a problem without much system and arrived at a solution more or less by chance. Goodyear's discovery of a way to vulcanize rubber, described on page 318, is a good example. In our time such problems are taken up by teams of scientists and engineers working together systematically in great laboratories. Such laboratories are run by universities, by the federal and state governments, and especially by many large manufacturing companies. By teamwork in the laboratory and by international cooperation, scientists increase man's knowledge of, and his control over, the world in which he lives.

As you have studied the growth of America in the twentieth century, you have seen over and over again how important scientific research has been in solving our problems. In developing industry, in conserving natural resources, in finding better farming methods, and in improving health, Americans have turned to their scientists for help. The scientists have not always known the answers to questions, but often they have found them. In doing so, they have made great contributions to American life. The airplane, the motion-picture machine, the radio, and television are just a few of the twentieth-century inventions we owe to the scientists. Perhaps some members of your class will investigate these and other inventions and report to the class on them.

Summary

In the first half of the twentieth century, life in the United States was greatly changed. The health of the people improved. Epidemic diseases like yellow fever that used to take many lives every year were wiped out. The battle against tuberculosis, cancer, and infantile paralysis was fought in many laboratories and hospitals. Doctors had many new methods and drugs to help the sick. Americans improved their diet. Unfortunately, some Americans could not afford to take advantage of all these health aids.

A good deal of leisure time and many forms of recreation helped make the lives of Americans easier and more interesting. The movies, radio, television, sports, and hobbies, and, above all, automobiles enabled Americans to "have a good time." More education for more people helped in building better lives. Most children of 1900 had only a grammar school education, while most children of 1950 attended high school. From high school more students than ever before went on to colleges and universities. Adults continued their education in extension courses and by much reading of newspapers, magazines, and books.

One result of more education was that more Americans were interested in literature and the arts. Americans seemed to like writers and artists who presented the many sides of American life. The most popular form of music was jazz, though many Americans enjoyed symphony music and operas. In the middle 1900s American artists won places for themselves in the international world of art, and American scientists won honors in the international scientific world. The work of scientists became closely cooperative. Most scientists did their work in the laboratories of universities, government bureaus, or large manufacturing companies.

Science, education, music, literature, and the other arts all helped Americans to build more comfortable and more satisfying lives in the twentieth century.

For a Quick Review

1. Mention several ways in which scientific research has brought longer life and better health to the American people.

2. What are the problems in bringing the best medical service to all the people? What solutions have been proposed?

3. Name some of the most popular recreations of Americans today.

4. How have schools been improved in the twentieth century?

5. What are some of the ways in which Americans continue their education after they leave high school?

Learning to Study More Easily

COLLECTING INFORMATION THROUGH INTERVIEWS

In Chapter 31 you read how Americans in general live their daily lives, get an education, and spend their leisure time. How well does this account fit the people of your community? How many museums and parks does your city have? What kinds of magazines and books do the people in your neighborhood read? What proportion of the boys and girls who are in school in the fifth grade stay to graduate from your high school? No textbook can answer such questions for each individual community. You and your classmates, however, can obtain the answers. You can obtain information from various people. Then you can pool the information and see how your community compares with the general trends in American life.

To collect information through interviews, you and your classmates will need to plan together in advance. Here are some questions that may help you plan.

1. What is the major question you are trying to answer? Perhaps it is: How do the people of our community spend their leisure time?
2. What kinds of information will help you to answer this question? In other words, what subquestions should you ask? To investigate the use of leisure time, for example, you might find out about such things as time spent watching television, circulation of books from the public library, number and kinds of magazines and books sold at newsstands, and attendance at sports events.
3. What people can furnish information on the questions you are investigating? The list of people will depend, of course, on the questions. To continue with the example of leisure time, you might interview the managers of the local movie houses, an official at the public library, the owners of newsstands, and so on.

   To prepare for such interviews, make a card-file listing of the persons from whom your group expects to get information. Put the name of each on a separate card. Then write on the card the exact questions the class has decided should be asked of that individual. When the student goes for the interview, he can ask the questions.
4. How and to whom will you present your findings? Through oral reports, panel discussions, written reports, or bulletin-board displays? You can collect and organize your information more efficiently if you know how you will use it.

As you plan your investigation, check frequently with your teacher. You will need an O.K. from your school officials before you carry out your plan.

The people your group is likely to want to interview are busy men and women. To save their time and yours and to make your investigation go smoothly, do these things:

1. Arrange each interview well in advance, scheduling a definite time and place.
2. Be at the interview place on time. Know exactly what you expect to do. Your class may wish to rehearse some imaginary interviews to get practice in beginning and ending such conferences easily.
3. After the interview show your appreciation for it by writing a note of thanks. Ask your teacher to check it with you before you mail it.

32 *Your American Adventure*

During the Second World War a boy who looked much older than his 14 years enlisted in the Army. His parents reported his true age and he was dismissed from the service. Before he was sent home his commanding officer had a talk with him.

"Jim, why did you lie about your age and cause all this trouble?" the officer asked.

"I wanted to do my part. After all, we're in a war," Jim answered. "I guess I'll have to admit I thought it would be exciting, too."

"You must realize," said the officer, "that even in wartime your most important job is to go to school. You and the other Americans your age are going to be running this country in a few years. The country needs what I call practicing citizens—people who find out the facts about problems, think about them, and then act to solve them. You can start in school to do a lot of learning, a lot of thinking, and some acting on these problems."

"But, sir, isn't the most important thing to win the war?" asked Jim.

"Of course, we must win the war," replied the officer, "and we're going to win it. But winning the war will not alone solve many of our serious problems. They will be with us long after the war is won. You and others your age are going to have to deal with them when you are grown up. Your most important duty is to prepare to deal with them intelligently. Your job now is at home and at school, learning to be a good citizen."

What serious problems did the officer have in mind? They are the problems your country will face as you grow up. In this chapter we shall discuss four of them. We shall begin each problem by summarizing its history. Understanding the development of problems in the past is the first step toward solving problems in the future. The past, the present, the future—all are parts of one continuous American adventure.

1 *Democracy Must Continue to Grow*

As you have followed the American adventure through the years, you have watched the idea of democracy grow. In colonial times, as compared with today, you found little democracy. The people were divided into definite social classes. A person was usually expected to live out his life in the class into which he happened to be born. The son of a wealthy man had a good education. The son of a skilled craftsman might learn to read and write. After all, he had to keep his accounts. But his education seldom went any further than that. Most people received no education. In colonial times a property owner could vote and hold office, if he owned enough property or paid a certain amount of taxes. A man who did not own property usually had no share in running the government. His part was to obey the laws that were made by somebody else.

Even in those early days, however, there were Americans who insisted on more democracy, including equal rights for all. Life, liberty, and the pursuit of happiness, said the writers of the Declaration of Independence, are the rights of all mankind. All men, they said, are born free and equal. These were ideals. They represented what some people hoped would come true someday. Thomas Jefferson knew very well that these ideals did not describe what actually existed in 1776. These ideals are so high that, although we have worked toward them ever since, we have not reached them completely in practice—almost two centuries later. But we have made great progress. Certainly people in the United States today come much nearer than at any earlier time in our history to enjoying equal rights and opportunities. It is probably correct to say that our people come nearer to enjoying equal rights and opportunities than any other people in the history of the world.

The idea of democracy. The idea of democracy today is much broader than it was two centuries ago. At first those who talked of democracy thought mostly about political democracy. That is, they talked about giving more people the right to vote and hold office—a share in running the government. They wanted to protect individual rights such as those that are listed in the Bill of Rights.

Today we think these rights are extremely important, of course, and we are still working to improve our political democracy. In addition, however, we think of democracy as having other sides. For example, democracy has come to mean that every young person should have a chance to go to school and obtain the education that will make his life more useful and happier. It has come to mean that everyone should have opportunities for earning a living and for enjoying good health. It has come to mean that everyone should have a chance to serve his community and his nation. In other words, democracy today includes the ideal that every person shall have a chance to make as great a success of his life as his ability and hard work will permit.

Democracy today emphasizes the importance of individuals, persons like you and your friends. It is a part of democracy that each person, with his particular abilities, opinions, and ambitions, is to be considered as an individual. Each person is to be judged by what he is and what he can do rather than by where he came from or who his parents are.

So it is that democracy means much more today than it did when the American adventure began. Let us retrace some of the steps through which we Americans have expanded our idea of democracy.

Gains in political democracy. As you have read, more and more people gradually have gained a share in our government. In colonial times only property owners had the right to vote and hold office. In the Revolutionary period the Patriots used arguments for liberty, equality, and the rights of the individual as reasons for breaking away from the mother country. After the Revolution many people who did not have equal rights demanded that the Patriots' arguments be carried out in practice. These people demanded the right to vote and to hold office. In the 1800s, especially in the 1820s and 1830s, most states abolished the property requirement. They gave the right to vote and hold office to all white male citizens over 21. The Fourteenth and Fifteenth Amendments were added to the Constitution to assure Negroes the right to vote. The campaign for woman suffrage, begun just before 1850, reached its goal 70 years later. Thus an ever-increasing part of the American people has gained a voice in the government.

Democracy in the Words of Famous Americans

Democracy means not "I am as good as you are," but "You are as good as I am."

REV. THEODORE PARKER

As I would not be a slave, so I would not be a master. This expresses my idea of democracy. Whatever differs from this, to the extent of the difference, is no democracy.

ABRAHAM LINCOLN

I believe in democracy because it releases the energy of every human being.

WOODROW WILSON

All the ills of democracy can be cured by more democracy.

ALFRED E. SMITH

Democracy is based upon the conviction that there are extraordinary possibilities in ordinary people.

REV. HARRY EMERSON FOSDICK

Democracy is a process, not a static condition. It is becoming, rather than being. It can easily be lost, but never is fully won. Its essence is eternal struggle.

JUSTICE WILLIAM H. HASTIE

¶ What do you think democracy is? Perhaps each member of your class will want to frame his or her own definition, using no more than 35 words.

METRO-GOLDWYN-MAYER

Defending freedom. You have read about the arrest of John Peter Zenger, in 1734, for publishing criticisms of the royal governor of New York. This movie scene shows him at his trial. The jury decided he was not guilty. Zenger, a German-born American, was an early fighter for freedom of the press. Why is it an important freedom?

Personal rights. Gradually Americans have won the guarantee of equal personal rights. When the states were formed during the Revolution, many of their constitutions included a bill of rights. (Virginia's constitution is an example. Other states followed Virginia's lead.) When the federal Constitution was written, it protected the rights of citizens. (See Article I, Sections 9 and 10.) Soon after the Constitution was ratified, the Bill of Rights was adopted, (Amendments I–X). Read these parts of the Constitution and discuss the meaning of each one. What rights of the individual did each one guarantee? In the 1860s slavery was ended, and another important step toward equal rights was taken. (See Amendments XIII, XIV, XV.) In the twentieth century the American people have continued their efforts to assure to each individual such rights as freedom of speech, freedom of worship, and equal protection under law.

Educational opportunities. During the 1800s our communities opened up public elementary schools. Beginning in the 1800s, and more rapidly in the 1900s, they established public high schools. Community colleges and state universities make a college education available to those who are prepared for it. How did the growth of public schools make opportunities more nearly equal for young people? How did the spread of education help protect the rights of individuals? Review pages 331–334, 451–452, and 640–642 for help in considering these questions.

Reform. Since the early 1800s we have seen that many reformers have tried to improve American life. Some of them worked to clean up city slums and relieve poverty. Some of them tried to help immigrants to get acquainted with their new country, learn American ways, and make their contributions to American life. Do you remember Jane Addams and her work at Hull-

House? Others worked to get for women the right to own property or the opportunities to choose occupations that had formerly been followed only by men. There was Susan B. Anthony, a leader in the woman's rights movement. How were these reformers helping toward the goal of equal rights and wider opportunities for all citizens? Skim through pages 340–341 and 445–451 if you need to refresh your memory on this topic.

Wider government service. As you studied the American adventure, you saw that the people have called on local, state, and national governments to undertake new activities to help citizens. Health services, such as those provided by visiting nurses in many cities and states, furnish one example. Another is social security legislation, providing unemployment insurance, old-age pensions, and payments to widows with young children. Can you give examples to show how these and other expanded services of the government have increased opportunities for many people?

Contributions of immigrants. When one group of immigrants after another came to America during the 1800s and early 1900s, each group met some of the same difficulties. The Irish, the Germans the Scandinavians, the Italians, the Slavic groups, and the others faced the same problems. What were the difficulties the newcomers faced? Why do you think these difficulties arose?

As the members of each group, in turn, got jobs and helped to build America, the other Americans gradually accepted them as fellow citizens. The older Americans realized that the newcomers and their children had much to contribute. We think of their music, for example, and their beautiful art work, interesting customs, and delicious foods. You have read of the immigrants and the children of immigrants who became leaders in sports, business, politics, the arts, and in other kinds of activity. Have people been especially interested that Sam Gompers was an immigrant or that Willie Mays is a Negro whose forefathers had been slaves? Or were they more interested in what Sam and Willie could do? What connections can you show between the story of newcomers in America and the nation's progress toward equal rights and broader opportunities?

Continuing our progress toward democratic ideals. It is clear that the American adventure of the past has been an adventure in progress toward freedom and equality for Americans. It is equally clear that we have not yet realized those ideals. We must continue to strive toward them in the future.

Voting. There are still many citizens who are denied the right to vote. There are many more citizens who can vote but fail to do so. In presidential elections, for example, usually less than 60 per cent of eligible voters actually vote. Even fewer vote in state and local elections. Our government is supposed to be run by majority opinion. But how can we know what the majority opinion is when only a fraction of the eligible voters take the trouble to vote? How can we solve this problem and continue our progress toward government by all the people? That is one challenge that you will meet in your American adventure.

DEPARTMENT OF AGRICULTURE

Learning by doing. A 4-H Club member is brushing his calf, which he raised as a club project (see page 536). Through this experience the boy is learning to raise livestock. His little brothers will soon have projects of their own.

Personal rights. Every now and then someone tries to deny equal personal rights to an individual or to a group of individuals. Special officers in the United States Department of Justice have been appointed to help protect the rights of persons. Various private organizations work toward the same end. Here again we have not achieved the ideal. The continued protection of personal rights will be another challenge in your American adventure.

Educational opportunity. We are far from realizing the democratic ideal of equal educational opportunity for American girls and boys. Too many young people who are eager and able to learn have to leave school to go to work. Many schools lack adequate laboratories, libraries, health services, and vocational guidance. Old school buildings have to be repaired or replaced. As our population increases, additional schools must be built for the larger number of children. This will be one of the most important challenges of your American adventure: to keep our public school system improving and expanding to meet higher standards and a growing population.

Duties of democratic citizenship. Such matters, you may say to yourself, are problems that concern congressmen and governors and mayors, not ordinary citizens. If that is what you think, you cannot be more wrong. Every American citizen has duties as well as rights. If he does not perform his duties, he will not long enjoy his rights.

He obviously has the duty to vote, though too many citizens fail to do so. But a citizen's duty only begins with voting. He should take an active interest in political affairs. He should make his views known by expressing them to friends and by writing them to

CLEVELAND PUBLIC SCHOOLS

School broadcast. Some schools have radio stations where students present programs for the school and, sometimes, for the community. What are the advantages to the school? What do the students who take part in the broadcasting gain from their work?

"What work shall I choose?" A guidance counselor is helping this girl find out about several kinds of work that might be suited to her abilities and interests. Have you investigated fields of work that you might like to enter?

CLEVELAND PUBLIC SCHOOLS

Craftsman. Before the time of machines and factories, craftsmen like this one made products for the home by hand. What changes came with the use of machines in factories?

newspapers and to government officials. Best of all, he can become a working member of the political party of his choice.

The private citizen can contribute to the continued progress of democratic education. He can be active in a Parent-Teacher Association. He can serve as a member of the local board of education. He can strengthen democracy by encouraging the clubs or other organizations to which he belongs to follow democratic practices. When another citizen's personal rights are being threatened, he can stand up and speak for democracy.

Duties of young Americans. Still, you may say, these are problems for grownups; they have nothing to do with you now. If you think so, you are wrong. For you have your democratic responsibilities in the school, in the home, in the groups to which you belong. If you get into the habit of meeting your responsibilities now, you will be likely to meet them as a grownup.

Do you participate in school elections? Do you take part in student government? Do you follow democratic practices at home? Do you stand up for the democratic ideals in the groups to which you belong? Do you protest when another boy or girl is being denied equal rights or equal opportunity? Remember, if you stand by today while someone else is being denied his rights, you will be denied your rights tomorrow.

2 *The American People Must Maintain a High Standard of Living*

An outstanding story of the American adventure has been the tremendous increase in the amount of goods produced by the American people. The increased production has meant that the people have been able to live well. Americans enjoy the highest standard of living in the history of the world.

The early farming period. The first settlers in the European colonies, you remember, had to obtain food and supplies from the mother country. They had to work hard for many years before they could take care of their own needs. Pioneers on one frontier after another for 200 years went through this stage of hand-to-mouth existence. The older communities, meanwhile, were able to produce a surplus, which they exported. In return they obtained manufactured goods, with which they made their lives more comfortable.

In the colonial period and in the days

of the early republic, most Americans earned a living by farming or by shipping. Manufacturing—of clothing, for example, or of wood and iron products —was done by craftsmen in their little shops or by families in their homes.

The spread of machine production. The great change came when men invented machines to do the work of human hands. Then men set up rows of machines in factories and hired workers to tend them. The change began in the spinning and weaving of cloth. The sewing machine made possible the large-scale manufacturing of clothing and shoes. Using a new, inexpensive way of manufacturing steel, men produced enough steel to make an endless variety of products, from battleships to farm fences. Machine tools turned out large quantities of interchangeable parts. These parts were bolted or welded together to make plows, harrows, reapers and binders, locomotives, railroad cars, and other products. Power was supplied first by water, then by steam, then by electricity.

Men and machines working together produced huge quantities of goods that could be sold at low prices. People in every part of the country could afford to buy them. Railroads spread over the country to bring the goods to the people. Manufacturers had the whole country as a market. To obtain money for building larger factories to supply this ever-expanding market, they organized big corporations.

New problems. This tremendous growth of manufacturing created new problems. Our country was using up its natural resources too rapidly. We had to begin to conserve our wood and water, our minerals and our topsoil. Factories were built in cities and Americans had to solve the problems of city life—sanitation and health, protection of life and property, transportation, housing, recreation, and so on.

Factory workers had to organize unions to obtain equal bargaining power with the big corporations. Business became so powerful that it threatened to control federal, state, and local governments. Reforms had to be carried out to keep the control of government safely in the hands of the people.

Advance in the 1900s. The twentieth century added a new chapter to the story of expanding production. The moving assembly line speeded up the making of products. One result was the enor-

Oil refinery. A way to conserve minerals is to use them efficiently. Modern refineries use scientific processes to make the most products possible from each barrel of petroleum.

STANDARD OIL CO. (N.J.)

20TH CENTURY-FOX

Pioneer waste. Cutting forests and burning the timber enabled pioneers to plant their crops. But a valuable resource was thus wasted and the way was opened for later soil erosion.

Water power. The same dams that prevent destructive floods also produce water power for electricity. This is the Grand Coulee Dam in the state of Washington. The story of its construction and the benefits it brings to the Columbia River area would make an interesting report.

BUREAU OF RECLAMATION

mous growth of the automobile industry. New industries were started, such as the making of airplanes, movies, radio, and television. With the aid of the science of chemistry, men even made new materials, like plastics, that nature had neglected to make.

In the twentieth century the problems of our industrial world became more difficult, and our solutions for some problems were improved. Our country became more dependent on other countries for raw materials and for customers. The countries of the free world depended on us for goods and for help in improving their own agriculture and manufacturing. We lived in an interdependent world. Hard times in other countries could cause hard times among us. To protect our people from dangers beyond their control, our government set up unemployment insurance, old-age pensions, minimum-wage and maximum-hour laws.

Our future prosperity. What about the future? Our population will continue to increase. Our country will have to increase its production in order to supply this larger population. But that will not be enough. Production must grow faster than population, so that all Americans will have more goods to use and enjoy. Our country must continue to help the other nations of the free world until they are able to support themselves. For these purposes we must continue to advance—in inventions, in the training of skilled workers and efficient leaders, in the use of atomic energy and other discoveries of science. We can believe that the progress of the past will look small compared to the achievements of the future.

Your part in tomorrow's adventure. The United States is a young country. The American adventure has hardly more than begun. There are no more frontiers on the edge of settlement in the West. But there are twentieth-century frontiers for your American adventure. You can find some of these frontiers in the great industrial laboratories, in atomic-energy plants, in university libraries. You can find them wherever the organization of industry and the production and distribution of its products can be improved. You can find an important frontier in the effort to improve relations between labor and management. You can find a frontier in the underdeveloped countries of the world, teaching American know-how to other peoples.

You have already done some thinking about what you will be when you grow up. In a few years you will have to begin making decisions. What part will you play in making your America prosperous and strong? Will you raise wheat with tractors and combines? Will you make automobiles or bridges or houses? Will you transport goods or sell them? Will you be a secretary or a teacher? Will you work in a laboratory, trying to improve products or to harness atomic energy? Will you run a bank or a big corporation? Will you write books or paint pictures or plan and build new and beautiful buildings?

Remember that in playing your part in the American adventure you will have two aims. One will be to build a full and happy life for yourself. The other will be to cooperate with others for the peaceful progress of your country and of the world.

Entertainment on the frontier. Unlike many of us today who rely upon television, radio, or the movies to entertain us, frontier families had to make their own entertainment.

3 *The Arts and Sciences Add to Our Enjoyment of Life*

By reading a book, seeing a movie, or watching a television program, you can join in many adventures. Some of them actually happened. Some might have happened. Some probably could not happen. You can, in imagination, travel to foreign countries and share in the lives of distant peoples. When you do so, you are using the arts to expand your personal world. And this is only one of many ways you can use literature, the theater, and the other arts to make your world bigger and more interesting. What are some of the other ways you use the arts for pleasure?

When you turn a knob and click on your radio, record player, or television set, you are about to enjoy one of the practical uses of modern science. When you sit down to dinner in midwinter and your mother serves strawberry shortcake made of quick-frozen strawberries for dessert, you are enjoying another kind of modern scientific development. In what ways that you can think of does modern science increase your comfort and enjoyment of life?

The arts and sciences in a democracy. We have said that democracy has many sides, many goals for all the people to share. Making life more interesting, more enjoyable, for every person is one of the goals of democracy. Helping all Americans to understand, appreciate, and use the arts and sciences is one way of working toward the goal of more enjoyable living. If we review our progress toward that goal, it may help us see the promises that the arts and sciences hold for your American adventure.

Limited enjoyment of the arts and sciences. During colonial days and in the early years of our nation, the majority of the people did long, hard days of work. They had little leisure for reading, going to plays, or enjoying music, for example. Indeed, many people could not read and lived far away from the nearest theater or concert hall. America was a new country just being built. Many people, especially on the frontier, had to work hard to get food, shelter, and clothing. Only the wealthy had time to read books and money for plays and concerts. They had beautiful pictures and fine decorations in their homes. But most men and women had none of these things.

In the mid-1800s many people worked in mills and mines and factories. These workers had no time or money for enjoying the arts and sciences. But in this period, as you have seen, American life began to change.

Growing opportunities. In this period the opportunities for education increased. Public schools were built, and children were compelled to attend them. They learned to read, and reading is a doorway to the understanding of the arts and sciences. At the same time the same inventiveness that produced machines for farm and factory also produced machines for lower cost printing. You remember that the first penny newspaper came out in the 1830s. The rotary press and the Linotype made possible the printing of books and newspapers in large numbers at low prices. Just as Americans were learning to read, these machines put reading material into their hands.

Americans took a deeper interest in the world around them. And workers in the arts responded to that new interest. Writers wrote books, artists painted pictures, and musicians composed music that the people enjoyed. (See pages 335–338, 453–456, and 644–649.)

The twentieth century. In the twentieth century, opportunities for Ameri-

Music at home. Pioneer families of the 1800s, living miles apart, had to find recreation at home. Scenes like this, from the movie *Romance of Rosy Ridge,* were common.

METRO-GOLDWYN-MAYER

Television. The TV set brings into the living room music, drama, sports, and news. The television industry has grown rapidly since the first commercial broadcasts in 1939.

ALLEN B. DUMONT LABORATORIES, INC.

POCKET BOOKS, INC.

Low-priced books. Paper-covered books costing from 25 to 75 cents make it possible for more people than ever before to own and enjoy books.

Nature study. The boys are part of a class that is studying plants and insects. By learning about nature, they will be more fully equipped to understand and enjoy the world around them.

COMMUNITY CONSOLIDATED DIST. 10, WOODSTOCK, ILL.

cans to enjoy the arts expanded rapidly. Most people worked shorter hours and had more leisure. At the same time they earned more and could afford books, works of art, music, and the theater. Many children received a high school and even a college education. When they grew up they could understand and enjoy the arts. They could practice the arts themselves.

Again science made its contribution in the nick of time. Scientific laboratories produced movies, radio, television, and improved methods of printing in color. These new inventions brought plays, music, information, and a variety of entertainment to the wider and ever-growing American audience.

The American adventure, as you have seen, has meant a growing feeling of equality among our people. It has also meant a larger share of the good things of life for our people. The wider enjoyment of the arts and sciences has been part of the feeling of equality and of the higher standard of living.

Your American adventure. What part will the arts and sciences play in your American adventure? Will you plan your education so that you will be prepared to get as much enjoyment out of them as possible?

Your education can serve you in three important ways. It can prepare you for earning a living. It can prepare you for good citizenship. It can prepare you for the intelligent enjoyment of books, plays, music, painting, and other forms of art. Is your education preparing you for the full, rich life that comes with the achievement of these three aims? You can make that kind of a life your American adventure.

GLENS FALLS INSURANCE CO., GLENS FALLS, N.Y.

Burgoyne's surrender. The victory at Saratoga (see page 138) helped the 13 states win independence. In the Revolutionary period, affairs in the United States were closely connected with affairs in other countries.

4 *World Leadership Is a Challenge to Our Nation*

The American adventure has taken place in a world of many nations. At times in their history the American people have been deeply interested in their relations with foreign countries. In other periods they have paid little attention to what foreign nations were doing. What made the difference? What can we learn from the past experience of our nation in the field of foreign affairs? Before we consider these questions, let us look back at some of the high points in the story of our relations with other parts of the world.

Early American interest in world affairs. In the colonial period the leaders and the educated people in the North American English colonies were eager for news from the mother country. Laws passed in England might change their daily living. The colonists were interested in what happened among European nations. If England went to war in Europe, they (and their ships on the high seas) would be in it, too. In short, the English colonists were interested in affairs outside their own country because European affairs directly affected their lives.

In the Revolutionary period American affairs were still closely tied in with those of European nations. The Americans depended on France, Spain, and Holland for aid in winning their independence. You will remember that France actually lent money, provided supplies, and sent armed forces to assist the American cause. American leaders carefully watched European rivalries during this period. They knew that they were likely to find their friends among England's enemies.

Foreign affairs of the young republic. At the end of the Revolution the new United States had as neighbors British Canada, Spanish Florida, and Spanish Louisiana. These neighbors kept the American leaders (and sometimes the people) concerned about the attitudes of European nations. As you know, the European nations were at war much of the time from 1792 to 1815. American leaders decided that the United States should take no part in Europe's wars. Do you remember Washington's neutrality proclamation and, later, Jefferson's embargo? (See pages 193 and 195.) What was the purpose of each?

Although determined to remain neutral, American leaders and many of the people continued their interest in international affairs as long as Europe was at war. They had reason to do so, since the wars affected the United States.

One direct effect was felt by Americans living in the Mississippi Valley. Do you remember the demand of western farmers for the right of deposit at New Orleans? What did international affairs have to do with it? What action resulted? What was its effect on our nation? (See pages 212–219.)

The European wars had other effects on Americans. Eventually the United States fought Great Britain in the War of 1812. How did the wars in Europe help cause the War of 1812? European affairs also played a part in bringing the War of 1812 to an end. (See pages 194–200.) It is easy to see why Americans were deeply concerned with foreign affairs during these first years of national independence.

A period of little interest in world relations. Soon, however, the situation changed. In Europe, in 1815, the great powers made a peace that lasted for many years. There was not another general European war until 1914, when the First World War began. In the Western Hemisphere the position of the United States soon became safer and stronger. Within a decade after the War of 1812, our nation had no threatening neighbors along its borders and no fear of attack from abroad. What arrangement had been made with Canada that has promoted peaceful relations ever since? What had happened to Florida? What did the Monroe Doctrine show about the relations of the United States with the other American nations and with those of Europe? You can refresh your memory on these points by skimming pages 202–205, and 217–219. All these events made it possible for our people to turn to developing their country, paying little attention to the outside world.

Through much of the middle 1800s, the American people almost forgot about their relations with other nations, except during boundary disputes and during the Mexican War. The people were busy occupying their part of the continent, developing its resources, and solving the problem of national union. Of course, Americans carried on trade with many countries, including China and Japan. The United States exchanged ambassadors with the other countries of the world and made treaties with them. But our relations with other nations seldom held the spotlight

NATIONAL LIFE INSURANCE COMPANY, MONTPELIER, VT.

Occupying the land. The pioneer, building a log cabin, squares a log to make it fit. In the 1800s Americans had little time for interest in the rest of the world.

as far as our people were concerned. International relations went fairly smoothly with peace prevailing. The big debates of national politics were about problems at home.

Renewed attention to world affairs. Meanwhile the United States was growing into a great industrial country. As you remember, by the late 1800s, the American people made huge quantities of goods in factories. Farmers used machines to produce bigger crops. The United States exported its surplus goods and imported raw materials and other products. As they carried on a world-wide trade, the American people again became concerned with events in other parts of the world. Just before and after 1900, the United States obtained overseas territories and built the Panama Canal. Naturally, this expansion increased American interest in world events. (See pages 468 and 485–500.)

When the First World War came in Europe, the American people thought they could keep out of it. They tried to remain neutral. As a neutral, however, the United States found itself facing many problems. Some of them were like the ones Americans leaders had faced in the day of Jefferson and Madison—interference with American trade, for example. Other problems, such as submarine warfare, resulted from the changed times. Eventually the United States entered the war on the side of the

Allies. The reasons for this were complex, as you read on pages 509–510, but we can draw two conclusions about them. First, the United States had developed world-wide interests and close contacts with other countries. Therefore any major war affected it directly—so directly that it was increasingly difficult for our country to remain neutral in a general war. Second, the American people felt that a victory for the Allies would be a victory for democracy. Once in the war, our nation made important contributions of supplies, armaments, and soldiers.

World leadership. After the First World War the American people seemed to want to keep out of international affairs as much as possible. They preferred to live mainly to themselves, as they had done during much of the nineteenth century. The United States refused to join the League of Nations. Before long, however, the government began to cooperate in League activities. Individual Americans took part in the work of the League. Before long, also, the United States led in a disarmament conference and in other plans to build world peace. It appeared that the American people preferred to withdraw from the world, but the facts compelled them to take part in world affairs. They needed markets and raw materials. Hard times in other parts of the world would bring hard times to the United States. We lived in an interdependent world, and we had to help keep it peaceful and prosperous. (See pages 518, 547, and 594.)

The world-wide interests of our people, as well as American opposition to dictatorship, caused the United States to be drawn into the Second World War. After that war the United States was the wealthiest and most powerful country in the world. It turned out more manufactured goods than all the rest of the world combined. This time it was a leader in organizing the world for peace. It was one of the founders of the United Nations. The American people had learned that to enjoy peace they must work for peace throughout the world.

After the Second World War the great powers of the world became divided into two groups—the democratic, anticommunist countries on the one hand and the communist countries on the other. The United States was recognized as the strongest nation of the free world, and became its leader. What has the United States done to strengthen the free world against communism? (See pages 592–600.)

Your American adventure. You are living in a world divided between communist and free nations. What can the American people do to preserve prosperity and peace in such a divided world?

In order to save the free nations from communism, we must be strong. If you are a boy, when you are five or six years older you will be called on to serve in the armed forces. That will be your personal part in keeping America strong.

In order to strengthen the underdeveloped nations of the free world, we must help them expand their industries, improve their health, and raise their standard of living.

In order to oppose and overcome communism, we must know what the free world stands for. It stands for re-

COMMUNITY CONSOLIDATED DISTRICT NO. 10, WOODSTOCK, ILL.

Studying foreign affairs. Today Americans realize that their lives are affected by happenings in other parts of the world. These young Americans, studying about events in Asia, illustrate our interest in international affairs. How do you find out about important world events?

spect for the individual, for his right to freedom of thought, freedom of speech, and freedom of worship. It stands for the equality and prosperity of all peoples. It stands for equal opportunity. We believe that the weak have the same right to justice under the law as the strong. We believe that the way to settle a dispute is by conference and compromise, not by force.

Do you recognize in these principles the faith of democracy? Have you learned that the American adventure of the past has been largely a slow but steady progress in making these ideals work? Then you are ready for the conclusion that part of your American adventure will be to help other peoples accept these democratic ideals and make them work.

Summary

The American adventure is one—in the past, in the present, and in the future. What you have learned about the problems of the past will help you in meeting the same problems in the future.

The development of democracy has meant a gradual growth of respect for the individual and his rights. It has meant greater political democracy. It has meant more nearly equal opportunity for every person in education and in earning a living. The American adventure has been an advance toward real democracy. That advance will continue in the future.

The American adventure has also been an advance in comfortable living and good health. Americans live longer

This is the land. This map shows the mountains, lakes, and rivers, the lowlands, plains, and plateaus of our country. On it we can read a large part of the story of conservation. Rivers tumbling down the mountains cause flood and soil erosion. We build dams to hold back the water and use it for transportation, irrigation, and electric power. In the mountains are the main forest areas, which we must save along with the wildlife they shelter.

On this map we can also read much of the story of the settlement of our country. The jagged Atlantic coast harbored the little vessels of the early settlers. Settlement spread over the Piedmont and then slowed up at the mountains. Once across the Appalachians, the settlers could float down the Ohio and the Mississippi. West of the Mississippi are the Great Plains and the Rocky Mountains. This area was settled after railroads were built.

than they used to. The American people produce and consume more goods than any other people in the history of the world. We produce enough to help other nations. We must remain prosperous, not only for our own happiness, but for the safety and happiness of the free world.

A high standard of living includes leisure and taste for the appreciation of the arts and sciences. The increase of leisure, the spread of education, and new inventions have brought appreciation of the arts within the grasp of all Americans. The future should bring wider participation in and enjoyment of the arts and sciences. That is part of the idea of democracy.

In the twentieth century the United States has become the leader of the free world against communism. It must remain strong to help keep the free nations strong. Americans must understand and support the principles of democracy. With those principles we must win the hearts and minds of the peoples of the world. In that way we shall surely defeat communism.

The American adventure of tomorrow promises to be more challenging and more exciting than the American adventure of the past.

Unit Roundup

HIGH POINTS OF THE UNIT

In Unit 9 you have read about problems that face the American people today, problems that will be part of your American adventure. A useful way to review what you have learned about these problems is to take part in a panel discussion of one of them.

Start by deciding how many panels the class can prepare and choose the most important problems for discussion. Each student should suggest problems that he or she thinks should be considered by a panel. List these topics on the blackboard. Decide through group discussion which topics should be presented. Check the final list to make certain that there is no duplication and that each problem included is a major one.

Before you prepare for your discussion, review the suggestions for panel discussions given on page 630.

EXPAND YOUR VOCABULARY

Review the words and phrases given below in preparation for a "definition spelldown."

Agricultural Extension Service
Americanization program
census
contour plowing
consolidated school
Dust Bowl
foreign-born
4-H Clubs
human resources
interdependence
melting pot
minority
natural resources
prejudice
restriction
skyscraper
soil erosion
tenement
topsoil
water power

HISTORY IN THE MOVIES

1. The film *Conservation of Natural Resources* presents information about the use of water power, forest, and soil resources

in the United States. Study it, looking for answers to the following questions: (*a*) What problems are pointed out concerning the use of natural resources? (*b*) What suggestions are made for conserving the resources? (*c*) Do the suggestions for conservation of resources seem to be in line with the definition of conservation as "wise use"?

2. The film *Wastage of Human Resources* tells how we waste the abilities of some of our people and how we can prevent such waste.

3. Studying the film *The Flag Speaks* will be an interesting way to review some important steps in the growth of democracy. You will also learn how to display our flag and some important facts about its history.

WITH CRAYON, RULER, AND PASTE

1. Make one of the graphs suggested below. Before you begin, you should decide whether a bar graph, a line graph, or a picture graph will present the data best. You will need to consult a statistical reference such as *The World Almanac* or *Historical Statistics of the United States*. (*a*) The number of immigrants who came to the United States in 1880, 1890, 1900, 1910, and 1920. (*b*) The percentage of foreign-born persons in the United States in 1920, 1930, 1940, and 1950. (*c*) College enrollments in the United States in 1920 and 1950.

2. Bring the class time line up to date, deciding as a group what events to show on it.

3. Draw a series of cartoons to show how different our daily lives would be if all the household appliances and conveniences that modern science has developed since 1900 were suddenly taken away.

4. Draw a series of cartoons to show what difference it makes in your life whether there is cooperation or fighting among nations.

5. Make a chart showing some of the important rights and duties of citizenship in our democratic nation. You could use these headings: Rights of Citizens, Period When Won, Duties of Citizens, How to Be Carried Out. What title will you give the chart?

PUT ON A PLAY

1. Plan and present a series of skits to show contributions made to American life by various racial and nationality groups.

2. Present a radio roundup on soil conservation. Through brief interviews, roving-reporter descriptions, and skits, show why conservation is needed and how it is being accomplished.

3. Plan a series of scenes that present some of the problems to be solved if all citizens are to enjoy democratic rights.

4. Give an unrehearsed pageant that traces the development of one of the following topics (or an aspect of it) in United States history:

Enriching American life through the arts and sciences
The growth of interdependence within the nation and the world
Growing to world leadership

STORIES THERE WAS NO ROOM TO TELL

1. Choose one of the persons mentioned below, or another who interested you as you studied Unit 9, as the subject for a biographical report.

Marian Anderson   Ferde Grofé

Stephen Vincent Benét	Sinclair Lewis
Aaron Copland	Carl Sandburg
George Gershwin	Gladys Swarthout
	Lawrence Tibbett

2. Prepare a floor talk on one of these topics:

The Grand Coulee Dam
The history of professional football
The March of Dimes and the battle against polio
The Metropolitan Opera—on stage, radio, and television (You may substitute a major symphony orchestra.)
Vacation season in a national park
The work of a public health nurse

USE YOUR IMAGINATION

1. Write a series of letters that might have been sent to his relatives in Europe by a young immigrant who had come to the United States to make his fortune in the early 1900s. Space the letters over a two-year period and tell in them the problems the young man probably met and solved in finding a job, a place to live, and new friends.

2. Write a newspaper editorial on one of the important problems discussed in Unit 9—one about which citizens of the United States will probably have to make a decision in the future. Indicate what solutions have been proposed and the solution that you would recommend.

SHOW IT ON A MAP

1. Make a map of your own state, showing important cities, main railroad lines, and any of the following that are applicable in your state:

coal deposits	major water-power developments
copper, lead, or zinc deposits	national parks
iron deposits	oil fields
irrigation projects	steel mills

2. On an outline map of your state or region, including surrounding states, show by picture symbols or other devices the larger nationality and racial groups that have settled there. Beside each symbol put the date or dates when the greatest numbers of that particular group came.

YOUR COMMUNITY GROWS WITH THE NATION

1. Make a list of 10 persons, either immigrants themselves or children of immigrants, who have been important in the history of your city or state. Prepare a brief biographical sketch of each one.

2. Prepare a report on "Health regulations in my community." Investigate the sanitary laws that must be observed by dairies, grocery stores, meat markets, and restaurants. Investigate the regulations concerning quarantine and vaccination.

3. How does your school help you to learn to be healthy? In what classes do you study health rules, diet, recognition and avoidance of disease, and so on? What might be done to reduce the amount of sickness and to improve student health in general?

4. Find out how people in your community spend their leisure time. You might begin by interviewing people in charge of recreational facilities. (See suggestions on page 651.) You could make a survey among the students of your school to find out what leisure-time activities are most popular and what recreational facilities (parks, movies, and so on) they use the most. Summarize your findings in an article for the school newspaper.

5. Make a graph for your state, showing

its population by decades. Compare the rate of population increase in your own state with that in the country as a whole.

6. What opportunities are there in your community for people to continue their education after they have finished high school? Is there a junior college? A college? Are there evening courses so that persons employed in the day can attend? Are there classes or lecture series sponsored by the public library or another such agency?

Summarize your information in a bulletin-board display entitled "Open Doors to Education," giving for each "open door" information about who may attend, cost, and other such facts.

7. Investigate the opportunities in your community to enjoy music, paintings, sculpture, and other works of art. Is there a symphony orchestra, an art gallery, or an art museum? Does the public library have a fine-arts division? Does your school have a collection of prints and reproductions of works of art?

FURTHER READING

Books about Interesting People

Amelia Earhart, Heroine of the Skies by Doris Shannon Garst. Messner, 1947.

Babe Ruth by Martin Weldon. Crowell, 1948.†

Mr. Bell Invents the Telephone by Katherine B. Shippen. Random House, 1952.

Our Foreign-born Citizens by Annie E. S. Beard and Frederica Beard. Crowell, 1946. Biographies of 48 great Americans, including Einstein, Merganthaler, Rockne, and Van Loon.

We Have Tomorrow by Arna Wendell Bontemps. Houghton Mifflin, 1945. Biographies of American Negro leaders.

Stories of Adventure and Everyday Life

Assorted Sisters by Florence Crannell Means. Houghton Mifflin, 1947. The scene is a settlement house in Denver.

Blue Willow by Doris Gates. Viking, 1940. Dust storms cause Janey's family to go to California to make a new start.

Melindy's Medal by Georgene Faulkner and John Becker. Messner, 1945. Life in a new housing project.†

Petar's Treasure: They Came from Dalmatia by Clara I. Judson. Houghton Mifflin, 1945. A family from Dalmatia makes a new home in Mississippi. Find other interesting stories by this author.

Teresita of the Valley by Florence Crannell Means. Houghton Mifflin, 1943. Experiences of a Spanish-American girl in a new school.

Triumph Clear by L. L. Beim. Harcourt, Brace, 1946. Experiences of a girl polio patient at Warm Springs Foundation.

Other Interesting Accounts

Great Heritage by Katherine B. Shippen. Viking, 1947. Using our natural resources wisely.

Modern Medical Discoveries by Irmengarde Eberle. Crowell, 1954. Learning about vitamins and the "wonder drugs."

North Star Shining: A Pictorial History of the American Negro by Hildegarde Hoyt Swift. Morrow, 1947. Includes Stories of great American Negroes.

Story of Baseball in Words and Pictures by John Durant. Hastings House, revised edition, 1949. The development of the great American game.

The Land Renewed by William R. Van Dersal and E. H. Graham. Oxford, 1946 Saving our land.

Declaration of Independence

When, in the course of human events, it becomes necessary for one people to dissolve the political bands which have connected them with another and to assume, among the powers of the earth, the separate and equal station to which the laws of nature and nature's God entitle them, a decent respect to the opinions of mankind requires that they should declare the causes which impel them to the separation.

We hold these truths to be self-evident: That all men are created equal; that they are endowed by their Creator with certain inalienable rights; that among these are life, liberty, and the pursuit of happiness. That to secure these rights, governments are instituted among men, deriving their just powers from the consent of the governed; that whenever any form of government becomes destructive to these ends, it is the right of the people to alter or to abolish it and to institute a new government, laying its foundation on such principles, and organizing its powers in such form, as to them shall seem most likely to effect their safety and happiness. Prudence, indeed, will dictate that governments long established should not be changed for light and transient causes; and accordingly all experience hath shown that mankind are more disposed to suffer, while evils are sufferable, than to right themselves by abolishing the forms to which they are accustomed. But when a long train of abuses and usurpations, pursuing invariably the same object, evinces a design to reduce them under absolute despotism, it is their right, it is their duty, to throw off such government and to provide new guards for their future security. Such has been the patient sufferance of these colonies; and such is now the necessity which constrains them to alter their former systems of government. The history of the present king of Great Britain is a history of repeated injuries and usurpations, all having in direct object the establishment of an absolute tyranny over these states. To prove this, let facts be submitted to a candid world.

He has refused his assent to laws, the most wholesome and necessary for the public good.

He has forbidden his governors to pass laws of immediate and pressing importance, unless suspended in their operation till his assent should be obtained; and, when so suspended, he has utterly neglected to attend to them.

He has refused to pass other laws for the accommodation of large districts of people, unless those people would relinquish the right of representation in the legislature—a right inestimable to them and formidable to tyrants only.

He has called together legislative bodies at places unusual, uncomfortable, and distant from the depository of their public records, for the sole purpose of fatiguing them into compliance with his measures.

He has dissolved representative houses repeatedly, for opposing, with manly firmness, his invasions on the rights of the people.

He has refused for a long time, after such dissolutions, to cause others to be elected; whereby the legislative powers, incapable of annihilation, have returned to the people at large for their exercise; the state remaining in the meantime exposed to all the dangers of invasion from without and convulsions within.

He has endeavored to prevent the population of these states; for that purpose obstructing the laws for the naturalization of foreigners, refusing to pass others to encourage their migration hither, and raising the conditions of new appropriations of lands.

He has obstructed the administration of justice, by refusing his assent to laws for establishing judiciary powers.

NOTE: Spelling, capitalization, and punctuation have been modernized.

He has made judges dependent on his will alone, for the tenure of their offices and the amount and payment of their salaries.

He has erected a multitude of new offices, and sent hither swarms of officers to harass our people and eat out their substance.

He has kept among us, in times of peace, standing armies, without the consent of our legislatures.

He has affected to render the military independent of, and superior to, the civil power.

He has combined with others to subject us to a jurisdiction foreign to our constitutions and unacknowledged by our laws, giving his assent to their acts of pretended legislation:

For quartering large bodies of armed troops among us;

For protecting them, by a mock trial, from punishment for any murders which they should commit on the inhabitants of these states;

For cutting off our trade with all parts of the world;

For imposing taxes on us without our consent;

For depriving us, in many cases, of the benefits of trial by jury;

For transporting us beyond seas to be tried for pretended offenses;

For abolishing the free system of English laws in a neighboring province, establishing therein an arbitrary government, and enlarging its boundaries, so as to render it at once an example and fit instrument for introducing the same absolute rule into these colonies;

For taking away our charters, abolishing our most valuable laws, and altering, fundamentally, the forms of our governments;

For suspending our own legislatures and declaring themselves invested with power to legislate for us in all cases whatsoever.

He has abdicated government here, by declaring us out of his protection and waging war against us.

He has plundered our seas, ravaged our coasts, burned our towns, and destroyed the lives of our people.

He is at this time transporting large armies of foreign mercenaries to complete the works of death, desolation, and tyranny, already begun with circumstances of cruelty and perfidy scarcely paralleled in the most barbarous ages and totally unworthy the head of a civilized nation.

He has constrained our fellow citizens, taken captive on the high seas, to bear arms against their country, to become the executioners of their friends and brethren, or to fall themselves by their hands.

He has excited domestic insurrections among us and has endeavored to bring on the inhabitants of our frontiers the merciless Indian savages, whose known rule of warfare is an undistinguished destruction of all ages, sexes, and conditions.

In every stage of these oppressions we have petitioned for redress in the most humble terms; our repeated petitions have been answered only by repeated injury. A prince whose character is thus marked by every act which may define a tyrant is unfit to be the ruler of a free people.

Nor have we been wanting in attentions to our British brethren. We have warned them, from time to time, of attempts by their legislature to extend an unwarrantable jurisdiction over us. We have reminded them of the circumstances of our emigration and settlement here. We have appealed to their native justice and magnanimity; and we have conjured them, by the ties of our common kindred, to disavow these usurpations, which would inevitably interrupt our connections and correspondence. They, too, have been deaf to the voice of justice and consanguinity. We must, therefore, acquiesce in the necessity which denounces our separation, and hold them, as we hold the rest of mankind, enemies in war, in peace, friends.

We, therefore, the representatives of the United States of America, in General Congress assembled, appealing to the Supreme Judge of the world for the rectitude of our intentions, do, in the name and by the authority of the good people of these colonies, solemnly publish and declare: That these united colonies are, and of right ought to be, free and independent states; that they are absolved from all allegiance to the British crown and that all political connection between them and the state of Great Britain is, and ought to be, totally dissolved; and that, as free and independent states, they have full power to levy war, conclude peace, contract alliances, establish commerce, and do all other acts and things which independent states may of right do. And, for the support of this declaration, with a firm reliance on the protection of Divine Providence, we mutually pledge to each other our lives, our fortunes, and our sacred honor.

The Constitution

of the United States

Preamble. We the people of the United States, in order to form a more perfect union, establish justice, insure domestic tranquillity, provide for the common defense, promote the general welfare, and secure the blessings of liberty to ourselves and our posterity, do ordain and establish this Constitution for the United States of America.

ARTICLE I
Legislative Department

SECTION 1. Congress

All legislative powers herein granted shall be vested in a Congress of the United States, which shall consist of a Senate and a House of Representatives.

NOTE: This text of the Constitution has been prepared from the official text published by the Government Printing Office. Spelling and capitalization have been modernized. The headings in boldface type and footnotes have been added for your convenience.

SECTION 2. House of Representatives

Term, election of Representatives. 1. The House of Representatives shall be composed of members chosen every second year by the people of the several states, and the electors in each state shall have the qualifications requisite for electors of the most numerous branch of the state legislature.

Qualifications. 2. No person shall be a Representative who shall not have attained to the age of twenty-five years, and been seven years a citizen of the United States, and who shall not, when elected, be an inhabitant of that state in which he shall be chosen.

Apportionment of Representatives, direct taxes. 3. [Representatives and direct taxes shall be apportioned among the several states which may be included within this Union, according to their respective numbers, which shall be determined by adding to the whole number of free persons, including those bound to service for a term of years, and excluding Indians not taxed, three-fifths of all other persons.[1]] The actual enumeration shall be made within three years after the first meeting of the Congress of the United States, and within every subsequent term of ten years, in such manner as they shall by law direct. The number of Representatives shall not exceed one for every thirty thousand, but each state shall have at least one representative; and until such enumeration shall be made, the State of New Hampshire shall be entitled to choose three, Massachusetts eight, Rhode Island and Providence Plantations one, Connecticut five, New York six, New Jersey four, Pennsylvania eight, Delaware one, Maryland six, Virginia ten, North Carolina five, South Carolina five, and Georgia three.

Vacancies. 4. When vacancies happen in the representation from any state, the executive authority thereof shall issue writs of election to fill such vacancies.

Officers of House, power of impeachment. 5. The House of Representatives shall choose their Speaker and other officers; and shall have the sole power of impeachment.

Section 3. Senate

Number of Senators, term. 1. The Senate of the United States shall be composed of two Senators from each state, chosen [by the legislature thereof,[2]] for six years, and each Senator shall have one vote.

2. Immediately after they shall be assembled in consequence of the first election, they shall be divided as equally as may be into three classes. The seats of the Senators of the first class shall be vacated at the expiration of the second year, of the second class at the expiration of the fourth year, and of the third class at the expiration of the sixth year, so that one-third may be chosen every second year; [and if vacancies happen by resignation or otherwise, during the recess of the legislature of any state, the executive thereof may make temporary appointments until the next meeting of the legislature, which shall then fill such vacancies.[3]]

Qualifications. 3. No person shall be a Senator who shall not have attained to the age of thirty years, and been nine years a citizen of the United States, and who shall not, when elected, be an inhabitant of that state for which he shall be chosen.

Officers of Senate. 4. The Vice-President of the United States shall be president of the Senate, but shall have no vote, unless they be equally divided.

5. The Senate shall choose their other officers, and also a president pro tempore, in the absence of the Vice-President, or when he shall exercise the office of President of the United States.

Impeachment trials. 6. The Senate shall have the sole power to try all impeachments. When sitting for that purpose, they shall be on oath or affirmation. When the President of the United States is tried, the Chief Justice shall preside: and no person shall be convicted without the concurrence of two-thirds of the members present.

Punishment in case of conviction. 7. Judgment in cases of impeachment shall not extend further than to removal from office, and disqualification to hold and enjoy any office of honor, trust or profit under the United States: but the party convicted shall nevertheless be liable and subject to indictment, trial, judgment and punishment, according to law.

Section 4. The Two Houses

Power to regulate elections. 1. The times, places and manner of holding elections for Senators and Representatives shall be prescribed in each state by the legislature thereof; but the Congress may at any time by law make or alter such regulations, except as to the places of choosing Senators.

[1] Repealed by Section 2 of Amendment XIV.

[2] Changed by Amendment XVII.

[3] Changed by Amendment XVII.

Annual meeting. 2. The Congress shall assemble at least once in every year, and such meeting shall [be on the first Monday in December [4]] unless they shall by law appoint a different day.

SECTION 5. **The Separate Houses**

Admission of members, quorum. 1. Each house shall be the judge of the elections, returns and qualifications of its own members, and a majority of each shall constitute a quorum to do business; but a smaller number may adjourn from day to day, and may be authorized to compel the attendance of absent members, in such manner, and under such penalties, as each house may provide.

Rules of order. 2. Each house may determine the rules of its proceedings, punish its members for disorderly behavior, and with the concurrence of two-thirds, expel a member.

Record of proceedings. 3. Each house shall keep a journal of its proceedings, and from time to time publish the same, excepting such parts as may in their judgment require secrecy; and the yeas and nays of the members of either house on any question shall, at the desire of one-fifth of those present, be entered on the journal.

Adjournment. 4. Neither house, during the session of Congress, shall, without the consent of the other, adjourn for more than three days, nor to any other place than that in which the two houses shall be sitting.

SECTION 6. **Privileges of Members**

Salary, privileges of members. 1. The Senators and Representatives shall receive a compensation for their services, to be ascertained by law and paid out of the treasury of the United States. They shall in all cases, except treason, felony and breach of the peace, be privileged from arrest during their attendance at the session of their respective houses, and in going to and returning from the same; and for any speech or debate in either house, they shall not be questioned in any other place.

Holding other offices forbidden. 2. No Senator or Representative shall, during the time for which he was elected, be appointed to any civil office under the authority of the United States, which shall have been created, or the emoluments whereof shall have been increased, during such time; and no person holding any office under the United States shall be a member of either house during his continuance in office.

SECTION 7. **Method of Making Laws**

Tax bills. 1. All bills for raising revenue shall originate in the House of Representatives; but the Senate may propose or concur with amendments as on other bills.

Bill into law. 2. Every bill which shall have passed the House of Representatives and the Senate, shall, before it becomes a law, be presented to the President of the United States; if he approve he shall sign it, but if not he shall return it with his objections to that house in which it shall have originated, who shall enter the objections at large on their journal, and proceed to reconsider it. If after such reconsideration two-thirds of that house shall agree to pass the bill, it shall be sent, together with the objections, to the other house, by which it shall likewise be reconsidered, and, if approved by two-thirds of that house, it shall become a law. But in all such cases the votes of both houses shall be determined by yeas and nays, and the names of the persons voting for and against the bill shall be entered on the journal of each house respectively. If any bill shall not be returned by the President within ten days (Sundays excepted) after it shall have been presented to him, the same shall be a law, in like manner as if he had signed it, unless the Congress by their adjournment prevent its return, in which case it shall not be a law.

Veto power of the President. 3. Every order, resolution, or vote to which the concur-

[4] Changed by Amendment XX.

rence of the Senate and House of Representatives may be necessary (except on a question of adjournment) shall be presented to the President of the United States; and before the same shall take effect, shall be approved by him, or being disapproved by him, shall be repassed by two-thirds of the Senate and House of Representatives, according to the rules and limitations prescribed in the case of a bill.

Section 8. Powers Granted to Congress

Enumerated powers. The Congress shall have power

1. To lay and collect taxes, duties, imposts, and excises, to pay the debts and provide for the common defense and general welfare of the United States; but all duties, imposts, and excises shall be uniform throughout the United States;

2. To borrow money on the credit of the United States;

3. To regulate commerce with foreign nations, and among the several states, and with the Indian tribes;

4. To establish an uniform rule of naturalization, and uniform laws on the subject of bankruptcies throughout the United States;

5. To coin money, regulate the value thereof, and of foreign coin, and fix the standard of weights and measures;

6. To provide for the punishment of counterfeiting the securities and current coin of the United States;

7. To establish post offices and post roads;

8. To promote the progress of science and useful arts by securing for limited times to authors and inventors the exclusive right to their respective writings and discoveries;

9. To constitute tribunals inferior to the Supreme Court;

10. To define and punish piracies and felonies committed on the high seas and offenses against the law of nations;

11. To declare war, grant letters of marque and reprisal, and make rules concerning captures on land and water;

12. To raise and support armies, but no appropriation of money to that use shall be for a longer term than two years;

13. To provide and maintain a navy;

14. To make rules for the government and regulation of the land and naval forces;

15. To provide for calling forth the militia to execute the laws of the Union, suppress insurrections, and repel invasions;

16. To provide for organizing, arming and disciplining the militia, and for governing such part of them as may be employed in the service of the United States, reserving to the states respectively the appointment of the officers, and the authority of training the militia according to the discipline prescribed by Congress;

17. To exercise exclusive legislation in all cases whatsoever, over such district (not exceeding ten miles square) as may, by cession of particular states, and the acceptance of Congress, become the seat of government of the United States, and to exercise like authority over all places purchased by the consent of the legislature and the state, in which the same shall be, for the erection of forts, magazines, arsenals, dockyards, and other needful buildings; and

Implied powers (elastic clause). 18. To make all laws which shall be necessary and proper for carrying into execution the foregoing powers, and all other powers vested by this Constitution in the government of the United States, or in any department or office thereof.

Section 9. Powers Denied the Federal Government

Denied to Congress. 1. The migration or importation of such persons as any of the states now existing shall think proper to admit shall not be prohibited by the Congress prior to the year 1808; but a tax or duty may be imposed on such importation, not exceeding $10 for each person.

2. The privilege of the writ of habeas corpus shall not be suspended, unless when

in cases of rebellion or invasion the public safety may require it.

3. No bill of attainder or ex post facto law shall be passed.

4. No capitation, or other direct, tax shall be laid, unless in proportion to the census or enumeration herein before directed to be taken.

5. No tax or duty shall be laid on articles exported from any state.

6. No preference shall be given by any regulation of commerce or revenue to the ports of one state over those of another: nor shall vessels bound to, or from, one state be obliged to enter, clear, or pay duties in another.

Public money. 7. No money shall be drawn from the treasury, but in consequence of appropriations made by law; and a regular statement and account of the receipts and expenditures of all public money shall be published from time to time.

No titles of nobility. 8. No title of nobility shall be granted by the United States: and no person holding any office of profit or trust under them, shall, without the consent of the Congress, accept of any present, emolument, office, or title, of any kind whatever, from any king, prince, or foreign state.

Section 10. Powers Denied the States

Powers absolutely denied. 1. No state shall enter into any treaty, alliance, or confederation; grant letters of marque and reprisal; coin money; emit bills of credit; make anything but gold and silver coin a tender in payment of debts; pass any bill of attainder, ex post facto law, or law impairing the obligation of contracts, or grant any title of nobility.

Concerning tariff duties. 2. No state shall, without the consent of the Congress, lay any imposts or duties on imports or exports, except what may be absolutely necessary for executing its inspection laws: and the net produce of all duties and imports, laid by any state on imports or exports, shall be for the use of the treasury of the United States; and all such laws shall be subject to the revision and control of the Congress.

Powers denied, except with consent of Congress. 3. No state shall, without the consent of Congress, lay any duty of tonnage, keep troops, or ships of war in time of peace, enter into any agreement or compact with another state, or with a foreign power, or engage in war, unless actually invaded, or in such imminent danger as will not admit of delay.

ARTICLE II
Executive Department

Section 1. President and Vice-President

Term of President and Vice-President. 1. The executive power shall be vested in a President of the United States of America. He shall hold his office during the term of four years, and together with the Vice-President, chosen for the same term, be elected as follows:

Election of the President. 2. Each state shall appoint, in such manner as the legislature thereof may direct, a number of Electors, equal to the whole number of Senators and Representatives to which the state may be entitled in the Congress; but no Senator or Representative, or person holding an office of trust or profit under the United States, shall be appointed an Elector.

[The Electors shall meet in their respective states, and vote by ballot for two persons, of whom one at least shall not be an inhabitant of the same state with themselves. And they shall make a list of all the persons voted for, and of the number of votes for each; which list they shall sign and certify, and transmit sealed to the seat of government of the United States, directed to the president of the Senate. The president of the Senate shall, in the presence of the Senate and House of Representatives, open all the certificates, and the votes shall then be counted. The person having the greatest number of votes shall be the President, if such number be a majority of the whole number of Electors appointed; and if there be more than one who have such majority, and have an equal number of votes, then the House of Representatives shall immediately choose by ballot one of them for President; and if no person have a majority, then from the five highest on the list the said house shall in like manner choose the President. But in choosing the President the votes shall be taken by states, the representation from each state having one vote; a quorum for this purpose shall consist of a member or members from two-thirds of the states, and a majority of all the states shall be necessary to a choice. In every case, after the choice of the President, the person having the greatest number of votes of the Electors shall be the Vice-President. But if there should remain two or more who have equal votes, the Senate shall choose from them by ballot the Vice-President.[5]]

3. The Congress may determine the time of choosing the Electors, and the day on which they shall give their votes; which day shall be the same throughout the United States.

Qualifications. 4. No person except a natural-born citizen, or a citizen of the United States, at the time of the adoption of this Constitution, shall be eligible to the office of President; neither shall any person be eligible to that office who shall not have attained to the age of thirty-five years, and been fourteen years a resident within the United States.

Presidential succession. 5. In case of the removal of the President from office or of his death, resignation, or inability to discharge the powers and duties of the said office, the same shall devolve on the Vice-President, and the Congress may by law provide for the case of removal, death, resignation, or inability, both of the President and Vice-President, declaring what officer shall then act as President, and such officer shall act accordingly, until the disability be removed, or a President shall be elected.

[5] The method of electing the President and Vice-President was changed by Amendment XII.

Salary. 6. The President shall, at stated times, receive for his services, a compensation, which shall neither be increased nor diminished during the period for which he shall have been elected, and he shall not receive within that period any other emolument from the United States, or any of them.

Oath of office. 7. Before he enter on the execution of his office, he shall take the following oath or affirmation: "I do solemnly swear (or affirm) that I will faithfully execute the office of President of the United States, and will to the best of my ability, preserve, protect and defend the Constitution of the United States."

Section 2. General Powers of the President

Military powers, supervision of executive departments, pardons. 1. The President shall be Commander in Chief of the Army and Navy of the United States, and of the militia of the several states, when called into the actual service of the United States; he may require the opinion, in writing, of the principal officer in each of the executive departments, upon any subject relating to the duties of their respective offices, and he shall have power to grant reprieves and pardons for offenses against the United States, except in cases of impeachment.

Treaties, appointments. 2. He shall have power, by and with the advice and consent of the Senate, to make treaties, provided two-thirds of the Senators present concur; and he shall nominate, and by and with the advice and consent of the Senate, shall appoint ambassadors, other public ministers and consuls, judges of the Supreme Court, and all other officers of the United States, whose appointments are not herein otherwise provided for, and which shall be established by law; but the Congress may by law vest the appointment of such inferior officers, as they think proper, in the President alone, in the courts of law, or in the heads of departments.

3. The President shall have power to fill up all vacancies that may happen during the

recess of the Senate, by granting commissions which shall expire at the end of their next session.

SECTION 3. **Other Duties of the President**

He shall from time to time give to the Congress information of the state of the Union, and recommend to their consideration such measures as he shall judge necessary and expedient; he may, on extraordinary occasions, convene both houses, or either of them, and in case of disagreement between them, with respect to the time of adjournment, he may adjourn them to such time as he shall think proper; he shall receive ambassadors and other public ministers; he shall take care that the laws be faithfully executed, and shall commission all the officers of the United States.

SECTION 4. **Impeachment**

The President, Vice-President and all civil officers of the United States, shall be removed from office on impeachment for, and on conviction of, treason, bribery, or other high crimes and misdemeanors.

ARTICLE III
Judicial Department

SECTION 1. **Federal Courts and Judges**

1. The judicial power of the United States shall be vested in one Supreme Court, and in such inferior courts as Congress may from time to time ordain and establish. The judges, both of the Supreme and inferior courts, shall hold their offices during good behavior, and shall, at stated times, receive for their services, a compensation, which shall not be diminished during their continuance in office.

SECTION 2. **Jurisdiction of United States Courts**

General jurisdiction of federal courts. 1. The judicial power shall extend to all cases, in law and equity, arising under this Constitution, the laws of the United States, and treaties made or which shall be made, under their authority;—to all cases affecting ambassadors, other public ministers and consuls;—to all cases of admiralty jurisdiction;—to controversies to which the United States shall be a party;—to controversies between two or more states;—[between a state and citizens of another state[6]];—between citizens of different states;—between citizens of the same state claiming lands under grants of different states, and between a state, or the citizens thereof, and foreign states, citizens or subjects.

Supreme Court. 2. In all cases affecting ambassadors, other public ministers and consuls, and those in which a state shall be a party, the Supreme Court shall have original jurisdiction. In all the other cases before mentioned, the Supreme Court shall have appellate jurisdiction, both as to law and fact, with such exceptions, and under such regulations as the Congress shall make.

Rules concerning trials. 3. The trial of all crimes, except in cases of impeachment, shall be by jury; and such trial shall be held in the state where the said crimes shall have been committed; but when not committed within any state, the trial shall be at such place or places as the Congress may by law have directed.

SECTION 3. **Treason**

Definition, evidence required. 1. Treason against the United States shall consist only in levying war against them, or in adhering to their enemies, giving them aid and comfort. No person shall be convicted of treason unless on the testimony of two witnesses to the same overt act, or on confession in open court.

Punishment. 2. The Congress shall have power to declare the punishment of treason, but no attainder of treason shall work corruption of blood, or forfeiture except during the life of the person attainted.

[6] Amendment XI limits this clause to cases in which a state sues citizens of another state.

ARTICLE IV
Relations of the States

SECTION 1. **Acceptance of Acts of States**

Full faith and credit shall be given in each state to the public acts, records, and judicial proceedings of every other state. And the Congress may by general laws prescribe the manner in which such acts, records, and proceedings shall be proved, and the effect thereof.

SECTION 2. **Status of Citizens**

Privileges. 1. The citizens of each state shall be entitled to all privileges and immunities of citizens in the several states.

Extradition. 2. A person charged in any state with treason, felony, or other crime, who shall flee from justice, and be found in another state, shall on demand of the executive authority of the state from which he fled, be delivered up, to be removed to the state having jurisdiction of the crime.

Fugitive slaves. 3. [No person held in service or labor in one state, under the laws thereof, escaping into another, shall, in consequence of any law or regulation therein, be discharged from such service or labor, but shall be delivered up on claim of the party to whom such service or labor may be due.[7]]

SECTION 3. **New States and Territories**

New states. 1. New states may be admitted by the Congress into this Union; but no new state shall be formed or erected within the jurisdiction of any other state; nor any state be formed by the junction of two or more states, or parts of states, without the consent of the legislatures of the states concerned as well as of the Congress.

Power of Congress over U.S. possessions. 2. The Congress shall have power to dispose of and make all needful rules and regulations respecting the territory or other property belonging to the United States; and nothing in this Constitution shall be so construed as to prejudice any claims of the United States, or of any particular state.

[7] Amendment XIII abolished slavery.

SECTION 4. **Guarantees to the States**

The United States shall guarantee to every state in this Union a republican form of government, and shall protect each of them against invasion; and on application of the legislature, or of the executive (when the legislature cannot be convened) against domestic violence.

ARTICLE V

The Process of Amendment

The Congress, whenever two-thirds of both houses shall deem it necessary, shall propose amendments to this Constitution, or, on the application of the legislatures of two-thirds of the several states, shall call a convention for proposing amendments, which, in either case, shall be valid to all intents and purposes, as part of this Constitution, when ratified by the legislatures of three-fourths of the several states, or by conventions in three-fourths thereof, as the one or the other mode of ratification may be proposed by the Congress; provided that no amendments which may be made prior to the year 1808 shall in any manner affect the first and fourth clauses in the ninth section of the first article; and that no state, without its consent, shall be deprived of its equal suffrage in the Senate.

ARTICLE VI

General Provisions

Public debt. 1. All debts contracted and engagements entered into, before the adoption of this Constitution, shall be as valid against the United States under this Constitution, as under the Confederation.

Supreme law of the land. 2. This Constitution, and the laws of the United States which shall be made in pursuance thereof; and all treaties made, or which shall be made, under the authority of the United States, shall be the supreme law of the land; and the judges in every state shall be bound thereby, anything in the Constitution or laws of any state to the contrary notwithstanding.

Oath of office. 3. The Senators and Representatives before mentioned, and the members of the several state legislatures, and all executive and judicial officers, both of the United States and of the several states, shall be bound by oath or affirmation, to support this Constitution; but no religious test shall ever be required as a qualification to any office or public trust under the United States.

ARTICLE VII

Ratification of the Constitution

The ratification of the conventions of nine states, shall be sufficient for the establishment of this Constitution between the states so ratifying the same.

Amendments to the Constitution

AMENDMENT I

Religious and Political Freedom Guaranteed

Congress shall make no law respecting an establishment of religion, or prohibiting the free exercise thereof; or abridging the freedom of speech, or of the press; or the right of the people peaceably to assemble, and to petition the government for a redress of grievances.

AMENDMENT II

Right to Bear Arms

A well-regulated militia, being necessary to the security of a free state, the right of the people to keep and bear arms, shall not be infringed.

AMENDMENT III

No Quartering of Soldiers

No soldier shall, in time of peace, be quartered in any house, without the consent of the owner, nor in time of war, but in a manner to be prescribed by law.

AMENDMENT IV

No Illegal Search

The right of the people to be secure in their persons, houses, papers, and effects, against unreasonable searches and seizures, shall not be violated, and no warrants shall issue, but upon probable cause, supported by oath or affirmation, and particularly describing the place to be searched, and the persons or things to be seized.

AMENDMENT V

Individual's Rights in Trials

No person shall be held to answer for a capital, or otherwise infamous crime, unless on a presentment or indictment of a grand jury except in cases arising in the land or naval forces, or in the militia, when in actual service in time of war or public danger; nor shall any person be subject for the same offense to be twice put in jeopardy of life or limb; nor shall be compelled in any criminal case to be a witness against himself, nor be deprived of life, liberty, or property, without due process of law; nor shall private property be taken for public use without just compensation.

AMENDMENT VI

Rights of the Accused

In all criminal prosecutions the accused shall enjoy the right to a speedy and public trial, by an impartial jury of the state and district wherein the crime shall have been committed, which district shall have been previously ascertained by law, and to be informed of the nature and cause of the accusation; to be confronted with the witnesses against him; to have compulsory process for obtaining witnesses in his favor, and to have the assistance of counsel for his defense.

AMENDMENT VII

Trial by Jury

In suits at common law, where the value in controversy shall exceed twenty dollars, the right of trial by jury shall be preserved, and no fact tried by a jury shall be otherwise re-examined in any court of the United States, than according to the rules of the common law.

AMENDMENT VIII

Bail, Punishment

Excessive bail shall not be required, nor excessive fines imposed, nor cruel and unusual punishments inflicted.

AMENDMENT IX

Rights Retained by the People

The enumeration in the Constitution, of certain rights, shall not be construed to deny or disparage others retained by the people.

AMENDMENT X

Powers Reserved to the States

The powers not delegated to the United States by the Constitution, nor prohibited by it to the states, are reserved to the states respectively, or to the people.

AMENDMENT XI

Suits against States (1798)

The judicial power of the United States shall not be construed to extend to any suit in law or equity, commenced or prosecuted against one of the United States by citizens of another state, or by citizens or subjects of any foreign state.

AMENDMENT XII

Election of President and Vice-President (1804)

The Electors shall meet in their respective states, and vote by ballot for President and Vice-President, one of whom, at least, shall not be an inhabitant of the same state with themselves; they shall name in their ballots the person voted for as President, and in distinct ballots the person voted for as Vice-President, and they shall make distinct lists of all persons voted for as President, and of all persons voted for as Vice-President, and of the number of votes for each, which lists they shall sign and certify, and transmit sealed to the seat of government of the United States, directed to the president of the Senate;—the president of the Senate shall, in the presence of the Senate and House of Representatives, open all the certificates and the votes shall then be counted;—the person having the greatest number of votes for President shall be the President, if such number be a majority of the whole number of Electors appointed; and if no person have such majority, then from the persons having the highest numbers not exceeding three on the list of those voted for as President, the House of Representatives shall choose immediately, by ballot, the President. But in choosing the President, the votes shall be taken by states, the representation from each state having one vote; a quorum for this purpose shall consist of a member or members from two-thirds of the states, and a majority of all the states shall be necessary to a choice. [And if the House of Representatives shall not choose a President whenever the right of choice shall devolve upon them, before the fourth day of March next following, then the Vice-President shall act as President, as in the case of the death or other constitutional disability of the President.[8]]—The person having the greatest number of votes as Vice-President, shall be the Vice-President, if such number be a majority of the whole number of Electors appointed, and if no person have a majority, then from the two highest numbers on the list, the Senate shall choose the Vice-President; a quorum for the purpose shall consist of two-thirds of the whole number of Senators, and a majority of the whole number shall be necessary to a choice. But no person constitutionally ineligible to the office of President shall be eligible to that of Vice-President of the United States.

AMENDMENT XIII

Slavery Abolished (1865)

Section 1. Neither slavery nor involuntary servitude, except as a punishment for crime whereof the party shall have been duly convicted, shall exist within the United States, or any place subject to their jurisdiction.

Section 2. Congress shall have power to enforce this article by appropriate legislation.

[8] Changed by Amendment XX.

AMENDMENT XIV

Citizenship, Representation (1867)

Section 1. All persons born or naturalized in the United States, and subject to the jurisdiction thereof, are citizens of the United States and of the state wherein they reside. No state shall make or enforce any law which shall abridge the privileges or immunities of citizens of the United States; nor shall any state deprive any person of life, liberty, or property, without due process of law; nor deny to any person within its jurisdiction the equal protection of the laws.

Section 2. Representatives shall be apportioned among the several states according to their respective numbers, counting the whole number of persons in each state, excluding Indians not taxed. But when the right to vote at any election for the choice of Electors for President and Vice-President of the United States, Representatives in Congress, the executive and judicial officers of a state, or the members of the legislature thereof, is denied to any of the male inhabitants of such state, being twenty-one years of age and citizens of the United States, or in any way abridged, except for participation in rebellion, or other crime, the basis of representation therein shall be reduced in the proportion which the number of such male citizens shall bear to the whole number of male citizens twenty-one years of age in such state.

Section 3. No person shall be a Senator or Representative in Congress, or Elector of President and Vice-President, or hold any office, civil or military, under the United States, or under any state, who, having previously taken an oath, as a member of Congress, or as an officer of the United States, or as a member of any state legislature, or as an executive or judicial officer of any state, to support the Constitution of the United States, shall have engaged in insurrection or rebellion against the same, or given aid or comfort to the enemies thereof. But Congress may by vote of two-thirds of each house, remove such disability.

Section 4. The validity of the public debt of the United States, authorized by law, including debts incurred for payment of pensions and bounties for services in suppressing insurrection or rebellion, shall not be questioned. But neither the United States nor any state shall assume or pay any debt or obligation incurred in aid of insurrection or rebellion against the United States, or any claim for the loss or emancipation of any slave; but all such debts, obligations, and claims shall be held illegal and void.

Section 5. The Congress shall have power to enforce by appropriate legislation the provisions of this article.

AMENDMENT XV

Right of Suffrage (1870)

Section 1. The right of citizens of the United States to vote shall not be denied or abridged by the United States or any state on account of race, color, or previous condition of servitude.

Section 2. Congress shall have power to enforce this article by appropriate legislation.

AMENDMENT XVI

Tax on Income (1913)

The Congress shall have power to lay and collect taxes on incomes, from whatever source derived, without apportionment among the several states, and without regard to any census or enumeration.

AMENDMENT XVII

Direct Election of Senators (1913)

Section 1. The Senate of the United States shall be composed of two Senators from each state, elected by the people thereof, for six years; and each Senator shall have one vote. The electors in each state shall have the qualifications requisite for electors of the most numerous branch of the state legislatures.

Section 2. When vacancies happen in the representation of any state in the Senate, the executive authority of such state shall issue writs of election to fill such vacancies: provided that the legislature of any state may empower the executive thereof to make temporary appointments until the people fill the vacancies by election as the legislature may direct.

Section 3. This amendment shall not be so construed as to affect the election or term of any Senator chosen before it becomes valid as part of the Constitution.

AMENDMENT XVIII

Prohibition (1919)[9]

Section 1. After one year from the ratification of this article the manufacture, sale, or transportation of intoxicating liquors within, the importation thereof into, or the exportation thereof from, the United States and all territory subject to the jurisdiction thereof for beverage purposes is hereby prohibited.

Section 2. The Congress and the several states shall have concurrent power to enforce this article by appropriate legislation.

Section 3. This article shall be inoperative unless it shall have been ratified as an amendment to the Constitution by the legislatures of the several states, as provided by the Constitution, within seven years from the date of the submission hereof to the states by the Congress.

AMENDMENT XIX

Woman Suffrage (1920)

Section 1. The right of citizens of the United States to vote shall not be denied or abridged by the United States or by any state on account of sex.

Section 2. Congress shall have power to enforce this article by appropriate legislation.

[9] Repealed by Amendment XXI.

AMENDMENT XX

Presidential Term of Office (1933)

Section 1. The terms of the President and Vice-President shall end at noon on the twentieth day of January, and the terms of Senators and Representatives at noon on the third day of January, of the years in which such terms would have ended if this article had not been ratified; and the terms of their successors shall then begin.

Section 2. The Congress shall assemble at least once in every year, and such meeting shall begin at noon on the third day of January, unless they shall by law appoint a different day.

Section 3. If at the time fixed for the beginning of the term of the President, the President-elect shall have died, the Vice-President-elect shall become President. If a President shall not have been chosen before the time fixed for the beginning of his term, or if the President-elect shall have failed to qualify, then the Vice-President-elect shall act as President until a President shall have qualified, and the Congress may by law provide for the case wherein neither a President-elect nor a Vice-President-elect shall have qualified, declaring who shall then act as President, or the manner in which one who is to act shall be selected, and such person shall act accordingly until a President or Vice-President shall have qualified.

Section 4. The Congress may by law provide for the case of the death of any of the persons from whom the House of Representatives may choose a President whenever the right of choice shall have devolved upon them, and for the case of the death of the persons from whom the Senate may choose a Vice-President whenever the right of choice shall have devolved upon them.

Section 5. Sections 1 and 2 shall take effect on the fifteenth day of October following the ratification of this article.

Section 6. This article shall be inoperative unless it shall have been ratified as an amendment to the Constitution by the legislatures of three-fourths of the several states within seven years from the date of its submission.

AMENDMENT XXI

Repeal of Prohibition (1933)

Section 1. The Eighteenth Article of Amendment to the Constitution of the United States is hereby repealed.

Section 2. The transportation or importation into any state, territory, or possession of the United States for delivery or use therein of intoxicating liquors, in violation of the laws thereof, is hereby prohibited.

Section 3. This article shall be inoperative unless it shall have been ratified as an amendment to the Constitution by conventions in the several states, as provided in the Constitution, within seven years from the date of the submission thereof to the states by the Congress.

AMENDMENT XXII

President Limited to Two Terms (1951)

No person shall be elected to the office of the President more than twice, and no person who has held the office of President, or acted as President, for more than two years of a term to which some other person was elected President shall be elected to the office of the President more than once.

But this article shall not apply to any person holding the office of President when this article was proposed by the Congress and shall not prevent any person who may be holding the office of President, or acting as President, during the term within which this article becomes operative from holding the office of President or acting as President during the remainder of such term.

Maps

Charts and Graphs

Study Skills

General Book List

Useful Reference Books

American History Atlas edited by A. B. Hart, D. M. Matteson, and H. E. Bolton. Denoyer-Geppert, 1953. The development of the United States reported through maps.

World Atlas by J. Paul Goode. Rand McNally, 1953. A general reference atlas.

Hammond's American History Atlas. Hammond, 1951. Maps and charts showing events and developments in American history.

Historical Statistics of the United States 1789–1945 prepared by the Bureau of the Census. Government Printing Office, 1949. Statistics about the growth of our nation since its formation—population, trade, manufacturing, mining, farming, and so on.

Information Please Almanac edited by John Kieran. Doubleday, published annually. A standard statistical reference and book of facts.

Statistical Abstract of the United States prepared by the Bureau of the Census. Government Printing Office, published annually. A summary of important statistics concerning the United States today—population, industry, trade, farming, and so on.

The World Almanac and Book of Facts edited by Harry Hansen. *New York World-Telegram and The Sun,* published annually. A summary of important statistics collection of facts.

Britannica Junior: The Boys' and Girls' Encyclopaedia. Encyclopaedia Britannica. (15 volumes)

Compton's Pictured Encyclopedia. Compton. (15 volumes)

World Book Encyclopedia. Quarrie Corporation. (19 volumes)

Current Biography. Who's News and Why. H. W. Wilson, 1940 to date, annual cumulation of monthly issues. Brief biographies of living persons.

Dictionary of American Biography edited by Allen Johnson, Dumas Malone, and Harris E. Starr. Scribner, 1928–1936. (21 volumes) Short biographies of leaders in various fields of American life. If these volumes are not in your school library, try your public library.

Dictionary of American History edited by James Truslow Adams. Scribner, 1940. (5 volumes) Short accounts of events in American history. If you do not find this set in your school library, go to the public library to use it.

Books about Leaders in American Life*

America's Greatest Inventors by John C. Patterson. Crowell, 1943.

Art in the New Land by Charlie M. Simon. Dutton, 1945. Biographies of American artists from colonial days to the present.

Book of Americans by Rosemary C. Benét and Stephen Vincent Benét. Farrar, 1933. Verses about famous Americans, Columbus to Woodrow Wilson.

In Calico and Crinoline: True Stories of American Women, 1608–1865 by Eleanor M. Sickels. Viking, 1935. Short biographies of 18 American pioneer women.††

Lays of the New Land: Stories of Some American Poets and Their Work by Charlie M. Simon. Dutton, 1943. Biographies of outstanding poets from William Cullen Bryant's day to the present.

Pioneer Art in America by Carolyn S. Bailey. Viking, 1944. American crafts and craftsmen; chapters on Whittier, Currier and Ives, Stephen Foster, and Grant Wood.†

Presidents in American History by Charles A. Beard. Messner, 1953. Short biographies of our Presidents.

Twelve Daughters of Democracy: True Stories of American Women, 1865–1930 by Eleanor M. Sickels. Viking, 1941. Biographies of 12 women who have contributed to American life during the last century.††

Books about Many Sides of American Life

American Costume Book by Frances H. Haire. Barnes, 1934. A helpful reference on dress in different periods.

American Past: A History of the United States from Concord to Hiroshima, 1775–1945 by Roger Butterfield. Simon and Schuster, 1947. This picture history includes 1,000 photographs, cartoons, paintings, and so forth.

Americans and Their Songs by Frank Luther. Harper, 1942. Popular songs from early days and the stories behind them.

America's Stamps: The Story of One Hundred Years of U.S. Postage Stamps by Maud Petersham and Miska Petersham. Macmillan, 1947. The stories behind our stamps.

Growing Up with America edited by May L. Becker. Lippincott, 1941. Thirty-two stories of American life from colonial times to the present.†

Historic Models of Early America and How to Make Them by C. Maginley. Harcourt, Brace, 1947. Directions for making models of tools, houses, vehicles, and so on, that our ancestors used.

Homespun Playdays by Carolyn S. Bailey. Viking, 1942. Stories of Americans at play from colonial times to the mid-1800s.†

Long May It Wave: The Story of the Flag by Leslie Thomas. Morrow, 1941. A history of our United States flag and of earlier flags of American history.†

Make Way for the Mail by John J. Floherty. Lippincott, 1939. How our postal service has developed from colonial times until today.

Modern Wonder Books of Ships by Norman V. Carlisle and Eugene Nelson. Winston, 1947. The development of ships from those of early times to the superliners of today.

Modern Wonder Books of Trains and Railroading by Norman V. Carlisle. Winston, 1946. A history of railroading and of the people who built our railroads.

Primer for America by Robert P. Tristam Coffin. Macmillan, 1943. Ballads about Americans and their way of life.††

School Bell Rings by Evelyn R. Sickels. Scribner, 1942. Stories about school life in America from 1775 to 1863.†

Trails West and the Men Who Made Them by Edith Dorian. McGraw-Hill, 1954.

Yankee Doodle's Cousins by Anne Malcolmson. Houghton, 1941. Characters in our American folklore, real and legendary.†

* A † beside a title means easy reading, and †† shows that the book is difficult, while no symbol indicates that the book is average in ease of reading.

Presidents and Vice-Presidents

President	State	Term	Party	Vice-President	State
George Washington (1732–1799)	Virginia	1789–1797		John Adams	Massachusetts
John Adams (1735–1826)	Massachusetts	1797–1801	Federalist	Thomas Jefferson	Virginia
Thomas Jefferson (1743–1826)	Virginia	1801–1809	Republican	Aaron Burr	New York
				George Clinton	New York
James Madison (1751–1836)	Virginia	1809–1817	Republican	George Clinton	New York
				Elbridge Gerry	Massachusetts
James Monroe (1758–1831)	Virginia	1817–1825	Republican	Daniel D. Tompkins	New York
John Quincy Adams (1767–1848)	Massachusetts	1825–1829	Republican	John C. Calhoun	South Carolina
Andrew Jackson (1767–1845)	Tennessee	1829–1837	Democrat	John C. Calhoun	South Carolina
				Martin Van Buren	New York
Martin Van Buren (1782–1862)	New York	1837–1841	Democrat	Richard M. Johnson	Kentucky
William Henry Harrison (1773–1841)	Ohio	1841	Whig	John Tyler	Virginia
John Tyler (1790–1862)	Virginia	1841–1845	Whig	....	....
James K. Polk (1795–1849)	Tennessee	1845–1849	Democrat	George M. Dallas	Pennsylvania
Zachary Taylor (1784–1850)	Louisiana	1849–1850	Whig	Millard Fillmore	New York
Millard Fillmore (1800–1874)	New York	1850–1853	Whig	....	....
Franklin Pierce (1804–1869)	New Hampshire	1853–1857	Democrat	William R. King	Alabama
James Buchanan (1791–1868)	Pennsylvania	1857–1861	Democrat	John C. Breckinridge	Kentucky
Abraham Lincoln (1809–1865)	Illinois	1861–1865	Republican	Hannibal Hamlin	Maine
				Andrew Johnson	Tennessee

Andrew Johnson (1808–1875)	Tennessee	1865–1869	Republican	....	....
Ulysses S. Grant (1822–1885)	Illinois	1869–1877	Republican	Schuyler Colfax	Indiana
				Henry Wilson	Massachusetts
Rutherford B. Hayes (1822–1893)	Ohio	1877–1881	Republican	William A. Wheeler	New York
James A. Garfield (1831–1881)	Ohio	1881	Republican	Chester A. Arthur	New York
Chester A. Arthur (1830–1886)	New York	1881–1885	Republican	....	....
Grover Cleveland (1837–1908)	New York	1885–1889	Democrat	Thomas A. Hendricks	Indiana
Benjamin Harrison (1833–1901)	Indiana	1889–1893	Republican	Levi P. Morton	New York
Grover Cleveland (1837–1908)	New York	1893–1897	Democrat	Adlai E. Stevenson	Illinois
William McKinley (1843–1901)	Ohio	1897–1901	Republican	Garret A. Hobart	New Jersey
				Theodore Roosevelt	New York
Theodore Roosevelt (1858–1919)	New York	1901–1909	Republican	....	....
				Charles W. Fairbanks	Indiana
William Howard Taft (1857–1930)	Ohio	1909–1913	Republican	James S. Sherman	New York
Woodrow Wilson (1856–1924)	New Jersey	1913–1921	Democrat	Thomas R. Marshall	Indiana
Warren G. Harding (1865–1923)	Ohio	1921–1923	Republican	Calvin Coolidge	Massachusetts
Calvin Coolidge (1872–1933)	Massachusetts	1923–1929	Republican	....	....
				Charles G. Dawes	Illinois
Herbert Hoover (1874–)	California	1929–1933	Republican	Charles Curtis	Kansas
Franklin D. Roosevelt (1882–1945)	New York	1933–1945	Democrat	John N. Garner	Texas
				Henry A. Wallace	Iowa
				Harry S. Truman	Missouri
Harry S. Truman (1884–)	Missouri	1945–1952	Democrat	....	....
				Alben W. Barkley	Kentucky
Dwight D. Eisenhower (1890–)	New York	1952–	Republican	Richard M. Nixon	California

States, Territories,

Name	*Date of admission to Union*	*Population*	*Area (sq. mi.)*	*No. of Represent-atives in Congress*	*Capital*	*Largest city*
Alabama	1819	3,061,743	51,609	9	Montgomery	Birmingham
Arizona	1912	749,587	113,909	2	Phoenix	Phoenix
Arkansas	1836	1,909,511	53,102	6	Little Rock	Little Rock
California	1850	10,586,223	158,693	30	Sacramento	Los Angeles
Colorado	1876	1,325,089	104,247	4	Denver	Denver
Connecticut	1788	2,007,280	5,009	6	Hartford	Hartford
Delaware	1787	318,085	2,057	1	Dover	Wilmington
Florida	1845	2,771,305	58,560	8	Tallahassee	Jacksonville
Georgia	1788	3,444,578	58,876	10	Atlanta	Atlanta
Idaho	1890	588,637	83,557	2	Boise	Boise
Illinois	1818	8,712,176	56,400	25	Springfield	Chicago
Indiana	1816	3,934,224	36,291	11	Indianapolis	Indianapolis
Iowa	1846	2,621,073	56,280	8	Des Moines	Des Moines
Kansas	1861	1,905,299	82,276	6	Topeka	Wichita
Kentucky	1792	2,944,806	40,395	8	Frankfort	Louisville
Louisiana	1812	2,683,516	48,523	8	Baton Rouge	New Orleans
Maine	1820	913,774	33,215	3	Augusta	Portland
Maryland	1788	2,343,001	10,577	7	Annapolis	Baltimore
Massachusetts	1788	4,690,514	8,257	14	Boston	Boston
Michigan	1837	6,371,766	58,216	18	Lansing	Detroit
Minnesota	1858	2,982,483	84,068	9	St. Paul	Minneapolis
Mississippi	1817	2,178,914	47,716	6	Jackson	Jackson
Missouri	1821	3,954,653	69,674	11	Jefferson City	St. Louis
Montana	1889	591,024	147,138	2	Helena	Butte
Nebraska	1867	1,325,510	77,237	4	Lincoln	Omaha
Nevada	1864	160,083	110,540	1	Carson City	Reno
New Hampshire	1788	533,242	9,304	2	Concord	Manchester
New Jersey	1787	4,835,329	7,836	14	Trenton	Newark

and Possessions

Name	Date of admission to Union	Population	Area (sq. mi.)	No. of Representatives in Congress	Capital	Largest city
New Mexico	1912	681,187	121,666	2	Santa Fe	Albuquerque
New York	1788	14,830,192	49,576	43	Albany	New York City
North Carolina	1789	4,061,929	52,712	12	Raleigh	Charlotte
North Dakota	1889	619,636	70,665	2	Bismarck	Fargo
Ohio	1803	7,946,627	41,222	23	Columbus	Cleveland
Oklahoma	1907	2,233,351	69,919	6	Oklahoma City	Oklahoma City
Oregon	1859	1,521,341	96,981	4	Salem	Portland
Pennsylvania	1787	10,498,012	45,333	30	Harrisburg	Philadelphia
Rhode Island	1790	791,896	1,214	2	Providence	Providence
South Carolina	1788	2,117,027	31,055	6	Columbia	Charleston
South Dakota	1889	652,740	77,047	2	Pierre	Sioux Falls
Tennessee	1796	3,291,718	42,246	9	Nashville	Memphis
Texas	1845	7,711,194	267,339	22	Austin	Houston
Utah	1896	688,862	84,916	2	Salt Lake City	Salt Lake City
Vermont	1791	377,747	9,609	1	Montpelier	Burlington
Virginia	1788	3,318,680	40,815	10	Richmond	Richmond
Washington	1889	2,378,963	68,192	7	Olympia	Seattle
West Virginia	1863	2,005,552	24,181	6	Charleston	Huntington
Wisconsin	1848	3,434,575	56,154	10	Madison	Milwaukee
Wyoming	1890	290,529	97,914	1	Cheyenne	Cheyenne
District of Columbia		802,178	69			
TERRITORIES AND POSSESSIONS						
Alaska		128,643	586,400	1	Juneau	Juneau
American Samoa		18,937	76		Pago Pago	Pago Pago
Guam		59,498	206		Agaña	Agaña
Hawaii		499,794	6,435		Honolulu	Honolulu
Canal Zone		52,822	553		Balboa Heights	Balboa Heights
Puerto Rico		2,210,703	3,423		San Juan	San Juan
Virgin Islands of U.S.		26,665	133		Charlotte Amalie	Charlotte Amalie

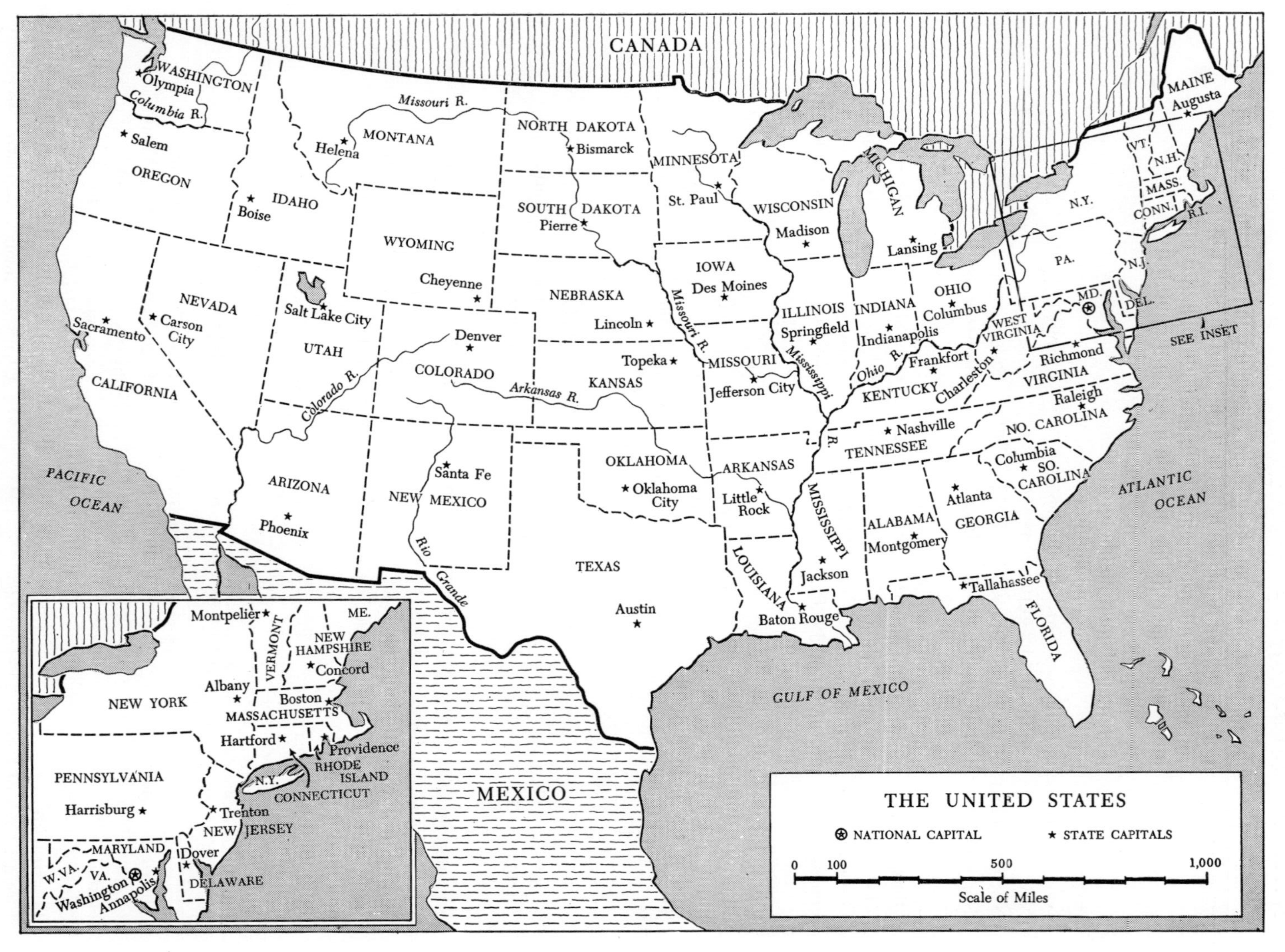
THE UNITED STATES
NATIONAL CAPITAL
STATE CAPITALS
0
100
500
1,000
Scale of Miles
CANADA
MEXICO
PACIFIC OCEAN
ATLANTIC OCEAN
GULF OF MEXICO
SEE INSET
WASHINGTON
Olympia
Columbia R.
OREGON
Salem
CALIFORNIA
Sacramento
NEVADA
Carson City
IDAHO
Boise
MONTANA
Helena
Missouri R.
WYOMING
Cheyenne
UTAH
Salt Lake City
Colorado R.
ARIZONA
Phoenix
COLORADO
Denver
Arkansas R.
NEW MEXICO
Santa Fe
Rio Grande
NORTH DAKOTA
Bismarck
SOUTH DAKOTA
Pierre
NEBRASKA
Lincoln
KANSAS
Topeka
OKLAHOMA
Oklahoma City
TEXAS
Austin
MINNESOTA
St. Paul
IOWA
Des Moines
Missouri R.
MISSOURI
Jefferson City
ARKANSAS
Little Rock
LOUISIANA
Baton Rouge
WISCONSIN
Madison
ILLINOIS
Springfield
Mississippi R.
MISSISSIPPI
Jackson
MICHIGAN
Lansing
INDIANA
Indianapolis
OHIO
Columbus
Ohio R.
KENTUCKY
Frankfort
TENNESSEE
Nashville
ALABAMA
Montgomery
GEORGIA
Atlanta
FLORIDA
Tallahassee
WEST VIRGINIA
Charleston
VIRGINIA
Richmond
NO. CAROLINA
Raleigh
SO. CAROLINA
Columbia
PA.
N.Y.
MD.
DEL.
N.J.
CONN.
R.I.
MASS.
VT.
N.H.
MAINE
Augusta
NEW YORK
Albany
Montpelier
VERMONT
ME.
NEW HAMPSHIRE
Concord
Boston
MASSACHUSETTS
Hartford
Providence
RHODE ISLAND
N.Y.
CONNECTICUT
PENNSYLVANIA
Harrisburg
Trenton
NEW JERSEY
Dover
DELAWARE
MARYLAND
W.VA.
VA.
Washington
Annapolis

Historical Holidays

January 8	Anniversary of the Battle of New Orleans (Louisiana)
January 19	Robert E. Lee's Birthday (Alabama, Arkansas, Florida, Georgia, Kentucky, Louisiana, Mississippi, North Carolina, South Carolina, Tennessee, Texas); Lee-Jackson Day (Virginia)
January 30	Franklin D. Roosevelt Day (Kentucky, Virgin Islands)
February 11	Edison Day
February 12	Abraham Lincoln's Birthday (Arizona, California, Colorado, Connecticut, Delaware, Illinois, Indiana, Iowa, Kansas, Kentucky, Maine, Maryland, Michigan, Minnesota, Missouri, Montana, Nebraska, Nevada, New Jersey, New Mexico, New York, North Dakota, Ohio, Oregon, Pennsylvania, South Dakota, Tennessee, Texas, Utah, Vermont, Washington, West Virginia, Wisconsin)
February 14	Arizona Admission Day (Arizona)
February 22	George Washington's Birthday (most states)
March 2	Texas Independence Day (Texas)
March 15	Andrew Jackson's Birthday (Tennessee)
March 17	Evacuation Day (Suffolk County, Massachusetts)
March 25	Maryland Day (Maryland)
March 30	Seward's Day (Alaska)
April 12	Halifax Day (North Carolina)
April 13	Thomas Jefferson's Birthday (Alabama, Missouri, Nebraska, Virginia)
April 14	Pan American Day
April 19	Patriot's Day (Maine and Massachusetts)
April 21	San Jacinto Day (Texas)
April 26	Confederate Memorial Day (Alabama, Florida, Georgia, Mississippi)
May 8	VE Day

May 10	Confederate Memorial Day (North Carolina and South Carolina)
May 20	"Mecklenburg Declaration of Independence" Anniversary (North Carolina)
May 30	Memorial Day (most states); Declaration Day (Maryland); Confederate Memorial Day (Virginia)
June 3	Jefferson Davis's Birthday (Alabama, Florida, Georgia, Mississippi, South Carolina, Texas, Virginia); Confederate Decoration Day (Kentucky, Louisiana, Tennessee)
June 14	Flag Day (Pennsylvania)
June 17	Bunker Hill Day (Suffolk County, Massachusetts)
June 20	West Virginia Day (West Virginia)
July 4	Independence Day (all states)
July 13	Nathan Bedford Forrest's Birthday (Tennessee)
July 24	Pioneer Day (Utah)
August 14	VJ Day; Victory Day (Rhode Island); World War II Memorial Day (Arkansas)
August 16	Bennington Battle Day (Vermont)
September (*first Monday*)	Labor Day (all states)
September 9	Admission Day (California)
September 12	Defender's Day (Maryland)
September 17	Citizenship Day (I Am an American Day); Constitution Day
October (*first Monday*)	Missouri Day (Missouri)
October 11	General Pulaski's Memorial Day
October 12	Columbus Day
October 18	Alaska Day (Alaska)
October 31	Nevada Day (Nevada)
November (*first Tuesday after first Monday*)	Election Day (most states)
November 11	Veterans' Day (formerly Armistic Day) (most states)
November (*last Thursday*)	Thanksgiving Day (all states)
December 15	Bill of Rights Day

Acknowledgments

WE WISH to express appreciation to William B. Fink, of the State University Teachers College, Oneonta, New York, and Mrs. Buena Stolberg, of the junior high school in Webster Groves, Missouri, for their advice concerning the text and study helps; to A. Faryar, of the United Nations, for helpful suggestions on the section of the book dealing with the UN; to Mrs. Louise Field, Research Associate of the Twentieth Century Fund, for help in preparing charts and graphs; to the staff of the Union College Library for innumerable services; and to Miss Eunice B. Merriss and Miss Helen Morey, librarians at the Greenwich, Connecticut, Public Library, for checking the bibliographies.

We acknowledge permission to reprint the following copyright material:

The pronunciation system used is that which appears in *Webster's New International Dictionary,* Second Edition, copyright, 1934, 1939, 1945, 1950, by G. & C. Merriam Co., and is used by permission.

Page 313, "S-t-e-a-m-boat a-comin'." From *Life on the Mississippi* by Mark Twain; used by permission of Harper & Brothers.

Page 334, Teaching in Frontier Michigan. From *The Story of a Pioneer* by Anna Howard Shaw; used by permission of Harper & Brothers.

Page 369, Southern Life in Wartime. From *Reminiscences of Peace and War* by Mrs. Roger A. Pryor, 1905; permission of The Macmillan Company.

Page 407, Refrigerator Cars. Reprinted with permission from *Scientific American,* July 17, 1869.

Page 424, John Henry. From *John Henry: Tracking Down a Negro Legend* by Guy B. Johnson; permission of The University of North Carolina Press.

Page 615, An American View. Reprinted from *War Songs* by Struthers Burt; copyright 1942 by Charles Scribner's Sons; permission of the publishers.

Page 646, "Birches." From *Mountain Interval* by Robert Frost. Copyright, 1916, by Henry Holt and Company, Inc. Copyright, 1944, by Robert Frost.

Page 648. From *The People, Yes* by Carl Sandburg, copyright, 1936, by Harcourt, Brace and Company, Inc.

To the Teacher

FROM THE beginning of the planning and thinking that produced this book, it was our purpose to tell the history of the United States as the story of the American adventure. To the Americans who participated, it was the great adventure. It was adventure to the explorers, the first settlers on the seacoast, the pioneers who pushed the frontier westward, and to the millions who followed in their footsteps. It was adventure to the men who built our roads and railroads and raised our cities. It was adventure to the political leaders who expressed the popular will and to the reformers who broadened the principles and practices of democracy. It was adventure to all Americans who worked to achieve a more comfortable life in freedom. While tracing this past, the book points ahead to the continuing American adventure with new frontiers that the pupils will share tomorrow.

To tell this story, we have used an essentially narrative style, enlivening the account with dramatic incidents, descriptive passages, biographical sketches, and the clash of personalities, sections, and issues. We have endeavored to convey to the pupil a sense of adventure throughout.

The illustrations, including the line drawings, maps, and charts enhanced by color, portray visually and vividly the theme of adventure. Through performing the unit-end activities, the pupils will find themselves, in imagination, participants in the adventure of the American past. Through the recordings and films listed separately in a teacher's manual, so that they may be frequently revised, the pupils may hear and see many of the dramatic incidents of the American adventure. Thus the history of their country will become part of their inner experience.

We have told the American story as an adventure in freedom. For young people growing up, an understanding of their country's past, a patriotic pride in its unique achievements, and the hope of their own participation in the American adventure are democracy's strongest safeguard.

Index